HOFFMANN: AUTHOR OF THE TALES

Portrait of Hoffmann
Pencil Sketch Made by Wilhelm Hensel
in the Summer of 1821

HOFFMANN:
AUTHOR OF THE TALES

BY HARVEY W. HEWETT-THAYER

1971
OCTAGON BOOKS
New York

Reprinted 1971

by special arrangement with Princeton University Press

OCTAGON BOOKS

A DIVISION OF FARRAR, STRAUS & GIROUX, INC.

19 Union Square West

New York, N. Y. 10003

LIBRARY OF CONGRESS CATALOG CARD NUMBER: 73-120629

Manufactured by Braun-Brumfield, Inc.
Ann Arbor, Michigan

Printed in the United States of America

To

A.M.T.

PREFACE

DURING a part of the nineteenth century E. T. A. Hoffmann was not only one of the most popular authors in Germany but his name was often mentioned on the continent of Europe, especially in France and Russia, with the great masters of world literature. His stories were translated into the chief European languages, and his influence on other writers was widespread. In recent decades Hoffmann has emerged from a temporary obscurity, and the author of the "Tales" appears again as a writer of genuine distinction, close to a major figure in his country's literature. And yet in English there has been hitherto no comprehensive account of his life and work—only a few specialized articles and the brief introductions to translations or to two or three tales edited for school use.

The present book is planned as an introduction to Hoffmann, for both the general reader who wants to know something of foreign literatures and the student. To the latter reader the footnotes are primarily addressed. With the former in mind, I have translated the quotations from the German, but in a great many cases I have given the original text in the footnotes, particularly when the passage seemed to be of special significance either in itself or for a quality in the language that could not readily be reproduced in English. Doubtless I have been somewhat arbitrary in my choice, but I wished to keep the notes within bounds. Often, when the full original text is not given, I have inserted a German word or phrase in brackets after the translation. For those acquainted with German this may contribute something to a further appreciation of the passage. An apology may seem fitting for the unusual amount of purely descriptive material—such as the analyses of the stories themselves—but this procedure seemed essential for the reader who has not read Hoffmann's tales. Hoffmann as musician and critic of music unquestionably deserves a more comprehensive treatment than the brief account in the Epilogue, which is obviously derivative. This important phase of Hoffmann's activity could be adequately evaluated only by a competent scholar in the history of music.

In the preparation of this work I have drawn extensively on Hoffmann's letters and diaries, and I am also deeply indebted to the research of German scholars, especially to Georg Ellinger, Carl Georg von Maassen, and Hans von Müller. From monographs and articles by other scholars I have obtained information on Hoffmann's life and work and many stimulating suggestions; the references in the notes may serve as an acknowledgment. To my friends, Professors Herbert S. Murch and Bernhard Ulmer, of Princeton University, Harold S. Jantz, of Northwestern University, and William Dighton, of Queens College, who have read chapters of the manuscript, I would express my gratitude for helpful advice on many points; to Professor Ulmer I am especially indebted for his invaluable assistance in reading the proof. It is a pleasure also to acknowledge my obligation to the libraries that have generously and courteously served me and placed their resources at my disposal. In addition to the Princeton University Library, I am indebted to the libraries of Columbia, Chicago, Iowa, Minnesota, Pennsylvania, Toronto, Wellesley, the New York Public Library, the Library of the Metropolitan Museum of Art, and the Library of Congress. In several chapters I have incorporated substantial parts of articles that have appeared in the *Germanic Review,* and I am grateful to the editors for their kind permission to reprint this material here.

The references in the footnotes to Hoffmann's works are to Grisebach's edition. In the quotations from Hoffmann's *Briefwechsel* and *Tagebuch,* the original spelling has been retained.

HARVEY W. HEWETT-THAYER

Princeton, N.J.
March 29, 1948

CONTENTS

ILLUSTRATIONS

Portrait of Hoffmann. Pencil Sketch Made by Wilhelm Hensel in the
Summer of 1821. Reproduced from *Briefwechsel* II.   *frontispiece*

The following are works by Hoffmann: *facing page*

PART I · HIS LIFE

CHAPTER 1

KÖNIGSBERG

THE ancient city of Königsberg lies near a great lakelike arm of the Baltic Sea; long lines of sand dunes separate the so-called Fresh Haven (Frische Haff) from the open ocean. Winds from the cold northern seas sweep over the gloomy forests of fir and pine that cover the sandy shores. Upon this remote land the shadow of winter with its long, dark nights hangs perpetually; even of more sunny German regions Heine could say that "our northern summer is only a winter painted green." In the thirteenth century the territory of which Königsberg became the capital was wrested from Slavic tribes by the crusading knights of the Teutonic Order. For a time Teuton and Slav lived as master and slave, but in the course of centuries the enmities arising from this relationship were wiped out and forgotten, and the blood of the two races mingled. When the world without is somber and forbidding, man is led to turn introspectively to the world within, and the tendencies that seem native to the Slav—withdrawal and meditation, the mystic consciousness of the unseen world—blended with the more sturdy and practical qualities of the Germanic conquerors.

It would be rash to maintain that German Romanticism stems exclusively or even primarily from the Russian borderlands, taking root in congenial soil and fertilized by a transfusion of Slavic blood. The romantic temper is a universal trait, not confined to any one people or to any time or place. And yet undeniably three great progenitors of the Romantic Movement in Germany were East Prussians, Hamann, Herder, and Kant, each contributing his part to the initial impulse that stirred the slumbering spirit in other parts of the country. All three were educated at the University of Königsberg, Kant becoming in time the most illustrious member of the university faculty. To Herder, Hamann communicated his somewhat nebulous but still germinal ideas of nature as opposed to artifice, the greatness of primitive literatures, and the authority of the emotions. These Herder developed more systematically into the creed of the first outburst of German Romanticism, the Storm and Stress of the 1770's and 1780's. From Königsberg Kant first challenged the arrogance of eighteenth century rationalism and prepared the soil for the growth of romantic philosophy. Kant was born, lived, and died in Königsberg, never wandering, it was said, more than a few miles from the city gates, though his spirit knew no bounds except the stars in the night sky.

And on January 24, 1776, a child was born in Königsberg, in the Französische Gasse, who was to become one of the world's great romantic storytellers. About a week later, on February 2, the baby was christened to bear the name of Ernst Theodor Wilhelm Hoffmann.[1] His father and mother were cousins: Christoph Ludwig Hoffmann had married Luise Albertine Doerffer, the daughter of his mother's sister.[2] Christoph was a lawyer of ability and a talented musician, but he was capricious and unstable, and there were constant temperamental clashes with his wife who had inherited and absorbed the disciplined sobriety and regard for routine that prevailed in the Doerffer household. Of their disagreements, which Hoffmann later called a "comedy of domestic dissension" (Hauskreuzkomödie), he must have learned largely from gossip in his grandmother's house, for he was only between two and three years old when the ill-assorted marriage was dissolved. Luise Hoffmann returned to her mother's home in the Junkergasse, almost under the shadow of the great royal palace which had once been the headquarters of the Teutonic Knights. Before long—after three or four years—Christoph Ludwig Hoffmann removed to the town of Insterburg, taking with him the older of the two little boys; Ernst, the younger, remained with his mother in Königsberg. With this departure Hoffmann's father disappears almost completely from his life, save as an indistinct but still treasured memory of one who, as he thought, could have understood him in a household where he felt himself so much an alien—"a poor father is still always much better than anyone else to bring one up, however good that one may be."

It was not an exhilarating environment into which the little boy

1 For the change of name to Ernst Theodor Amadeus, cf. p. 45.

2 The presence of Slavic blood in Hoffmann's inheritance is indicated by the genealogical records, but to what extent his origins were Slavic, or even Magyar, as has been suggested, remains undetermined. The *Genealogisches Handbuch bürgerlicher Familien (Deutsches Geschlechterbuch)*, published by B. Koerner (Berlin, 1900), VII, pp. 163-75, gives an account of the East Prussian Hoffmann family, and shows that E. T. A. Hoffmann was seventh in line from a certain Jan von Bagienski, who came from Poland in the latter part of the sixteenth century (earliest date, 1585). One of Bagienski's sons married a Hoffmann, and the sons of the latter used Bagi(e)nski and Hoffmann "abwechselnd," in time "Hoffmann" replacing entirely the original Polish name. The wife of the original Bagienski had a German name; with these exceptions the genealogical tables give the names of no other wives. If they were all German, the Polish blood became somewhat diluted in seven generations. Jan von Bagienski may also have been part German. Hitzig said that the name "Voetheri" was of Hungarian origin, a statement that has never been confirmed.

1. Self-Portrait, Giving Explanation of Physiognomic Details

2. Self-Portrait

was thus projected.[3] Hoffmann's grandfather Doerffer, who had been a jurist of parts and a man of prominence in the community, had died two years previously. His wife, Hoffmann's grandmother, had apparently made no effort to master her grief and lived in a kind of cloistered seclusion; even in her own house she remained almost exclusively in her own apartments—her meals were served to her there. And now the prodigal daughter began to participate in this withdrawal.[4] Ernst, as he was called in the family, saw almost nothing of his mother, though she lived till toward the end of his days at the university. The elements of her character which probably precipitated the disruption of her marriage were doubtless intensified in the strange type of widowhood that was now her lot; she was weak, ineffective, and complaining, at times subject to.mild hysterical outbursts. She had no influence whatever on the development of her son, though he pays her a touching tribute of affection at the time of her death.

Otherwise the family consisted of a maiden aunt and a bachelor uncle. The possible presence of a second aunt has been a moot point in Hoffmann biography. The strangely contradictory qualities attributed to an Aunt Sophie have formed an insoluble enigma, and the shadowy figure of another aunt who could thus remove something of Sophie's inconsistency seemed to take shape from the autobiographical sections of *Kater Murr* and *Der Musikfeind*. This is the gentle "Tante Füsschen" of the Kreisler reminiscences who held the little boy on her lap, singing with marvelous voice to the accompaniment of the lute: "Staid men who can write and do sums and doubtless more besides have shed tears in my presence at the mere memory of her playing on the lute." Her early death left its imprint on the mind of the boy—he was childishly rebellious at this first evidence of our common mortality. Most biographers have regarded "Tante Füsschen" as a purely imaginary figure of Hoff-

---

[3] Hoffmann himself was later keenly conscious of the defects of his youthful upbringing: "Ja ja—in meiner ersten Erziehung, zwischen den vier Mauern mir selbst überlassen, liegt der Keim mancher von mir hinterher begangenen Thorheit" (*Briefwechsel*, I, p. 190), or in the autobiographical pages of *Kater Murr*: "Gewiss ist es aber, dass, wenn Kreisler über die trostlose Verlassenheit in seinen Knabenjahren klagt, wenn er das zerrissene Wesen, das ihn oft in seiner innersten Natur verstört, jener Zeit zuschreibt, wohl das Verhältnis mit dem Oheim in Anschlag zu bringen ist. Er konnte den Mann, der, Vaterstelle zu vertreten, berufen und der ihm mit seinem ganzen Tun und Wesen lächerlich erscheinen musste, nicht achten." x, p. 104.

(All such references as this latter to just a volume and page number, without author and title, are to Grisebach's edition of Hoffmann's works.)

[4] Hippel, who went in and out of the Doerffer house for ten years, reported that he saw Hoffmann's mother and grandmother hardly more than three or four times.

mann's creation, and the genealogical tables of the Doerffer family
that Hans von Müller has unearthed from various sources make no
mention of her.[5] But Hoffmann's story of "Tante Füsschen" in
Kater Murr has an unmistakable ring of authenticity, especially in
view of his acknowledged methods in the literary use of his own
past. Until further information is available, one may hazard the
guess that she was a relative living in the Doerffer family whom
the little boy quite naturally called "aunt."[6] The older aunt, the
real Aunt Sophie, was without musical interests, without imagination, and was perhaps narrowly domestic and limited in her intellectual horizons, but she loved little Ernst, and to her he owed whatever there was of "home" in the gloomy house in the Junkergasse.

As Ernst emerged from babyhood, the upbringing of the boy de-
volved upon his mother's brother, Otto Wilhelm Doerffer, the only
male member of the household. Not in Ernst's eyes alone was this
tutelage a major calamity. His uncle Otto was at this time a fussy,
pedantic old bachelor, who was vegetating on into middle life without employment or ambitions, and quite devoid of ideas. Like his
father he had been trained in the law, but unlike his father, who
carried on the profession with eminent success, he retired, it is said,
after his first failure in pleading a case before an open tribunal.[7]
Ernst was about five or six years old when his uncle ceased to have
any real occupation. His uncle kept an ever-watchful eye upon the
growing boy and strove to inculcate in him the same habits of
extreme orderliness, the same extravagant regard for traditional

[5] In the third and supplementary volume of the *Briefwechsel*, Hans von Müller
promised to publish a full explanation of all his sources, but vol. III has not yet appeared.

[6] Ellinger thinks the case of "Tante Füsschen" in the main a matter of "freie poe-
tische Erfindung, vielleicht beeinflusst durch die Schilderung, die Rousseau im ersten
Buch seiner Bekenntnisse von dem Einflusse entwirft, den seine Tante auf die Entwicklung seiner Leidenschaft für die Musik ausgeübt hat" (*Werke*, IX, p. 264).
Schaukal, on the other hand, accepts "Tante Füsschen" without question as a real
aunt (*E. T. A. Hoffmann: Sein Werk aus seinem Leben*, p. 7). According to Harich
(*E. T. A. Hoffmann: Das Leben eines Künstlers*, p. 19), Hans von Müller had found
in the autumn of 1918 proofs of the existence of "Tante Füsschen" and permitted him
to make use of the fact in his biography, although at that time Müller had not published his findings. In the various publications of Hans von Müller since that date
which have been available to the present writer, the question of "Tante Füsschen"
has not been raised.

[7] This story is derived from Hippel. According to Hans von Müller, Otto Wilhelm
Doerffer's opponent before the court was the elder Hippel, and after his defeat he
seized the opportunity of a change in the structure of the courts to secure his retire-
ment. It was on this occasion that Hoffmann's father was transferred to the court at
Insterburg. Cf. "Aus E. T. A. Hoffmanns Herzensgeschichte 1796-1802," in *Deutsche
Rundschau*, CXXXVII, pp. 252-60, and *Das Kreislerbuch*, p. xi.

conventions and outward conformity that governed his own life and made of it a satisfaction—of a certain kind—to himself, if indeed to no one else. His life was regulated by an ironclad routine. The days were divided with scrupulous exactitude into specified hours and even minutes, and devoted to unproductive pursuits, to "sleeping, eating, and drinking, and then again to sleeping and eating, with a little reading and music to aid digestion." From this discipline there was in the earlier years no possible escape, for uncle and nephew occupied the same sleeping room and spent the waking hours in the common living room.

Hoffmann's keen and precocious intelligence soon fathomed his uncle's weaknesses and viewed with contempt the futility of the life he led. He became aware—perhaps dangerously aware—of his own superiority. Uncle Otto presented an array of vulnerable points, though for the most part he was too dull to feel the barbs of mockery or to perceive the source of practical jokes played upon him. The lively ingenuity of the nephew invented various methods of teasing and mystifying his well-intentioned tormentor. Even in his university years Hoffmann continued to satirize the then doddering old gentleman. Making a pun on the initials of his name, Ernst nicknamed him the "O Weh" uncle or refers to him as "Der dicke Sir" (the stout gentleman).

That the loneliness of Hoffmann's boyhood and his guardian's smug complacency did not develop in him a greater tendency to the morose or to the sly and cunning, that with unconscious poise he could find vent for his ebullient spirits in his mockery of the ludicrous and at the same time accept and assimilate what there was of value in his uncle's training, offers testimony to the solid integrity of the boy's character. To be sure, the substantial achievements that are gained in life by regularity of effort and unremitting application to one's tasks were not conspicuously evident in the case of his uncle Otto, but little Ernst had the perception to acknowledge the validity of the precept and ignore the example. When the time came, he was an industrious student and throughout life a reliable and diligent worker.

In Hoffmann's character this solid trait which responded to his uncle's discipline and was manifest in a conscientious performance of all official duties, was linked incongruously with a pronounced artistic temperament. In the discussion of Zacharias Werner among the "Serapion Brothers" Theodor (Hoffmann) contends that the hysteria of a mother is not inherited by her sons but brings forth in them an exceedingly lively, indeed an eccentric, imagination, and unmistakably applies this theory to himself. Something of his musical talent he presumably inherited from his father, who was a skillful performer, especially on the viola da gamba, though he was erratic and perhaps irreverent in his treatment of a musical score. But his uncle Otto was also a lover of music and himself knew how to "handle the spinet with barbaric virtuosity." Musical evenings formed a constant feature of life in the Doerffer house, affording the small boy an infinite relief from the daily monotony. Friends arrived with their instruments—viola da gamba, viola d'amore, flute, French horn and the like—and together they attacked the music of the masters. Ernst was admitted to these performances—he was supposed to profit from them—and sat quietly on a stool in his Sunday suit. At first his own musical gifts seemed entirely dormant, and the musical evenings only tickled his sense of the ludicrous, while he watched the fantastic grimaces of the amateur musicians as they drew the bow or puffed out their cheeks. His uncle gave Ernst his first lessons in music, and when both interest and proficiency seemed to justify it, provided professional guidance in the person of Podbielski, an organist in one of the churches (Domkirche) who in all probability later contributed to the figure of Meister Abraham in *Kater Murr*. The boy received instruction for the piano and organ and in musical theory. A local artist of some renown was also summoned to instruct Ernst when he showed unusual aptitude for drawing.

To one of his relatives, though not of the immediate family circle, Hoffmann looked up with warm affection, even with reverence. This was his great-uncle, Christoph Ernst Voetheri, his grandmother's brother. Out of his former service as a lawyer in Königsberg, the old gentleman had retained the position of legal adviser to several great landholders in the country roundabout, and was accustomed to spend some time each year on their baronial estates. He was fond of taking his grandnephew with him on these expeditions, both as companion and in time as an assistant. Hoffmann's story *Das Majorat* (The Entail) is founded on such a visit and presents both a charming portrait of the old gentleman and a not less pleasing picture of the relation between uncle and nephew.

As a boy Hoffmann was markedly small for his age. When he began to attract attention by his musicianship, at twelve or thirteen, the skill of his playing was emphasized by the impression that he was a lad of eight. He remained diminutive in stature; he had heavy, bushy dark hair, a rather low forehead, and a prominent nose. His lack of personal comeliness was relieved, or some might perhaps say, heightened, by piercing dark eyes. The extraordinary mobility of his facial muscles changed the appearance of his countenance with amazing rapidity, from somber gravity to uproarious merriment; perhaps most characteristic was a certain impishness. The movements of his body were similarly swift, and he gave the impression of being always in motion. Hoffmann was conscious of his physical inferiority; to him it was like a striking birthmark, and at times it burrowed painfully into his inner self. There is doubtless a faint subjective note in his portrayal of the grotesque figure of Klein Zaches. Whatever resentment, however, Hoffmann might have cherished against the gods for not bestowing upon him the gift of pulchritude was met by a strong countervailing sense of humor. In his first love affair—a boyish admiration for Amalie Neumann, a schoolgirl whom he used to meet on the street but to whom he never spoke—he wished that he might be even uglier, even the very paragon of ugliness, so that she might at least look at him.[8]

Naturally school days brought some relief from the galling dullness of the Doerffer household; at least during school hours Hoffmann was no longer in the house. At the age of six he was sent to the "Deutsch-reformierte Schule" (Burgschule),[9] which was under the expert guidance of a certain Stephan Wannowski, a Polish gentleman of the Protestant faith. In these days of progressive education it may be merely a senile nostalgia which leads some elderly men to deplore the passing of the type to which the "German Reformed" School in Königsberg belonged. It was a "one-man school,"

[8] Hoffmann executed a number of sketches of himself, one or more of which are reproduced in editions of his works; cf., in Maassen's edition, the frontispieces to vols. I, IV, VI, VII, VIII; also Illus. 1, 2. With considerable plausibility Eberhard Meyer argues that the sketch with phrenological notations on the visible parts of his face and head is probably the most accurate. Cf. "Aus dem literarischen Nachlasse Immermanns," in *Schriften des Vereins für die Geschichte Berlins*, Heft 150 (Berlin, 1917), pp. 447-51 (cf. Illus. 1). For portraits by others, see the picture of Hoffmann and Devrient in the wine room of Lutter and Weg(e)ner (Maassen, IV, p. lx), which Maassen thinks may have been derived from a sketch by J. P. Lyser; the portrait by Wilhelm Hensel (cf. Frontispiece), and that used as the frontispiece of Maassen III, which, if at all accurate in expression, caught the sitter in an unusually amiable mood. Öhlenschläger described Hoffmann as "ein burlesk phantastischer Elfe." Cf. the Danish author's *Briefe in die Heimat auf einer Reise durch Deutschland und Frankreich*, translated by Georg Lotz, Altona, 1820; quoted by C. G. von Maassen, in *Der grundgescheute Antiquarius*, I (1920), pp. 119-20.

[9] Cf. Hans von Müller: "Die Königsberger Burgschule und ihr Rector Wannowski," in *Altpreussische Monatsschrift*, XLIV (1907), pp. 599-605, reprinted in *Materialien zu einer Biographie E. T. A. Hoffmanns*, Berlin, 1907.

for much of the instruction was given by the rector, Dr. Wannowski himself, and all of it was permeated by his personality. The study of the classical languages and literatures, primarily Latin, formed the center of instruction, but in the hands of Dr. Wannowski it became the vehicle not only for mental discipline but also for orientation in universal culture, for the acquisition of aesthetic standards and moral equilibrium. The lectures on philosophy that the learned doctor delivered to the boys were illuminating and practical discourses on the art of living, founded on the best thoughts in human history and spiced with corroborative illustrations, often drawn from personal experience. The power of Dr. Wannowski's personality and the intensity of his convictions kept the eyes of every boy fastened on the master's face.

At the beginning Ernst's scholastic performance did not satisfy the family in the Junkergasse. Like most boys of strong individuality and marked artistic gifts, he limited his efforts to the subjects that interested him. For several years, also, no friendly intimacies sprang up between him and his comrades in the school. He was a prisoner permitted for a few hours daily to leave his cell for work in the outside world and he did not speak the same language as his fellow workers. The other boys fought shy of him, for they were afraid of his tongue.

This situation was radically altered a few years later when in 1787 Theodor Gottlieb Hippel entered the school. The two boys had met by chance the previous year and a mutual attraction even then gave promise of the solid friendship that was to last through Hoffmann's life. Hippel was Hoffmann's senior by only a month, and the two youths possessed that combination of similarities and divergences upon which the most stimulating and abiding friendships are founded. Hippel was the son of a rural pastor in the village of Arnau, a few miles distant from Königsberg, in those days seemingly much farther away. The two boys were both virtually motherless—Hippel, an only child, actually so from his fifth year. But whereas Hoffmann was subjected to the irritating and unintelligent guidance of his uncle, which prompted him to constant mockery, Hippel grew up in the companionship of an indulgent father whose solicitude for his only child tended to develop in him a touch of softness and ineffectuality, while Hoffmann exhibited to the world a precocious independence and a superficial callousness. They were kinsmen in the liveliness of their imagination and their sensitivity to beauty, though Hoffmann's spirit was far deeper and richer. Although appreciative of music, Hippel was without musical talent. Love of nature was instinctive in the son of the country pastor, while Hoffmann was incorrigibly urban. Not the release from city pavements but the unbroken companionship with his friend made the holiday visits to the rural seclusion of the pastor's living so precious and memorable. It is merely a derivative echo from Rousseau, coupled with the torturing perplexities of his last days in Königsberg, that prompted Hoffmann to write to Hippel: "You see nature coming to life again, every little blade of grass springing forth, every swelling bud unveils for you the spirit of life—you breathe more freely in the purified air." His heart was ever in the town.

When Uncle Otto proposed that Hippel, always an exemplary student, should come to the house and assist Ernst as a kind of mentor and unofficial tutor in studies where he was lamentably deficient, doubtless Ernst thought the plan almost too good to be true. On Wednesday afternoons, when the "O Weh Onkel" was accustomed to make his stately visits on his friends, the two boys could have the living room to themselves; later the plan included Saturday afternoons as well. They studied diligently for a time, but later when "Aunt Sophie" brought tea for them, they threw their Latin or Greek texts aside and purloined forbidden volumes from Uncle Otto's bookshelves, Rousseau's *Confessions* in a German translation being perhaps the favorite choice. They made music also and when weather allowed they played games in the garden—games such as imaginative boys in all lands invent for their pastime. They were medieval knights and held tournaments, filching swords from two statues, made of wood and painted to resemble sandstone, representing Mars and Minerva. As adolescents they evinced an interest in a girls' boarding school over the garden wall and conceived the plan of digging a tunnel under the wall to provide access to it. In the sweat of their brows they had dug a trench of considerable dimensions when it was accidentally discovered by Uncle Otto. The boys were ready with an explanation: the trench was being prepared for the reception of an exotic American plant. Uncle Otto did not wait for the arrival of the imaginary shrub, but secured the service of two workmen to fill in the trench. That two laborers were required might indicate the magnitude of the conspirators' accomplishment, and Uncle Otto was either generous or strangely obtuse in not providing for this work in another way. Now and then the boys admitted two other youths to their intimate circle—Faber, who could play duets with Ernst, and Matuszewski, a budding artist.

Many years later, in the story *Der Artushof*, Hoffmann introduced
the latter among the artist friends of the hero in Italy.

The devotion of the two youths to one another was in no way
affected by the difference in their external prospects. Hoffmann faced
adversities and uncertainties, particularly in the profession that
in time circumstances forced upon him. Hippel had not only a doting
father but an influential and very wealthy uncle whose name he bore.
In those days Theodor Gottlieb Hippel was one of the outstanding
men in East Prussia. From small beginnings he had risen through
energy and ambition to eminence in the community; positions and
titles of distinction were showered upon him. Though somewhat
veiled in anonymity, he was also an author of repute; his novels
Lebensläufe in aufsteigender Linie and *Kreuz- und Querzüge des
Ritters A bis Z*, somewhat in the manner of Lawrence Sterne, are
still of significance in the history of German fiction. In addition,
Hippel's uncle was a bachelor. In the course of time he secured a
patent of nobility which covered not only himself but his immediate
kin, so that the humble village pastor and young Hippel, still a
schoolboy, became nobles of the Holy Roman Empire. Hoffmann's
friend was heir presumptive to his uncle's vast wealth and in time
would succeed to the great baronial estate that the elder Hippel was
to acquire. With his uncle's interest and support young Hippel was
destined, not for the career of a struggling barrister, but for service
in the state. He later became a capable official in the service of his
country, remembered perpetually in Prussian history as the author
of the famous appeal "An mein Volk" which Frederick William III
issued at the beginning of the war against Napoleon. Hoffmann's
letters to Hippel, particularly in their young manhood, not only are
a chief source of information as to the events of the period but they
reveal also the inner life of the man: "to you I can appear without a
mask," he wrote in 1796. In them he disclosed the emotional and
romantic tendencies of his nature, and the letters themselves show a
romantic style in the process of development.

At the age of sixteen Hoffmann entered the university of his native
city as a student of law. His remarkable versatility, particularly his
musical talents, had raised questions in his own mind as to the choice
of a career. "I have to force myself to become a lawyer," he wrote
to Hippel in May 1795, and only a little later, when he had finished
his legal studies, he wrote: "If it depended upon myself alone, I
would become a composer and would have the hope to attain distinction in that field while in the one I have chosen I shall remain an

eternal bungler." But family tradition and economic caution dictated his acquiescence in plans made by others. Nearly all of his immediate relatives had been lawyers, though the family tree shows a sprinkling of clergymen in earlier generations, his grandfather Hoffmann, for instance. To expect a living at the outset from musical composition ran counter to all precedents. Yet the strong pull toward the life of a creative artist did not deter Hoffmann from solid and conscientious application to the study of law. Indeed, he became interested in his studies and attended the lectures from the beginning with a regularity exceptional among German students. The discipline of his uncle Otto, joined to a certain tenacity and toughness in his own character, was bringing forth good fruit.

Externally, the transfer from school to university brought little change in the young man's way of living; it was merely the substitution of another place and other subjects of study. He still lived at home and in no way participated in the traditional habits and age-old customs of German students. His friend Hippel had entered the university a year in advance, and, destined for the career of a statesman, he extended the range of his academic interests beyond purely legal studies. However much Hippel might have preferred the quiet room in the Doerffer house and the tested comradeship of the past years, as a young nobleman with brilliant prospects he naturally accepted or even sought companions among the young cavaliers of the university circles and entered into the sports popular among German university men. Only two or three times did he succeed in persuading Ernst, who had no taste for sports, to join him in horseback riding—and with droll results. The habit of study together had been abandoned when Hippel left school to enter the university, but the two young men still met frequently in more or less formal fashion to discuss matters over a bottle of wine; they often amused themselves by conversing in rhymes.

Hoffmann's friendship with Hippel lasted throughout his life. It was a solace for Hoffmann, a kind of prop even though circumstances forced them apart for years at a time. Now and then there were slight misunderstandings and long gaps in their correspondence, but the friendship was never really broken, defying both separation and growing disparity of interests. In story after story Hoffmann introduces two devoted friends of varying temperament, not in any case really portraits of Hippel and himself, but reminiscent of their relationship. In *Die Räuber*, written only about a year before Hoffmann's death, the two friends are beginning a trip to

Italy together—a trip which remained the unfulfilled dream of the two Königsberg comrades.

In the summer of 1795 Hoffmann completed his work at the university and, having passed the first examination for admission to the bar, was ready for professional employment. Along with his professional studies he had pursued his old aesthetic interests, had read Winckelmann and copied treasures from Herculaneum which he found pictured in the Royal Library. He was even ambitious to obtain commissions for portraits, and two paintings from French history upon which he had labored with enthusiasm he sent by his uncle's manservant to Hippel's wealthy uncle, hoping that the latter would buy them for his growing collection. Unfortunately, to Hoffmann's embarrassment and chagrin, the elder Hippel misinterpreted the gesture and thought them a gift from his nephew's friend.

Hoffmann's initial experience as a composer dates from his boyhood. After reading Rousseau's *Confessions* he essayed to imitate the French master and compose an opera while lying in bed, but the boy fell asleep and in some way set fire to the curtains in the room. After this fiasco his ambitions apparently lay dormant for a time, but toward the end of his university years they were awakened, and obviously in a more mature form. On February 24, 1795, he wrote to Hippel: "It gives me pleasure to see your father listening to me while I play my little songs and rondos; I have composed a 'Romanze' to the Empress of Russia." In October he was composing music for the Cathedral Scene in *Faust I* and planning to write a score for Goethe's little play *Claudine von Villabella*; he also wrote music for songs in Goethe's *Lila*. But as musical composition did not, and indeed could not at first, prove remunerative, Hoffmann turned to an occupation more immediately promising: he began to give lessons in music. He was by no means in financial need, but he was eager to begin his emancipation from family control and possess funds that were really his own.

In the exercise of this new vocation, Hoffmann unwittingly plunged himself into an emotional martyrdom that tortured a long period of his young manhood. He fell passionately in love with one of his pupils, unfortunately a married woman, Frau Dora (Johanna Dorothea) Hatt, whom he called "Cora" after the heroine of a popular play by Kotzebue. She was more than nine years older than Hoffmann, and had married, at the insistence of relatives, a man nearly three times her age, one who could neither appreciate her

beauty nor understand her delicate sensibilities. The young teacher
of music and his pupil met on the common ground of artistic sensitivity and response. As Hippel wrote in his brief biographical sketch
of his friend: "A new world had arisen before him but at the same
time he had fallen into an ocean whose waves cast him anchorless this
way and that. He had won a heart that he could call his own but
still not possess; in daily visits lay the daily separation, and with
fullness of happiness the certainty of inevitable loss was mingled.
With the goblet of love's joy the bitterest of torments were meted out
to him." The hopelessness of the relation weighed heavily upon
Hoffmann; his love was a consuming fire that burned in the very
depths of his being.

The exceptional versatility of Hoffmann's later career was still
further foreshadowed during these university years, for he began
his work as a writer of fiction. How was it possible for a young man to
carry on legal studies to a successful, even distinguished, conclusion,
paint pictures, compose music, give instruction in music, and at the
same time write a long three-volume novel? The enigma is explicable
only on the assumption that the gods occasionally bestow diverse
gifts and the requisite energy to make use of them. Only the title of
this novel is known, *Cornaro, Memoiren des Grafen von S.* In
sending parts of the novel for Hippel's criticism, Hoffmann queries:
"Is the whole not a bit bizarre [buntschäckigt]?" It seems probable
that Hoffmann's adjective is correctly chosen, if, as has been reasonably conjectured, the immediate impulse to write *Cornaro* was supplied by Grosse's famous thriller *Der Genius* (The Tutelary Spirit).
When the publisher to whom Hoffmann sent the manuscript returned
it after a time, explaining that its anonymity was a barrier to publication, the youthful author was especially indignant at its soiled
condition, perhaps because it could not, thus uninviting, be sent out
again. Nothing daunted, he began another novel, *Der Geheimnisvolle* (The Man of Mystery), a title prophetic of later tales. A few
pages from the manuscript which Hoffmann included in a letter to
Hippel provide no hint as to the content of the story and might
indeed have been a part of the letter itself, had it not been for Hoffmann's introductory words and the quotation marks, for the fragment is from a letter to a friend in glowing asseveration of com-
radely devotion.

The months following Hoffmann's departure from the university
form a period of peculiar perplexity and despair. After his examinations ("Auskultator," July 22, 1795) for entrance into the

legal service of the Prussian government he waited long in understandable irritation for official action, and the work to which he was eventually assigned at the Königsberg courts brought him little but vexation. Conditions in the Doerffer household became more intolerable. The irritating qualities of his uncle Otto were inevitably more pronounced at sixty than at forty-five. And teasing him had ceased to be diverting: "Der dicke Sir is used up as a subject for my mockery and is too pitiful for my contempt." Into these days also fell the death of his mother, news of his father's serious illness, and a disturbing visit from his worthless older brother.[10] Music was his only consolation: "I should despair without my piano." He attended parties and balls, such festivities as Königsberg offered, but was bored. Apparently his relations with "Cora" became the subject of town gossip, however strict the effort to keep them secret. One might infer from a passage in one of his letters that he feared a challenge from her husband. Finally at a masquerade party early in 1796 some scandalous outbreak occurred. Hoffmann calls it a "bull-fight" (Stierszene), but the letter to Hippel in which he says he described the affair is missing in their correspondence. Either Hippel destroyed it or deleted the offending passages from one of the letters he preserved. This incident had, so Hoffmann wrote, "more serious consequences than I thought at the beginning." He saw no alternative but flight.

He proposed at first to go to Marienwerder, where his friend Hippel was living, but the family objected—perhaps Marienwerder was not far enough away. Then he suggested Glogau, and a letter was dispatched to another brother of his mother's, who occupied a prominent legal post there. His uncle, Johann Ludwig, who had been one of Hoffmann's sponsors at baptism, expressed his willingness to assist his nephew. Thus all was arranged for his departure, though silence was to be preserved until immediately before the date: "Then many will turn up their noses and gape, and either praise the fugitive or condemn him, according as the glass of their mood is

---

10 Of Hoffmann's older brother, Karl Wilhelm Philipp, three years older than Ernst, not much is known. On July 10, 1817, Hoffmann wrote a letter to him which was left unfinished and never sent. The content of the letter indicates that no communication had passed between them in many years. The letter itself was prompted by a letter from his brother, written in Cannstadt in Silesia, which he had recently received. At the beginning of the previous winter Hoffmann had been visited by a youth who told him that he was his brother's son and that his father was dead. The young man presented evidence of his identity, and Hoffmann gave him some money since he seemed to be in desperate straits.

polished through which they look at it."[11] This was late in February and the flight was set for early May. Time could not move fast enough for Hoffmann.

[11] "Denn werden manche Nase und Maul aufsperren, und den Flüchtling entweder loben oder verdammen, je nachdem das Glas ihrer Laune, wodurch sie's ansehn, geschliffen ist." *Briefwechsel*, I, p. 96.

CHAPTER 2

THE YOUNG LAWYER AND HIS PROFESSION

WITH boyish enthusiasm Hoffmann looked forward to the journey. At twenty-one he had never been more than a few leagues from his birthplace, a radius determined by the location of the country estates he had visited with his great-uncle. To him the journey was a high adventure, an escape into the great world; though the destination was Glogau, the road he was to travel was a road without an end. The wind-swept shores of the Baltic would recede into the distance and a sunnier clime would rise before him. Even in the passing of a few milestones—as it would seem to us today—he expected to discover, along with a radically altered climate, a change in the character of the people: close-lipped, long-faced northerners would yield place to the warmhearted, merrymaking men of the southland. Hoffmann seemed to think that Glogau was situated on the shores of the Mediterranean.

And yet when the time came, the separation from all he had ever known, the parting from one who had made his life in the immediate past a blissful torment, overwhelmed him. "I fled from my native city in a kind of stupor or intoxication," he wrote. Parting made him weak as water, and he was ashamed of the tears that he strove to keep back. "Then a desperate merriment took possession of me, and three times in succession I pulled on my trousers hindside before." The journey by post coach lasted several days, including an enforced week end in Posen to wait for a connection. Some incidents of the trip Hoffmann described in the style of Lawrence Sterne, whose *Sentimental Journey* was one of his favorite books. Hoffmann and Hippel had jestingly called one another Yorick and Eugenius.

A cordial welcome awaited the wanderer in Glogau. His Doerffer relatives there did at least something to justify the anticipated distinction between the north and the south. Not only was his uncle Johann Ludwig a prominent legal official but his house was a center of hospitality and social diversion. Hoffmann calls his aunt "an excellent woman," and the three young people, two daughters and a son, he found intelligent, lively, and amiable, although at the beginning his comment on the two daughters was somewhat critical. The household was then in a flutter of excitement in preparation for the marriage of the older daughter. The new cousin was immediately made one of the family and even complained that these agreeable

's acquaintance. Without more substantial evidence, this
ion of "M" remains merely a conjecture. Still less, despite
letter, could "M" have been Minna Doerffer, the younger
cousins, to whom he did become engaged some time later,
was a Roman Catholic. The irony that later forms so
element of Hoffmann's literary style, the capacity for
t and droll criticism of himself, appear in the narration
in which he almost declared his love:

ly I was in the company of this girl, in the happiest mood.
gtime sun, just setting, still cast its last rays through the
verything was in such a lovely atmosphere. Her form
hover in the motes that the sunbeams made visible, and
er toward her I felt her soft breath on my glowing cheek.
py and I wanted to tell her so. The word died upon my lips
ck six o'clock, and the flute music of the clock played
'Forget Me Not' in solemn tones. Her long eyelashes
und I sank back in my chair—two, three lines, I thought
ds:

nk dass ich's sey, wenn's laut in Deiner Seele spricht
giss mein nicht!'

lness vanished, and a fever chill cooled the glow that had
in me. Finally the notes became silent. 'It's past,' I said.
replied in muffled tones. I was about to throw myself at her
I thought of. . . ."[1]

ef friend of Hoffmann's Glogau days, outside of his uncle's
as an official in the Excise and Customs Bureau named
He is the only one here who thinks it worthwhile to attach
me." Hampe was an accomplished musician, later taking

war ich mit jenem Mädchen zusammen—in der frohsten Laune—die
e FrühlingsSonne warf noch die lezten Strahlen durchs Fenster—alles
eblicher Haltung—ihre Figur schien in den Atomen, welche der Strahl
chte, zu schweben, und ich fühlte halb zu ihr hinüber gebogen ihren
uch auf meiner glühenden Wange—ich war glücklich und wollt's ihr
Wort erstarb mir auf der Zunge, als es sechs schlug, und die FlötenUhr
che Vergissmeinnicht in feyerlichen Tönen spielte—die lange Wimper
senkte sich, und ich fiel in meinen Stuhl zurück—zwey, drey Verse, ich
e Worte:

enk dass ich's sey, wenn's laut in Deiner Seele spricht
ergiss mein nicht!'

nn schwand dahin, und ein Fieberfrost kühlte die Gluth, welche in mir
war! Endlich schwiegen die Töne—Es ist vorbey, sagt ich!—Ja—
sie dumpf—ich wollte ihr zu Füssen stürzen, da dachte ich an. . . ."
, I, p. 143. The attribution of the song "Vergissmeinnicht" to Mozart is

relatives would not let him alone
in all their social engagements.
cousin Ernst Ludwig, a jolly co
him, and he was downhearted lat
to enter the university. After th
families—or in those desiring t
household frequently spoke Frenc
musical, an accomplished singer,
mon diversion in the family. Hof
sins, probably also with friends,
marktsfest zu Plundersweilen. In

But new work, new companion
at once subdue the emotional fern
Hatt had induced. He tried to c
inconsistent with the carefree m
Reason told him that there was
"this despairing relinquishment
for a worn-out graybeard, not for
right to make demands of fortun
of reason. He confided in his uncle
further correspondence with "Co
mann's letters possible "exhibits"
disregarded this admonition an
neutralizing the softening influe
ceived her portrait, doubtless a
in Nova Zembla," with no warm
copy to which his "glowing fanc
October he began longingly to
companying his uncle on a trip
following year he was again in his
firm resolve to venture the utter
that separated him from the wom
a method of securing her divorce f
the tragicomedy of hopeless love a

According to the familiar adage
spaces and the human heart provi
A young lady in Glogau whom H
a temporary apprenticeship in th
the initial letter, it was all too easy
Rohrer, the Polish lady whom he
thetical visits to relatives in Glo

Hoffman
identifica
the initia
of his tw
for "M"
marked
detachme
of a scen
"Rece
The spri
window;
seemed t
leaning c
I was hap
as it str
Mozart's
drooped,
of the wo

'D
Ve

All joyf
risen wit
'Yes,' she
feet—the
The cl
family,
Hampe:
himself t

[1] "Neulic
untergehen
war so in
sichtbar m
sanften H
sagen—das
das Mozar
ihres Auge
dachte an

Aller Froh
aufgestiege
erwiederte
Briefwechs
incorrect.

Die Exorcisten.

3. "Die Exorcisten," One of the Series of Caricatures on the Napoleonic
Period

4. Sketch of a Soldier Shooting Down Unzelmann's Wig

up music as a profession. The two young men assisted the loyal people of Glogau in preparing a festival play to be performed in grateful recognition of the King's recovery from the measles. Hampe wrote the music and Hoffmann painted the scenery, appropriately enough, the temple of Aesculapius; the text was by another hand. Among the townsfolk participating was "Mlle. Doerffer" (Minna).[2] Other Glogau acquaintances were Julius von Voss, later a prolific novelist and dramatist, whom Hoffmann encountered in 1807-1808 in Berlin, and the Gräfin Lichtenau, the former mistress of King Frederick William II, who became the wife of Hoffmann's friend Holbein. For a time Hoffmann saw a good deal of the painter Molinari, who was engaged in the interior decoration of the Jesuit church. Though, as Hoffmann suggests, the legal authorities for whom he officially labored might have regarded it as a breach of professional decorum, he assisted Molinari in this work, an episode which he used in the story *Die Jesuiterkirche in G.* Association with a professional artist reawakened in Hoffmann's mind the question of his calling and provoked dreams of success as a painter. Molinari had spent much time in Italy and was soon returning there: "I unfortunately not," Hoffmann wrote. Italy was and remained his dreamland. Again and again he planned the journey southward; the trip is mentioned repeatedly in the correspondence with Hippel, and with the typical longing of the northerner for the southlands. The scenes of several of Hoffmann's stories are laid in Italy, in Venice, Naples, or Rome, and so accurate, so intimate, are the descriptions that one refuses to believe that he never walked the streets.

In the early summer of 1798 Hoffmann passed the second examination for legal posts under the government—the "Referendar" examination. Perhaps as a reward for his success he was granted a furlough and journeyed over the mountains to Dresden. It was his first pleasure trip, and they were few indeed in Hoffmann's life. His descriptions of scenery in the Silesian mountains, especially of the Zacken waterfall, have been cited as refutation of the prevailing opinion that he had little feeling for nature. They are unquestionably the product of an observing eye, to a certain extent the eye of an artist who sees with accuracy and understands how to assemble the elements into an artistic composition. But the inner vision that probes beneath the surface and makes the landscape a personal inter-

2 Cf. Hans von Müller: "Drei Arbeiten Hoffmanns aus den ersten Regierungsjahren Friedrich Wilhelms III," in *Deutsche Rundschau*, CLXVI (January 1916), pp. 57-85.

pretation is missing. One would not deny to him an appreciation of beauty in nature, but nature was not to him a living voice, not the intimate companion of his pilgrimage.

The Dresden Gallery was, on the other hand, an apocalyptic revelation; Hoffmann's dreams and visions had come true. To this experience he reverted again and again. Correggio's "Holy Night" "lifted him into Heaven" and before Raphael's Madonna he stood in reverence and awe. A few years later, in the barren wastes of· his Polish exile, he exclaims: "When shall I wander again in the fields of Paradise, when shall I see Dresden again?" To the artist in him the gallery was both a discouragement and an incentive. He could perceive the wide chasm that still separated him from the great masters, and he resolved for the time being to renounce color altogether and ground himself in the initial mastery of draftsmanship.

Presumably about this time—perhaps when he had passed the examinations for professional advancement—Hoffmann became engaged to his cousin Minna Doerffer (Sophie Wilhelmine Konstantine); no exact date is available.[3] Soon the Glogau Doerffers were thrilled by the official announcement that Hoffmann's uncle, Johann Ludwig, was to be transferred from provincial Glogau to a higher court in Berlin. Since Hoffmann was indubitably a very able young lawyer and now was betrothed to Minna, it was but natural that he should accompany his uncle's family to the Prussian capital, where a place was found for him as "Referendar" at the "Kammergericht."

Hoffmann arrived in Berlin on August 29, 1798. It was his first residence in a large city, and he reached out with both hands to grasp the new opportunities that were offered him—the opera, theater, concerts, and exhibitions of painting. Although his interest in music had slumbered a bit during the days in Glogau, save as a social asset in the circles where his uncle's family moved, it was now awakened in full force and he made some acquaintances of value in the musical and theatrical world. And Hoffmann aspired to be something more than an appreciative listener. His ambition to participate creatively

[3] The researches of Hans von Müller have made this engagement not only plausible but a well-nigh certain fact in Hoffmann biography. In his review of Harich's life of Hoffmann (*Zeitschrift für Bücherfreunde*, N.F., xiii, 1921, pp. 69-71), Müller is much too modest in emphasizing the conjectural aspects of his discovery. He says he has presented certain obscure periods in Hoffmann's development in separate studies (Arbeiten) in narrative style, "wiederum in schärfstem Gegensatz zu den Meinungen des 19. Jahrhunderts und mehr auf Grund von zum Teil gewagten Kombinationen als von aufgefundenen Dokumenten; so 1908 Hoffmanns Verhältnis zu der Cousine, die ich Minna nenne." But Hoffmann himself speaks of "Minna D" in a letter, and Müller's researches prove beyond the shadow of a doubt that the second of the Glogau cousins was thus called in the family.

took the shape of a "Singspiel," or drama with music, the text and music of which he had completed by March 1799. In charming naïveté he sent the manuscript of his little opera, *Die Maske*, to the Prussian Queen. The letter which accompanied it has not been preserved, but apparently he sought to interest Her Majesty in securing a performance of the operetta. An official reply suggested that he apply to the director of the Royal Theater.

Accordingly Hoffmann wrote to Iffland, who held that post, offering his play and filling nearly half the letter with fulsome flattery, the remembrance of which must have been galling in later years. When, belatedly, Iffland gave the play what consideration he thought it merited and decided to return it, the author was no longer "in loco," as runs the notation on Hoffmann's letter in the archives of the Royal Theater—he was already at his new post in Posen. The copy of *Die Maske* that Hoffmann sent to Queen Luise was found in 1922 in the library of the former Royal Palace in Berlin. It consists of four slender volumes, each of the three acts bound separately and the text in a fourth; the binding is neatly painted in sepia, doubtless by Hoffmann himself. Against the list of dramatis personae Hoffmann boldly, if not impudently, placed the names of the Berlin opera personnel whom he wished to take the roles, including among the really eminent, "Herr Fortuno," the stage name of his friend Holbein, who was a new and rather insignificant member of the company. The name of author and composer is nowhere indicated; thus the work was naturally catalogued as "anonymous." *Die Maske* is the only complete work in dramatic form which has been preserved. The scene is contemporary Athens, but with the exception of a German painter all the characters are Italians. It is probably mere coincidence and hence of slight moment that certain motifs used in later works, such as the jealousy of two brothers, appear in *Die Maske*.[4] At this time also Hoffmann composed a group of six songs which he tried unsuccessfully to get published.

From the social life in which the Doerffer household was soon busily involved Hoffmann could not remain aloof, especially in his new status as the betrothed of a daughter of the house. To his great

---

[4] The text of *Die Maske* was published by Friedrich Schnapp (Berlin, 1923), who found it in the library. He included three selections from the musical score and some interesting facsimiles, for example, of Hoffmann's letter to Iffland. The binding is in imitation of the volumes that the hopeful author sent to his Queen. The first account of *Die Maske* was published by Hans von Müller in *Drei Arbeiten Hoffmanns aus den ersten Regierungsjahren Friedrich Wilhelms III*; cf. note 3.

satisfaction his old comrade Hippel joined him in Berlin in the latter part of the following year. Hoffmann urged him to come to the great city, setting forth its attractions in brilliant colors and slyly suggesting that Hippel was burying himself in a remote corner of the world and leading a humdrum life as a country gentleman. Hippel was reminded of his own earlier plans, and, perhaps mindful of his uncle's hopes, responded to the message, deciding to prepare himself for service in the government. For two months the old friends were again in constant companionship, studying together as they had years before in the Doerffer living room in Königsberg, though now it was no longer Hippel who served as pilot. They took the examinations for the third advance in rank, the "Assessor" examination, Hoffmann obtaining a mark of exceptional excellence. In the early spring of 1800 Hoffmann was rewarded with a position in the legal administration of Prussian Poland and was sent to the city of Posen. The two friends left Berlin together and traveled by a rather circuitous route in order that they might visit Dresden, where Hoffmann could guide his friend to the glories of the great gallery.[5]

In Posen Hoffmann occupied bachelor quarters for the first time and was no longer directly or indirectly under the supervision of relatives with whom he lived. In Königsberg this control had imposed a galling servitude; in Glogau and Berlin he had acquiesced inevitably out of consideration for those whom he loved and respected, but it was nevertheless an unremitting discipline. Inevitably perhaps, Hoffmann was tempted to make full if not prodigal use of this new freedom. The young men connected with the civil administration of Poland, the parts of the old Polish kingdom recently acquired by Prussia, formed a decidedly merry crew, or "brotherhood" as Hoffmann called them, and for a time he was unquestionably one of the merriest. He was always scrupulous in the performance of professional obligations, but out of hours, so to speak, he plunged into a career of very dubious diversion. Perhaps conscious of frivolities that his friend would condemn he wrote to

---

[5] The whole period of Hoffmann's association with his uncle Johann Ludwig, which ended with his departure for Posen, presents an inner struggle between the artist and the burgher. To advance in the profession which he had chosen more or less under duress, it was essential that he devote his energies to an activity that was at variance with the inner artistic urge. But it is hard to agree with Schenck that his uncle tried to influence him into the pathway of the Doerffer traditions. Johann Ludwig had received the troubled nephew into his household and, apart from the relations that developed between Hoffmann and his daughter, doubtless felt morally bound to provide for him every opportunity for training and advancement in his profession, but the record affords no evidence of anything resembling the exercise of personal influence.

Hippel only once during his stay in Posen. In the autumn of the following year his grandmother died and he journeyed to Königsberg. Hippel, whom he arranged to meet in Danzig, hardly recognized in him the intimate friend of former years and was inexpressibly shocked at the change:

"An unwonted merriment which degenerated almost into buffoonery and a delight in the obscene caused one to suspect that some sort of change which had come over his heart, had turned him to the vulgar and especially to a certain lasciviousness which could not help being so much the more ruinous for him since the southern violence of his temperament always led him to extremes."[6]

Later, in retrospect, Hoffmann confessed that at the time he had become "what school principals, parsons, uncles, and aunts call dissolute; wine in the process of fermenting never tastes well, and I was then in ferment; a conflict of emotions, purposes, and so forth, raged within me, and I wished to benumb myself into insensibility." It is not difficult to perceive at least one of the perplexities that he sought to silence in a chaos of unworthy pleasures, a perplexity that was fundamental, ineradicable—his choice of a profession. At the outset he had indeed surrendered and was faithful to the law, by no means lacking interest in his work. But there was still the insistent voice within him fortifying the conviction that nature had intended him for something quite different. Could he never obey this higher call? Doubtless the local success of his music for Goethe's *Scherz, List und Rache* in a one-act version loosened the chains that bound him and opened the prospect of a more congenial activity. This play was performed during the New Year's period 1800-1801 and repeated several times later.[7]

[6] "Eine ungewöhnliche Lustigkeit, die fast in Possenreissende Skurrilität ausartete, und das Wohlgefallen am Obscönen liessen ahnen, dass irgend eine Veränderung, die sein Herz betroffen, ihn dem Gemeinen und besonders einer gewissen Lascivität zugewandt habe, die für ihn um so verderblicher seyn musste, als die südliche Heftigkeit seines Temperaments ihn immer auf Extreme führte." *Briefwechsel*, I, pp. 26-27.

[7] In 1902 Hans von Müller called attention to the fact that the attribution of this music to Hoffmann rested upon a "Randnote" in Hitzig's life of Hoffmann, where no source was indicated. Cf. "Hoffmann-Reliquien," in *Die Musik*, I (June 1902), pp. 1651-66. Of course, in view of Hitzig's many years of close intimacy with Hoffmann, the fact could have been communicated orally. Twenty years later Müller received information that seemed a partial confirmation of Hoffmann's work. A note from Jean Paul to Goethe (June 1801), in the Goethe-Archiv in Weimar, brought to Goethe's attention music for *Scherz, List und Rache*, given to Jean Paul by a young musician in Berlin: "Reichardt und andere Kenner geben ihm durch ihr Urtheil den Muth, das Ihrige zu wünschen" (cf. Hans von Müller: *E. T. A. Hoffmann und Jean Paul*, pp. 35, 39-40, 89, 102). Jean Paul had just married Caroline Mayer, one of Minna Doerffer's closest friends. Hoffmann mentions the score of *Scherz, List*

Probably also in his early days in Posen Hoffmann began to be troubled by the possible unwisdom of another choice, his betrothal to Minna Doerffer. As early as October 6, 1800, he wrote to Hippel that he was anticipating a visit to Berlin in the immediate future; he lamented certain aspects of his bachelor existence and was thinking of marriage—a plan which his uncle Otto opposed as something "too hasty and juvenile." Previous to his departure from Berlin he had been in almost daily association with Minna for nearly four years, and it would be mere guesswork to suggest that this journey was designed, perhaps unconsciously, to test the validity of the attachment after less than a year of absence. Perhaps in the meantime a counter attraction in Posen had begun its influence. Certain it is that within a little more than a year, probably early in 1802, he broke the engagement, obviously, then, an act of matured deliberation. After a long silence, indeed after his marriage, Hoffmann wrote to Hippel (January 25, 1803): "Perhaps by chance you have received news from B[erlin] of the tragic end of the second love episode in my life?" and in the next letter: "If I were writing this autobiography with the conscientiousness of Rousseau, who was willing to step before the judgment seat of the Eternal with his Confessions under his arm, Minna D. would in friendly fashion offer me her hand—not in reconciliation, no—because I was guiltless— when everybody cursed me and censured my faithlessness. I have forcibly annulled a relationship which would have made her and myself unhappy."[8] These are the only direct references to his engagement in the correspondence with Hippel, who must have known of the engagement during his stay in Berlin, but various passages in the letters from Glogau suggest that Hoffmann's rigid devotion to professional work was in part prompted by the prospect of marriage.

His decision to break the engagement may be interpreted, though perhaps not conclusively, in terms derived from several of his later stories, notably *Der goldene Topf*, as a protest of the artistic spirit

und Rache in his review of Beethoven's Egmont music and in the third of the *Briefe aus den Bergen*, but without reference to the name of the composer. The composition was credited to him in Brockhaus' *Conversations-Lexikon* (1818-1819).

8 "Vielleicht hast Du durch Zufall einige Nachrichten von dem tragischen Ende der zweiten Liebesepisode in meinem Leben aus B[erlin] erhalten?" "Schriebe ich diese SelbstBiographie mit der Gewissenhaftigkeit Rousseaus der mit seinen Bekenntnissen unter dem Arm vor den Richterstuhl des Ewigen treten wollte, so würde Minna D. mir die Hand—nicht zur Versöhnung nein—weil ich schuldlos war—als mich alles verwünschte und den treulosen schalt—freundlich bieten.—Ich habe mit Kraft ein Verhältniss vernichtet, welches sie und mich unglücklich gemacht haben würde." *Briefwechsel*, I, pp. 187, 190-91.

against the fetters of ordinary domesticity. Minna was a clever, well-educated young woman, apparently also a forceful personality, and six months older than her cousin. Already in Glogau, but incomparably more in Berlin, she was immersed in an ocean of social activities into which Hoffmann would inevitably have been drawn. Outside of his professional duties he would have been subjected to the strait jacket of social conventions, a torture chamber from which there would have been no escape. On the one hand there is, or seems to be, freedom and on the other acquiescence in rigid, meaningless formulas. The conflict between the artist soul and bourgeois living is a real one, and some of the great masters of fiction have portrayed it. Hoffmann extricated himself in time.[9]

Hoffmann's lodgings in Posen were in the same house with one of his colleagues, the Regierungsrat Johann Ludwig Schwarz, to whose autobiography, *Memorabilia from the Life of a Businessman, Author, and Humorist,* one is indebted for information on a period of Hoffmann's life when his letters are few. Schwarz was himself, as the title of his autobiography indicates, well equipped for friendship with the newcomer, and his wife reviewed books for literary periodicals and wrote several novels. Hoffmann moved into a congenial environment. For the celebration of the beginning of the new century Schwarz and Hoffmann prepared a cantata for performance in Posen, Schwarz writing the text and Hoffmann the music. It was given on the night of December 31, 1800, and was received with at least local esteem. Schwarz sent a copy of the cantata to Queen Luise. Remembering *Die Maske*, did Hoffmann perhaps propose it as a jest?[10]

At the home of a colleague, Kriminalrat Gottwald, Hoffmann met Maria Thekla Michalina Rohrer (Polish, Trzinska), whom he

[9] Minna Doerffer never married. She lived for many years in the family of her Berlin friend Adelheid von Gerlach (Frau von Bassewitz) in Potsdam and Halle. She died in 1853 (cf. Hans von Müller: *E. T. A. Hoffmann und Jean Paul*). Despite the breaking of the engagement, Hoffmann seems to have maintained friendly relations with his uncle and his cousin Ernst. In Bamberg he wrote twice to Minna's mother, May 30 and September 11, 1809, and in 1816 he sent portraits of their common uncle and aunt, Otto Wilhelm and Sophie, to a "verehrte Cousine," whether to Minna or to her older sister (Frau Henriette Korn), whose marriage took place soon after Hoffmann's arrival in Glogau, is not evident from the letter, which gives no address. Hans von Müller assumes Minna to have been the recipient, but Ellinger suggested the older sister to Max Morris, the publisher of the letter (*Euphorion,* xx [1913], p. 366). The letter implies some communication between Hoffmann and his cousin in the time previous to the letter and a knowledge of and perhaps an interest in Hoffmann's success with *Undine.*

[10] Cf. note 4. Schwarz's autobiography was entitled: *Denkwürdigkeiten aus dem Leben eines Geschäftsmanns, Dichters und Humoristen,* Leipzig, 1828.

married in 1802. She was the sister of Gottwald's wife and a daughter of a former secretary of the city government when Posen was still a Polish city.[11] She was called by the third of her three baptismal names or by the endearing diminutive "Mischa." Michalina was at this time nineteen or twenty years old, a young woman of rare beauty, with slender figure, dark brown hair, and deep blue eyes. She had neither intellectual gifts nor wealth, but she had a loving, faithful heart, and through varying and distressful fortunes she remained a devoted companion to her capricious and at times desperately impoverished husband. With her Hoffmann could enjoy just as much of normal domesticity as he desired and otherwise walk his own pathways and dream his own dreams. A year and a half after marriage, he wrote to Hippel: "I should have to despair, or rather I should long since have given up my post, were it not that a dear, dear wife sweetens all the bitterness that I am compelled to drink here to the dregs, and strengthens my spirit so that it can bear the dead weight of the present and even retain strength for the future."[12]

The Prussian civil authorities stationed in Posen were not on the best of terms with the military—a not unusual phenomenon! Drawn mostly from the aristocracy, the army officers disdained both the government officials and the solid citizenry of the town. The situation was materially exacerbated by the arrival of a new military commandant, General von Zastrow, who with contemptuous arrogance drew the lines of social exclusiveness even more rigidly. The social world of Posen was deeply resentful, and after a time several of Hoffmann's friends concocted an audacious plot by way of vengeance. Hoffmann was induced to sketch a series of caricatures which were manifolded and distributed at a great ball on Shrove Tuesday 1802. Two of the conspirators, disguised as picture vendors, attended to the distribution in such a way that at first a caricature did not fall into the hands of the person caricatured. Thus there was general merriment, but later, when the sketches were passed around, there was a change of mood. General von Zastrow was represented as

[11] Doubtless Hoffmann was placing the matter in the best possible light when in a letter to Hippel nearly a year after his marriage he raised Michalina's father to the rank of a former "Stadtpräsident." In the combined last will and testament of Hoffmann and his wife, her name appears as Maria Tekla Michalina; in the church record of her death it is given as Marie Thecla Michielina, *Briefwechsel*, II, p. 754.

[12] "Ich müsste verzweifeln, oder vielmehr, ich würde längst meinen Posten aufgegeben haben, wenn nicht ein sehr liebes liebes Weib mir alle Bitterkeiten, die man mir hier bis auf die Neige auskosten lässt, versüsste, und meinen Geist stärkte, dass er die Centnerlast der Gegenwart tragen, und noch Kräfte für die Zukunft behalten kann." *Briefwechsel*, I, p. 187.

a regimental drummer; with two teaspoons he was beating on a tea-pot hung about him like a drum, and calling out, "Au thée! au thée!" Other despised officers and titled personages were similarly held up to ridicule. Hoffmann's talents had not been hidden under a bushel, and the identity of the artist was as plain as that of his victims. Indeed he must have been naïvely unsuspecting if he fancied there could be any mystery about it. The irate general immediately dispatched a denunciation of the offending civil servant to the authorities in Berlin—it was rumored, by express messenger that very night.

Hoffmann was at that moment a candidate for promotion to the rank of "Regierungsrat." The civil authorities had to take some notice of his flagrant misdemeanor, but in view of his unquestioned attainments were doubtless loath to carry the punishment too far; it is not impossible that they were secretly sympathetic to his misbehavior. The promotion was granted but Hoffmann was transferred to Plock. This town on the Vistula had recently become a more important outpost of Prussian administration through the transference there of offices formerly at Thorn. After a journey to Plock in search of living quarters, Hoffmann returned to Posen to make Michalina his bride. The Roman Catholic ceremony took place on July 26, 1802, in the Corpus Christi Church.

Despite its new political importance Plock was hardly more than a dull Slavic village and it seemed to Hoffmann to be on the very border of the civilized world. His stay there was, he wrote, "an exile which is destroying my very soul," and again: "Were I only out of this damned hole!" "I wander here in a swamp among thorn bushes which tear my feet till they bleed"; extreme effort is required not to sink completely into the morass. This sentiment he expressed in a bitter caricature: the people of Plock are represented as buried in mud and slime; Hoffmann alone, through supreme energy, keeps his head above it, but from Olympian heights his superior officer reaches with a mighty pole and tries to force him down into the bog. "Now I live as a saint doing penance," he wrote, "or rather as any Christian should live—in the hope of a future life." He worked "like a horse" among the dust-covered documents of the court and tried to resist their power to bury him.

Yet this exile had a salutary influence. The utter absence of social life such as he had enjoyed in Posen left vacant hours which his restless spirit sought to fill. He studied musical theory and according to Hitzig began to write an essay on the sonata as a musical form;

and he turned with renewed interest to musical composition. This interest was in part stimulated by the music in the cloister churches in Plock. He was able to perceive the excellence of a musical score, of a mass, for example, even though the singers "shrieked like owls." He was deeply moved by an Incantus in G minor, and yet the nun sang the part "so that one could only to a certain degree make head or tail out of it [nur einigermassen so dass man daraus klug werden konnte]." And he began to compose masses for performances in these cloisters. An advertisement by the music publisher Nägeli in Zürich offered a prize for a piano composition. Hoffmann presented a "Grosse Phantasie für das Klavier" and signed himself "Giuseppi Dori aus Warschau"; in spite of Nägeli's unfavorable comment he then sent him a sonata, as a proof "that just censure does not offend me." A few acquaintances in Plock evinced some interest in music, and with three of them Hoffmann founded an instrumental quartet, but as with the music in the nunneries his own satisfaction came largely from the music he heard with the inward ear rather than from the performance of the ambitious amateurs. He was "enraptured by the heavenly harmonies of Haydn," though the playing was abominable, beneath all criticism, "like everything else in this horrible hole." Activity with paint and brush was resumed. Industriously he copied the pictures of ancient vases in the Hamilton collection,[13] and he wrote to Hippel that he had made great progress in painting and had attained something like perfection in getting a likeness. He would, he said, paint portraits of Hippel, his wife, and children, when he came to see them. But only a few weeks later he became discouraged and wrote that he had put his painting aside.

Literary ambitions stirred again. He wrote an essay on the use of the classical chorus in the drama, with particular reference to Schiller's *Die Braut von Messina* (The Bride of Messina), then recently published. It was entitled "Sendschreiben eines Klostergeistlichen an seinen Freund in der Hauptstadt" (Letter of a Cloistered Friar to his Friend in the Capital City), and appeared in Kotzebue's magazine, *Der Freimüthige*, September 9, 1803. For the first time Hoffmann saw his work in print. "Twenty times I gazed upon the magazine with sweet loving glances of paternal joy"; "happy prospects for a career in literature," are the entries in his

---

[13] Either *Collection of Etruscan, Greek, and Roman Antiquities from the Cabinet of William Hamilton*, Naples, 1766-1767, or *Antiquités étrusques, grecques, et romaines gravées par F. A. David*, Paris, 1787. For an account of the residence in Plock, cf. Hans von Müller: "E. T. A. Hoffmann in Plock," in *Deutsche Rundschau*, CLVII, pp. 418-45; CLVIII, pp. 84-117.

diary. The thoroughness with which he always prepared for his work is already evident in this first publication; he scanned the classics for information as to the music of the ancients.

He also wrote a play for a prize that Kotzebue was offering in the same periodical—a comedy, *Der Preis* (The Prize), in which he cleverly used the competition itself as a theme for his play. The text itself is lost, but an outline of the plot appeared in the report of the contest. The letter to Kotzebue accompanying the comedy is amusing as the work of an unpracticed hand in such matters, a mixture of half-concealed pride and self-depreciation. Hoffmann calls his play a "bungler's job," and he adds a curious postscript: "If the whole work should be regarded as a slip of the pen, the author would dedicate it to that one of the Areopagus [that is, the jury for the prize] who has curls or curls his hair—it is on fine soft paper."[14] As the prize was fairly substantial, one hundred Friedrichs d'or, Hoffmann's interest in competing was doubtless in part prompted by the chronic financial stringency in his household affairs. The report on the competition was printed in the issue of *Der Freimüthige* for February 11, 1804. Fourteen plays were examined, but none was found worthy of the award. Hoffmann may have felt some satisfaction that no one else won the prize, and he had considerable reason for gratification in the treatment of his play in the report: "Among all the contestants the author of this comedy, with the possible exception of No. 4 [a play called *Harlekins Wiedergeburt*] has the most talent for writing comedy; the public can probably expect good things [viel Gutes] from the author."[15]

In view of Hoffmann's literary ambitions at the time, it may seem strange that he did not respond to this encouragement; he did indeed try, but without success, to get his play published. The two dramatic fragments, *Der Renegat* and *Faustina*, also written in Plock, as "Singspiele" or operetta texts, may represent a further attempt to unite an interest in dramatic form with his cultivation of musical composition. Of the former, five scenes of the first act are preserved;

[14] Hoffmann uses the same expression in a letter written at about the same time. He is appealing to Hippel to use whatever influence he may have in certain quarters to rescue his friend from the exile in Plock, and encloses a letter to a superior official, which can be sent, if circumstances seem favorable, but if not, "it can, if S[chleinitz] or someone in the family wears curls, be used for curl-papers. It is fine white paper, and the assurances as to zeal in service will certainly make the hair curl splendidly." Schleinitz, president of the Kammergericht, had married a sister of Hippel's father-in-law.

[15] *Der Freimüthige: Ein Unterhaltungsblatt,* herausgegeben von A. von Kotzebue und G. Merkel, II (1804), Literarischer und artistischer Anzeiger . . . No. 6, pp. xxi-xxiv.

the scene is laid in Algiers and the little play was probably suggested by Mozart's *Abduction from the Seraglio*. The fragment *Faustina* contains only the dramatis personae and two pages of text; eighteenth century Venice was to have been the background of the play, and the leading characters prominent Italian musicians of the day— the German composer Hasse, and Faustina Bordoni, the great Italian singer who became his wife.[16] These fragments, together with *Die Maske*, written previously in Berlin, and the one act of *Prinzessin Blandina*, a Märchen comedy in the manner of Tieck, written in Leipzig in 1814, constitute Hoffmann's sole use of the dramatic form.[17] In spite of dramatic situations in his stories and his keen sense of dramatic effect, as evidenced both in his writings on the drama and in his work at the Bamberg theater, it seems plain that he did not find the form of the drama congenial for his own creative work.

During Hoffmann's residence in Plock his uncle Johann Ludwig died in Berlin and his aunt Sophie in Königsberg. In a quizzical letter to Hippel, Hoffmann ponders upon the eternal question— the inscrutable ways of divine wisdom in allowing death to take one person and leave another—his uncle Johann Ludwig, a useful worker with family and friends, and his other uncle, Otto Wilhelm, a "lonely, forsaken old bachelor, on whose continued existence nothing depends, who accomplishes nothing in any field and is bored from the hour when he rises in the morning till at the stroke of nine he goes to bed again. Why did *he* have to remain alive?" From his aunt Sophie Hoffmann expected to receive an inheritance that would relieve an acute financial embarrassment, by no means the last in the Hoffmann household. Impatiently he waited for news and then set out posthaste for Königsberg. The old house in the Junkergasse which had once been like a prison cell was now filled with memories that time had softened, and the "O Weh Onkel" of other days, once fussy and imperious, was merely a pitiful, broken old man. A chance meeting with the daughter of "Cora" Hatt set chords of emotion faintly stirring "in sweet unknown melody." "Cora" herself was dead. This

---

[16] "Der Renegat" and "Faustina" were first published from the manuscript by Hans von Müller in *Die Musik*, III (1903). "Zwei unvollendete Singspiele von E. T. A. Hoffmann." They are reprinted in Ellinger's edition of Hoffmann's works, xv, pp. 20-34, and in Harich's edition, XII, pp. 491-511.

[17] One might include as dramatic work *Die Pilgerin* and *Wiedersehen*, two "prologues" which Hoffmann composed for special court festivities in Bamberg, and, with less assurance, the revision of dramatic texts into opera libretti. Hoffmann's share in the dramatizing of Fouqué's *Undine* was doubtless considerable, as is suggested by his correspondence.

meeting was a dramatic close to these days, the last Hoffmann ever spent in his native city. Time moved "at snail's pace" in Plock while he waited for his release. Eventually, in part through the efforts of Hippel and connections Hippel had gained by his marriage, the authorities decided to transfer Hoffmann from Plock to Warsaw.

One of the most important "happenings" of Hoffmann's stay in Plock was his decision to keep a diary. The entries, beginning October 1, 1803, continue, with long interruptions indeed, into the year 1815, and naturally form an invaluable source for the biographer. The diary is a curious document, quite unlike most journals which have ever seen the light in printed form. It was not intended for any eyes but his own, though there is evidence of his expectation that Michalina might cast a prying if not suspicious eye upon it. Hoffmann interjects phrases in Latin, French, and Italian, and in Plock already he began to write German words and sentences in Greek letters, all this, after the pattern of Samuel Pepys, obviously calculated to cheat feminine curiosity. The diary contains multitudinous bits of information not recorded elsewhere—dates, references to the work of a day (musical or literary), the books he read, his meeting with friends and acquaintances. The earlier entries while he used a notebook for the purpose are longer and more detailed; later entries, by far the larger part, were made in the calendar type of diary, where there was little room for expansion.

Often the record of a day or a series of days consists of a single jotting which designates the content of the time or describes his mood, such as: "Oct. 18, 19, 20, 21, 22, 23, 24, 25—Dies tristes et miserables," or more cryptically: "January 25, 26, 27, 28, 29, 30, and 31. Ohe! Ohe!!!" He employs a considerable number of adjectives, often without the word "mood" to describe his state of mind, as "fantastic," "pleasant," "morose," or "mood of exaltation"; occasionally the single word "nothing" or "dies ordinarius." Following his youthful admiration for Rousseau's *Confessions* he intended to rival his master's pitiless candor in the disclosure of himself. With amusing but tantalizing frankness he writes: "On May 11 precisely at 8:30 I was an ass." Frankness is also exemplified in the constant acknowledgment of conviviality; the pages are plentifully sprinkled with entries concerning the wines and punch that made an evening memorable and even the amount consumed: "Drank Bishop's punch afternoon and evening." In the dubious effort to deceive Mischa he frequently used an ideograph, a diminutive goblet —Mischa was indeed naïve!

The Hoffmanns arrived in the former Polish capital in April 1804 and found quarters in the Fretagasse, up three flights. Warsaw was, to be sure, a royal city, but as such its external appearance was somewhat disconcerting, a princely capital but at the same time a Slavic market borough. Spacious and elegant public buildings, the palaces of officials or the very rich stood cheek by jowl with wretched little hovels. Hoffmann found the city "noisy, mad, wild, confusing."

"It is astonishingly lively in Warsaw, especially in the Fretagasse, for here there is a thriving trade in flour, groats, bread, and green vegetables.... Close under my window certain differences have arisen between three female flour vendors, two pushcart men, and a boatsman's boy. All appealed to the tribunal of the huckster who carries on his trade in the cellar below in the midst of his wares—during this time the bells of the parish church, of St. Benno, and the Dominican Church (all close at hand) were ringing, and in the churchyard of the Dominicans (directly above me) the hopeful catechumens were beating two old kettle drums; responding to their mighty instinct, the dogs of the whole neighborhood barked and howled—at that moment Wambach, the equestrian performer, came merrily riding along to Janissary music—out of the New Street a herd of pigs came to meet him—great friction in the middle of the street—seven pigs are trampled down. Great squealing! Oh!—Oh! the whole invented for the torture of the damned!"[18]

Hoffmann was sitting at the piano composing a sonata. In this untimely interruption he compared himself to Hogarth's "Enraged Musician," and throwing down his pen he escaped into the park.

As ever, he was professionally correct, but now he began openly to cultivate a subordinate career as a musician. He soon became a leading, if not the leading, figure in the musical life of the Polish city. The time and energy required for his legal duties were grudg-

[18] "Lebhaft ist es in Warschau erstaunlich, vorzüglich in der FretaGasse, da hier Mehl, Grütz, Brodt und GrünzeugHandel ganz ausnehmend blüht. . . . Dicht unter meinem Fenster entstanden zwischen drey Mehlweibern, zwey Karrenschiebern und einem SchifferKnechte einige Differenzien, alle Partheyen plaidirten mit vieler Heftigkeit an das Tribunal des Höckers, der im Gewölbe unten seine Waaren feil bietet—Während der Zeit wurden die Glocken der PfarrKirche—der Bennonen—der DominikanerKirche (alles in meiner Nähe) gezogen—auf dem Kirchhofe der Dominikaner (gerade über mir) prügelten die Hoffnungsvollen Katechumenen zwey alte Pauken, wozu vom mächtigen Instinkt getrieben die Hunde der ganzen Nachbarschaft bellten und heulten—in dem Augenblick kam auch der Kunstreiter Wambach mit JanitscharenMusik ganz lustig daher gezogen—ihm entgegen aus der neuen Strasse eine Heerde Schweine—Grosse Friction in der Mitte der Strasse—sieben Schweine werden übergeritten! Grosses Gequike. —O!—O!—ein Tutti zur Qual der Verdammten ersonnen!" *Briefwechsel*, i, p. 206.

ingly given, for his professional tasks were "a loathesome chrysalis which strove to confine the fair pinions of the artistic spirit until they break through." In part by his efforts the Musical Society or Academy of Music in Warsaw was founded and took possession of an old dilapidated palace, the Mniszek Palace. Here through interior reconstruction a spacious hall was provided where Hoffmann, for the first time an orchestral leader, conducted the music of Mozart, Gluck, and Beethoven. His talents as a mural painter were employed in the decoration of the new home of the Academy. Those who came to consult him on legal matters often found their authority seated high on a scaffold with paints and brushes, but when he descended they encountered in him the keenest of legal minds.

Previous to their departure from Plock, the Hoffmanns had received Mischa's little niece as a member of the family. Her father, Gottwald, one of Hoffmann's companions in Posen, had been caught in misappropriation of funds, had been arrested, but had escaped from prison into the unknown, with a severe sentence hanging over his head. A year after the arrival in Warsaw Hoffmann's first and only child was born, a little daughter whom they named Cäcilie. At the time he was composing a solemn mass for full orchestra and in honor of the newcomer he gave it to the nuns of St. Bernard's cloister for performance on St. Cecilia's Day.

Life in Warsaw was in pleasant contrast with the dull existence in Plock. The city fascinated Hoffmann with its strangeness and its variety; it offered much also in the way of entertainment, such as the theater, both Polish and German. Also, he soon found himself a member of a very congenial group—young men interested in literature and music, among them friends of enduring value and significance. It was here that Hoffmann met Julius Eduard Itzig, a most devoted and generous friend throughout the remainder of his life and his first biographer. Later, when baptized into the Christian Church, he changed his name to Hitzig, the name by which he is usually known. Hitzig arrived in Warsaw a few months after Hoffmann and was also employed in the legal administration of Prussian Poland. They lived next door to one another, and on the same floor, so that they talked to one another out of neighborly windows, and Hitzig listened with delight to Hoffmann's piano playing, often late in the night.[19]

[19] Other members of the group were Kuhlmeyer, solicitor to the Prussian government; Morgenroth, a violinist, also there in government service, but poised, as it were, for escape into professional work as a musician; and Heinrich Loest, later a

Here too Hoffmann met Zacharias Werner whom he had known slightly in boyhood. The Werners had lived on an upper floor in the same house with the Doerffers in the Junkergasse. Zacharias' father was a professor in the university and had served as one of the godfathers at Hoffmann's baptism. The mother, who had become a widow in Hoffmann's boyhood, exercised a curious fascination upon him, which was perhaps the beginning of his absorbing interest in abnormal mental states, for she was insane. She suffered from fantastic delusions, and at times thought herself the Virgin and her son the Saviour of the world.[20] Hoffmann's acquaintance with Werner in those days was only casual, for Zacharias was eight years older— an impassable gulf in boyhood. Werner was a man of extraordinary gifts, which, save for his unbalance and his excesses, might have gained for him a place of high distinction in German literature; as it is, his dramas must still be reckoned with in any estimate of dramatic writing during the Romantic Period. At this time he was, like Hoffmann, in government service, as secretary of the Prussian "Kriegs- und Domänenkammer," but he had already achieved a reputation in the literary world, had published a volume of poems and the drama *Die Söhne des Tals* (The Sons of the Valley).

During these days Werner was working on a new play, *Das Kreuz an der Ostsee* (The Cross by the Baltic Sea), a tragedy with the historical and legendary background of the conflict between the Teutonic Knights and the heathen people of East Prussia. For the first part of this drama, *Die Brautnacht* (The Bridal Night), Werner induced Hoffmann to write music for choruses and for the accompaniment of a certain scene; in a letter to Hippel, Hoffmann described this part of the play in detail. Werner wished to send the play to Iffland, director of the Royal Theater in Berlin, for presentation and tormented his collaborator day and night to finish the music at a stipulated time (Er lag mir immer auf dem Halse und quälte mich). It was doubtless of value to Hoffmann, though hardly recognized at the time, to participate, as it were, in the birth throes of a literary work. But he had already begun to perceive the faults in Werner's character: "Werner is a sad proof," he said, "of how the most superb endowment can be slain by a stupid upbringing and

---

poet of some note. Hans von Müller's monograph *Heinrich Loest über Hoffmann*, Köln, 1922, I have been unable to examine.

[20] That Werner's mother suffered from this particular delusion in Werner's youth rests solely on Hoffmann's statements. Düntzer assigns it to the latter part of her life. Cf. H. Düntzer's life of Werner in *Zwei Bekehrte* (Leipzig, 1873), p. 39.

how the liveliest fancy must learn to crawl, if it is drawn down by an inferior environment."[21]

In 1806 the roar of cannon began to resound nearer and nearer over the Polish plains. As Hoffmann was always indifferent to all political concerns until he himself became entangled in them, one might almost say that he awoke one morning and found the Prussian government overthrown and Napoleon's troops in possession of the city. Prussia's Polish empire, obtained in the three successive divisions of that unhappy country, had crumbled. This overturn deprived all Prussian officials of their positions and their livelihood. With or without the sanction of the Berlin authorities, they divided the local treasury among themselves, perhaps, as Hitzig records, so that it would not fall into the hands of the enemy, and went their own ways. For the sake of economy Hoffmann moved his family into the palace of the "Musical Society," "under the roof," as it stands at the heading of a letter. For a time at any rate, the improvident musician could live on the money taken from the Prussian treasury.

The work of composition had not been abandoned during his more exciting life in Warsaw. At the end of the first year, in April 1805, Hoffmann's musical setting for Brentano's *Die lustigen Musikanten* (The Jolly Musicians), written the preceding December, was performed in the German theater in Warsaw.[22] Another operetta (Singspiel) *Der Kanonikus von Mailand*[23] and a mass for full orchestra were composed in the year 1805. Now, relieved of professional obligations, Hoffmann plunged into an astonishing productivity as a composer, in quantity and range rivaled only by the years in Bamberg—overtures, sonatas, motets, canzonets, his harp quintet and piano quintet. Since the new French regime in no way interfered, he continued to conduct the concerts in the great hall; his own "First Symphony in E Major," composed in 1806, was performed several times.

But a less precarious existence for himself and his family had to be

[21] Schenck's opinion that Zacharias Werner exercised a strong influence on Hoffmann in Warsaw, an influence he never outgrew, seems quite unsubstantiated by any available evidence, certainly not by Hoffmann's letter to Werner, June 28, 1806, to which Schenck refers.

[22] According to Hans F. Schaub, the playbill of the performance called the composer of the music simply "einen hiesigen Dilettanten." Schaub was reviewing the first *German* presentation of the operetta, in Hamburg, 1924 "Eine E. T. A. Hoffmann Ausgrabung," in *Allgemeine Musikzeitung*, LV, pp. 149-50.

[23] Hoffmann hoped to place *Der Kanonicus von Mailand* on the Berlin stage and sent the score to the great actor Bethmann, hoping he would influence Iffland to produce it; at the same time he wrote to Werner, then in Berlin, to enlist his support. Cf. *Briefwechsel*, II, pp. 16-20.

sought, for this way of living could not go on indefinitely. With this aim in view, Hoffmann sent his wife and the two children—for Mischa's niece was still with them—to Mischa's mother in Posen (January 1807), and determined to try a hazard of new fortunes in the musical world. A serious illness delayed his departure. Yet even while critically ill Hoffmann was dreaming his new melodies, and in convalescence he wrote to Hitzig: "Since the time when I could begin work in composition, I often forget my cares, even the whole world. For the world of a thousand harmonies which is built up at my piano in my room is irreconcilable with any other world outside." The dream world was the real world after all. Hoffmann wanted Hitzig to remind Werner—both were now in Berlin—that he was still counting on Werner's writing a "Faust" for him to set to music; he would, he said, be unwilling to give up this "favorite" idea of his; indeed even now, sitting at the piano, he was composing music for "Faust."

Hoffmann remained in Warsaw a little over six months after the beginning of the French occupation. Hitzig urged him to try Vienna and provided him with letters to his wealthy relatives there. Above all others Hoffmann would have preferred the imperial city on the Danube with its musical traditions and its animated musical life. Yet he had misgivings: to a Prussian, Austria was a foreign country, and, almost penniless, he might have difficulty in bridging over the period until he could establish himself there. Berlin was musically far less promising, particularly after the collapse of Prussian fortunes in the war with Napoleon, but he had friends there to help him. Eventually the question was decided quite apart from his own choice. The Prussian officials still lingering in Warsaw were suddenly confronted with the necessity of swearing allegiance to a foreign government or leaving the country within a week. As a man of honor Hoffmann could accept only the second alternative, but the authorities refused him a passport to Vienna. After a visit with his family in Posen he arrived in Berlin on June 18, 1807.

The year that followed—Hoffmann's second residence in Berlin—presents a bleak and tragic picture. Only a couple of months after his arrival he received news that his little two-year-old daughter was dead and his wife seriously ill. Also, his efforts to secure a living even for himself were unrewarded; what chance was there for an artist to gain a footing in a defeated and impoverished city like Berlin? He toiled and waited; he trod the pavements in alternate hope and despair. He tried every expedient, sought in vain to get orders for portraits, to earn a pittance by offering caricatures for sale,[24] or to sell some of his compositions. He even appealed to the King, seeking to obtain money he thought due him through the loss of his position in Warsaw—a loss surely by no fault of his own. Though officially his plea was rejected, he did receive a small sum from Stein, then the Prussian chancellor.[25] In time starvation came to knock at the door; Hoffmann wrote to Hippel that for five days he had eaten nothing but bread; half insane from worry, he was wandering in the Tiergarten when an acquaintance found him there and shared with him what little he himself had. Hitzig was living in Potsdam and was in the main ignorant of his friend's extremity.

In these unhappy days Zacharias Werner again crossed Hoffmann's pathway. The needy musician sought the privilege of composing music for a drama by Werner which was to be performed in Berlin. It seems a pardonable bit of envy when in a letter to Hippel Hoffmann records the honors which had been bestowed upon his former friend.[26] Since he had left Warsaw, Werner's star had risen: he had been presented to the King of Bavaria, had associated on terms of intimacy with the Duke of Gotha, and was at the time visiting in Goethe's house in Weimar—Goethe had received him most cordially and commented favorably on his works. A little later Werner returned to Berlin. He hinted mysteriously that he had plans for the future in which Hoffmann would play a part, but in the meantime Hoffmann busied himself from morning till night preparing drawings for Werner's *Attila*, expecting if successful to receive four or five Friedrichs d'or, a sum of sovereign importance in his plight. The capricious Werner, however, gave the order to another artist. Werner himself earned a good deal of money, and what Hoffmann calls his "filthy greed" was especially disgusting; it did not belong in the "soul of an artist."

A few years later when Hoffmann is trying his own wings as a man of letters, he discusses Werner in the dialogue of *Berganza*. Werner is the dog's specimen of a "speckled" (gesprenkelt) char-

24 Several of these caricatures which had fallen into the hands of Kunz and are now in the Staatsbibliothek in Bamberg were recently published by Leopold Hirschberg: *Sammlung grotesker Gestalten nach Darstellungen auf dem K. National-Theater in Berlin*, Berlin [1922].

25 Cf. Hans von Müller: "E. T. A. Hoffmann als 'Regierungsrat' und als 'verjagter Offiziant,'" in *Mitteilungen des Vereins für die Geschichte Berlins*, xxxix (1922), pp. 58-65.

26 Letter of December 12, 1807. Cf. Hoffmann's entry in his diary more than a year later, in Bamberg (May 26, 1809): "Werner hat vom Fürsten Primas eine Pension von 1000 fl. erhalten—eine Nachricht die sonderbar auf mich wirkt—welcher Fürst wird künftig [was] für mich thun."

acter. To men of this type one cannot deny intelligence, depth, or even spiritual qualities, but they surrender willingly to the common vulgarities of everyday living, are egotistic, selfish, poor husbands and parents (Werner was divorced from three wives), and faithless friends; some sin on their part, if only a violation of good taste, betrays the innate lack of taste. Unfortunately Hoffmann himself violates good taste in exposing, while Werner is still living, the tragic situation in the Werner household and the insane delusions of Werner's mother.[27]

Berganza was written during a time of great emotional turmoil, and Hoffmann dipped his pen in acid. Later, in the discussions of the Serapion Brothers, he saw Zacharias Werner with more kindly eyes. To be sure, less than a decade had passed, but time is a relative concept, especially in the shaping of human character, and in these years Hoffmann had lived more than many men do in half a lifetime. He had matured and mellowed, and death itself was only a brief span distant. Since Hoffmann's last meeting with him Werner had forsaken his wayward ways and at times dissolute habits, and had developed into a reality the affectation of religious devotion and Christian mysticism which had intermittently characterized him. In Rome he had abjured the Protestant faith, had studied Roman Catholic theology and been consecrated a priest. The churches in Vienna where Werner was to preach were thronged, and his fame was spread abroad by the people of different lands who attended the famous Congress. He died in 1823, only a year after Hoffmann.

Hoffmann's adverse criticism was altered not only by time and distance but also by Werner's own humble acknowledgment of his weaknesses in the preface to *Die Mutter der Makkabäer* (The Mother of the Maccabees), which, though written at an earlier period, was the last of his dramas to be published during his lifetime (1820). Hoffmann forgets the disparaging comment that he voiced in his letters to Hippel from Warsaw and remembers only the happy time when Werner was his friend. He even characterizes him as the most good-humored and amiable man imaginable; even the fantastic flourishes (Schnörkel) of his appearance and of his nature con-

---

[27] "Er hielt sich für einen Auserwählten Gottes, der die Geheimnisse einer neuen geläuterten Religion verkünden solle; mit innerer Kraft, die ihn das Leben an den erkannten Beruf setzen liess, hätte er ein neuer Prophet, oder was weiss ich, werden können; aber bei der angebornen Schwächlichkeit, bei dem Kleben an den Alltäglichkeiten des gemeinen Lebens, fand er es bequemer, jenen Beruf nur in Versen anzudeuten, ihn auch nachgerade zu verleugnen, wenn er seine bürgerliche Existenz gefährdet glaubte." I, p. 135.

tributed to make him a most attractive and delightful companion in whatever environment he might be found. At the session of the Serapion Club Theodor (Hoffmann) produces a drawing of Werner, dating apparently from their days in Warsaw, and his companions of the brotherhood are much impressed by the humor, the roguish wit, the human qualities of his face, joined to the evidences of a mystic bent, and they propose to make him an honorary member of the club.

Hoffmann bases his revaluation upon the psychological problem involved in Werner's youth, the peril to a sensitive and imaginative spirit in the constant association with an insane mother who stamped upon the malleable mind of the boy her frenzied notions of his divine unlikeness to other men. Werner stood, as it were, between his mother's fantastic dreams for his future and his own highly developed sensual nature. Hoffmann has now a sympathetic understanding for the human struggle in the life of his erstwhile friend.

In his need Hoffmann appealed to Hippel for a loan, reluctantly, for Hippel was himself far from wealthy at the time. Through adverse circumstances and the political overturn his great inheritance had dwindled away. In the summer of 1807 Hoffmann inserted an advertisement in the *Allgemeiner Reichsanzeiger*, setting forth without false modesty his attainments as a musician and composer and his acquaintance with the theater; he desired a position as director of music or as producer in a theater. Though in the meantime he was offered a place as assistant in a music publishing house in Leipzig, he delayed making a decision until the results of the advertisement should appear. He much preferred to be active in the production of music than to be concerned merely with publishing the work of others; in addition, the salary was inadequate and the long and rigid hours of service that were stipulated would have been intolerably irksome. From Lucerne and Bamberg came answers to the advertisement, and negotiations were entered upon with Graf Soden,[28] the director of the Bamberg theater. In the spring of 1808 a definite offer was made and accepted: Hoffmann was to commence work on the first of September. Despite the thoughtful invitation of

[28] Graf Soden requested Hoffmann to compose music for an opera text he had written, *Der Trank der Unsterblichkeit,* and for a play with music (Melodram), *Joseph in Ägypten;* Hoffmann sent the finished score of the former to Soden on February 27, 1808. In the *Zeitschrift für Bücherfreunde* (N.F., xvi, 1924, pp. 104-9) Oskar Krenzer published the only letter yet discovered out of Hoffmann's correspondence with Soden. It contains interesting comment on the use of the chorus in drama, on the "Melodram," showing that Hoffmann had continued to reflect upon the problem of the *Sendschreiben eines Klostergeistlichen* and related questions.

Graf Soden that Hoffmann spend the intervening period on his estate near Bamberg, Hoffmann elected to pass the summer with his old friend Hampe in Glogau. Not only was Hampe a friend whose companionship he much prized, but this arrangement made it both easier and less costly to journey on to Posen in order to accompany Michalina to her new home.

The days of suffering and despair in Berlin were not without some lasting values. With hopes centered in a career as a musician, Hoffmann devoted much of his time to composition, and some of his work at the time may be reckoned among his most distinguished compositions, for example, a Requiem, and six songs for the church; three of the latter, "Ave Maris Stella," "O Sanctissima," and "Salve Regina," appear as compositions of Kreisler in *Kater Murr*. Disappointment attended most of his efforts to dispose of his compositions, but three canzonets with Italian and German words and piano accompaniment were published by Werkmeister in Berlin and were favorably reviewed by the *Allgemeine musikalische Zeitung* (June 23, 1808), the reviewer referring to Hoffmann as already "Musik-Direktor" in Bamberg; indeed, in the issue of June 9, the journal had announced Hoffmann's appointment with comment upon his competence for the position.[29] Thus his name was beginning to be known in the musical world.[30]

From Hoffmann's correspondence it is evident that he became acquainted, however casually, with some of the prominent men of letters in Berlin.[31] It would have been strange if his old friend Hitzig had not interested himself in furthering such acquaintance. Hitzig had become associated with the publisher Reimer and was presently (1808) to establish himself as bookseller and publisher. Previous to his residence in Warsaw, he had associated with literary groups in Berlin

[29] "Man kann dieser Bühne zur Acquisition eines so gründlichen Komponisten, so erfahrnen Singmeisters und überhaupt so talentvollen, gebildeten und achtungswürdigen Mannes, Glück wünschen."

[30] Hitzig's statement that Nägeli in Zürich published two piano sonatas and a harp quintet lacks confirmation; the notice of Hoffmann's appointment in the *Allgemeine musikalische Zeitung* mentioned "drey grosse charakteristische Klaviersonaten" soon to appear "bey Nägeli."

[31] Cf. letter to Hippel, December 12, 1807: "Fichte und Schleiermacher sind wieder hier. . . . Varnhagen, Chamisso, Winzer, Robert sind Dir gewiss unbekannte Namen, indessen nenne ich sie Dir, als junge höchst talentvolle Leute, die uns gewiss viel, viel gutes liefern werden"; letter to Hitzig, 1807: "Gestern war ich von 7½ bis 8½ bey Mad. Levi, wo viele Leute *Thee* mit *Rum* tranken und vernünftige Gespräche führten, von 9 Uhr bis 11½ bey Winzer eingeladenermassen, wo wieder viele Leute *Rum* mit *Thee* tranken—ich lernte Bernhardi (hat ein hübsches Gesicht), Schleiermacher, vor allen Dingen aber den Componisten Schneider kennen." *Briefwechsel*, ɪ, p. 222; ɪɪ, pp. 34-35.

and now increasingly extended his connections with the literary world, becoming a close friend of most of the Romantic authors there. For Hoffmann this stay was a kind of initiation into the artistic world of the Prussian capital, and he had not long to wait before he himself belonged in that world.[32]

[32] For a rather unsympathetic account of Hoffmann during this stay in Berlin, cf. Friedrich Holtze: "Ernst von Tettau und E. T. A. Hoffmann," in *Mitteilungen des Vereins für die Geschichte Berlins*, xxxix (1922), pp. 53-58.

CHAPTER 3

IN the spring of 1793 two youths, Ludwig Tieck and Wilhelm Heinrich Wackenroder, set forth from Berlin to pursue their studies at the University of Erlangen in southern Germany. Like minstrels or artisans of the Middle Ages, they journeyed on foot. The emotional response to their experiences gradually increased to a culmination point when they reached the medieval cities of Bavaria. The great northern plain lay behind them, flat, dull, and sunless, the abode of sterile rationalism, and before their longing eyes the diversified landscape of the Southland rose, colorful and picturesque, with its ancient walled towns, crumbling castles, its cathedrals and churches where a mystic religious faith still held sway in alluring contrast to the sober, white-washed Protestantism of Berlin. And Bamberg was one of the cities of their pilgrimage. This journey of Tieck and Wackenroder was a milestone in the history of German Romanticism.

Hoffmann's pilgrimage to southern Germany was a decade and a half later, but it aroused a similar enthusiasm in the new Prussian wanderer. In Poland he had already read something of Tieck, probably of Wackenroder, and the year in Berlin had brought him into preparatory association with some of the local Romantics. By nature sympathetic to much in Romantic doctrine, Hoffmann had absorbed what was most congenial to him, to be transformed in the course of time into emotional and spiritual values that were all his own.

Bamberg lies in a charming valley, surrounded by lovely wooded hills; through the city runs the little river Regnitz in two branches. Upon a slope in the center of the town rises the superb medieval cathedral, one of the great monuments of Romanesque architecture. Without and within it is adorned with some of the most glorious carvings of the medieval sculptor, and memories of emperor, knight, and saint haunt its shrines. Other churches there are also—Romanesque, Gothic, and Baroque, with their monuments and treasuries of other days—and princely structures, largely of the Baroque period, for Bamberg was not only the seat of a prince-bishop but the residence of a Bavarian duke. If Hoffmann's dream of Italy was never realized, he could still feel that Bamberg was both literally and figuratively halfway there.

Hoffmann and Michalina arrived in Bamberg on September 1,

1808, and Hoffmann entered upon a most significant period of his life, in many ways determining the course of the years to come and leaving ineradicable scars of emotional experience. Unfortunately for the biographer, out of the four years and a half he spent in Bamberg there are irritating gaps in the diary, including one whole year and half of another. At first lodgings were found in the house of a dyer at Zinkenwörth 56, but before long the Hoffmanns moved to No. 50 in the same street, into the house of one Warmuth, who played the trumpet in the court orchestra.[1] It was a very modest apartment, one large room occupying the whole of the third floor and a tiny chamber under the roof, but in prospect at any rate Hoffmann was happier than he had ever been before. The long tyranny of legal statutes and technicalities seemed at an end. At last he was established as a musician and to the new work he could devote his undivided energies. About this time Hoffmann began to substitute "Amadeus" for "Wilhelm" in his name, out of admiration for Wolfgang Amadeus Mozart,[2] and one is tempted to connect the change with this entrance into really professional life as a musician. Legally, of course, his name remained unchanged; he used the names given him in baptism in his later professional life at the courts in Berlin, and he appears as Ernst Theodor Wilhelm in his last will and testament. But the name taken in sentiment or in caprice has clung to him almost to the complete rejection of his real name.

But professionally Hoffmann soon found conditions that dampened his enthusiasm and outraged his artistic ideals.[3] During the negotiations with Hoffmann, Graf Soden, director of the Bamberg

[1] Cf. C. G. von Maassen: "E. T. A. Hoffmanns Bamberger Wohnung," in *Süddeutsche Monatshefte* iv² (1907), pp. 426-30; Oskar Krenzer: *Hoffmann in Bamberg*, Bamberg, 1922.

[2] This explanation of the unofficial change of name is generally accepted. One can perceive a characteristic jest in Hoffmann's own explanation as reported by Hippel: that the initial "W" was "ein Schreibfehler auf einem der ersten Manuskripte, und da ich einmahl mit dem 'A' coursire und die Münze gangbar ist, so mag ich nichts daran ändern." This obviously does not betray why the "A" was converted into "Amadeus." In *Kater Murr* Kreisler gives St. Chrysostom's Day, January 27, as the date of his birth, the birthday of Mozart.

[3] Cf. Werner Mausolf: *Hoffmanns Stellung zu Drama und Theater*, Berlin, 1920; Carl Schaeffer: *Die Bedeutung des Musikalischen und Akustischen in E. T. A. Hoffmanns literarischem Schaffen*, Marburg, 1909; and especially Rudolf Köppler: *E. T. A. Hoffmann am Bamberger Theater*, Bamberg, 1927. Köppler regards Hoffmann's strictures on the Bamberg orchestra entirely unjustified; as orchestral conductor Hoffmann was then merely an amateur, with only the Warsaw experience behind him; Köppler thinks, apparently, that in pique Hoffmann transferred his own incapacity to the orchestra. He seeks also to defend Cuno against Hoffmann's criticism; the failure of the theater was largely due to war-time conditions, which drove the wealthy patrons from the city, not to Cuno's stupidity and mismanagement.

theater, had surrendered his position to "a certain Heinrich Cuno" and left Bamberg for Würzburg. Upon acquaintance Cuno proved to be an "ignorant, conceited windbag" and in his hands the whole enterprise, a combined theater and opera house—as was, and still is, customary in small cities—was tottering to disaster. The orchestra that Hoffmann was to direct was wretched; with dubious tact Hoffmann wrote to his friend, the violinist Morgenroth, that the concert-master Dittmeyer "plays at least twelve times worse than you"; the bassoons sounded like "combs," the horns like "jews-harps," and the violins like pasteboard covers. Some of the players were possessed of boundless conceit and were never happier than when turning things upside down. There was a monstrous to-do about the directing of the orchestra—whether the director should stand in front playing the violin or direct from the piano. Hoffmann expected too much from the Bamberg audiences and in time was sorely disillusioned, though they doubtless differed little from the so-called musical public everywhere; some were capable of keen and intelligent appreciation and others covered their real ignorance and indifference by a cloak of irritating pretence. Within two months Hoffmann withdrew from his duties as director of music, though he retained the now empty title as of possible value in the future. He composed, however, incidental music for the performances—ballets, marches, choruses, and the like. The compensation was niggardly and was not always paid.[4]

To provide for a decent existence Hoffmann sought pupils in music and found them apparently in considerable numbers, as he says, "among the best families." With an exclamation point he notes in a letter to Hitzig that he is instructing five countesses. To a musician, particularly to a creative artist, such an occupation is likely to be a dismal financial stopgap. Whatever real satisfaction may be obtained from a few gifted pupils is swallowed up in struggles with the incompetent and the indolent. But Hoffmann faced the situation with courage.[5]

[4] In the spring of 1809, when Hoffmann foresaw the coming collapse of Cuno's enterprise, he heard from a friend in Dresden, presumably Morgenroth, that the position of director of music in Breslau was to be vacant. Hoffmann wrote to Breslau, but apparently the matter ended with his inquiry. Cf. Georg Jensch: "Ein verschollenes Klaviertrio von E. T. A. Hoffmann" in *Zeitschrift für Musikwissenschaft,* II (October 1919), pp. 23-43. Hoffmann resented the advice of a friend (Seckendorf) that he renounce music and establish himself in legal practice.

[5] He also earned an honest penny by small commissions in purchasing music for his pupils from the firm of Breitkopf und Härtel. Cf. Hans von Müller: "E. T. A. Hoffmann als Musikalienhändler," in *Süddeutsche Monatshefte* IV2 (December 1907), pp. 666-79.

In still another way he sought to add to his income. One of the connections with the musical world tentatively established during the unhappy Berlin days now bore fruit. From Berlin he had sent some of his musical compositions to Dr. F. Rochlitz, the general musical director for the great publishing house of Breitkopf and Härtel, until recently one of the chief publishers of music in the world. Dr. Rochlitz thought well of the compositions, but they were not accepted for publication. Now from Bamberg Hoffmann wrote to Rochlitz, offering his services as a regular contributor to the *Allgemeine musikalische Zeitung* of which Rochlitz was the editor. His appeal was successful and during the following years he published articles and reviewed numerous musical works in this journal, then the most important periodical of the kind in Germany. With his letter to Rochlitz he sent the manuscript of *Ritter Gluck*, partly a highly imaginative story, partly an interpretation of Gluck as a composer of opera. It appeared in an early issue of the journal (March 1809), and thus was the beginning of Hoffmann's career as a writer of fiction. The following year he sent Rochlitz the first of the *Kreisleriana* in which he painted the first strokes on the portrait of the eccentric musician, the most interesting creation of his genius, and at the same time a baffling portrait of himself. Some of his musical compositions were published by Breitkopf and Härtel and by Nägeli in Zürich, bringing him an occasional but ever-welcome honorarium.

But fortune had still in store a satisfying employment in Bamberg. In September 1809 Soden had—probably reluctantly—assumed again the responsibility for the Bamberg theater, but surrendered his post to a new organization, formed by prominent citizens, which was intended to supply financial backing for the undertaking. About a year and a half after Hoffmann's arrival, Franz von Holbein, whom Hoffmann had known during his first residence in Berlin, was invited to the post of director, quite possibly at Hoffmann's suggestion. He immediately asked Hoffmann to work with him as theater composer, theater architect or designer and decorator, thus engaging in his service something of Hoffmann's rare versatility. He also secured excellent talent for the performances, and a resplendent period in the annals of the Bamberg stage began.

Hoffmann wrote music, designed and executed the *décor* for play after play. He became absorbingly interested in the mechanics of stage production and was modestly proud of his success in inventing novel scenic effects, such as the castle in *Käthchen von Heilbronn*, which burns and falls in ruins before the eyes of the spectator, or the supernatural apparition of the cross in Calderon's play *Die Andacht zum Kreuz* (La Devoción de la Cruz). He was also influential in the choice of plays for the repertoire—Shakespeare's *Hamlet*, the German classics, Goethe, Schiller, and Lessing, Kleist's *Käthchen*, and the more important dramas of Iffland, Kotzebue, and others; the latter were what the taste of the time demanded, however low in the scale of dramatic values they seemed to Hoffmann. Particularly noteworthy were the splendid performances of several plays of Calderon in the translation of August Wilhelm Schlegel.[6] His hope to produce some of Shakespeare's comedies was never realized. Hoffmann earned a place among the great producers in the history of the German stage.

The brilliance of Hoffmann's conversation soon rendered him a welcome guest in Bamberg society, though at first invitations were probably sent in the expectation that he would "favor" the company with some musical selections. To preserve his position and further his interests, such invitations had to be accepted, however stupid the gathering, however distressing to accompany on the piano the young ladies of Bamberg who could not sing. The torture of these hours is revealed in the *Kreisleriana*. The ready tongue that had alienated him from boyhood companions now answered the bidding of a mature, incisive mind in witty and whimsical sallies, often a shade too sharp and pungent. His evenings he spent regularly, when not invited into Bamberg society, in convivial companionship at the "Rose," a tavern the name of which is spread large over the pages of his diary. The company often drank far into the night, Hoffmann entertaining the others by his scintillating wit and occasionally by daring caricatures. He was the center of the group and provided stimulus for the merrymaking, infectiously transmitted to others who without him might have been rather dull fellows. By common consent the master of ceremonies, he relentlessly showed the door to all whose stupidity proved incorrigible. Not infrequently he passed hours at the tavern alone in the afternoon over his work and his wine. In pleasant weather he often walked out to a country tavern by the riverside in the little village of Bug (Buch).

His most constant companion was C. F. Kunz, who united the seemingly incongruous professions of wine merchant and proprietor

---

[6] Hoffmann may have been encouraged to bring the Spanish dramatist to the Bamberg stage by Goethe's production of Calderon's *Der standhafte Prinz* (El Príncipe constante), January 30, 1811.

of a lending library.[7] Many of his books he obtained in exchange for his wines, and Hoffmann once wrote to Hitzig, then a bookseller and publisher in Berlin, proposing a barter of this sort and recommending a fiery Burgundy such as he remembered to have been a favorite with Hitzig. Toward the end of his stay in Bamberg, Hoffmann signed a contract with Kunz according to which the latter was to publish Hoffmann's literary work, for Kunz was adding to his other professions that of book publisher. The contract is preserved; in it appears for the first time the title of Hoffmann's collection of tales, the *Fantasiestücke in Callots Manier* (Fantasy Pieces in the Manner of Callot). Other friends were the physicians Marcus and Speyer, uncle and nephew, and for a time the eminent actor Leo. Marcus and Speyer were both scholars in medicine and medical theory, interested in new developments, especially in those concerning the relations between the mind and the body. Dr. Marcus was head of the insane asylum St. Getreu, and, like the famous Dr. Koreff, whom Hoffmann was to know intimately in later Berlin days, he made use of hypnotism in his treatment of certain ills. Also like Dr. Koreff, he doubtless stimulated in Hoffmann the interest in curious and occult phenomena of mind and body which is manifested in so many of his tales. Dr. Marcus was also a man of wide cultural interests; he was the leader in the plan for the reorganization and regeneration of the Bamberg theater. Hoffmann prized highly the friendship of both uncle and nephew.

Presumably Hoffmann also saw something of F. G. Wetzel, who came to Bamberg at the end of 1809 as editor of a local journal. Later Wetzel assisted Kunz in his work as a publisher. In a letter to Kunz, Hoffmann asks whether Wetzel has not made certain changes

---

[7] As is noted later, Hoffmann's regard for Kunz gradually diminished after his departure from Bamberg, until there was something like a real break between them. Kunz's reminiscences of Hoffmann were first published in the periodical *Phönix* in 1835 under the title "Supplemente zu E. T. A. Hoffmanns Leben," and then reprinted in his book *Aus dem Leben zweier Dichter* (1836). In the *Phönix* Kunz published some letters from Hoffmann to himself as additions to the reminiscences (1837). Kunz proved himself in many ways unworthy of Hoffmann's friendship. In the reminiscences he sought to exploit his relations with men of distinction, and demonstrably emended or perhaps even forged communications from Hoffmann in such a way as to emphasize their intimacy and claim a share in his literary development—such, for example, as his alleged participation in the selection of Fouqué's *Undine* as a text for an opera. He showed lack of consideration for the feelings of others in the publication of personal gossip, and at times treated Hoffmann's memory with scant reverence. But, as the diary gives ample evidence, they were in close, almost daily, companionship during Hoffmann's stay in Bamberg, though even then there were disagreements. Cf. letter to Dr. Speyer, May 1, 1920, *Briefwechsel*, II, pp. 399-409, also II, pp. 84, 85, 163-64, 190, 211, 319.

in his manuscript, and in another letter he sends greetings to Wetzel
and submits to Wetzel and Kunz the question of descriptive chapter
headings in *Der goldene Topf*. Wetzel was probably the author of
the appreciative and intelligent review of *Der goldene Topf* in the
Heidelberger Jahrbücher der Literatur. His authorship of *Die
Nachtwachen von Bonaventura*, one of the most characteristic but
still baffling products of the Romantic Period, is still open to
question.[8]

In her husband's social life Michalina participated very little.
Hoffmann spent a large part of his time outside the apartment, and
the accounts he gives in letters to Hitzig of her contentment and of
their quiet domesticity are highly colored. There is record of an occasional walk together, an afternoon in the tavern at Bug, a dinner
invitation in which Michalina is included—for example, a birthday
party for Kunz—that is about all. Since the death of Cäcilie, who
might have cemented their union, husband and wife had to a certain
extent grown apart. Hoffmann continued to respect his wife, to be
fond of her indeed, and to appreciate her faithfulness. In his conversation he often attributed to her fictitious cultural attainments and
was indignant if others seemed in any way to suggest skepticism—it
was a little game he played.[9] She remained to the end the mistress of
his household and he cared as best he could for her well-being. There
is no really trustworthy evidence that he was ever technically unfaith-
ful to her, yet his heart was prone to wander elsewhere, and his
conscience, doubtless in remembrance of the Gospel injunction, leads
him once in remorseful frankness to write in his diary the words
"adultery in thought" (geistiger Ehebruch).

For an overmastering passion seized him: he fell in love again with
one of his pupils, this time not a married woman but a young girl. The
passion was equally hopeless, and there is no evidence that he ever
thought of it otherwise, as he did in the case of "Cora" Hatt, but his

    [8] *Die Nachtwachen von Bonaventura* was for many years—and with considerable
assurance—attributed to Schelling, also to Caroline (Schlegel) Schelling, and indeed
to Hoffmann himself. Cf. R. M. Meyer: in *Euphorion*, x (1903), pp. 578-88 and Gottfried Thimme: *Euphorion*, xiii (1906), pp. 159-84. For Wetzel's authorship, cf. Franz
Schultz: *Der Verfasser der Nachtwachen von Bonaventura*, Berlin, 1909, and for
Brentano's, Erich Frank: "Clemens Brentano der Verfasser der Nachtwachen von
Bonaventura," in *Germanisch-Romanische Monatsschrift*, iv, pp. 417-40, and Frank's
introduction to a new edition of the *Nachtwachen*, Heidelberg, 1912. A discussion of
the possible influence of some of Wetzel's works on Hoffmann would lead too far
afield: Schenck's parallels are far from conclusive (*E. T. A. Hoffmann: Ein Kampf
um das Bild des Menschen*, pp. 86-95).
    [9] Ellinger very generously and, perhaps one may say, gallantly, comes to Mischa's
defense: as an unpretentious woman with natural feelings and reactions she may in
her opinions have often hit the nail on the head.

infatuation bore him on irresistibly like a mountain torrent. Julia
Marc lived in Bamberg with her widowed mother; Herr Marc had enjoyed the title of "Consul," and the widow was usually addressed in
Bamberg society as the "Frau Consulin." Hoffmann's friend Dr.
Marcus, who had retained the original spelling of the name or had
Latinized it, was Julia's uncle, and Dr. Speyer her cousin. Mother
and daughter moved in the best circles and in such a way as to suggest considerable affluence. Julia was possessed of a thrilling,
matchless voice and a fine musical intelligence, and she responded
admirably to Hoffmann's instructions. Not only did they meet at
the house of Frau Marc, but she sang under Hoffmann's guidance or
in duets with him at concerts and informal musical evenings in
Bamberg society, and they danced together at numerous balls. The
vigor of his infatuation was not lessened by his characteristic capacity for detachment and self-criticism. That he was a married man of
thirty-five and Julia a girl of only fifteen[10] at the beginning of his
enchantment was a fact by no means lost from view—"irony about
myself, somewhat as in Shakespeare where people dance about their
open grave," yet to be ridiculous in his own eyes was only a momentary curb on his emotions. For a time there was a slight coolness in
his relations with Dr. Speyer, whom Hoffmann suspected of influencing the Marc family against him: "Speier [Speyer] is a
wretched knavish Mephistopheles," he wrote in his diary.

The entries in Hoffmann's diary with reference to Julia, almost
daily for many months, may seem absurd, but they have still a tragic
undertone. To screen the situation from Mischa's inquisitive eyes he

[10] Juliana Eleanora Marc was born March 18, 1796. It has seemed expedient to
retain the spelling "Marc," since it is the form most frequently employed in Hoffmann literature. There would be equally good reason for writing "Mark," the spelling that Hoffmann uses exclusively in his diary. From grandnephews of Julia,
Maassen gathered information concerning the family, including material derived
from family papers. It appears that the names "Marc" and "Mark" were used somewhat interchangeably, especially in different branches of the family. After Julia's
separation from Gröpel she married a cousin, Dr. Louis Marc; her second marriage
was a very happy one. They lived in Arolsen, and she was apparently much admired, both for her social gifts and her occasional participation in local musical
events. Her tombstone reads: "Julie Marc, geb. Mark, geb. den 18ten März 1796,
gestorben den 16ten März 1863." Cf. C. G. von Maassen: *Der grundgescheute Antiquarius*, II, Heft 2-3 (January 1923), pp. 71-84, "Julia Marc-Reliquien"; and Hans
von Müller in Appendix to *Briefwechsel*, II, p. 635. Kunz calls Hoffmann's infatuation for Julia Marc an inexplicable mystery. According to him, Julia was pretty,
blooming (blühend), and amiable, but her coloring was more Netherlandish than
Italian and her "plumpness" more "à la Rubens" than "à la Raphael"; she possessed a good understanding and a childlike spirit, but she was without a poetic
spark. What Hoffmann says of her is only a reflection of himself. Cf. Funck (Kunz):
Aus dem Leben zweier Dichter, p. 87.

used a symbol for Julia, "Ktch," an abbreviation for Käthchen and a reference to Käthchen von Heilbronn, the heroine of Kleist's play of that name. Hoffmann spoke of this drama as one of three in all dramatic literature that had most moved him, and it was brilliantly performed in Bamberg under his direction. It is improbable that Julia Marc bore any strong resemblance to Käthchen von Heilbronn except in Hoffmann's imagination. She belonged to aristocratic and relatively sophisticated circles in a ducal city, while Kleist's heroine, despite her Cinderella-like emergence at the end of the play as the daughter of the emperor, is a simple bourgeois maiden, whose whole being is absorbed, mysteriously and supernaturally, in selfless love. Perhaps the name Hoffmann gave Julia meant merely what in his dreams he wished her to be. For days in succession the brief entries in the diary, often only three or four lines, end with the symbol repeated several times with exclamation points. The entries for the third and fifth of February 1811 are typical—except for the words "at home":

[Feb] "3 A.M. Lesson at Marc's—then to Holbein's—P.M. likewise—then to Buch [Bug]—back late—to the theater—highly vexatious mood—excessively romantic and capricious—De profundis clamamus—Evening drank punch at the 'Rose.' "

[Feb] "5 A.M. Lesson at Marc's—P.M. at Kunz's—then to Holbein's—at home—to the children's ball—Ktch: plus belle que jamais et moi—amoureux comme quatre vingt diables—excited [mood]—to Kunz according to invitation—Drank [symbol] in the evening—good humor. (Finished the sextet.)"

On the twenty-eighth of the same month, he writes: "Either I shoot myself like a dog or I shall go mad."

Not only did Hoffmann visit the home of the Marcs for the frequent music lessons but he was also often there for tea or for an evening. Probably Frau Marc became aware of his attitude toward her daughter, and in view of the ardor of his feelings he must have been a consummate actor to be able to conceal them. Once he passed a dreary evening there, for, he says, Frau Marc had purposely sent Julia to the theater. It appears evident that she sought to make him conscious of his social inferiority; one day Hoffmann records "an infamous, murderously vexatious quarrel" with her, adding the words "depreciation" and "wounded pride." On the next day he spoke to Holbein of his firm resolve to leave Bamberg. At times a possible escape to Italy dangled before his eyes; early in January 1812 he writes: "There must, there must be a decision made—Roma

—Roma tu eris mihi salutaris," and "Italia" in huge letters. He repeats the beginning of the Latin phrase a few days later, and "Ktch-Ktch-Ktch," "ruin hovers over me and I cannot avoid it." The ardent lover struggles with his passion; an evening at the Marcs passes without the customary flood of emotion, and he writes humorously: "Käthchen on the wane." On the theory that "one stroke of lightning may put out another," he tries the fruitless experiment of a flirtation with one of the actresses or with the wife of his friend Kunz; on April 19, 1812, he writes: "Inamorato nella S[i]g[nora] K[unz] come il diavolo," but only a few days later: "Indifference toward the Inamorata because Ktch was so surpassingly beautiful when I met her." With his musical genius he labored to do her honor. For her he composed three Italian canzonets, finishing them in the feverish agitation of a painful illness so that they might greet her on her birthday; to her also he dedicated six Italian duets, and the arias "L'acciar ti rendo" and "Mi l'agnero tacendo." The latter appears in *Kater Murr* as the favorite song of Kreisler and Julia Benzon. Mischa was not unaware of her husband's infatuation, and his diary records unhappy domestic incidents.

But what from the beginning was destined to happen, happened. The house of the Frau Consulin, with its glitter and social distinction, was founded on the sands. To save the family fortunes from bankruptcy, it was essential that Julia should marry wealth. On March 26, 1812, Hoffmann writes the fatal words on the margin of his diary: "Gröpel Hamburg merchant arrived." A few days later, dining with Dr. Speyer at the "Rose," he hears the rumor that this visitor is to marry Julia. Gröpel, however, departs within a brief time, and no announcement is made. The wretched and suspicious lover displays unwarranted resentment, and Julia punishes him with coldness and reserve, though he blindly characterizes her conduct toward him as "intolerable rudeness." Yet a reconciliation soon follows, and, as the weeks go by and no evidence of a betrothal is forthcoming, the old relations are resumed. Perhaps clutching at straws, Hoffmann finds Julia more inclined to intimacy than before, though he cannot forget the unconfirmed report. He writes the word "esperanza" in his diary, not a "hope" for himself but a hope that the rumored marriage will not take place. On August 8, however, Gröpel returns, and the betrothal is announced. Two days later Hoffmann writes in Italian: "It's all over (the blow is struck). The lady has become the betrothed of that accursed shop-keeper, and it seems as if all the poetry and music in my life are extinguished—it is necessary for me to form a resolution worthy of a man such as I believe myself to be. This was a devilish day."[11]

And yet he still goes to the house, and Julia sings his own duets with him, as he says, "con molto espressione," adding in Italian: "The ass of a fiancé is very jealous and this fact causes me much pleasure." A few weeks later, September 6, the Marcs arrange a picnic at Pommersfelden to which a considerable company is invited, including Hoffmann and Mischa.[12] Both Gröpel and Hoffmann drink too much, and an unpleasant if not disgraceful scene occurs. Gröpel, grabbing at Julia for support, falls reeling to the ground, and Hoffmann, unmindful of Julia's presence, flings an opprobrious epithet at him. The Hamburg merchant is led off and put to bed. After a sleepless night Hoffmann writes a letter of profound apology to Frau Marc: he was not himself, did not know what he was doing, his state was akin to madness. She replies curtly the next day, canceling the music lessons, and a few days later reinforces this mild rebuke by a note that virtually forbids him the house.

On September 17 Hoffmann wrote in the diary: "The symbol Ktch will appear no more," but he was in error. In the following weeks he saw Julia now and then—it was inevitable in the little city—and they both sang at the rehearsals and in the performance of Mozart's *Requiem*. Even if in reality he was merely trying to deceive himself, he could write: "It is really all over, only a certain afterglow of exotic romantic visions makes me still take notice of her." On December 3 Julia Marc was married "to that cursed shop-keeper" (con questo maledetto mercante). But the newly wedded pair did not leave Bamberg immediately. Now that Julia was actually safe in the bonds of matrimony and her own financial emergency relieved, Consulin Marc could relent. On December 12 Hoffmann was invited to the house for the evening and the following day, at the home of common friends, he met "Mark [meaning the Frau Consulin], Gröpel et Consorten"; on the eighteenth Hoffmann made a farewell visit to Julia "pour jamais." It was really "forever"; two days later Julia's departure is recorded, and Hoffmann never saw her again.

Julia Marc moves softly through the pages of Hoffmann biography in dim outlines like the figure of a dream. In essence she seems

[11] "Il colpo e fatto! La donna e diventa la sposa de questo maledetto asino di mercante e mi pare che tutta la mia vita musicale e poetica e smorzata—bisogna di prender une risoluzione degna d'un uomo come io credo d'esser—quest' era un giorno diabolico."
[12] Cf. Funck (Kunz), pp. 90-93.

to be a peerless voice, which nature had placed appropriately in a body of surpassing loveliness. Of her little is known except what is to be inferred from Hoffmann's diary and from the tales in which he, as an artist, makes use of his memories. She doubtless revered him as the great teacher who had opened up to her the sublime realm of melody, even for her own participation. In the course of time she unquestionably became aware of his adoration: "She knows all, or rather suspects," Hoffmann wrote. Whether her affections were ever really involved will remain an unsolved problem. Hoffmann once used the word "sphinx" with reference to her, and he pondered deeply over her words: "You don't know me, my mother does not either—no one—I have to lock up so much deep within me. I shall never be happy."

Though Hoffmann never saw her or heard her voice again, Julia did not disappear from his life and work; for a time even the cryptic symbol occurred in the pages of his diary. Fairly early in this strange love affair the poet spirit within him perceived, though somewhat dimly, the eternal values that lay beneath the months of trial: "I believe that something poetic lurks [spukt] behind this demon, and to this extent Ktch would be regarded only as a mask."

Indeed the experience never entirely faded but took on a new meaning. In almost immediate reminiscence, conceived as a kind of poetic farewell, he wrote the little sketch *Ombra Adorata,* one of the *Kreisleriana.* "Ombra adorata" are the first words of an aria in a forgotten opera on the theme of Romeo and Juliet. The symbolism of the title is obvious. Soon he presented the experience more at length and in a radically different mood in *Nachricht von den neuesten Schicksalen des Hundes Berganza* (Report on the Latest Fortunes of the Dog Berganza). Hoffmann linked his narrative to one of Cervantes' *Novelas Ejemplares, El casamiento engañoso* (The Deceitful Marriage), to which there is attached a long conversation between two dogs, Scipio and Berganza.[13] In later tales this devotion, at the time seemingly unrewarded, reappears in ever-changing guise, to receive its final form, its culmination, in the unfinished novel *Kater Murr.* The poet's dream, the artist's ideal, is incorporated in the person of his loved one, but the object of the

---

[13] In his reminiscences of Hoffmann, Kunz printed, apparently from his archives, several pages of the original manuscript of *Berganza,* which with unusual discretion Kunz had omitted from publication as too virulent and too transparently a satire upon the Marc connection. Cf. Maassen's edition, I, pp. 456-62 and the "Lesarten" in Ellinger's edition, xv.

endless quest, the goal of longing, must never be attained, for the vision would fade away into the light of common day.

Years afterwards, when Hoffmann heard of Julia's desperate unhappiness in her marriage with Gröpel and of her separation from him, he wrote to her cousin Dr. Speyer, May 1, 1820: "If you find it advisable and expedient to mention my name in the M[arc] family or to speak of me at all, in a moment of cheerful sunshine tell Julia that her memory lives in me—if one can even call that memory only with which the mind and soul are filled, that which in mysterious stirring of the higher spirit brings to us the fair dreams of rapture, of happiness, which no arms of flesh and bone are able to grasp and hold firm. Tell her that the angelic vision of all the kindness of heart, all the heavenly charm of real womanly perception, and childlike virtue, which shed its beams upon me in that unhappy time of Stygian darkness, cannot leave me in the last breath of my life— indeed then for the first time the released spirit will see in genuine existence that being which was [once] its longing, its hope, and its consolation." Apparently Dr. Speyer not only found the sunny hour appropriate for the communication but gave Julia either the letter or a copy of the passage that had been written for her, for in her copy of Hitzig's life of Hoffmann she inserted these lines from Hoffmann's letter.[14]

On the threshold of womanhood Julia had awakened a passion in the breast of a strange, enigmatic musician who later became a famous man of letters. Pain and distress were for a time her lot, but in mature life she could look back and understand, could be grateful for a brief interlude in her life when she could give to a man of genius something that no one else could give. She even forgave his caricature of her mother in *Berganza*: "It came about in the confusion of his spirit, in a heart torn asunder in love and anxiety for me."

The daily obligations as well as the often empty pocketbook kept Hoffmann anchored in Bamberg, however much his romantic spirit

---

[14] "Finden Sie es gerathen und thunlich meinen Nahmen in der Familie M[arc] zu nennen oder überhaupt von mir zu reden, so sagen Sie in einem Augenblick des heitern Sonnenscheins Julien, dass ihr Andenken in mir lebt—darf man *das* nehmlich nur Andenken nennen, wovon das Innere erfüllt ist, was im geheimnissvollen Regen des höheren Geistes uns die schönen Träume bringt von dem Entzücken, dem Glück, das keine Aerme von Fleisch und Bein zu erfassen, festzuhalten vermögen—Sagen Sie ihr, dass das Engelsbild aller Herzensgüte, aller Himmelsanmuth wahrhaft weiblichen Sinns, kindlicher Tugend, das mir aufstralte in jener Unglückszeit acherontischer Finsterniss, mich nicht verlassen kan beim lezten Hauch des Lebens, ja das *dann* erst die entfesselte Psyche jenes Wesen das ihre Sehnsucht war, ihre Hoffnung und ihr Trost, recht erschauen wird, im wahrhaftigen Seyn!" *Briefwechsel,* II, pp. 404-5. Cf. also reference to *Der grundgescheute Antiquarius* in note 10.

might long for wandering in the Bavarian or Swabian countryside. Nuremberg was not far away and he managed to get a few days of absence for a visit there. In the spring of 1811 he made a pilgrimage to Bayreuth, in part at any rate to see Jean Paul, whose work he had so much admired. From Hoffmann's reticence on the subject, it seems probable that the visit was not entirely pleasurable. Jean Paul's wife had been an intimate friend of Minna Doerffer in Berlin, and in view of the broken engagement of her friend she may have regarded Hoffmann as a faithless renegade. This attitude on his wife's part may have influenced Jean Paul's reception of his visitor. But she herself showed no resentment at the time: "His wife recognized me but does not think of *odiosa*," he wrote in his diary.[15]

Kunz was a devotee of the hunt, a sport which he thought beneficial to his health. Despite his lifelong aversion to physical exercise and all kinds of sport, Hoffmann decided to try his hand at it, oddly enough thinking he would find something "poetic" in it. Under the tutelage of Kunz, he practiced the use of a gun in yards and gardens as a preliminary apprenticeship, and then went forth to a forest preserve to which Kunz had access. The forester and gamekeeper tried to provide satisfactory targets for his marksmanship. He participated in the sport a good many times and apparently looked upon his career as a hunter in a mood of uproarious good humor, though the practical results were rather meager. The bird on the branch flew away, the rabbits scuttled off unharmed, though the amateur marksman was certain that his aim had been accurate. Once the rest of the party whistled for Hoffmann but he did not come; they found him about to aim at three rabbits, but he was trying to make up his mind which one to choose. Another time with obvious glee he enters in his diary, "Shot a deer," but an indiscreet if honest bystander insisted that the forester had really fired the shot, though he generously gave the credit to the amateur huntsman. Kunz says that Hoffmann was too lively and too fanciful for a hunter.

The last months in Bamberg were in part devoted to work on the opera *Undine*, externally at any rate the outstanding success of Hoffmann's career as a composer. Fouqué's little story was pub-

---

[15] This visit to Bayreuth was not, however, the first meeting of Hoffmann and Jean Paul. In the late summer of the previous year (1810), Jean Paul had been in Bamberg, and Kunz had invited Hoffmann and Dr. Marcus to meet him at dinner. From Kunz's account of the dinner, it would seem that Hoffmann had not at that time made a very favorable impression on the honored guest. Cf. Kunz's *Erinnerungen aus meinem Leben in biographischen Denksteinen: Jean Paul Friedrich Richter* (Schleusingen, 1839). This section of Kunz's reminiscences of Jean Paul is reprinted in W. H. Schollenheber's *E. T. A. Hoffmanns Persönlichkeit*, München, 1922.

lished by Hitzig in 1811. Hoffmann was enraptured with the story
and saw in it a "glorious" theme for an opera. He wrote to Hitzig
(July 1, 1812) about it and apparently a plan began at once to
take shape in his mind, for less than two weeks later he wrote again,
asking whether Hitzig could not find among his literary friends
someone who would undertake to furnish the libretto. Perhaps remembering a sonnet he had produced for Julia's birthday, Hoffmann
remarked: "You know versifying is not at all easy for me."[16]
Whether or not he had at the time the sly hope that Hitzig, who
was a close friend of Fouqué's, might induce the author of the story
itself to prepare the text of the opera—this was what actually happened, to Hoffmann's inexpressible satisfaction. It is, however, evident from the correspondence between Fouqué and Hoffmann that
the latter's share in the preparation of the text was not negligible.

Already early in the summer of 1812, six months before the marriage of Julia Marc, Holbein had given up the Bamberg theater and
taken a similar position at Würzburg. Thus Hoffmann was again
adrift on the seas of uncertain fortune. He had now no reliable
source of income, merely the wavering support from private pupils
and the spasmodic returns from his own writing and composition.
He could have followed Holbein to Würzburg, but, to quote a letter
to Hitzig (November 30), he was so content with the leisure resulting from his withdrawal from the theater that despite Holbein's
wish he could not bring himself to take up the "toilsome business of
directing the mechanical and aesthetic part of the performances."
Yet two months later he wrote Breitkopf and Härtel that he expected to begin work in Würzburg the middle or the end of March.
At the time suggested, however, he was still in Bamberg and wrote
(March 23) to the same publishing firm, "Not for all the world in
the present war conditions would I have gone to the *Fortress* Würzburg." Apparently he thought Würzburg a danger spot when war
clouds were rising. These were perhaps only surface reasons; doubtless in the tortured months of summer, autumn, and early winter
Hoffmann was in no mood to make important decisions or face a
new situation.

Early in the new year, however, a new prospect opened up which
possibly accounts for his hesitation in accepting the post in Würzburg. Rochlitz and the publisher Härtel recommended him as music

---

[16] For a list of the poems that Hoffmann at various places incorporated in his
stories and comment on the use made of them, cf. Allen W. Porterfield: "E. T. A.
Hoffmann as a Lyric Writer," in *Modern Language Quarterly*, II (1941), pp. 43-58.

director to Joseph Seconda, the manager of an opera company that performed in Leipzig in winter and in Dresden in summer.[17] In March the negotiations were completed and Hoffmann was ready to leave Bamberg for his new work.

The years September 1809 to April 1813, which Hoffmann spent in Bamberg, were filled with high hopes and sad disillusionments. Only for brief periods was he financially in even relatively easy circumstances. At times, if we can believe the record of his diary, he was desperately in need; once, he says, he sold his old coat "just to be able to eat." It was a time of unsettled political conditions and the wars of the Napoleonic era with all their repercussions were often, as it were, at the gates of the city. On such occasions the "best" families fled, and for a time Hoffmann had few pupils or none at all. In 1809 both Austrian and French troops were about the city and in the summer of 1812 the great Emperor himself with his Empress held entry into Bamberg, and a great illumination was arranged in their honor. Napoleon was then on the first stages of his fatal journey to Moscow.

It is not to be denied that Hoffmann himself was seriously at fault for his financial embarrassments. He was extravagant and improvident; despite household economies his manner of living was highly indiscreet for a man of his income. Unfortunately, since Frau Cauer, the mistress of the "Rose," gave credit, Hoffmann accumulated a fearsome indebtedness; she is said to have remarked that his departure from Bamberg made her several thousand gulden poorer, though it is uncertain whether this statement refers to his debts to her or her prospects for the future, or perhaps both. Hoffmann had long dreamed of a tidy competence from the Doerffer estate in Königsberg. Soon after the death of his uncle Otto, the executors sent him five hundred thalers, a first payment of his inheritance. Hoffmann greeted the receipt of this payment with childish delight, even though it was barely enough to pay his debts; later installments were swallowed up in daily needs. The estate of the Doerffers had suffered serious reverses and had dwindled to a shadow of the affluence Hoffmann had expected.

The kind of life Hoffmann led was also unquestionably not conducive to physical well-being, and it told upon him. The diary bears witness to frequent hours and days, even successive days, of illness,

---

[17] In March 1810 Hoffmann had asked Rochlitz to recommend him for this position with Seconda, but his application came too late; Seconda had already engaged F. Schneider, whose resignation left the directorship with Seconda in 1813 again vacant.

paralyzing headaches, and digestive malaise; he had indeed in Warsaw suffered from a hardening or atrophy of the liver.

But when all this is admitted or even underscored, one is confronted with the amazing, breath-taking record of Hoffmann's productivity. His days seemed to be filled with private lessons, with somewhat irregular but often exacting work in the theater; he participated in rehearsals and performances of most of the miscellaneous musical activities in Bamberg; he was a much-sought guest in the society of the town, and spent countless hours in tavern conviviality. When did he find time to wedge in his own work? The list of musical compositions during these years is prodigious, especially if it includes work begun but not finished till later, like *Undine*, or other work that never saw the light. A list is significant as showing not only the quantity but the range of his musical compositions:

The operas, *Dirna* and *Aurora und Cephalus*; stage music for an allegory *Das Gelübde*, for Soden's play *Julius Sabinus*, for Stegemayer's *Herr Rochus Pumpernickel*, Seyfried's *Saul, König von Israel*, Castelli's *Roderich und Kunigunde*, Calderon's *Die Brücke von Mantible*; marches for Kotzebue's *Das Gespenst* and choruses for *Die Spanier in Peru*; arias for the Singspiel *Das Geheimnis*; chorus for Holbein's *Der Brautschmuck*; choruses and marches for Schiller's *Die Braut von Messina*; chorale for Fouqué's *Ida Münster*; music for songs in Maler Müller's *Golo und Genoveva*; Prologue, *Die Pilgerin*, Prologue, *Wiedersehen*, Prologue for the Carolina Festival; Waltz for the Carolinentag; Ballet, *Arlequino*; a Miserere; piano sonata; piano trio in C major; six Italian canzonets, three Italian canzonets, three Italian canzonets, six Italian duets; recitative and aria *L'acciar ti rendo*, aria *Mi lagnero tacendo*.

One must then take into account the articles written for the *Allgemeine musikalische Zeitung*, often demanding concentrated examination and detailed analysis of structure and form in musical composition. For this periodical Hans von Müller has reckoned that Hoffmann must have written at least one hundred reviews in a period of six years, a large part of which was spent in Bamberg.[18] These articles are of permanent significance in the history of musical

---

[18] For a detailed account of Hoffmann's contributions to the *Allgemeine musikalische Zeitung*, cf. Hans von Müller: "E. T. A. Hoffmann als Musikschriftsteller für Breitkopf und Härtel," in *Süddeutsche Monatshefte*, v¹ (1908), pp. 28-64, 283-95. Müller questions the authenticity of some reviews that have been attributed to Hoffmann and have appeared in collections of his musical writings. E. Kroll also subjects the list to a test of authenticity and makes similar rejections, cf. "E. T. A. Hoffmann als Musikkritiker," in *Signale für die musikalische Welt*, LXVIII (1910), pp. 289-92, 332-33, 411-14.

criticism. From the French he translated a technical work on violin playing. Further, the diary contains frequent references to his painting. He spent several weeks on the frescoes of the Altenburg; for his friend Dr. Marcus he executed murals for a "salon" in the garden; he painted an allegorical picture for the "Casino" in Bamberg, a curtain for the theater in Würzburg, and day after day he records "painted" when he was at work on his portraits. And, finally, his career as a writer of fiction had really begun, as *Ritter Gluck, Don Juan, Berganza,* and several of the *Kreisleriana* bear evidence.[19]

[19] Hans von Müller thinks that *Ritter Gluck* was written in Glogau in the summer before Hoffmann's arrival in Bamberg. Ellinger assigns it to the Bamberg period. Köppler (cf. note 3) would place it in the Berlin residence—1807-1808.

CHAPTER 4

WITH THE SECONDA OPERA TROUPE

AFTER farewell dinners Hoffmann and his wife set out for Dresden at six o'clock on the morning of April 21, 1813. It was not at all a propitious time for travelers to be on the road. The rebellion against Napoleon's domination which had been stirring since the catastrophe of the Russian campaign had gained momentum to the point where Prussia formally declared war on March 16, with Russia as the principal ally. The territory through which the two wanderers had to pass was already in part occupied by troops of the contending armies. The first day went by without incident, but in Bayreuth, where the night was spent, they were strongly urged not to venture farther. On the second day they had to pass the outposts of the army of the Rhine Confederation, and during the two following days they were in the midst of marching troops—Prussian, Cossack, Kalmuck, Bashkir, and others. The roads were gay with the various uniforms, and often clogged with batteries, cannon, and supply wagons so that progress was impeded. They found the inns overflowing with Prussian Hussars, Russian dragoons, and Cossacks, and to secure a place to lay one's head was a desperate venture. All night long the troops filed by on the roads outside; there was something uncanny, terrifying, in the nocturnal tumult with the commands and outcries often in a strange tongue.

On April 25 the Hoffmanns arrived in Dresden. The city was occupied by the Allies. Both the Emperor of Russia and the Prussian King were there, and that very day the Emperor of Russia had been greeted with a great ovation in his honor. Satirical verses against Napoleon appeared as transparencies in the windows. The whole night was filled with noisy merrymaking, resounding hurrahs and Russian folk songs; Prussian and Russian officers embraced one another on the street, and the taverns were filled with motley, clamorous throngs.

Hoffmann expected to appeal to Seconda, the general manager, at once for financial assistance, at least for reimbursement of the traveling expenses, which in the circumstances had mounted unreasonably, but heard to his dismay that Seconda was still in Leipzig. A letter was dispatched the next day, describing the acute distress into which the Hoffmanns were plunged. Hoffmann's childlike in-

nocence in money matters is nicely illustrated when he records a
remittance of seventy thalers: "Which relieved me of all care. Great
joy! Happy mood!"

A welcome surprise awaited him the next day after their arrival.
In the popular garden resort, the "Linkisches Bad," he met Hippel,
whom he had not seen in nine years. Hippel was at the time attached
as one of the counselors to the staff of Hardenberg, the Prussian
chancellor, and had accompanied Hardenberg to Dresden in the
train of the Prussian King. This chance meeting restored the old
boyhood friendship, which had slumbered somewhat during the
Bamberg years. In the nature of things Hoffmann and Hippel were
no longer the ardent youths who had once sworn eternal devotion to
one another, but Hoffmann writes that his friend is still the same
old friend—that beneath the Star of the Red Eagle Order his heart
still brims over with the same friendly affection as five and twenty
years before.

Dresden had once seemed a "paradise" to him, and its loveliness
was hardly impaired in his eyes even at this time, though it was
thronging with thousands of soldiers and rent with the tumult of
marching cavalry, infantry, and artillery, the shouting of commands, and the outcries of the surging crowds of onlookers. Morgenroth, a friend of his Warsaw days, relieved Hoffmann's financial
distress for the time being and promptly introduced him to the
musical life of the Saxon capital. With intense satisfaction he
heard the splendid renderings of masses in the Roman Catholic
Court Church, and attended with interest and pleasure—but not un-
critically—the performances of an Italian opera company. In the
evening he joined kindred spirits in the Dresden taverns.

But all these new experiences could not stifle Hoffmann's professional anxiety. He consulted Franz Seconda, Joseph's brother,
who was manager of a theatrical company in Dresden. In view
of the unrest in and about the city he advised Hoffmann to leave for
Leipzig at once. At the beginning of May Hoffmann made futile
efforts to follow this advice, yet he could not obtain a pass; and
"there was no post, no diligence, no horses." How could such a
journey be undertaken when open hostilities might break out in the
vicinity at any moment? On May 6 the Prussian and Russian troops
began to evacuate the city; the Prussian chancellor and his assistants left the following day; the two monarchs had already departed.
Hoffmann writes: "The most horrible disquiet and anxiety, when
shall I get to Leipzig?" On the eighth the retiring troops destroyed

the bridges over the Elbe. Suddenly there was the thunder of cannon close at hand; the French were approaching from the other side of the city, and at five in the afternoon the great Emperor himself entered the town. Soon the King of Saxony, an ally of Napoleon, returned to his capital, greeted noisily by the fickle crowd.

In the midst of all this confusion and war alarms Hoffmann wandered about the town, an interested and even fascinated spectator. Relying, as he says, on his swiftness of foot, he crept up to dangerous posts of observation. The Russians still occupied the opposite bank of the Elbe, Dresden-Neustadt, and there was constant shooting back and forth across the stream. French soldiers clambered upon the roof and tower of the Court Church near the riverbank, and from that lofty outpost shot at the Russians on the other side. "There could be no thought of mass or vespers," Hoffmann wrote. He watched the fighting, heard the bullets hissing and striking against the walls; once he was himself hit by a rebounding bullet which, he says, wounded only his boot flap, leaving a blue scar on his leg; he visited the market place where a Russian shell fell, causing more consternation than damage.

Without recognition of the strange complexity of Hoffmann's character, one might be shocked at the lack of emotional response, when the country of his birth is at war, fighting for its very existence, but there is little or no evidence of profound concern in his diary. Despite the dangers and miseries of war, which he indeed records, "no meat, no bread," he sets in his diary day by day the words "cheerful" or "happy mood." It would have been strange if he had felt much inclined to work in these circumstances, but before long he found a quiet little room, four flights up, which he called "romantic" and "poetic"—where he could close his eyes and stop his ears to what was going on outside, the temporary vagaries of human beings in their stupidity, and concern himself with the things that are not seen but are eternal.

Finally, after the middle of May the position of the contending forces made it possible to fulfill Seconda's earlier request and leave for Leipzig. Hoffmann and Mischa departed with the post-coach on May 20, but near Meissen, only a short distance from Dresden, one of the horses became frightened and the heavily laden coach was overturned. One of the twelve passengers was instantly killed. Though himself bruised and shaken up, Hoffmann succeeded in dragging Mischa out from under the trunks and boxes. Blood was flowing from her head, and for the moment he thought her lifeless, but the wound on her forehead was not at all serious and with a day of rest she was able to continue the journey to Leipzig, where they arrived on the afternoon of May 23. He was pleasantly greeted by Seconda and warmly indeed by both Rochlitz and Härtel. He began work at once. The orchestra was one of the best in Germany and, though the singers were not all of the highest quality, both rehearsals and performances afforded high satisfaction. Hoffmann now occupied a post of genuine distinction in a city famed for its cultivation of music; he felt "like a fish in the water, moving joyous and free in the right element."

The performances, however, did not continue long without disturbance. At the beginning he found Seconda as Rochlitz had described him, "a nice, honest, stupid man," but he was timid and lacking in resourcefulness; he lost his head completely whenever matters did not run smoothly in their accustomed grooves—and this inevitably happened during the Napoleonic wars. A week or so after Hoffmann's arrival the military operations began to move in the direction of Leipzig, and the city fathers were overhasty in declaring the city in a state of siege. Seconda threatened to close the theater and dismiss the entire company, "to go wherever we wanted to go," but the troupe was more enterprising and courageous and decided to continue for two weeks, assuming responsibility for the venture.

In the meantime the armistice was declared which lasted from June 4 to August 12. To the surprise and delight of everyone Seconda was invited to bring the company to Dresden and to play in the Court Theater—with extraordinary privileges as to the use of scenery and costumes. On June 24 the company left for the Saxon capital. In a letter to Dr. Speyer, Hoffmann gave an entertaining account of the traveling party, which consisted not only of the regular members of the troupe but of "1 theater barber, 2 scene shifters, five maids, nine children, two newly born and three still at the breast, five dogs, a parrot that scolded continually at everything, four monkeys, and a squirrel."[1]

This time Hoffmann found modest but charming quarters on the edge of the city. From the vine-draped windows he could look up the valley of the winding Elbe toward the picturesque region called, very inappropriately, Saxon Switzerland; in the other direction,

---

[1] The diary for June 24 and 25 presents a different account of the journey: "Auf einem elenden Leiterwagen die abscheuligste Reise nach Dresden in der ungemüthlichsten Stimmung gemacht."

only a few steps from the door, he saw "glorious Dresden with its domes and towers." Work began immediately with rehearsals for the performances. He found the orchestra decidedly inferior to the one he had directed in Leipzig. These days mark the beginning of discord in his relations with Seconda, who seemed to blame Hoffmann for the incompetence of the orchestra, and uncomplimentary adjectives steal now into the diary when Seconda is mentioned: "he is an uncouth ass." One of the first operas performed was the *Sargino* of Paer, now completely forgotten; Hoffmann notes that he occupied the very spot where the composer himself had directed the first performance of the opera; and personal memories came over him too, for in other days Julia Marc had sung an aria from *Sargino*. Mozart's *Don Juan, Die Entführung aus dem Serail* (The Abduction from the Seraglio), and *Die Zauberflöte* (The Magic Flute) and Gluck's *Iphigenie in Tauris* were given, and indeed many other operas, most of which are now merely names in the history of opera. Some were produced to Hoffmann's satisfaction, and others, according to his diary, indifferently or badly.

Two days in the week the Seconda troupe surrendered the theater to the Italian company, which was still in Dresden. The two rival companies stood, however, on a friendly footing, and Hoffmann saw much of the Italian director and the singers; he spoke both French and Italian. In compliment to him one of his own compositions, a duet, was interpolated in an Italian opera, and the Italian director proposed to write a German song to be similarly inserted in one of the performances of Hoffmann's German troupe; but Hoffmann was skeptical: "he understands about as much German as I do Chinese."

Dresden was still occupied by the French troops. In honor of the Emperor the city prepared a prodigious celebration on August 10— fireworks and the thunder of cannon, so that the windows rattled and the houses shook: "our prima donna sang her aria with cannon obligato." The jovial citizens who enjoyed a spectacle took time by the forelock, for the armistice ended on August 12, and they could not afford to wait for Napoleon's birthday on August 15.

Hostilities were at once resumed, and Dresden was for a time a chief center of military operations. A few days later, August 22, Hoffmann saw fit to move into the center of the town, for the little suburban cottage was in the firing line of an important entrenchment. The diary contains daily reference to the fortunes of war, and, when the battle surged in and around Dresden, terse but often eloquent notes of an eyewitness. Hoffmann intended to edit and amplify the diary for publication as *Drei verhängnisvolle Monate* (Three Fateful Months), but only a small fragment of the work was ever completed. Much supplementary information as to his adventures and his emotional response is found in his correspondence.

Hoffmann records the comings and goings of Napoleon during the time when Dresden was the Emperor's headquarters. On August 26, the first day of the Battle of Dresden, the Emperor rode over the bridge, which had been restored: "Riding the same little dun horse; he cast his head violently this way and that and had a certain manner about him that I had never noticed before"; or again, "With the fearful look of a tyrant and with the voice of a lion the Emperor roars to his adjutant, 'Voyons!'" The wounded and the dying are brought into the city. For his walks in and about the city Hoffmann found a companion in Keller, a comedian in the opera company, and with foolhardy enterprise they crept to points of vantage, standing one time only fifty paces behind the French outposts when a Russian artillery attack was launched. Often he made his observations with a spyglass from an attic window or even from the dome of the Frauenkirche (Church of Our Lady).

Incidents of the bombardment are related with startling but pregnant brevity. Hissing and crackling, a bomb passed over Hoffmann's head as he was about to enter the door of his house; another tore a part of the roof from the house opposite and broke in bits the three windows of the first floor, so that wood and bricks came rattling down to the pavement. Before their eyes soldiers and citizens were torn in pieces. One day Hoffmann records that he crept softly out the rear door and through the alley to the rooms of his friend Keller which looked out on the New Market: "We were looking pleasantly enough out of the window, with a glass of wine in our hands, when a bomb fell on the market place and exploded; at the same moment a Westphalian soldier who was just about to pump water fell down dead, his head shattered, and at quite a little distance a well-dressed burgher fell, he seemed to try to pull himself up again, but his body had been torn open, and he too fell back dead." Keller dropped his wine glass. "I emptied mine and exclaimed: 'What is life that it cannot stand a fragment of glowing metal, how weak is human nature!'"[2] Artillery roared about the city till the very earth trembled, and at night the heavens were red with fire. On August 29,

2 *Tagebücher*, pp. 301-2 (Drey verhängnissvolle Monathe).

when the Battle of Dresden was over, Hoffmann visited the battlefield outside the town, a sight of horror that burned itself into his brain. His thrilling little sketch *Vision auf dem Schlachtfeld bei Dresden* (Vision on the Battlefield of Dresden) is the literary version of the experience.

During all this time there were naturally no performances in the Court Theater, but when the immediate danger was over, they were resumed, even though fighting continued in the vicinity and later there was expectation of a renewed attack by the allied troops. The city did not surrender to the Austrians and Russians until November 11. Many days passed when Hoffmann could think of little except the exciting events occurring around him—it could not be otherwise. At times he sought peace in the art gallery, "far removed from the turmoil of war, in another world." This second residence in Dresden, as one may view it in the pattern of Hoffmann's whole life, shows the beginnings of a change, a shift, in the beckonings of his genius. Doubtless quite unconsciously he was facing the problem of allegiance to one or the other of his talents. There was never an open conflict between the musician and the man of letters, but gradually the latter assumed the ascendancy.

He was, as he says, "inhumanly busy." The task as musical director of the opera company was exacting. He wrote for the *Allgemeine musikalische Zeitung* and, more important still, was making gratifying progress on the score of *Undine*. Yet more and more did the creative spirit within him turn to literary work and impose obedience upon him. According to the contract, Kunz in Bamberg was ready to publish Hoffmann's first book, the first two volumes of the *Fantasiestücke in Callots Manier*. Hoffmann had originally proposed "Bilder nach Hogarth"; it will be remembered that he likened himself to Hogarth's "Enraged Musician" when he was interrupted in the composition of a sonata by the din in the Warsaw streets. Kunz suggested Callot instead of Hogarth. In a Bamberg collection Hoffmann saw and admired the work of this seventeenth century Frenchman and was ready to accept the substitution. For the first volume he wrote a brief essay on Callot, hardly more than a page, a kind of dedication or apostrophe, as it were, and an acknowledgment of kinship of spirit. In describing Callot, Hoffmann is in part characterizing himself: "Even the commonest subjects from everyday life—his peasant dance, for which musicians are playing, seated like birds in the trees—appear in the shimmer of a certain romantic originality, to the wondrous delight of anyone whose spirit is inclined to the fanciful."[3]

Kunz induced Jean Paul to write a foreword to introduce the new writer to the literary world. At first Jean Paul refused; he did not wish to write any more words of introduction for other people's books, and doubtless his personal opinion of the new storyteller was colored by his wife's prejudices, but after reading the manuscript he consented, even with some enthusiasm. Had it not been for the magic of Jean Paul's name and the purely practical or even sordid value of it on a title page, Hoffmann would have preferred no introduction whatever. In the beginning he stipulated that the work should appear anonymously; he was still a musician and not a man of letters. "I do not want to be named," he wrote to Kunz, "since my name should become known to the world through a successful musical composition and not otherwise." Later, however, he wrote giving permission both for the use of his name and for reference to his profession as musical director. Hoffmann was not entirely satisfied with the tone of the introduction; though sufficiently laudatory, it seemed too much concerned with his personality, and he wished it dropped in a second edition.

In Dresden he finished the tale *Der Magnetiseur* and wrote *Der Dichter und der Komponist* (The Poet and the Composer), an essay in the form of a dialogue, with narrative elements derived from his own experiences in the beleaguered city. But above all, these months in Dresden are ever memorable in the life of Hoffmann for the beginning of *Der goldene Topf*. With one leap, as it were, he gained the summit of his powers as a creative artist, and he himself was conscious of it. To Kunz he wrote: "May God only let me finish the 'Märchen' as I have begun it—I have done nothing better, the rest are rigid and dead beside it."

He was often ill during these months. Not only was proper food lacking while the city was besieged but presumably the presence of thousands of wounded soldiers imperiled the health of the town. Somewhat cynically he records the three steps of the epidemic that was prevailing: "Dysentery, typhoid, death"; "only two days ago I was still so ill that I really thought of becoming a fair angel." During this second residence Hoffmann extended his acquaintance to include some prominent authors of the Saxon capital and passed evenings in the company of Friedrich Schulze, Theodor Winkler,

---

[3] I, p. Cf. also Richard von Schaukal, "Hoffmann und Callot," in *Germanisch-Romanische Monatsschrift*, xi (1923), pp. 156-65.

and Friedrich Kind in the Café Eicheltraut. All three enjoyed at the time a quite unmerited reputation and are now deservedly forgotten save as footnotes to literary history. Under the pen name of Friedrich Laun, Schulze wrote numberless stories; Hofrat Winkler as "Theodor Hell" was editor, author, and translator. Kind, the leader of the so-called Dresden Romanticists, depends largely on Weber's music for an abiding place in the halls of fame: he wrote the libretto for *Der Freischütz.*

On December 9 the company returned to Leipzig for the winter, as had been customary. Hoffmann found rooms in the "Goldenes Herz," where he had lived during his previous residence, and externally the coming months promised little change. But there were marked differences. The disagreements with Seconda multiplied and became more acrimonious. Seconda was officious and unreasonable, though he could be surprisingly affable and generous at times. Hoffmann felt friendless and said he was living "the life of an anchorite." The only new companionship that he particularly esteemed was that of Adolph Wagner, who according to Hoffmann could speak seventeen hundred languages. Despite this phenomenal linguistic attainment, Adolph Wagner is chiefly remembered today, if indeed he is remembered at all, as an uncle of Richard Wagner. Friedrich Wagner, Richard's father, Hoffmann knew also, though not intimately during the earlier stay in Leipzig (he had died in the meantime). He was also acquainted with Ludwig Geyer, to whom by some the paternity of Richard Wagner has been attributed.

Much more time than formerly Hoffmann spent at home, not merely from lack of congenial companionship elsewhere but under the inexorable spell of new literary plans that began to ripen in his mind. He continued work on *Der goldene Topf,* finishing it on February 15, but turned aside at times as other ideas seemed to demand instant attention. The story *Die Automate* appeared in part in the *Allgemeine musikalische Zeitung* and as a whole in the *Zeitung für die elegante Welt*; this was one of the leading periodicals of the time and the presence of Hoffmann among the contributors is evidence of his increasing repute in the world of letters. A request from Cotta, publisher of the equally important journal *Das Morgenblatt,* for a contribution offers further evidence. The satirical sketch *Schreiben des Affen Milo* (Letter of the Ape Milo) was published in Rochlitz' journal, and the short tale *Erscheinungen* (Visions) with a background of war-time Dresden was written at this time but did not appear until some years later. Another work that he proposed to Kunz in these days for inclusion in the third volume of the *Fantasiestücke*, "Szenen aus dem Leben zweier Freunde," was probably a continuation of the idea involved in *Der Dichter und der Komponist*, a series of conversations on artistic topics connected by a thread of narrative.[4] On March 4 he noted in his diary "Idea for the book Die Elixiere des Teufels" and he began writing the following day. In almost exuberant spirits he wrote to Kunz of his plans for the new work. *Die Elixiere des Teufels* was Hoffmann's only completed longer work of fiction, his one novel. Work on the novel was interrupted while he wrote the gruesome tale of *Ignaz Denner*, earlier projected as "Der Revierjäger" (The Game Warden), and the fanciful little play *Prinzessin Blandina*, though of the latter he wrote only one act.

In "Quarrel with Seconda," recorded on February 25, he uses a forceful word, "Zank," which had not appeared previously, and the next day Seconda gave him the official notice for the termination of his services in twelve weeks "a dato."[5] He continued to conduct the performances though he was eager to end the "intolerable connection": "I cannot rid myself of a certain disquiet which torments me and, most important, makes all my literary work difficult for me." He was also seriously ill in these days, contracting a severe cold from

[4] The part of *Die Automate*, the musical discussion between Ludwig and Ferdinand, which Rochlitz published in the *Allgemeine musikalische Zeitung*, February 9, 1814, was presented as a "Fragment" from these "Scenes." Rochlitz says they are to be included in the third volume of the *Fantasiestücke*, to be published "perhaps still in this year"; the reader of the journal will remember the two friends whom the war brought together after long separation (*Dichter und Komponist*). It is probable that Rochlitz' statements are founded on oral communication with Hoffmann. Nothing further was written on the "Scenes," but when *Die Automate* is read before the Serapion Brothers, the identity of Ferdinand with the poet in *Der Dichter und der Komponist* is acknowledged.

[5] The immediate circumstances attending the break with Seconda are given in a letter from Hoffmann to Rochlitz which Felix von Lepel first published (in abridged form in *Signale für die musikalische Welt*, xciii (January 16, 1935), pp. 33-34. The letter is dated March 7, 1814. "Nicht verhehlen kann ich's, dass meine Verhältnisse bei dem hiesigen Theater bei der täglich zunehmenden Grobheit und Indolenz des Hrn Seconda sich merklich verschlimmerten, und dass ich oft alle Fassung und Gleichmut des Geistes aufbieten musste um nicht auf diese oder jene Art loszubrechen." Then he tells of the performance of the *Wandernde Schauspieler* during the entr'acte of which Seconda rebuked him "auf die pöbelhafteste Weise" in the presence of all the actors and the "mutes." The next day he was considering whether it was possible for him in honor to continue in his work when Seconda's message arrived. He asked Rochlitz' advice. The following day Rochlitz called on Hoffmann, finding him in the pitiful circumstances that he later described in the obituary reminiscences in the *Allgemeine musikalische Zeitung*. The publication of this letter puts the affair in quite a different light from the impression obtained from Hans von Müller's note to Hoffmann's letter to Hitzig, June 8, 1814: "Hoffmann war am 25. Februar während einer Probe grob gegen Seconda geworden, und dieser hat ihm darauf am 26. gekündigt." *Briefwechsel*, ii, p. 213.

rehearsals in a frigid theater. He called himself a living thermometer and for the first time in his life submitted to the then popular remedy of bleeding; through this and "through seven thousand eight hundred and forty other remedies I escaped pneumonia and perhaps death itself."

Early in April Seconda asked Hoffmann to accompany the troupe to Dresden for the summer engagement. Though the time that Seconda had set had not run out, Hoffmann resented this request as an impertinence after Seconda's curt dismissal, refused to go, and remained in Leipzig, at least for the time being merely a man of letters. Again he was without salary and thrown upon his own resources, the varying rewards of his miscellaneous work. To be sure during the whole of this year occasional remittances were received from the settlement of the Doerffer property in Königsberg, relatively small in amount but of vital importance. Unfortunately Hoffmann was obliged to treat these payments as income and not as capital.

Hoffmann continued to write occasionally on musical topics to the end of his life, but with the completion of *Undine* his work as a composer was substantially at an end. At the request of a Leipzig publisher he composed in July 1814 a "Battle Symphony" (Schlacht-Symphonie) in honor of the Battle of Leipzig the preceding October, but apparently he regarded it as unworthy of his name, for it was issued under the pseudonym of Arnulpf Vollweiler. The few later compositions are really negligible. For the same publisher who commissioned him to compose the "Battle Symphony" he drew a series of patriotic caricatures. Both in England and Germany Napoleon and his era were extensively caricatured. During the stress of war and the unhappy periods of intermittent peace this formed an outlet for the emotions, and after his downfall ridicule of the great conqueror could be circulated in Germany with impunity. Hoffmann executed several caricatures and his description of them in a letter to Kunz is interesting:

"1. How Lady Gallia is through the might of the allies finally freed from the devil that had possessed her. Cf. Illus. 3.

"2. How Lady Gallia recompenses her physicians for the damages which she caused them during her paroxysm and still promises special gifts.

"3. [Issued by another publisher] The exequies of the universal monarchy, where the King of Westphalia appears among the mourners smelling Vinaigre à quatre voleurs, because he is not feeling well."[6]

Hoffmann was much entertained by the product of his satirical pen, and remarked with satisfaction that the caricatures were being sent over to England.

This work was done on order, and Hoffmann was under the necessity of earning a bit here and there wherever he could, but he doubtless approached the task with some personal inclination. Reference has already been made to his seeming indifference in the early weeks of the War of Liberation. A passage in one of his letters written in Dresden might even be interpreted to mean that as long as Dresden was safe and life within the city undisturbed, it was immaterial to him which side won the victory: among his Dresden friends he regrets that interest in the progress of the war excludes more important subjects of conversation. Yet it was impossible for him to resist entirely the surge of patriotic emotion that swept over most of Germany, especially his own fatherland. The force of the movement for freedom from a foreign yoke may be measured by its effect upon the poet Rückert, by nature a scholarly recluse, who was nevertheless caught up by the torrent and participated in the war through his fiery poems—the only way possible for him. In the *Vision auf dem Schlachtfeld bei Dresden* Hoffmann voiced the common hatred of the foreign conqueror, but his letters and diary, by and large, provide scant evidence of deep feeling, of the patriotic fervor that moved most of his fellow countrymen. Only a few passages now and after Waterloo express his joy in the victory that brought peace and freedom. It would be quite unjust to suggest that he was thinking only of himself, of the interruption of his own plans and activities, but he was listening to the eternal harmonies that his spirit tried to grasp.[7]

At the close of *Der Dichter und der Komponist*, written in Dresden in September and October 1813, he tried perhaps to reconcile two

---

[6] "Abbildung, wie Dame Gallia von dem Teufel, der sie besessen, endlich durch verbündete Macht glücklich befreit wird."

"Abbildung, wie die Dame Gallia ihren Aerzten den Schaden ersezt, den sie ihnen während des Paroxismus verursacht, und noch besondere Geschenke verspricht."

"The exequies of the universal monarchy. Feierliche Leichenbestattung der Universalmonarchie." (The first words are in English.)

"Letzeres Blatt, auf dem der König von Westphalen im Leichengefolge an Vinaigre à quatre voleurs riecht, da ihm schlimm worden, u.s.w. ist ergötzlich." *Briefwechsel*, II, pp. 202-3.

[7] For an attempt to establish Hoffmann's patriotic "Gesinnungen," particularly in the later years of his life, cf. H. Pröhle: "Zur Ehrenrettung Ernst Theodor Wilhelm Hoffmanns," in *Die Grenzboten*, L (January 1891), pp. 121-28.

points of view. The two old friends, Ludwig the composer and
Ferdinand the poet, the latter temporarily a warrior, have for a time
forgotten the war and have discussed the relation between the author
of a text and the musician who sets the words to music. Ferdinand
takes up his sword and helmet, preparing to leave, and "now
equipped like the god of war" stands before his friend who has just
voiced the artist's lament: "What is going to become of art in this
rude tempestuous time? Will it not die away like a tender plant
which turns in vain its withered head toward the dark clouds behind
which the sun has disappeared?" But Ferdinand sees outside the
clouds gleaming with the red of dawn; the lazy children of nature
esteemed not her gifts and trod them capriciously beneath their feet,
and angry Mother Nature awakened war from its sleep to frighten
Nature's children back to their mother.

As the siege of Dresden provided an effective background for *Der
Dichter und der Komponist,* the war-time adventures inspired the
little tale *Erscheinungen.* It forms a companion piece to the *Vision
auf dem Schlachtfeld bei Dresden,* and except for the slight plot the
experiences of the hero are presumably Hoffmann's own, as an eyewitness to the departure from Dresden of twelve thousand French
troops under General Mouton (Graf von Loben) to attack the
Russians encamped on the surrounding hills. It is a historical fact
that the Russians were in some secret way informed of the coming
French sortie, and Hoffmann invents a pretty fable to account for
their foreknowledge: A Russian nobleman disguised as an old
beggar, standing on the bridge hat in hand, as the French forces
pass over, and a beautiful Russian girl, now a servant in a Dresden
household, who, it is to be inferred, swims down the Elbe out of the
closely guarded city to give her fellow countrymen the warning, and,
more remarkably still, swims back up stream, like a water nixie, and
climbs up over the parapet of the bridge. The narrator of the night's
adventure is Anselmus, the hero of *Der goldene Topf.* The emotional
impact of the war is suggested at the first meeting of the friends
who become the Serapion Brothers, and in *Der Zusammenhang der
Dinge* one of the characters, deeply chagrined over the collapse of
his Prussian fatherland, seeks to continue the struggle against
Napoleon by participating in the Spanish campaign. Other references to the Napoleonic wars, as in *Der Elementargeist,* are purely
casual.

An unexpected visit from Hippel in early July was the first step
toward a new change in Hoffmann's fortunes. Hippel had been on a

holiday trip to Switzerland and passed through Leipzig on his way to Berlin. Though now retiring at his own urgent request to a relatively minor post in his East Prussian fatherland, Hippel had in the past years occupied a place of distinction among the advisers of the chancellor and enjoyed a wide acquaintance with prominent officials in the Prussian government. Hoffmann hoped that he might use his good offices to secure for him some position in the Prussian capital. From a passage in a letter to Kunz, one might infer that he had in mind a place in the musical world, perhaps as director of an orchestra. But whatever direction Hippel's efforts may have taken, it is a post in the legal administration for which he indicates a prospect when he writes to Hoffmann a few weeks later.

In Warsaw Hoffmann had closed the ponderous tomes and tied up the legal documents, as he supposed, forever; he was to realize the dream of his youth and live by his music. It was surely caprice or an overgenerous interpretation of motive that led him later to suggest that, conscious of his musical abilities, he had refrained from competing for another legal position with scores of other Prussian officials in Poland who like himself had been cast adrift. Now, in the meantime, he had made his little journey in the world as a professional musician, had experienced its uncertainties, had tasted its bitterness, but little of its triumphs. As far as he could look forward, in any situation to which he might aspire, he would be subjected to the whims, the arbitrary power of a superior, perhaps one of an uneven and undependable temperament. Already before his open quarrel with Seconda he had refused an appointment as director of music in his native city of Königsberg. One could think of a multitude of reasons for his refusal; an inadequate salary is suggested by Hoffmann's irony: "They were willing to give me 258,430 Thalers salary." Following the line of procedure that Hippel had begun for him, he entered into correspondence with Kircheisen, the Minister of Justice, and early in September was offered a position as assistant at the "Kammergericht," the Supreme Court of Judicature, or Highest Court of Appeals. The appointment proposed was for six months only and was without salary but it held some hope, nevertheless, of a permanent and honorable activity. In his general situation at the time, as he wrote to Hippel, he had no right to a choice, and on September 24 he left for Berlin, the "safe haven" into which his old friend Hippel was guiding him.

More than a year had passed since Hoffmann's departure from Bamberg, but in the last days in Leipzig the vision of Julia Marc again haunted him. Whether or not because of the exercise of his creative imagination—the scenes of passionate love in *Die Elixiere des Teufels*—the old mood awakened and asserted its former right "to involve me in Fantasmatis."

In the spring of 1814, several months before the departure for Berlin, the first two volumes of the *Fantasiestücke in Callots Manier* were published, bearing the subtitle *Blätter aus dem Tagebuche eines reisenden Enthusiasten* (Leaves from the Diary of a Traveling Enthusiast). Except in Jean Paul's foreword, the name of the author was not indicated. The two small volumes contained *Ritter Gluck, Don Juan, Nachricht von den neuesten Schicksalen des Hundes Berganza,* six of the *Kreisleriana,* and *Der Magnetiseur.* Now with these volumes before the public Hoffmann was equipped as a man of letters with solid credentials to present to the literary world of the Prussian capital.

CHAPTER 5

THE LAST RESIDENCE IN BERLIN

NEW FRIENDS AND OLD

UPON their arrival in Berlin the Hoffmanns established themselves on the top floor of a house in the Französische Strasse, the second parallel street to the east of Unter den Linden. The following summer they moved to a third-floor apartment in a house on the corner of Taubenstrasse and Charlottenstrasse, where they remained until the death of Hoffmann seven years later. Three of the rooms were on the Charlottenstrasse side of the house and looked out on the Gendarmenmarkt, one of the most familiar scenes in Berlin. Here in the center stood the Royal Theater, flanked on either side by a large Baroque church, the French Cathedral, and the New Church. In the immediate vicinity were the cafés and wine rooms that played a prominent part in the life of Hoffmann during the following years.

Hoffmann drew for Kunz an amusing sketch of the house and the neighborhood, showing not only the rooms of the flat—Hoffmann and Mischa lying in their beds in the sleeping room, even the position of a mousetrap—but also the location of the buildings roundabout. The actor Devrient lived next door, and he and Hoffmann are looking out of neighboring windows, blowing clouds of tobacco smoke at each other. On the Taubenstrasse a coach with prancing steeds is bringing Baron Fouqué of Nennhausen to town. Behind one of the churches market women are offering vegetables for sale; along the Markgrafenstrasse on the other side of the theater walk Tieck, Bernhardi, and Brentano; at a restaurant Herr Kunz from Bamberg is inspecting a menu two yards long—Hoffmann was then anticipating a visit from his Bamberg friend, which never took place. Several characters from Hoffmann's stories are walking the streets: the student Anselmus (*Der goldene Topf*), Dr. Dapertutto and Giulietta arm in arm (*Das verlorene Spiegelbild*); a dog runs along the Charlottenstrasse and an ostrich promenades on the Markgrafenstrasse; a monkey sits atop the Royal Theater; and inside the theater Graf Brühl, the director, stands thoughtfully, hand at his chin, while a group of authors prostrate themselves in supplication before him; Kreisler is seen talking to Bernhard Anselm Weber, the leader of the orchestra.[1]

[1] Reproduced in *Briefwechsel*, II.

The volumes of the *Fantasiestücke* had provided a kind of literary accolade which assured Hoffmann entrance into the charmed circle of Berlin society. At last he could bask in the sunshine of literary fame. On the day after Hoffmann's arrival Hitzig, who in this very year disposed of his business interests and returned to the courts, gave a dinner in honor of the newcomer, followed by a "tea" or a kind of reception. In letters to Hippel and Kunz, Hoffmann describes the dinner, which was at "the best" restaurant and given in the "best" way. He lists the guests: "Ludwig Tieck, Fouqué, Franz Horn, Chamisso, Bernhardi, der Professor Moretto, der Maler Veith." Hoffmann was justified in feeling flattered by the presence of so distinguished a group—which it would perhaps have been difficult to match at that time anywhere in Germany. In the evening two popular singers, the twin sisters Marcuse,[2] sang from Hoffmann's and Fouqué's opera *Undine*, as yet unpublished and unperformed. As a jest Hoffmann was introduced as "Dr. Scholz from Rathenau," and only after the music did Fouqué announce that the "Kapellmeister Johannes Kreisler is here among us"—everyone in those days was reading the *Kreisleriana* in the *Fantasiestücke*. It was a happy moment in Hoffmann's life.

This dinner provided a kind of formal introduction into the life of the coming years. By virtue of Tieck's presence—and perhaps one may include Bernhardi's—the early group of Romantic writers, the "Romantic School," was represented in the company. Otherwise, though the difference in age was immaterial, the guests belonged to the later phase of the Romantic Period, to the last phase indeed. The first fervor of Romanticism had died away. There was no one now like Novalis to embody the profound spiritual qualities of the Romantic revival. Tieck had recently published the first two volumes of his *Phantasus*, the swan song of his Romanticism, and he was soon to turn to a new type of literary activity, the *Novellen*; the shadow of nineteenth century realism was about to fall upon the author of *Franz Sternbalds Wanderungen* and the Romantic Märchen. After varied experiences August Wilhelm Schlegel was again living at the château of Mme. de Staël in Switzerland, and his brother Friedrich had for some years resided in Vienna, lecturing on literature and entering upon a career in Austrian governmental service. Tieck's

---

[2] Cf. Friedrich Holtze: "E. T. A. Hoffmann und die Schwestern Marcuse," in *Schriften des Vereins für die Geschichte Berlins*, Heft 43 (Berlin, 1910), pp. 3-19. The author refers to the Kreisler-Wallborn letter in which the two singers are introduced, and presents evidence to show that the singer Bettina, of *Das Sanctus*, was Elisabeth Marcuse.

presence at Hitzig's dinner was a happy accident; now living at Ziebingen near Frankfurt on the Oder, he was only an occasional visitor in Berlin and in a few years removed to Dresden.

Fouqué illustrates to a certain extent the tendencies of decaying Romanticism. In 1811 he had published his masterpiece, the charming little story of *Undine*, the water nymph who weds a mortal man in order to gain an immortal soul; the beauty and pathos of this tale have not faded with the years. But in 1813 the novel *Der Zauberring, ein Ritterroman*, pointed down the slippery path to a lifeless antiquarianism. Yet at this time Fouqué was undoubtedly the most illustrious figure among the men of letters in Berlin. He was a nobleman, Baron Friedrich de la Motte Fouqué, a soldier and a polished courtier. Hoffmann had become acquainted with Fouqué through their correspondence concerning *Undine*, and now a personal friendship developed. Hoffmann spent happy holidays at Nennhausen, Fouqué's country estate, or a group of friends met Fouqué at Potsdam for a dinner, as it were, sharing with him the distance between Berlin and Nennhausen.

Only the year before, in 1813, Chamisso had written his one story, *Die wundersame Geschichte von Peter Schlemihl* (The Strange Story of Peter Schlemihl), the fantastic and entertaining tale of the unfortunate man who sold his shadow to the devil; it has not lost its freshness even today. His poetry still appears in all anthologies of German verse; its appeal is less strong than it once was, and yet it is far too much to say that the genuine though perhaps commonplace sentiment of the cycle *Frauen-Liebe und Leben* is kept alive merely by Schumann's music. Hoffmann conceived a warm regard for the creator of Peter Schlemihl, and he appears directly or indirectly in more than one of Hoffmann's tales. There was, however, a long interruption in their companionship, for in 1815 Chamisso embarked on a Russian scientific expedition which lasted for three years and carried him around the world as its official botanist. It was commonly supposed that the original intent had been, among other achievements, to find the North Pole by the way of Bering Strait. Hoffmann drew a clever sketch bearing the legend: "Schlemihl journeys to the North Pole and is received by the same in friendly fashion."

Bernhardi, whom Hoffmann had met during his previous stay in Berlin, had attained a place of some merit among the early Romanticists, and was the former husband of Tieck's brilliant but erratic sister Sophie. Franz Horn, another of the guests, was a novelist, dramatist, and poet, with a considerable reputation at the time; his works on German literature and his studies of Shakespeare are still of interest and significance as appraisals of values in the early part of the nineteenth century. Hoffmann may have felt an especial satisfaction in meeting him, for he had already published a volume on Gozzi; enthusiasm for Shakespeare Hoffmann shared with most literate Germans of the time, but an acquaintance with the Italian dramatist was far less common.

Philipp Veit, the painter, was a son of Dorothea Schlegel by her first husband; Dorothea was the daughter of the famous Moses Mendelssohn, friend of Lessing, and was thus an aunt of the great musician. Taking her two little boys with her, she had deserted her husband for the sake of Friedrich Schlegel, whom she married a little later. She had been baptized first into the Protestant Church, and then with Friedrich Schlegel embraced a fervent, perhaps one may say, an ostentatious, Roman Catholicism. Philipp Veit had participated in his mother's religious pilgrimage, and the strong religious tendencies òf his painting were already manifest even before he joined the so-called "Nazarenes" in their Roman cloister.

In his art Philipp Veit was an exponent of the early Romantic conceptions such as are incorporated, for example, in Tieck's *Franz Sternbalds Wanderungen* and Wackenroder's *Herzensergiessungen eines kunstliebenden Klosterbruders*. Hoffmann and Veit met at least occasionally until the young painter's departure for Rome. Making allowances for personal differences, they were still agreed in basic conceptions: the artist's function is that of a priest; the creative impulse is of divine origin, and the still small voice must be obeyed. According to Eberhard Meyer, the guest presented to Hoffmann as "Professor Moretto" was Karl Georg von Winterfeld(t); if this was the case, Hitzig's invitation was felicitous. Like Hoffmann, Winterfeldt was trained both in law and music; for a time he was also connected with the Kammergericht, and later gained fame as a musicologist.[3]

For the absence of Contessa from the festive board one can only conjecture that illness prevented his acceptance of an invitation; he was often ill in these days. He was a friend of Hitzig's even from their student days together, and Hitzig as host for the evening must have been aware of qualities in Contessa that would make for a close friendship with his guest. For Contessa, though by nature retiring and averse to boisterous mirth, had much in common with Hoff-

---

[3] Cf. Eberhard Meyer: "Aus dem literarischen Nachlasse Immermanns," in *Schriften des Vereins für die Geschichte Berlins*, Heft 50 (1917), pp. 447-51.

mann. He was a talented performer on the violin, a painter of landscapes, a clever amateur actor and mimic, and though his literary
work hitherto had been mainly in other fields—the polite comedy in
the French tradition—a bent for the occult and the mysterious was
already apparent.

A few months after Hoffmann's arrival, Clemens Brentano came
to Berlin and remained there for about four years. Brentano was
the son of an Italian merchant in Frankfurt on the Main and Max-
imiliane von La Roche, who played a brief but significant role in the
life of the youthful Goethe. For a time Hoffmann saw him frequently
—he was naturally interested to meet the author of *Die lustigen
Musikanten*, the play which had prompted one of his earliest musical
compositions. He could not be otherwise than quickened by contact
with a man of Brentano's exceptional gifts, for in natural endowment
Brentano outshone all the men of letters with whom Hoffmann associated in Berlin. His lyric poetry is marked by depth of feeling and
by delicate and playful fancy. He had written dramas as a follower
of Tieck—brilliant satirical plays and dramas of medieval pag-
eantry. His erratic novel *Godwi* had made a considerable sensation,
and he could talk with Hoffmann of his own exquisitely fanciful
Märchen, still in manuscript, and of the narrative of medieval life
Aus der Chronika eines fahrenden Schülers (From the Chronicle
of a Wandering Scholar), a part of which he was in these very
days preparing for publication. Not a decade had passed since
the two friends, Clemens Brentano and Achim von Arnim, had
published their matchless collection of folksongs and ballads, *Des
Knaben Wunderhorn* (The Boy's Magic Horn), exemplifying one
of the most fruitful activities of the Romanticists, the revivifying of
the German past.[4]

It was not, however, until the following summer that the closest
friend of Hoffmann's last years came to Berlin—the actor Ludwig
Devrient. After the death of Iffland, director of the Royal Theaters,
to whom Hoffmann had once offered *Die Maske* for production, Graf
Brühl was appointed to this important and influential post. Graf
Brühl was an amiable, capable, but somewhat complaisant and easy-
going official. Commendably intent on securing an effective personnel

[4] It may be assumed that Hoffmann met Achim von Arnim, then Brentano's
brother-in-law, through his marriage with Bettina Brentano. Arnim was a country
gentleman in the Mark but was often in Berlin, and there is evidence that Hoffmann
agreed to collaborate with the two friends in a series of *Briefe über das neue
Theater*; cf. Reinhold Steig: *Achim von Arnim und die ihm nahe standen.* 1: *Achim
von Arnim und Clemens Brentano* (Stuttgart, 1894), pp. 343-45.

for the Berlin stage, he engaged distinguished or promising actors
from theaters in different German cities. Devrient came from the
theater in Breslau. He belonged to a famous family of actors, perhaps the most famous in German theatrical history. Though there
are diverse opinions as to his merits, Ludwig Devrient was probably
the greatest actor of his time in Germany, playing with equal power
great tragic roles and humorous parts. Hamlet and Falstaff were,
for example, among his most successful roles.

He was fond, perhaps inordinately fond, of jovial company, and
Hoffmann found in him a companion after his own heart. Together,
or with other comrades, they spent evening after evening in the
famous wine cellar of Lutter and Weg(e)ner, almost next door to
Hoffmann's dwelling place. Hoffmann drew a sketch of them sitting
over a bottle of wine, a sketch which is often reproduced in biographies of Hoffmann. There, often forgetting professional and personal
cares, they gave free play to wit and humor. In days when either
was ill—and Hoffmann was often ill—they visited each other, and
almost from the beginning, recognizing a kinship strong as that of
blood, they addressed one another with the pronoun of the second
person singular, reserved in German for members of one's family
and intimate friends—and Hoffmann was exceptionally sparing in
his use of it.

Hoffmann was a candid and even remorseless critic of his friend's
performance on the stage, and in all probability the great actor
relied more on Hoffmann's praise or censure than on the combined
professional criticism of the Berlin journals. An amusing anecdote
is related. After a performance in the theater Devrient was accustomed to join Hoffmann in their favorite wine room.[5] At the beginning Hoffmann usually employed an odd, silent method of
expressing his opinion: he pinched Devrient in the leg, the vigor of
the action being graded according to the measure of his approval.
Once the actor returned from the theater, having played Falstaff
in *Henry IV*. The plaudits of the audience were still ringing in his
ears. He stepped up to Hoffmann in expectation of commendation,
but Hoffmann sat silent, his elbows on the table, biting his nails.
Devrient paced the room in rage; finally, poking his friend in the
ribs, he uttered an indignant, "Hm?" Hoffmann replied quietly:
"You played like a pig." Devrient, now thoroughly angry, grabbed

5 For an entertaining though perhaps apocryphal account of Hoffmann and a group
of friends at Lutter and Wegner's cf. "Tafelrunde bei E. T. A. Hoffmann," in
Deutsche Rundschau, cxc (1922), pp. 184-89.

hold of his friend and exclaimed, "Satan, I am going to tear you to bits!" Hoffmann answered calmly: "Sit down and listen. You played the first part like a god, but because you played the second part in the same fashion, you played—just as I said." Then he explained his meaning more fully: "You remember, don't you, that Falstaff in the first part is in the main the one who is teased and made a fool of, but in the second part he does the teasing and the fooling, and so must be quite a different fellow? But you did not bring this out, and therefore you played as . . ." "The devil, you're right!" exclaimed Devrient, and requested the management to have *Henry IV* given again.[6]

The circle of close friends underwent the inevitable changes that time brings in all human relationships.[7] Hitzig never wavered in his friendship, though the two old companions saw somewhat less of one another as the years passed. It would be unjust to use the word "jealous" in connection with as noble and selfless a man as Hitzig, but he disapproved of some aspects of Hoffmann's strong friendship for the actor Devrient and he was alarmed lest Hoffmann's fondness for alcoholic stimulants might receive too much encouragement through Devrient's influence. The fruitful acquaintance with the artist Veit was soon terminated by Veit's departure for Rome. Brentano left Berlin in 1818, but in this year Chamisso returned from his world journey and cordial relations were at once resumed. After July 1816 Contessa lived on the country estate of his friend Ernst Houwald, but this was only a day's journey from Berlin, and Contessa often joined his old friends in the Prussian capital. Naturally Hoffmann, now a prominent man of letters, had many acquaintances in the literary, musical, and artistic circles who could not be reckoned among his intimate friends, such, for example, as Friedrich Tieck the sculptor, brother of Ludwig Tieck. Now and then he was honored by invitations to the more exalted circles, and dined at the palace of the Prussian chancellor. He had become one of the celebrities of the town, and visitors sought him out, for example, the Danish author Öhlenschläger and the Swedish traveler Atterbom, the latter coming with an introduction from Ludwig Tieck.

An outstanding addition to the company of Hoffmann's early intimates was the renowned Dr. Koreff, who returned to Berlin in 1816.

[6] Related in Grisebach, i, p. lxvi, first printed in the *Hamburger Jahreszeiten* (1846).
[7] Two other close friends of Hoffmann in Berlin were Freiherr von Lüttwitz and L. A. von Rebeur, the latter one of his very few "Duzfreunde." Cf. Hans von Müller: "Aus Hoffmanns Berliner Freundeskreis," in *Frankfurter Zeitung*, June 25, 1901.

Koreff was a professor on the medical faculty of the University of Berlin and personal physician to Hardenberg, the Prussian chancellor. Through the latter connection he wielded at times a strong if not sinister influence upon matters of state. As a physician he was one of the chief experimenters in the use of mesmerism or hypnotism in medical therapy, an activity that naturally aroused Hoffmann's interest and curiosity.

The picturesque figure of Graf Pückler-Muskau, later Prinz Pückler-Muskau, also appears in the pages of Hoffmann biography. Despite his aristocratic birth, his lordly estates, and his association with the princely world, he was unconventional, and constantly shocked and outraged the circles to which he belonged. Absurdly extravagant and ever in debt, he attracted attention through his exhibitions of horsemanship, his fabulous entertainments, amorous adventures, and absurd boyish pranks. From his estates, where later his gardens became famous throughout Europe, he often came to Berlin, a striking and flamboyant figure in the society of the Prussian capital. Here he became a suitor for the hand of Gräfin Lucie Pappenheim, daughter of Chancellor Hardenberg. Even after their marriage he never concealed from her his passionate love for the countess' protégée or foster daughter, the mysterious Helmine Lanzendorf. Helmine is a fascinatingly enigmatic figure in the social history of the times; her origins are still an unsolved problem. Even the widowed King of Prussia paid court to her, desired to make her his morganatic wife, elevating her to appropriate princely rank, and he did bestow upon her a patent of nobility. In all probability it was the mystery of Helmine Lanzendorf that supplied material for Hoffmann's story of *Das öde Haus*. Pückler-Muskau aspired to a diplomatic career, and for a time hoped through the influence of the chancellor to receive an appointment as minister to Constantinople or Madrid, the very thought of which inflamed his romantic imagination. It was even suggested that he might take Hoffmann with him; diplomacy might have stretched Hoffmann's extraordinary versatility to the breaking point. Hoffmann used the term "geistesverwandt" of Pückler-Muskau, "kindred in spirit," meaning, it may be assumed, that they had in common the fertile and eccentric imagination, a fondness for striking jokes, and contempt of conventions.

A MEDLEY OF NEW FORTUNES

But beside these new experiences, personally gratifying and encouraging, there hangs a picture of quite a different hue. The "har-

bor" was by no means as safe and tranquil as is suggested in Hoffmann's grateful acknowledgment of Hippel's assistance. Letters to
his friend written in the months following his arrival in Berlin, September 26, 1814, disclose discouragement and grave apprehension.
"It is something genuinely characteristic of my life," Hoffmann
wrote, "that I am always compelled to do what is radically opposed
to the real deeper principles of my being." He had believed himself
forever freed from service in the courts, but found himself working without pay as a kind of apprentice at tasks where his competence had long since received the official stamp. He feared a possible transfer back to Poland, which he loathed, though in a later
letter it seemed a possible refuge from financial worries. Although
it was for the time being hardly more than a happy dream, he still
hoped that the projected performance of *Undine* might release him
for service in a musical appointment in Berlin. Were it not for the
obligation to provide reasonable comfort "for my dear wife, after
what she has gone through with me," he would again play the role
of a "musical schoolmaster" rather than "warble in the juridical
treadmill."

As heretofore, Hoffmann was scrupulously attentive to his professional duties at the courts, as irksome as they often proved to be.
His work there was not only faithful and reliable, but really distinguished, as the annual reports of his superiors demonstrate.[8]

[8] Cf. Felix Hasselberg: "Hoffmann als Kammergerichtsrat, Urteile des Senatspräsi-
denten v. Trützschler über Hoffmanns dienstliche Tätigkeit in den Jahren 1814 bis
1821," in *Mitteilungen des Vereins für die Geschichte Berlins*, xxxix (1922), pp.
60-65. With some explanatory material and quotations from Hoffmann's correspondence, Hasselberg cites from the yearly reports of Hoffmann's superior, made
to the King and to Kircheisen, the Minister of Justice. As a member of a judicial
body, Hoffmann could hardly have been rated higher than he appears in these reports.
On December 24, 1815, Trützschler wrote: "Ungern, sehr ungern werde ich dagegen
den RegierungsRath Hoffmann verlieren, wenn er in einem anderen Wirkungskreise
fixirt werden soll. . . . Die eigenthümliche Präcision, womit er arbeitet, thut der Gründ-
lichkeit keinen Abbruch, u. wenn es auf eine zarte Behandlung des Gegenstandes, auf
eine lichtvolle Darstellung u. elegante Ausführung ankommt, so würde ich mich vergeb-
lich nach jemandem umsehen, der es ihm zuvorthäte." By 1818 (report of January 2)
he could say: "Unter den wirklich activen Mitgliedern nimmt . . . der K. G. Rath Ernst
Theodor Wilhelm Hoffmann 40 J. alt und jetzt gerade die Hälfte seiner Lebenszeit im
Dienst, würdig den ersten Platz ein. Selten ist die Kunst rasch u. mit der höchsten
Präcision zu arbeiten, mit dem Talent, tief in den *Geist* der Gesetze einzudringen, in
so hohem Grade vereinigt, wie bey ihm u. nicht oft lässt ihn die Lebendigkeit seines
Geistes eine die Form u. Verfassung geltende positive Vorschrift übersehen. Ich
würde sein ausgezeichnetes Talent schlecht zu benutzen verstehen, wenn ich ihn mit
Diebes- und ContraventionsSachen, u. anderer losen Kost ermüden wollte. Aber in
schwierigen Sachen, wobey sein Geist Nahrung findet, thut es ihm an klarer
Darstellung u. scharfsinniger Entwicklung keiner zuvor. Sachen dieser Art versteht
er meisterhaft von allen Seiten zu beleuchten. . . ." In accordance with his seniority,
Hoffmann began not long after his appointment at times to preside at the sessions—a

Occasionally he excused delay in the delivery of a manuscript on the score of compelling work. His professional life, he says, drags after him like a prisoner's block, and "I believe that it is once for all a punishment for my sins that I could not continue in the free air and had to go back to my prison, just like a pampered bird in a cage to which food has so long been handed out that it can no longer find its nourishment in the open." Though he did not directly charge his superiors with purposeful misuse of his time and energies, it is evident that in his opinion work was piled on him inconsiderately.

The question of daily bread would in time become desperate. To be sure the executors of the Doerffer estate had not as yet quite reached the bottom of the barrel. On January 4, 1815, Hoffmann received three hundred thalers but this time there was no question of discretion in his use of his inheritance, for he was forced to spend it for the necessities of life. Obviously he could not toil indefinitely without a regular salary, though he notes the expectation of some incidental fees. He renewed his claim to salary lost to him through the collapse of the Prussian government in Poland, but apparently his quest of a situation in a "foreign country"—that is, in Bavaria —was a black mark in the eyes of Prussian officialdom. He implored Hippel's aid in effecting a transfer—to the office of the chancellor or to the Department of the Interior. Until his permanent appointment to the Kammergericht nearly two years after his arrival in Berlin, he was still reluctant to continue work at the courts and sought a position as "Expedient" or "forwarding clerk" in some ministry, and he was actually thus employed for a time in the summer of 1815. He desired to avoid the responsibilities of a more exalted position, receive a secure if modest living, and—most important—gain free time for his work as a creative artist.[9]

Since so many of Hoffmann's hopes were built upon Undine, it was inevitable that he should make an effort to secure the production of the opera. In this he was ably seconded by Fouqué, who began to approach Brühl in the late winter of 1815; it is said that Fouqué

---

task that he fulfilled with great distinction. In the report of January 10, 1819, Trützschler emphasizes Hoffmann's complete control of the court during a period when he himself was absent. Even in Plock, where the dreariness of his exile might have tempted him to indifference, the official estimates of his abilities and his exemplary use of them anticipate the opinions given above. Cf. the reports of the very rigid Präsident von Beyer quoted by Hans von Müller in "Hoffmann als 'Regierungsrat' und als 'verjagter Offiziant,'" in Mitteilungen des Vereins für die Geschichte Berlins, XXXIX (1922), pp. 58-60.

[9] Cf. Hans von Müller: "E. T. A. Hoffmann als Ministerialsekretär in spe," in Mitteilungen des Vereins für die Geschichte Berlins, XLII (1925), pp. 6-11.

through his high social standing interested members of the royal family. On May 3, 1815, Hoffmann wrote a letter to Fouqué, signed Johannes Kreisler, saying he had heard from the "best source," in spite of Brühl's silence, that the opera had made a thorough sensation and was to be produced. A little later he wrote to Kunz that he was seeing Brühl often and the opera was to be performed in the autumn, though only a few days later he still informed Fouqué that it would be produced in the winter. He was apparently both amused and irritated by Brühl, who seemed to regard him as a "budding dilettante": "he does not credit me with any knowledge of the production of a play." Hoffmann was authorized to consult the great architect Schinkel in the preparation of the scenery.

The performance of *Undine* was delayed until the following summer, when it was given in the Royal Theater on the Gendarmenmarkt on August 3, 1816, enjoying thus the signal honor of being chosen for the King's birthday. *Undine* was at least moderately successful with the public; within about a year it was performed fourteen times, a mark of considerable esteem in a crowded repertoire. In his correspondence Hoffmann exaggerated the number of performances and probably the crowds that thronged the theater. The opinions of the professional critics were varied and on the whole less favorable than the popular approval, though of course the commendatory review by the composer Weber far outweighed the mass of journalistic criticism.

The role of Undine, the water sprite, was sung by Johanna Eunike. She was apparently superbly fitted for the part—eighteen years old, a young woman of great beauty and charm and a thorough musician. Hoffmann remained on a friendly footing with her until his death. He sent her a copy of *Kater Murr* with a dedicatory sonnet and from his deathbed the story of *Meister Floh*, accompanied by a tender little note. He was inexpressibly grateful to her for her share in the realization of his dream. Though memories of Julia Marc may have been awakened, for once again youthful beauty and a marvelous voice were united, the parallel would seem to end there. The conjecture that Johanna Eunike was the successor of Julia Marc in Hoffmann's affections is a sentimental distortion of the biographer. There is no real evidence to support it, surely not that one of his "Letters from the Mountains" was written as if to her; this was merely a kind of dedication to one whom he admired.

That after a year of some success *Undine* vanished completely from the footlights is in part explained by the disastrous fire of

July 29, 1817, which destroyed the theater and its contents, including the scenery, costumes, and some of the musical scores of *Undine*.
The opera had been given two days before, the last opera to be performed in the old Royal Theater, and was to have been given the
following evening. The theater was not rebuilt for a couple of years.
Brühl suggested that *Undine* might be performed in the great opera
house, but Hoffmann thought that his intimate opera, like those of
Mozart, would be lost in the larger building. In addition, the management may have been reluctant to replace the scenery and costumes, for Hoffmann implies that they were especially costly. It is
possible, further, that the immense popularity of Weber's *Der Freischütz*, performed a few years later, may have dimmed the chances
for a revival of *Undine*; it was similarly a romantic opera founded
on German folklore.[10]

The destruction of the theater was a personal adventure for Hoffmann. He lived directly opposite it, and was in grave danger, as he
says in a letter "of being again completely ruined." The roof of the
house caught on fire twice, all the windows in the rooms facing the
Charlottenstrasse were broken, and the paint on the window frames
and doors dripped from the heat. Hoffmann was seated at his table
writing when his wife entered with the alarm: "neither she nor I lost
our heads for a second; when the firemen, joined by some of our
friends, beat on the door, we had, with the help of the cook, already
carried curtains, beds, and most of the furniture into the rear rooms
which were much less endangered; there they remained, for I did
not wish them carried out till the last moment." Hoffmann's caution
was justified, for his neighbors, who were overhasty in removing
their household goods to the street, had articles ruined and stolen:
"I did not lose even a teacup." In a letter to Adolph Wagner he
enlarged with characteristic fancy upon one episode of the fire: "The
credit of the State wavered when the wig room stood in flames and
five thousand wigs flew up; Unzelmann's wig in *The Village Barber*
with its long queue hovered over the bank building like a threatening
meteor," but the State was saved by a courageous huntsman of the
Guard, "who brought down the aforesaid monster with a well-aimed
rifle-shot after several fire hose had in vain been directed at the wig
as it rose *ad altiora*." Hoffmann supplied an amusing sketch of this
heroic act (cf. Illus. 4): he assisted the firemen and took a hand with

10 Cf. Wilhelm Pfeiffer: *Über Fouqué's Undine*, Heidelberg, 1903; H. Pfitzner:
"E. T. A. Hoffmanns *Undine*," in *Süddeutsche Monatshefte*, III (1906), pp. 370-80.
Pfeiffer gives the text of the opera.

the hose, binding-up a "wounded hose" with his wife's apron, according to one letter, silk, in another, gingham.

The preparations for the production of *Undine* involved Hoffmann in a vengeful conspiracy which is perhaps hardly to his credit, however justified was the punishment of the victim. Joseph Fischer, a bass singer, refused to take the part of Kühleborn, Undine's implacable uncle, on the plea that the music was not singable. Fischer was possessed by an almost incredible vanity. He was a vocal exhibitionist rather than an artist and practiced by preference a pyrotechnic vocalism, which, according to competent critics, distorted and smothered the original score. All this inevitably aroused Hoffmann's distaste. For his prime satisfaction Fischer depended upon applause and was incensed and enraged when in the course of time his weaknesses were observed and he heard evidence of disapproval. In childish petulance he wrote a long communication which was published in Gubitz' periodical *Der Gesellschafter*, complaining of this affront to his artistic accomplishments, recounting his triumphs in faraway cities, and stressing applause as the very meat and drink of the artist. A devastating rejoinder appeared in *Der Freimüthige*; the anonymous author was probably Hoffmann.

In the spring of 1818 Gubitz arranged a miscellaneous performance as a benefit for the "Society for the Relief of Helpless Warriors." One of the numbers was to be a song by Joseph Fischer. For the course of events one is unfortunately mainly dependent on Gubitz' autobiography published many years later.[11] He suspected interference and obtained the services of four policemen to maintain order, for he had heard that Hoffmann and his "gang" (Schwarm) were to gather in the restaurant of Lutter and Wegner ready to descend upon the theater. When Fischer appeared on the stage, a terrific uproar arose; he began to sing but was completely drowned out by the tumult. Cries of, "Kneel down and beg pardon," resounded through the house. Gubitz contended that Hoffmann had inserted in the newspapers the day before a story of a French actor who had been thus humiliated. The curtain was lowered, only to let loose a more violent pandemonium, the audience taking sides. This

11 Cf. F. W. Gubitz: *Erlebnisse, nach Erinnerungen und Aufzeichnungen* (Berlin, 1868), 2 vols., II, pp. 87-105. Gubitz makes Fischer's wife primarily responsible for her husband's indiscreet complaint in Gubitz' weekly. In these years Gubitz was commendably engaged in other philanthropic enterprises; he published a series of stories called "Gaben der Milde," donated by the authors and to be sold for the benefit of the wounded soldiers and the orphans of the late war; both Hoffmann (*Erscheinungen*) and Brentano contributed works to this project.

was the end of Fischer's career in Berlin. It did not, however, end Gubitz' animosity toward Hoffmann. In his autobiography he tried to besmirch Hoffmann's character, repeating certain gossip as to Hoffmann's conduct during his residence in Berlin 1807-1808, which attributed to him an illicit relation with a married woman and foisted upon him an illegitimate child.[12] It is possible that Tusmann in *Die Brautwahl* is Hoffmann's humorous portrait of his adversary.[13]

The first of May 1816 Hoffmann received a permanent appointment at the Kammergericht. In view of his patent as "Regierungsrat" dating from 1802, the regulations governing priority soon made him chairman of the court, presiding in the absence of the "President." Probably at times during the succeeding years the ghost of his unforgotten dreams disturbed his rest. Whether or not he would have accepted a position as leader of an orchestra is an unanswered question. The harbor was now relatively safe, and he would have hesitated to sail out again on uncharted seas. He had an established position and the kind of social life that satisfied and stimulated him. As a high civil functionary he was privileged or doubtless on occasion under obligation to wear a uniform, for there is record of his dining at the house of the Prussian chancellor and of his appearance at functions in the palace of the King. Hitzig remarks that Hoffmann in this uniform looked like an Italian colonel.[14]

---

[12] Gubitz, *op. cit.*, I, pp. 246-52. In an article entitled "Ein anonymes pornographisches Werk von E. T. A. Hoffmann," in *Zeitschrift für Bücherfreunde*, N.F., III, pp. 82-95, Paul Margis accepts these charges against Hoffmann's character, but Margis is in this instance a special pleader, since he is trying to prove Hoffmann to be the author of an anonymous pornographic novel, *Schwester Monika*, and reviews Hoffmann's life with this intent. In the same number of the periodical, both Hans von Müller and C. G. von Maassen scornfully and thoroughly demolish Margis' main argument as to the authorship of the novel in question. For a full account of the rumors concerning Hoffmann's life in Berlin during 1807-1808, cf. Gottfried Fittbogen: "Auf der Suche nach E. T. A. Hoffmanns Sohn," in *Das literarische Echo*, XXIV (1922), pp. 1272-76. The acquaintance of Kreisler and Rätin Benzon, antedating the beginning of *Kater Murr*, some critics have associated with Hoffmann's friendship for this nameless lady in Berlin. Kreisler's tribute to Rätin Benzon (x, 67) for her kindness to him at a time of distress may of course stem from Hoffmann's remembrance of this lady's kindness in his own time of distress, but it is not an essential hypothesis, for Hoffmann required this earlier acquaintance in the development of his plot. Fittbogen has proved that Gubitz' account of Hoffmann's illegitimate child is false; one may admit the fact of his friendship for an unnamed lady and dismiss the story of illicit relations as probably a malicious fabrication. Gubitz also regarded Hoffmann's influence over Devrient as seriously detrimental; he was the tempter who indirectly undermined the great actor's constitution.

[13] Cf. F. Holtze: "Einleitung" to the text of *Die Brautwahl* in *Schriften des Vereins für die Geschichte Berlins*, Heft 43, pp. 46ff.

[14] For a description of the civilian uniform devised for the greater dignity of certain officials on state occasions, cf. F. Holtze: "E. T. A. Hoffmann als Hofmann," in *Mitteilungen des Vereins für die Geschichte Berlins*, XLII (1925), pp. 11-14.

The odious political conditions that arose in Germany at the end of the Napoleonic wars forced upon Hoffmann a very unwelcome assignment. After the Congress of Vienna, mainly under the malign and sovereign influence of Metternich, the so-called "Period of Reaction" set in. Liberalism had cherished vain hopes, encouraged by the patriotic flame that had flared up and burned brightly for a decade past, but now the faintest spark was ruthlessly extinguished. Everything that savored of liberalism was mercilessly crushed. Spies reported on the lectures of university professors and watched suspiciously the merrymaking of students. Thousands were apprehended and sent off to prison terms for trifling infractions of suppressive laws or on prejudiced or fraudulent evidence. The wearing of a certain ribbon was treason.

The Prussian King appointed a special legal commission (Immediat-Kommission) for the investigation of activities alleged to be subversive and hence a peril to the state. Hoffmann was one of the members of the commission. He possessed a keen legal intelligence and a rigid sense of correct procedure, and he was incensed at the arbitrary methods, the contempt of laws, and the personal animosities that developed in this unhappy era. On one point he agreed with the authorities: action should be taken against crazy outbursts of a few hotheads, such, for example, as the murder of Kotzebue, but he utterly condemned the measures now being taken not "against deeds but against opinions." Unfortunately the King not only authorized the commission from the courts but a little later under the influence of fanatics established a "Ministerial Commission" as well. A resultant conflict of jurisdiction and authority was a foregone conclusion, even if the "Ministerial Commission," aided by the King, had not definitely tried to assert its superiority over the other commission.

The most famous case upon which Hoffmann in his capacity as a member of the Special Commission rendered an opinion and a protest was that of "Father Jahn," the founder of the "Turnverein" movement. In many ways Jahn was a ridiculous fanatic, preaching ultraviolent and exclusive nationalism, and Hoffmann looked upon him in amused contempt; Jahn and his chauvinistic nationalism are held up to ridicule in *Klein Zaches*. But he had not forfeited his rights under the law. In his management of this case Hoffmann showed courage and even audacity. Jahn was arrested on the basis of evidence presented by spies and informers, and the matter was brought before the Special Commission. After a thorough investiga-

tion Hoffmann drew up a report showing that the specific charges
against Jahn were without foundation, and accordingly the commission recommended the release of the prisoner, who had already
been in jail for nearly eight months.

The Ministerial Commission was strongly under the influence of
a certain Kamptz, Commissioner of Police in the Department of the
Interior, a fanatical zealot to whom all means were legitimate if by
them those cherishing liberal opinions could be smoked out and
brought to punishment. Under Kamptz's whip the Ministerial Commission disagreed with the recommendation of the Special Commission, and on the King's command Jahn was sent to the fortress of
Kolberg. To secure public approval Kamptz had an announcement
inserted in the newspapers that the guilt of Jahn had been established. This outrageous untruth aroused Jahn in his fortress imprisonment to make a formal demand that the High Court investigate the source of this false report. Here a conflict of principles was
involved; Kamptz would have to be summoned before the court. The
Minister of Justice, Kircheisen, who appointed Hoffmann to the
court, was wary and ordered a halt to the proceedings on the ground
of official immunity; even the chancellor took a hand. But Hoffmann
stood his ground: the highest officials of the state, he said, are not
outside the law; they are, on the contrary, subject to it just as other
citizens; "only the King has the right, from higher reasons of state,
to stop the course of legal proceedings."[15] And the King did interfere,
but not in the interest of justice. Hoffmann served on the Special

---

[15] For a brief account of the Jahn Case by a contemporary, cf. Wilhelm Dorow:
Erlebtes aus den Jahren 1813-1820 (Leipzig, 1843), I, pp. 202-9, and for the documents, including Hoffmann's formal opinion rendered in the case and the King's
letter to the Kammergericht, cf. II, pp. 179-200 (Der Prozess des Dr. Jahn wider den
Geheimen Ober-Regierungsrath von Kamptz). From Hoffmann's report, p. 199:

"Wir bemerken hierbei ehrerbietigst, dass wir dem gemäss unsern Standpunkt
nicht verkennen und uns frei von jeder ungeziemenden Anmassung fühlen, wenn
wir diejenige Pflicht nämlich:

"Jedermann ohne Ansehen der Person und Unterschied des Standes nach Vorschrift
der Gesetze und nach unserer besten Kenntnis und Überzeugung unpartheiische rück-
sichtslose Justiz zu administriren, welche wir als die heiligste in unserm Amtseide
beschworen haben, mit der strengsten Gewissenhaftigkeit, mit der unerschütter-
lichsten Treue zu erfüllen streben und auf Überzeugung beharren, dass nur Se.
Majestät Der König unmittelbar die Macht haben, aus höhern Staatsgründen den
Gang des Rechts zu hemmen.

Berlin, den 14. Februar 1820."

Cf. also Gottfried Fittbogen: "E. T. A. Hoffmanns Stellung zu den 'demagogischen
Umtrieben' und ihrer Bekämpfung," in *Preussische Jahrbücher*, CLXXXIX (1922),
pp. 79-92. Fittbogen maintains that Hoffmann's lack of political interests made him
peculiarly valuable, rendering him an impartial investigator. Cf. further F. Holtze:
"500 Jahre Geschichte des Kammergerichts," in *Schriften des Vereins für die Geschichte Berlins*, Heft 47, pp. 193-99.

Commission for nearly two years (October 1819 until the summer of 1821), and then obtained his release. But the story did not end with his release.

For the deplorable sequel to this controversy, Hoffmann himself must bear a part of the blame. To find relief from vexing personal relationships in satirical thrusts was a practice firmly rooted in Hoffmann's youth, when, for example, he teased the "O Weh Onkel" and concocted (on paper) an elaborate plan for the "canonization of Uncle Ott." In the second volume of *Kater Murr*, which was written immediately after his release from the Special Commission, he satirized one of his most bitter opponents in the activities of the commission, but still somewhat discreetly. Even in those days it would hardly have been possible for Tzschoppe, his victim, to take official notice; to recognize himself in Hoffmann's story—in the guise of a Spitz dog—might have acted as a boomerang and made him ridiculous. But Hoffmann now carried his satire a step beyond discretion.

Toward the end of 1821 Hoffmann began to send installments of his new story *Meister Floh* to Friedrich Wilmans, a publisher in Frankfurt on the Main, and early in January 1822 he delivered the third of these installments, which was to prove fateful for its author. In this section of the story, after the two heroes have been arrested, a certain Knarrpanti takes up the case against one of them, following a procedure that forms a close parallel to the methods of Kamptz: flimsy charges, confiscation of private papers, personal animosity, arrogance, and incredible stupidity. It is conceivable, though improbable, that the offensive material might have been overlooked, if Hoffmann himself had kept silent. But he betrayed his satirical purpose, perhaps even boasted of it in the company of his friends, who inconsiderately told their friends, who were not necessarily the friends of Hoffmann, and so it became the talk of the town.

Kamptz determined to prevent the publication of *Meister Floh*. A messenger, armed with the authority of the Prussian state, was dispatched to Frankfurt to request of the Free City the surrender of all material in any way involved—the manuscript itself, parts already in the hands of the printer, and correspondence with the author. Diplomatic courtesy dictated compliance with this request, and Wilmans was directed to hand over the documents, though some Frankfurt officials questioned Prussia's right to exercise censorship in the Free City of Frankfurt. Naturally Hoffmann did not remain in the dark about all this and in frantic distress he wrote to Wilmans,

giving directions for deletions in the manuscript. It was too late;
the documents in the case had already been delivered up, and to
them Wilmans innocently added this letter, presumably thinking
that the deletions proposed in the letter might satisfy the Prussian
authorities and end the matter. However indignant Hoffmann might
be at the perversions of justice for which Kamptz was responsible
and however morally justified in using the potent weapon of ridicule
in combatting them, he found himself now in real peril: his enemies
were powerful, and his position at the courts might be taken from
him.

Through the proper channels the full account of Hoffmann's
crime—as seen by Kamptz—was placed before the chancellor, with
the suggestion that the offender might properly be punished by
transfer to some other post; the remote East Prussian town of
Insterburg was mentioned, where Hoffmann's father lived after his
departure from Königsberg. It was Hoffmann's good fortune that
Hippel was in Berlin at the time as a member of a governmental commission, and in his old friend's behalf Hippel interviewed high officials, even Kamptz himself.

But another momentous factor began to play its part in the affair,
beyond the control of the King's ministers or the King himself.
Hoffmann's health, which had been giving more and more cause for
concern, now, in his overwhelming anxiety, took a marked turn for
the worse. Neither he nor his friends could manufacture, in order
to gain time, the swoons into unconsciousness when he attempted to
rise from his bed. Through the malicious arrangement of Tzschoppe,
his enemy in Hardenberg's office, an official demand was issued for
a hearing within twenty-four hours. The executor of this royal order
was met at the door by Hippel and Hoffmann's physician, who
affirmed that Hoffmann was physically unable to meet the requirement; with the confirmation of another physician a formal statement of Hoffmann's condition was sent to the authorities. In the
course of two weeks the patient recovered sufficiently to prepare a
detailed and masterly defense of his conduct and to submit to the
ordeal of examination in his own house. This was conducted by the
"President" of the court, who was friendly to Hoffmann and called
attention in his report to Hoffmann's superior attainments in the
law and to his invaluable services. These documents were added to
the mounting pile in the "Hoffmann case" and passed from hand

to hand among the competent officials.[16] The King recommended a reprimand and no further action, but no action of any kind was ever taken. Even the most vengeful enemy may stay the hand of the executioner when it is obvious that death is already waiting at the door of the cell without being officially summoned. Hoffmann's illness was now so pronounced that there could be no question of further service either in Berlin courts or in faraway Insterburg. With proper excisions *Meister Floh* was released for publication. At the time when he surrendered the manuscript the crafty Wilmans had required a substantial deposit to make sure its return.[17]

The record of Hoffmann's health forms a wavering, fluctuating line, but ever in a downward direction. He was excessively sedentary in his habits, and physical exercise was rare and spasmodic—the hunting expeditions with Kunz stand practically alone in the years of his manhood. He would have done well to take a leaf from the book of "Father Jahn," whom he so mockingly ridiculed. His daily routine in Berlin was of a type to undermine the stoutest constitution, and Hoffmann's was already weakened. There were long and arduous hours at the courts, social engagements, followed by evenings in the wine cellar of Lutter and Wegner; and often, with mind alert and imagination enkindled, he returned home to sit at his desk and write till early dawn. Probably he was himself aware, apart from Hitzig's friendly warnings, of the way in which he was burning his candle, but to him there was no other way.

In the spring of 1818 Hoffmann was dangerously ill for weeks, and again in the spring of the following year his illness was so alarming and his bodily strength so sapped that he was obliged to secure a leave of absence from his duties at the courts. He and Mischa spent the better part of three months at Silesian watering places, principally at Warmbrunn. An illness which came upon him in the autumn of 1821 was the beginning of the end—an atrophy of the liver and what was apparently a degeneration of the spinal marrow. And when in early

16 Cf. Georg Ellinger: "Das Disziplinarverfahren gegen E. T. A. Hoffmann," in *Deutsche Rundschau*, cxxviii (1906), pp. 79-103. The text of Hoffmann's "Verteidigungsschrift" is pp. 97-100.

17 From the archives in Berlin the offending passages in *Meister Floh* have been restored in Hans von Müller's edition of the story (Berlin, 1908). One illustration may serve. Knarrpanti confiscated the papers of his prisoner Peregrinus Tyss, "Wasch- und Küchenzettel nicht ausgenommen," and, finding in an old diary the sinister words "Entführung" and "entführt," concludes that Peregrinus is an abysmally depraved character. The other judge insists on seeing the context and discovers that the words in question refer to Mozart's opera and to *Wilhelm Meister*. To Knarrpanti this only proves Peregrinus' slyness in thus concealing his base designs.

January the intense anxiety over the affair of *Meister Floh* filled his days and nights, a host of physical ills took possession of him. During the succeeding months, January to June, there were days that seemed brighter, when there was surcease of pain, but there was never really any hope.

His legs became paralyzed and gradually also his hands. Doubtless impelled by the torturing consciousness of his financial position, which now verged on bankruptcy, he went on with his work. After a time only an occasional note was written by his own trembling hand. He dictated to his nurse and amanuensis from his sickbed, even from his deathbed, not only the last part of *Meister Floh* but a new story, *Die Genesung*, and the beginning of another, *Der Feind*. He had the courage even to promise a date for the completion of the third volume of *Kater Murr*[18] and to discuss plans with the publisher Max in Breslau concerning a new long novel, the most ambitious from his pen, *Schnellpfeffers Flitterwochen vor der Hochzeit* (Schnell-pfeffer's Honeymoon Before the Wedding).[19] But no word was ever written on either.

In pathetic little notes Hoffmann begs Hitzig for assistance in reading and revising the manuscript of *Meister Floh* before sending it to Wilmans: he has no strength to do it himself and is filled with deathly terror (Himmel-Angst) that the reader may detect in this last section the weakness of the sick author: "in this case it were advisable to let the whole matter drop." "I am wretched still," he writes to Wilmans, "that is, the body, but not the spirit which is fresh and strong." He bore his physical pains with heroic fortitude and even to the end retained his sense of humor and jested about his illness.

On March 26, 1822, Hoffmann and Michalina wrote a combined last will and testament, each making the other the heir "in case it should please God to end our union and call one or the other out of temporal things" (dieser Zeitlichkeit):

"We . . . have now for twenty years lived continuously in a truly

[18] In September 1821 he informed Dümmler the publisher that the third part of *Kater Murr* ("da ich nun nicht mehr abbreche") could be ready by the New Year; in January 1822 he wrote to Carl Schall that it was to appear at Easter time.

[19] The conjecture that *Schnellpfeffers Flitterwochen vor der Hochzeit* was to be an autobiographical novel and was to reflect especially his life in Posen has been constantly repeated and indeed accepted as more than a conjecture, but it has not much to support it. The fragmentary note that Hitzig printed from Hoffmann's "Nachlass" indicates a purpose to utilize some personal memories of his youth, and nothing more. On the basis of the odd title it has been repeatedly stated that he proposed to center the novel in his Posen days and his acquaintance with Mischa previous to his marriage; this is a mere guess with little foundation.

contented and happy marriage. God has given us no children who still live, but otherwise has presented us with many joys, yet also tested us with heavy and hard suffering, which we have borne with steadfast courage. Each has ever been the support of the other, as indeed married people are who love and honor one another with a faithful heart, as we have done."[20]

In April Hippel left for his East Prussian home. The old friends who had studied and played together as boys met for the last time. At first Hoffmann refused to believe in the necessity of Hippel's departure and was resentful, but he then relented, spoke hopefully of meeting again, but wept bitterly. Hoffmann died on June 25, 1822. He was buried in a new cemetery belonging to the Jerusalemerkirche in the parish of which the Hoffmanns lived. The street on which the cemetery is situated has borne various names, but is most familiarly known as the Königgrätzerstrasse. Both the death notice in the newspaper and the tombstone record his name as E. T. W. Hoffmann, which was still his legal name, but the parish record of the church preserves the "A"—Amadeus—which he had chosen in love for the master of music.[21]

THE LITERARY WORK OF THE LAST YEARS

The creative imagination is an indwelling "demon," like Faust's spirit world, which, once summoned, cannot be banished without a

[20] "26. März 1822. Wir, nehmlich ich der KammerGerichtsRath Ernst Theodor Willhelm Hoffmann und ich Maria Tekla Michalina gebohrne Rohrer haben nun bereits seit Zwanzig Jahren in einer fortdauernden wahrhaft zufriedenen glücklichen Ehe gelebt. Gott hat uns keine Kinder am Leben erhalten aber sonst uns manche Freude geschenkt, doch uns auch mit sehr schweren harten Leiden geprüft, die wir mit standhaftem Muth ertragen haben. Einer ist immer des andern Stütze gewesen, wie das Eheleute sind, die sich, so wie wir, recht aus dem treusten Herzen lieben und ehren." *Briefwechsel*, II, p. 514.

[21] Shortly after the death of her husband, Michalina left Berlin and returned to the home of her mother in Posen, where she lived till about 1835, with the exception of a year that she spent with her niece Michalina von Lekszyski in Ostrowo. This niece was the former Michalina Gottwald who had lived with the Hoffmanns in Plock and Warsaw, after the defalcation of her father; she was now married to an official in the Prussian service. Leaving Posen, Hoffmann's widow resided in Breslau till (circa) 1849, when she removed to the Silesian watering place of Warmbrunn, where she died January 27, 1859. In view of Hoffmann's debts Mischa formally renounced all claim to his estate. With characteristic selfless endeavor Hitzig busied himself in her behalf, and for many years, till his own death in 1849, he was unwearied in his devotion to her well-being. The proceeds from his biography of Hoffmann, and from the *Letzte Erzählungen*, which he published at his own expense, were set aside for her benefit, and, ignoring her public renunciation of Hoffmann's estate, he repeatedly extracted sums from various publishers of her husband's works. Hippel also remembered the widow of his old friend and used his influential connections to secure her a small pension. For further details cf. *Briefwechsel*, II, pp. 539-96, 738-97.

struggle. Despite the urgency of professional tasks, despite the multifold distractions of the new environment, Hoffmann could not entirely disobey the voice within: "I cannot abandon art," he wrote to Hippel. In the early days the Café Manderlee in the Markgrafenstrasse was the spot where he met his literary friends and for a time it threatened to replace the "Rose" of Bamberg in his diary. In time the company gathered frequently in Hoffmann's home, where both Hoffmann and Michalina were adepts in brewing fragrant and stimulating punches. These meetings formed the prototype for the later gatherings of the "Serapionsbrüder."

A curious cooperative plan soon came into being among these friends, a novel the chapters of which were to be written in turn by Hoffmann, Hitzig, Chamisso, and Contessa.[22] The plan resembled the familiar pencil and paper game in which a poem, perhaps a "limerick," is composed by a group, each contributing a line in accordance with a predetermined rhyme scheme; there was to be no collusion between the authors, and each had to attach his chapter as best he could to the work of his predecessors. Chamisso began the game with a startling incident or coincidence: a roofer falls from a tower and breaks his neck and his wife gives birth to trillings, three boys indistinguishable from one another; the fortunes of the three boys were to form the substance of the novel. Unfortunately, *Der Roman des Freiherrn von Vieren* never progressed beyond the initial stages, though both Hoffmann and Contessa adapted the material they had prepared to other uses. Naturally the departure of Chamisso on his long journey around the world was a barrier to the completion of the project. Later Hoffmann, Fouqué, and Contessa twice united in a cooperative plan, though of a different type: each contributed one tale to a volume of *Kindermärchen* which Reimer published in 1816 and to a similar collection the following year. Hoffmann's stories were *Nussknacker und Mausekönig* (Nutcracker and Mouse-King) and *Das fremde Kind* (The Stranger Child). The former is one of the most delightful of his works, showing his skill in weaving a tale equally fascinating to children and grownups.

As Hoffmann's reputation grew apace, he began to be besieged by editors requesting contributions. In the latter part of the eight-

[22] For an account of this scheme and of its predecessor, *Die Versuche und Hindernisse Karls,* the combined work of Varnhagen von Ense, Neumann, and Fouqué, with Chamisso as a prospective fourth contributor, cf. Helmuth Rogge: *Der Doppelroman der Berliner Romantik,* Leipzig, 1926; also Ludwig Geiger: *Aus Chamissos Frühzeit: ungedruckte Briefe nebst Studien* (Berlin, 1905), pp. 118-208.

eenth century and in the early nineteenth a principal feature of the yearly book market was the publication of annual "gift-books"; they appeared year by year in countless numbers and under a great variety of titles. Much of the fugitive verse of these decades, the shorter narratives, essays, and even plays, first appeared in the pages of these annuals. Hoffmann contributed stories to Fouqué's *Frauentaschenbuch*; to the *Urania*, published for many years by Brockhaus in Leipzig; to the *Taschenbuch zum geselligen Vergnügen*; and several others. The importunity of editors and Hoffmann's chronic financial embarrassment combined at times to drown out the voice of his artistic conscience, which was by nature keenly active, and inferior stories were produced, though it is not too much to say that no tale is negligible or lacking in characteristic qualities. Hoffmann was quite aware that he was prostituting his talents; on August 30, 1816, he wrote to Hippel: "I shall never write another *Goldener Topf*."[23] Hoffmann's salary, when he was finally given a permanent position, was modest but by no means contemptible and it was later substantially increased,[24] yet he could always find a corresponding outlet for any increase in his income. His letters disclose a rather sharp sense of business method and somewhat devious bargaining habits with the various publishers—he was not averse to pitting one publisher against another and stating optimistic terms that he was wont to receive.[25]

The first fruit of the new Berlin companionship was *Die Abenteuer der Sylvesternacht* (The Adventures of New Year's Eve), which he read aloud to his friends on the evening of January 13, 1815. The content of the tale was linked to Chamisso's *Peter Schlemihl* and thus he paid tribute to the work of his new friend. It was plainly imperative, however, that he should return to *Die Elixiere des Teufels* and finish the novel, the first volume of which had been ready for the printer previous to his arrival in Berlin. He found a publisher for it and set to work on the second volume; the first volume was published

[23] Two years later he wrote to Helmina von Chézy (October 16, 17, 1818) that he was honored and disconcerted by her favorable opinion of his works: "da ich bis jezt, das Märchen vom goldenen Topf vielleicht ausgenommen, nichts von eigentlicher Bedeutung geliefert." *Briefwechsel*, II, p. 314.

[24] Cf. Felix Hasselberg: "Hoffmann als Kammergerichtsrat," in *Mitteilungen des Vereins für die Geschichte Berlins*, XXXIX (1922), pp. 60-65.

[25] Cf. his letters to publishers in the *Briefwechsel* and especially Maassen's account of Hoffmann's relations with the publisher Schrag in Nuremberg, whose firm issued Fouqué's "Frauentaschenbuch," in *Von Büchern und Menschen: Festschrift Fedor von Zobeltitz zum 5. Oktober 1927 überreicht von der Gesellschaft der Bibliophilen*, Weimar, 1927, under the title "E. T. A. Hoffmann, Leonhard Schrag und das Frauentaschenbuch," pp. 145-64; this article contains letters not in the *Briefwechsel*.

in the autumn of 1815 and the second at Easter of the following year.

Most of the new stories—and the best of them—which were written during the first two years in Berlin were "Künstlernovellen," stories of the artist in relation to life: *Die Fermate, Der Artushof, Die Jesuiterkirche in G., Das Sanctus,* and *Rat Krespel.* The most vital aspect of the problem had already been suggested in *Der goldene Topf*: is there any place in the world of everyday for the man of artistic gifts; can he ever find a home for his dreams in the world of commonplace reality? Among the tales of the first years in Berlin, *Der Sandmann* stands somewhat apart; though clumsily put together the story presents in arresting fashion the mysterious problem of demonic possession, of insanity, or, in Freudian terms, the perpetuation of a childhood complex. As in the Dresden days Hoffmann could still be torn for a time from his political apathy by startling events in the great world. In *Der Dey von Elba* he portrayed the effect of the news that the great Emperor had escaped from his island solitude. The subtitle of the short essay, *Send-schreiben des Türmers in der Hauptstadt an seinen Vetter Andres* (Letter from the Tower Watchman in the Capital to his Cousin Andres) shows the apt method Hoffmann uses in placing the account in the words of a trained observer.[26]

The numerous stories of the remaining years, 1817-1822, are to a certain extent those conditioned by editorial insistence and Hoffmann's improvidence, but among them the great peaks stand out— the summits of his later achievement, *Klein Zaches, Kater Murr, Prinzessin Brambilla,* and *Meister Floh,* and of a different type but still masterpieces of the narrator's art, *Das Majorat* and *Das Fräulein von Scuderi.*

The contract with Kunz for the publication of the *Fantasiestücke* was still valid, and accordingly Hoffmann sent *Der goldene Topf* when completed to make the third volume, which appeared in the autumn of 1814, and made plans for a fourth volume. A slight coolness had arisen between the two Bamberg friends; in Bamberg their friendship had evidently not been unclouded, for on May 18, 1812, Hoffmann wrote in his diary: "Unpleasant quarrel with Kunz which probably has separated us forever; at bottom I am rather glad of it." He thought, and with reason, that Kunz had acted inconsiderately if not dishonestly when he declined to publish Hoffmann's account

---

[26] Cf. Hermann Kügler: "Zum 'Traum des Domküsters Andreas Otto,' " in *Mitteilungen des Vereins für die Geschichte Berlins,* XLI (1924), pp. 32-36.

of his war-time experiences in Dresden and then without a word issued the *Vision auf dem Schlachtfeld bei Dresden*. That Kunz rejected *Ignaz Denner* as unworthy of inclusion in the fourth volume of the *Fantasiestücke* naturally intensified the estrangement.[27]

The *Fantasiestücke* established a precedent for similar collections of Hoffmann's tales, whether or not they had been previously published. Thus the two volumes of the *Nachtstücke* were issued in 1816 and 1817. The success of these collections doubtless prompted the publisher Reimer, in February 1818, to suggest to Hoffmann still another gathering of his scattered stories. Hoffmann replied cordially and mentioned four works already published in the annuals and proposed to add two more to make a round half dozen for a "nice little volume." It was a happy thought on Hoffmann's part to raise the question of placing the stories in a "frame" after the "fashion of Tieck's *Phantasus*." The device was, of course, an old one, but he probably mentioned Tieck's work as the most recent use of it; the third and last volume of the *Phantasus* had appeared only two years before this. In the *Phantasus* a number of friends are met together at a country house, partly by invitation and partly by accident, and several of the group read their works aloud, both stories and plays; the reading is accompanied by discussion on the part of the whole company. The "framework" in Tieck's *Phantasus* develops into a story in itself, but Hoffmann probably thought only of the discussions. In his reply to Reimer he assumes that the publisher will be among the "three thousand guests" invited that very day to a tea at the house of Obermedizinalrat Rust, and suggests, if this is the case, they could discuss the matter there. It may then be presumed that the plans for the *Serapionsbrüder* were agreed upon over the teacups at the house of Medizinalrat Rust.

There are four volumes of the *Serapionsbrüder*, two published in 1819—at Easter and in the autumn—and one in 1820, and in 1821. At the first meeting four friends were present—Lothar, Theodor, Cyprian, and Ottmar—while Sylvester and Vinzenz were discussed as prospective members at the third meeting and appeared at the fourth. Lothar, Theodor, and Cyprian represent, generally speaking, delicately graded aspects of Hoffmann's own personality: Lothar is more realistic in his views and is somewhat inclined to skepticism; Theodor is Hoffmann the musician, and Cyprian is an out-and-out romantic and mystic. Ottmar is Hoffmann's old friend

[27] Cf. note 7 to Chapter 3.

Hitzig, more of a realist, more skeptical than Lothar; he is ever calling his companions back to earth. He censures Cyprian for writing a book based on the "deepest Catholic mysticism" (*Die Elixiere des Teufels*), for his "insane delight in insanity"; he "hates everything that coming from within to outward expression behaves in an unaccustomed or strange fashion." With prosaic skepticism he interrupted the solemn séance of some friends who were raptly watching an experiment with a ring hanging on a string and moving, it was expected, according to the will of the spectators; Ottmar scornfully insisted that the movement was owing to a current of air. There is subtle self-criticism when Theodor censures Cyprian for looking into the "shuddery deeps of nature," but he still often looks in there himself. And Lothar reproves both Theodor and Cyprian for introducing the absurd subject of ghosts. Sylvester is Contessa and Vinzenz is Dr. Koreff.[28]

Though all the stories are the work of Hoffmann and the major part of them assigned to his three representatives, he distributes his tales with discrimination both to his own personalities and to Ottmar and Sylvester, in the latter case showing especial care in selecting stories of his own imagining which might be appropriate to the literary tendencies and prejudices of his two friends, though there is perhaps a bit of malicious humor in attributing to Ottmar-Hitzig a harrowing ghost story; Ottmar excuses himself indeed and confesses that he has tried to imitate the style of Sylvester-Contessa. Why Hoffmann assigned only one story, *Die Königsbraut*, to Vinzenz-Koreff is open to conjecture, but Vinzenz is a lively and sparkling participant in the discussions, and the story is perhaps the wittiest, surely the most hilarious, in the four volumes.

There is some evidence that the group of friends who occasionally met together went for a time under the name of the "Seraphinen-brüder." The origin of the name is doubtful, as well as the shift to "Serapionsbrüder," though we may accept Hitzig's narrative, particularly since it agrees in essentials with Hoffmann's story in the first volume. A meeting of the intimate circle of Hoffmann's friends was held on the invitation of Chamisso soon after his return from

---

28 It is difficult to agree with Maassen that Cyprian may also stand in part for Koreff on the strength of his interest in abnormal mental states, for Hoffmann participated in these interests and in the same fashion as is recorded of Cyprian. All the other evidence points to Hoffmann, and Cyprian was present at the first meeting, while Vinzenz, who is unquestionably Koreff, did not appear until the fourth. Still less defensible is the conjecture of some critics that Cyprian is Chamisso and Lothar is Fouqué.

his three-year absence—and on November 14, which is St. Serapion's
Day. In view of this meeting in honor of Chamisso's return and soon
after the agreement with Reimer, it is perhaps difficult to find
adequate reason for the exclusion of Chamisso from the Serapion
Brothers. It may be admitted, of course, that, apart from *Peter
Schlemihl*, Chamisso was not a storyteller, but neither was Hitzig nor
Koreff. The absence of Fouqué is more easily explained; though he
lived till 1843 and continued to write, his work after *Der Zauberring* (1814) seemed to Hoffmann flat and spineless. "Don't you
notice," he wrote to Kunz in 1818, "a striking weakness in Fouqué's
recent works? His knights have been associating with Prussian
Uhlans and officers of the Guard." Probably Hoffmann wished to
avoid further complication through the addition of other partic-
ipants; he had chosen the six with utmost care for his purpose.

The discussions of the Serapion Brothers are by no means limited
to criticism of the stories. Hoffmann works in, for example, a
comparison of old and new church music, an essay in the form of a
dialogue between himself as Theodor and himself as Cyprian, with
occasional interruptions by other members of the group. This illuminating study of church music in two different periods he worked
over from an article published some time previously in the *Allgemeine
musikalische Zeitung*. Hoffmann was doubtless happy in finding a
device that gave him opportunity to ventilate his opinions on various
topics that found no natural place in his other writings.

At the time when the four friends—Lothar, Theodor, Cyprian,
and Ottmar—come together for their first meeting, twelve years
have passed since similar gatherings. They are somewhat embarrassed
in one another's presence, for they know they are not the same.
The whirlpool of time has caught them up and tossed them about;
days of excitement and of "bloody terror" lie behind them—an allusion to the wars of 1813-1815. Can Lothar again bring them to the
same boisterous merriment by reading Tieck's *Zerbino* to them? or
Cyprian bring in some fantastic poem or high-flown opera for which
Theodor can compose music on the spot, and thunder away, seated
at the rheumatic piano, as twelve years before? Though "what has
once been can never, never come back," they are still friends and
propose to meet weekly as before and read their stories for common
discussion. The meetings are indeed resumed, though there are long
intervals between them, such, for example, as the months of Theodor's
serious illness—Hoffmann's illness in the spring of 1819.

The name "Serapion" Hoffmann introduces through a short nar-

rative of personal adventure on the part of Cyprian. Losing his way
while walking in the mountainous region near B(amberg), he came
upon a hermit in monk's garb, whose personality interested him.
Returning to the city he discovered that the hermit was a certain
Graf P., a nobleman, diplomat, and poet, once beloved in social
circles for his graces and his wit. He had suddenly disappeared and
was later found preaching in the villages of the Tyrolese mountains
as the monk Serapion. When forcibly brought back, he became a
raving madman. Through the treatment of Dr. S(peyer) in B(amberg) he lost his violence, but persisted in the delusion that he was
Serapion, who suffered martyrdom under the Emperor Decius. Regarding him as hopelessly insane but harmless if left alone, Dr. S.
allowed or connived at his escape from the hospital, and Serapion
built himself a little cottage beside a ravine and lived there as a
pious anchorite, giving helpful advice to peasant folk who visited
him.

Cyprian decided to take a hand, read extensively in works on
insanity, and armed with knowledge thus acquired went forth to cure
the hermit. He was, however, amazed at Serapion's intellectual vigor.
The hermit quite outmatched him in logical dialectic: time is a
purely relative concept that the individual bears within him; to him
it may seem only three hours since he was executed at the command
of the Emperor Decius; this is the Theban desert and the city of
Alexandria is not far distant. He defied Cyprian to convince him
of the contrary, even if he were to take him to B., as is proposed: "If
one of us is mad, it is just as likely to be you as I." Cyprian learned to
love and revere the gentle old man with his strangely twisted wisdom.
From his characterization of the stories that Serapion was wont to
tell him, the "Serapionist principle" is derived, which is supposed to
provide a canon for the storytelling of the brotherhood. Ottmar
discovers that it happens to be St. Serapion's Day, and they take
the saint for their patron.

In describing Serapion's stories, Cyprian first emphasizes their
highly imaginative quality, the ardor of Serapion's fancy; the characters appear with "plastic fullness" and in "glowing life." Most
noteworthy is the impression that Serapion has actually seen what
he relates. Ellinger and others have overstressed this quality of
direct observation and have evaluated Hoffmann's tales according to
this part of the "Serapionist Principle," the accurate observation
of reality. Harich avers that Hoffmann himself would apply the
principle only to stories of a lesser order and is really criticizing

merely the milk-and-water Romanticists, who are prone to let reality slip out of their hands. Both critics have apparently forgotten the "fiery fancy" which was the first characteristic of Serapion's tales and that the "direct observation" of Serapion included what is seen with the eye of the mind. In other words, the fantastic must be presented as if seen by an accurately observing eyewitness. This idea is repeatedly affirmed in the discussions of the brotherhood. For example, their common friend Leander is rejected for membership in the club, in spite of his cleverness, intelligence, and wit, for he does not have the "Serapionist Principle"; everything he creates he has thought out with mature reflection, weighed out as it were, but he has not really seen it. "It is not that reason has control of his fancy, it has entirely replaced it." And Sylvester is welcomed as a worthy member because he puts his visions (das innere Gebilde) in words and writes nothing that he has not truly felt and seen in his soul.

Three years after Hoffmann's death, a last collection of his stories appeared, *Die letzten Erzählungen von E. T. A. Hoffmann.* With characteristic generosity Hitzig arranged for the publication and paid for it in the hope that something might be gained for the support of Hoffmann's widow. All of the stories had been published previously in periodicals. The *Letzte Erzählungen* contained several numbers that had appeared before the last volume of the *Serapionsbrüder* was issued but for one reason or another had not been included there.[29] The other tales were written later, *Die Räuber,* an audacious but not ineffective use of Schiller's plot, *Die Geheimnisse, Des Vetters Eckfenster,* the botanical story *Datura Fastuosa, Die Genesung,* and *Meister Johannes Wacht.* The last three were not published until after Hoffmann's death.

The exceedingly promising fragment *Der Feind,* a story that Hoffmann left unfinished at his death, was published in the *Frauentaschenbuch auf 1824.* The three chapters that Hoffmann wrote give no uncertain promise of a major work of his ripened art. For his background he returned to old Nuremberg, which he had

---

[29] The legal problems of *Die Marquise de la Pivadière* may have seemed inappropriate for the discussion of the brotherhood, or he may have rejected it on the same grounds as Hitzig in compiling the *Letzte Erzählungen,* as merely a retelling in German of the French original; *Die Irrungen* was indeed available but was only half a story, to be completed the following year in *Die Geheimnisse; Der Elementargeist,* which Hoffmann began early in 1821, was probably not yet ready when the manuscript of the *Serapionsbrüder* was sent to the press. It is more difficult to assign reasons for the omission of *Die Doppeltgänger;* it was published this very year, 1821, in *Feierstunden,* a reworking of material he had written several years before for his share of the cooperative novel *Der Roman des Freiherrn von Vieren.*

portrayed so effectively in *Meister Martin der Küfner*. It is the time
of Albrecht Dürer's highest achievement and his supreme fame, and
Dürer himself was to be the principal character. Apparently the
plot of the story was to be centered in the relations past and present
between Dürer and a rival painter Irmshöfer, who years before had
fled from Nuremberg, taking with him the daughter of a patrician
family. It is evident that he deserted her and their child in Italy. A
few years later the child and the dying mother were accidentally
found in Naples by a Nuremberg merchant, who after the mother's
death brought the five-year-old boy back home. Despite the enmity
between him and the boy's father, the reasons for which are not as
yet disclosed, Dürer took the little boy into his home and brought him
up as a foster son, now a youthful artist of great promise. The plan
for the story is broadly laid, indicating at any rate a "Novelle" of
substantial length. In vivid and objective portrayal Hoffmann has
rarely equalled the opening scene in a Nuremberg tavern, where
the sturdy citizens of the old city are gathered, each individualized
with master strokes, or the brilliant second chapter, where the people
of Nuremberg, as at the end of Wagner's *Meistersinger*, are gathered
on the "Hallerwiese" toward the close of day, for promenade, youthful sports, and general merrymaking. The moving throng, the individuals in the crowd, are presented with a skill that suggests the
Goethe of "Vor dem Tor." Though Dürer himself does not appear at
all in the first chapter, only very briefly in the second, and likewise
briefly at the end of the third, the author knows how to keep the
focus directly or indirectly upon him. It is another tragedy of
literary history that death intervened to prevent the completion of
Dürer's portrait, the portrait that Hoffmann the artist could have
drawn.[30]

As already noted, *Die Genesung* was one of the works that Hoffmann dictated from what was virtually his deathbed. That a dying
man should write a story entitled "The Recovery (of Health)" invites a symbolic interpretation. Over the trivial round of social life
in his brother's house, the endless teas, artificial, shallow, inane, Graf
S. . . . broods until an insane melancholy takes possession of him, a
"fixed idea" that as a punishment for man's degeneracy, for man's
constant cultivation of the superficial, nature has erased the color
"green" from the earth. A young physician, who is in love with a

[30] Max, the publisher in Breslau, to whom Hoffmann had transferred a large part
of his publishing interests, hoped that Tieck would complete *Der Feind*, a task
that Tieck was not in the least likely to undertake.

niece of the Count, undertakes to effect a cure through mesmerism. A coach brings the party to a lovely spot in the forest, the Count himself in mesmeric slumber; the test will be in his awakening, to find the trees still green and the birds singing. Hoffmann employs his old device of a personal narrator: a friend who walking in the wood is perplexed in seeing the coach arrive in the secluded glade, and then, after explanations, joins the party as a spectator of the experiment. The story does not indicate, as some perhaps wishfully have interpreted it, that Hoffmann on his deathbed had gained a new understanding of external nature, that in his city flat he longed for the "green" of the forests. "Green" is only a symbol, and he is merely reiterating his old contempt for artificiality and shallowness. To be sure Hitzig reports Hoffmann's outcry in the last springtime of his life that he had as yet "seen no green tree this spring," but the green trees that he longed to see were those along the streets and in the parks of Berlin. Hoffmann loved life as Heine did on his "mattress grave," and the springtime "green" was a sign of life renewed. One may associate this expression of regret on Hoffmann's part with an anecdote that Hitzig relates of Hoffmann's last birthday. In reaction to the sentiment that Schiller expressed in the familiar line, "Das Leben ist der Güter höchstes nicht" (Life is not the highest of our possessions), Hoffmann burst out with a vigor he had not displayed the whole evening: "No, no, to live, live, only to be alive, under whatever circumstances it may be."[31]

The contributions to the *Allgemeine musikalische Zeitung*, which for a number of years past had formed a substantial part of Hoffmann's activity, now virtually ceased. Soon after his arrival he wrote a paper for Rochlitz' journal on musical affairs in the Prussian capital, *Briefe über Tonkunst in Berlin*, but in spite of the suggestion in the title there was only one of them, and only once again, in 1819, did an article of his appear in the familiar pages, *Der Baron von B*, which presently was taken up into the *Serapionsbrüder*. Rochlitz was to be sure no longer the editor of the journal, yet he maintained an interest in it, and this defection of a valued contributor may have aroused his displeasure, for he wrote of Hoff-

---

[31] In this connection, Hoffmann would have felt a prophetic irony if he had recalled his words after the death of his mother: "Das grosse Studium des Todes ist uns verhasst, weil unser verzärtelter Geist sich nur an blühenden Rosen weidet, deren Dorn er fürchtet—Ach Freund, wer nicht den Tod sich bey Zeiten zum Freunde macht, und auf vertraulichen Fuss mit ihm umgeht, dem macht er zuletzt seine Visite immer auf die quälendste Art." Letter to Hippel, *Briefwechsel*, I, p. 100.

mann less sympathetically than one would expect from the cordial friendship of the Leipzig days.[32]

The last years apparently produced little in the way of musical criticism. It is possible that he wrote a considerable number of reviews for Berlin journals in addition to the few that are known, but as yet they lack positive identification.[33] When early in 1820 the renowned Italian musician Spontini was appointed general musical director in Berlin, Hoffmann greeted the newcomer with cordial welcome in *Gruss an Spontini.* Personal acquaintance, even friendship, only deepened his regard for Spontini's musicianship. In the latter part of the same he translated into German the French text of Spontini's opera *Olympia* and the following summer he wrote a review of the performance for the *Zeitung für Theater und Musik*; in February he had already reviewed Spontini's *Lalla Rookh.*[34]

[32] Cf. Friedrich Rochlitz: *Für Freunde der Tonkunst*, 4 vols. Leipzig, 1824-1832; Vol. II (1825), pp. 3-34. The account of Hoffmann is in a section called "Bildnisse" and is in the main a reprint of the article which appeared after Hoffmann's death in the *Allgemeine musikalische Zeitung* for October 9, 1822. For his "Bildnis" of Hoffmann, Rochlitz wrote several introductory paragraphs and then took his original paper, reworded some passages, and made additions. In this process the general estimate of Hoffmann is altered. He speaks rather contemptuously of Hoffmann's work at the Bamberg theater: "Auf H's Betrieb versuchte man sich mit Allem: dem Höchsten und Niedrigsten, dem Würdigsten und dem Fratzenhaftesten; selbst Heiligen-Geschichten, und in denselben Himmel und Hölle nach alten Kirchenbildern, wurden dargestellt," referring evidently to the performances of Calderon. For the quarrel with Seconda he casts the blame entirely on Hoffmann. In the "Nekrolog" he censured Hoffmann for his faithlessness in his friendship with Zacharias Werner; here the censure is sharpened, "kaum verzeihlich." He attributes to Hoffmann an unreasonable and even angry resentment at any criticism of his work and describes in detail his wrath at Rochlitz' review of the first two volumes of the *Fantasiestücke* (*Allgemeine musikalische Zeitung*, August 17, 1814, columns 541-50), which was in the main favorable. On the other hand, Hitzig asserts that Hoffmann never read reviews of his works and was quite indifferent to criticism. Rochlitz' biographical details are unreliable and he speaks of Hoffmann's stories with a certain condescension. He ceased to be the editor of the *Allgemeine musikalische Zeitung* in 1818, but continued his contributions; cf. Hans von Müller in *Süddeutsche Monatshefte*, v¹ (1908), p. 56.

[33] Cf. Felix Hasselberg: "Ein unbekanntes Kreislerianum," in *Mitteilungen des Vereins für die Geschichte Berlins*, XLIV, pp. 127-28. Hasselberg has scanned the files of the *Vossische Zeitung*, 1815-1822, and thinks he has discovered a large number of reviews by Hoffmann, of which he presents one as a sample—the account of a concert by the violinist Karl Möser. Further findings are evidently taken up in the following article, which the present writer has been unable to examine: "Neue E. T. A. Hoffmann-Funde. Unbekannte Opern- und Konzertkritiken aus den Jahren 1815 bis 1821," ermittelt und mitgeteilt von Felix Hasselberg, in the *Königsberger Hartungsche Zeitung*, February 19 and October 28, 1928. Cf. also Hans von Müller: "Die neueren Sammlungen von E. T. A. Hoffmanns Werken und Privataufzeichnungen," in *Zeitschrift für Bücherfreunde* N.F., XVIII (1926), pp. 1-16.

[34] Cf. Hans von Müller: "Hoffmann contra Spontini," in *Die Musik*, VII (December 1907), pp. 338-52; Giuseppe Radiciotti: *Spontini a Berlino*, Ancona, 1925; Charles Bouvet: *Spontini*, Paris, 1930; Hans Kuznitzky: "Weber und Spontini in der musikalischen Anschauung von E. T. A. Hoffmann," in *Zeitschrift für Musikwissenschaft*,

These reviews plunged Hoffmann into the foolish controversy then raging in Berlin as to the respective merits of German and French-Italian opera; the Berlin world of those days was divided into two hostile camps, reminiscent of Wieland's Abdera and the lawsuit over the donkey's shadow.

Hoffmann's two reviews of Weber's *Der Freischütz* were sincerely appreciative but not uncritical. He had met Weber in Bamberg, and in Berlin they had become friends; Weber thought very highly of *Undine* and reviewed it favorably in the *Allgemeine musikalische Zeitung*. Unluckily, Weber was offended by Hoffmann's reviews of *Der Freischütz*, thus ending a connection that Hoffmann had valued. During these last years Hoffmann became a member of a choral and social organization, "Die jüngere Liedertafel," and the last of his musical compositions were two songs for this club.[35] It was perhaps only a fancy on the part of one mortally ill that in the last months of his life Hoffmann turned again to *Undine* and borrowed the complete score from the library of music of the Royal Theaters. He had wished a different prelude, had thought that the water-nixie nature of his heroine had not been sufficiently brought out, and Fouqué had prepared a text, but Hoffmann's music was never written.

---

x (February 1928), pp. 292-99. According to Hoffmann's letter to Hippel, June 24, 1820, he undertook the translation of *Olympia* reluctantly at the express wish of the King ("weil es der König gewünscht"). Yet the letter of Graf Brühl, June 5, 1820, very politely, even hesitatingly, expresses the hope that Hoffmann might be willing to assume the task; Brühl makes no mention of the King and says the suggestion came from Spontini himself.

35 Cf. Hans von Müller: "E. T. A. Hoffmanns letzte Komposition," in *Die Musik*, XLIII (June 1912), pp. 3349-52. The day after the burial of Hoffmann, the society had a memorial meeting. A song by Friedrich Förster, "Nachruf an unsern Freund E. T. A. Hoffmann" was sung; Förster was the author of the songs referred to above.

PART II · HIS WORKS

CHAPTER 6

THREE FUNDAMENTALS:
PHILOSOPHY, RELIGION, AND POLITICS

PHILOSOPHY

AN understanding of the Romantic Period, or specifically of the work of Hoffmann and of the perplexities that run, often tragically, through his tales, is impossible without some knowledge of the philosophic thought preceding and contemporary with Romantic writing. The rationalism of the eighteenth century had penetrated into the remotest corners of everyday thinking. Much that was wholesome, even salutary, was accomplished in this Age of Enlightenment, the "Aufklärung," as the Germans call it, but in the course of time the doctrines of rationalism seemed to degenerate into a drab utilitarianism, a mere recipe for getting on in the world. The phrase "a healthy human understanding" became widely current, coupled with the implication that it covered all man needed for success and happiness in this world. The high priest of rationalism in this debased form was the Berlin bookseller and publisher Friedrich Nicolai, whom the youthful Tieck pilloried with his biting satire.

Toward the end of the century a murmur of dissent began to be heard and the Romantic Movement came into being. Rationalistic theories seemed to leave no room for the poetic and spiritual side of man's nature and to confine the imagination in a strait jacket. There were those who in thought anticipated the words of Shelley in his *Defence of Poetry*: "Reason is to the imagination as the instrument to the agent, as the body to the spirit, as the shadow to the substance." It was the good fortune of the Romanticists that a school of philosophic thinking arose to give them a foundation for their revolt.

In Hoffmann's youth Immanuel Kant was the most distinguished citizen of Königsberg. He must have been a familiar figure to Hoffmann from his boyhood on, for he lived not far away in the little city, and it is said that the people of the town could set their clocks by the regularity of Kant's walk to the university and his return. As a student of law, Hoffmann did not register for Kant's courses of lectures, though it was the fashion for students to do so irrespective of the technical subjects in which they were enrolled. Yet after the custom of German students everywhere Hoffmann probably "sampled" Kant's lectures by occasional attendance; indeed he must have done so, for according to Hippel he admitted that he could not understand them. But Hoffmann did not need to listen to Kant's voice to be affected by Kantian ideas; they were in the air, and it is inconceivable that Hoffmann and Hippel did not discuss them in their frequent meetings over a bottle of wine.

It would be presumptuous to attempt a survey of the philosophy of Kant, Fichte, and Schelling in a few sentences,[1] but some points where the philosophy of the time most influenced literature, particularly the work of Hoffmann, may be briefly summarized. In his first "Critique" Kant set limits to the range of the human intellect, thus undermining the arrogance of the rationalists. There is a world of phenomena, Kant said, which we apprehend through our senses but behind these phenomena lie the things in and of themselves—their essential being—which we can never grasp; we have no organs for comprehending them; we are separated from them by "barriers of brass."

The philosopher Fichte, associated with members of the Romantic School by ties of personal friendship, went a step farther than Kant. He denied the very existence of the phenomenal world except as we ourselves apprehend it. It seems to exist, he said, but its existence depends upon us; it is the product of our sense perceptions. Schelling was even more intimately linked with the little group of young men who formed the nucleus of the newly developing Romantic Movement. He did not deny the existence of nature apart from our apprehension of it, but taught that nature and spirit are identical—nature is visible spirit and spirit invisible nature. In Schelling's teachings there is only one substance, which is God, the Divine Absolute, and the visible world consists of multiform emanations from this Divine Substance, which differ in attributes but are still essentially one since they are parts of an identical whole. Hence man is one emanation; a flower or a mineral are other forms. Man is nature become self-conscious, but still in essential being is akin to the flowers and the stones. He emerges for a time as a self-conscious being, but after a little while is reabsorbed into the unity of the

---

[1] Cf. Hinrich Knittermeyer: *Schelling und die romantische Schule*, München (1928); for the influence of Schelling and his followers upon Hoffmann, especially important are Gustav Egli: *E. T. A. Hoffmann: Ewigkeit und Endlichkeit in seinem Werk*, Zürich-Leipzig-Berlin, 1927, and Karl Ochsner: *E. T. A. Hoffmann als Dichter des Unbewussten*, Leipzig, 1936. Cf. also Wilhelm Schmidt: "Fichtes Einfluss auf die ältere Romantik," in *Euphorion*, xx (1913), pp. 435-58, 647-81; xxi (1914), pp. 251-70.

Divine Being. There is as a consequence in each man a vital core that stands in relationship to the One Soul. Romantic literature is inextricably interwoven with these philosophic concepts.

There is no direct evidence of Hoffmann's acquaintance with the writings of Fichte. During his second residence in Berlin (1807-1808) he mentions in a letter to Hippel that Fichte and Schleiermacher are "again" in Berlin. This was the winter when Fichte delivered his famous addresses to the German nation (*Reden an die deutsche Nation*) which made him a figure of national significance outside of academic circles. In a later letter he mentions meeting Schleiermacher, but personal acquaintance with Fichte is nowhere recorded. Fichte had died before Hoffmann's return to Berlin in 1814. Yet if Hoffmann had never read Fichte's works, the Fichtean ideas had gained wide currency and were doubtless discussed in his hearing. Admiring Jean Paul as a novelist, he may have dipped into his criticism of Fichte's theories in the *Clavis Fichtiana* or perceived the disparagement of them involved in some of his novels.[2] In Dresden he became absorbed in Schelling's *Weltseele* (World-Soul).[3]

If we accept the philosophy of Fichte that we create our world, that it has no existence apart from our apprehension of it, then the world of sense perceptions is quite negligible save for our interest in it, since it exists only in us. William Lovell, the hero of Tieck's novel, said: "Things are because we thought them. . . . Why doesn't the world fall in chaotic fragments? We are the fate that holds it upright. . . . Virtue exists only because I have thought it." In other words, the normal distinction between the subjective and the objective has ceased to be valid, and the world of objective reality has become purely subjective. Novalis, the most profoundly philosophic spirit among the early Romantics, was aware of the full range of this theory; he placed it in the form of an equation: "The ego is equal to the non-ego," or again, "We dream of journeys through the universe; but is not the universe within us? The deeps of our spirit we do not know. The mysterious pathway leads within. In us or nowhere is eternity with its worlds, the past and the future."

A distinctive, perhaps *the* most distinctive, aspect of German Romanticism is intimately related to these trends of philosophic

[2] Cf. note 5, in Part II, Chapter 7.

[3] An earlier acquaintance with Schelling might perhaps be inferred from an entry in Hoffmann's diary on April 17, 1812: ". . . im Novalis gelesen und sehr erbaut worden (Studium der Naturphilosophie—Schelling)," but this probably means merely that he knew of Schelling and, aroused by the reading of Novalis, thought of looking up Schelling's "Naturphilosophie."

thought. Close to the center of German Romanticism lies the awareness on the part of its chief representatives that beneath the mass of sense perceptions, which make up the world of our everyday life, the physical things around us, there exists a deeper meaning, an inexplicable substance, a relationship which, if not supernatural, is at least supersensuous. In this conviction they were antirationalistic. They did not, however, reject science or scientific investigation, but they were still unsatisfied with the deepest probings of which the human intellect is capable. Nor did dogmatic religion in the narrow sense meet their longing to penetrate beyond the barrier. They were unwilling to accept material things as only material things— the primrose by the river's brim was more than a primrose by the river's brim. From this awareness their exalted conception of the poetic function is derived; what is denied to the rationalistic thinker, to the scientist, is vouchsafed to the poet. By a divine intuition the poet catches glimpses here and there of the spiritual world which surrounds us, or, in the thought world of a Schelling, can perceive the relationship of the individual to the divine all-embracing Substance from which all things are derived. Novalis is the supreme exemplar of this lofty view of the poet's service.

A philosophy that denies objective reality, that allows the individual to create his world, or rather maintains that he does and must create it, is obviously a boon to the dreamer. The world of dreams is just as real as the world of his sense perceptions, since he creates them both. Without hesitation he can choose the world in which he prefers to live. To many of the Romanticists these philosophical theories provided a sanction for their dreaming, for their otherworldliness. But not to all. To Heinrich von Kleist, one of the most gifted authors of the period, the philosophic limitation of man's intellectual powers came as an overwhelming catastrophe: if there is no possibility of attaining truth, if all our learning is only relative, a mere approximation, what is the value of all our striving? And to Hoffmann the philosophy of his times brought a perplexing doubt as to the reality of things. Is there any reality? What is mere seeming, and is there any difference between seeming and being? With these devastating questions Hoffmann plays in one story after another, and despite the rollicking humor of the tales it is a somber play. The more tragic his feeling was, the more grotesque were the forms in which he clothed his uncertainty.

In the use of one strange device some of the Romanticists went a step farther than was really sanctioned by their philosophical guides.

This device has been conveniently called the disintegration of personality, and is a modification of the philosophy of the "Ego." In the Fichtean system, the Ego creates its world and hence is the one reality. What is then left if we deny the existence of the Ego, that is, as a self-conscious, integrated personality? The Romanticists pondered much upon problems of palingenesis and metempsychosis —the rebirth of a personality in a later day, perhaps not in entire forgetfulness of a former life, perhaps in consciousness of this, echoing Rossetti's words: "I have been here before." The phenomenon called the disintegration of personality involves the separation of an individual into two or more contemporaneous personalities; or, more intriguing still, a personality may be shared by two people. On the theory that our sense of identity depends upon the association of memories uniting our experiences, there might then be postulated the possibility that certain experiences seemingly forgotten and buried in the subconscious self might combine to form a counterpersonality, a rival ego. The motif of double identity is of frequent occurrence in Romantic fiction—a double personality in one man, or a personality divided between two people, each having a partial personality of his own and a personality in part shared.

In a novel by Hoffmann's acquaintance Achim von Arnim, this division of personality between two characters is explained by a blood transfusion. Partly for narrative interest, Hoffmann and others attach the idea to two people who have a strange personal resemblance to one another and participate in one another's thoughts and deeds. Medardus, the leading character in *Die Elixiere des Teufels* becomes uncertain whether he is still the runaway monk Medardus or whether he is really Viktorin the man whom he thinks he has killed; and Viktorin thinks he is the monk Medardus. Medardus on his wedding day hears a tumult in the street and looking out sees this other self being borne to execution for crimes he himself has committed and this other self has confessed. In *Die Doppeltgänger* (The Doubles) two young men, identical in appearance, in voice, and manner, are in love with the same girl, though only one of them has ever seen her; the other by mysterious telepathy—or collusion has created her out of his dreams, even to a knowledge of her name. In this case Hoffmann attributes the resemblance to occult prenatal influence—as in Goethe's *Die Wahlverwandtschaften*; the mother of one of the youths, though entirely innocent, has been in love with the father of the other.

But the use of doubles was for the Romanticists not merely a method of entertaining the reader with startling and perplexing or amusing incidents; it was not a Shakespearean *Comedy of Errors*, though Brentano's *Die mehreren Wehmüller* increased the confusion by adding a third to the doubles. The integrity of the individual had been brought into question long before the Romanticists toyed with the idea of the disintegration of personality. The question was inevitable when one began to reflect upon the nature of self-consciousness and the problem of divided personality. All this is obviously quite apart from the common conception of two natures struggling within the human being—the aspiring and the sensual-earthly. The moment that the consciousness of personality is undermined, the whole structure of reality is likewise undermined. In his young manhood Hoffmann was tormented by the concept of self-duplication. Though he found the idea of "doubles" in the novels of Jean Paul and later in Fouqué's *Der Zauberring*, his own employment of the concept is decidedly individual.[4] The contemporary cult of mesmerism lent support to these speculations. The mesmerized subject might lose the awareness of his own individuality; he responded not to his own will but to the will of another.

Antirationalism was a native element in Hoffmann's make-up. He was early conscious of a conflict with rationalistic thinking, years before he became a kind of antirationalist crusader. At eighteen he wrote to Hippel stressing the rights of the emotional side of human nature and tried to establish a balance between the "head" and the "heart" as the real goal of education, and a month later he wrote: "As long as we remain in the flesh and cannot sever our senses from our spirit, we must not banish our unreasoned enthusiasms [Schwärmerei] from us. To us they are what colors are to a painting; they exalt every idea that busies our minds; with each thought of happiness they spread over us a beneficent sensation of gentle rapture." In a later letter he quotes from Herder the lines: "Who would not dig himself his own grave, were it not for the sweet delusion?"[5] If the sweet delusion is all there is, why not cling to it?

Hoffmann himself was not a philosophical thinker, though he pondered in perplexity over certain philosophical problems. For the systematic philosophy of the schools he had little appreciation, except as it might touch the fundamental questions of human living in which he was personally concerned. Were it not for the spur to the

    [4] Cf. Margot Kuttner: *Die Gestaltung des Individualitätsproblems bei E. T. A. Hoffmann*, Düsseldorf, 1936; Wilhelmine Krauss: *Das Doppelgängermotiv in der Romantik*, Berlin, 1930; Martin Roehl: *Die Doppelpersönlichkeit bei E. T. A. Hoffmann*, Rostock [1918]; Max Dessoir: *Das Doppel-ich*, zweite Auflage, Leipzig, 1896.
    [5] Cf. Herder (Suphan), xxix, p. 59.

imagination in Schelling's *Weltseele* (*Von der Weltseele*) one might
be surprised that Hoffmann's patience endured the ordeal of reading
it. He loved, however, to wander in the twilight borderlands of
speculative thought and found in G. H. Schubert perhaps his most
congenial companion for such voyaging. Schubert's *Ansichten von
der Nachtseite der Naturwissenschaften* (Views of the Nocturnal
Side of the Natural Sciences) was published in 1808; the substance
of the book had been delivered as lectures in Dresden in the winter
of 1807-1808, and it is probable that the memory of them was still
vivid in the minds of Hoffmann's friends there a few years later. It
is possible that in his Bamberg days Hoffmann learned something
of Schubert's ideas through Wetzel, who had been a close friend of
Schubert's, but in view of the very meager record of Hoffmann's
acquaintance with Wetzel, it seems hardly probable.[6] According to
a letter of July 26, 1813, Hoffmann hopes to receive a copy of
Schubert's book through Kunz's aid: "Now that I have finished
with the study of Schelling's *Weltseele*," he says, "I can go on to it."
Schubert was a devoted pupil and lifelong friend of Schelling, and it
was perhaps a natural step to turn to him after the *Weltseele*. Hoffmann acknowledges the receipt of the work and comments upon it
in the same letter to Kunz with which he dispatches the last section
of *Der Magnetiseur*.[7] Schubert's *Symbolik des Traums* (Symbolism

[6] Wetzel had been Schubert's most intimate friend in their university days; in the
years preceding his arrival in Bamberg he had lived in Dresden and associated with
the Dresden group of Romantic writers, and hence may have discussed with Hoffmann the content of Schubert's lectures, but there is no evidence of it. The relations
between the two men could hardly have been intimate; Hoffmann mentions Wetzel
only twice in his diary. The silence of Hoffmann is hardly challenged by the statement of Wetzel's daughter Constanze many years later: "Der Musikdirektor und
Dichter Hoffmann war des Vaters Freund und besuchte uns oft." Constanze was
only three years old when the family moved to Bamberg and only five and a half
when Hoffmann left for Dresden. If Hoffmann had been a frequent visitor, it would
have surely appeared in his diary. To be sure, the diary for the year 1810 is entirely
missing, but the entries from 1811 to the time of Hoffmann's departure are abundantly sprinkled with references to his daily companionships and visits to the houses
of his friends. Trube thinks the relations between the two men did not advance above
the level of "einer beobachtenden und abwartenden Bekanntschaft"; cf. Hans Trube:
Friedrich Gottlob Wetzels Leben und Werk, Berlin, 1928; F. A. Koethe: "Ernst
Theodor Wilhelm Hoffmann und Friedrich Gottlob Wetzel," in *Blätter für literarische Unterhaltung* (1837), pp. 385-86, 389-90, 393-94, 397-98.

[7] There would seem to be no foundation for Max Pirker's assertion that "Der
Magnetiseur ist mit Elementen aus Schuberts Ansichten durchsetzt" (*Euphorion*,
xvii [1910], p. 443). *Der Magnetiseur* was begun May 19, 1813, and it was July 26 when
Hoffmann wrote to Kunz, seeking his aid in obtaining Schubert's book. On August
19, when the last section of *Der Magnetiseur* was being sent to Kunz, he wrote:
"Schuberts Ansichten pp habe ich erhalten und bin begierig auf alles, was der
geniale Mann geschrieben und schreibt"; it is evident that his acquaintance with
Schubert dates from the preceding days. The same reasoning would rule out Pirker's

of Dreams), showing the author a faraway predecessor of Freud, was published by Kunz in 1814, the first book to be issued in his new publishing venture.

The highly imaginative and poetic style of the first lecture in Schubert's *Ansichten* is reminiscent of Novalis' *Hymnen an die Nacht* (Hymns to the Night), and in choosing a title for the publication of his lectures Schubert may have had Novalis' poems in mind, as well, perhaps, as the astronomical designation for the side of a planet that is turned away from the sun. In view of the fanciful and emotional tone, one is puzzled by Hoffmann's criticism of the book as "ingenious [scharfsinnig] rather than poetic." The influence of Schubert's work on Hoffmann was considerable but may easily be overestimated. It is, indeed, possible to collect a long series of passages, for example, from *Der goldene Topf* and from Schubert's *Ansichten*, which show striking similarities in thought and expression. In some cases "borrowing" may be admitted; *Der goldene Topf* was finished before *Die Symbolik des Traums* was published. Other stories may be combed for further evidence of Schubert's influence. In general the passages afford indubitable proof of an intellectual and aesthetic kinship between Hoffmann and Schubert. Even in the *Ansichten* Hoffmann could probably find little in the realm of ideas that was really new to him, rather a brilliant presentation, a codification, or amplified confirmation, of ideas that had long been surging in his own spirit. For example, *Der Magnetiseur* was begun on May 19, 1813, some weeks before Schubert's book was in his hands. The direct and indirect references to Schubert in Hoffmann's writings are numerous; Schubert remained a kindred spirit, offering continual stimulus in the presentation of ideas, in the use of imagery and illustrative incident.[8]

Attention has sometimes been called to the presence in Hoffmann's works of concepts resembling the philosophic thinking of Jakob Boehme, the mystic Silesian cobbler, though naturally in Hoffmann's case adjusted to his purposes as an artist. Despite the profuse ref-

---

suggestion that Hoffmann found the "germ" of *Der goldene Topf* in the myths contained in Schubert's *Ahndungen einer allgemeinen Geschichte des Lebens*, Leipzig, 1806; cf. Pirker's review of P. Margis: "E. T. A. Hoffmann: Eine psychographische Individualanalyse," Leipzig, 1911, in *Euphorion*, xx (1913), pp. 251-61.

[8] For details with reference to Hoffmann's use of Schubert, cf. Wilhelm Lechner: *Gotthilf Heinrich Schuberts Einfluss auf Kleist, Justinus Kerner und E. T. A. Hoffmann*, Münster, 1911; P. Sucher: *Les Sources du merveilleux chez E. T. A. Hoffmann*, Paris, 1912; Hans Dahmen: *E. T. A. Hoffmanns Weltanschauung*, Marburg a/L, 1929; F. R. Merkel: *Der Naturphilosoph Gotthilf Heinrich Schubert und die deutsche Romantik*, München, 1912, and the works of Egli and Ochsener, cf. note 11.

erences to his reading, Hoffmann nowhere mentions Boehme;[9] if he had struggled with *Aurora* or *De Signatura Rerum*, it seems probable that he would have recorded the fact. As Boehme's thought had become widely diffused among those of a mystical turn of mind, Hoffmann might well have absorbed some of it without being aware of the ultimate source.[10] Some knowledge of Swedenborg's thought may also be assumed; Hoffmann refers to the Swedish seer in both *Der Magnetiseur* and *Der goldene Topf*.

Ricarda Huch, one of the most penetrating and illuminating students of German Romanticism, has said of the Romantic writers, but with especial reference to Hoffmann, that they were "homeless" in their bodies; they did not feel at home there: "the immediate homeland of the human being is his body and whether he feels happy or wretched in this environment determines his feeling of having a home on this earth."[11] Hoffmann was such a homeless one, and art, the work of the creative imagination, was his escape from his physical self and his environment into his real home. His own stories formed a method of withdrawal into the spiritual world of his imagination. The intense subjectivity of his tales was long overlooked, for it was far from as patent as in the case of a Novalis or a Tieck. Longing, a passionate personal longing, for a happier, a more beautiful, world is a perpetual undertone in everything he wrote. The artist soul is cramped and confined in the world of everyday, is held a prisoner in bonds by the crudity of material things. There is no refuge but in a world of dreams. "My kingdom is not of this world," is Hoffmann's favorite quotation from Scripture.

RELIGION

While the Romanticists took counsel with their philosophers and

[9] Cf. E. Ederheimer: *Jakob Boehme und die Romantik*, Heidelberg, 1904.

[10] Hypothetically a line of succession from Boehme to Hoffmann might be established: the mystic French philosopher Louis Claude de St. Martin (1743-1803), "le philosophe inconnu," as he called himself, was demonstrably indebted to Boehme and he translated the *Aurora* into French. In turn Schubert translated St. Martin's *De L'Esprit des choses* into German, and Adolph Wagner, Hoffmann's friend in Leipzig, the same author's *L'Homme de désir*. Boehme's ideas may have taken this pathway in reaching Hoffmann. In 1801 Zacharias Werner wrote to Hitzig that he had been reading a volume of Boehme's works "mit frommer unschuldiger Andacht" and discovered in Boehme "das Original oder Vorbild der jetzt Mode werdenden Dichtkunst." Werner's appreciation may have provided another and early channel for Hoffmann's acquaintance with Boehme's thought. Cf. J. E. Hitzig, *Lebens-Abriss Friedrich Ludwig Zacharias Werners* (Berlin, 1823), pp. 23-25; also Felix Poppenberg, *Zacharias Werner und die Romantik* (Berlin; without date, but 1893); H. Düntzer, *Zwei Bekehrte* (Leipzig, 1873), pp. 23-24.

[11] Cf. Ricarda Huch: *Ausbreitung und Verfall der Romantik* (Leipzig, 1902), p. 201.

applied the new ideas to works of their creative imagination, they could not forget that they were also children of religious faith. The eighteenth century was not only the "Age of the Enlightenment"; it witnessed also the flowering of pietism. Novalis defined philosophy as "a homesickness to be at home everywhere," and to him and his kind philosophy in its broader range included religion as perhaps a longing to be at home in heavenly places or indeed as the most important branch of philosophy. An account of the author's religious beliefs and of his relationship to the Church, Catholic or Protestant, or indeed both, forms an integral part of the biography of most writers during the Romantic Period. From this generalization Hoffmann stands, or seems to stand, apart as a conspicuous exception. The biographies and special monographs as a rule either do not raise the question or state that religion played no role in his life.

In the Doerffer household of Hoffmann's youth, the most rigid of traditional forms prevailed, including those of an ecclesiastical nature. Hoffmann's grandfather on his father's side and his great grandfather on his mother's were rural clergymen in East Prussia. In one of his earliest letters to Hippel, Hoffmann wrote: "As religious devotion and piety, which have always ruled in our family with a golden scepter, it was required that we should be sorry for our sins and go to Communion."[12] He was thus in his youth forced to an outward religious conformity. In Otto Wilhelm Doerffer he had ever before him day and night, since they shared a common bedchamber, an unlovely example of religious hypocrisy—a punctilious observance of an external show of religious living that ill concealed a pettiness of conduct, a hollowness of character, and a lack of Christian sympathies. The presence of the Werner family in the same house furnished a potent warning against all forms of religious fanaticism.

And yet in his biographical sketch Hippel says that Hoffmann, even in the period of the most extravagant mischievousness (ausgelassener Mutwillen), in school days or student life, never made any sarcastic remarks or whimsical utterances (launigte Äusserungen) concerning those to whom he owed respect. In this connection, Hippel mentions Dr. Wannowski, the rector of the school, from whom Hoffmann received his first formal instruction in religion—the Court Preacher Schulz, who probably prepared him for the rite of confirmation, and Hippel's own father, the village pastor in Arnau. Hippel records further that in their days of close comradeship

---

[12] *Briefwechsel*, I, pp. 44-45. Letter of December 7, 1794.

Hoffmann avoided all conversation on religious or political matters; he would break off any conversation that would lead to such topics, and according to Hitzig this aversion continued throughout Hoffmann's life.[13] Hoffmann's silence in the long letters to Hippel is even more significant, for the letters, after the fashion in earlier friendships, contain a deep revelation of his inner being, a frank unburdening of his spirit.

Hoffmann's interest in the Roman Catholic Church is an evident reaction to the circumstances of his upbringing. It is probable that he was first drawn to the Roman Church through the spirit of contradiction. Protestantism was all around him, apparently a particularly arid variety in his own household. Königsberg was an emphatically Protestant city; the Roman Catholic population was insignificant, and Hoffmann states that the youthful Kreisler had to journey twenty or thirty leagues to hear real Catholic church music. And it was probably the music of the Church that formed the introduction. In regard to his musical setting for certain stanzas of the *Dies Irae*, he wrote to Hippel expressing a hardly concealed wish that he were "in a Catholic place" where certain changes might fit his composition for production in church.

In Glogau Hoffmann lived for the first time in a community with a large Roman Catholic population, though he resided in the Protestant family of his uncle. In the Polish "provinces" he was placed in an almost completely Roman Catholic environment. He married a Roman Catholic wife by the rites of the Church. Leaving Poland, after a little more than a year in Protestant Berlin, he spent four years and a half in Roman Catholic Bamberg. Thus for a long period he was immersed in circumstances in which Roman Catholicism became a daily intimacy. He attended services in Catholic churches; he frequently sang in their choirs, both in Warsaw and in Bamberg, and composed music for the Roman liturgies. In Bamberg he marched in the Corpus Christi procession, and the profound impression derived from a visit to the Capuchin monastery, especially his reverence for the aged monk Pater Cyrillus, have a wider significance than as a mere source for *Die Elixiere des Teufels*.

The very morning after his arrival in Dresden Hoffmann heard mass (requiem) in the Catholic Court Church. He wrote Hippel from Glogau on Sunday, January 22, 1797, as from his window he

[13] "Der Widerwille gegen solche Gespräche ist ihm an sein Ende geblieben; man konnte ihn damit bannen." Hitzig: *Aus Hoffmanns Leben und Nachlass* (Berlin, 1823), I, p. 14.

watched the procession of villagers wending their way into town for church service, and in his words there is an unmistakable touch of envy of the simplicity and fervor of their faith. His respect for the religious feelings of devout Catholics is admirably attested by the passages in which he interprets certain plays of Calderon as performed on the Bamberg stage and comments on the impossibility of Protestant actors playing in such dramas with real success. These plays are founded on basic principles that are deeply rooted in the very being of Roman Catholics; they present experiences alien and incomprehensible to Protestants. Such human relationships to the Divine Hoffmann never treated with ridicule or viewed with skepticism. The scorn of the "Aufklärung" doubtless involved a resentment that the simple consoling faith of other days had been undermined. The words of Alexander's father-in-law in *Ein Fragment aus dem Leben dreier Freunde* expresses this idea, with which in all probability Hoffmann agreed: "In the old days we had a simple pious faith, we recognized the other world but also the foolishness of our own minds; then came the Age of Enlightenment, which made everything so clear that because there was nothing but clarity one saw nothing and plumped one's nose against the nearest tree in the forest."[14]

Despite minor errors, Hoffmann's writings show intimate acquaintance with Catholic liturgies, with Catholic beliefs and practices, and with the monastic orders. His work as a composer for Catholic services imposed upon him the necessity of first understanding and then participating in the devotional life of a Roman Catholic. In his essay *Alte und neue Kirchenmusik* he asserts without reservation that an attitude of worshipful devotion is a necessary part of the composer's equipment when he approaches the composition of a mass. The whole tone of this essay demonstrates that Hoffmann regarded the composition of a mass as a religious experience. Further, the story *Das Sanctus* implies that respect, if not religious reverence, is also required of singers who participate in the rendering of a mass.

Kreisler's interview with the Abbot in *Kater Murr* is doubtless in essence autobiographical. The Abbot's invitation to Kreisler to enter the monastery is then a reflection of an incident or incidents in Hoff-

---

[14] "In alter Zeit hatten wir einen frommen schlichten Glauben, wir erkannten das Jenseits, aber auch die Blödigkeit unserer Sinne, dann kam die Aufklärung, die alles so klar machte, dass man vor lauter Klarheit nichts sah und sich am nächsten Baum im Walde die Nase stiess." vi, p. 141.

mann's life, when he was asked to embrace Catholicism, though no biographer has interpreted it as such. The circumstances of his life brought him for many years into frequent and friendly contact with members of the clergy. It is reasonable, if not inevitable, to assume that at times the doors were cordially but discreetly opened for the entrance of the musician into a closer relationship with the Church. Kreisler's reply is significant: he acknowledges that he has at times cherished such a "whim" as contained in the Abbot's suggestion, but he shrinks back in awe (Schauer), for such a step would be taken at the cost of many a conviction that he "drew in with his mother's milk."[15] Among the convictions derived from his Protestant upbringing was a lingering conception of worldliness and insincerity on the part of the Roman clergy. A love of splendor and elegance and of luxurious living is subjected to unfavorable comment in *Die Jesuiterkirche in G.* and in *Kater Murr*. The Abbot in *Kater Murr* is a precise portrait of a superior ecclesiastic, as Hoffmann conceived them—cultivated, erudite, fond of dignified living, a zealous and untiring champion of the rights of his order. Yet Hoffmann records that one might suspect a monkish slyness behind his simple unctuous words which seemed to come from "the most devoted heart."

In various passages Hoffmann suggests insincerities and unworthiness among monks or clergymen. There is a secret door in *Das Fräulein von Scuderi* which the sly monks had contrived to facilitate a clandestine exit from the sequestered discipline of the monastery. Brother Hilarius in *Kater Murr* comments on the difficulty of a musical score that will keep the eyes of the monks so closely fastened to the notes that they cannot squint at the pretty girls in the congregation. In *Die Elixiere des Teufels* Hoffmann presents contrasting figures among the clergy and the devotees of religious orders: on the one hand the humble, tolerant Prior, incomparably devout, gentle, and wise, and Pater Cyrillus, a figure of exalted purity of character, who suffered martyrdom for the faith; on the other a group of timeservers and intriguers, whose chief activity is the pursuit of preferment, providing worldly power and luxury. The two knaves in *Datura Fastuosa*, one of them a runaway monk, are secret emissaries of the Jesuit Order. The weakness of the flesh is a Biblical conception to which Hoffmann more than once refers, and he has every sympathy with human frailty. What he portrays as in-

---

[15] One may dissent radically from Pfeiffer-Belli's opinion that these convictions were merely those of a rationalist. Cf. W. Pfeiffer-Belli: "Mythos und Religion bei E. T. A. Hoffmann," in *Euphorion*, xxxiv (1933), pp. 305-40.

sincerity, timeserving, or downright hypocrisy on the part of ecclesiastics or members of religious orders is a Catholic counterpart for Otto Wilhelm Doerffer's example in the world of Protestant faith.

The period of Hoffmann's main interest in the Roman Catholic Church coincides with the time when he was composing music for its services. The culmination of these tendencies was reached when he marched in the Corpus Christi procession in Bamberg; this act was a purely voluntary expression of himself, and it is inconceivable that a man of Hoffmann's character would have done it for any other reason. But gradually professional considerations turned his musical activity away from the Church,[16] and his departure from Bamberg brought him, after a brief and troubled residence in Dresden and Leipzig, back to Berlin, to spend the remaining years of his life in an outspoken Protestant environment.

Most of Hoffmann's tales were written after he left Bamberg, though he still made use of the Bamberg scene, and certain experiences of his residence there continued to hold him in thrall. Some of his stories, taken chronologically, seem to provide an indirect record in reminiscence of his spiritual wanderings. In *Don Juan*, written in Bamberg, and in *Die Elixiere des Teufels*, perhaps conceived there and begun not long after his departure, Hoffmann stands closest to the Roman Catholic influences that surrounded him during the previous years. In each of these narratives he presents a decidedly Christian, indeed Roman Catholic, conception of sin; and in *Die Elixiere des Teufels* a more unequivocably Roman Catholic doctrine of repentance and salvation. In essence *Die Elixiere des Teufels* is the novelist's exposition of Catholic dogma, conceived and partly executed when he was still strongly under its influence. In later years, according to Hitzig's report,[17] Hoffmann spoke critically of *Die Elixiere*. That his sympathy with Roman Catholicism diminished after his return to a Protestant environment is the most plausible explanation of his disapproval.

That most of Hoffmann's stories ignore the religious aspects of human living is a plain parallel to his avoidance of conversation on religious subjects, and doubtless has the same source. Most of his characters betray no direct influence of religion upon their views of life, though they may call upon God or the saints, or their church

---

[16] "Der Freund hatte stets eine grosse Kirchenmusik im Kopfe; ich stimmte mit meinem von ihm geforderten Rat für eine grosse Oper und setzte ihm meine Gründe auseinander." Kunz, *Aus dem Leben zweier Dichter*, p. 74.

[17] Hitzig, *op. cit.*, note 13, II, p. 166.

attendance is recorded. On the other hand, several of his figures definitely derive their purity of purpose, their upright, unspotted lives, from their religious faith—for example, the Justiciary in *Das Majorat*, a portrait, to be sure, of Hoffmann's great-uncle Voetheri; Fräulein von Scuderi in the story bearing her name; and Andres in *Ignaz Denner*.

A few years after his return to Berlin, Hoffmann wrote *Der Kampf der Sänger* (The Contest of the Minstrels, written in 1817). At first blush this tale may seem like an effort to present, while telling a story, a picture of medieval religious faith—a picture that might challenge comparison with Brentano's *Aus der Chronika eines fahrenden Schülers*, the most successful evocation of the medieval religious spirit that Romanticism produced. Yet, despite the use of Roman Catholic symbolism and medieval supernaturalism—which indeed the story demanded—it is distinctly Protestant in essence. Wolframb's encounter with Nasias is a case in point. The pious singer merely smiles at the proposals made to provide protection for him—the holy water, the consecrated candles, the musk that a Capuchin had worn in a bag on his breast. Wolframb does not rely at all on such traditional elements of churchly protection. It is the fervor of his piety, the simplicity of his faith, the nobility of his character, that win the victory over the assaults of the evil spirit; he needs only "what a pure, pious spirit is capable of carrying in itself." Though in *Kater Murr* Hoffmann returns to his Bamberg backgrounds, the religious sympathies that underlie *Die Elixiere des Teufels* have in the main disappeared. In the long monastic episode referred to above he is distinctly critical. To only one part of the Abbot's long discourse does he seem to give unqualified assent: that the monastery may afford an asylum for those who cannot find a place in the outside world where they really belong.[18] Kreisler dissents from the Abbot's comparison between the pious days of old and the degeneration of the present; he thinks the idea "monkish" and holds that a pious, childlike mind, "to which the convulsive ecstasy of an intoxicating ritual remains alien" has no need of signs and miracles and ecstasies to practice real Christian virtue.

The rise of Protestant feeling in Hoffmann culminates, significantly enough, in his last finished story, *Meister Johannes Wacht.*

---

[18] Note characters in Hoffmann's stories who renounce the world and find peace in monastic seclusion: both of the main characters in *Das Gelübde*, Natalie in *Die Doppeltgänger*, the heroine of the intercalated story in *Das Sanctus*, of *Die Marquise de la Pivadière* and even Medardus in his remorseful return to the cloister (*Die Elixiere des Teufels*).

The hero is a sturdy, even bigoted, Protestant in Catholic Bamberg toward the end of the eighteenth century. Only in this story does Hoffmann discuss openly an antagonism between Protestantism and Catholicism. Johannes depends upon the power of God within him; "the true religion" is firmly rooted in his breast. After tragedy and sorrow have entered his household, he withdraws to his room, where he finds mercy and consolation in communion with God and comes forth in full power to carry on. In his youth he had imbibed in Augsburg an almost fanatical Protestantism; hence, Hoffmann says, his prejudices can be pardoned. His wife, born in a Catholic family, had defied her relatives, forfeited a rich inheritance, withstood in unshakable courage the tormenting insistence (Eindringen) of the Church, and had married Johannes, but Hoffmann is careful to add that her change of faith had been one of "pure, ardent devotion."

Hoffmann's early silence on religious questions can rightly be interpreted only as resulting from profound perplexity, surely not from indifference. The problems of man's relationship to an unseen world troubled him, but ideas that had been implanted in his mind made it difficult for him to accept a formal religious creed. However, it is quite possible to overemphasize the influence of rationalism. In the early days it was unquestionably not merely rationalistic skepticism that sealed his lips; if he had been secure in his unbelief, he would have been the last to curb the expression of it. Indubitably he was held in check by religious teachings and by the lofty example of those whom he unreservedly revered.

Hoffmann had a deeply religious nature. He was keenly conscious of the invisible world that constantly impinges upon our world of visible and material reality. He pondered much on the problem of the dualism of good and evil. But, despite the intensity with which he portrayed the power of evil, there is no question whatever of his belief in a Divine Power which is superior to evil. "The eternal Power" (die ewige Macht), with a considerable variety of modifiers, is a frequent expression in his writings and his fondness for it may be derived from a feeling that it did not involve the theological accretions associated with the word "God."

He dreamed of an invisible Church which unites those whose spirit finds no satisfaction in purely material things and with endless striving seeks a higher and nobler realm. Again, one may cite Hoffmann's favorite quotation from Scripture: "My [their] kingdom is not of this world." The phrase "the invisible Church" (die unsichtbare Kirche) appears in one of his earliest stories (*Der Magnetiseur*,

1813) and is used in frequent repetition through the years of his literary activity. Even though at times he introduces the expression in such a way as to suggest a dependence upon popular tales of secret leagues, this cannot obscure the sincerity with which he incorporates in these words a devoutly religious concept. In a letter to Kunz, November 17, 1813, he gives an extract from *Der Dichter und der Komponist* on which he was then engaged: "The golden gates are opened and in a single beam knowledge and art enkindle the holy striving which unites men into a church."[19]

In accounting for the decline of religious music, for the lack of true feeling, and the shallowness of most modern music written for the Church, Hoffmann deplores what he regards as the influence of French thought, especially in the period immediately preceding the French Revolution—skeptical rationalism and levity. In this connection, he speaks of "the impious denial of the Power that rules over us, which alone gives success and strength to our working and to our works, of the mocking contempt for redemptive piety" which swept over Germany at the time. Now, he thinks, a time has come, "in which the impotence of all mistaken striving, of all preoccupation with earthly activity for earthly ends," is plainly evident, a time "in which the spirit, as if illumined by a ray from Heaven, recognizes its home, and through this recognition gives courage and strength to bear the afflictions of earth, indeed to withstand them."[20]

And for Hoffmann music was a door that opened into this more

---

[19] "Die goldenen Thore sind geöffnet und in *einem* Strahl entzünden Wissenschaft und Kunst das heilige Streben, das die Menschen zu einer Kirche vereinigt," *Briefwechsel*, II, p. 169. These words are not in the published version of *Der Dichter und der Komponist*; for them Hoffmann apparently substituted the following: "Ja, in jenem fernen Reiche, das uns oft in seltsamen Ahnungen umfängt, und aus dem wunderbare Stimmen zu uns herabtönen und alle Laute wecken, die in der beengten Brust schliefen, und die nun erwacht, wie in feurigen Strahlen freudig und froh heraufschiessen, so dass wir der Seligkeit jenes Paradieses teilhaftig werden—da sind Dichter und Musiker die innigst verwandten Glieder einer Kirche. . . ." VI, p. 82.

[20] "Dass dieser Leichtsinn, dieses ruchlose Verleugnen der über uns waltenden Macht, die nur allein unserm Wirken, unsern Werken Gedeihen und Kraft gibt, die spöttelnde Verachtung der heilbringenden Frömmigkeit von jener Nation herrührte, die so lange Zeit auf unglaubliche Weise der verblendeten Welt in Kunst und Wissenschaft als Muster galt, liegt am Tage. . . ." "Diese Zeit, in der sich die Ohnmacht alles verkehrten Strebens, aller Befangenheit im irdischen Treiben um irdischen Zweck so deutlich offenbart, in der der Geist, wie durch einen Himmelsstrahl erleuchtet, seine Heimat erkennt, und in dieser Erkenntnis Mut und Kraft erwirbt, die Bedrängnisse des Irdischen zu ertragen, ja ihnen zu widerstehen." "Alte und neue Kirchenmusik," in *Allgemeine musikalische Zeitung*, XIV, p. 577. In the revision of this article in connection with material from other reviews for insertion, as the dialogue in the *Serapionsbrüder*, this passage was omitted. It is reprinted in E. Istel: *E. T. A. Hoffmanns Musikalische Schriften* (pp. 231-32) and in Ellinger (p. 202).

glorious realm where the human spirit communes with the Divine; in many passages scattered throughout his writings music is designated as the interpreter of the Divine. Kreisler defends his music against the strictures of Pater Cyprianus, the ascetic bigot:

"Is it sinful to praise the Eternal in the language which He has Himself given us, so that the heavenly gift may awaken in our breast the rapture of ardent devotion, indeed the knowledge of the other world, is it sinful to mount up on seraph's wings of song above everything earthly and in pious longing and love strive up toward the Highest?"[21] But it would be an error to regard music as Hoffmann's religion; for him it was merely the chief human means for communion with the Divine.

Brentano implicitly censured Hoffmann for the irreligious nature of his stories. In January 1816 he wrote to Hoffmann: "For some time I have had a horror of all poetry which mirrors itself and not God. . . . Dear Hoffmann, why didn't you let poor Spiecker [Spikher in *Das verlorene Spiegelbild*] find his innocence again, and indeed through Jesus?" This letter was apparently never sent, probably, Hans von Müller suggests, because Brentano communicated the contents personally. Since for a time Brentano and Hoffmann saw one another fairly frequently in Berlin, probably Brentano, ardent but childlike propagandist, made his protest more than once. Years before this, indeed before there were any stories of Hoffmann's to criticize, Zacharias Werner had written to Hoffmann from Weimar: "Just think of God a little!" (Denken Sie ein bisschen an Gott.) This is the only exhortation on record, but once again, in view of Werner's nature, it was probably not the only one delivered. A few months after Werner's letter Hoffmann wrote to Hippel somewhat ironically: "Our [friend] Werner arrived here day before yesterday. . . . I assured him that now and then I had thought of God a little." Werner thought Hoffmann godless, and Hoffmann thought slightingly of Werner's type of godliness.

Mischa told Hitzig that Hoffmann on his deathbed asked her to fold his hands and then murmured: "One must also think of God." The story may be authentic or the product of Mischa's wishful imagination, but Hoffmann's words, if he really uttered them, do not mean

---

[21] "Ist es sündhaft, die ewige Macht zu preisen in der Sprache, die sie uns selbst gab, damit das Himmelsgeschenck die Begeisterung der brünstigsten Andacht, ja die Erkenntnis des Jenseits in unserer Brust erwecke, ist es sündhaft, sich auf Seraphsfittigen des Gesanges hinwegzuschwingen über alles Irdische und in frommer Sehnsucht und Liebe hinaufzustreben nach dem Höchsten. . . ?" x, p. 362.

that he had neglected the thought of God until that last moment. He had been thinking of Him all his life.

POLITICS

The discussion of politics was also banned in Hoffmann's presence. It is hardly too much of a generalization to say that he avoided religion as a topic of conversation because he stood in awe of matters that others held sacred, that he himself, too, held sacred in his own way, but he shunned politics because political discussions bored him. Only in stress of circumstances that moved most of his contemporaries to vigorous partisanship and active participation did he display a fugitive interest in what was going on in the political world.[22] An account has already been given of Hoffmann's attitude during the Napoleonic wars and the meager impact of war experiences and war-time interests upon his writings; in many ways he resembled Goethe in his reaction to the events of the early nineteenth century. In *Die Irrungen* and *Die Geheimnisse* he is not belittling the heroic resistance of the Greeks at the beginning of their war for independence or disapproving the interest of many Germans in the Greek cause. His satire is directed against maudlin sentiment and ostentatious sympathy with the Greeks. Baron Theodor von S. makes elaborate preparations for his journey to Greece, including what he supposes to be a modern Greek costume; his expedition becomes the talk of the town, especially at the "aesthetic teas," but he gets only as far as Zehlendorf, a few miles from Berlin, now virtually a part of the city, where he accidentally discovers that the newspaper which had prompted his feverish activity was a year old.

There is no evidence that he ever gave serious thought to the relative merits of different systems of government. *Don Carlos* was indeed fervently admired in his youth, but the political problems presented there—Schiller's elucidation of governmental theories—apparently provoked no response; it was only the personal situation, the love of a young man for a woman who could never be his wife. Though living in a monarchy he never compared the monarchical system, absolute or limited, with a democracy or a republic, and he

---

22 In the *Kreisleriana* (*Höchst zerstreute Gedanken*) Hoffmann implies that interest in politics is, in normal circumstances, incompatible with the life of the artist: "Welcher Künstler hat sich sonst um die politischen Ereignisse des Tages bekümmert —er lebte nur in seiner Kunst, und nur in ihr schritt er durch das Leben; aber eine verhängnisvolle schwere Zeit hat den Menschen mit eiserner Faust ergriffen, und der Schmerz presst ihm Laute aus, die ihm sonst fremd waren." This passage stands by itself in the "Scattered Thoughts," and there is no indication of whom he is speaking. I, p. 51.

accepted things as they were without investigation, save as a monarch might govern wisely or foolishly. He is in no way concerned with the administrative side of princely activities, whether conservative or liberal; he is interested in rulers as human beings whom a peculiar fortune, the nature of which he declines to examine, has placed in a position apart from their fellow men.

He was, then, not politically a democrat. To him all that mattered was the character of a man, his intellectual gifts, his personal integrity, and the rightness of his emotional response. But he was fundamentally democratic in his views of human relations. His satire is constantly leveled at every kind of sham, pretense, and shallowness. Already in Posen he had taken his revenge upon aristocratic exclusiveness by his fateful caricatures, and later as a man of letters he dipped his pen in caustic ink whenever it was a question of social distinctions and aristocratic pretensions.

The duodecimo principalities in the Germany of Hoffmann's day offered capital targets for good-humored satire. Here Jean Paul had blazed a trail for Hoffmann to follow. The rulers of these diminutive realms constituted, to be sure, a social class of which Hoffmann knew little through firsthand observation, and he could allow his imagination full scope. Only in Bamberg did he come casually into contact with court circles of this type. Not long after his arrival the Princess of Neufchâtel was in Bamberg, visiting her mother the Duchess (Herzogin in Bayern), and for her name-day Cuno requested Hoffmann to prepare a "Prologue" for presentation in the theater. In a letter to Hitzig, Hoffmann gave an ironical account of the episode: "I threw together some very ordinary sentimental stuff, composed equally sentimental music, and it was produced, not sparing lights, horns, echoes, mountains, rivers, bridges, trees with names carved on them, flowers, wreaths. From the mother of the Princess I received, together with gracious words, fifty Carolins for the emotional experience I had provided for her. . . . At a certain place in the 'Prologue' 'I went, I flew, I plunged into her arms!' (an uncommonly fine climax) mother and daughter embraced with tears in the ducal box, and the audience applauded rather ironically." The piece was repeated the next evening, and at the same passage the ducal personages again embraced one another with tears. The "Prologue" was entitled *Die Pilgerin* (The Pilgrim). Hoffmann says he is now in a certain fashion introduced at court, sings in the court concerts, and has been invited to instruct the young Duchess in singing, the wife of Duke Pius, son of Duke Wilhelm, later when she recovers from her catarrh, which, according to the court marshal, is usually in March. It was then in November, but there is no further mention of the Duchess' singing lessons.

In *Kater Murr* and, somewhat less completely, in *Die Elixiere des Teufels* the novelist draws full-length portraits of a prince. In the case of Prince Irenäus (*Kater Murr*) Hoffmann is not so much attacking rank as such as ridiculing petty pride in noble blood and inherited traditions. He rarely allows Prince Irenäus to appear without administering a satirical thrust. The Prince's head is utterly empty except for the consciousness of his hereditary rank and reverence due to rank; what has been customary in princely families, especially in his own, belongs among the immutable cosmic laws. He is not haughty; to be haughty requires a certain modicum of intellect, even if a distorted one. It does not seem at all strange that Prince Irenäus should beget an imbecile son, though in the proposed reconstruction of family relationships an attempt has been made to relieve him of the parentage of Prince Ignatius and transfer it to some unknown person.

Somewhat reluctantly he permits the wandering Kreisler to remain at Sieghartsweiler. He is disturbed that Kreisler arrived on foot and is appeased only by Meister Abraham's discreet lie that Kreisler had a carriage waiting for him in the park. In his effort to combat the Prince's scruples Abraham assures him that Kreisler had formerly lived in quite different circumstances—had been privileged to dine at princely tables. The veil of secrecy that Kreisler wishes drawn over his past provides the Prince with an excuse to think him of noble blood, and he then proceeds to add the particle "von" to Kreisler's name. Thus equipped, the musician is permitted to stay in the principality. He admits to Rätin Benzon that prince as well as commoner may put on a dressing gown and wear a nightcap; a prince "cannot put out of his mind such bourgeois matters as marriage, the joys of fatherhood, and the like, and it is at least pardonable that he should surrender to them in moments when the state and his concern for the observance of the proprieties at court and in the land do not claim his whole being." The monologue of the court physician after an interview with Princess Maria, wife of Prince Irenäus, is stronger testimony to Hoffmann's scorn of princely pretense than his ridicule of the Prince: "She would like to convince others, and herself indeed, that the cement [Kitt] with which nature fastens body and soul together is of a particular kind, when it is a question of fashioning something princely, and is in no way to be compared with what she uses in the case of us poor children of earth of bourgeois origins." Elsewhere it is said of the Princess Maria that heart and intellect have become atrophied through rigid observance of court etiquette.

The reigning prince in *Die Elixiere des Teufels* is a contrasting figure. The characterization of his qualities, which Hoffmann puts in the mouth of the director of the princely art gallery, may approximate Hoffmann's own ideal of a monarch. The Prince has consistently exemplified the maxim that his subjects are not there for his sake, but rather that he is there for their sake. Complete freedom of speech is granted. Taxes are exceedingly moderate, and prices as a consequence are low. The police are hardly in evidence at all (das gänzliche Zurücktreten der Polizei), and the citizen as well as the stranger is not in the remotest fashion molested by official zeal; there are no troublesome soldiers (die Entfernung alles soldatischen Unwesens), and strangers enter the country without the annoyance of police formalities customary in other lands. He is a lover and a genuine connoisseur of the arts—every artist of ability, every gifted man of learning, is welcome at court; the degree of his distinction is the only test of his ancestry.

Medardus, to whom this tribute to the Prince is directed, soon has the good fortune to encounter the Prince walking in the park. The Prince sees in him a stranger, engages him in conversation on painting and music, graciously shows him the beauties of the park, and then invites him to the court to play faro. Medardus hesitates to accept the privilege of appearing in court circles, confessing that he does not belong to the nobility. The Prince scoffs at his scruples: "What is nobility!" [Was Adel! Was Adel!] he exclaims. "I have convinced myself that you are a man of intelligence and education; knowledge ennobles you and qualifies you for entrance into my society." At court there are musical evenings and literary gatherings, the Prince presiding while others read their works. At his first meeting with the Prince, Medardus had noted a certain glibness in the discussion of art which betrayed a lack of real depth, and one evening a learned physicist reads a paper of profound significance at which the Prince is visibly bored. The Prince is also a composer, and at the first concert of the court orchestra Medardus finds one piece of music conventional and tedious, but luckily he does not advance an opinion before he discovers that it is the work of the Prince. Much later the clever and wise court physician characterizes the interest of the Prince in science and the arts as mere coquetry. To be sure, many artists and scholars of bourgeois birth may be seen about the court, but those of finer feelings, who are unable to look upon conditions there with a kind of serene irony, are seen seldom, or not at all. Whatever the effort to appear unprejudiced, there is always something in the attitude of the aristocracy toward the bourgeoisie that suggests condescension or toleration of what is unfitting—that a man of common origin should be there at all. No man of proper pride can endure the situation when an artist in an aristocratic assemblage is really the only one who has to do the condescending and to suffer what is intellectually common and tasteless.

In *Klein Zaches* also the novelist chose a petty principality for the scene of his story. Life there is portrayed with genial humor, and the satire is not less pungent, though the tiny realm lies on the borders of the fairy-tale world. The rulers spend their days in a welter of trivialities, which, for lack of something significant, they magnify into matters of critical concern. Prince Demetrius ruled his miniature country in such a way that his subjects were quite unaware of being ruled, but the first words of his successor, Prince Paphnutius, were: "I am going to rule," and his first and most far-reaching act was the introduction of "die Aufklärung," to be announced by great placards posted throughout the land. It may be inferred that Hoffmann was breaking a lance for the "invisible reign" of Prince Demetrius, though his criticism of Prince Paphnutius is mainly directed against the promulgation of the "age of reason" and the ruthless suppression of all opponents, including the forcible expulsion of the fairies from the realm. He elevated Andres, his body servant, to the position of prime minister as a reward for faithful service in lending his master six ducats when in an inn he had once been out of funds. In this incident the satirical mood is evident, though it would be hazardous to conclude that Hoffmann is satirizing arbitrary and incongruous appointments to positions of responsibility in the state.

In other tales there are incidental thrusts at the narrow-mindedness and inflated self-esteem of the aristocracy. The father of young Baron Euchar (*Der Zusammenhang der Dinge*) is much alarmed when one of the tutors attributes Euchar's inexplicable conduct to the possession of a "poetic soul"; he fears Euchar may have inherited his nature from his mother, whom the most splendid court festivities left with nothing but headache and distaste, and he is relieved when a Gentleman of the Bed Chamber declares the tutor an ass and assures him that genuinely noble blood flows in Euchar's veins, that his nature is "baronial" and not "poetic." From the relations between aristocrat and commoner in many instances no conclusions could be drawn. Hoffmann does not condemn even indirectly the Graf von Vach (*Ignaz Denner*) because he does not reward Andres more liberally for saving his life or investigate later the real value of the position to which he has appointed him. It is not the gulf between classes that renders the marriage between Princess Angiola and the artist Berthold so tragic in its consequences (*Die Jesuiterkirche in G.*). Hoffmann is not attacking the aristocracy in making Baron S. (*Die Irrungen*) an absurd brainless coxcomb—he might as well have been a rich commoner. On the other hand, the novelist creates noblemen of quite a different stamp: the Baron in *Das Majorat* has no pride of rank; he regards the bourgeois Justiciary not merely as his equal but as his superior and seats him in the place of honor at the table, irrespective of the rank of other guests. In *Die Doppeltgänger* there is a high-minded ruler, devoted to the welfare of his people and beloved by them; that the heir apparent is a man of a very different stripe is a matter of concern to his subjects but this prompts Hoffmann to no criticism of the system. In several of Hoffmann's tales men of noble birth appear as human beings moving in their own circles, and there is no comment favorable or unfavorable upon their relations with the bourgeoisie.

Hoffmann was not a conscious critic of the organization of society in his day and by no means a social reformer. It is, of course, obvious that no one writes stories of contemporary life without implied social comment. Hoffmann was both amused and indignant that some men assume an attitude of superiority over their fellows on the basis of their birth rather than upon personal merit and act with complacent arrogance toward them, but he does not inquire into historical factors that have produced aristocratic privilege or condemn an hereditary monarchy and the arbitrary distribution of princely favors upon which an aristocratic system is built up. And yet when an arbitrary government invaded his own domain he was capable of righteous wrath and open rebellion. The persecution of liberal thought, the use of spies and informers, the arrest and imprisonment of worthy citizens upon slender or utterly false evidence, aroused his fury, and he acted without thought of self, as a government official in defending the rights of the individual. As has been related elsewhere, Hoffmann's fearless championship of legal rights and the resultant circumstances contributed indirectly to his early death.

The satire so abundantly scattered throughout Hoffmann's tales

is directed against the petty foibles of mankind, the absurd incon-
sistencies, and especially the pretensions of individual men and
women. Caustic are his comments from the days of *Berganza* on
when it is a question of musical enthusiasms and musical appreciation; the musical culture of Bamberg seemed at times to be a transparent hoax. Literary pretensions Hoffmann dissected with the
scalpel of his wit. He had perhaps an unreasoning and surely an
ungallant prejudice against women authors, and doubtless would
have applied to them the famous dictum of Dr. Johnson concerning
women preachers. The aesthetic pretensions of the socially prominent
were belabored in season and out of season, especially the literary
and musical teas where the people of the social world condescended
to their superiors. The pretensions of wealth were equally chastised
with the pretensions of rank.

Hoffmann died at forty-six. If the Biblical limit of years, three
score and ten, had been granted him, they would have carried him
on through the Young German Movement to the very verge of the
Revolution of 1848. Indeed, some authorities date the end of the
Romantic Period with the death of Hoffmann. Had he lived, he
might have learned something of Young German doctrines—the
participation of literature in political and social questions. A receptiveness to such influences is faintly indicated in Hoffmann's stories
of the last period, even though a really radical change in his work
would have been unlikely; he would never have lost his interest in
the spiritual problems of the artist's life or in the impinging of a
world of mystery upon the world of everyday. Something of a new
direction is suggested in his last writing, somewhat indefinitely in
Des Vetters Eckfenster, the last work published during his lifetime,
and more conclusively in *Meister Johannes Wacht*, written in the
last months of his life and offered to the publisher Max only four
days before his death.

Meister Johannes Wacht may seem at first like a reworking of
material already used in *Meister Martin der Küfner*, a suggestion
perhaps that in these last days the seemingly inexhaustible fertility
of invention had been squandered and he could turn only to old
themes. The external resemblance is undeniable. Meister Johannes
is, like Meister Martin, a craftsman, in this case a carpenter and
builder, of excellent reputation in the community and possessed of
considerable wealth. The story centers in the question of a daughter's marriage; Martin will bestow his daughter's hand only on a
cooper; Johannes Wacht is possessed by an insensate prejudice

against lawyers, and the suitor in question is a lawyer. But Johannes is a much more complicated character, and psychologically Hoffmann penetrates much farther into his inner life. As noted above, he is a devout Protestant in a Roman Catholic community, and his religious convictions support him in time of trial. Whereas Meister Martin merely stood squarely on his personal dignity in the presence of a count, Johannes interests himself in popular causes: "Unshakable in magnanimity, fidelity, and his feelings as a burgher, he became with each year more and more a man of the people." His scorn of lawyers is bound up with his conviction that they all seek a shameful profit from what is most sacred, most honorable; that is, they deceive and wrong the people who seek their aid: "You are going to carry on a trade with the law, as with some base ware for sale on the public market, and weigh it out with false scales to the poor peasant or the oppressed burgher, who whined in vain before the throne of the rigid judge, and get paid with the bloody penny, which the poor man bathed in tears hands out to you."[23]

Johannes Wacht is one of Mother Nature's favored children, for she has given him integrity of character and an understanding heart: "Pondering and determining the fate of her children, Nature pursues her own dark, inscrutable way, and what conventions, or opinions, or considerations, passing for valid in our narrow life, try to establish as the true goal of existence, is to her only the impertinent play of foolish children who fancy themselves wise. The Mother of Life does not choose for her favorites the palaces of the great or the splendid apartments of princes. So she allowed our Johannes, whom one can call a particular recipient of her favors, to see the light of the world upon a wretched straw pallet in the workshop of an impoverished master turner."[24]

The tale has a happy ending, but the sympathetic reader feels a hidden pathos. In these last weeks of his life Hoffmann turns back to

[23] "Mit dem Recht willst du Handel treiben, wie mit einer feilen schnöden Ware auf öffentlichem Markt, und es zuwägen mit falscher Wage, den armen Bauern, dem gedrückten Bürger, der vor des starren Richters Polsterstuhl vergebens winselte, und dich zahlen lassen mit dem blutigen Heller, den der Arme dir, in Tränen gebadet, hinreicht." xiv, p. 119.

[24] "Die Natur verfolgt, ihrer Kinder Schicksal erwägend und bestimmend, ihren eignen dunklen, unerforschlichen Weg, und das, was Konvenienz, was im beengten Leben geltende Meinungen und Rücksichten als wahre Tendenz des Seins feststellen wollen, ist ihr nur das vorwitzige Spiel sich weise dünkender betörter Kinder. . . . Nicht die Paläste der Grossen, nicht fürstliche Prunkgemächer, wählt die Mutter des Lebens für ihre Lieblinge. So liess sie unsern Johannes, der . . . wohl einer ihrer begünstigsten Lieblinge zu nennen, auf dem elenden Strohlager in der Werkstatt eines verarmten Drechslermeisters zu Augsburg, das Licht der Welt erblicken." xiv, pp. 103-4.

Bamberg, where fertile and troubled years were spent. In memory he wanders about the old city, recalls the pleasant walk to Bug (Buch), the fountain of Neptune on the market place, even the type of beauty characteristic of the maidens of the town, and the excellencies of the Bamberg cuisine. To the youthful Jonathan Engelbrecht, suitor for the hand of Johannes' daughter, he once more lends some subjective notes of character or experience. He is a young lawyer and also a poet. When it seems as if his love for Nanni is hopelessly blocked by her father's obstinate prejudice, his friend, the old Domizeller, interprets the experience in terms that Hoffmann in retrospect might have used of himself in his relationship to Julia Marc: this unhappy experience is the prose that is to be overcome with bitter sorrow, "but you have conquered and can devote yourself to the poetry of it." On his deathbed Hoffmann has not forgotten Julia Marc.

CHAPTER 7

THE DEVELOPMENT OF HOFFMANN'S STYLE

AS Hoffmann absorbed into himself something of the philosophic thinking of his time and transformed it into terms that he could understand and use, he also responded to literary influences. In his extensive but rather capricious reading he noted ways in which others wrote and, doubtless in the main unconsciously, employed similar methods and devices. The originality of his own work is not appreciably lessened.

He was somewhat scornful of source-mongers; a review of *Klein Zaches* in the *Heidelberger Jahrbücher der Literatur* disclosed a number of alleged borrowings, and a year later in the preface to *Prinzessin Brambilla* Hoffmann thanked the reviewer for giving him occasion to look up his sources and thus enrich his knowledge. The pursuit of sources and parallels is an interesting game of detection, in which various hands have participated. The findings of the investigating sleuths are not always in agreement, and they are occasionally farfetched or merely ingenious. In many cases, of course, the parallels presented are in themselves of interest and significance, even though Hoffmann's use of the "source" is dubious. He possessed a most fecund imagination of his own, which was capable of creative work without dependence on models. In many cases he did respond to a stimulus, perhaps a mere hint, which he worked over into something inimitably his own.[1]

An indication of a source or sources is often given in the text itself, as if in conscientious acknowledgment of indebtedness.[2] For example, he mentions Lewis' novel *The Monk* in *Die Elixiere des Teufels,* though his dependence on the English novelist is really slight. The case of *Der Elementargeist* is similar though his indebtedness is greater; as in *Die Elixiere des Teufels* one of the characters has recently been reading *The Monk,* so in *Der Elementargeist* Jacques Cazotte's *Le diable amoureux* is mentioned and discussed.[3] In the comment of the Serapion Brothers after a story

[1] Cf. especially Sucher, Dahmen, Reimann (Bibliography) and notes in editions of Hoffmann's works, particularly those of Ellinger and Maassen.

[2] In this connection it is strange that Hoffmann never refers to Zimmermann's famous book *Über die Einsamkeit,* to which he is demonstrably indebted.

[3] Cf. Johann Cerny (Czerny): *Jacques Cazotte und E. T. A. Hoffmann* in *Euphorion,* xv (1910), pp. 140-44; Hans von Müller in *E. T. A. Hoffmann und Jean Paul,* pp. 38-39; Müller extends the influence to *Die Maske, Datura Fastuosa,* and *Meister Floh.*

has been read, there is frequent and probably purposeful indication of books consulted. Thus after the reading of *Doge und Dogaressa* Lothar remarks that Ottmar has had Le Bret's History of Venice before him and adorned his rooms with pictures of streets and squares to prompt his imagination and correct his descriptions. That the initial impulse for the writing of *Die Bergwerke zu Falun* came from a brief passage in Schubert's *Ansichten von der Nacht-seite der Naturwissenschaften* is disclosed by Ottmar's comment. He thinks Schubert's brief narrative, a few sentences only, more moving than Theodor's fully developed story.

To spur his imagination to activity, particularly when in haste to meet obligations entered into with publishers, Hoffmann scanned old chronicles or collections of anecdotes. Thus Wagenseil's *Chronik von Nürnberg* yielded him part of the plot for *Das Fräulein von Scuderi*, and the appendix to the *Chronicle*, describing the Meister-singer, provided material used in *Meister Martin der Küfner* and *Der Kampf der Sänger*; much later he drew on Wagenseil in writing the unfinished tale *Der Feind*. From Hafftitz' curious work *Microchronicon Marchicum*, or, as Hoffmann called it, *Micro-chronicon berolinense*, he obtained material for *Aus dem Leben eines bekannten Mannes* (*Der Teufel in Berlin*) and *Die Brautwahl*. For many of his stories he studied works of curious old medical lore or the numerous contemporary books on mesmerism and related phenomena. Hoffmann's brief notes to Krailowsky, the proprietor of a lending library in Berlin, reveal his meticulous care in building up the historical and topographical backgrounds for his tales.[4] Where many a novelist might say to himself that it really did not matter, that by evasion or a slight vagueness in the descriptive passages criticism could be avoided, Hoffmann spent endless effort in obtaining exactitude even in the minutest detail. With the supplementary assistance of maps and pictures, his extraordinary visual imagination could create an illusion of firsthand acquaintance. He asks Krailowsky for books of travel in Sweden when he is writing *Die Bergwerke zu Falun*, and when preparing for *Das Fräulein von Scuderi* requests several descriptive books on Paris, also Voltaire's *Siècle de Louis XIV* and the novels of Mme. de Genlis; similar preparation is made in books on Rome when *Signor Formica* is in the making. He wanted Dr. Speyer to read *Der Magnetiseur* before the

---

[4] Cf. Hans von Müller: *E. T. A. Hoffmann und sein Leihbibliothekar*, Leipzig, 1904 (Privatdruck).

story was printed so that he might test it from the medical standpoint.

The early admiration for Jean Paul left palpable traces in the style of Hoffmann's letters to Hippel; the extravagant expression of sentiment is quite in the vein of Jean Paul, also the fanciful designations for postscripts and appendices in his correspondence. Yet the cult of friendship and the luxuriant expression of it flourished in the eighteenth century before Jean Paul's day, and Hoffmann might have adopted the exuberance of others, if Jean Paul had not at the time happened to be the most popular model. But the lavish display of sentiment gradually fades out in Hoffmann's case before he began his career as a man of letters. A study of the use of motifs in Jean Paul and Hoffmann reveals many parallels, in some of which the direct influence of the older novelist seems clearly demonstrable: the juxtaposition of contrasting characters, one an idealist and dreamer, the other a practical realist, the fondness for eccentric figures and unusual situations, the "humours" of the human being, the question of double personality, and irregularity in the arrangement of material. These devices and traits are marked characteristics of Jean Paul's work, and they left their traces in Hoffmann. Yet again, it should be noted that most of these motifs were to be found in the German novel before Jean Paul. Though by his foreword to the *Fantasiestücke* Jean Paul gave a certain endorsement to Hoffmann's writing, he later spoke disparagingly of Hoffmann and his ,work and regarded him as a crass imitator, primarily of Tieck and of himself. In sending a copy of the second part of *Kater Murr* to Jean Paul, January 19, 1822, Hoffmann says that if Jean Paul had read his works, he would have been convinced of his deep respect for him, and further: "that your work has penetrated into my inmost being and had its effect upon my way of carrying on my own work [Gestaltung]." It had been years since Jean Paul had sponsored Hoffmann's first venture into the world of books; in the meantime the author of the *Fantasiestücke* had become a famous and popular author, but no word had passed between them. When Hoffmann's last illness was already gripping him, he turned back to the beginning and remembered Jean Paul's not ungracious patronage of his first flight. One is not inclined to attach great importance to the wording of this letter.[5]

[5] For discussion of Hoffmann's relations with Jean Paul, cf. Robert Herndon Fife Jr.: "Jean Paul Friedrich Richter and E. T. A. Hoffmann: A Study in the Relations of Jean Paul to Romanticism," in *Publications of the Modern Language Association*, xxii (1907), pp. 1-32; J. C(z)erny: *Jean Pauls Beziehungen zu E. T. A. Hoff-*

The first work of fiction mentioned in Hoffmann's letters is *Der Genius* (The Tutelary Spirit), by Julius Grosse (1794), which was translated into English under the alluring title of *The Horrid Mysteries*. The youthful Hoffmann was profoundly impressed by this novel, as indeed was the youthful Tieck at almost the same time, the imprint upon the latter amounting to a temporary mental and emotional disturbance close to insanity. *Der Genius* was one of the flood of sensational romances that spread over Europe in the latter part of the eighteenth century. In *Northanger Abbey* Jane Austen includes *The Horrid Mysteries* among the seven "Gothic" tales that Miss Thorpe recommends to Catherine Morland. Like Walpole's *Castle of Otranto*, it has entirely lost its savor; the pleasant goose flesh that an earlier generation enjoyed while reading it no longer responds to the stimulus. In time Hoffmann learned to take similar material—the occult, the mysterious, even the frankly sensational —and mold it into something essentially different.

In the eighteenth century there was a widespread renewal of interest in secret societies, especially in Free Masonry, and a conviction developed that great and noble ends could be achieved by such brotherhoods.[6] The soil was thus prepared for the fanatic or the charlatan to pose as the possessor of ancient secrets, of arcana cherished by learned and holy men of old and handed down through their disciples; by subtle advertising of such wares the new prophet could entice the credulous into an organization. Thus the society of the Rosicrucians, which led a shadowy life in the previous century, appeared here and there in organized secret groups and in varied der-

---

mann, Mies, 1907, 1908; Hans von Müller: *E. T. A. Hoffmann und Jean Paul,* Köln, 1927; Paul Nerrlich: *Jean Paul und seine Zeitgenossen* (Berlin, 1876), pp. 253-56. Jean Paul's later opinion may be illustrated by L. Rellstab in his "Blätter der Erinnerung," in *Morgenblatt* (October 28, 1839), pp. 1030-31. Rellstab is telling of a visit to Jean Paul in August 1821, and Jean Paul discusses recent authors who have achieved fame and popularity. "Die meisten sind ewig abwärts sinkende Sonnen, die bei ihren Aufgängen culminirt haben. So auch Hoffmann. Ich führte ihn durch eine Vorrede in's Publikum ein und machte, dass er in Deutschland gelesen wurde. Ich war der Meinung, sein erstes Werk werde nicht die Spitze seines Geistes seyn, sondern er werde höher steigen. . . . Sonst [i.e. apart from his musical criticism] aber ist in dem ersten wie in den folgenden Werken das Beste Nachahmung und Plünderung, besonders von Tieck und mir. . . . Er wiederholt sich selbst und steigert seine Ausartungen, so dass ich jetzt einen ordentlichen Widerwillen an seinen Büchern habe." For further utterances of Jean Paul with reference to Hoffmann, cf. Cerny, *op. cit.,* note 3, and Maassen's article "Hoffmann im Urteil seiner Zeitgenossen," in *Der grundgescheute Antiquarius,* ii. Maassen thinks that Jean Paul was envious of Hoffmann's popularity. Hitzig, on the other hand, reports that Jean Paul spoke to him of Hoffmann in 1822 with some appreciation.

6 Cf. Ferdinand Josef Schneider: *Die Freimaurerei und ihr Einfluss auf die geistige Kultur in Deutschland am Ende des XVIII. Jahrhunderts,* Prag, 1909.

ivation from the more or less legendary seventeenth century source. Inevitably the novel reflected this contemporary trend. The popular novelist, seeking sensational material, preferred to introduce secret leagues whose purposes were sinister or perverse, for the activities of such a secret organization could be employed for the creation of suspense, for enthralling mysteries, and hidden crimes. Thus the so-called "Bundesroman," the "novel of a League," flourished for a season. Even Goethe was not immune to contemporary fashions and his *Wilhelm Meisters Lehrjahre* (Wilhelm Meister's Apprentice-ship) is in part a "Bundesroman"; the hero is secretly watched over and guided by members of a secret league until he "learns to live" and is himself inducted into the "Tower." *Der Genius* represents the darker side of the genre.

Hoffmann's delight in *Der Genius* would naturally lead him to seek other novels of the class. Presumably in this way he became acquainted with the seventeenth century work of the Abbé de Mont-faucon de Villars, *Comte de Gabalis ou Entretiens sur les sciences secrets*.[7] Though hardly a novel, it is in part narrative and could introduce him to a superb figure of such a "Magus" giving instruction to a possible disciple in his mystic lore. He found there a full and detailed account of the elemental spirits (Elementargeister) which play an important part in some of his tales, beginning with *Der goldene Topf*.[8] The existence of a league of this sort implies a search for appropriate members, a recruiting agency; thus the league pursues its purposes, exalted or infamous, by extending a fine-spun, invisible net. As a consequence it requires an agent or agents to lure a candidate, or victim, into the net. In Goethe's novel the Abbé is such a messenger, who has his eye on Wilhelm from Wilhelm's youth. That Hoffmann was influenced by elements of the "Bundesroman" is doubtless undeniable.

On the other hand, however, it is improbable that even in his early days he was unreservedly committed to the ideas and methods of the "Bundesroman." His enthusiasm must have been somewhat tempered by the satirical parody of the leagues in the older Hippel's novel *Kreuz- und Querzüge des Ritters A bis Z*. The raillery of Hippel's work would have appealed to him; it is also inconceivable that Hoffmann was unacquainted with a novel written by a man he him-

---

[7] Cf. Erika Treske: *Der Rosenkreuzerroman "Le Comte de Gabalis" und die geistigen Strömungen des 17. und 18. Jahrhunderts*, Berlin, 1933.

[8] Cf. Oswald Floeck: *Die Elementargeister bei Fouqué und anderen Dichtern der romantischen und nachromantischen Zeit*, Heidelberg, 1909.

self knew and the uncle of his closest friend.[9] His opinion of the
novelist Cramer is also an indication that he had quite outgrown his
youthful admiration for the sensational fiction of the "Bundesroman" type—long before his own career as a storyteller began. In
1803 his diary records a most damning comment on Cramer as "beneath all criticism," though in his schoolboy days he looked upon him
as "the first genius under the sun."

For the outstanding qualities of his tales Hoffmann did not need
to go to the "Bundesroman," and by and large he would not have
found them there. He derived them from other sources, or indeed they
were the children of his own mind, not stepchildren adopted into his
family. The chief resemblance to the "Bundesroman" is the presence
in many of the tales of a figure who acts as agent, a "go-between,"
or "Mittler," influencing the lives and controlling the destiny of
others, whether merely as a mesmerist of phenomenal if not downright supernatural powers or as a non-human being in human form,
like the salamander Archivarius Lindhorst. But they were not representatives of secret leagues, and had the "Bundesroman" not
presented a ready-made pattern, Hoffmann would have found the
creation of such characters essential to the stories he was to tell
and would have himself invented them.

In Hoffmann's young manhood the influence of the earlier Romanticists—Novalis, Tieck, Wackenroder, and others—was like a subtly
diffused atmospheric condition, a stimulating spring breeze that
awakens to new life. Here and there his writings show plainly his
dependence upon the work of his immediate predecessors; indeed
he makes no effort to conceal it. Hoffmann was a lifelong admirer of
Ludwig Tieck. Probably *Die Bergwerke zu Falun* would not have
been written as Hoffmann wrote it without Tieck's *Der Runenberg*
or *Das fremde Kind* without *Die Elfen*; he planned a continuation
of Tieck's unfinished story *Abraham Tonelli*. Direct and indirect
allusions to Tieck's plays and stories are numerous, and in the critical writings, the dialogues on dramatic art, Hoffmann more than
once supports his own opinions through reference to Tieck's views,
particularly to the comment and the discussions in *Phantasus*. Tieck
taught him that the Märchen could without loss be transferred to a
contemporary setting. In the use of "Romantic Irony," for example
in *Prinzessin Blandina*, he was unquestionably following Tieck's

9 Hoffmann refers to Hippel's novels in his defense in the *Meister Floh* case and
indirectly to the title of one of them (*Kreuz- und Querzüge des Ritters A bis Z*) in
Kater Murr. Hippel is mentioned together with Hamann in the letter to Jean Paul,
January 30, 1822.

Märchen comedies: the characters step out of their roles and speak *in propria persona*, as in *Der gestiefelte Kater* and *Die verkehrte Welt*, though Tieck was by no means the first to employ the device. But of course neither Tieck nor Hoffmann confined the Romantic conception of irony to an external formula that is calculated to startle the reader. This was merely an exuberant form of irony by which the author demonstrated his superiority to the work of his imagination by destroying suddenly the illusion he had created. In the writings of the Romanticists, irony was a subtly pervasive spirit informing the work of the poet. It was a kind of intellectual exaltation, or rather the evidence of it. The author was in his work but stood above it, and through irony he expressed his release from the bondage under which most men live and think. Hoffmann's conception of the artist, the divine mission of the poet, musician, and painter, owes much to Tieck, Wackenroder, and Novalis.[10]

There are echoes of Novalis both in ideas and in the poetic imagery with which they are expressed. In *Berganza*, where Hoffmann still stands upon the threshold of his literary activity, there is mention of Novalis and of the Blue Flower, the most enduring of his poetic concepts: "Only to one who is sanctified [geheiligt] does the Blue Flower unfold its chalice," and Berganza quotes his former master Kreisler as saying of Novalis: "The purest beams of poesy shone in his childlike spirit, and his life was a hymn which he sang in glorious tones to the Highest Being and to the holy wonders of nature."

Though the dramatic form was almost completely alien to Hoffmann's genius, he acknowledged the guidance of the Italian dramatist Gozzi in certain elements of his storytelling.[11] When Hoffmann

[10] "Es giebt keinen höheren Zweck der Kunst, als in dem Menschen diejenige Lust zu entzünden, welche sein ganzes Wesen von aller irdischen Qual, von allem niederbeugenden Druck des Alltagslebens, wie von unsaubern Schlacken befreit, und ihn *so* erhebt, dass er, sein Haupt stolz und froh emporrichtend, das Göttliche schaut, ja mit ihm in Berührung kommt." *Berganza*, I, p. 128. Cf. Käte Friedemann: "Die romantische Kunstauffassung," in *Zeitschrift für Ästhetik und allgemeine Kunstwissenschaft*, xviii (1925), pp. 487-525.

[11] Cf. Hedwig Hoffmann Rusack: *Gozzi in Germany*, New York, 1930; H. Dahmen: "E. T. A. Hoffmann und Carlo Gozzi," in *Hochland*, xxvi (1929), pp. 442-46. Dr. Rusack gathers all the allusions to Gozzi in Hoffmann's works and traces his influence in Hoffmann's stories. For example, she finds in *Il re cervo* the germ for the magic microscope in *Meister Floh*. In Gozzi's *fiaba* a magician gives to King Deramo a magic bust which by a laugh discloses the insincerity of the ladies among whom the King might choose a bride; when, by this method, he discovers the real love of Angela, he destroys the bust, for he will never yield to the temptation to test her love. Hoffmann enlarges the use of the microscope over that of Gozzi's bust and subtly ennobles the attitude of Peregrinus Tyzz over that of the King: Peregrinus refuses to test the love of Rosa Lämmerhirt at all. Ellinger had mentioned the fact of Hoff-

became acquainted with Gozzi is indeterminate, but his first reference, in a letter to Hippel from Warsaw, September 26, 1805, suggests both understanding and admiration already fully developed. He is speaking of the production of Brentano's little play *Die lustigen Musikanten* in April of that year; Hoffmann's music for the play was composed the previous December. In this drama Brentano introduced figures taken from Gozzi's revival of the familiar "masks" of the "Commedia dell' Arte"—Truffaldino, Tartaglia, Pantalone. "But, holy Gozzi," Hoffmann exclaims, "what monsters were made out of the fascinating figures created by jovial caprice."[12] It may well be that Hoffmann was attracted to Brentano's play by the very elements derived from Gozzi. In the same letter to Hippel he states that during the previous year he has earnestly applied himself to the study of Italian and planned the following winter to perfect himself in the oral language and to acquire knowledge of the dialects, "Venetian, Neapolitan, etc." In this letter he brings his acquisition of the language into connection with the proposed trip to Italy, but it would seem possible that his study was also prompted by a desire to read Gozzi in the original with complete understanding. A wish to become acquainted with the Italian dramatist may, further, have been stimulated by his reading of Tieck.

It was the rare union of the grotesquely comic with the serious, the daring use of fantastic supernaturalism, the bizarre and seemingly capricious arrangement of material, which endeared Gozzi to him and placed the Italian high in the Pantheon of Hoffmann's literary divinities. In several of his works there is unmistakable evidence of Gozzi's influence. In a letter to Kunz, August 19, 1813, he acknowledges the "ghostly" presence of Gozzi in *Der goldene Topf*; details in his narratives are taken over from Gozzi but worked over in Hoffmann's manner. Indeed the part of *Prinzessin Brambilla* which specifically concerns the theater constitutes a purely imaginary Roman parallel to Gozzi's Venetian rebellion against the popularity of Chiari and Goldoni and his sponsorship of a return to the spirit, at least, of the "Commedia dell' Arte."

Of Kreisler it was said that nature in forming him had tried a new recipe—and it turned out a failure. One must indeed be cautious

---

mann's probable indebtedness to *Il re cervo*, but without details. In 1810 Hitzig published an edition of Gozzi in the original Italian; it seems probable that Hoffmann urged the publication on his friend. Some acquaintance with the "Commedia dell' Arte" on Hoffmann's part is indicated as early as November 1795 (*Briefwechsel*, I, p. 78).

[12] *Briefwechsel*, I, p. 209.

in accepting Kreisler as a portrait of the author. But in Hoffmann as in Kreisler incongruous elements were joined which never fused into a coherent unity. Nature had bestowed on him an artist's soul, filled with inexpressible longing for beauty, for ultimate and eternal values, a longing which found its most nearly perfect satisfaction in music, his own dreams of melody, and the supreme musical creations of the great masters.

But nature at the same time had given Hoffmann an acute sense for the phenomena of his mundane environment. In his youth he spoke of having "too much reality" (zu viel Wirklichkeit). The so-called world of reality forced itself upon him, even the minutiae of everyday existence. He possessed a keen vision for the detail of ordinary living, and the humdrum facts gripped him every time he opened his eyes. They were not observed with will or purpose; he did not wander about the streets, notebook in hand, gathering material for eventual use—he had no need of doing so.

These two elements of his being are equally characteristic of his stories—the other world, the world of dreams, and the world of our everyday. In his tales he achieved the artistic union of the two elements that he never brought to pass in his own life and being. We may say of him as Lowell said of Poe: "In his tales he has chosen to exhibit his powers chiefly in that dim region which stretches from the very limits of the probable into the weird confines of superstition and unreality. He combines in a very remarkable way two faculties which are seldom found united: a power of influencing the reader by the impalpable shadows of mystery, and a minuteness of detail which does not leave a pin or a button unnoticed." "The analyzing tendency of his mind balances the poetical and enables him to throw a wonderful reality into his most unreal fancies."[13] The outer world and the inner world are united by a strange reciprocal relationship; the outer world "acts as a lever" which raises in us the power to see the inner world and is thus essential to our comprehension of it.[14]

[13] Cf. James Russell Lowell: "Our Contributors No. xvii, Edgar Allan Poe," in *Graham's Magazine*, xxvii (February 1845), pp. 49-53.

[14] The use of concrete reality by the Romanticists as a stepping-stone to the higher or spiritual reality is succinctly expressed by Hilde Cohn: "Die Bewegung der Romantik bedeutet innerlich den Weg zur Unendlichkeit, der durch die Endlichkeit führt" (*Realismus und Transzendenz in der Romantik*, Heidelberg, 1933, p. 6). For a divergent view of Hoffmann's combination of Romanticism and realism, cf. Rodolfo Bottacchiari: "Romanticismo e Realismo in E. T. A. Hoffmann," in *La Cultura*, i (1922), pp. 245-68. The Italian critic thinks Hoffmann by nature a realist, as he finally demonstrated in *Des Vetters Eckfenster*; the philosophical conception of the identity of the two worlds—that of sense perception and that beyond our senses

5. Design for the Dust-Cover of *Kater Murr*

6. The "Mad Kreisler"

If the novels that Hoffmann wrote during his student days were available for present examination, they would doubtless show a strong, if not slavish, dependence upon the sensational mystery stories popular at the time. They would probably bear witness to his interest in the occult, as is suggested by the title "Der Geheimnisvolle," and demonstrate the irresistible stirrings of the spirit within him that had not yet found a characteristic medium of expression. Years elapsed before his creative powers ripened and became entirely his own, something inseparable from his personality, when he could cast away borrowed plumes and write as only he could write. In the meantime, music filled his hours, and the creative impulse was still confined to the world of harmony. And music remained to the end in his mind the one supreme method whereby the human spirit feels and expresses its relation to the Divine.

But Hoffmann began to regard literature as a parallel form, another way of expressing this relationship. The symphony was the perfect vehicle; the opera was decidedly a lesser genre, even though his chief success in music was in that field; words confine the imagination, though by them the opera gains in ready intelligibility. And Hoffmann really began his career as a writer of fiction by way of musical criticism. His first "story" is a musical essay disguised in the form of a narrative. In *Ritter Gluck* the narrator meets a strange old musician whom he accompanies to his lodgings. Hoffmann leaves the reader in doubt whether this chance acquaintance is merely a pathetic lunatic who imagines himself to be Gluck or is in reality Gluck or the spirit of Gluck reincarnated. To the narrator he explains a score of Gluck's from sheets that are absolutely blank, as in a later tale, *Der Artushof*, a half-mad painter sits before a blank canvas on which he sees a great masterpiece. In sending *Ritter Gluck* to Rochlitz, Hoffmann called it "an essay."

In *Don Juan*, the immediate successor of *Ritter Gluck*, the narrative element has increased in significance. A traveler attends a performance of Mozart's opera given in a theater which is a part of the hotel in which he is staying. After he has listened enraptured to the music of the first act, he hears a rustling and looking up finds that the singer who has played the role of Donna Anna has joined him in the box he is occupying. In the conversation that follows the singer reveals to him the deeper meaning of the opera, which becomes transformed and transfigured when she resumes her part. At midnight,

---

—led him to attempt an externalization of his dreams, to reduce them to concrete, graspable terms, and in this he was not entirely successful.

since the door is open from the inn, he steals back to the box, intoxicated by the loveliness of the remembrance, and at two o'clock he feels her presence there and hears her voice. He learns in the morning that the glorious singer who had sung the part of Donna Anna had died at that hour.

Just as music is produced to have an effect upon the hearer, to elicit an emotional response or even an intellectual satisfaction, so Hoffmann contrived his tales with a similar purpose—they were to produce an effect on the human spirit, on the emotions, the imagination. Edgar Allan Poe, a literary kinsman if not indeed a disciple of Hoffmann, describes a method of storytelling that, if not derived from a study of Hoffmann, can yet be applied to his German predecessor. In his review of Hawthorne's *Twice-Told Tales* Poe wrote: "A skillful literary artist has constructed a tale. If wise, he has not fashioned his thoughts to accommodate his incidents, but having conceived with deliberate care a certain unique or single effect to be wrought out, he then invents such incidents—he then combines such events as may best aid him in establishing this preconceived effect." And in greater detail Poe analyzes his own procedure in the "Philosophy of Composition": "I prefer commencing with an *effect*. . . . I say to myself, in the first place, 'of the innumerable effects, or impressions, of which the heart, the intellect, or (more generally) the soul is susceptible, what one shall I, on the present occasion, select?' Having chosen a novel, first, and secondly a vivid effect, I consider whether it can best be wrought by incident or tone—whether by ordinary incidents and peculiar tone, or the converse, by peculiarity of both incident and tone, afterward looking about me (or rather within) for such combinations of events or tone, as shall best aid me in the construction of the effect." In the essay referred to above, Lowell noted this quality in Poe: "His mind reaches forward to the effect to be produced."

This method as described by Poe is abundantly illustrated in Hoffmann's stories, for example in *Das Majorat* (The Entail). At the beginning he places a description like an initial determinative chord or series of chords, foreshadowing the nature of the composition. He paints a picture of wild and awesome desolation surrounding the crumbling castle of R - - - sitten, with effective contrast supplied by the smiling, fruitful landscape close at hand; in one place one hears only the ominous croak of the ravens and the whirring scream of the storm-boding sea gulls, and in the other the little birds sing their morning songs. This passage is followed by a series of incidents that create a weird and ghostly terror. Hoffmann has gained the effect he had in mind.

The substance of Hoffmann's major tales is created by two different processes of the imagination that he himself described; in combination they formed to him the practice of Romantic writing. "That which is experienced or felt in life leads us out of life into the realm of the infinite." That is, the everyday experiences of human living, the material things of daily contact, are full-laden with symbolic, transcendent significance. Only the poet can open the eyes of the blind to see their glory. The second process is the reverse of the first: "The inspired poet brings the miraculous phenomena of the spiritual world into life," or the idea is perhaps more concretely expressed in the description of the author, really himself, in the introductory chapter to the *Fantasiestücke*: "An author to whom the forms of everyday life appear in his inner romantic spiritual world and who presents them then in the gleam that flows around them there."[15] These two processes meet in a focal point and constitute Hoffmann's method of approach to human living, *sub specie aeternatatis*. It was a blind aberration of critical insight that for decades saw in Hoffmann only a teller of weird but meaningless tales and so praised the more pedestrian of his stories.

Accurate observation with the "seeing eye," such an eye as he attributes to Callot, was a first clause in Hoffmann's creed. In 1820 he wrote a fictitious letter to the editor of a Berlin periodical *Der Zuschauer* (The Spectator), in which he says: "You doubtless know already how all too gladly I look on, and observe, and then put down in black and white what I right vividly have perceived."[16] In one form or another this idea occurs repeatedly in Hoffmann's opinions on literature—for example, in the conversations of the Serapion Brothers, or more succinctly in *Des Vetters Eckfenster* (My Cousin's Corner Window), the last work to be published during his lifetime.[17]

According to the habit formed long before, in *Berganza*, in *Der Dichter und der Komponist*, and in *Seltsame Leiden*, Hoffmann clothes his ideas in an imaginary narrative with dialogue. The

---

[15] xv, p. 10; vi, p. 83. "Ein Dichter oder Schriftsteller, dem die Gestalten des gewöhnlichen Lebens in seinem innern romantischen Geisterreiche erscheinen, und der sie nun in dem Schimmer, von dem sie dort umflossen, wie in einem fremden wunderlichen Putze darstellt." i, p. 10.

[16] "Sie wissen es nehmlich wohl schon, wie gar zu gern ich zuschaue und anschaue, und dann schwarz auf weiss von mir gebe, was ich eben recht lebendig erschaut." *Briefwechsel*, ii, p. 421.

[17] "Des Vetters Eckfenster" appeared in *Der Zuschauer* in the spring of 1822, only a few months before Hoffmann's death.

"cousin" is an author, really Hoffmann himself, endowed with an unusual and lively fancy and given to jesting in a humorous fashion all his own. Now, however, the cousin is paralyzed. Illness has no power to check the "quick wheeling" of his imagination, but the evil demon of his malady has blocked the pathway that thought must pursue in order to take form on paper. The window opens on the Gendarmenmarkt, the same scene upon which Hoffmann in illness and health looked out during the years of his Berlin life.

It is market day. The square with the Royal Theater and the two great churches is thronged; every conceivable kind of goods is offered for sale; and the Berlin populace of all classes is milling about. A spyglass is at hand, and the cousin gives the narrator a lesson in acute observation, though he admits it is an art that is hardly to be learned. The cousin knows that not a spark of talent for writing glows in the narrator's breast, but the first requirement for authorship is "an eye that really sees": "Yonder market place offers nothing to you but the sight of a dappled, thought-confusing throng of people engaged in meaningless activity, but to me there develops from it a most manifold panorama of the life of the people, and my spirit, a valiant Callot or a modern Chodowiecki, executes one sketch after another, the outlines of which are often bold enough." Thus challenged, the narrator notes the mistresses and servants, the vendors of socks, teacups, spoons, knives, geese, charcoal, and so on, the infinite details of costume, the movements, gestures, and facial expression. To this the cousin adds the imagined circumstances of their home life, the endless variety of character, all visible to the inward eye of his fancy.

Hoffmann saw much more than a motley throng on the market place. His observation penetrated beyond the externals of personal appearance or imagined conduct to the mind of man; his characters are grounded in psychological verity. Indeed, his insight into the relation between mind and conduct is uncannily in agreement with the findings of scientific research in the century after his death. His descriptions of abnormal mental states and of the action resulting therefrom have been declared professionally accurate by competent psychiatrists.[18] This logic of behavior lends a conviction of reality even to the most eccentric conduct of his characters. He succeeds, further, in combining precise observation of detail with consistency

[18] Cf. Dr. Otto Klinke: *E. T. A. Hoffmanns Leben und Werke vom Standpunkte eines Irrenarztes,* Braunschweig und ˙ ɔipzig (no date, but preface dated December 1902).

of behavior in such a way that the miraculous becomes for the time being entirely credible. In this respect there is no difference between the so-called "real" world and the world of dreams, since the latter is placed on an equal plane of reality. Hoffmann objectifies his dreams to the point where the two worlds merge completely. One could collect from his letters and diary a long series of insignificant incidents or observations and show how he made use of them, lending them significance in his tales.

Closely akin to this acuteness of observation of everyday reality is Hoffmann's predilection for contemporary backgrounds, involving reference to definite localities, cities, streets, squares, restaurants, to local hairdressers, shopkeepers, and music teachers, all called by their real names. Even in the Märchen, where the supernatural prevails, the fantastic phenomena are projected against the background of contemporary life in Berlin, Dresden, or Frankfurt. After Ottmar's reading of his story *Ein Fragment aus dem Leben dreier Freunde* Theodor-Hoffmann remarks that Ottmar had excellent reason for placing the scene in Berlin and naming familiar streets and squares, for through the definite location of the scene the whole work acquires the appearance of historical veracity, which assists the laggard imagination, and gains uncommonly in vividness and freshness for the reader who is acquainted with the place. Similarly, after the reading of *Die Brautwahl* the practice is warmly defended. In other days it was customary, even the rule, to take the Märchen of Scheherazade as a model and transplant everything that could be called a Märchen to the Orient. In this way "one created a world that hovered unsteadily in the air and disappeared before our eyes. . . . The foot of the heavenly ladder on which one will climb into higher regions must be firmly fixed in life, so that every man is enabled to climb up too ; if clambering ever higher and higher he finds himself then in a fanciful magic realm, he will believe that this realm still belongs in his life, and is really the most wondrously glorious part of it."[19]

Hoffmann's method of telling a story—his technique in the narrower sense—is at times somewhat indirect and devious. He was indeed a capable craftsman, but not a supreme master in the manage-

[19] "Die Sitten des Morgenlandes nur eben berührend, schuf man sich eine Welt, die haltlos in den Lüften schwebte und vor unsern Augen verschwamm. . . . Ich meine, dass die Basis der Himmelsleiter, auf der man hinaufsteigen will in höhere Regionen, befestigt sein müsse im Leben, so dass jeder nachzusteigen vermag. Befindet er sich dann, immer höher und höher hinaufgeklettert, in einem fantastischen Zauberreich, so wird er glauben, dies Reich gehöre auch noch in sein Leben hinein, und sei eigentlich der wunderbar herrlichste Teil desselben." VIII, pp. 90-91.

ment of his material. Despite the originality of his storytelling, his technique is still under the influence of his predecessors in fiction. Among the novelists whom he most admired in his youth were Sterne and Jean Paul. It may, of course, be maintained that Sterne's seemingly haphazard method of narration—for example, in *Tristram Shandy*—was really a most refined and subtle form of art, that Sterne gains his general effect with conscious artistic intent through the very violation of all chronology and the inclusion of most multifarious material. The reading public of Hoffmann's day was not at all offended by the incoherence and willful caprice of Jean Paul's novels, which were, to be sure, only more exuberantly formless than much of the fiction of the time—and perhaps were acclaimed for that very reason. It is of course a far cry from the vagaries of Sterne and the irritating diffuseness of Jean Paul to the relative compactness of Hoffmann's tales, but now and then they are somewhat lacking in shapeliness and are less comely in their form than they are masterly in other elements of the narrator's art.

It was the fashion of the eighteenth century to enhance the reality of the imagined material by such devices as the pretence that the letters or diary had been found in an old trunk in the attic, or to interpolate extracts from diaries or long first-person narratives till the story resembled a Chinese nest of boxes. Such indeed was *Der Genius,* the first novel that Hoffmann mentions in his letters. It would doubtless be going too far to risk even a guess that he derived from *Der Genius* the involved technique that he followed in some of his stories. There were too many other novels built on a similar pattern, such as Lewis' *The Monk,* which unquestionably supplied something to the construction of *Die Elixiere des Teufels*; and the most popular thriller of a somewhat later date, Maturin's *Melmoth the Wanderer,* equally popular in England and on the Continent, follows the pattern in an even more exaggerated form.

Hoffmann's shorter tales lend themselves less satisfactorily to this type of fictional technique. *Der Sandmann, Ignaz Denner,* and *Das öde Haus* are examples of irregular order of narration; instead of a simple story in chronological sequence of events, the material is broken up and related in the reverse order. In these tales and some others, the formula closely approximates a mannerism; at the end the reader finds the antecedent circumstances upon which the mysterious happenings of the earlier narrative depend. Obviously this method may be employed for the creation of suspense, and justifiably employed to that end, but Hoffmann follows the pattern too closely, though it would be a rash hand that would venture to reshape these tales and arrange the material differently, without losing the effect which Hoffmann had in view.

Hoffmann was deeply impressed by the stories of Heinrich von Kleist.[20] In Kleist he found an almost incomparable master of the short narrative, standing largely isolated in his generation of fiction writers. In such stories as *Das Erdbeben in Chili* and *Die Verlobung in St. Domingo* he could admire a conciseness without undue condensation, not one word too many or one word too few—an economy of means to an end that was exceedingly rare in the Romantic Period and uncommon at any time. Though the technique of Kleist's stories presented a model that Hoffmann might have desired to follow, the whole bent of his genius ran counter to an acceptance of this discipline. It is indeed possible that some of the stories that are told with restraint and with an approach to terseness, such as *Das Fräulein von Scuderi*, show the influence of Kleist's example. At all events, Hoffmann accepted the challenge of Kleist's *Die Marquise von O.* and wrote a story *Das Gelübde* on the same strange theme, a psychological problem of startling originality: a woman has been attacked when in a state of unconsciousness or hallucination and the paternity of her child became a torturing question or an incredible delusion.

With considerable frequency Hoffmann employed the device of a personal narrator who is a chance spectator of the action and then perhaps through the operation of curiosity thus aroused comes into possession of added information—what went before and what came afterward—so that a more or less perfectly rounded tale is built up. If the reader becomes interested both in this observer for his own sake and in the process by which he acquires his information, while at the same time he follows the main thread of the story, the novelist has perhaps gained an appreciable advantage over the simpler form of impersonal narrative. For example, in *Die Jesuiterkirche in G.* the use of this artistic method is highly effective; the life story of Berthold the painter is much enhanced in its appeal through the "framework" of the "Traveling Enthusiast" who accidentally happens on the scene, becomes acquainted with Berthold, and then pieces the fragments of his life together. *Das Majorat* exhibits an even more skillful interweaving of two narrative threads; on the occasion

---

[20] Cf. W. Orth: *Kleist und Hoffmann.* Opladen, 1920. Orth calls attention to their common dependence on the nature philosophy of Schubert and the investigations of Reil on mental phenomena, and upon the fiction of Julius Grosse. He notes the use of the same or similar motifs in Kleist and Hoffmann and the divergences of treatment and style; he finds many traces of Kleist's influence in Hoffmann's works.

of his visit to the castle of R - - - sitten, the first person narrator is
not only an observer of a situation that excites his interest, but
through his love for the Baroness is himself for a time in danger of
becoming involved in it, standing as it were upon the threshold of a
world where he might participate in the doom that hangs over the
whole baronial family. The technique of *Rat Krespel* runs closely
parallel to that of *Die Jesuiterkirche in G*; the narrator becomes
acquainted with Krespel and his daughter, and learns from various
sources the strange story behind the occurrences of which he himself
is a witness.

At times Hoffmann allows a whimsical mood to take possession of
the storyteller's art. In bringing *Der goldene Topf* to an end, the
author takes the reader into his confidence: he has no words to describe the beauty and bliss of the island whither the hero has departed with his bride. Luckily he receives a note from the Archivarius, who in some magic fashion was aware of his predicament: if
the author wants to write the last chapter, the Archivarius invites
him to descend the cursed five flights of stairs (in Dresden Hoffmann
lived up four flights) and come to his house, where writing materials
lie waiting in the blue palm room. Thus we have an interview between
an author and one of his characters—a device already used by
Clemens Brentano in *Godwi* and anticipating by a century the
strange technique of Unamuno's *Niebla* (Mist). Lindhorst receives
him cordially, brings a bowl of flaming arrack, throws off his dressing gown, climbs into the bowl, and vanishes in the flames. Hoffmann
tastes of the delicious drink, and the last chapter is written. The two
stories *Die Irrungen* and *Die Geheimnisse* form really one con-
secutive narrative, published in the *Berlinischer Taschenkalender*
in the issues for 1821 and 1822. In *Die Geheimnisse* Hoffmann
adopted the curious technical device mentioned above and extended
its use. Some of the characters in *Die Irrungen* are filled with discomfiture at the publication of the story and indignantly voice
their protests to the author. Accordingly Hoffmann, under the
cipher Hff., enters the story as a character and takes a hand, albeit
a feeble one, in the action. The mysterious sky-blue reticule—the
loss of which occasioned most of the trouble in *Die Irrungen*—falls
by chance into his hands, and as Hff. he deciphers the fragmentary
and in part illegible manuscript that it contained, using these fragments to make up the greater part of the second tale.

The arrangement of material in the unfinished novel *Kater Murr*
may seem eccentric to the point of lunacy, and in the whole realm

of fiction it would be difficult to find a parallel. The *Godwi* of Clemens Brentano seemingly carried eccentricity to the limits of the whimsical, but Hoffmann in *Kater Murr* has outdistanced his friend. The two volumes of the novel, all Hoffmann wrote, are composed of two separate narratives that in irregular segments alternate throughout the book—the autobiography of the cat and a narrative in the third person taken from the life of the musician Kreisler, the one-time owner of the cat. The combination of the two is the result of an accident that Hoffmann explains in his foreword. For use as a pad or as blotting paper while writing his own life Kater Murr had filched pages from a book in his master's library, the biography of Kreisler, which apparently had been privately printed and circulated, since it was not in the book trade. When Hoffmann as editor took the manuscript to Mr. Dümmler the publisher—who had bought Hitzig's business when Hitzig returned to the courts—the leaves from the life of Kreisler remained unnoticed. Mr. Dümmler agreed to take the work, though he had never before published the writings of a cat, and the typesetter went to work, incorporating the pages of the Kreisler biography wherever they happened to fall. Since the error was not discovered until it was too late to disentangle the medley, the book was issued still containing the results of the cat's vandalism. The Kreisler narrative begins or breaks off in the middle of a sentence just where it chanced that the cat tore the pages out of the book. The life of the cat can indeed be coherently put together by omitting the "blotting paper" sheets, but the corresponding process of deleting the cat's story leaves a collection of fragments fortuitously selected by Kater Murr. The latter process has indeed been carried out by Hans von Müller and published with other Kreisler material in *Das Kreislerbuch*, but this indubitably does violence to Hoffmann's purpose in arranging the strange juxtaposition of two narratives.

If it is taken literally, the nickname "Gespenster-Hoffmann" (Specter-Hoffmann) which trailed the novelist down through the nineteenth century is hardly deserved, for genuine "spooks" are not really a characteristic feature of his stories, though he does introduce them. The supernatural elements in Hoffmann's tales, which might be covered by a broader definition of the name, are by and large, eerie, weird, mystical, often also an imagined extension of phenomena that are subject to scientific examination and proof. They provoke a not unpleasant thrill of apprehension, or, in greater potency, a touch of real fear or perhaps terror, but rarely horror. Indeed some of his excursions into the supernatural are carried on in a mood of lighthearted curiosity or even jollity. Yet Hoffmann defends the introduction of the genuinely horrible into literature. The question is introduced at a meeting of the Serapion Brothers as a preliminary to Cyprian's narrative *Vampyrismus* or, as Harich entitles it, *Die Hyänen* (The Hyenas).[21] Sylvester contends that the use of so ghastly a theme as vampirism must degenerate into a portrayal of the horrible, the revolting. Both Theodor and Cyprian oppose Sylvester's vehement condemnation: such a theme does not necessarily descend to the offensive and the disgusting, for, if the author has "poetic tact," even such a subject, in itself perhaps intrinsically revolting, may still arouse "the deep thrill [Schauer] of that mysterious terror which dwells in our own breast and when touched by electric shocks from the dim spirit world, convulses our minds without upsetting [verstören] them." "The lever of fear, terror, or horror" may be employed to stir the human spirit to its very depths. As examples of such poetic control of sinister material, Theodor refers to Shakespeare and to Tieck's story *Liebeszauber* (Love Charm), and Lothar adds Kleist's *Das Bettelweib von Locarno* (The Beggar Woman of Locarno).

At times Hoffmann contrives a startling union of the comic with the fearful; he manipulates the material so that the humorous itself is changed into the fearful or even the horrible. This is a unique element in his style. *Der Sandmann* affords an example: the automaton Olimpia with her mechanical movements and monosyllabic utterance is a droll conception, but Nathanael, ardently in love with the doll, reading his poems to her, is a tragic figure, and in the final scene where the automaton is bandied about, used as an offensive weapon, and its eyes drop out, the comedy becomes tinged with horror. In *Ignaz Denner* the storyteller quite forgot his Shakespeare; he sought an effect through the accumulation of horrible and revolting details, and failed. Behind the horrible there must stand something inexplicably exalted, some utmost reach of human nature, which deflects the impact.

A considerable number of his stories Hoffmann placed against a historical background, in some cases indeed, the immediate past, as the siege of Dresden in *Erscheinungen* and the Peninsular War in

[21] The discussion is prompted by a reference to Lord Byron; Sylvester calls *The Siege of Corinth* a masterpiece, full of the most vivid pictures and original ideas, but the introduction of the horrible in *Der Vampyr* has kept him from even reading the story; the mere idea involved in it sent ice-cold shivers over him. *The Vampyre* of William Polidori, Byron's physician, was falsely attributed to Byron and translated into German as his work; Hoffmann refers again to it as the work of Byron in his review of Weber's *Der Freischütz*, xv, p. 187.

Der Zusammenhang der Dinge. The scene of some of his tales is laid in a historical epoch, though historical events are not utilized, as in *Meister Martin der Küfner.* Numerous stories as a whole or in part take place in a foreign land, particularly in Italy. Hoffmann's extreme diligence in gathering and shaping his historical, topographical, and cultural material has been mentioned elsewhere; he was acutely aware of the novelist's obligation in this regard. But the use of material thus collected he deemed even more important, as is shown in the discussions of the Serapion Brothers, especially of *Der Zusammenhang der Dinge.* There is a peculiarly characteristic quality in historical material which the author vainly seeks to grasp if he hovers about in a vacuum. Unless he possesses the requisite skill to work up the material, he does not produce the color of real life; he dips into the paint pot, and the result is a confused hodgepodge of color streaks. That is, the novelist cannot communicate the sense of reality in historical or foreign scenes simply by dabs of "local color." The novelist must grasp and present historical truth, though the events themselves may belong entirely to his imagination. The word "grasp" (erfassen) is of profound importance; it meant to Hoffmann a complete absorption in the material he had collected so that he could reproduce scenes from the historical past as if he had been an eyewitness and present them with the vividness of contemporary actuality. This process is illustrated in such stories as *Signor Formica, Doge und Dogaressa,* and *Meister Martin der Küfner.* But he supplies no sovereign method of attack upon material collected, no formula or recipe to produce the desired results, for the process is guided by a kind of secret clairvoyance that is vouchsafed to but few. Indeed it has been shown that certain matters connected with the life of Salvator Rosa, which Hoffmann apparently imagined and put into *Signor Formica,* are historically true, though there is no record of them in the sources Hoffmann used.

Most of Hoffmann's tales were published either with no descriptive "tag" or with the simple words "eine Erzählung"—a story or narrative. *Signor Formica* was the only one described as a "Novelle," though in a letter to Kunz he speaks of *Der Magnetiseur* as expanding under his hands into a "Novelle" of considerable dimensions. In the second half of the eighteenth century the word "Novelle" began to be used in Germany but for the most part without any clear definition. Hoffmann was probably acquainted with the attempts of the Schlegels to define and delimit the term as covering a separate literary genre—the familiar definitions of Tieck and of Goethe were not published till a few years after Hoffmann's death. It is probable that Hoffmann did not attach any great importance to his designation of *Signor Formica* as a "Novelle," and indeed other tales fit more neatly into the common definitions of the genre. Before reading the story at a meeting of the Serapion Brotherhood, Ottmar states that he has tried to imitate the tone, the easy but pleasing breadth of the old Italian "novelas," particularly those of Boccaccio, but has doubts of his success. At the end Vinzenz finds the chief resemblance to Boccaccio in the amount of space devoted to "beating people up."

Hoffmann's prose is always fluent and clear though he never attained the limpid clarity of his masters, Goethe, or Novalis, or even Tieck, but he never descended to the annoying turgidity of Jean Paul, another of his masters. His style is by no means uniform, since without effort, by instinct as it were, he modified the method of expression in accordance with the type of story he was telling. One needs merely to compare the prose style of *Die Elixiere des Teufels* or *Ignaz Denner* with that of *Klein Zaches* or *Die Brautwahl*. In *Tristram Shandy* another of his masters remarked that: "Writing, when properly managed (as you may be sure I think mine is) is but a different name for conversation"; Sterne meant, of course, "good conversation," and with that emendation one may apply Sterne's principle to many of Hoffmann's stories: an excellent raconteur is telling a tale and knows how to cultivate a pleasant personal relationship with his hearers.

The musician Hoffmann is evident in the subtle cadences of the sentence, even as the structure of musical composition, of counterpoint, can be traced in many of his stories. He had an odd habit, which one may be tempted to censure as an irritating mannerism, of repeating the first words of a direct quotation after "said he" or the like has interrupted it: " 'Sehen Sie wohl,' unterbrach Albertine den geheimen Kanzlei-Sekretär, 'Sehen Sie wohl,' "; " 'nimmermehr,' rief Albertine, 'nimmermehr heirate ich, etc.' " This repetition is in all probability a legacy of Hoffmann's processes in musical composition. When the substance of the story requires or invites, he delights in elaborate use of tone color, of onomatopoeia; a good illustration is the song of the three serpents in the lilac tree (*Der goldene Topf*):

"Zwischendurch — zwischenein — zwischen Zweigen, zwischen schwellenden Blüten, schwingen, schlängeln, schlingen wir uns— Schwesterlein—Schwesterlein, schwinge dich im Schimmer, schnell,

schnell herauf, herab—Abendsonne schiesst Strahlen, zischelt der Abendwind, etc."[22]

The use of irony is a marked characteristic of Hoffmann's style. Several of the *Kreisleriana* are written throughout in an ironical tone, in the simpler form of ironic discourse, where the author says precisely the opposite of what he really means; but later the irony of Hoffmann's tales becomes more subtle. His address to the guild of scene shifters and stage mechanics (*Der vollkommene Maschinist*), giving them instructions how to defeat the intentions of the playwright, and the *Gedanken über den hohen Wert der Musik* are illustrations of the early use of irony. In the tales, especially in the Märchen, the follies, vagaries, and stupidities of human living are set forth with much more subtle irony. More subtle still is the irony involved in the circumstances of the stories themselves, an indirect comment on "life's little ironies." *Ein Fragment aus dem Leben dreier Freunde* offers a good example. The three friends are in a well-known restaurant in the Tiergarten. A young girl of arresting beauty enters, as if seeking someone, and then a young man hastily slips through the throng to press into her hand a note which she hurriedly conceals. Presently she joins an older man and woman, evidently her father and mother, at a neighboring table, seizing, however, the first opportunity when their attention is engaged to draw forth the bit of paper and read its contents. "Then the friends saw how the blood mounted to the face of the poor girl, how great tears came into her lovely eyes, how her breast rose and fell from inward anxiety; she tore the little piece of paper into a hundred fragments, and slowly, as if each one of them were some fair hope, hard to renounce, she gave them to the winds." The three impressionable youths were much exercised over this occurrence and speculated upon the tragic situation apparently involved, comparing the girl to Ophelia and Emilia Galotti. Eventually, however, two years later, the content of the fatal communication is revealed: the hat she had ordered from a milliner would not be ready for the occasion when she hoped to wear it. In the use of so-called Romantic Irony, Hoffmann is on the whole more sparing than his predecessor and model Tieck, and the frequent asides to the reader are by no means always examples of it. There is often no breaking of the illusion; indeed, these talks with the reader may serve to increase the conviction of reality in the narrative as told.

Any account of Hoffmann's method of work must face the per-

[22] Compare Carlyle's quite skillful translation of this passage.

sistent legend of his dependence upon alcoholic stimulants. Wine has been made the key word in explaining the fertility of his imagination; the eccentric dance of his puppets could be set in motion only through the spur of alcoholic stimulation.[23] The theory has been tempting to some investigators, who assume and then exploit a hypothetical relation between genius and abnormality, or any type of aberration from the norm. The legend started with the well-meaning but sober-minded Hitzig, who expressed disapproval of his friend's convivial habits. Hitzig was commendably exercised about Hoffmann's health, had good grounds for his anxiety, and was quite justified in the conviction that Hoffmann's manner of life was injurious to his physical well-being. Hitzig admits, however, that the gatherings about the fragrant punch bowl in Hoffmann's home— in which he himself participated—were not characterized by any kind of excess; Hoffmann's colleagues, so to speak, in the literary world, met for the discussion of topics interesting to them all, and in the circumstances the punch bowl was an inevitable accessory. It was apparently the constant and late evenings spent in the wine rooms of Lutter and Wegner that excited Hitzig's concern. Yet there is no proof that even there Hoffmann ever drank immoderately; indeed, the contrary is far more likely. Had no insidious physical weakness been already preying upon him, had his life otherwise been judiciously regulated, such relaxation would doubtless have been a minor or negligible drain upon his bodily resistance.

Among the *Höchst zerstreute Gedanken* in the *Kreisleriana* there is a brief but pertinent paragraph on the subject. "There is a good deal of talk," Hoffmann says, "about the inspiration that artists derive from the use of strong drink; musicians and poets are named who can work only in this way. . . . I don't believe it—but it is certain that spirituous liquors promote the more active transformation of one's ideas in the happy state of mind, I might say, in the fortunate constellation, when the mind passes over from reflection to creative work. It is not exactly a fine figure, but in this case the imagination

[23] Cf. Arvède Barine (Cécile Vincens): *Poètes et nevrosés, Hoffmann, De Quincey, Edgar Poe, Gerard de Nerval*, Paris, 1898; the article on Hoffmann was originally published in a series of "Essais de littérature pathologique," in the *Revue des deux Mondes, Le Vin-Hoffmann*, cxxxii (1895), pp. 307-48. Cf. Ellinger's review in the *Zeitschrift für deutsche Philologie*, xxxiii, pp. 550-54. The essay is filled with inaccuracies and as an account of Hoffmann's life is so completely negligible that one wonders why Ellinger (whom she calls Essinger) thought it worth-while to review it. Both Klinke and K. F. van Vleuten ("Edgar Allan Poe," in *Die Zukunft*, xliv, pp. 181-90) deny on scientific examination of the evidence both excessive drinking on Hoffmann's part and any determinative influence of alcohol on his writing. Cf. also Dr. Bl-A. Cabanès: *Grands Névropaths, Malades Immortels*, Paris (1920), iii, pp. 9-36; Cabanès refers to two other French medical studies of Hoffmann.

seems to me like a mill wheel which the stream turns with increasing force—a person pours wine on it, and the motive power within turns more rapidly." He provides an illustration: when punch is prepared involving the lighting of cognac, arrack, or rum, the spirits of the elements—salamanders, gnomes, water nymphs—come into play in his fancy. Yet he does not end his brief comment without a warning: "the spirit that is born from light and subterranean fire and controls man so boldly, is dangerous, and one cannot trust its affability, for it quickly changes its bearing and becomes a fearful tyrant instead of a beneficent, agreeable friend."[24] In the *Serapionsbrüder* Lothar-Hoffmann insists that for no work is a clear, calm mind so indispensable as for one that shoots out in all directions "into the blue with playful, orderless caprice but should and must bear in itself a solid kernel"—a good characterization of Hoffmann's own Märchen.

Since Hoffmann was both musician and painter, one would assume that his auditory and visual sensations were especially acute, that both his ear and his eye were phenomenally sensitive. He himself adds the sense of smell: "Not so much in dreams as in the condition of delirium which precedes falling asleep—particularly when I have been hearing a good deal of music—I find a blending of colors, tones, and odors. It seems to me as if they were all produced through the beam of light in the same mysterious way and then were obliged to combine together into a wonderful harmony. The perfume of the dark-red carnation has a strange, magical effect upon me; involuntarily I sink into a dreamy condition and hear then as if from far distance the deep tones of a tenor clarinet swelling in force and then dying away."[25] This is one of the "Very Scattered Thoughts" in the first cycle of the *Kreisleriana*. At the end of the second cycle, in *Johannes Kreislers Lehrbrief*, Hoffmann reverts to the experience

[24] "Man spricht so viel von der Begeisterung, die die Künstler durch den Genuss starker Getränke erzwingen—man nennt Musiker und Dichter, die nur *so* arbeiten können. . . . Ich glaube nicht daran—aber gewiss ist es, dass eben in der glücklichen Stimmung, ich möchte sagen, in der günstigen Konstellation, wenn der Geist aus dem *Brüten* in das *Schaffen* übergeht, das geistige Getränk dem regeren Umschwung der Ideen befördert.—Es ist gerade kein edles Bild, aber mir kommt die Fantasie hier vor, wie ein Mühlrad, welches der stärker anschwellende Strom schneller treibt—der Mensch giesst Wein auf, und das Getriebe im Innern dreht sich rascher!"—"dass der Geist, der von Licht und unterirdischem Feuer geboren, so keck den Menschen beherrscht, gar gefährlich ist, und man seiner Freundlichkeit nicht trauen darf, da er schnell die Miene ändert und statt des wohltuenden behaglichen Freundes, zum furchtbaren Tyrannen wird." I, pp. 51-52.

[25] "Nicht sowohl im Traume, als im Zustande des Delirierens, der dem Einschlafen vorhergeht, vorzüglich wenn ich viel Musik gehört habe, finde ich eine Übereinkunft der Farben, Töne und Düfte. Es kommt mir vor, als wenn alle auf die gleiche geheimnisvolle Weise durch den Lichtstrahl erzeugt würden, und dann sich zu einem wundervollen Konzerte vereinigen müssten. Der Duft der dunkelroten Nelken wirkt mit sonderbarer magischer Kraft auf mich; unwillkürlich versinke ich in einen

as if some critic had challenged him: "It is no empty figure, no
allegory, when the musician says that colors, odors, and beams of
light appear to him as tones, and he sees a wonderful harmony in
their intertwining. Just as, in the words of a sagacious physicist,
hearing is an internal seeing, so to the musician seeing becomes an
internal hearing, that is, becomes the innermost consciousness of the
music, which vibrating in unison with his spirit, resounds from everything that his eye comprehends."[26]

Thus Hoffmann perceives and analyzes his own double or triple
synesthesia. The essential unity of all sense perceptions was a natural
corollary of Romantic thinking, and Romantic literature from its
inception in the work of Novalis, Tieck, and their companions explored intensively and extensively the phenomena of synesthetic
experience, the simultaneous excitation of different sensations, and
the interchange from one area of sensation to another.[27] Undeniably
at times they toyed with the idea when the reality was not present. In
many cases it would be impossible to draw a sharp dividing line
between the genuine psychological experience and the purely asso-
ciative or even rhetorical combinations of sensory experience. A
metaphor involving different sense perceptions may be the product
of intellectual effort or imitation of another's experience. There is,
however, no reason to doubt the accuracy of Hoffmann's own account

---

träumerischen Zustand und höre dann, wie aus weiter Ferne, die anschwellenden
und wieder verfliessenden tiefen Töne des Bassetthorns." I, p. 46. Cf. also *Briefwechsel*, II, p. 352.

[26] "Es ist kein leeres Bild, keine Allegorie, wenn der Musiker sagt, dass ihm
Farben, Düfte, Strahlen, als Töne erscheinen, und er in ihrer Verschlingung ein
wundervolles Konzert erblickt. So wie, nach dem Ausspruch eines geistreichen Physikers, Hören ein Sehen von innen ist, so wird dem Musiker das Sehen ein Hören von
innen, nämlich zum innerlichsten Bewusstsein der Musik, die mit seinem Geiste
gleichmässig vibrierend aus allem ertönt, was sein Auge erfasst." I, p. 321. The physicist to whom Hoffmann refers was J. W. Ritter, the young Jena scientist who, like
Novalis, united genuine scientific interests with romantic perceptions. Cf. *Frag-
mente aus dem Tagebuch eines jungen Physikers*, Heidelberg, 1810; Ellinger, xv,
p. 186.

[27] Cf. Paul Margis: "Die Synaesthesien bei E. T. A. Hoffmann," in *Zeitschrift für
Ästhetik und allgemeine Kunstwissenschaft*, v (1910), pp. 91-99; Heinz-Richard
Stock: *Die optischen Synaesthesien bei E. T. A. Hoffmann*, München, 1914; O.
Fischer: "E. T. A. Hoffmanns Doppelempfindungen," in *Archiv für das Studium der
neueren Sprachen*, CXXII (1909), pp. 1-22; M. Katz: *Die Schilderungen des musikalischen Eindrucks bei Schumann, Hoffmann und Tieck*, Giessen, 1910; and in *Zeitschrift für angewandte Psychologie*, v (1911), pp. 1-53; Ernst Glöckner: *Studien zur
romantischen Psychologie der Musik mit besonderer Rücksicht auf die Schriften
E. T. A. Hoffmanns*, München, 1909. According to Margis, Hoffmann's synesthetic
experiences were both primary and secondary; that is, the striking of a tone was
not immediately connected with the idea of a color but later, after the excitement
of the psychic organism by music, in tranquility colors were united to tones in the
conception; the synesthesia of colors or odors with tones was, however, simultaneous
or primary. This observation, if correct, shows the preponderance of the musical in
Hoffmann's sensory experience.

Cavallerie oder Infanterie? —

7. Canonicus Stöhr

8. Pasquin

of sensory phenomena. The intensity of his experience of sensation, especially of sound and sight, stamps the examples of synesthesia with peculiar vividness and reality. This is true when the metaphors are startling, even when our duller spirits are unable to follow him— when, for example, Kreisler writes to Baron Wallborn that on a certain occasion he was wearing a coat of a C minor color and a cape of E major, it is not a vapid jest on Hoffmann's part, though we cannot probe into the sensation that prompted the metaphor.

Music was ever in Hoffmann's mind, even when he was occupied in alien fields. The application of musical terms in simile and metaphor to other than musical subjects is a hallmark, the unmistakable fingerprint of Hoffmann's style. Already in his younger years it appears in letters to Hippel: from Glogau he wrote comparing the possible content of his letter to a piano concerto, and in another letter he asserts with droll humor that his cousin Ernst Ludwig, his roommate, is snoring in F minor. In his literary work it is impossible to determine whether or not the use of the figure was preceded or accompanied by synesthetic experience. A further reference to Kreisler's letter to Baron Wallborn may afford an illustration: "Unresolved discords cried out most unpleasantly into my inmost being, but just as the serpent-tongued sevenths were about to sweep down into a very light world of friendly thirds, then Your Excellency had departed."[28] For these linguistic vagaries Kreisler apologizes: people say that music has enwebbed him to such a degree and transformed him into a chrysalis that he can no longer extricate himself—that to him everything takes on the form of music.

Though Hoffmann had a keenly observant eye and described the external surfaces of things with uncanny accuracy and himself stood in reverence before the paintings of the masters, his own eye failed him and he turned to the ear when it was a question of finding a symbol for the highest experiences of which man is capable. It is then not the visual but the auditory symbol that he seeks.[29] He would not have written as the English poet:

"I saw Eternity the other night
Like a great Ring of pure and endless light."

He would find a symbol for eternity or infinity in terms of harmony.

[28] "Unaufgelöste Dissonanzen schrieen recht widrig in mein Inneres hinein, aber eben als all die schlangenzüngigen Septimen herabschweben wollten in eine ganz lichte Welt freundlicher Terzen, da waren Ew. Hoch- und Wohlgeboren fort—fort . . . ." I, p. 286.

[29] For the preponderance of auditory experience and auditory symbols in Hoffmann, cf. Carl Schaeffer: *Die Bedeutung des Musikalischen und Akustischen* in *E. T. A. Hoffmanns literarischem Schaffen*, Marburg, 1909.

CHAPTER 8

HOFFMANN AND THE OCCULT

AN interest in the occult, in the unexplained and inexplicable
aspects of nature and human experience, was basic with
Hoffmann. It was doubtless present in his boyhood, an in-
alienable part of his being, however futile may be the search for
sources in his inheritance. If more were known of his father, the
paternal character might supply something more than the vague
hint of the irresponsible and the irrational.

As boys Hoffmann and Hippel busied themselves with Wiegleb's
Natural Magic, particularly in winter when play in the garden became impossible. As the title implies, there is nothing supernatural,
nothing unexplained, in Wiegleb's work, but there is much that
might seem so, or at least highly mystifying to the uninitiated, and
thus could prove enthralling to an imaginative youth. From Wiegleb
the pathway may lead to the unknown and the inexplicable. Wiegleb's work was fitted with a curious and somewhat misleading title
page: *Johann Nikolaus Martius: Unterricht in der natürlichen
Magie, oder zu allerhand belustigenden und nützlichen Kunststücken,
völlig bearbeitet von Johann Christian Wiegleb* (Instruction in
Natural Magic, or for all sorts of entertaining and useful tricks,
completely revised by Johann Christian Wiegleb), Berlin und Stet-
tin, 1779-1805. The real treatise by Martius was originally published in Latin (1700), but was later translated into German and
apparently enjoyed a considerable sale.[1]

Wiegleb's work is, however, not a revision of Martius at all, but a
substitution, and he expanded Martius' single volume eventually to

[1] The title of Martius' original work was *Dissertatio de magia naturali ejusque
usu medico ad magice curandum,* Erfordiae (Erfurt), 1700. The title page of the
German translation read: "Jo. Nicol. Martii Med. Doct und Practici zu Braunschweig
Unterricht von der MAGIA NATURALI und derselben medicinischem Gebrauch auf
magische Weise, wie auch bezauberte Dinge zu curiren Welchem beygefüget Ein
Neu eröffnetes Kunst-Cabinet und Antonii Mizaldi Hundert Curieuse Kunst Stücke
mit einem Nötigen Register." Franckfurt und Leipzig, Bey Christoph Gottlieb
Nicolai, 1717. Number 178 of the "Kunst-Cabinet" gives directions for the preparation of a "Tinctur," "die alle Metallen vollkommen machet / auch schwere Kranck-
heiten heilet / und den Menschen bey langem Leben erhält." The edition of 1719
bore a slightly different title: *Unterricht von der wunderbaren Magie und derselben
medicinischem Gebrauch auch von zauberischen und miraculosen Dingen: Sympathie,
Spagyrik, Astrologie, etc.* Martius' book was an eighteenth century successor to the
similar publication of Wolfgang Hildebrand in the preceding century: *MAGIA NA-
TURALIS, DAS IST KUNST und Wunderbuch, begriffen wunderbahre Secreta,
Geheimnisse und Kunstücke,* 3rd Edition, Erffurdt, 1663-1666.

twenty. Even as a youth Hoffmann may well have been amused by Wiegleb's preface as exemplifying eighteenth century rationalism of the Nicolai type, in part from the mouth of Nicolai himself. The work of Martius was out of print, says Wiegleb, but there were still demands for it; Nicolai, the publisher, knowing perfectly the worthlessness of the book and unwilling, simply for his own profit, to delude the public with a reprint, "thought rather of an arrangement whereby he might please the lovers of natural magic without doing so at the expense of sound human understanding."[2] Accordingly he decided to get together an entirely different collection of "tricks" (Kunststücke), based upon the most recent physical and chemical knowledge. It seems odd that he did not regard it as "deceiving" to retain a portion of the old title.

The first volume began with a rationalistic essay by Professor J. P. Eberhard of Halle "Über die sogenannte Magie" (Concerning So-called Magic). The rest of this volume and the following volumes of the long series present then a numberless multitude of experiments, games, tricks, and the like: they are grouped under such headings—repeated in each volume—as electrical, magnetic, optical, chemical, arithmetical, tricks, and chapters on tricks with cards. In Hippel's biographical sketch of Hoffmann he mentions only one example of the practical use that they made of Wiegleb's instructions, the attempt to raise a silken balloon, several feet in diameter, which Hoffmann's aunt Sophie had sewn together for them: "A few drops of hydrochloric acid which accidentally fell on the ball while it was being filled" gave the experiment a tragicomic end. By inference from the Kreisler biography in *Kater Murr* one may add optical tricks, the preparation of secret inks, and perhaps the manufacture of a portable organ. Years later in dreary Plock, Hoffmann records in his diary under the date of October 2, 1802, that he spent the whole evening foolishly enough (läppischer Weise) in reading Wiegleb and determined sometime to try his hand at the construction of an automaton.

There is no proof that Hoffmann was acquainted with the works of

---

2 "Dachte vielmehr auf eine Vermittelung, die Liebhaber der natürlichen Magie zu vergnügen, ohne solches auf Unkosten des gesunden Menschenverstandes." "Auf diese Art wollte er nun das Publikum von jener abgeschmackten Schrift ablenken und ihm dafür eine weit bessere und nützlichere in die Hände bringen, wodurch *zumal* in gewissen teutschen Provinzen, wo leider noch Aberglauben genug herrscht, geläuterte Begriffe und abergläubische Possen vertrieben werden könnten." The boys' attempt to construct a balloon was founded on Wiegleb's chapter "Die aerostatischen Maschinen" (VII, pp. 179-212, edition of 1793); the account of automatons which later excited Hoffmann's interest is II, pp. 231-50, edition of 1782.

the Romantic School—Tieck, Wackenroder, Novalis, and the Schlegels—before the time of his residence in Warsaw. He was, to be sure, living in Berlin in the days when Wackenroder's *Herzensergiessungen* and Tieck's *Sternbald* had recently been published there and were being widely discussed, and in spite of the rigors of preparation for his examinations he was eagerly receptive to the cultural opportunities that the Prussian capital had to offer. Yet Hitzig implies that in Warsaw he first called the new Romantic literature to Hoffmann's attention, and Hoffmann himself wrote to Hippel of *Sternbald* as a newly discovered world of delight. It would seem probable that Zacharias Werner as well as Hitzig had a share in directing their common friend to the new literary movement. Yet a fondness for supernatural mysteries could have found some satisfaction in minor products of the romantic spirit before the emergence of the Romantic School gave a deeper meaning to research in the shadow side of human life. As time went on, Hoffmann's curiosity led him to examine countless books that dealt with the occult and the mysterious, and the reaction against rationalism had brought forth a well-nigh inexhaustible supply of them.

The period of Hoffmann's literary activity was one of widespread interest in mesmerism, or animal magnetism, in somnambulism, clairvoyance, and kindred phenomena. Even alchemy had not yet lost its fascination, and the flamboyant symbolic language used in earlier books on alchemy still captured the imagination. These aspects of the occult are fundamental elements in a large number of Hoffmann's tales. Two of his most intimate friends in Bamberg, the physicians Marcus and Speyer, experimented in mesmeric or hypnotic therapeutics, and Dr. Koreff in Berlin, a member of the Serapion Brotherhood, was one of the most noted exponents of the practice. It is not demonstrable that Hoffmann studied the works of Mesmer himself or of Puységur, who was Mesmer's chief follower in France, though he unquestionably knew them through their later expositors.

Of the writers on "animal magnetism" Hoffmann was personally acquainted with Kluge[3] and probably also with Hufeland. Kluge was a physician and alienist in Leipzig and served as the official physi-

---

[3] Apart from Schubert, whose work was not technical, Hoffmann's chief sources of information were: Kluge's *Versuch einer Darstellung des animalischen Magnetismus als Heilmittel*, Berlin, 1811; Reil's *Rhapsodien über die Anwendung der psychologischen Curmethode auf Geisteszerrüttungen*, Halle, 1803; Bartels' *Grundzüge einer Physiologie und Physik des animalischen Magnetismus*, Frankfurt am Main, 1812; and Hufeland's *Über Sympathie*, Weimar, 1811.

cian for the Seconda troupe; Hoffmann mentions him with respect.[4] Hufeland left Jena and joined the medical faculty of the University of Berlin in 1812.[5] Doubtless Hoffmann's knowledge of mesmerism and related subjects was to a large extent derived not from books but through friends in the medical profession. Already in Bamberg, as he records in his diary, he had seen a "Somnambule," the current designation for one under mesmeric influence, but adds the significant word "Doubts." Probably Dr. Marcus or Dr. Speyer had invited Hoffmann to the hospital for this purpose. It may also be assumed that through his friend Dr. Koreff in Berlin he was present at mesmeric séances and observed the phenomena about which at the time everyone was talking. He is probably using Ottmar as a mouthpiece in the *Serapionsbrüder* when Ottmar says of Vinzenz (Dr. Koreff): "He is the most zealous exponent of magnetism, and I cannot deny that I have heard from his lips the most penetrating [scharfsinnig] and profound things that can be said on this obscure subject."

The prospective entrance of Vinzenz into the Serapion Brotherhood serves as a natural introduction of the subject of mesmerism, and Hoffmann's reasoned evaluation of its use in therapy can be derived from the discussion. Lothar relates an incident that is intended to show his profound disbelief in the curative powers of magnetism: he was tormented by an unendurable nervous headache; by chance Vinzenz dropped in, and promised immediate relief: "What? . . . nothing more than that? That's easy enough. In ten minutes I will banish your headache wherever you wish, into the back of the chair, into the inkwell, into the spittoon—out of the window." But the ministrations of Vinzenz had no effect; the pains continued, though Vinzenz insisted that the patient was merely deluded by a deceitful echo.

Discussion of the abstract theory, Lothar maintains, is futile, for an empirical test proves the falsity of the method. By way of illustration, he goes on to tell of a knotty problem that a king of England

---

[4] Maassen (IV, p. 281) questions the identification of this Leipzig physician with the author of the treatise. He bases his opinion on the amusing satire in the *Seltsame Leiden* on the psychic cures of a theater physician there and assumes that the physician in question is none other than the Dr. Kluge who attended the Seconda troupe; indeed, in a letter to Kunz, December 28, 1813, Hoffmann states that this physician treated all ailments from the psychic point of view. Maassen thinks Hoffmann would not have jested as in the *Seltsame Leiden* about the author of a book to which he so often refers. It seems improbable that Hoffmann would have suffered from any such inhibition.

[5] According to Varnhagen, Hufeland was one of those (Eichhorn, Schleiermacher) who interceded for Hoffmann at the time of the trouble over *Meister Floh*.

once set before the members of the Academy: does a bucket of water containing a fish weigh more than the bucket without the fish? The members of the Academy were ready with their learned answers when someone craftily proposed to weigh the buckets and find out. Yet to the discomfiture of Lothar and to the amusement of the others it is disclosed that on another occasion, in a nervous illness, Lothar had turned to magnetism for relief. The others are disinclined to accept Lothar's excuse that this was only a proof of his weakness, as when men of intelligence, dissatisfied with the results of regular medical care, take refuge in the ministrations of old women, in simples, and the like.

Cyprian, the most romantic of the three Hoffmanns in the Brotherhood, explains magnetism as the potentiated force (Kraft) of the psychic principle, which is capable of complete control over the physical; one cannot deny the power of the psychic principle or close one's ear "to the wondrous chords [Anklänge] that resound into us and out of us, to the mysterious music of the spheres, which is the changeless life principle of nature itself."[6] Lothar admits that the doctrine of magnetism must exercise an infinite charm over everyone of poetic spirit; he himself has been, and still is, stirred to the depths of his soul: "But who can wish wantonly and presumptuously to penetrate into the deepest secrets of nature, who may desire to know or even to catch a glimpse of that mysterious bond which unites body and spirit and thus determines our existence?"[7] Magnetism is based, or is supposed to be based, on such knowledge, but as long as such a knowledge is really impossible, its doctrines, derived from individual observations, often mere illusions, resemble the vague gropings of one born blind. He does not deny the existence of the magnetic power, that the alien psychic principle is incorporated into a fluid, "or whatever one may call it," into an agency "which goes

[6] "Was ist der Magnetismus, als Heilmittel gedacht, anders als die potenziierte Kraft des psychischen Prinzips, die nun vermag das physische ganz zu beherrschen, es ganz zu erkennen, jeden, auch den leisesten abnormen Zustand darin wahrzunehmen und eben durch die volle Erkenntnis dieses Zustandes ihn zu lösen. Unmöglich kannst du die Macht unseres psychischen Prinzips wegleugnen, unmöglich dein Ohr verschliessen wollen den wunderbaren Anklängen, die in uns hinein, aus uns heraustönen, der geheimnisvollen Sphärenmusik, die das grosse unwandelbare Lebensprinzip der Natur selbst ist." VII, pp. 10-11.

[7] "Wer mag frevelig und vermessen eindringen wollen in das tiefste Geheimnis der Natur, wer mag erkennen, ja nur deutlich ahnen wollen das Wesen jenes geheimnisvollen Bandes, das Geist und Körper verknüpft und auf diese Weise unser Sein bedingt. Auf diese Erkenntnis ist aber doch der Magnetismus ganz eigentlich basiert, und solange dieselbe unmöglich, gleicht die aus einzelnen Wahrnehmungen, die oft nur Illusionen sind, hergeleitete Lehre davon, dem unsichern Herumtappen des Blindgebornen." VII, p. 11.

out from the magnetizer and, streaming forth, seizes the mental powers [geistige Potenz] of the one magnetized." It produces thus a state which deviates radically from all human life and being, but this is unhealthy, an abnormality, and as such is highly dangerous.

The remainder of the discussion is occupied almost completely by a long narrative in which Theodor, Hoffmann more peculiarly himself, relates his own experiences in mesmerism. The account is not factual autobiography, except probably in the essentials. If Hoffmann had become interested in mesmerism during his university years through a friend in the medical department, or had then "read everything" on which he could lay his hands, there would have been some reflection of this interest in his letters, and at no time was he grieving over the death of a sister—this is pure fiction. On the other hand, the two experiences upon which he has formed his opinions are quite probably founded on fact. In the first place, he participates repeatedly in mesmeric séances conducted by a sincere and reputable physician, though they are allowed to become somewhat of a fashionable spectacle; he seems to witness surprising evidences of clairvoyant power. But in the end Theodor is convinced that the subject under hypnotic spell is diabolically clever and is deceiving even the physician himself. Later, Theodor is privileged to attend another and quite different exhibition of mesmeric force. All the trappings of the spectacular are eliminated; there is apparently no loophole for charlatanism to creep in, and the test is carried out in a thoroughly sober and scientific spirit. The genuineness of the cure effected appears to be unequivocally demonstrated.[8] Theodor takes thus a middle ground in the controversy, a position substantially in agreement with Lothar.

From the active and conscious mesmeric agent, exercising his power over a subject in his presence, it is but a step to much more dubious manifestations of occult forces. Once the existence of a magnetic fluid is recognized—acting in an analogous fashion to electricity or magnetic relations and attraction between mineral

---

8 It seems probable that the spectacular séance was one conducted by Dr. Koreff in Berlin. From the narrative it is plain that the second adventure was with Dr. Marcus in Bamberg, perhaps amplified by later opportunities to observe the work of Dr. Hufeland in Berlin. Ellinger notes (xv, p. 214) that in view of the definite location of the second experience in Bamberg, the first case must fall into Hoffmann's second residence in Berlin (1807-1808), but, since Hoffmann first saw a "Somnambule" in Bamberg, he thinks that Hoffmann himself could not have seen the first séance as described, had possibly heard of it from others, and inserted it as an experience of his own. But Hoffmann's alteration of the chronological sequence was essential to the effective contrast, which was a part of Theodor's argument, and if this is recognized, Ellinger's conjecture becomes superfluous.

substances—the range of activity that the credulous or perhaps the perverse imagination may assign to it is limitless. A mesmerist may project the magnetic fluid over an indeterminate space and control a subject in the faraway. Unconscious and unintentional influences may be assumed possible. Persons at a distance may be mysteriously attracted to one another as by a magnet, or as the moon draws the sea, through some secret power within, of which the individual may be entirely unaware. Such extensions of the magnetic theory account for a multitude of puzzling phenomena, such as clairvoyance, thought transference, and presentiments. Though not always suggesting the quasi-scientific explanation of magnetism, Hoffmann makes frequent use of these occult phenomena in his tales.

The cult of magnetism had by 1813 sufficiently engaged Hoffmann's attention to become the theme of one of his earliest stories. Indeed *Der Magnetiseur* may even be regarded as his first story that is really a story, for *Ritter Gluck* and *Don Juan* are at bottom musical essays adroitly attached to a narrative in the first person, and *Berganza* is a curious compound of dialogue and narrative, chiefly interesting as containing Hoffmann's first criticism of the drama in Germany and his most vitriolic version of the episode of Julia Marc.

The opening of *Der Magnetiseur* was palpably suggested by the first chapter of *Heinrich von Ofterdingen*. As in Novalis' story, a father, the Baron, quotes the same familiar saying as the father of Heinrich: "Träume sind Schäume" (Dreams are but foam), while Ottmar, the son, regards the old saying as the password (Weidspruch) of the materialists and looks upon dreams as a possible gateway into mysterious realms. At first Hoffmann spoke of the tale as "Träume sind Schäume," but changed to the present title. With considerable ingenuity Ottmar twists the adage to extract from it a new meaning agreeable to his romantic prepossessions: the "foam" is the noble essence, as of champagne; "see how the thousand tiny bubbles rise like pearls in the glass and swirl about on top in the foam; these are the spirits which impatiently free themselves from earthly fetters; and thus the higher spiritual principle lives and works in the foam. . . . Accordingly the dream may be produced from the foam in which our life spirits spurt up joyfully and freely, when sleep takes possession of our external life, and this dream may then begin a higher intensive life in which we not only sense all the phenomena of the distant spirit world but really learn to know them, a life in which we hover over space and time."[9]

In addition to the Baron and Ottmar, the party gathered around the evening fire includes Maria, the Baron's daughter, and Franz Bickert, an elderly painter, long a family friend and house guest.[10] Ottmar's ecstatic defense of the mission of the dream world leads his father to remark that he seems to hear Ottmar's friend Alban speaking. This is the storyteller's device for introducing the "magnetizer" who is also a guest in the house, but has not yet joined the group by the fire. He is a physician of distinction and an ardent practitioner of the new magnetic therapy. Ottmar had met Alban during his university years and fallen a prey to his dominant personality. He had invited Alban to his father's country estate, where Alban had decided upon his fiendish plan to subjugate Maria to his secret powers; previous to the opening of the story he had cured Maria from a serious nervous collapse, which it is plain he himself had induced. The discussion of magnetism which begins after the mention of Alban's name foreshadows the action of the story, though all try to steer clear of a subject on which there is such a wide divergence of opinion. Apart from Ottmar's enthusiastic support, the views of the Baron and Bickert suggest in general outline those which Hoffmann later placed on the lips of the Serapion Brothers; that is, in addition to affording to the charlatan a clear opportunity for a field day, the use of mesmeric power is so imperfectly understood that it is a peril for one to toy with it: "It is well for you if nature allows you with your clumsy hands to pluck at her veil and does not punish your curiosity with your destruction."

The Baron, though intellectually opposed, is at the moment emotionally receptive to serious discussion of mysterious phenomena, because on this day, the ninth of September, memories crowd

---

[9] "Sieh die tausend kleinen Bläschen, die perlend im Glase aufsteigen und oben im Schaume sprudeln, das sind die Geister, die sich ungeduldig von der irdischen Fessel loslösen. . . . Es mag daher auch der Traum von *dem* Schaum, in welchem unsere Lebensgeister, wenn der Schlaf unser extensives Leben befängt, froh und frei aufsprudeln, erzeugt werden und ein höheres intensives Leben beginnen, in dem wir alle Erscheinungen der uns fernen Geisterwelt nicht nur ahnen, sondern wirklich erkennen, ja in dem wir über Raum und Zeit schweben." I, p. 140.

[10] For the fourth volume of the *Fantasiestücke* Hoffmann planned a number to be entitled *Des Malers Franz Bickert Allegorien im gothischen Styl*, which was never written. The work is mentioned in the correspondence with Kunz and in the "Billet des Herausgebers an Justizrath Nikomedes," which was printed at the end of *Der Magnetiseur* in the first edition of the *Fantasiestücke*. In *Der Magnetiseur* Bickert shows some traits in common with Hoffmann, but he is hardly a self-portrait, as has been maintained.

upon him of strange occurrences in his youth. At the Military Academy he had met a mysterious Danish Major who exercised an uncanny power of drawing men to him and controlling their wills, partly through the peculiar fascination of his eyes. The Baron became his slave. Among the common people it was reported that the Major had entered into a pact with the devil. The death of the Major was attended by inexplicable, ghostly phenomena, in the case of the Baron by a hideous and awful dream. This inserted narrative may seem at first a maladroit interruption, having no integral connection with the main story; but it serves, of course, to heighten the tenseness in the atmosphere and calls attention to one fact that is to be held in memory: the Baron is haunted by an arresting resemblance between Alban and the Danish Major who has been dead these many years, a resemblance especially in the strange non-human eyes. The Baron's story is followed by a brief narrative of Ottmar's in defense of his friend Alban, which contributes vitally to the development of the plot: Alban had beneficently cured a strange mental twist in the betrothed of Theobald, one of his friends and disciples. But at the end of his story Maria falls in a swoon on the breast of the old painter. She perceived a resemblance to her own case: Was Alban entangling her through secret hellish powers, to make her his slave and force her, thinking only of him, to forget Hypolit, her own betrothed? As if by magic Alban appears, coming, so the Baron is convinced, through locked doors, like the Danish Major, and restores the girl to consciousness.

After this episode Hoffmann continues his story by a method popular in the eighteenth century novel and still common in his day. He inserts, in the first place, a long letter from Maria to Adelgunde, a sister of her betrothed, giving with extreme candor a detailed account of her relations with Alban. In her dreams she had been visited from childhood by a benign figure who had released her from the terror of nightmare visions; in Alban she recognized this dream personality as a living being. At first unwilling to submit to magnetic treatment, to lose consciousness in the heightened fervor of the somnambulistic state, she in time surrenders completely, and is now, it seems, irrevocably subject to Alban's control. He knows every thought of her mind; indeed he governs all her thinking: "I know that Alban thinks these divine thoughts in me, for he is then himself in my being like a higher animating spark, and if he departs —which is only spiritually possible, because bodily separa ion is a matter of indifference—then all is dead. I can live only in this existence with him and in him." She fancies that only through Alban can she love Hypolit more strongly and sincerely.

This letter is followed by a fragment of a letter from Alban to his friend Theobald, which, though couched in part in metaphysical language, is a counterpart of Maria's letter. "To draw Maria entirely into myself, so to entwine her whole existence, her very being into mine, that separation must destroy her—that was the thought which, filling me with rapture, expressed only the fulfillment of Nature's desires." He assures his friend that he is no ridiculous sentimental lover; it is only the immediate recognition of the secret spiritual tie between himself and Maria. As Hoffmann first wrote this letter of Alban's, it contained a detailed theory of magnetic influences as Hoffmann interpreted them, at least for the purposes of the tale; he had, as he wrote to Kunz, worked arduously, seriously, on this section, but rejected it in order to hold more closely to the story. One may perhaps regret the loss of those early probings into mesmeric beliefs and practices, yet at the same time one notes with satisfaction the development of an artistic conscience, which had been so conspicuously lacking in *Berganza,* the inchoate predecessor of *Der Magnetiseur.*

At the end Hoffmann complicates his storytelling technique further by the introduction of a new personal narrator, the executor of the Baron's estate. By accident he arrives upon the scene when the body of Bickert, the old painter, is being borne to the grave, and after the burial he accompanies the pastor to the lonely, deserted castle where Bickert continued to live after the death of the whole family. Sections of Bickert's diary are then introduced which reveal in stark outlines what has happened since the first narration was broken off. Maria falls dead before the altar as she is to be married to Hypolit; the latter, regarding Ottmar as responsible for the whole tragic chain of circumstances, challenges him to a duel and is himself slain. Ottmar enters the army and is killed in battle. On the fatal ninth of September the Baron dies in the arms of his old friend. This collection of calamities is kept from tipping the scales into the ludicrous only by the pathetic eloquence of the old artist who remains in the castle and wanders from room to room where those who loved him had lived. Hoffmann wrote to Dr. Speyer that at the end of the tale he "raged away among living people like a Genghis Khan, but it simply had to be so."

In this story the author takes the current belief in mesmerism as a foundation, but carries the hypnotic powers far beyond the bounds of tested experience into the region of the supernatural. The narrative about the Danish Major is plainly intended to suggest a parallel, where the events boldly transcend human experience. Between the lines Hoffmann leads the reader to infer that Alban, like the Danish Major, has consciously or unconsciously éntered through mesmerism into a connection with the world of evil, or indeed that he is the sinister Major simply in a new and different form.

Years afterwards, in one of his last stories, *Der Elementargeist*, Hoffmann resurrected the Danish Major and transformed him into an Irish Major named O'Malley. Two officers, intimate friends of old, are by an unexplained telepathy reunited after the Battle of Waterloo in a remote Belgian manor house. Most of the story is the first-person narrative of one of them: he becomes the victim of devilish intrigues on the part of O'Malley, who, more unmistakably than his Danish predecessor, is in league with the devil. Through picturesque incantations and hocus-pocus O'Malley conjures up the beguiling form of a female salamander, surpassingly beautiful, and the officer, passionately in love, is saved from the final step of surrendering his immortal soul by the interposition of his faithful old servant. *Der Elementargeist* is one of Hoffmann's weaker productions; his heart was not in it, and the elaborate settings—midnight necromancy at a ruined castle in an impenetrable forest, the magic doll, or Hebrew teraphim, which serves as a symbol of love, the miraculously sudden appearances and disappearances and dissolutions (a shot is fired at the Major and he simply evaporates)—are in their crude and conventional sensationalism quite unworthy of Hoffmann's imagination. They are not convincing even within the magic realm that Hoffmann bids us enter. Paul Talkebarth, the shrewd and faithful old servitor, humorous and wise beneath the cloak of simple, doglike devotion, saves the tale from insipidity.

Count S - - - - i, the "Sinister Guest" in the story of that name (*Der unheimliche Gast*), is an adept in mysterious arts, possessed of extraordinary powers that may be classed as mesmeric or covered by the indefinite extension of the mesmeric principle. Angelika lies ill from the shock at the report of the death of a young officer to whom she is betrothed. Marguerite, the governess, secretly the Count's confederate, continually whispers his name in her ears and at times the Count himself appears and stares for a long time at the sleeping girl; on her wedding day Angelika falls into a strange swoon which the physician definitely calls a "magnetic condition." The Count is also capable of exercising his powers at a distance and of receiving messages by telepathy. Once in Naples he had gained magnetic influence over the betrothed of a Russian general, Boleslav, and taken her from him, subsequently slaying her through mysterious remote control; and he continually pursues his former rival with nightly terrors, which appear for the time being as ghostly, for Boleslav supposes that he has killed him in a duel. Some of his activities, however, are merely fiendish but, unfortunately, quite human intrigues. In contrast with *Der Magnetiseur* Hoffmann provides a happy ending for this tale. Structurally the story is defective, since it fails to supply counter activities, particularly of a supernatural nature, which defeat the foul intent of the Count and permit the joyous reunion of the lovers. One expects a disclosure of some mystic source for the dream in which Angelika sees her lover, earlier reported slain, returning to her safe and sound; one demands an explanation, even if in itself a mystery, of the sudden death of the Count on the very day that he is to be married to Angelika.

Die Automate (The Automatons) followed *Der Magnetiseur* after a short interval, presenting a somewhat similar theme—the inexplicable employment of psychic powers that transcend the limits of space and penetrate into the secret recesses of the human spirit. Hoffmann wrote *Die Automate* in Leipzig while still working on *Der goldene Topf* and intended it for publication in the *Allgemeine musikalische Zeitung*. The story is awkwardly constructed and bears the weight of several loosely related themes that prove a heavy burden for so short a narrative; in addition it has no real conclusion. To the story in the narrower sense Hoffmann adds a long discussion of the mechanical production of music, of the music of nature, and of the spirit of man in relation to the interpretation of music. From Hoffmann's rather apologetic letter to Rochlitz, one suspects that this section was included, or at any rate allowed to expand, in order that *Die Automate* might qualify for the pages of a musical journal. Rochlitz as editor apparently thought differently about it and published only this part of the narrative as a fragmentary essay in the form of a dialogue. The entire story, however, saw the light the same year (1814) in the *Zeitung für die elegante Welt*; later it was taken up into the *Serapionsbrüder*.

The exceedingly slight plot introduces a theme that Hoffmann was later to work out in rich and memorable forms: a love once passionately experienced, though irrevocably forfeited in the eyes of the world, remains an eternal possession. Here the theme is casually, almost incongruously, inserted, but its very presence is testimony to the still vivid memories of Julia Marc. More closely related to the central subject of *Die Automate* is the general discussion of mechanical likenesses of human beings. Ludwig, one of the protagonists, envisages the possible construction of marionettes that could execute a complicated dance figure with a human partner, but the very thought fills him with nameless horror. And more terrible still is the related thought that there may be little or no difference between the two dancers—which one is real and which a mere mechanical toy? This tragic dilemma contains the germ of Olimpia, the fateful automaton of *Der Sandmann*, written the following year.

The fancy of man has long been intrigued by the possibility of creating a being resembling man and giving it a semblance of human life; the mandrake root becomes an "Alraune" or a pure mechanism is fabricated and then magically endowed with some human capacities, as in *Frankenstein*. In Plock, as already noted, Hoffmann reread Wiegleb and conceived the plan of constructing an automaton. In the second volume of Wiegleb the author gave a long description of a mechanical chess player which was exhibited extensively in Europe and before exalted personages. The chess player was dressed as a Turk. That Hoffmann examined automatons whenever opportunity offered is probable. The purely mechanical aspect of their construction, the artful deceptiveness of their accomplishments, fascinated him.[11]

As one would anticipate, the automaton of Hoffmann's story is of a different and inexplicable sort. The whole town is excited over the exhibition of the "Talking Turk," an extraordinary mechanism in the form of a turbaned Turk, which gives answers to questions involving the most intimate secrets of the questioner, even replies in foreign tongues with which the questioner is familiar, though the question has been put in German. The revelations of the Turk set the little city into a pleasant but uncomfortable flutter. Two friends, Ludwig and Ferdinand, are somewhat unwillingly drawn into the whirl of interest and visit the exhibition. To one of them the answer given involves knowledge of events in his past life that have remained unknown to everyone but himself, an episode that had constituted the most profound experience he had known. The skeptical youth is dumfounded and overwhelmed. The power of the Turk far exceeds

---

[11] On October 10, 1813, Hoffmann records seeing an exhibition of automatons in Dresden, and he is doubtless making use of his own experience when Ludwig says: "Von den höchst wunderbaren Automaten im Danziger Arsenal war mir viel erzählt worden, und vorzüglich deshalb unterliess ich nicht hineinzugehen, als ich mich vor einigen Jahren in Danzig befand," vii, p. 85.

the familiar tests of professional "mind-reading." It is demonstrated that no one could possibly be concealed inside the figure, and the showman is often in another remote part of the room, talking with other people when the answers are given. Rumor connects the automaton with a mysterious Professor X whom the two young men visit. He shows them a group of automatons of his construction, which gives rise to the discussion of mechanical music mentioned above, but nothing is disclosed beyond the amazingly skillful adjustment of mechanical devices. Later they discover that the professor, an adept in physics and chemistry, maintains a laboratory in a villa outside the town. Walking past, they hear a voice of wondrous beauty singing the same Italian song that Ferdinand had once heard in a dream; this dream had been the center of the incident about which he had questioned the Turk, with the intent of unmasking his pretensions. As became Hoffmann's unvarying habit, he carries the marvelous, at any rate slightly, beyond the bounds of any possible explanation, and leaves it precisely where he found it. Apparently in this case, through some form of mental telepathy, the professor controlled the Turk and dictated his answers, though he was never present in the room. But, of course, this is not an explanation.

In *Das öde Haus* (The Deserted House) the Countess, regarded as mentally deranged, governs by some unexplained telepathy the actions of her former lover, now her brother-in-law. Words spoken half in jest to the singer Bettina in *Das Sanctus* have a mysterious power to deprive her of her singing voice. The case is discussed as an inexplicable psychic phenomenon, and a cure is sought by psychic means—the parallel tale of a Moorish singer at the time of the conquest of Granada, which Bettina overhears. Old Margareta in *Doge und Dogaressa* had once enjoyed a wide reputation for her remarkable cures, administering remedies compounded of herbs and using secret salves, but she also employed a peculiar stroking of the hands, apparently a kind of unconscious hypnotism, and she is equally uncertain of the sources of her prophetic gift, of which she is superstitiously afraid.

In various other tales Hoffmann introduces mesmeric phenomena or similar manifestations of occult powers where, however, it does not form such an integral element in the story. The figure of Chiara in *Kater Murr* shows Hoffmann's continued interest in phenomena of the type, externally mechanical but still inexplicably clairvoyant. In Chiara, the little gypsy girl, the magician Severino perceived at first glance extraordinary psychic powers, and she became the "Invisible Maiden" whose voice was projected by ventriloquism from the "crystal ball." With this exhibition Severino gained fame and fortune, though, of course, the mere trick of ventriloquism could not explain the answers that Chiara gave to the questioners of the crystal ball; her knowledge of the secret thoughts of others, of events outside her personal experience, transcended natural phenomena. Even when locked up in a cabinet, she knows of Severino's death, which occurred in a house some distance away. After the death of Severino, Chiara enters the employ of Meister Abraham, then a traveling showman, and becomes his wife. Later, after she has been mysteriously spirited away and Abraham has no knowledge of her whereabouts, her voice speaks again from the "crystal ball."

To Hoffmann the dream world was the real world after all. "Sancho thought," he says, "that God should honor the one who invented sleep; he must have been a clever fellow; and yet more honor is owing to the one who invented dreams, but not the dream which rises only when we lie under the soft covering of sleep. No! the dream that we dream our whole life long, that often takes upon its pinions the oppressive burden of earthly things."[12] In *Prinzessin Brambilla* he asks the reader: "What difference did it make that you awoke from the dream? Did not the unutterable rapture remain with you, which in external life surges through the soul like a stinging pain? And everything around you seemed barren, sad and colorless? And you fancied that the dream was your real existence, that what you had formerly regarded as your life was only the misunderstanding of a deluded mind."[13] "There is a higher kind of dreaming," says Ottmar in *Der Magnetiseur*, "in which man may draw into himself rays from the world-spirit that nourish and strengthen him with divine power." Again and again Hoffmann speaks with special emphasis of the "delirium" in the moment of falling asleep, that is, the transitional period when the world of seeming reality meets the world of

[12] "Sancho meinte, Gott solle den ehren, der den Schlaf erfunden, es müsse ein gescheuter Kerl gewesen sein; noch mehr mag aber wohl der geehrt werden, der den Traum erfand. Nicht *den* Traum, der aus unserm Innern nur dann aufsteigt, wenn wir unter des Schlafes weicher Decke liegen—nein!—*den* Traum, den wir durch das ganze Leben fort träumen, der oft die drückende Last des Irdischen auf seine Schwingen nimmt, vor dem jeder bittre Schmerz, jede trostlose Klage getäuschter Hoffnung verstummt, da er selbst, Strahl des Himmels in unserer Brust entglommen, mit der unendlichen Sehnsucht die Erfüllung verheisst." xi, p. 54.

[13] "Half es, dass du aus dem Traum erwachtest?—Blieb dir nicht das namenlose Entzücken, das im äussern Leben, ein schneidender Schmerz, die Seele durchwühlt, blieb dir das nicht zurück? Und alles um dich her erschien dir öde, traurig, farblos? und du wähntest, nur jener Traum sei dein eigentliches Sein, was du aber sonst für dein Leben gehalten, nur Missverstand des betörten Sinns?" xi, p. 24.

higher reality; at such times the conscious waking self is for a transitory moment placed in contact with another, a spiritual world, which in view of the barriers of mortal flesh the human spirit may not really enter yet. The significance of this intermediate period between waking and sleeping had been noted by Schubert.[14]

Though Hoffmann weaves many dreams into the substance of his tales, they are perhaps fewer in number than one might expect from these utterances, and only occasionally are they employed as decisive elements in the structure of the plot. In *Der unheimliche Gast* Angelika has once had a terrifying dream, the details of which she cannot recall, but the terror itself remained. Yet it all comes back to her out of the hidden depths of her being, when the "sinister guest" finally becomes a suitor for her hand; it had been a fearful burning beam of light which pierced her heart, and she recognizes it now in the beam which springs from the eyes of Count S - - - i, the suitor. The dream of Elis Fröbom in *Die Bergwerke zu Falun* is manifestly of supernatural origin, serving to direct his conduct and guide his life to its tragic end. In *Das Majorat* the old Justiciary dreams what the narrator, his nephew, is experiencing at the same time. The unraveling of the mystery in this tale is dependent on the somnambulism of old Daniel; Hoffmann uses also the familiar superstition that the criminal unconsciously but irresistibly is drawn to the place of the crime, and that questions can extract the truth from a sleepwalker. Hermelinda (*Das Gelübde*) is made aware in a dream of the precise moment of her lover's death. The dream of Ludwig in *Der Zusammenhang der Dinge* is employed with humorous effect; he dreams prophetically of his misfortunes at the ball the coming evening, and incongruously applies to this trivial affair the famous lines from Schiller's *Wallenstein*: "The spirits of great fates walk on before them, etc." The dreams of Eugenius in *Datura Fastuosa* are without mysterious implication; Hoffmann simply anticipates the modern psychologist and reveals the subconscious self of his hero: that hidden beneath the dry, pedantic exterior of the young scientist there lies a passionate eroticism. In the second part of *Die Elixiere des Teufels* the novelist records fairly numerous dreams. In keeping with the altered experience of Medardus, most of them are the subconscious voice of awakening conscience; in the form of visions his

14 In view of the question of Poe's relation to Hoffmann, it is interesting to note Poe's emphasis upon "those mere points of time, where the confines of the waking world blend with those of the world of dreams," "the point blending between wakefulness and sleep" in the production of fancies that are beyond expression in words. Cf. *Marginalia, Complete Works* (Harrison Edition), xvi, p. 88.

past rises to accuse him, or in feverish fantasies the question of divine forgiveness agitates him. The warning dreams of Hedwiga and Julia in *Kater Murr* would defy the explanation of the psychologist and verge plainly on the supernatural—while Meister Abraham falls naturally to sleep and dreams of his past happiness.

It is perhaps idle to conjecture why Hoffmann in his stories made so little of the most familiar of folk superstitions, the belief in ghosts.[15] Deep within him lay the faith in a spirit world that surrounds us; to its voices we may listen in moments of especial privilege. And yet the spirits of the departed, whether in recognizable shape—like the ghost of Hamlet's father or of Banquo—or manifesting their presence by various signs, appear relatively rarely in his pages. It is quite probable that ecclesiastical concepts of the other world stayed Hoffmann's pen; it was a territory of thinking upon which he was ever loath to express an opinion or to seem to express an opinion. Perhaps even more, he was deterred by the general crudeness of most beliefs in ghostly manifestations.

Near the beginning of *Das Majorat*, after Hoffmann has conjured up an atmosphere of uncanny terror through the description of the mysteriously crumbling castle and the wild voices of the night storm, Theodor, the first person narrator, feels a soft shudder, like the thrill "which one senses at a vividly related ghost story, and which one enjoys feeling." And Theodor's apprehensions are well founded. Distressing sounds are heard; whimperings as of an animal in pain; the door is suddenly thrown open and the ghost of old Daniel, though invisible, is heard to shuffle across the room to the walled-up door, the scene of his crime.

Again, in the opening scene of *Der unheimliche Gast*, Hoffmann makes a similar preparation for spectral appearance, though the setting is altered radically and only the intensity of the night storm, weirdly whistling down the chimney, creates in the little company about the tea table a receptiveness to the ghostly thrill, but Hoffmann in the end disappoints us. The group discusses the common belief in ghosts, and two or three anecdotes are narrated involving ghostly phenomena. The wife of the Colonel is skeptical, regards the whole subject as childish nonsense, and wishes to turn the conversation into more pleasant and profitable channels. At the other extreme is the young lawyer Dagobert, who insists that such a faith is firmly rooted in our nature; the stories of phantom appearances

[15] Cf. the *Gespensterbuch* of Apel-Laun, Leipzig, 1810-1812, one of the sources for Hoffmann's investigations in occult phenomena.

naturally find "an eternal and profound echo in our souls, for the responding strings lie in our inmost being," "it is not possible to deny the world of spirits that surrounds us." In the midst of the conversation the door opens, and, unannounced, the "sinister guest" enters. But he is not a ghost at all. He is a Sicilian gentleman, courtly in manner and distinguished in appearance, though still inexplicably sinister, apart from the context provided for his entrance.

The nameless story which editors have entitled *Eine Spukgeschichte* (A Ghost Story) is a brief narrative related by Cyprian at a meeting of the Serapion Brotherhood. At a birthday party one of the two young daughters of Colonel von P. plans to enliven the company as evening draws on by impersonating the "White Lady," a legendary ghost of the estate of whom she has heard the gardener tell stories, but in her preparations for the prank she encounters the White Lady herself, and is found by her companions in a swoon. From this time on, at nine o'clock every evening—an unconventional hour for ghosts—the specter appears. The jovial physician, who is called to attend the young girl in the resultant mental and physical state, conceives the clever idea of setting all the clocks, even the village clock, back for an hour, so that nine o'clock will pass while the girl supposes that it is only eight, but the ghost in question is not to be outwitted by this childish trick, and appears as usual. In the *Spukgeschichte* the ghost is seen by only one person, like Banquo's ghost, though others may be present; yet all see a plate, which the girl hands to the specter, pass through the air and settle down on a table as if invisible hands had placed it here. The identity of the phantom is not disclosed, nor are the reasons why it so maliciously set about to bring ruin on a whole family. The absence, however, of these normal elements of a ghost story is easily explained; the events are related orally, and the story was not prepared for formal submission to the members of the club. In the discussion that follows, Theodor contributes an anecdote about a musician who is persecuted by an invisible spook, playing in masterly fashion on his piano.

The case of the Danish Major in *Der Magnetiseur* hardly falls under the classification of ghostly phenomena. He is, to be sure, seen leaving the barracks in full panoply, opening and closing the gate of the enclosure with a clatter which resounds far and wide through the night, yet he is lying dead in his own room; his door is securely locked from the inside, the main door of the barracks and the outside gate are also locked. But the Major is presumably in league with the devil and possessed of supernatural powers, including perhaps that of reappearing in another form, that of Alban. The ghost of Alexander's aunt (*Ein Fragment aus dem Leben dreier Freunde*) is, however, genuine. At midnight she wanders through the rooms of her dwelling, with groans and sighs, even going to a cupboard and taking medicine for digestive ills. The friends to whom Alexander narrates his adventures are amazed, since they supposed that the denizens of the other world were freed from such mundane troubles. At times Alexander catches a glimpse of his aunt's long, pointed nose or of her long, thin fingers, when he is investigating the contents of trunks and boxes. Alexander has been a pronounced rationalist and is shocked at his sudden descent into the role of a "ghost-seer." He assures his friends that his aunt had been mentally sound. She had been betrothed, and all preparations for the marriage had been made, even to the arrival of the clergyman, but the bridegroom never appeared. The day of this tragedy she celebrated each year by donning her bridal garments and waiting for the faithless lover; a similar motif appears in *Das öde Haus* and, incidentally, in Dickens' *Great Expectations*. Altogether the effect of her presence is more comic than terrifying. The two "revenants" in *Die Brautwahl* and the two magicians in *Meister Floh*, both long registered as "dead," are also humorously portrayed.

The most common German word for insanity, "Wahnsinn," and its derivative adjective are of frequent occurrence in Hoffmann's tales, but they are employed in a vast majority of cases in conversation or in narratives in the first person, and most often in the non-technical sense, in the diminished potency of casual speech—when the speaker feels that circumstances are too perplexing or too complicated for normal endurance or when one wishes to characterize what seems to be irrational conduct or utterance. But Hoffmann also uses the word in its more exact and technical meaning. He pondered much on the phenomena of the mind, upon his own mental state, and was at times himself terrified at the thought of madness. On January 6, 1811, he wrote in his diary: "Why do I sleeping and waking think of madness so often? I should think that mental purgation might work like a blood-letting." Was the writing of stories for Hoffmann a kind of physic for the mind?

In the conversation of the Serapion Brothers, the word occurs repeatedly in its full technical meaning; the insanity of St. Serapion, their patron, provides occasion for it. Hoffmann's interest in mental abnormality is both represented and stoutly defended in the utterances of Cyprian, the most mystic of the Hoffmann trio. "I always believed," he says, "that in the abnormal, nature vouchsafes to us glimpses into her most terrible depths, and, in fact, even in the horror which has often seized me in this odd relationship [with the mad hermit], vague hints, presentiments, and visions rose before me which strengthened and animated my spirit to an especial exhilaration."[16] In another passage he maintains that "some measure of madness, or folly, is so deeply rooted in human nature that one cannot come to know human nature better than through a careful study of the insane and the mentally deficient. We do not have to seek them out in madhouses, they run across our path daily; best of all, we can carry on our study in our own selves, where that precipitate from the chemical process of life is present in sufficient quantity."[17] This doubtless forms an accurate statement of Hoffmann's own attitude and of the fundamental reasons for his constant occupation with questions of abnormality. And Cyprian-Hoffmann persists in his point of view despite the scorn of the practical Ottmar-Hitzig and the milder disagreement of the more balanced, more skeptical Hoffmann in the person of Lothar.

In his stories Hoffmann works as a creative artist, not as a scientist, though it has been shown that his description of mental states and strange neuroses are professionally accurate, indeed in some ways anticipating the investigations of later days.[18] Hoffmann's

[16] "Immer glaubt' ich, dass die Natur beim Abnormen Blicke vergönne in ihre schauerlichste Tiefe, und in der Tat, selbst in dem Grauen, das mich oft bei jenem seltsamen Verkehr befing, gingen mir Ahnungen und Bilder auf, die meinen Geist zum besonderen Aufschwung stärkten und belebten." VI, pp. 28-29.

[17] "Will ich nur beibringen, dass einiger Wahnsinn, einige Narrheit so tief in der menschlichen Natur bedingt ist, dass man diese gar nicht besser erkennen kann als durch sorgfältiges Studium der Wahnsinnigen und Narren, die wir gar nicht in den Tollhäusern aufsuchen dürfen, sondern die uns täglich in den Weg laufen, ja am besten durch das Studium unseres eigenen Ichs, in dem jener Niederschlag aus dem chemischen Prozess des Lebens genugsam vorhanden." IX, p. 14.

[18] Cf. Otto Klinke: *E. T. A. Hoffmanns Leben und Werke vom Standpunkt eines Irrenarztes*, Braunschweig und Leipzig, 1903. Klinke analyzes Hoffmann's physical and mental characteristics and comments in detail on the abnormal figures and strange occurrences in his stories. The tales stand the test of scientific examination: "Es ist wirklich staunenswert, mit welcher minutiösen Genauigkeit sich Hoffmann in diese wissenschaftlichen Fragen vertieft hat." To the alienist much of the seemingly supernatural is capable of interpretation in terms of mental phenomena. We may or may not accept this point of view, but the varied nature of Hoffmann's appeal to readers is shown in that his works may serve as "Quellen" for the investigation of a professional psychiatrist. Cf. also Ellinger's objection to Klinke's psychiatric explanation of phenomena in *Die Elixiere des Teufels* (introduction to his edition). And yet Ellinger says that Dr. Dapertutto on a certain occasion uses a phial containing Prussic acid, which produces the effect described (*Das verlorene Spiegelbild*). Ellinger seems to be adopting Dr. Klinke's methods. Hoffmann may, of course, have

aesthetic interest is aroused mainly if not exclusively when he can imagine something occult and mysterious behind the phenomena of mental derangement; when what seems like mental unbalance, like insanity, results from unknown forces within and without. The sober rationalist might perhaps study Tieck's *Der blonde Eckbert* as a case history of developing madness, but the author unquestionably did not intend it as that, and the reader for whom Tieck wrote will scornfully reject the interpretation and discern elements in the story quite irreconcilable with it. Among Hoffmann's tales *Der Sandmann* forms the closest parallel to Tieck's story in this regard.

Hoffmann begins his story with three long letters. Nathanael, a student at the university, writes to his friend Lothar, the brother of Clara, his betrothed. As is explained later, Lothar and Clara are orphaned children of a distant relative whom Nathanael's mother took into her home after the death of her husband. Nathanael has been thoroughly perturbed by a recent experience: in a Piedmontese peddler of barometers, David Coppola, who comes to his rooms, he recognizes the old lawyer Coppelius, the most sinister figure in his childhood memories, and he proceeds to narrate the events of the past—though it may seem strange that Lothar, living in the family from boyhood, should not have heard of them. Upon Nathanael's father this Coppelius had had some mysterious hold; his mother held the visitor in aversion and in awe, and the children were terrified at his presence. Since he often came in the evening for his secret meetings with his father, Nathanael identified him with the Sandman of the nursery tale, to which however the nurse of Nathanael's sister had made gruesome additions—the Sandman not only induced sleep but would scatter sand in the children's eyes until they fell out. As he grows older Nathanael's curiosity is piqued by these nocturnal visits and he slips in, hides behind a curtain, and watches. His father and Coppelius are conducting some sort of experiment over a great cauldron; he is horrified to see his father's face distorted into a like-

---

read of these effects in the medical journal (1813) to which Ellinger refers, but Dr. Dapertutto's activities were outside the range of ordinary chemistry. Ochsner (*E. T. A. Hoffmann als Dichter des Unbewussten*) carries Hoffmann's scientific clairvoyance beyond the date of Klinke's study to include the investigations of mental phenomena made by scholars in recent years, notably the work of Jung. In his monograph, Ochsner advances the opinion that Medardus (*Die Elixiere des Teufels*) is a victim of paranoid schizophrenia, and the whole story of the various appearances of Viktorin as his "double" may be derived from this mental condition. Apparently any objections that the reader might raise against this theory—such as that the mad monk is seen by others, for example, in the house of the forester—could be met by the fact that Medardus is himself relating the story of his life.

ness to Coppelius himself. Coppelius cries out for, "More eyes, more eyes!" In his terror the boy betrays his presence. Coppelius seizes him and holds him over the cauldron until his father begs for his release. This hideous experience is followed by a long illness. In the meantime Coppelius has disappeared and the father regains his former happiness and serenity. After a year Coppelius returns and that night Nathanael's father is killed by an explosion in the improvised laboratory. The city authorities conduct investigations, but Coppelius is not to be found.

Clara answers this letter, though Nathanael had not intended it for her eyes. Her letter is employed to interpret Nathanael's delusions from the standpoint of a cool, balanced, and healthy mind; she argues with admirable sanity and with loving concern; "All that was horrible and terrifying about the affair took place only in your mind; the genuine actuality of the external world had doubtless little share in it";—"only the belief in the hostile power can in fact make it hostile to you." She urges him to put the whole matter out of his mind and plans to visit him and ban the ugly Coppelius with her laughter. A second letter from Nathanael to Lothar shows a much calmer frame of mind. He is somewhat ironical about Clara's deep, philosophical letter, the logic of which he attributes to Lothar's instruction. This second letter serves also to introduce two other characters, Spalanzani,[19] the professor of physics, and his beautiful daughter Olimpia; Nathanael has seen her only once ·sitting by a table, apparently asleep although her eyes are open.

The remainder of the story is a narrative by an unnamed friend of Nathanael's. A fortnight after the last of the three letters, Nathanael comes home for a holiday, at first happy to be with those he loves, but soon the inward unrest manifests itself again. In vain Clara remonstrates with him: "As long as you believe in him [Coppelius], he exists and is active; only your belief is his power." Her common-sense attitude irritates Nathanael. Formerly he had written charming little tales to which Clara had listened with delight; now his work is somber and formless, incomprehensible; he thinks that Clara's lack of appreciation betrays a cold, prosaic disposition, and he calls her a "damned lifeless automaton." His harsh and envenomed treatment of Clara enrages Lothar, and a duel is averted only by Clara's timely interference.

19 Hoffmann has used the name of a distinguished Italian scientist of the eighteenth century (correctly spelled Spallanzani); in Spalanzani's construction of the automaton, Hoffmann may have been satirizing certain experiments of the Italian scientist, but it seems equally possible that he merely liked the sound of the name.

On his return to the university, Nathanael finds the house where he had formerly roomed burned down and secures new lodgings directly opposite the house of Spalanzani. Soon there is another visit from Coppola, who this time is selling spectacles, which to Nathanael's reminiscent horror he calls eyes; he spreads them, strangely sparkling and shimmering, upon the table. Nathanael is spellbound with terror. In the end he buys a small spyglass to rid himself of his tormentor. With this he watches with ever-growing fascination the strangely inert form of Spalanzani's daughter across the way, sitting by the window. This episode in Nathanael's life has become familiar through Offenbach's opera. His whole being is absorbed in this new passion, and Clara is forgotten. He is a guest at the ball through which Spalanzani introduces his daughter to local society; he becomes a visitor in the house and reads his poems to Olimpia, charmed rather than repelled by her monosyllabic utterance. One day as he enters the house he hears an uproar and finds Spalanzani and Coppola tugging and pulling, amid shrieks and curses, at a woman's form, the body of Olimpia. Finally Coppola twists the figure out of Spalanzani's hands and raises it to wield a mighty blow at his antagonist. He then rushes down the stairs with the automaton over his shoulder, but the eyes drop out; Spalanzani picks them up and throws them at Nathanael. The dispute over Olimpia had arisen because Spalanzani had stolen from Coppola the eyes used in the construction of the automaton. Madness grips Nathanael and he would have throttled Spalanzani, had not the tumult drawn rescuers to the scene.

After a long illness Nathanael awakens in his own home to new life and the renewal of the old love. The dark shadows of the past seem entirely lifted. One day Nathanael and Clara are out walking and climb a tower to get a view; Nathanael takes from his pocket the spyglass that he had bought from Coppola and levels it at Clara. Madness again seizes him; he tries to throw Clara from the tower, but Lothar saves her; in the crowd below Nathanael spies his ancient enemy, the lawyer Coppelius, and hurls himself over the parapet to his death.

The career of Nathanael from childhood to this tragic end might supply an interesting case for the modern psychiatrist. An incident in childhood retained in the subconscious self rises to distort his life and constitutes his doom; the story becomes thus a "case history" of developing insanity. But Hoffmann unquestionably would not allow this interpretation or see the events of the story in this light; he does not admit any rational explanation of Coppelius and his power over Nathanael. Similarly, the insanity of the Countess Angelika in *Das öde Haus* is bound up with the operation of nameless occult forces. In *Der unheimliche Gast* the other characters repeatedly call Marguerite insane, but she is really acting in collusion with a fiendish mesmerist and is under the spell of his inexplicable powers.

On the other hand, Amalia in *Die Räuber* does become indubitably insane under the impact of tragic circumstance and without any suggestion of mysterious forces at work. In *Die Elixiere des Teufels* Viktorin also is unquestionably mad when he reappears in the guise of a monk; but the story does not enlighten us as to the cause, whether under the operation of unknown powers which govern the destiny of the family, or, more realistically, from heredity, or merely as a result of his fall from the cliff. The case of Hermogen in the same novel is much less positive; he is overwrought and irrational, perhaps only temporarily, as the result of an appalling and corroding experience; he has been seduced by his stepmother. Nettelmann (*Fragment aus dem Leben dreier Freunde*), who fancies himself the King of Amboina, is a subordinate figure in the story whom Hoffmann introduces in order to supply parallel adventures to Alexander's account of the ghost of his aunt; Hoffmann does not concern himself further with the mental vagaries of Nettelmann. Prinz Ignatius (*Kater Murr*) is regarded in the story as mentally unbalanced, and Hoffmann somewhat humorously suggests medical terms that might be applied to his malady—"Paranoia fatuitas, Stoliditas." The modern diagnosis would probably be simply a case of "arrested development"; the Prince has the mind of a ten-year-old boy, delighting in childish pranks and brutal pleasures. The problem of Kreisler, Hoffmann's partial portrait of himself, deserves a chapter for itself.

From Novalis and Tieck Hoffmann derived at least a literary interest in the occult forces in nature that at times reach out and control the lives of men, in the conception of an elemental kinship or even identity between plants or minerals and human beings. In his own way he followed these literary congeners of Schelling's philosophical writings and expressed similar ideas in the Märchen. In other stories he rarely invaded this realm of mystic speculation. But the mineral world of *Heinrich von Ofterdingen* and *Der Runenberg*, with its benignant or malign allurement, appears as the root idea of *Die Bergwerke zu Falun*. The sailor Elis Fröben arrives in Göteborg from a voyage to the East Indies. Hoffmann describes with zest the merrymaking in the port on the arrival of the great ship, but Elis finds that his mother, the only remaining member of his family, has died in his absence, and he has no heart for the festivities. In this mood he meets an old miner who describes to him the beauty of the miner's life—a poetic rhapsody taken at times almost bodily from the fifth chapter of Novalis' novel. A strange dream, also reminiscent of passages in *Heinrich von Ofterdingen,* lures him on; in it he visits the mineral world and beholds the face of a mighty woman, the "queen," as the old miner explains, and as he looks upon her countenance he feels that his very self melts away into the glistening stone. The call is irresistible and he wanders, half unconsciously, on the road to Falun. Here he finds work in the mines, gains the favor of Persohn Dahlsjö, manager and wealthy shareholder, and falls in love with Ulla, Dahlsjö's daughter. One day when he is alone in the depths of the mine, the miner appears to him, now more or less openly betraying supernatural connections. He warns Elis that he will be punished for his faithlessness—he is working there valiantly for the hand of Ulla, not from devotion to the mineral world. The old miner, as is presently disclosed, is Terborn, who more than a century earlier had been one of the first to develop the mines and lived on in legends of his mysterious pact with the power which rules in the bosom of the earth, now and then appearing with admonitions to a later generation. In distress at the rumor that Ulla is the betrothed of another, Elis descends into the mine, where now his earlier dream becomes waking reality: a blinding light seems to pass through the mine shaft and the walls become "transparent as crystal," so that he looks into paradisiacal fields of glorious metal trees and plants on which hang fruits and flowers of sparkling gems, and sees there the mighty queen and her maidens. But the vision is interrupted by the appearance of Dahlsjö, who has come in order to deny the rumor of Ulla's betrothal and express his approval of Elis' suit. Even though a day is set for the wedding, Elis is tortured by inexplicable foreboding. An icy hand seems to grasp his heart, and he talks confusedly of marvelous treasures that lie concealed in the deeps. But the rich veins of metal he has discovered the others cannot find; he alone, he says, understands the secret signs, the meaningful writing which the hand of the queen herself has engraved on the rocky clefts. The very morning of the wedding Elis tells his bride that he is going down into the mine to procure her a wedding gift— the sparkling cherry-red Almandin, more precious than the carbuncle. But he never returns. Fifty years later his body is found, miraculously preserved, and only a gray old woman, hobbling on crutches, recognizes Elis Freböm.

Before Chamisso started on his expedition around the world in 1815, Hoffmann obtained from him some suggestions for a botanical story. Chamisso had already begun his modest career as a botanist and on his return he became the custodian of the Royal Herbarium.[20] If Hoffmann had written the story at that time, one may perhaps assume that he would have founded it on some inexplicable connection between man and the vegetable world, such as is suggested, for example, in Tieck's *Der Runenberg*. The plan for a botanical tale lay dormant for several years and the storyteller turned back to it only about a year before his death. *Datura Fastuosa* was published in the *Taschenbuch für Liebe und Freundschaft auf 1823* in the autumn of 1822. If haply the original plan was as here conjectured, *Datura Fastuosa* contains no hint of it. That material was being used at the same time—in Märchen form—in *Meister Floh*. In *Datura Fastuosa* a student of botany, living in the house of his revered professor and working in his experimental greenhouses, marries the widow of the professor after the latter's death, though she is old enough to be his mother. The marriage is proposed by the widow herself to avoid the possible scandal of his remaining there. He endures the ridicule of his fellow students and even fights a duel. Later he falls into the clutches of an infamous siren, of the international spy type, at whose behest he undertakes to murder his wife through the odor of the Datura Fastuosa, but he discovers the wiles of the enchantress just in time. Magic methods for the cultivation of tropical plants in an extreme northern clime and the existence of this death-dealing flower are meager substitutes for the mystic kinship of man and flower.

Hoffmann's attitude toward occult phenomena was an unstable compound of belief and skepticism. This dichotomy corresponds to the two sides of his nature and the two-fold influences of his youth —the lingering rationalism of the eighteenth century with which he was early surrounded, which he could never entirely erase, no matter how he ridiculed it; and, on the other hand, the romantic tendency to speculation in the unknown and the unknowable, the desire to believe in that which defies man's understanding. When Kreisler rushes into Meister Abraham's cottage in breathless terror

---

[20] Cf. Hoffmann's letter to a professor of botany, Lichtenstein, asking him for a book on botany, and particularly for the name of a plant; Datura Fastuosa was probably supplied by Professor Lichtenstein. *Briefwechsel*, II, p. 295.

because he has seen his double walking beside him, Abraham explains the miraculous phenomenon: it was merely the operation of a convex mirror, but Kreisler "was annoyed, as everyone is, when the miraculous in which one has believed is explained away. Man is more pleased with the deepest horror than with the natural explanation of what has appeared to him as ghostly: he just will not be satisfied with this world; he demands to see something from another world which has no need of a body to reveal itself to him."[21] In his tales there is no real consistency in his acceptation or rejection of mysterious happenings. He was one of those who chafed under rationalistic limitations and refused to accept them. As an artist he perceived the multiplicity of uses to which supernatural, or, at any rate, inexplicable occurrences could be put. The occult lured him aesthetically, and this would have been valid reason enough for his use of it, even if he had regarded the phenomena he portrayed with utter disbelief. It is necessary to draw a line between a purely intellectual attitude, which may be even radically skeptical or perhaps mildly neutral, and on the other hand an emotional response, which would temporarily submerge an intellectual conviction.

Diligent and ingenious investigation of Wiegleb's *Natural Magic* has shown that many of Hoffmann's miraculous happenings are adaptations of Wiegleb's tricks: Ignaz Denner makes a light in the dark forest by uncorking a bottle, or a cigar is lighted with one's fingers, or it seems so. This is an interesting discovery on the part of the detectives, but beyond all question Hoffmann did not intend any such natural explanations of his mysterious phenomena to be made, as the chemist or physicist might supply. In *Die Brautwahl* by strange prescience Hoffmann anticipated these scholarly revelations: to certain skeptical people the magician Leonhard accords full permission to assume that he is merely a very clever sleight-of-hand performer and to seek an explanation of all the strange events (Spukereien) in Wiegleb's *Natural Magic* or somewhere else.[22] Equally futile is the attempt to explain the mysterious events in

---

[21] "Und ärgerte sich, wie jeder, dem das Wunderbare, woran er geglaubt, zu Wasser gemacht wird. Dem Menschen behagt das tiefste Entsetzen mehr als die natürliche Aufklärung dessen, was ihm gespenstisch erschienen, er will sich durchaus nicht mit dieser Welt abfinden lassen; er verlangt etwas zu sehen aus einer andern, die des Körpers nicht bedarf, um sich ihm zu offenbaren." x, p. 148.

[22] When Fabian, the skeptical student, says to Prosper Alpanus: "Ich bin ein aufgeklärter Mensch und statuiere keine Wunder," Alpanus replies, ". . . bin ich gleich nicht eben ein Zauberer, so gebiete ich doch über hübsche Kunststückchen," and Fabian retorts scornfully: "Aus Wieglebs Magie wohl oder sonst!" v, p. 56 (*Klein Zaches*).

terms of hallucination or kindred phenomena, however much Hoffmann makes use of scientific or quasi-scientific investigation of
mental vagaries: the ghost of Daniel is a genuine ghost, and Emanuel
Spikher has actually lost his reflection in the mirror.

It was reported that Hoffmann now and again late at night
aroused his wife from her slumbers and bade her sit beside him, for
he was terrified of the spirits that his imagination had called into
being. Reason was powerless to calm his trepidation. Hoffmann possessed neither a set of rigidly certified beliefs like a creed, which
he could recite in unquestioning adherence, nor a corresponding
body of disbelief. That he believed in the supernatural is beyond all
question, though he refused to put himself on record as to the precise
limits of belief and disbelief. In the meantime there remained the
fascinating borderland where his creative genius might wander at
will. There are more things in heaven and earth than we have
dreamed of.[23]

[23] "Man sagt, das Wunderbare sei von der Erde verschwunden, ich glaube nicht
daran. Die Wunder sind geblieben." II, p. 217.

CHAPTER 9

THE ARTIST AND HIS WORLD

IN view of all this I cannot help loving musicians, and since their kingdom is not at all of this world, they appear like citizens of an unknown, distant city, queer in what they do and the way they do it—ridiculous indeed, for Hans makes fun of Peter because he holds his fork in his left hand while Hans his whole life long has held his fork in his right."[1] The dog Berganza is speaking of musicians, for he has been Kreisler's dog, but he would doubtless have extended to all artists this characterization of their apartness.

In early youth Hoffmann was conscious of his own isolation, and this consciousness, compounded of genuine alarm and secret satisfaction, did not diminish as the years brought to him a widening acquaintance with the world. Even at the beginning it became more and more acute through the well-meant efforts of the Doerffer household to force conformity upon him. He was like an eaglet in a pen with common barnyard fowl; he would fain beat his head against the blue dome while his companions crow and cackle over a newly laid egg. On January 25, 1796, only a few months before his departure from Königsberg he wrote to Hippel:

"A feeling of exaltation bears me up on bold pinions. . . . I would like to force my way through the column of gnats, through the machinelike men that beset me roundabout with their dull commonplaces. . . . When I reflect upon it, I am not happy that at times my brain works in somewhat eccentric ways—this eccentricity plainly degrades me in the eyes of all about me, and people who divide everything into numbers and handle them like an apothecary often want to place their orthodox toll-gate before me or throw their official yoke around my neck."[2]

[1] "Ich kann die Musiker um des allen nur lieben, und da überhaupt ihr Reich nicht von dieser Welt ist, erscheinen sie, wie Bürger einer unbekannten fernen Stadt, in ihrem äussern Tun und Treiben seltsam, ja lächerlich, denn Hans lacht den Peter aus, weil er die Gabel in der linken Hand hält, da er, Hans, seine Lebtage hindurch sie in der rechten Hand gehalten." I, p. 102.

[2] "Ein erhebendes Gefühl trägt mich empor auf kühnen Fittigen . . . und ich möchte mich durch die MückenKolonne, durch die MaschinenMenschen, die mich umlagern mit platten Gemeinplätzen, gern durchschlagen . . . dass es zuweilen etwas exzentrisch in meinem Gehirnkasten zugeht, daüber freue ich mich eben nicht beym Besinnen—dies exzentrische sezt mich offenbar herunter in den Augen aller die um mich sind—und Leute, die alles in Nummern theilen und Apothekerartig behandeln, möchten mir manchmahl ihren orthodoxen Schlagbaum vorhalten, oder ihr offizinelles Krumholz um den Hals werfen." *Briefwechsel*, I, p. 93.

In his boyhood Hoffmann was tortured by the conviction that hardly anyone really knew him and understood him, and in later years of struggle and success it was only here and there that he found real companionship among those with whom he lived his life. The barnyard fowl with wings but still incapable of flight refused to believe that the eagle's wings brought him a little nearer to the stars. Kreisler, in whom Hoffmann put more of himself than into any other of his characters, was likewise conscious of the chasm that yawned between himself and those who lived within the sound of his music. Even their shallow scorn of him seemed in itself a compliment. As he remarked to Berganza: "The man whose whole effort in life is concentrated in the labor of getting better things to eat and drink, and not to have any debts, calls everyone mad who sacrifices happiness, prosperity, even life itself, to a great and holy idea . . . and this censure really exalts him. . . ."

The position of the artist in the rude world of everyday was to Hoffmann a personal problem. In the first of his Märchen he recorded his pondering and his convictions, more memorably perhaps than in any of the later tales but less concretely in view of the Märchen form; and Anselmus, though possessing the soul of an artist, is not presented clearly as a man of letters, a musician, or a painter. Consequently, some of the later tales face the problem more directly, and in others Hoffmann touches upon the status of the artist, even though it is not the central theme. In Hoffmann's opinion the artist is set apart from other men by his very nature; he can never be like them and live with them as they live with one another. His real home is in the world of his dreams, and that he persistently lives there seems an affront to his environment. The forces of ordinary existence are strongly equipped with offensive and defensive weapons; the artist, to be sure, has a sword and a shield, but what is he among so many? It is ever a one-sided combat which ends in defeat or ignominious compromise: "They went to battle but they always fell." And yet, as Hoffmann indicated in *Der goldene Topf*, the bourgeois life has its own compensations. However Hoffmann may satirize its narrowness and complacence, bourgeois living has its lure in a kind of narrow security, its freedom from the torments and ills of the spirit. As long afterwards Meister Abraham says to Murr: "If you knew the way the world runs, you would perceive that the Philistine, who always pulls in his antennae, is the best off."

Der goldene Topf was finished only a few months before Hoffmann's final departure for Berlin and published in the autumn after his arrival. Beginning in January of the following year (1815) Hoffmann wrote a number of "artist" stories, in which he explored more precisely the theme presented symbolically in the great Märchen. To be sure, the first story written in these days does not attack the fundamental problem, though the hero is an artist, and the second tale indeed forms a rather frail introduction to the series, dragging in at the end a vital question in the life of an artist, which apparently applies in no essential way to the artist in the story. *Das verlorene Spiegelbild* (The Lost Reflection in the Mirror) is a part of *Die Abenteuer der Sylvesternacht* (The Adventures of New Year's Eve), Hoffmann's first literary work after his return to Berlin; he read it aloud to Chamisso, Hitzig, and Contessa on the evening of January 13. The "adventures" are presented as extracts from the diary of the "Traveling Enthusiast." In the first adventure *Die Geliebte* (The Loved-One), he unexpectedly encounters Julia and her husband at an evening reception; memories surge upon him, and without hat or cloak he rushes from the house. In the restaurant where he takes refuge, which supplies the title for the second adventure (*Der Keller*), he meets Peter Schlemihl, the hero of Chamisso's story, and another figure equally strange, who matches the reluctance of the shadowless Schlemihl to stand with a light behind him by a demand that the mirror in the room be veiled. Chance plays into the hands of the narrator a manuscript containing the life of this man, Emanuel Spikher, who no longer casts a reflection in a mirror. Spikher was a German artist of promise who takes leave of his faithful wife and his little boy and journeys to Italy for the perfecting of his talent. There he falls into the clutches of a devil-woman, Giulietta, whose beauty and fascination made him her captive. In love for her he sells his "mirrored image," but when, under the influence of the infamous Dr. Dapertutto, who was in league with the devil, she demanded the murder of his wife and child and his immortal soul, Spikher, like Chamisso's hero, employed the Scriptural command to the Tempter. Returning to Germany, where his loss was soon discovered, he became a homeless wanderer, seeking forever the temptress of other days, to demand of her the return of his mirrored self.

The story of Emanuel Spikher is plainly conceived as a symbol, a kind of literary precipitate of the meeting with Julia in the first episode. One might say that Hoffmann, having tried wistful renunciation, has determined to experiment with resentment, no longer against Julia's mother, as in *Berganza*, but against Julia herself;

he may be able thus to erase the whole disturbing experience from his mind. In the first scene Julia seems in the beginning to view him simply as a casual acquaintance of other days: "her face seemed distorted in scornful ridicule, and yet when his errant glances touched her, a beam seemed to float over to him from the glorious past, out of a life full of love and poesy." "I wish you were sitting at the piano," she says, "and were singing softly of past happiness and hope." A goblet of wine passes from her hand to his, and for a moment they are together as of old, while by the hands of a master the "Andante" from Mozart's sublime *E Major Symphony* is being played. At that moment a clumsy lout with protruding frog's eyes and spider legs wavers in. She rises, and in the voice of a stranger she says: "Should we not rejoin the company? My husband is looking for me. You were right amusing, my good friend, still in good spirits as of old." It is significant that Hoffmann named the malign enchantress Giulietta. Did Julia steal his "mirrored image"; is he like Spikher a homeless wanderer, seeking to regain the vision, the ideal that she has taken from him?

The second of the artist series, *Die Fermate* (The Hold) was published in the autumn of 1815 in the *Frauentaschenbuch auf 1816* and later in the *Serapionsbrüder*, where it is assigned to Theodor. The story is without tragic undertones, for a musician is narrating reminiscences of his youth, and whatever struggles there were, or misunderstandings, are now forgotten in the glow of remembrance. Blithely Theodor, the hero, tells of the beginnings of his career. As later in *Doge und Dogaressa*, the novelist ties his story to a picture in a Berlin exhibition, in the case of *Die Fermate*, a painting by J. F. Hummel[3] in the autumn exhibition of 1814. A description of the painting begins the story: an arbor at an Italian "locanda," one lady playing a guitar, another singing, while an Abbate, acting as director of the music, waits with uplifted baton for the singer to finish her cadenza; in the rear of the picture the host is entering with wine. That the Abbate is distracted by the arrival of the host and gives an untimely signal to the accompanist to strike the final chord, can hardly have been suggested by the picture, but is supplied by Theodor, one of two friends standing before it. Italian scenes and Italian days rise before his eyes; he seems to smell the

---

[3] Hummel's painting is reproduced in an article on the artist by Georg Hummel in *Mitteilungen des Vereins für die Geschichte Berlins*, XLI (1924), p. 5, and more satisfactorily in C. G. von Maassen: *Der grundgescheute Antiquarius*, II (1923), pp. 68–69.

fragrance of Italian wines; he contrasts the cold sobriety of the very air that breathes around them with the land where joy in living is cultivated. But more than all, he is emotionally stirred because the painting presents an episode out of his own life; even the figures are accurate portraits. He proposes to his friend to repair to Tarone's restaurant, and there, over a bottle of Italian wine, Theodor tells his story—*Die Fermate*.

In constructing the setting for the first scenes Hoffmann made abundant use of his own youth: the provincial society of the remote little city, the curious old uncle with his love of music, the amateur concerts—taken from the musical evenings in the Doerffer house—the city trumpeter with his companions, the old organist at the piano, the tax-collector who played the flute so mightily and exerted himself so in breathing that he constantly blew out the candles on the stand. From boyhood Theodor had wished to do little else than strum his uncle's old piano; the queer old organist had been summoned to give him instruction in piano, organ, and musical theory, and later, because of his accurate sense of time, he was allowed to beat the drum at the concerts. Though there is no real evidence of her existence, it is probable that Demoiselle Meibel is a real figure out of Hoffmann's youth in Königsberg—a former singer of recognized merit, now far past her prime, who after much begging would consent to sing, "in a horrible squeaking voice, with all sorts of ludicrous flourishes and coloratura passages, while her extraordinary headdress, fastened with a bouquet of Italian porcelain flowers, trembled and nodded."

The town is thrown into excitement by the arrival of two Italian singers, sisters named Lauretta and Teresina. A concert with the local orchestra is planned, though the players are nearly all rank amateurs. At the rehearsal everything goes awry, for the musicians have not the faintest notion of how to accompany the singers—Lauretta "shrieked, raged, and wept" with anger and impatience. The organist at the piano, indignant at her reproaches, rises and leaves the room; others are about to follow, but Theodor saves the day, persuading the ruffled musicians to remain, and seats himself at the piano to direct the players. How often had Hoffmann directed an orchestra from this position! The concert itself was a thrilling event, the audience was in raptures, save for Demoiselle Meibel, who took a pinch from her snuffbox—the shape of a pug dog—and maintained that Italian shrieking was not really singing at all.

From this time on during the stay of the singers, Theodor is

constantly with them, playing their accompaniments and learning
to love Italian music, which had not been a part of the old organist's
instructions. This artistic privilege is linked to the growth of a
personal attachment to the singers—he is never certain to which,
and his dismay at the thought of impending separation is assuaged
only by their proposal that he go with them as their official accompanist. Theodor gives a most entertaining account of their
departure—the carriage packed to the brim with two rather
"robust" young women, a stout serving woman, a barking pug dog,
a dozen boxes, bags, and baskets. Hoffmann probably has in mind
the departure of the Seconda troupe from Leipzig. Theodor himself
accompanies the carriage on horseback; in time, however, the steed
is seized by the "queer idea" of running back home and all of
Theodor's efforts to move forward with the carriage are unavailing;
the animal dances in circles, and on the application of the spurs
throws his rider to the ground. To Theodor's chagrin he is taken into
the carriage, and Teresina rides the stubborn beast without difficulty.
Equally diverting are the later experiences. An Italian tenor joins
the company, complicating the emotional relationship of Theodor to
the two sisters. Once at a concert in the very moment when Lauretta
is already enchanting the audience and expects a thundering ovation
for the coloratura pyrotechnics which she is to interpolate at the end
of the selection, Theodor, possessed by some evil spirit—whether
in malicious caprice or from revulsion in suddenly perceiving the
shallow artificiality of the coming exhibition—strikes the final chord,
thus giving the signal to the orchestra to break in with its fortissimo;
the picture is thus in part anticipated. When, without intention to
eavesdrop, Theodor accidentally hears the two ladies discussing him
with the Italian tenor in contemptuous terms, he writes a stinging
note of farewell and goes his way. Years afterwards, now a musician
of repute, he is journeying in Italy and happens on the very scene
that the artist Hummel has portrayed. The past is forgotten, and a
happy reunion takes place in the Italian "locanda."

At the beginning weaving in memories from his own youth in
Königsberg, Hoffmann proceeds with episodes from the life of a
musician—his own as it might have been. With the first words of his
narrative Theodor suggests a turning point which was permitted to
him but not to Hoffmann: "Finally I cast all else aside and gave
myself up completely to 'noble musica.'" Theodor could abandon
"all else," but Hoffmann was fettered for a large part of his life to
an alien service; Theodor could visit the land which Hoffmann wor-

shiped from afar but never saw. In Theodor's attitude toward the two Italian singers and their art, Hoffmann probably had something of Julia Marc in mind, but he transforms the tragedy of that relationship into comedy. Neither Lauretta nor Teresina was anything more than an accomplished Italian singer, capricious, volatile, and essentially shallow, and, apart from the initial value of his friendship for them, the opening of new vistas in music and the initiation into a semiprofessional practice of music, they became to him merely cheerful shades in the Elysian fields of youth; his relation to them was tenuous, fragile, and had no abiding significance.

As a consequence there is something incongruous in the more serious reflection with which the story ends. In his thought at first Julia Marc has taken the place of the Italian sisters:

"Every composer remembers doubtless a mighty impression that time does not efface. The spirit living in the tone spoke, and that was the creative word which suddenly wakened the related spirit that was reposing within him; it beamed forth with might and could never more pass away. Certain is it that, thus stimulated, all melodies which come forth from within seem to us to belong only to the singer who cast into us the first spark. We hear these melodies and merely write down what she has sung. It is, however, the inheritance of us weak men, that while clinging to the clod of earth, we would fain bring down the heavenly into our wretched mundane limitations. Thus the singer becomes our loved one, our wife, it may be! The magic is destroyed and the inner melody, once proclaiming things of glory, is turned into a lament over a broken soup dish or an ink spot on new linen."[4] At the end another story is evidently hovering in Hoffmann's mind, one which he wrote before a year had passed, *Die Jesuiterkirche in G. Die Fermate* was the first tale that Hoffmann wrote directly for one of the popular annuals, and it is possible that he purposely kept the story, which otherwise might have developed a deeper undercurrent, in a mood of blithe, even humorous, reminis-

---

[4] "Jeder Komponist erinnert sich wohl eines mächtigen Eindrucks, den die Zeit nicht vernichtet. Der im Ton lebende Geist sprach und das war das Schöpfungswort, welches urplötzlich den ihm verwandten im Innern ruhenden Geist weckte; mächtig strahlte er hervor und konnte nie mehr untergehen. Gewiss ist es, dass, so angeregt, alle Melodien, die aus dem Innern hervorgehen, uns nur der Sängerin zu gehören scheinen, die den ersten Funken in uns warf. Wir hören sie und schreiben es nur auf, was sie gesungen. Es ist aber das Erbteil von uns Schwachen, dass wir, an der Erdscholle klebend, so gern das Überirdische hinabziehen wollen in die irdische ärmliche Beengtheit. So wird die Sängerin unsere Geliebte—wohl gar unsere Frau! Der Zauber ist vernichtet und die innere Melodie, sonst Herrliches verkündend, wird zur Klage über eine zerbrochene Suppenschüssel oder einen Tintenfleck in neuer Wäsche." VI, pp. 73-74.

cence. But he allowed something quite different, the subjective note, to creep in at the end.

The story which follows *Die Fermate* in chronological order, *Der Artushof*, adumbrates some of the ideas suggested in the last words of *Die Fermate*, but does not attack the question squarely, forming thus a kind of transition to the tragedy of *Die Jesuiterkirche in G.* The title, *Der Artushof*, is taken from the superb fifteenth and sixteenth century building in Danzig, long used as a meeting place for merchants and business men and as a kind of stock exchange. Hoffmann begins his story with a fine description of the great interior hall with its tall supporting granite columns, with its splendor of wall paintings and wood carving.

Temporarily fate has anchored young Traugott there as an assistant to a rich businessman, Elias Roos—really as a kind of partner, since Traugott's substantial fortune is in the business. In view of the obligations that this fact involves, Elias Roos tolerates Traugott's ineptitude in business transactions and has even arranged a marriage between him and his daughter Christina, though Traugott's utter incapacity for mercantile matters fills him with voluble disdain. Traugott dawdles over his tasks and is quite capable of handing to Elias Roos an "Aviso" of great financial importance which he has not written at all but covered with drawings and meaningless sketches. Christina is first cousin of the Veronika of *Der goldene Topf*, a pretty, worthy maiden of outstanding domestic virtues; her almond tarts always turned out well, her butter gravy always properly thickened: "If the neighbor's house were on fire, she would first feed her canary and lock up the linen before she sped to the office to inform her father that his house was also on fire."

Traugott's eyes are ever wandering from his random occupation with business documents to the paintings on the walls, particularly to one portraying a burgomaster of olden days on horseback and a youth of wondrous beauty, "almost feminine in appearance," holding the bridle; "the form, the face of the man aroused in him an inner shudder but a world of sweet presentiments gleamed from the countenance of the youth." Involuntarily one day he copies these two figures on the "Aviso" he is supposed to be writing. He hears a muffled voice behind him: "Good, fine, that's the way I like it; something can come of that." Looking around he sees the very figures of the picture before him, though they are soon lost in the milling crowd. By chance two business associates of Elias Roos from Königsberg, uncle and nephew, happen upon the scene as Traugott innocently hands the drawing to Elias Roos, as if it were the business communication which was intrusted to him to compose. The presence of the two men mollifies the indignation of the merchant, particularly when the elder of the visitors, himself a collector of engravings, drawings, and the like, praises Traugott's talents and on the spot urges him to abandon the counting house and prepare for a career as an artist. The younger visitor on the other hand presents a very dour view of the artist's life, warning Traugott of its financial insecurity and the consequent deprivations. But the advice of the elder visitor, though timely, was unnecessary, for the glimpse of the two figures, a vision as it were, had quivered through his being with the force of lightning, and now "he saw plainly what hitherto had been only premonition and dream." A second visit of the strange pair to the Artushof gives Traugott an opportunity to do the old man a favor, one quite contrary to ordinary practices in the business world. The old man is an eccentric artist and the youth is presented as his son. Eventually the painter agrees to take Traugott as a pupil; Traugott leaves his desk in the Artushof and renounces the hand of Christina, even though the wedding day had been already set.

Berklinger, the artist, explains the miraculous resemblance in the wall painting; he himself had painted the picture in his early days, using himself as a model for the central figure of the burgomaster and his son for the page—the painting was really two or three centuries old. On the occasion of Traugott's first visit to the artist's home, the latter exhibits a work just finished upon which he has been engaged for a year, "Paradise Regained," a companion piece to the "Paradise Lost" of the previous year. Ecstatically and ever more incoherently, the old man explains the details of the picture, even addressing some of the figures in it in meaningless ejaculations. The canvas is really utterly blank; yet the artist sees there his unrivaled masterpiece. With tactful ambiguity Traugott admits that he has never seen a painting like it, but earlier works of the artist excite his genuine interest and admiration. Among them is a portrait of a young girl of surpassing beauty, closely resembling Berklinger's son; the latter hurriedly informs Traugott that it is his sister Felicitas and implies that she is dead. Traugott, who is drawn more and more to the artist's son, discovers accidentally that he is really the daughter of the artist—the youth is Felicitas in masculine disguise. The old man chances to come upon the scene at the moment of Traugott's discovery, and in incomprehensible wrath thrusts the young man out of the house. In accordance with a prophecy, Berklinger

believes that he will instantly die the moment that his daughter falls
in love and has thought to ward off possible suitors through this masquerade.

The following day Traugott finds that both father and daughter
have disappeared; he seeks with untiring zeal for some clue to their
whereabouts, finding only the cryptic words: "Gone to Sorrento."
In Italy his search is unrewarded, though he pursues phantom
rumors this way and that. Gradually the odd sentimental purpose
of his Italian journey is dimmed by Italy itself and by acquaintances
in the world of artists there, indeed, in time, by the success of his
own work. Finally rumors reach his ears of an old painter and his
daughter, the description of whom seems to tally with the lost pair.
He seeks them out; they are not Berklinger and Felicitas, though
the daughter Dorina bears an amazing resemblance to the missing
girl. He soon becomes an intimate friend, living in the family until
the father warns him of the equivocal position in which Traugott
is placing his daughter.

Later, the death of Elias Roos, in whose firm Traugott's paternal
inheritance is still invested, requires his presence in Danzig. There
the mystery of Berklinger's disappearance is solved; a friendly
town councilor owned a villa not far from Danzig which he had
fancifully named "Sorrento" and there he had benevolently hidden
the fugitives. In the meantime the tragedy that Berklinger feared
has occurred; Felicitas has had a suitor, and her father has died
according to the prophecy. The girl, shocked by the manner of her
father's death, then scorned her lover, but later married a lawyer,
a "Kriminalrat" in Marienwerder. Felicitas, as the wife of this official, has ceased to cast a spell over Traugott. He winds up his
affairs and returns to Italy and to Dorina.

Der Artushof is less charmingly conceived, less buoyantly narrated than its immediate predecessor. Hoffmann would seem to have
had two ideas for the story, neither of which is fully realized. One
of them is the Julia motif: when Traugott sees the portrait of
Felicitas, he finds in her "the loved one of his soul, whom he has
long borne in his heart and recognized only in presentiment," but
the loved one is not lost, can never be lost, for she remains his eternal
inspiration. After Traugott's return to Danzig, when he learns of
the marriage of Felicitas, he exclaims: "No, she is not that, not
Felicitas, the heavenly vision which enkindled an infinite longing in
my breast, in pursuit of which I journeyed to a faraway land, ever
seeing it before me, my gleaming star of hope," and "I never lost

you, you remain forever mine; for you are indeed the creative art which lives in me." Hoffmann expresses these ideas in *Die Automate*, and later in *Die Doppeltgänger*, and by implication in *Die Brautwahl*. To this conception the novelist has added another idea, the relation of a man to a woman who is not the ideal of his inspiration but will satisfy the demands of his non-spiritual nature. It may be a question whether the invention of Dorina is not a tactical error and Traugott's return to her a disturbing note, if not really inconsistent with the main theme, still a jarring element lessening its force. The marriage with Dorina is, one may admit, reasonable and altogether human, but the suspicion arises that Dorina and her wonderful resemblance to Felicitas formed a tempting tidbit for the readers of a popular annual.

Die Jesuiterkirche in G. (The Jesuit Church in G.) is the story that seemed to be promised in the closing paragraph of *Die Fermate*. Here too Hoffmann has set the main story within a frame, but in this case the frame is more significant and more closely interlocked with the picture it contains. As a narrator Hoffmann introduces the "Traveling Enthusiast" from the *Fantasiestücke*, who is delayed for several days in G(logau) by an accident to his carriage. To seek relief from the tedium of this interruption in his journey he seeks out a certain Professor Aloysius Walter of the local Jesuit Seminary of whom he has heard a friend speak. The professor is a cultivated and decidedly worldly ecclesiastic, one of Hoffmann's chief portraits of the Roman clergy. On his first visit the conversation turns to church architecture, prompted by what the narrator has seen on the way; they discuss the fitness of different styles—Gothic, Renaissance, Baroque—for church buildings, and appropriately enough the professor proposes a visit to the Jesuit church, where he says an artist is at work on the interior decoration.

The narrator can hardly explain the curious effect that the artist, Berthold, has upon him, for the words he speaks, the expression of his face, suggest some deep pain burrowing within, a life shattered by some secret woe. His interest is further stimulated, and incidentally the interest of the reader, by a veiled altar painting and by the apparent unwillingness of the professor to discuss the artist. That night the clear cool air after a storm invites the narrator, even after midnight, to take a walk. Seeing a light in the Jesuit church, he enters, finds Berthold still at work, and, in the absence of Berthold's assistant, offers to take the place of this menial. He is more and more captivated by Berthold's strange personality, by his bizarre but still searching opinions on art, and his philosophy of life. And Berthold's words at parting add to the fervor of his curiosity: "Could you for a moment of your life have a serene spirit, if you were conscious of a horrible, inexpiable crime?"

The following morning the professor again takes the traveler to the church, and now unveils the altar piece—the Virgin and St. Elizabeth in a garden, the Christ-child and St. John the Baptist playing with the flowers, at one side in the background a man on his knees in prayer; only the Virgin and the two children are in finished form. To the astounded visitor the painting suggests even the Raphael of the great Madonna in Dresden. But he notes that the man at prayer has the face of the artist Berthold. The professor explains that the painting had been presented to the church, that Berthold on his arrival in G(logau) had fallen in a swoon on seeing the picture, and with horror and aversion had refused the professor's proposal that he complete the painting. The professor is plainly not interested in Berthold and is indifferent to his fate; but, perceiving the intense interest of the narrator, he remembers that a former seminarian had become attached to the painter and had written down from his own lips the story of his life. With callous indifference he now places this manuscript in the traveler's hands. "I know," he says, "that you are not a writer. The author of the *Fantasiestücke in Callots Manier* would have pruned it sadly after his mad fashion and then immediately had it printed. I don't expect that of you." The central section of the story is then the content of this manuscript.

Upon the insistence of his teacher, Berthold's parents had sent him to Italy—"the sprouting plant must have more sunshine in order to thrive, bear bloom and fruit." Even though in D(resden) many excellent original works could be studied, only in Italy would Berthold's talent really become alive, "in the land where art flourishes." Reluctantly Berthold listens to his new friends in Rome and turns from landscape painting, hitherto his devotion, to historical subjects, which they regard as the highest themes for the artist. Later in Naples, the famous Philipp Hackert, Goethe's friend, accepts him as a pupil, but neither in Hackert's landscapes—faithful transcriptions from nature—nor in his still-lifes can Berthold find pure satisfaction. By chance he makes the acquaintance of an old painter, a Greek from the island of Malta, an eccentric artist standing apart from contemporary fashions, whom Hackert calls mad since he cherishes fantastic opinions and has built up a system of art which is quite untenable. In the opinion of this new mentor the mere copying of nature is not art, though of the highest technical perfection; whether landscapes or historical paintings, such work remains forever like copies of a book written in a tongue foreign to the copyist. Perfection of reproduction is not art; the artist must penetrate the depths that lie behind the phenomena of nature, so that by his work, as in that of the great masters, one is lifted up into a higher realm. And the old painter sees in Berthold the spark that might be kindled into flame.

This new and disturbing message simply brings to the surface the slumbering discontent with his own performance, in spite of the acclaim of his friends. He throws his brushes aside and wanders aimlessly, feverishly, about in the vicinity of Naples. Nature, which he wishes to comprehend in the meaning of the Maltese artist, still refuses to divulge its secrets, becomes to him a "threatening monster." The companionship of another artist, Florentin, brings him some measure of consolation, and he tries his hand at the airy, graceful figures in which Florentin excels.

One day on the estate of a Neapolitan nobleman which was open to artists because of the superb views of Vesuvius and the sea, Berthold sees for one brief moment a woman of supernal loveliness, the ideal of which he has dreamed, and in ecstasy stretches his canvas to record the vision. His whole being is transformed; animated by a heavenly power, he begins to paint religious pictures, mostly of joyful and serene content, which are sought as altar pieces for chapels and churches. Even Hackert admits that his former pupil has found his real vocation. In each of these paintings he places the figure of his momentary vision. Attention is called to the likeness of this figure to a certain Princess Angiola, though Berthold himself disdains the suggestion.

Presently Naples is torn asunder by the revolution at the time of the French invasion during Napoleon's first Italian campaign. Wild mobs rove through the town, wreaking their capricious will upon people of the upper classes. Hoffmann presents vivid and memorable scenes of their fiendish activities. At the risk of his own life Berthold rescues the Princess Angiola from the plundered palace of her father, and they flee together. She has fallen passionately in love with her rescuer and is willing that her family should think her dead rather than lose Berthold. They make their way to Germany where Berthold hopes in M (evidently Munich) to establish his reputation by the very picture now unfinished in the Glogau church. But his strength is broken. The heavenly vision has become an earthly woman who is dependent on him for her daily bread; he tries to defy the paralysis of his powers, but in vain. When she now sits for him in the flesh, Angiola, once his ideal, becomes a mere wax figure on the canvas, staring at him with eyes of glass. His condition gradually approaches madness; in wild despair he curses her and the child she has borne him. His cruel treatment of wife and child arouses the indignation of the neighbors, and the authorities decide to intervene, but the little family has fled. Soon after this Berthold appears in N(eisse) in Upper Silesia, and there again begins the painting upon which his hopes had rested, but a serious illness stayed his hand. To defray his expenses, his effects are sold, including this unfinished painting, which later comes into the possession of the church in Glogau. On partial recovery he wanders forth into the unknown—a wretched invalid beggar.

Again the next night the traveler visits the church and assists Berthold at his work on the lofty scaffolding. He has drawn the conclusion that Berthold has murdered his wife and child, and is determined to discover the truth. In conversation with Berthold he implies that he is acquainted with his story and adroitly leads to the point where he boldly puts the fatal question. In reply Berthold asserts that his hands are clean of blood, and threatens to throw himself and his visitor down from the scaffolding if a further word on the subject is spoken.

A half year later a letter comes from the professor: soon after the departure of the "Traveling Enthusiast" Berthold had become cheerful and serene, and had completed the altar piece. Then he disappeared suddenly, and circumstantial evidence—his hat and walking stick beside the River O(der)—indicates that he has taken his own life.

For the story *Rat Krespel* (Councilor Krespel) Hoffmann himself never provided a title. It appeared first in Fouqué's *Frauentaschenbuch auf 1817* with a personal "cover letter" to the editor; later, when incorporated into the second volume of the *Serapionsbrüder*, it is not read from manuscript as are most of the tales, but is narrated orally by Theodor as a memory of personal experience. The French translation of Loève-Veimars bears the title "Antonie," and an English version is named "The Cremona Violin."

On Theodor's arrival in H, the town is all agog over the fantastic conduct of a certain Rat Krespel, whom many good citizens regard as manifestly insane. He is a jurist and diplomat of high repute, and, in return for services he had rendered, a reigning prince had

generously offered to foot the bill when Krespel proposed to build
himself a new house. In the construction of this dwelling Krespel
had exhibited his extraordinary whimsicality. He gathered the various
materials together on a vacant lot and one fine day summoned a
builder and workmen. To the consternation of the builder Krespel
produced no plans, and only the munificent pay induced the builder
to follow Krespel's personal directions—to erect blank walls until
orders to stop were given. Then Krespel went about with a walking
stick and designated the places where he wished the workmen to
knock out the masonry just laid in order to let in doors and windows.
The structure, when completed, was a masterpiece of whimsy—
windows here and there of all shapes and sizes. In the finished dwelling a splendid banquet was given by way of a "house-warming,"
but only the workmen were bidden; mason's assistants, carpenter
boys, and hungry hod carriers were regaled with partridge pies,
roast pheasants, and truffles. In the evening the wives and daughters
arrived, and there was dancing till dawn, Krespel himself playing
the violin and directing the musicians.

Theodor meets Rat Krespel at dinner in the house of Professor
M., where Krespel's unconventional but original behavior as dinner
guest excites Theodor's interest. Krespel's parrying of an inquiry
concerning "Antonie" piques his curiosity, which presently is even
more acutely aroused by information received from the professor.
Krespel had arrived in the town several years before and had taken
a house where he lived alone with an old housekeeper; everyone believed him to be a bachelor. Yet once, after he had been absent for
some months, the people of the town saw the house brilliantly lighted
and then heard music—piano, violin—and a woman's voice of surpassing beauty. Later, about midnight, one heard Krespel's voice
in violent and vehement tones, another masculine voice apparently
in remonstrance or reproach, and the voice of a maiden in broken
lament. Finally a young man stumbled down the steps sobbing,
threw himself into a carriage standing by the entrance, and drove off.
The old housekeeper did little to satisfy the inquisitive neighbors:
Krespel had brought home a beautiful young woman whom he called
Antonie; a young man then arriving was apparently her betrothed,
but Krespel evidently disapproved and demanded his immediate departure. Antonie remained a mystery. Krespel hardly allowed her to
appear at the window and on rare occasions when she accompanied
him outside the house he watched her with "argus eyes." Music was
not permitted in her presence, and though the marvelous voice of that

first evening was obviously hers, she never sang again, even in Krespel's house.

To Theodor the mystery is highly provocative. He dreams of Antonie; in dreams he hears her voice, even singing some of his own compositions, for Theodor, like Hoffmann, though a young lawyer, is a musician and composer. He resolves to play the gallant hero and free her from her bondage. From the professor he has heard of Krespel's odd hobby, the making of violins. It is Krespel's conviction that some secret lies hidden in the body of each fine instrument, and he purchases rare old violins at fabulous prices, and, after playing them, dissects them to discover the mystery of their tone. Through his own interest in music Theodor insinuates himself into the good graces of Krespel. On his first visit Krespel shows him his collection of violins—about thirty old instruments, among them one hanging higher than the others and bearing a wreath of flowers: "This violin," says Krespel, "is a very remarkable, wonderful instrument of an unknown master, apparently from the time of Tartini. I am convinced that something peculiar lies in the inner structure and that, were I to take it to pieces, a secret would be disclosed, after which I have long been seeking, but—just laugh at me if you wish—this dead thing to which I, myself alone, still give life and sound, often speaks to me out of itself in wondrous fashion, and it seemed to me, when I played it for the first time, as if I were only the magnetizer, who is able to arouse the sleeping one so that acting now of itself it proclaims its inner views in words. Don't believe that I am silly enough to accept in the slightest such chimeras, but it is still queer that I have never prevailed upon myself to cut that dumb, dead thing to pieces. And I am glad now that I have not done it, for since Antonie has been here, I sometimes play this violin for her, and she loves to hear it."[5]

[5] " 'Diese Violine,' sprach Krespel, nachdem ich ihn darum befragt, 'diese Violine ist ein sehr merkwürdiges, wunderbares Stück eines unbekannten Meisters, wahrscheinlich aus Tartinis Zeiten. Ganz überzeugt bin ich, dass in der innern Struktur etwas Besonders liegt, und dass, wenn ich sie zerlegte, sich mir ein Geheimnis erschliessen würde, dem ich längst nachspürte, aber—lachen Sie mich nur aus, wenn Sie wollen—dies tote Ding, dem ich selbst doch nur erst Leben und Laut gebe, spricht oft aus sich selbst zu mir auf wunderliche Weise, und es war mir, da ich zum ersten Male darauf spielte, als wär' ich nur der Magnetiseur, der die Somnambule zu erregen vermag, dass sie selbsttätig ihre innere Anschauung in Worten verkündet.—Glauben Sie ja nicht, dass ich geckhaft genug bin, von solchen Fantastereien auch nur das mindeste zu halten, aber eigen ist es doch, dass ich es nie über mich erhielt, jenes dumme tote Ding dort aufzuschneiden. Lieb ist es mir jetzt, dass ich es nicht getan, denn seitdem Antonie hier ist, spiele ich ihr zuweilen etwas auf dieser Geige vor. Antonie hat es gern—gar gern.' " VI, pp. 37-38.

On the occasion of his second visit, Theodor meets Antonie, who is assisting Krespel in the construction of a violin, and gradually he becomes a frequent visitor. One evening Krespel seems in an especially good humor, for he has discovered a certain irregularity, apparently purposeful, in the structure of a Cremona violin. Theodor regards the moment as propitious and directs the conversation to his own ends. By way of illustrating his contempt for certain modern trends in music—assured of Krespel's approval—he goes to the piano and sings, and then by way of proving his point, and to lure Antonie, he begins a glorious soul-stirring song of Leonardo Leo. Antonie rushes to the piano, opens her lips, but in that moment Krespel seizes Theodor by the shoulders and screams: "It would violate all good form and good manners, if I were to express aloud the vigorous wish that Satan should come out of hell and here on the spot gently strike off your neck with his glowing claw fists and in this way, so to speak, make short shrift of you. But apart from this you must admit that it is really very dark, and since today there are no street lamps, even if I were not to throw you down the steps, you might do harm to your nice legs. Just go right home, and remember in most friendly fashion your genuine friend, if perchance you should nevermore find me at home; you understand, don't you?"[6] And with these words he slowly forces Theodor out of the door, turning him about so that he cannot catch a final glimpse of Antonie. With broken spirit Theodor leaves the city, but, as ever happens, "the livid colors of the daydream grew pale, and yet Antonie—even her singing which I never heard—shone often into the very depths of my spirit like a gentle, comforting shimmer of roses."

On a journey two years later Theodor approaches the city. A mysterious, indescribable feeling of terror possesses him, a heavy weight it seems upon his breast, mounting even to physical pain, as he hears men's voices in a solemn chorale. A burial is taking place in the near-by churchyard. It is Antonie who is being borne to her grave. This is the prelude to his last meeting with Krespel, who even on this day is fantastically clad, wearing a violin bow as a

---

[6] "Gegen alle Lebensart, gegen alle guten Sitten würde es anstossen, wenn ich laut und lebhaft den Wunsch äusserte, dass Ihnen hier auf der Stelle gleich der höllische Satan mit glühenden Krallenfäusten sanft das Genick abstiesse, und Sie auf die Weise gewissermassen kurz expediere; aber davon abgesehen müssen Sie eingestehen, Liebwertester! dass es bedeutend dunkelt, und da heute keine Laterne brennt, könnten Sie, würfe ich Sie auch grade nicht die Treppe herab, doch Schaden leiden an Ihren lieben Gebeinen. Gehen Sie fein nach Hause; erinnern Sie sich freundschaftlichst Ihres wahren Freundes, wenn Sie ihn etwa nie mehr— verstehen Sie wohl? nie mehr zu Hause antreffen sollten!" vɪ, p. 40.

sword. Krespel invites him to his house, to the room where the collection of violins was hung. Each now bears a knot of crepe, but the violin of the old master is missing; in its place hangs a cypress wreath. "When she died," Krespel explains, "the sound-post broke in pieces with a resounding crash and the sounding board was rent asunder; the faithful violin could live only with her, in her; it lies with her in the coffin."

The insensate laughter, the outcries, singing, and dancing of Krespel convince Theodor that he is stark mad, and that behind his conduct lurks a secret guilt, that indeed in the last analysis he is in some way responsible for Antonie's death. With the bravado of a young man established at a court of law, he resolves to disclose the crime, even to tax the perpetrator with it to his face. But this quixotic enterprise turns out quite differently from his expectations; after Krespel has told his story Theodor turns his steps from the house with pity and respect for the old man in his tragic loneliness.

Traveling in Italy in search of precious old violins, Krespel met and married a renowned singer, Angela. Their temperaments were, however, in constant collision, and when one day she snatched from his hands a Cremona violin he was playing and smashed it to fragments, he rose in wrath, threw her out of the window, and, without looking back, left the house and returned to Germany. He was troubled by the rashness of his deed, particularly because Angela was at the time an expectant mother, but in time he learned not only that a daughter had been born to him but also that this defenestration had worked a miraculous change in his wife's character; her flashes of unrestrained passion had yielded to a calm docility. Though in the following years husband and wife corresponded amicably, he never saw her again. Angela's fame became international, and while singing in a German city, she had died; Krespel hastened to bring his daughter to his own home. From the lips of a physician he learned that disease and phenomenal musical gifts were inextricably united in Antonie's very being, that death was certain, even relatively imminent, if she continued to sing. He was thus unwilling to surrender her to the young composer to whom she had become betrothed, even though the latter loved her for her own sake and promised never to allow her to sing a note; Krespel wisely regarded this promise as of dubious fulfillment. Antonie gave herself up to her father's will and was placidly content in his companionship. In a mysterious way she identified herself with his most treasured violin, and when he played it, she heard her own voice singing—that voice of incredible beauty had passed over into the violin, the voice that Theodor never heard but which the professor had described. Beside her singing that of the most renowned vocalists seemed flat and expressionless; "never had I had a conception of the long sustained tones, those nightingale trills, the rise and fall in waves, this rising to the strength of organ tones, this sinking to the faintest breath."[7] On the night of her death Krespel had heard her singing, heard with it the playing of her former lover, in a dream; rousing himself from the spell that the dream cast upon him, he rushed to her apartment and found her lifeless.

It may be a question whether Hoffmann's story might not have been more effective without Krespel's narrative. In story after story, he adds this type of "flashback" which establishes the roots of later happenings in the soil of past days. That Antonie is Krespel's daughter was a natural inference from the outset, and the introduction of Angela, her mother, adds little of value—perhaps a bit of humor in the clash of two artistic temperaments, perhaps further insight into the character of Krespel himself. The identification of Antonie with the violin is already suggested by the simultaneous "death," perhaps more satisfactorily than by the longer development in Krespel's story. "It lies with her in the coffin"; the words would have formed an extraordinarily dramatic and moving end for Theodor's narration.

The story of Antonie is the most poignant of the artist tales, for the problem of the relation of the artist to life, which often allows even humorous byplay, is here transformed into the relation of the artist to life *and* death. The artist faces life at times courageously or timidly, with defiance or resignation; however bitter the contest, the possibility of victory is not utterly excluded, and he can still fight on. But how can art face death? Shall life itself be sacrificed to art —even for one heavenly moment of ecstatic self-expression—or shall art be sacrificed to mere existence? Through the two forces, an inexplicable, transcendent gift on the one hand and on the other a fatal physical fault in her nature, the shadow of death hangs over Antonie, if she yields to an impulse which is essentially a part of her being. At the imperious insistence of her father, she renounces her

[7] "Und ich muss Ihnen gestehen, dass gegen die Stimme, gegen den ganz eignen tief in das Innerste dringenden Vortrag der Unbekannten mir der Gesang der berühmtesten Sängerinnen, die ich gehört, matt und ausdrucklos schien. Nie hatte ich eine Ahnung von diesen lang ausgehaltenen Tönen, von diesen Nachtigallwirbeln, von diesem Auf- und Abwogen, von diesem Steigen bis zur Stärke des Orgellautes, von diesem Sinken bis zum leisesten Hauch." vi, p. 36.

lover and thus makes a choice between art and life; temptations are kept from her by the despotic rigor of her father's will. With glowing cheeks and flaming eyes she steps to the piano when Theodor tests his scheme of crafty enticement. The inner force of her divine gift was only slumbering, and, since Hoffmann doubtless intended us to interpret Krespel's dream as more than a dream, as in part reality—at any rate, to allow this possibility, Antonie eventually chooses a transitory exercise of her artistic gifts, with death at the end of the song, rather than a continuation of life without art.

Krespel himself is one of Hoffmann's major creations—with Anselmus, Klein Zaches, Kreisler, Meister Abraham, and Kater Murr. Despite his learning, his professional successes, his consolation in music, he is filled with bitter scorn for ordinary mundane activities, for the trivialities, the baseness, the narrowness of human living. And this scorn he expresses in fantastic behavior, in clever, burlesque leaps of fancy. These form a kind of safety valve to guard against serious explosions; they are a cloak for his real self. He is not insane, as the townspeople think; he is most terribly sane. There is much of Hoffmann in Rat Krespel.[8]

More ambitious than these varied attempts to portray the artist in relation to his world was the plan for a "Kunstroman," an artist-novel. On February 17, 1818, he wrote to the publisher Reimer of his intent. No sensible title has occurred to him; he says he has thought of "Künstlerleben" (The Life of Artists), but that is "commonplace and worn out." The novel was never written, yet the story of Kreisler in *Kater Murr* goes far to redeem his promise.

[8] The name "Krespel" and some elements of Rat Krespel's eccentricity are apparently derived from a character mentioned in Goethe's *Dichtung und Wahrheit* and further described in the correspondence of Goethe's mother. The latter was, of course, not available for Hoffmann, but Ellinger conjectures that details of Krespel's peculiarities may have been communicated to him by Clemens Brentano.

CHAPTER 10

THE MÄRCHEN

THE revolt against eighteenth century rationalism and classicism brought with it as a positive phase a new appreciation of the spontaneous and primitive in literature. Herder honored Ossian as the untutored voice of an ancient people and Shakespeare as the supreme dramatist, the native genius, and he collected the folk songs of all nations. The Romanticists were children of Herder in their admiration for the "poetry of the people." The collections of folk songs and folk tales, and new editions of and studies in the poetry of the Middle Ages, are a most significant by-product of Romantic literature. The most familiar collection, of course, is the work of the Brothers Grimm, *Kinder- und Hausmärchen*, known as "Grimm's Fairy Tales," for more than a century a beloved book in the nurseries of all lands. To be sure, Musäus had previously collected folk tales, *Volksmärchen der Deutschen* (1782-1786), but he had rewritten them in a sophisticated style; Wieland had written "Märchen," but they lack the naïveté of the real Märchen, are semi-ironic and artificially embroidered; he records the supernatural with detachment, with his tongue in his cheek. Only the Romanticists discovered the "soul" of the Märchen.[1]

To the Romanticists the Märchen was not merely a literary genre that possessed merit because of its primitivism, nor was it merely a weapon with which to combat the artificial. It was to them a supreme method of expressing truth; God has revealed unto babes the truths which He has concealed from the "wise and prudent." The essence of divine wisdom that eludes the philosopher in his logical thinking can be grasped by the intuition of simple minds and bodied forth symbolically in the form of a Märchen. To Novalis, for example, the Märchen was the "canon of poetry"; everything poetic must be like a Märchen—"all Märchen are only dreams of that homeland world which is everywhere and nowhere." The qualities of the old folk tales are eloquently expressed by Wilhelm Grimm in his introduction to the famous collection; they are derived from "that eternal foun-

---

[1] The bibliography of the Märchen is very extensive; for an excellent list of works on the subject, cf. the bibliography in Mimi Ida Jehle's *Das deutsche Kunstmärchen von der Romantik zum Naturalismus*, Urbana, 1935. Note particularly: R. E. Benz: *Märchendichtung der Romantiker*, Gotha, 1908; Hermann Todsen: *Über die Entwicklung des romantischen Kunstmärchens*, Berlin, 1906; R. Buchmann: *Helden und Mächte des romantischen Kunstmärchens*, Leipzig, 1910.

tain which bedews all life, even if it is only a single drop which a little cuplike leaf has caught, yet gleaming in the first red of dawn"; they are like children in their purity; "they have the same bluish-white, immaculate, shining eyes, which cannot grow any more, while the other parts of the body are still tender and weak, not fitted for the service of earth." Aspects of human living not susceptible to rational and scientific examination, feelings not describable in words, could be adumbrated in the form of a Märchen narrative.

But, while honoring the primitive Märchen, the Romanticists developed a Märchen type of their own—the "Kunstmärchen" (Art-Märchen) as a class differentiated from the "Volksmärchen." Tieck republished numerous old folk tales, some without change, in all their stark simplicity, others with subjective and lyrical embroidery. The retold folk tale was thus merging into the new type, the "Kunstmärchen" of which Tieck himself, in *Der blonde Eckbert* (Fair-haired Eckbert) and *Der Runenberg*, was the supreme master. In the "Volksmärchen" the supernatural is simple and unquestioned, is taken for granted. After reading of Cinderella's adversities, one is confronted with the bald statement: "Now Cinderella had a fairy godmother," and the phenomena of the godmother's supernatural appearances are never called into question. In the Kunstmärchen the supernatural takes the form, by and large, of mysterious and inexplicable forces, perhaps in external nature, which exert their power over human destiny. The boundaries between the natural and the supernatural are vague and shifting; the characters are never certain where these boundaries lie. Tieck says of "Der blonde Eckbert": "He could not find his way out of the enigma, whether he was now dreaming or had formerly dreamed of a wife named Bertha; the most miraculous mingled with the everyday"; or from *Der Runenberg*: "His whole previous life lay behind him in the far distance; the ordinary was so intermingled with the most strange that he could not possibly separate them."

The Volksmärchen is ever naïvely optimistic; as it begins with "Once upon a time," it ends with "And they lived happily ever after." The characters are rigidly divided into the totally good and the totally bad, and virtue is always rewarded with material blessings. The Kunstmärchen is often sinister in tone and tragic in outcome; human character is inextricably compounded of good and evil. The Volksmärchen tells a simple straightforward story without comment, but the author of the Kunstmärchen indulges in reflection and analysis of motive. A half century ago, H. H. Boyesen characterized the stories of Tieck with words worth quoting here, and with some modification for other authors and other tales they may be applied to the Kunstmärchen in general:

"We fondly believe that in an enlightened age like ours, when science mercilessly penetrates to the causes of every cherished mystery, the range of the terrible is gradually reduced to a mere vanishing quantity; but no amount of scientific reasoning can conquer the tremor which a timid person feels in a dark hall or in an empty church at midnight. The small territory of clear daylight fact which we have conquered for ourselves is on all sides surrounded by a far vaster realm of mystery, and whenever the gates are opened to this realm, our reason refuses to do our bidding,·and we are on the verge of insanity. It is on the boundary of these two realms of reason and mystery that Tieck has laid the scene of his fairy tales."[2]

The Romantic Kunstmärchen were not intricate and subtle allegories; they were symbolical narratives. Tieck's Märchen were intended to communicate a mood—such as awe or terror in the presence of unknown and mysterious forces—not to incorporate a concrete and graspable idea, though their content has tempted readers to make such an interpretation, for example, *Der Runenberg* as a parable of the love of money. Novalis left the exquisite little tale *Hyazinth und Rosenblütchen* without a "moral," though an explanation, albeit a metaphysical one, may be found in a verse posthumously published, and allegorical elements may be admitted in Kingsohr's Märchen in *Heinrich von Ofterdingen*, but the whole is a symbolical story demonstrating the ultimate triumph of the poetic imagination. In recent years perhaps such a story as Kafka's *Das Schloss* (The Castle) offers a modern parallel to the Romantic Kunstmärchen, though it seems more urgently to challenge the reader to seek an allegorical interpretation; one surrenders less easily to pleasure in the story as the evocation of a mood. Ricarda Huch's *Von den Königen und der Krone* (Of the Kings and Their Crown) may be a still more satisfactory illustration.

Hoffmann puts his Märchen to varied uses. The simplest of them were written for children, though he kept one eye on the adult reader. In others, despite their fanciful and humorous elements, he incorporated, as nowhere else in his writings, his profound ponderings upon the perplexing questions of man's relationship to life and to eternal values, or his comment in satirical form upon contemporary vagaries. In the preface to *Prinzessin Brambilla* he refers to Carlo

2 Cf. H. H. Boyesen: *Essays on German Literature* (New York, 1892), p. 341.

Gozzi's opinion of the Märchen as expressed in the foreword to his *Re de' Genj* (King of the Spirits), that a whole arsenal of absurdities and supernatural phenomena (Spukereien) is not sufficient to give a soul to the Märchen, which it can obtain only through a deep foundation, through a leading idea drawn from some philosophical view of life; Hoffmann adds that this is what he has tried to do in the story he is presenting. Thus a typical element in Hoffmann's tales is the indication of a perpetual conflict between the ideal and the real, the infinite and the finite, of the search for a dreamed-of paradise, and the finding of it, perhaps only in another world. The outstanding characteristic of Hoffmann's Märchen is the use of realistic and contemporary backgrounds, in a manner and to a degree of which Tieck never dreamed. Into this world of everyday Hoffmann projects a supernatural world of the traditional folk tale or more commonly of his own invention; he did not indeed disdain to include elements characteristic of the artificial stories of Wieland or to import motifs from the French Contes des Fées, from Hamilton and Perrault.

After Lothar has read his little fairy tale of *Nussknacker und Mausekönig*, Hoffmann allows the Serapion Brothers to discuss the story and to debate the nature of Märchen in general. Cyprian, who represents the more romantic side of Hoffmann, calls it "a venturesome undertaking to let what is thoroughly fantastic play over into everyday life, to throw absurd magic cloaks [Zauberkappen] over serious people, councilors of the supreme court, archivarii, and students, so that they, like fabulous spirits, creep in bright daylight through the most lively streets of the most familiar cities, and one may then become dubious as to the identity of each honest neighbor. It is true that a certain ironical tone arises inevitably from all this, which pricks the indolent mind, or rather with good-humored mien, like a malicious rogue, imperceptibly entices such a one into the alien region."[3] Theodor acknowledges that this "ironical tone might be a most dangerous cliff on which the charm of the

---

[3] " 'Doch bleibt es ein gewagtes Unternehmen das durchaus Fantastische ins gewöhnliche Leben hineinzuspielen und ernsthaften Leuten, Obergerichtsräten, Archivarien und Studenten tolle Zauberkappen überzuwerfen, dass sie wie fabelhafte Spukgeister am hellen lichten Tage durch die lebhaftesten Strassen der bekanntesten Städte schleichen und man irre werden kann an jedem ehrlichen Nachbar. Wahr ist es, dass sich daraus ein gewisser ironisierender Ton von selbst bildet, der den trägen Geist stachelt oder ihn vielmehr ganz unvermerkt mit gutmütiger Miene wie ein böser Schalk hinein verlockt in das fremde Gebiet.' 'Dieser ironische Ton,' sprach Theodor, 'möchte die gefährlichste Klippe sein, da an ihr sehr leicht die Anmut der Erfindung und Darstellung, welche wir von jedem Märchen verlangen, scheitern, rettungslos zu Grunde gehen kann.' " VI, p. 250.

invention and presentation—which we demand of every Märchen—
may be wrecked. . . ." Lothar, who perceives that Cyprian has in
mind *Der goldene Topf* of "our distant friend," cites Tieck as the
great master of the Märchen, and from the discussion in Tieck's
Phantasus he derives the characteristic qualities of the genre: "A
quietly progressing tone of narration, a certain innocence of presentation, which like gently fanciful music enthralls the soul without
noise or tumult. A work of fancy should leave behind it no bitter
taste, but an after-enjoyment, an echo."

Hoffmann's Märchen are peculiarly his own, are at bottom unlike
anything else in literature. Accordingly it would seem desirable,
indeed unavoidable, to give an account of them in considerable
detail. The first of his Märchen was *Der goldene Topf* (The Golden
Pot). The plan for this tale is mentioned in a letter to Kunz, August
19, 1813; Hoffmann writes: "Don't think of Scheherazade and the
Arabian Nights. Turban and Turkish trousers are completely
ruled out." And yet the story is to be miraculous and magical
(feenhaft), though daringly involved in ordinary life. Much later, in
the *Serapionsbrüder* Hoffmann characterized the *Arabian Nights*
as being precisely of this type; the characters and the settings were
familiar and everyday to people for whom the stories were originally
told; they are exotic only to the Western world. Before leaving
Bamberg, Hoffmann had been captivated by James Beresford's
Human Miseries, translated into German as *Menschliches Elend* by
Adolph Wagner, who a little later became one of his closest friends
in Leipzig, and he intended to write a story illustrating Beresford's
curious type of pessimism.[4] Now in Dresden he deepens and enriches
the conception by bestowing upon the hero something more of himself—the soul of an artist, the poet's spirit, and the external adventures become then the symbols of the perpetual conflict between
the soul of man and the physical necessities and annoyances of everyday life. In *Der goldene Topf* as in the later Märchen, *Prinzessin*

---

[4] In his reminiscences of Hoffmann, Kunz tells of Hoffmann's absorbing interest
in Beresford's work which he found in Kunz's library. Hoffmann's impulse to write
a story based upon Beresford was further supported by acquaintance with a man
in Bamberg whose career seemed to offer an excellent example of the theme. Kunz
dissuaded Hoffmann from his purpose probably because the identity of this illustrative "specimen" would have been too obvious. In a letter of August 19, 1813, Hoffmann refers to Kunz's advice: "Auch werden Sie bei Lesung (*Der goldene Topf*)
des Ganzen wahrnehmen, dass eine frühere in Bamberg gefasste Idee, die durch Ihre
sehr richtigen Bemerkungen und Einwürfe nur nicht zur gänzlichen Ausführung kam,
die Grundlage des Mährchens bildet."

Brambilla and *Meister Floh,* Hoffmann invents a myth with which
the events of the story are directly or indirectly intertwined.

Anselmus, the hero of *Der goldene Topf,* is akin to Hoffmann;
he has the soul of an artist, of a poet, but is ever in conflict with the
physical things of everyday life, is an unlucky wight with whom
everything seems to go awry. These misfortunes are illustrated by
petty occurrences: if he has a new coat he spatters candle grease on
it or tears it; if he attempts to be gallant, he stumbles over a stool;
if he accompanies a lady on the street, he is so absorbed in the effort
to be courteous that he leads her through puddles of muddy water.
It has been shown that most of Anselmus' trifling misadventures are
adapted from incidents in Beresford's book. Anselmus is an im-
pecunious student, earning a meager livelihood by giving private
lessons or performing trifling jobs as secretary. The scene is the
Dresden of Hoffmann's own day, and the story opens on a holiday,
the Feast of the Ascension. Hastening forward in the direction of
"Das Linkische Bad," a pleasure resort which Hoffmann himself
often visited, Anselmus upsets the basket of an old huckster woman,
and the contents, apples and cookies, roll away hither and thither as
spoil for the street urchins. The hideous old hag berates Anselmus
soundly for his awkwardness, while he pours into her lap the few
pennies he has saved for the holiday. An uncanny terror takes
possession of him and he flees from her.

Under a lilac tree by the river bank he tries to regain his composure. But ere long he hears strange voices in the tree, hears music as
of crystal bells. Looking up he sees three green-gold serpents weaving about in the branches. He tries to explain the phenomenon
realistically as the effect of the evening sun, but it cannot be explained away, for the music continues and he sees one of the serpents
raise its head toward him; he seems also to see two wonderful blue
eyes looking longingly at him. Anselmus stands beneath the tree in
inexpressible rapture. At sunset he hears a strange gruff voice ut-
tering words in some foreign tongue and sees the three serpents wind
down from the lilac tree and hasten off toward the river. On the way
back Anselmus encounters the assistant Principal of the school he
is attending, accompanied by his two daughters and the Registrator
Heerbrand. They are returning from an excursion and invite the
student to spend the evening at the Principal's house. The friends
are much exercised about Anselmus' mental condition, but the
evening passes pleasantly; only now and then does Anselmus fall

into a reverie and forget the little circle around him in remembrance of the strange adventures of the afternoon. It is plain that the blue-eyed Veronika, the elder of the two daughters, looks on the student with particular favor.

These friends are eager to assist Anselmus, and Registrator Heerbrand has heard of remunerative employment for which he can recommend him. A certain eccentric gentleman, the Archivarius Lindhorst, whose real occupation is somewhat of a mystery in the community, wishes a scribe to copy manuscripts written in Arabic and other strange and complicated letters. The work must be done with the greatest care; if a blot of ink falls on a sheet, a whole new piece of parchment must be used, and if one should happen to fall on one of the original manuscripts, the Archivarius is capable of booting the careless copyist out of the window. The following day, after Anselmus has collected a supply of ink, pens, and paper, together with examples of his own calligraphy, he presents himself at the door of the Archivarius' mansion. As he is about to lift the door knocker, it turns into the head of the old apple woman, grinning maliciously at him; he reels back and seizes the bell cord which, however, winds itself about him like a giant snake, and he swoons. Luckily the Principal of the school is passing at the time and finds Anselmus lying senseless in the street with an old huckster woman by his side.

However alluring the pay, Anselmus refuses to repeat the experience, but the Registrator persists and contrives to bring Anselmus to a café which the Archivarius is wont to frequent. There they find him entertaining the solid burghers with a fantastic tale. This is the first part of the myth:

"The spirit looked upon the waters, and they moved and roared in foaming waves, and plunged with thunder into the abyss. . . . Like triumphant conquerors the granite cliffs lifted their heads with their jagged crowns, protecting the valley, until the sun took it into her maternal bosom and embracing it with her beams as with glowing arms, tended it and warmed it."

Then hundreds of seeds (Keime) slumbering in the barren sand awoke from deep sleep and burst into bloom:

"But in the midst of the valley was a black hill which rose and fell like a human breast when it swells with ardent longing. Out of the chasms vapors rolled upwards, and gathering together into mighty masses, they strove as foes to veil the face of the mother [the sun]. But she called upon the storm which rushed into the midst of them, dispersing them, and as the pure beam rested again upon the black hill, then in might of ecstasy a glorious lily broke forth, opening its fair petals like lovely lips to receive the mother's sweet kisses."[5]

Now the splendid youth Phosphorus enters the valley and awakens a passionate love in the breast of the lily. The youth promises to return her passion, warning her, however, that the spark which he communicates to her the spark is thought—will enkindle in her the highest bliss, but the highest bliss is hopeless pain, in which she will pass away, to bud anew in an alien form; the longing that fills her will tease and torture her. She scorns his warning, and Phosphorus kisses her; and as if permeated with light the lily bursts into flames out of which an alien being comes forth to roam through endless space. The youth Phosphorus bemoans his loss, for it was really an infinite love for the lily that brought him into the lonely valley. Out of the womb of a granite cliff emerges a black-winged dragon, which seizes the new being born of the lily, bears it to the hilltop, and enfolds it in his pinions. It becomes a lily again, yet retaining both the "thought" which tears its inmost soul asunder and the torturing love for the youth Phosphorus. Clad in gleaming armor Phosphorus conquers the dragon and frees the lily, which he embraces in glow of heavenly love. The flowers, the birds, even the granite cliffs, pay homage to the lily as the queen of the valley.

The unimaginative citizens of Dresden gathered about the table regard the story as a piece of "Oriental bombast" and ask for something "real" out of the experiences of the Archivarius on his travels, and they laugh inordinately when he insists that the story is true, that the lily was his great-great-great-grandmother. Only the youth Anselmus feels a mysterious thrill and trembles to the very core of his being. As the Archivarius leaves the café, Heerbrand introduces Anselmus as the young man proposed for his assistant, but the Archivarius simply nods and hastens away.

The episode of the three green snakes fills the waking and sleeping

[5] "Der Geist schaute auf das Wasser, da bewegte es sich und brauste in schäumenden Wogen, und stürzte sich donnernd in die Abgründe, die ihre schwarzen Rachen aufsperrten, es gierig zu verschlingen. Wie triumphierende Sieger hoben die Granitfelsen ihre zackicht gekrönten Häupter empor, das Tal schützend, bis es die Sonne in ihren mütterlichen Schoss nahm und es umfassend mit ihren Strahlen wie mit glühenden Armen pflegte und wärmte. . . . Aber in der Mitte des Tals war ein schwarzer Hügel, der hob sich auf und nieder wie die Brust des Menschen, wenn glühende Sehnsucht sie schwellt.—Aus den Abgründen rollten die Dünste empor, und sich zusammenballend in gewaltige Massen, strebten sie das Angesicht der Mutter feindlich zu verhüllen; die rief aber den Sturm herbei, der fuhr zerstäubend unter sie, und als der reine Strahl wieder den schwarzen Hügel berührte, da brach im Übermass des Entzückens eine herrliche Feuerlilie hervor, die schönen Blätter wie holdselige Lippen öffnend, der Mutter süsse Küsse zu empfangen." I, p. 189.

hours of the distracted student, and he wanders about in a kind of daze. Again under the lilac tree he sees distinctly the longing blue eyes fixed upon him and, grasping the trunk of the tree, he shouts his love for the little green serpent, but on that day, and day after day, there is silence in the lilac tree. But eventually the Archivarius appears there and addresses him in a gruff voice which Anselmus recognizes as the one at whose bidding the serpents left the tree. Anselmus is heartened by the attitude of the Archivarius toward him and explains the unhappy incident which had prevented him from further application for the position as copyist, and also the subsequent experiences under the lilac tree. The Archivarius replies in a matter of fact tone: "Yes, she [the old apple woman] is one of my chief enemies, but I had no idea she was the door knocker"; equally casually he explains that the three green-gold serpents are his daughters who had been celebrating the holiday in the lilac tree. Through a magic mirror which the Archivarius constructs out of beams of light streaming from a stone in a finger ring, Anselmus beholds the three serpents again, one of them gazing upon him with longing eyes of deep blue. Crying, "O Serpentina, O Serpentina," Anselmus is beside himself with lover's ardor. An engagement is made for him to begin work the next day.

Day by day now Anselmus is busy with the manuscripts of the Archivarius. The room in which he labors is of immense size. The walls are of palm-tree trunks; palms with gold-bronze stems and great leaves like sparkling emeralds and other tropical plants are growing there, among which strange tropical birds fly about and make music. Anselmus copies the manuscripts almost without effort, however intricate the script; it is as if some magic power were working through him. In ever-increasing ecstasy he sees the youngest daughter Serpentina. One day in shimmering garments she winds down in graceful turns from a palm tree and assumes the form of a young woman of surpassing beauty. She sits on the chair beside him and places her arm around his waist, but in his effort to return the caress his arm constantly slips off the strange, smooth texture of her glittering dress. Here she completes the mythic tale which the Archivarius had told in the café, attaching to it the fortunes of her own family. Thus Hoffmann for the first time introduces into his stories the familiar legends of the Elemental Spirits, which had recently achieved a new popularity in fiction through Fouqué's *Undine*, the story of a water sprite.

The Archivarius Lindhorst is really a salamander. Once in the long ago, walking in the lovely garden, he fell in love with the green serpent, the daughter of the lily, and stole her from the lily's calyx, but Phosphorus, the mighty Prince of Spirits in the wonderland Atlantis, who ruled over the Elemental Spirits, warned him against marriage. Yet he disregarded the admonition, and in the moment of his first embrace the loved one turned to ashes, from which a winged being flew away. Wild with grief and rage at his loss, he devastated the fair garden, and for his misconduct he was punished by Phosphorus with banishment from the salamanders, to become a prisoner of the earth spirits, until such time as, purified by longing, he may take on human form, though retaining knowledge of nature's secrets and access to the miraculous powers of kindred spirits. "In a lily bush he found again the green serpent, and the fruit of his union with her was three daughters who appear to human beings in their mother's form." But the Archivarius may return to his brothers in the realm of the salamanders when three youths are found who, enkindled with heavenly longing for the world of wonder, love the three serpent daughters. As dowry for these three daughters, a friendly earth spirit or gnome has provided three diamond-studded golden pots. Old Liese, the apple woman, is the implacable foe of the Archivarius, for she is descended from a feather out of the wing of the hostile dragon in the story earlier related, and her mother was a beet root.

Thus naturally she endeavors to frustrate the plans of the Archivarius for the marriage between Anselmus and Serpentina. This contest constitutes the main elements of the plot. In his sober moments Anselmus is drawn to Veronika, the daughter of the Principal, and is rent asunder by the two conflicting devotions. When in the company of Veronika, who is at least a human being, he cannot believe that in other moments he is possessed by an insensate passion for a serpent. Hoffmann is interested in the fortunes of Anselmus, not in the release of the Archivarius; otherwise there would be two more stories for him to tell.

Veronika is an everyday girl with everyday notions. She fancies herself the wife of Anselmus, when he has become "Hofrat"; she dreams of a dwelling in the Schlossgasse, on the Neumarkt, or in the Moritzstrasse, of fine clothes, and exalted society, but the course of her love seems not to be running smoothly. On the advice of a friend who comes to tea, Veronika seeks a fortuneteller. It is naturally none other than old Liese, who lives in an uncanny little house on the edge of the town. Veronika is not reassured either by the mysterious black cat who guides her into the dwelling or by the appearance of the old hag, with her wiggling, pointed chin, toothless mouth, bony hawk's nose, and gleaming cat's eyes. The room also is filled with strange animals—apes, guinea pigs, and the like—raising a monstrous confusion of meowing, squeaking, croaking, and peeping. Old Liese turns out to be, or claims to have been, a former servant in the family and is minded to be of assistance. She can, however, disclose the future only through a midnight incantation on the eve of the autumn equinox; and Veronika steals forth in the tempest to the crossroads where the ceremony is to take place. Hoffmann builds up here a most entertaining maze of elaborate hocus-pocus—the burning cauldron, the black cat, fire sparkling from the swinging of his tail, and similar more or less traditional phenomena of necromancy. He has already shown his knack at this type of description in *Berganza*. The incantation is interrupted, and no definite conclusions can be drawn, but Liese promises to aid Veronika, and the reader is aware of her personal reasons for doing so.

Finally, when Anselmus promises himself to Veronika—that is, to marry her after he has attained the dignity of "Hofrat"—an overhilarious party is held in the schoolmaster's dwelling. The guests throw the punch tureen and the glasses at the ceiling, and the floor is covered with the fragments. But the punch serves only to enflame the fancy of Anselmus, and the love of Serpentina again possesses him. The last trial now faces him; he is to copy a manuscript of extraordinary difficulty, and for that purpose is taken from his usual place to the azure-blue apartment, where the golden pot sat in glory on a column of porphyry. This time the secret power seems to fail him; the ink will not flow, and a great blot falls on the leaves of the precious manuscript. There is a flash as of bluish lightning; the trunks of the palm trees are turned into great snakes and wind their constricting folds about the poor student, and he loses consciousness. Upon recovering from the swoon, he finds himself in a glass bottle on a shelf in the library, and not alone, for five other bottles have similar occupants, obviously earlier copyists. However, their situation is quite different; they have never really loved Serpentina—a love which now overwhelms Anselmus in an agony of longing. Presently he hears a faint and disagreeable murmur and perceives that the coffeepot in the cupboard opposite gradually assumes the form of the old apple woman, and her black cat crawls out of the inkwell. She stands before him and reviles him; her neighbor, the rat who lives above in the attic, will gnaw the shelf in two and he will fall into her apron, and she will carry him to Mademoiselle

Veronika, whom he must marry. But Anselmus remains steadfast in his love for Serpentina. Soon the Archivarius appears and, aided by a gray parrot, he carries on a fearful struggle with the enemy, each side using to the utmost the fantastic magic arts that they control. Old Liese is defeated and lies now merely an old beet root on the floor. The glass bottle is shattered, and Anselmus falls into the arms of Serpentina. They live happily ever after on the island of Atlantis. Mindful of his obligations as a novelist, Hoffmann does not leave the reader in doubt as to the fate of other characters: the Registrator Heerbrand is awarded the title of "Hofrat," and Veronika becomes his bride.

It is, of course, possible to read *Der goldene Topf* with enjoyment merely as the product of a strangely fertile and eccentric imagination, and Hoffmann himself doubtless enjoyed it merely as that. But it is more than an idle, fantastic tale. Hoffmann has expressed in the story problems that perplexed him, though they are cleverly concealed in a fabric of humorous fancies. Reality and unreality are constantly and inextricably mingled, are indistinguishable: which element of the tale is real and which is fancy? And at the very center of the narrative, Hoffmann places another question which perpetually tortured him: how can a man of unusual gifts accommodate himself to the world of our everyday; how can he remain his real self when the forces of his environment constantly demand conformity at the expense of that higher self? This problem becomes peculiarly acute when it is a question of marriage—ordinary domesticity on the one hand beckoning in the person of the schoolmaster's daughter, and, on the other, the world of dreams in the strange household of the Archivarius. For the man of genius, the man gifted above his fellows, there is no satisfactory abiding place in the world of everyday reality; his only refuge is on the island of Atlantis. Though many of his early readers quite ignored the passage and failed to perceive this thought underlying Hoffmann's ingenious but perhaps preposterous tale, the author himself provided a clue. In the interview at the end of the story the Archivarius says to the author: "Be calm, my good friend, do not lament thus! Were you not yourself just now in Atlantis, and haven't you there at least a nice little farmstead as a poetic possession of your inner mind? After all, is the happiness of Anselmus anything other than life in poetry, to which the sacred harmony of all beings is disclosed as the deepest secret of nature?"

It must not be inferred that Hoffmann conceives the artist's life

as an easy one, that the decision to lead such a life does not involve
a renunciation of much that brings satisfaction. The bourgeois life,
as Hoffmann presents it, is not entirely devoid of dignity or even a
kind of charm; there is security in the quiet pathways of ordinary
living. The appeal of Veronika and all she stands for is genuine,
and Anselmus is legitimately attracted. In the heart of the artist
there is a wistful longing for the life in which he cannot participate
except at the surrender of his real self. Anselmus is a faraway progenitor of Tonio Kröger.

    The myth that Hoffmann has imbedded in the story of Anselmus
was of his own invention, but it expresses ideas that were current in
Romantic days. Parallel to the Biblical story of paradise and the loss
of paradise, the Romanticists played with the poetic conception of a
time when man lived in harmony with all nature, conscious of the
unity of nature, of his kinship with all other concrete manifestations
of divine creative power, and with the benign power itself. This
childlike harmony symbolized by the lily has been lost through
"thought," through the disintegrating forces of man's intellectual
arrogance. After successful combat with the dragon, the prose of
life, or in Hoffmann's day specifically, "Die Aufklärung," this
primeval harmony can be restored through poetry, through faith
and love. Though it may be conceded that Hoffmann found these
ideas in Schubert, that he borrowed from him some of his imagery—
the lily and Phosphorus, for example—the thought was common
property of the Romantic brotherhood, and some years before the
appearance of Schubert's book had been expressed in inimitable
beauty in Klingsohr's Märchen in *Heinrich von Ofterdingen*. The
story of Anselmus is intended to run parallel to the symbolic content
of the myth. The poet soul within him, for a time concealed, buffeted
about in conflict with the "malice of things," the "materia peccans,"
as Hoffmann calls it in the letter to Hippel, attains the cosmic harmony that man has lost; he learns to see in the things of earth the
shimmer of the Divine.[6] Two antipodal worlds seek to control the

---

    [6] Harich's theory that the "Golden Pot" is a symbol for the inheritance that Hoff-
mann expected to receive from the Königsberg relatives seems utterly untenable and
quite unworthy of the deeper meaning underlying the whole Märchen. The myth, as
Hoffmann doubtless intended, allows various interpretations, particularly of the
details, and it is probable that the storyteller invented details simply to embellish
his myth and had for them no symbolism in mind. The simpler interpretation given
above is one that may be most easily applied to the story of Anselmus, but it is
probable that more metaphysical speculations were operative in Hoffmann's mind
when he invented the myth. G. Egli (*E. T. A. Hoffmann: Ewigkeit und Endlichkeit
in seinem Werk*, Chapter 4) regards the myth as an embodiment of ideas derived
from Schelling's philosophy of nature, expressed in part in symbols taken from

hero and govern his life, the one represented by the Archivarius and the other by old Liese, the hostile principle.

The second Märchen *Klein Zaches genannt Zinnober* (Little Zaches Called Cinnabar) was written during the summer of 1818 and appeared in January of the following year. It is probable that the general conception of the story dates from the time of a serious illness in the spring, when the enforced absence from Hoffmann's judicial duties gave leisure for reflection and for the incubation of deeper projects than the fabrication of stories for the annuals. It is not necessary to assume a relation of cause and effect between illness as such and the development of the creative imagination.

In *Klein Zaches* more than in any other of his tales Hoffmann speeds his satirical shafts openly and directly against several objects of his distaste. Interwoven with the substance of the story is constant ridicule of the "Aufklärung," the Age of Enlightenment. It should be remembered that in Hoffmann's day the word "Aufklärung" was not a term found almost exclusively in textbooks of history and literature, but was bandied about in familiar conversation, not yet embalmed in learned treatises. The conflict that the word suggested was still in vivid remembrance, indeed in certain quarters was still going on.

The tiny principality in which the events of the story take place had once been an Arcadian paradise; surrounded by lofty mountains, with its fragrant forests, its flowery meadows, and merrily splashing fountains, it resembled a glorious garden where the people wandered as if for mere pleasure, free from life's burdens. Everyone knew that Prince Demetrius was the ruler, but no one was aware of any ruling.

Schubert: that is, the identity of nature and spirit, both a part of God or the Divine Absolute; since imperfect nature, and man as a part of nature, are divine, then to that extent God is imperfect and incomplete. But as nature develops from a lower form to a higher—a dimly recognized process of evolution—God approaches the divine completeness. The lily then represents the spark of the eternal spirit that is immanent in all created things, and fosters in them a longing for a development into more perfect forms; and Phosphorus is the force that activates this longing for a higher existence in the lower forms of life, destroys them by transforming them into a higher form. Death is at the same time a new birth. Thus a new being comes forth from the lily as its petals fade; the vegetable form of life becomes animal, symbolized by the green serpent. The dragon is the power of evil in a dualistic world, which excites the sensual appetites and binds to earth the being born of the lily. Sin thus temporarily checks the upward movement, but is still essential to the process of development, for the rise of man as an animal to man as a perfected being, since only through sin does man become conscious of the separation from the immanent spiritual ideal, and thus longing is again engendered to attain the higher form. And Phosphorus continues as the activating power until the dragon is conquered and bound. Cf. also F. Strich, *Die Mythologie in der deutschen Literatur von Klopstock bis Wagner*, Halle (1910), II, pp. 302-6; and Schenck, *op. cit.*, pp. 410-24.

These advantages had induced many excellent fairies to settle there, and in almost every village, and especially in the forests, pleasant marvels were constantly occurring.

But Prince Demetrius died, and Prince Paphnutius reigned in his stead. Paphnutius resolves really to rule. Once when he had mislaid his pocketbook, he had borrowed six ducats from his valet, and now in reminiscent gratitude he raises the valet to the rank of Prime Minister. The valet is a thoroughgoing rationalist and, falling at the feet of the Prince, he begs his lord to end the chaos prevailing in the principality and introduce the "Aufklärung."[7] The Prince is much moved and is about to issue an edict to be placarded throughout the realm, announcing that from this moment on the "Aufklärung" has been introduced. But the new Prime Minister interposes. Of course by the introduction of the new order, the forests will have to be cut down, the rivers made navigable, potatoes planted, the village schools improved, acacia and poplar trees set out, the youth taught to sing morning and evening songs in two voices, highways laid out, and vaccination introduced—yet certain matters must be attended to first. All people who cherish dangerous opinions and pay no heed to reason must be banished from the realm, especially the fairies. They are the enemies of the Enlightenment and are largely responsible for the almost complete darkness that prevails in the land; they carry on a pernicious trade in the miraculous and do not hesitate to spread among the people a secret poison in the name of poetry. They must be sent back to their homeland of Dschinnistan. To temper the indignation of the people who are fond of them, it is decided to leave a few of the fairies behind, but to rob them of all power to become harmful to the Enlightenment, to put some of them to a useful occupation, such as knitting socks for the army. And yet it was not possible to eliminate all "marvels"; as Balthasar, the student poet, Hoffmann's counterhero, remarks: "The loftiest, most glorious trees still spring up from wretched little seeds, and the most manifold fruits still grow, the flowers and the insects still wear the most glittering colors, even the most wonderful of written characters, though no one can read them or imitate them." Conditions are not changed in the little principality when Prince Barsanuph ascends the throne.

In the person of Mosch Terpin, Professor of Natural Science at the University of Kerepes, Hoffmann satirizes the soulless, experimental scientist, who has no interest or intelligence beyond the

---

[7] This scene is quite probably a good-humored parody of the interview between King Philip of Spain and Marquis Posa in Schiller's *Don Carlos.*

results of mathematical measurements. The Professor could explain "how it rains, thunders, lightens, why the sun shines by day and the moon by night, how and why the grass grows, and so on, so that every child could not help comprehending." All nature he had compressed together into a neat little compendium that he could have ready at hand and pull out of it the answer to any question, as out of a drawer. His reputation was first established by his proving after many physical experiments that darkness resulted primarily from lack of light. After his daughter has become the betrothed of Klein Zaches, now Prime Minister, he obtains the permission to carry on experiments in the princely wine cellars to show why wine tastes different from water and has other effects.

In the Order of the Green-Spotted Tiger Hoffmann ridicules the German love of titles and external baubles of distinction. This Order is invented as a special honor to Klein Zaches; it is graded in accordance with the number of buttons, so that Klein Zaches as the head of the Order is to wear the insignia of the Green-Spotted Tiger with Twenty-two Buttons. How to attach the elaborate insignia to the strangely misshapen body of the Prime Minister presents a problem. A council of the Order, with the assistance of two philosophers and a natural scientist who has recently returned from the North Pole (a sly reference to Chamisso), is convened to discuss the matter, and a thick bed of straw is strewn before the building in order that the rattle of vehicles should not disturb the deliberations. Elsewhere in the story the author ridicules the chauvinistic nationalism which developed in Prussia early in the nineteenth century, partly under the leadership of "Father Jahn." In the curious punishment that the magician metes out to the student Fabian for his persistent incredulity, Hoffmann touches satirically upon the problem of religious sects and the suppression of them.

Klein Zaches is a grotesquely ugly, idiotic dwarf child: "One might have taken him at first for a gnarled piece of wood; his head was set down between his shoulders, and in place of a back there was a pumpkinlike projection; directly beneath his breast hung two little legs as thin as hazel twigs, so that he looked like a split radish." At the beginning of the story his mother, a peasant woman, lies exhausted by the roadside, and her incredible offspring, crawling out of the basket in which she has been gathering faggots, mutters and meows like a cat on the edge of the path. A good fairy, Rosabelverde, one of the few left in the realm, happens to pass that way and is filled with compassion. Through exercise of her magic arts a strange but priceless boon is conferred upon the hideous little idiot: everything that is praiseworthy or is praised in his presence is attributed to him. He becomes, or rather seems to become, a child of extraordinary beauty and intelligence because he takes on the form and the character of the pastor's little boy. At a concert he is overwhelmed by the plaudits of the audience in view of his amazing virtuosity on the violin; he is credited with the authorship of a poem which Balthasar reads at a literary tea; he takes the oral examinations for a position in the administration of the principality, and, though his answers are only grunts and meows, he is given the position over his rival, whose answers have, of course, been attributed to him. He rises to the position of Prime Minister. On one occasion the author allows this fairy gift to take a strangely comic turn: the local zoo has recently secured a peculiarly excellent specimen of the ape; Zaches arrives in all his grandeur as Minister of State to inspect the new acquisition, but the visitors all crowd around him, commenting on the fine qualities of this representative of the monkey tribe. It seems doubtful, however, that Hoffmann planned, as has been suggested, to make Klein Zaches, to whom, really undeserving, all things are granted, as the antithesis of Anselmus, with whom things usually went awry.

After a period of tutelage at the home of a pastor, Zaches rides to the university town of Kerepes to begin his studies. On the way he encounters two students, Balthasar and Fabian. The role of the former runs in part parallel with that of Anselmus in *Der goldene Topf*. While Anselmus had a poet's soul, he was as yet largely unaware of his gift, but Balthasar is already a poet; he loves "Waldeinsamkeit"—that word of Tieck's debatable coinage—to wander in the forest, and surrender to his dreams; and he is desperately in love with the fair Candida, daughter of Mosch Terpin, the physicist. His friend Fabian is a skeptical rationalist, and he tries to wean Balthasar from his moody dreaming to a practical view of life. While Balthasar sees wonder everywhere, Fabian has a material explanation for all mysterious phenomena. The chariot of the magician Prosper Alpanus seems to Balthasar to be a crystal mussel shell drawn by two unicorns in golden harness and guided by a silver pheasant. Behind, as footman, sits a gold beetle with shining wings; the movement of the carriage spreads sweet music through the air. Fabian sees only a farcical mummery, a carriage painted with silver paint, horns absurdly fastened on the heads of two horses; the gold beetle is merely a sunshade, and a hand organ has been attached to the wheels. Balthasar and Fabian visit the magician on his country estate. And, as they walk up the tree-shaded path toward the house, Fabian asks scornfully whether his companion sees anything unusual or magical: to Balthasar the very trees seem to belong to some "strange unknown land" and the two unicorns are grazing on the lawn. They are met at the door by an ostrich as butler or porter, and a bite on Fabian's finger temporarily shakes his incredulity.

The extraordinary rise of Klein Zaches to highest honors arouses resentment among his rivals, those whose excellencies he has appropriated. Obviously some magic power is at work. It is with a view to probing the mystery that the two students visit Prosper Alpanus. The magician leads them into the library and takes down one after another of the great folio volumes containing pictures of all the different "Alraunen" (Wurzelmänner), earth-spirits (gnomes), and the like. As he touches the pages the "gnome" pictured there springs out of the book and pirouettes about on the marble table. The young men recognize no one of them as Zaches. The magician is positive that he cannot be the king of the beetles, or the spider marshal, and proposes an experiment to determine his identity. He takes his guests through many extraordinary apartments, where strange animals are reading, writing, painting, and dancing, to an egg-shaped room in semidarkness. There Prosper Alpanus produces a magic mirror which discloses Klein Zaches and Candida in a lover's kiss. At the bidding of the magician, Balthasar gives the mirrored Zaches a stout blow with a stick, and he sees his rival tumble and roll over on the floor. The magician perceives that Zaches is a human being exercising power under some magic spell. Two other victims of Zaches's ascendancy spy upon him in a garden by his house and see the fairy Rosabelverde combing his hair, thus renewing the potency of the three fiery red hairs in which apparently the magic power is seated.[8]

The benevolent fairy becomes aware of danger approaching her protégé and she visits Prosper Alpanus to intercede. The contest which follows is a most entertaining example of Hoffmann's exuberant fancy. The magician is finally victorious and Rosabelverde must submit to his decisions. He gives directions to the young conspira-

---

[8] Schenck and others interpret the magic powers of Rosabelverde as analogous to mesmerism. Hoffmann is, however, telling a fairy tale—in his own way to be sure—and this explanation of his intent would seem to violate the fairy-tale elements on which he bases the action. His art is decidedly the loser through such banal interpretation. For Walzel's theory that *Klein Zaches* was conceived as the reverse of Chamisso's *Peter Schlemihl*, cf. *Das literarische Echo*, 1911, xiii, p. 1239.

tors; at the very betrothal festival of Klein Zaches and Candida they seize Zaches and tear out the magic hairs; the charm is broken, and all now see only a grotesque little figure rushing from the room. The people of the town are likewise released from the spell and gather in rage about the palace where Zaches has taken refuge. In terror he runs from room to room, finally falling into a silver pot, where he is drowned. And yet the kind magician permits a last deception; in death the little impostor appears in all his false glory, and the populace weep at his bier. The peasant woman who was his mother is granted the perpetual privilege of supplying onions for the table of the Prince.

The experiment of the kind fairy has miscarried. She stands beside the dead body of this "stepchild of nature" and acknowledges her failure. She had hoped and believed that the fine external gift would send beams of light into his inmost spirit and awaken a voice there to tell him, "You are not what people take you to be, but strive to resemble the one on whose wings, lame and unfeathered, you mount up." Yet no inner voice was awakened, no inner transformation took place.

The magician Prosper Alpanus leaves for his faraway home, but in departing gives to Balthasar his estate, for he sees in him a representative of the real world, the world of dreams, to be left behind in the world that seems to be real. "I love youths," he says, "who as you, my dear Balthasar, bear love and longing in pure hearts, in whose inmost soul there still echo those glorious chords which belong to that distant land of wonders, which is my home . . . at times it is as if you understood the murmuring streams, the rustling of the trees, as if the flaming red of sunset spoke to you in comprehensible words! . . . In these moments you really understand the wondrous voices of nature, for out of your own spirit rises the divine tone that is enkindled from the wonderful harmony in the very deepest being of nature."[9] The marriage of Balthasar and Candida takes place at the country estate of the magician, and Rosabelverde provides a magic wedding gift which will banish forever all the ordinary and trivial cares of a domestic establishment.

[9] " 'Ich liebe' fuhr Prosper Alpanus fort, 'ich liebe Jünglinge, die so wie du, mein Balthasar, Sehnsucht und Liebe im reinen Herzen tragen, in deren Innerm noch jene herrlichen Accorde wiederhallen, die dem fernen Lande voll göttlicher Wunder angehören, das meine Heimat ist . . . dir ist es zuweilen so, als verstündest du die murmelnden Quellen, die rauschenden Bäume, ja als spräche das aufflammende Abendrot zu dir mit verständlichen Worten! . . . In diesen Momenten verstehst du wirklich die wunderbaren Stimmen der Natur, denn aus deinem eignen Innern erhebt sich der göttliche Ton, den die wundervolle Harmonie des tiefsten Wesens der Natur entzündet.' " v, p. 74.

In a letter to Hippel, Hoffmann called *Klein Zaches* "the most humorous" of his stories hitherto, and in sending a copy to Graf Pückler, "the product of a somewhat frolicsome semi-ironical fancy." But he added that it came into being from an inner necessity, indeed almost a physical necessity, and it is as little concerned with allegorical thinking as it makes use of literary models. A year later, in the preface to *Prinzessin Brambilla* he speaks of *Klein Zaches* as a "free, loosely wrought execution of a jocose idea." In this whimsical and fanciful tale Hoffmann, despite the disclaimer in the letter to Pückler, asks in essence several closely related questions, but finds no answer for them: Is seeming in the end identical with being? Is it possible with human eyes to distinguish between them? Is "seeming" after all the only reality, and a sham reality at that? Does external performance—what the world sees—ever really correspond to the spirit that produces it; is it in any way commensurate with it? Hoffmann was acutely conscious that in his own work, for example in music, he only remotely approximated the divine vision that shone within him. His inclusion of "physical necessity" in his letter to Pückler supports the opinion that in the grotesqueness of Klein Zaches he has incorporated something of his sensitiveness as to his own person. The theme of "seeming" and "being" was constantly occupying Hoffmann's thought. On quite a different plane he reverts to the idea in a much later story, *Der Zusammenhang der Dinge*; here he presents two contrasting heroes, but neither is really what he appears to be. Similarly *Der Musikfeind* is looked upon as an "enemy of music," though he is really the most musical of all.

A year after *Klein Zaches*, the third of the major Märchen was published, *Prinzessin Brambilla*. On the title page Hoffmann adds, "Ein Capriccio nach Jakob Callot," and in the preface begs the reader not "to lose the fantastic caricatures of Callot from sight," for they form the basis of the whole story. A portfolio of Callot's engravings had been given to Hoffmann by Dr. Koreff as a birthday present, January 1820, and they doubtless suggested the carnival background out of which Hoffmann ere long began to write his Märchen. Eight of the engravings were published with *Prinzessin Brambilla.*

Hoffmann's story is one of the most baffling, most subtly intriguing, products of the creative imagination. If one eliminates or discounts all the apparently supernatural elements in the tale, the story still remains an amazing account of an eccentric and wealthy Roman nobleman, Prince Bastianello di Pistoja, who concocts a scheme to

reanimate the contemporary theater. To his aid he calls in a certain
Celionati, a peddler of curious wares and a reputed necromancer—
or perhaps Celionati is merely the Prince himself in disguise. He
uses the Shrovetide festival, with its processions of masks, its street
dances, and the accompanying spirit of frivolity and unbridled merriment, as an appropriate background for his experiment. The stilted
and bombastic tragedy, represented by the plays of the Abbate
Chiari[10] and performed with exaggerated histrionics, is to be replaced by dramas of lighthearted humor; the traditional figures of
the "Commedia dell' Arte" are to be restored to the stage, and,
though gay and frolicsome, the new drama is not to be without deeper
meaning. Hoffmann is thus dramatizing the rise of Gozzi as the
regenerator of the Italian theater. He parodies this artificial tragedy
in passages from a new play by Chiari, "The White Moor," and the
contemporary school of acting in the stilted declamation, the strut-
ting and posing, the wild gestures, of the actor Giglio Fava. It is,
however, this very actor who is to be converted to the new type of
drama, and an actress, worthy of the regenerated drama, is to be
found in Giacinta, the little dressmaker, fabricator of carnival costumes, with whom Giglio is in love.

But the elimination of the supernatural is not so easy. One can, to
be sure, explain as an elaborate but calculated hocus-pocus the great
procession that enters the palace of Prince Bastianello, and the later
adventures of Giglio in the palace; the twelve snow-white unicorns,
riders with the feet of birds, the ostriches which turn the pages of
the monstrous folio with their beaks, as the old magician reads part
of the intercalated Märchen of the Lake of Urdar. At the time of
the procession Celionati explains to the crowd on the street that it
is the Princess Brambilla, great-granddaughter of King Cophetua,
who has come to Rome to seek her betrothed, the Assyrian Prince,
Cornelio Chiapperi; the Prince himself had arrived in Rome to have
a molar tooth extracted, but in some way or another has got lost.
Celionati urges the populace to look for him in their rooms, kitchens,
cellars, wardrobes, and bureau drawers. All this is, of course, quite
in the merry spirit of the carnival. Giglio, masked, meets Pantalon on
the Corso, none other than the missing Assyrian Prince; a duel ensues, and Giglio falls, but when his body is carried off it is found
to be merely a pasteboard figure filled with grandiose lines from the

[10] Hoffmann does not directly identify his Abbate Chiari with Gozzi's opponent;
he says: "Vielleicht ein Vorfahr des berühmten Chiari, der in Fehde trat mit dem
Grafen Gozzi und die Waffen strecken musste." xi, p. 56.

dramas of the Abbate Chiari—this, obviously a simple allegory: the actor who has mistaken the nature of his talents is dead, and his real self is now available for the resurgence of a significant drama. The story, or rather a part of it, thus interpreted and shorn of its mysterious elements, would still remain a brilliant, effervescent product of Hoffmann's imagination.

But the patriotic plan of Prince Bastianello di Pistoja for the betterment of the Roman stage is only a part of Hoffmann's tale, and Hoffmann plainly never intended a purely material solution of the events of the story as clever manipulations of a carnival masquerade. Much unquestionably remains that is incapable of any rational explanation. By what magic does Giglio fancy that the exalted Princess is in love with him, or that he has been transformed into the Assyrian Prince? And how is Giacinta, the simple dressmaker, sewing night and day on carnival costumes ordered by Signor Bescapi, the merchant of costumes, convinced that the Prince is her lover? Giglio has had various adventures in which Giacinta has played a part, but after some days he finds her in the same old room, up numberless flights, and now upbraiding him for his long absence; she has not seen him for days. Is the purse that Giglio finds in his pocket, well filled, really akin to the inexhaustible purse of Fortunatus, or has the crafty Celionati by some sleight of hand merely "practiced it" into his possession? And has the identical purse of Giacinta come from the same source? The magic spectacle which makes the walls of the palace transparent crystal to the eyes of Giglio; the gilded bird cage into which Giglio is thrust, like the glass jars in *Der goldene Topf*—all this cannot easily be interpreted as mere carnival tricks.

Hoffmann really employs the merrymaking of Shrovetide when in Rome all are masked, or may be masked, to raise again his ever-recurring questions as to the reality of experience: are not all men really phantoms, deceiving one another and themselves indeed with ever-changing masks? "Do you really know," says Celionati to the German artists gathered in the tavern, "that I am sitting here among you?" Both Giglio and Giacinta become uncertain as to their own identity and temporarily lead lives governed by the delusion. One may assume, to be sure, that the two conspirators—or the two in one, if Celionati is the Prince—have invented the Princess Brambilla and the Prince Cornelio Chiapperi for their own purposes, but the two phantoms take on a life of their own and play a part outside the will of their creators. Celionati remarks that Giglio is suffering from "chronic dualism," and illustrates the idea by narrating an extreme case: twin princes, joined together after the fashion of the famous Siamese pair, in whom the nature of the one seemed to pass over into the other in constant alternation; their thoughts ran cross-wise, and neither really knew whether what he had thought was actually his own thinking or that of his twin.

When Giglio is first convinced that he is the Assyrian Prince, and is dancing with the Princess, the author remarks that any capable philosopher could explain the matter so that schoolboys in next to the lowest form could not help understanding this experiment of the inner spirit; and he calls attention to an anecdote in Mauchart's *Repetorium of Empirical Psychology*: a Würtemberg official fell downstairs, drunk, and then expressed sympathy for his secretary that he, the secretary, had had such a hard fall.

The idea, clothed in Fichtean language, is expressed in the mystic chorus of the net-weaving ladies around the magician Ruffiamonte: the verses are in *terza rima*, but here translated in prose:

"Who is the Ego which can give birth to the Non-Ego out of the Ego, can split apart its own breast. . . ?"

And in a later chapter the magician reads the answer out of the magic book, again in *terza rima*:

"Italy! land whose cheerful, sunny heaven enkindles the joy of earth in abundant bloom! O Rome the fair, where merry tumult releases at carnival time, time of masks, the serious from the serious! Joyfully the forms of fancy create illusions upon the many-colored stage, little, rounded to egg-form; that is the world, the rule of graceful apparitions. The spirit can out of the Ego give birth to the Non-Ego, can split apart its own breast."[11]

The inner Märchen, "the Story of King Ophioch and Queen Liris" is related in part by Cclionati and is continued later in more

---

[11] (1) Wo mag die Macht anmut'gen Spukes walten?
          Wer ist der Ich, der aus dem Ich gebären
          Das Nicht-Ich kann, die eigne Brust zerspalten?   (xi, p. 82.)

       (2) Italien!—Land, dess heitrer Sonnenhimmel
            Der Erde Lust in reicher Blüt' entzündet!
            O schönes Rom, wo lustiges Getümmel,

            Zur Maskenzeit, den Ernst vom Ernst entbindet!
            Es gaukeln froh der Fantasei Gestalten
            Auf bunter Bühne klein zum Ei gerundet;

            Das ist die Welt, anmut'gen Spukes Walten.
            Der Genius mag aus dem Ich gebären
            Das Nicht-Ich, mag die eigne Brust zerspalten. (xi, pp. 112-13.)

fragmentary form by extracts read aloud by the magician in the
Pistoja palace. Hoffmann assures the reader that it is not a negligible episode; it is only apparently a bypath, for it leads directly to
the core of the whole story. King Ophioch is filled with melancholy;
he has lost the harmony of his being with the world of forest and
fountains, and his queen, though perpetually in senseless laughter,
cannot cheer him. His real malady is explained by the Magus Her-
mod, somewhat cryptically: "Thought destroys perception, but a new
perception is born, the foetus of thought, from the prismatic crystal which has been formed in the marriage conflict of the fiery flood
and the hostile poison." Through the magic arts of this magician the
Lake of Urdar comes into being, and in the mirrored surface of the
lake, reflecting nature roundabout, the king and queen recognize
themselves. But the end of the Märchen is not yet. Through the
machinations of an evil magician, the Lake of Urdar dries up and
disappears, and then is restored through the counteraction of the
real magician. As the king and queen behold in the magic mirror of
the lake themselves, their real selves in their relationships to nature,
so have Giglio and Giacinta looked upon the surface of the lake,
and seen themselves—they have become the chief representatives
of the new Roman stage, an allegory that needs no explanation: in
the widest significance of the term, the Lake of Urdar is the life-
giving sense of humor.

Die Königsbraut (The King's Betrothed, 1821) differs markedly
from the other Märchen. The others were constructed in such a
fashion as to bear the burden of Hoffmann's serious thought, and
carry it easily; one could even read them without becoming aware
of any meaning beneath the surface of the narrative, but *Die Königsbraut* runs its blithesome course without any real burden at all.
There is no symbolic myth as a somewhat puzzling point of reference. The story is indeed a remarkably entertaining and sustained
bit of persiflage. The ironical tone is not employed occasionally for
special effect but pervades the whole narrative; the type of irony,
even, at times, the diction, remind one of Tieck's satirical comedies.
The droll supernaturalism is conceived in a jesting mood and presented with amused detachment; no touch of the serious, as in the
other Märchen, underlies the waggery.

In the other Märchen the magician or the supernatural agent is
an impressive figure, however bizarre certain aspects of his appearance may be, and he serves to introduce the hero to a world of
spiritual significance. But in *Die Königsbraut* Herr Dapsul von

Zabelthau, who works day and night in the astrological tower, is really a bungler; his dabbling in cabalistic science, the casting of horoscopes, his attempts to control the course of events by magic arts, never quite succeed. He is repeatedly deceived and defeated by the Gnome-King, who pretends to be the Vegetable-King, Daucus Carota the First, and eventually turns the would-be magician into a mushroom. Herr Dapsul is one of the most delightfully comic characters in Hoffmann's gallery; other magicians are indeed presented humorously and in comic situations—for example, Swammerdamm and Loewenhöck in their duel with telescopes—but an element of the awesome still clings to them. There is nothing of this in the case of Herr Dapsul; although he is learned in Oriental languages and refers glibly to Paracelsus, Mirandola, Thomas Aquinas, Cassiodorus Remus, and the like, as a magician he is half quack. At the outset Hoffmann stamps his activities as a dealer in the small wares of mystery. With fine irony Hoffmann assigns interminable speeches to Herr Dapsul, rambling and incoherent, in which, for example, he displays his knowledge of the elemental spirits, of their desire to wed with humans, of the various subdivisions among the gnomes, and even of the sylph who with perplexing reticence has been in love with him for years. These speeches are delightful nonsense. Ännchen, his daughter, though of noble lineage, as the family name implies, is a buxom peasant lass, whose supreme passion is her vegetable garden, in which she herself wields a valiant spade—"even malicious envy must grant her that." To her betrothed, Amandus von Nebelstern, a university student, she writes childish missives with three or four postscripts. While pulling up a carrot in the garden, she finds a splendid topaz ring through which the root has grown. This begins the complication of the little plot; once upon her finger it cannot be filed off and binds her as the bride of the Gnome-King.

In Amandus, Hoffmann supplies a neat parody of his other heroes. Amandus fancies himself a poetic genius and writes grandiloquently of his lofty calling, but the specimens of his work that Hoffmann craftily inserts offer proof of Amandus' fundamental error. His poetical accomplishments are, however, effective in conquering his rival, the Gnome-King. Herr von Zabelthau tries with his magic arts to break the spell that the Gnome-King exercises, but he falls a victim to the superior magicianship of his foe. Amandus, however, needs merely to sing to the accompaniment of a guitar one of the twelve dozen poems he has written and composed, and the offending rival begins to writhe, groan, and whine, as if he had a fearful pain in his stomach; during the singing he becomes smaller and smaller, turns into a tiny carrot, and vanishes into the earth, and from the story. After her dreams of queenly glory are at an end through the unmasking of the pretender, Ännchen returns to the vegetable garden with renewed enthusiasm. "Now let's get to work," she exclaims, seizes the spade from the hand of the maidservant, and swings it in the air, accidentally striking Amandus on the head, "precisely where the 'Sensorium commune' is supposed to lie." This has the fortunate effect of awakening Amandus to the foolishness of his poetic ambitions; he buries himself in the works of the really great poets of ancient and more recent times and is so filled with a beneficial exaltation that there is no place left for his own "Ich." He arrives at the conviction that a poem must be something quite different from the confused "rubbish of words" which a solemn delirium had in his case brought to the light of day. In other words, he has become a sensible youth.

Die Königsbraut is extraordinarily rich in delicately woven and intricate fancies. Hoffmann's curious and fertile imagination has nowhere surpassed such superb phantasies as the arrival of the Gnome-King and his train, or the dance of the multitudinous little people—sometimes on their heads, sometimes on their feet, in the most graceful trochees, iambics, pyrrhics, anapaests, tribrachs, bacchics, antibacchics, choriambs, and dactyls. In the use of curious names for his personages—in which Hoffmann was ever a past master—here he quite surpasses himself; to names already mentioned one may add: Baron Porphyrio von Ockerodates, the incognito designation for the Gnome-King, the chief retainers of King Daucus Carota the First—Pan Kapustowicz from Poland, Herr Schwarzrettich from Pomerania, Signor di Broccoli from Italy, and Monsieur de Roccambolle from France—or the grandees of the fictitious Vegetable Kingdom, gathered around the throne—"die Salatprinzen mit den Bohnenprinzessinnen, die Gurkenherzoge mit dem Melonenfürsten, . . . die Kopfkohlminister, die Zwiebel- und Rübengeneralität, die Federkohldamen," all in the most resplendent garments of their rank and station.

Die Königsbraut was one of the few stories written directly for inclusion in *Die Serapionsbrüder* and as such was assigned to one of the group at the time when the story was written. It is presented as the work of Vinzenz-Koreff, and the figure of Amandus, the would-be poet, may well be a sly caricature of Koreff himself in his poetic endeavors.[12]

Hoffmann's agreement with Fouqué and Contessa to publish a volume of children's stories, "Kindermärchen," for the Christmas trade would seem to force upon him some modification of material and style to conform to the general purpose. Of this necessity Hoffmann himself was perhaps not thoroughly convinced. Even *Der goldene Topf* he regarded as suitable reading for youngsters, as he wrote to Hippel: "Your children must read the Märchen, even the younger ones; although children cannot possibly grasp the underlying thought, I have found out that their imagination is stirred by many of the scenes." Hoffmann's daughter Cäcilie was not yet two years old when he parted from her forever, and his love of children could find its satisfaction only in the children of his friends. To the children of Hitzig he was a beloved "uncle"; one Christmas he fabricated for them a splendid castle of pasteboard, the Burg Ringstetten in *Undine*, and cleverly arranged a lighting system within. Doubtless Hoffmann wrote his two Kindermärchen with Hitzig's children in mind, though unquestionably at times in the stories he lost them from sight. It will be remembered that Chamisso wrote, or said he wrote, the story of Peter Schlemihl, the man who sells his shadow to the devil, for the amusement of these same children. The two stories which had appeared in the successive volumes of the Kindermärchen in 1818 and 1819 were later taken up in the *Serapionsbrüder*, where they were both assigned to Lothar. After the first story has been read, Theodor raises the question whether it is really a Kindermärchen at all; children might take pleasure in individual details, but would be quite incapable of perceiving the fine threads that run through the whole and bind the apparently heterogeneous material together. Lothar defends his Märchen: it is a grave error to underestimate the capacities of intelligent children and put before them such nonsense as is found in many so-called Märchen; he has tested the little tale before competent judges—his sister's children—and is assured of its validity as a Kindermärchen. Did Hoffmann perhaps try the story out on Hitzig's children?

In *Nussknacker und Mausekönig* Hoffmann followed the beaten

---

[12] Specimens of Dr. Koreff's verse may be inspected in the work of Friedrich von Oppeln-Bronikowski: *David Ferdinand Koreff, Serapionsbruder, Magnetiseur, Geheimrat und Dichter*, Berlin und Leipzig, 1928. Maassen thinks that Hoffmann is satirizing the "brainless rhymsters of the time" without reference to an individual, though the name Amandus von Nebelstern is probably a parody of "Arthur von Nordstern," the pen name of G. A. E. von Nostitz und Jänckendorf.

pathway which many writers of children's stories have trod—toys come to life and play their parts according to the characteristics which the child mind assigns to them. The story begins on Christmas Eve at the house of Medizinalrat Stahlbaum, doubtless a reminiscence of festivals at the Hitzig home. "Uncle" Drosselmeier, with something of Hoffmann in his make-up, arrives, bringing a castle with its artificial lighting and, surpassing the Burg Ringstetten of Hoffmann's manufacture, with figures skillfully manipulated. Hoffmann attaches the plot, however, to another gift, a curious Nutcracker in the form of a grotesque little man with a big head and thin little legs. That very night after all the family are in bed except little Marie, a fierce battle takes place between the forces of the king of the mice, seven-headed with seven crowns, which appear from every nook and cranny in the room, and the children's toys, especially the toy soldiers of little Fritz. The attack is primarily directed against the Nutcracker, who, as it appears later, is really a prince. The famous Prussian general Gneisenau complimented Hoffmann on his skill as a military strategist in the deployment of the different troops, the placing of the batteries—a body of tin soldiers on Mama's footstool. All forces fought valiantly and the outcome was determined only through the external or "providential" interference on the part of Marie's slipper.

The next morning Marie refuses to believe that these happenings were merely a dream. "Uncle" Drosselmeier comes to see the children and begins to narrate the story of Princess Pirlipat and the mouse-queen, joining his tale to the content of Marie's "dream." From this point on, Hoffmann interweaves deftly the events in the household of the Medizinalrat, the dream world of Marie, and the "myth" that "Uncle" Drosselmeier invents. Thus he employs a pattern similar to that of the other type of Märchen.

Much of the tale is composed of "fairy-tale" stuff, charmingly conceived and presented. Often the language of metaphor is cunningly adapted to a child's thought. The children talk to their toys with childlike credulity and Hoffmann has imitated various noises with strange vocables to delight the heart of a child. Plainly also, the imagination that invented the fantastic happenings in *Der goldene Topf* is not at a loss when entering the fairy-tale world of children. To protect little Princess Pirlipat from the vengeful Frau Mausering, queen of the mice, six nurses sit around her bed, each holding a cat, stroking him to insure an uninterrupted purring during the whole night. The king wishes to do appropriate honors for a large body of visiting kings and princes, and with this in view arranges for a great sausage feast. Only the queen herself is capable of preparing the sausage meat; the kettle is of gold, the fire of sandalwood. The queen dons her damask apron, and the king stirs at times in the kettle with his golden scepter. Genuine Märchen material also is the enchantment of the princess, who can be restored to her former beauty only by a young man who has never shaved or worn boots but can with his own teeth crack the nut Krakatuk.

But now and then Hoffmann forgets that he is writing a fairy tale for children. A character exclaims: "O holy instinct of nature, eternally unfathomable sympathy of all beings!" and in company with the court astronomer the same character pores over many books that treat of "sympathy, antipathies, and other mysterious things" —the theories of animal magnetism are buzzing in his brain. In the kingdom of the dolls, Marie asks the Nutcracker what peculiar meaning is attached to the word "confectioner," and he replies that "confectioner" is the name of an unknown but awful power, which, it is believed, can make of a man whatever it wills. The mere mention of the name will quiet the greatest tumult; each one then thinks no more of earthly things, of digs in the ribs and blisters on the head, but meditates and queries: "What is man and what can become of him?" But, as Lothar implies in his defense of his story, it is of no consequence whether or not the child gets the allusion when in the midst of the battle the Nutcracker cries out, "A horse, a horse! my kingdom for a horse!" The exclamation is appropriate in the circumstances. Even though "Uncle" Drosselmeier appears in the purely "human" elements of the story, a friend of the family and the narrator of the intercalated fairy tale, there is something uncanny about him, something supernatural, and little Marie is vaguely conscious of it. Hoffmann is writing a story for children, but he is tempted to tell a quite different tale.

Hoffmann wrote to Kunz that he thought the second "Kindermärchen," *Das fremde Kind* (The Stranger Child), was closer to the type, was "purer and more childlike." It even begins with the familiar formula, "Once upon a time." In the *Serapionsbrüder* Ottmar agrees with Hoffmann's opinion, but remarks that it is still not entirely free from flourishes (Schnörkel), the meaning of which would be beyond the grasp of a child. One suspects that Hoffmann took Tieck's little story *Die Elfen* (The Elves) as his model, though Tieck's Märchen is much simpler and more poetic. The theme is the same: an elf or fairy child becomes for a time the beloved playmate of human children. But Hoffmann makes no use of the familiar motif, employed by Tieck, that such relations are abruptly broken when the pledge of secrecy is violated. In Hoffmann's tale the interruption is brought about by other means. Pepser, the king of the gnomes, had insinuated himself in disguise at the court of the fairy queen, but his identity and his nefarious intrigues are discovered, and he is banished from the realm. As "Magister Tinte," "Master Ink," he becomes tutor to the two children of Herr Brakel auf Brakelsheim, with whom the fairy child has been playing; the "stranger child" appears as a little boy to Felix and as a little girl to Christlieb. Pepser, or Master Ink, is now a bitter enemy of the fairy queen, and the child is in danger if the visits to the children are continued. Some of the details also run in close parallel with those of Tieck's story. Similar imagery is used in the description of fairy land or elf land; and, as in Tieck's tale, contact with the fairy child extends through two generations, for here the father had as a boy seen the "stranger child." The figure of Magister Tinte gives Hoffmann opportunity to exercise his skill in the grotesque, both when Magister Tinte appears as a strangely formed human being and when, metamorphosed into a huge bottle fly, he dives into the milk pan. With charming humor Hoffmann describes the household of the impoverished country nobleman, and the visit of a wealthy and lordly cousin with wife and children provides room for effective satire upon riches and worldly pretensions.

The symbolism of the story seems obvious, and is distinctly reminiscent of both Tieck and Novalis. It is not difficult to perceive in the fairy child a personification of the imagination, as in Tieck's Phantasus poem and in the Klingsohr Märchen of Novalis. The children had always loved the forest, where the birds sang to them, the trees whispered their messages, and the brooks murmured in almost understandable words; and they were ready for the child to lead them to even more radiant realms. Magister Tinte is the spirit of dry-as-dust rationalism; he keeps the children in the dull and stuffy "indoors," reciting empty words; he is first cousin to the "Schreiber" in Klingsohr's Märchen.

The harrowing circumstances attending the publication of *Meister Floh* (Master Flea), the last of the Märchen, have already been narrated. The title page reads: *Meister Floh, ein Märchen in sieben Abenteuern zweier Freunde*. It may have been a covert compliment to Wilmans, the Frankfurt publisher, that Hoffmann laid the scene of the story in that city. Even previous to the annoyance over the manuscript of *Meister Floh*, Wilmans had shown himself a patient and forbearing man of business; instead of a peremptory letter complaining of Hoffmann's dilatory habits, he sent an extraordinary reminder in the shape of a case of wine.

Some hints for the character of Peregrinus Tyss, one of the two heroes, Hoffmann may have derived from his friend Clemens Brentano. Like Brentano, Peregrinus was the son of a wealthy merchant in Frankfurt and was intended for a business career, but with sovereign caprice he washed his hands of the one commission that his father entrusted to him—perhaps a reminiscence of Brentano's erratic service in the business house of his father's friend in Langensalza. To the disgust of his tutors he displayed a marked distaste, as did Brentano, for "real systematic learning"; "he did not want to know anything of the real world"; "only the marvellous," what excited his fancy, appealed to him; in this "he lived and moved." When his tutors were endeavoring to teach him about the Hanseatic League, Peregrinus was completely absorbed in China and fancied himself treading the streets of Peking; this is perhaps an intentional parallel to Brentano's dreamland of Vaduz. Like Brentano, Peregrinus attended the University of Jena, though, to be sure, Brentano was enrolled as a student in other universities as well. At the end of Brentano's university days his father could have exclaimed with the words of the father of Peregrinus: "Hans the dreamer went away; Hans the dreamer comes back!" Peregrinus traveled much, even to India, though some contended that his journeys were only in his own imagination. Hoffmann may have had in mind Brentano's second matrimonial venture when he ascribes to Peregrinus the misogynous sentiment that "women simply play with us as a cat with a mouse; for our tender exertions we earn nothing but mockery and scorn."

The enveloping myth is more closely integrated with the main story than in the previous Märchen; indeed, most of the characters are taken from the myth and presented in another, temporary guise. Some of them exhibit a significant gradation in their consciousness of their former personalities. Georg Pepusch, a friend of Peregrinus at the University of Jena, is at times keenly conscious that he is really the Thistle Zeherit.[13] Dörtje Elverdink is in a state of be-

---

[13] Wherever they happened to strike his fancy, Hoffmann took names for his characters from his miscellaneous reading. Cf. Max Voigt: " 'Zeherit' in E. T. A. Hoffmanns 'Meister Floh,' " in *Germanisch-Romanische Monatsschrift*, VI, pp. 353-55. Voigt shows that Hoffmann found names for some of the characters in this Märchen in P. F. Arpe's *De prodigiosis naturae et artis operibus, Talismanes et Amulata dictis*, etc., Hamburg, 1717. He frequently went back in his memory for names: the

wilderment and by no means always sure that she is the Princess Gamaheh, possibly because she has passed through an intermediate transformation as part of the pollen of a tulip. Peregrinus Tyss is the King Sekakis, but of this he has no inkling, no remembrance, and his connection with the mythic world is most tenuous; only toward the end of the tale does one of the magicians reveal to him his real identity, which is confirmed later still by a dream, but he renounces his past completely and marries a merely human girl, Rosa Lämmerhirt, the daughter of his bookbinder, and "they live happily ever after."

By this gradation it seems evident that Hoffmann is playing upon the metaphysical natural philosophy of Schelling and his school. Georg Pepusch has external qualities resembling a thistle; he is surly (mürrisch) and peevish (störig), but beneath the surface is very human and reasonable. Dörtje Elverdink shines in opulent beauty, like a tulip, in her shimmering taffeta gown. One passage especially would seem to incorporate the metaphysical concepts of a Schelling. Meister Floh has given Peregrinus a miraculous microscope, one hundred and twentieth the size of a grain of sand; when one looks fixedly into the small box that contains it, the microscope leaps into the pupil of the eye, and one can read the thoughts of other people. In the mind of Dörtje Elverdink he saw:

". . . the strange web of nerves and veins which enters into the depth of the brain. But through this web bright gleaming silver threads were entwined, doubtless a hundred times as thin as the threads of the thinnest spider's web, which seemed to be without an end; for they crept like tendrils out of the brain into a Something which was indiscoverable even to the microscopic eye, and became entangled, perhaps thoughts of a more sublime sort, the others of a type easier to grasp. Peregrinus perceived flowers in confused color masses, which formed themselves into human beings, and then human beings which melted away into the earth and then gleamed forth as stones and metals. And in the midst of it, all sorts of strange animals were moving, which were transformed countlessly, and talked in strange languages."[14]

name "Lindhorst" occurs in one of the Königsberg letters, and in his diary he records a visit to the painter Et(t)linger in Dresden (*Kater Murr*). See also notes in the editions of Ellinger and Maassen.

[14] "Das seltsame Geflecht der Nerven und Adern, die bis in das tiefe Gehirn hineingingen. Aber durch dies Geflecht schlangen sich hell blinkende Silberfäden, wohl hundertmal dünner als die Fäden des dünnsten Spinngewebes und eben diese Fäden, die endlos zu sein schienen, da sie sich hinausrankten aus dem Gehirn in ein selbst

This microscope Peregrinus uses to excellent effect in extricating himself from the wiles of Dörtje and of the two magicians, Leuwenhöck and Swammerdamm. It permits Hoffmann also to include incidentally some amusing and telling satire upon the hypocrisy of social intercourse, analogous to the magic invisibility employed in the seventeenth century satire of Grimmelshausen and others. The magician Leuwenhöck fawns upon Peregrinus, but his real thoughts are: "I wish that the black-feathered Satan would hurl you ten thousand fathoms into the abyss." Peregrinus is fulsomely flattered by one who hopes to borrow money of him; he hears the inner comment of young ladies, when they meet the rich bachelor, but it does not correspond at all to the words their lips utter. The microscope also provides material for literary satire, for it discloses the emptiness of intellectual and artistic pretense—the young men of letters, who are bursting with fancies and fine phrases and are adored by the ladies, are shallow charlatans; the "women of letters" (schriftstellernde Frauen) have at their beck and call (am Schnürchen) all the profundities of human life, cultivate genuine philosophical opinions on human relationships and clothe them in fine words, but the microscope discloses that the intricate web of veins and nerves does not penetrate into the depth of the brain; Meister Floh, ever at hand, explains that these are not ideas at all, only words that are trying to become ideas. And yet at the end Peregrinus cannot bring himself to use the glass upon the thoughts of Rosa Lämmerhirt, who seems to love him, and really does love him with the heart of a simple child. His refusal to make further use of the microscope symbolizes his final emergence as a mere human being.

The story of *Meister Floh* is a complex fabric woven of everyday happenings and fantastic supernaturalism. The narrative proper begins, perhaps somewhat prosaically, with preparations for the Christmas festival. Peregrinus Tyss is wont to celebrate Christmas with all the traditional customs—a blazing Christmas tree and multitudinous gifts, mostly children's toys; he distributes the gifts later among the poor families of his acquaintance. At the opening he is in a shop buying toys; a strangely beautiful young woman stands beside him, Dörtje Elverdink, and Meister Floh, her most precious

dem mikroskopischen Auge unentdeckbares Etwas, verwirrten, vielleicht Gedanken sublimerer Art, die andern von leichter zu erfassender Gattung. Peregrinus gewahrte bunt durcheinander Blumen, die sich zu Menschen gestalteten, dann wieder Menschen, die in die Erde zerflossen und dann als Steine, Metalle, hervorblickten. Und dazwischen bewegten sich allerlei seltsame Tiere, die sich unzählige Mal verwandelten und wunderbare Sprachen redeten." xii, p. 75.

possession, escapes from her keeping into one of the packages which Peregrinus takes home. From this incident the story develops.

Dörtje Elverdink, as the Princess Gamaheh, daughter of King Sekakis and the queen of the flowers, in faraway Famagusta, once went to sleep in a lovely garden; the Leech Prince sees her lying in slumber and burns with love for her, which he expresses in a way peculiar to his kind—he bites her behind the ear and begins to suck her blood. The Thistle Zeherit, growing nearby and likewise flaming with love, tries to protect her, but suddenly the malicious Spirit (Genius) Thetis appears, seizes the Princess, and bears her away through the air. Luckily Meister Floh is a witness of these happenings and conceals himself in some Brussels lace which the Princess wears about her neck. Two magicians, Leuwenhöck and Swammerdamm, are standing on a tower observing the course of the stars through a magic telescope. Meister Floh is struck by a beam from the telescope and falls down through the air on Leuwenhöck's nose, thus becoming his prisoner. Through the enforced aid of Meister Floh, Leuwenhöck adds to his profession as maker of magic microscopes the proprietorship of an extraordinary troupe of trained fleas which he exhibits in Berlin and elsewhere. In the meantime the Princess is discovered in the pollen of a Haarlem tulip and the two magicians restore her to human form and to a limited existence as a human being. According to authentic records, one of the two magicians died in 1680 and the other in 1725, but they are still above ground practising their dubious craft.[15]

After the first scene in the toy shop the whole action of the tale revolves about the possession of Dörtje Elverdink and of Meister Floh. The flea is essential to the very existence of Dörtje, for in the somewhat imperfect transformation into a human body that the magicians have brought to pass, the blood is stopped after a time at the spot behind the ear where the Leech Prince bit her, and circulation can be restored only through the bite of Meister Floh. Her crafty love-making is an effort to get the flea away from Peregrinus. The contest is carried on by the two magicians, who are deadly rivals, by Georg Pepusch, the Thistle Zeherit, and eventually also

[15] Antony van Leeuwenhoek and Jan Swammerdam were Dutch scientists of respectable attainments, the former much interested in the manufacture of microscopes and the scientific use of them. In his satirical portraits of them here, as also in the figure of Mosch Terpin, Hoffmann is not decrying genuine scientific research, as some have held, but is, so far as the question arises at all, making a sly thrust at the uninspired and sapless pursuit of scientific knowledge.

by the malicious Spirit Thetis and the Leech Prince, who reappear as an old-fashioned dancing master and a French customs officer.

Meister Floh, sitting in the folds of Peregrinus' neck cloth or on top of his nightcap, becomes his guide and mentor, governing the main action through the wisdom of his counsels. Peregrinus conceives a friendship for his tiny companion and allows him complete freedom to exercise his natural proclivities on the necks of the fair ladies of his acquaintance. After Peregrinus' marriage the flea remains as a welcome guest in the household; on the birth of the first child he sits by Rosa's bedside and bites the nose of the nurse when she falls asleep. The government of the flea realm is described as in essence republican; the "master flea" is the head of the flea senate, but in spite of the republican system enjoys a considerable measure of dictatorial powers—that is, of course when he is at liberty and among his own people. In order that it may oversee the voting accurately, the senate must not consist of more than 55,999 members.

One character, Aline, Peregrinus' old housekeeper with her phosphorescent nose, Hoffmann unfortunately leaves in the limbo of unexplained mystery. She is obviously no mere human being and she has a mysterious connection with Dörtje Elverdink, who also bore the name Aline when, posing as the niece of the proprietor, she served as a kind of show woman in Leuwenhöck's exhibition of trained fleas. Though one may admit the implicit challenge to find a double for her in the myth, it seems forced to interpret Aline as the Mandragora Root which the Thistle Zeherit summoned to the aid of the expiring Princess.

Peregrinus bears in his bosom, as King Sekakis, the precious carbuncle stone, a talisman beyond all price; the magicians are unaware of its whereabouts. The carbuncle stone would seem to symbolize the capacity for purely human love. This Peregrinus experiences, and after the miraculous incidents which make up the story, a double wedding is celebrated in the country house of Peregrinus—Peregrinus himself with Rosa Lämmerhirt and Georg Pepusch with Dörtje Elverdink. But on the morning after the wedding the second pair is missing. The gardener reports that something strange has taken place in the garden; he has dreamed all night of a cactus grandiflorus in full bloom, and begs Peregrinus and Rosa to come and see. In the garden they find a cactus flower which has withered in the first rays of morning sun, and, lovingly entwined about it, a tulip, striped white and lilac, that has also died "the death of the flowers." At midnight Peregrinus had been wakened by the odor of flowers that permeated the house; "at midnight," Georg Pepusch had said, then blooms the thistle "in full splendor and power, and in love's death (Liebestod) there dawns the morning-red of the higher life." Is true love, then, the highest love, realized only in death? Or in some far-off clime, like the Atlantis of Anselmus and Serpentina, are the Thistle Zeherit and the Princess Gamaheh living in the happiness that the world cannot give? The kind of happiness that Peregrinus Tyss, though really a king, has quite renounced in favor of earthly felicity in the companionship of the bookbinder's daughter?

CHAPTER 11

"DIE ELIXIERE DES TEUFELS"

DIE *Elixiere des Teufels, nachgelassene Papiere des Bruders Medardus, eines Kapuziners* (The Elixir of the Devil: Posthumous Papers of Brother Medardus, a Capuchin Monk) is Hoffmann's one completed longer work of fiction, his one novel; *Kater Murr* was unhappily left unfinished. The project of using the career of a renegade monk to embody certain ideas that were occupying his mind at the time may have been suggested to Hoffmann by Matthew Gregory Lewis' novel, *The Monk*; Lewis' story is mentioned in Hoffmann's novel, and it is possible to discover a number of superficial resemblances in details. The novels are, however, radically different in character.[1]

For the external form of the novel Hoffmann chose, as the title implies, the familiar device that he employed in several of the shorter tales, a common method in eighteenth century fiction: a manuscript falls by chance into the hands of an editor who then publishes it. Here the unnamed editor visits the Capuchin monastery in B., a reminiscence of Hoffmann's own visit to the monastery in Bamberg, as related by Kunz. The Prior entrusts him with the papers of the monk Medardus; "really they should have been burned," the Prior says. After the introductory note, the editor intrudes only occasionally—to introduce an intercalated manuscript, that of the old painter, or to explain that at a certain point this manuscript becomes indecipherable. In the seclusion of the same cloister from which the monk Medardus had once made his escape into the wide world, he looks back upon his life, seeking to find—and finding—a meaning in it all. It seems possible that Ricarda Huch, a warm admirer of Hoffmann, may have derived from *Die Elixiere* the plan for

---

[1] For parallels between Lewis' novel and *Die Elixiere des Teufels*, cf. Ellinger's edition of *Die Elixiere* (Berlin, 1907) and the introduction to the novel in his edition of Hoffmann's works; also, Wilhelm Horn: "Über das Komische im Schauerroman, E. T. A. Hoffmanns *Elixiere des Teufels* und ihre Beziehungen zur englischen Literatur," in *Archiv für das Studium der neueren Sprachen und Literaturen*, CXLVI (1923), pp. 153-63; and H. Koziol: "E. T. A. Hoffmanns 'Elixiere des Teufels' und M. G. Lewis' 'The Monk'" in *Germanisch-Romanische Monatsschrift*, XXVI (1938), pp. 167-70. Accepting the general influence of Lewis' novel, Koziol tries to extend the borrowings to the diction; the parallel passages from the two novels are not at all convincing. For the possible but dubious influence of Brentano's *Romanzen vom Rosenkranz* upon Hoffmann's novel, cf. E. Reitz: *Hoffmanns Elixiere des Teufels und Clemens Brentanos Romanzen vom Rosenkranz*, Bonn, 1920, and Victor Michels in *Euphorion* XI, pp. 772-73.

her novel *Erinnerungen von Ludolf Ursleu dem Jüngeren*, where a monk in a Swiss cloister relates the tragic downfall of the family of the Ursleus.

Die Elixiere des Teufels is not a long novel, but it is packed with incidents that follow one another often in restless succession. For any adequate understanding of Hoffmann's plan—of the real intent of the novelist—it would seem necessary to supply an outline of the plot, or a selection, as it were, from the multifarious happenings, which will illustrate the main stages of Medardus' experiences with life.

The earliest memories of the monk are centered in the monastery of the "Heilige Linde"; to this place of pilgrimage in "cold, faraway Prussia" his father had wandered in response to a vision that had promised him there release from the intolerable burden of his sins. Here, on the very day of his father's death, the child Franz is born. Later his mother takes the little boy and journeys far to the south, and in a Cistercian nunnery brings little Franz to visit the Abbess, who had known his father; the Abbess generously provides for the education of the little boy and for his mother's well-being. He receives instruction from a devout parish priest and in time enters a seminary to prepare himself for the priesthood. Frequent visits to a Capuchin monastery incline him, however, to the monastic life, and as Brother Medardus he takes the vows of the order. In the letter to Kunz, thinking as often in musical terms, Hoffmann calls the first part of his novel "grave sostenuto," and on his hero's entrance into the cloister, an "andante sostenuto e piano."

Some years after his induction, Medardus becomes custodian of the sacred relics in the possession of the cloister. To one of them his attention is especially drawn—a flask of mysterious contents, which had once been given to St. Anthony as a part of the oft-pictured temptation of the saint.[2] The perils to body and soul which lurk within this fateful flask are impressively underscored; accordingly, Medardus seeks to guard himself from temptation by removing from the ring the key to the cupboard in which the flask is kept and hiding it from his sight. This simple precaution is, however, ineffective, for the key and the treasure that it might unlock prey upon his mind —like the bloody key in the hands of Bluebeard's wife—and after a time, to his nameless horror, another identical key appears on the ring. One day two somewhat skeptical and irreverent visitors, to

[2] Callot's "Temptation of St. Anthony" was in the Bamberg collection of Callot's work which led Hoffmann to name his first book *Fantasiestücke in Callots Manier.*

whom Medardus is showing the relics in the treasure room, seize the flask from Medardus' hands, uncork it, and drink of the contents before the scandalized but fascinated monk can prevent this act of desecration; even the strange aroma seems to set new impulses coursing in his veins.

When Medardus preaches in the cloister church, throngs come from far and near, drawn thither by his eloquence and the spiritual fervor of his discourse. The Prior calls him "the pride of the monastery." And pride indeed takes full possession of the young monk; conscious of his superiority, he arrogantly looks down on his fellows and chafes at the restrictions which his monastic vows have placed upon the full exercise of his abilities. For St. Anthony's Day, Medardus has planned a signal triumph of his oratory: a relic which the saint once has actually held in his hands is in his keeping and not far away from those who are listening to his voice. But suddenly he falters and stammers in the midst of his eloquence. A stranger wearing a dark violet cloak is leaning against a pillar and looking fixedly at him with eyes of unearthly power. In him Medardus recognizes a figure still vivid in his childhood memories—the inexplicable apparition of the artist who in olden days had executed the paintings in the cloister chapel at "Heilige Linde" and at times still haunted the spot. Those relentless eyes hold the trembling monk as by a magic spell; he cannot look away. Finally he shrieks: "I, I myself, am St. Anthony," and swoons in the pulpit. No one else has seen the stranger in the violet cloak. All power has now gone from Medardus; he is broken in body and spirit. Couldn't the devil's elixir restore his vigor of body and mind? Though he sees the warning face of the old painter as he unlocks the cabinet, he takes a draught of the fiery liquid, and then another. New life pulses through his body; he is himself again, returning to the cloister pulpit in even more dynamic force than before. Now the Prior and his old benefactress, the Abbess, reason with him; he is no longer the humble servant of God, but is thinking only of his own power and fame.

Medardus grows still more restless in the confinement of the cloister. His inner rebellion is heightened by a disturbing episode. In the confessional a young woman confesses her sin—her love for him. He does not see her face, but some mysterious power within him identifies her in her beauty with the painting of St. Rosalia above the altar. Sensual impulses stir within, and emotional torment seizes him; he resolves to flee. The discreet Prior, however, decides upon a venturesome expedient: like the Wittenberg Prior in Goethe's *Götz von Berlichingen,* who sent the restive Brother Martin on various errands in the outer world, Prior Leonardus hopes to curb the rebellion of the young monk by sending him on a mission to Rome. Medardus takes the elixir with him, and the musical notation for the following book is "allegro forte."

As he wanders on by mountain pathways, Medardus comes upon a man in uniform sleeping close by the edge of a precipice. He approaches and calls to him, but in the movement of waking the man plunges down into the abyss below. In his overwrought mental state Medardus thinks himself responsible for the accident and thus of himself as a murderer. Though the relationship is not disclosed till much later, the man was the half-brother of Medardus, Graf Viktorin, and the two are identical—in form, face, even in the strange cross-shaped scar on the neck, and in speech and bearing. Viktorin is not killed by the fall, and upon this identity important elements of Hoffmann's plot are founded. From this time on Medardus is never entirely free from the complications arising from this resemblance and the unacknowledged kinship; indeed at times the two half-brothers lose their sense of separate identity or exchange their personalities, one with the other. As Medardus says: "I am what I appear to be, and do not appear to be what I am; it is an inexplicable riddle to me, I am divided in my ego." The characters of Medardus and Viktorin form Hoffmann's most extended and most telling use of the motif of "doubles." Presently Viktorin's groom appears, but is not at all surprised to see his master, as he supposes, in monk's attire. With uncanny intuition Medardus interprets correctly the first words of the groom, and is immediately enmeshed in a web of deceit: he assumes the role of Viktorin, who in the disguise of a monk was planning an amorous adventure in the neighboring manor house; he relies upon his lively intelligence and his nimble tongue to assist him in the situation into which he is about to plunge.

As a matter of fact, it is a double role that he is to play. Euphemie, the young second wife of Baron F., owner of the manor house, has concocted a clever plot. From the capital city she has written that she is sending an ecclesiastic to serve as spiritual adviser to her stepson Hermogen, whose morose disposition and adolescent contrariness are giving the Baron much concern. By this ruse she is to gain entrance for her lover Count Viktorin, who will appear disguised as a monk. Medardus plays his double role with consummate artistry and sublime self-confidence. He gains, to be sure, no influence over Hermogen, who remains obdurate and unresponsive.

Hermogen is suffering from a searing disillusionment, an adolescent terror of life itself, born of an experience that he refuses to divulge: he has been seduced by his stepmother. But otherwise, with his social gifts and cultivated tastes, and the deceiving show of saintly piety, Medardus is soon a welcome guest in the Baron's household. Immediately recognized as the famous preacher, he invents a plausible excuse for his acceptance of the mission to young Hermogen. With Euphemie, who supposes him to be Viktorin, her lover, Medardus satisfies his long-suppressed sensual desires. But something subtly different, though still essentially carnal, has overpowered him at the first sight of Aurelie, the Baron's daughter by his first marriage. He sees, or thinks he sees in her, the young woman who confessed her sinful love of him, and she seems embarrassed and self-conscious in meeting him. The reality of this previous encounter remains a mystery, probably a purposeful one: was it merely a hallucination in which both of them participated? a mere trick of memory? or the work of unseen powers which plays havoc, as was intended, in the mind of Medardus, but is turned to good in the case of Aurelie? In her later letter to the Abbess, Aurelie interprets the incident as a vision which, through the aid of St. Rosalia, wrought in her a fundamental purification.

Recognizing her deep piety, Medardus tries to gain ascendancy over her by way of his priestly offices. Aurelie alternates between acceptance of his religious ministrations—insidious in their diabolical cleverness—and a secret repugnance and disgust. In a flood of passion he approaches her as they kneel together in prayer, and she repulses him in uncomprehended terror, thus only increasing the frenzy of his passionate determination. Euphemie grows jealous and attempts to poison Medardus, but by crafty sleight of hand he exchanges the wine glasses, and she herself is poisoned. From her dying presence Medardus rushes to Aurelie's apartment, but he is met by her brother Hermogen, who bars his entrance. Hermogen has long been suspicious of the monk's relations with his stepmother and of his designs upon his sister. Once before this he has lurked in ambush and with the strange perception often attributed to the mentally deranged he has thrown Medardus' infamy in his teeth: "I wanted to fight with you, but I have no sword; and you are a murderer for drops of blood drip from your eyes and cling to your beard." This time Medardus stabs Hermogen. The house rings with the outcry of the double murder, but Medardus escapes.

Viktorin's groom, hearing the tumult and fearing for his master's safety, appears on the route of Medardus' flight, bringing Viktorin's horse, civilian clothes, and luggage. Medardus hides his monk's robes in a hollow tree, dons the civilian garb, and rides away. After minor adventures, he arrives in an unnamed industrial city, and poses for a time as a gentleman on his travels—a man of wealth, social accomplishments, and fine intelligence. It is here that he meets the humorous, philosophical Italian barber, Pietro Belcampo, or Peter Schönfeld. In an exhibition of paintings that is arousing interest in the city, Medardus finds, to his amazement, scenes from the monastery of the "Heilige Linde" where his childhood was spent, and the portraits of his old friend, the Abbess, and of Aurelie; before these pictures he is sorely troubled in concealing his emotion. But a more formidable trial awaits him: in a social gathering he meets the painter, who is none other than the mysterious artist whose eyes still bore into the depths of his being. He steels himself to appear unconcerned, but when the conversation turns to the recent crimes in the manor house of Baron F., the painter rises and denounces the suave and elegant gentleman before him as the runaway criminal monk. In the uproar that ensues Medardus escapes from the company, and with the aid of Belcampo, the barber, from the city.

The scene shifts to a forester's dwelling deep in the forest where Medardus has taken refuge after an accident to the carriage in which he was traveling. The forest idyll is, however, tragically interrupted by the intrusion of an insane monk whom the forester and his sons have found and rescued from an almost animal estate. He insists that he is the monk Medardus who has left the cloister in B., and perpetrated the fearsome crimes at the manor of Baron F. He has lost his identity in that of Medardus, and Medardus, seeing in him again his extraordinary "double," wavers in doubt as to the reality of his own. After the monk has entered Medardus' room and drunk from the magic flask, his insanity takes a dangerous turn, and the forester brings him for confinement to the neighboring city, the residence of the reigning prince. Medardus soon follows and presently, through a series of fortunate encounters, becomes a favored figure at the princely court. Only the princess, who, as one later learns, is a sister of the Abbess, holds politely aloof; it is said that she sees in him a resemblance to one of whom she does not wish to be reminded.

A new lady in waiting is expected at the court, and Medardus is present at her first appearance; it is Aurelie. Her glance rests for a moment upon Medardus, and she staggers and swoons. He loses his self-control, becomes for a brief instant the insane monk, his double, utters a wild, mad, cynical laugh, and rushes from the apartment. Ere long, despite explanations and protests, he is arrested and imprisoned. Hoffmann the lawyer probably took professional satisfaction in the successive cross-questionings of the culprit, in differentiating the methods of representatives of the law. Medardus builds up for himself a plausible existence as a Polish gentleman who has valid reasons for maintaining an incognito, and he even finds excuses for his linguistic shortcomings when the second investigator suddenly shifts to Polish. He is also confronted with Brother Cyrillus, summoned from the monastery as a witness, who not only positively identifies him, using as indisputable evidence the cross-shaped scar on his neck, but pleads with him to repent and return to God. Medardus stands his ground: he has never seen Brother Cyrillus before. The insane monk, who is, of course, the missing Viktorin, is confined in the cell below; eventually he loosens the stones of the floor and thrusts through the opening a naked arm holding a dagger; in the horrible grinning face that next appears Medardus recognizes himself. The dagger which he takes from the monk is the very one with which he has stabbed Hermogen. By these tokens he sees some inscrutable force at work and by voluntary death he determines to end his life of deceit and crime, to confess all, and thus to conciliate Aurelie. The novelist leaves the reader entirely in the dark as to the reality of this encounter with the insane monk—whether an actual occurrence or a hallucination. After feverish visions of awful penance, Medardus awakens to find a Dominican monk standing beside his bed of straw. It is again the old-painter, this time appearing not with vain warning but with encouragement: there is still a goal toward which Medardus can strive, still a work to be completed for his eternal salvation. The presence of the painter in this disguise is unquestionably supernatural, and the incident is carefully separated from the overwrought visions that have preceded.

The release of Medardus and full exoneration follow the confession of his insane double that the crimes were of his doing. Medardus is received again at court, with increased cordiality in recognition of the false accusation made against him. Aurelie herself bestows especial favor upon him, for the charges were made through her identification. In time Aurelie and Medardus as the Polish gentleman Krczynski are betrothed. To have gained her love is to Medardus the summit of earthly happiness, but the mind of Aurelie struggles with constant perplexity, for she cannot banish from her consciousness the haunting resemblance between her betrothed and the man who has murdered her brother and her stepmother. With this problem she wrestles in secret, only to compensate for her doubts by more fervent expression of her selfless love.

The very morning appointed for the wedding, Medardus and Aurelie are together, waiting for the summons to enter the prince's presence before the ceremony. A tumult is heard outside, and they look from the window; the insane monk is being carried to the place of execution to pay the penalty for the crimes that Medardus has committed. The monk catches a glimpse of Medardus at the window and shrieks in mad challenge. Medardus is suddenly transformed into his other self—the madman on his way to death. He seizes Aurelie with fierce rage and cries out: "Insane foolish woman, I, I, your lover, your betrothed, I am Medardus, am your brother's murderer, and you the bride of the monk; with your whimpering will you call down destruction upon your betrothed? I am king. I will drink your blood!" He grasps his dagger and thrusts at Aurelie who has fallen to the floor. Then he rushes down the stairway, drags the monk from the cart, throws him to the ground, and, striking about him with his dagger in the midst of the crowd, makes his escape. In the forest something leaps upon his back with the clutch of a wild animal; it is the insane monk, his other self, who as by a miracle has also escaped. Horrible is the grasp of the madman's hands, more horrible still his half-human mutterings, containing one terrifying, intelligible idea—that they eternally belong together. Finally Medardus summons sufficient strength to cast the burden from him, but falls himself unconscious.

Months pass before he comes to himself in an Italian hospital for the insane. The mysterious Belcampo had found him naked in the forest and had brought him to safety in a foreign land. On complete recovery Medardus enters a Capuchin monastery near Rome. He confesses to the Prior without reservation and accepts with gratitude the heavy penance exacted from him. Later in Rome he excites wonder and reverence through the extent and the fervency of his public devotions, day after day in one church after another. Though the populace begins to regard him as a saint, at least in the making, there are those in high ecclesiastical position who distrust this ostentatious display of piety. He is summoned before the Pope himself, who is attracted by his striking personality and his sovereign intelligence. But, apparently recalling the parable of the Pharisee and the Publican, the Pope deprecates an unseemly parade of religious devotion. When after a time it is whispered about that the Pope is planning to appoint Medardus to high office, even to be his own father confessor, Medardus arouses the envy of scheming and unscrupulous churchmen.

The faithful and ubiquitous Belcampo, informed by chance of impending danger, warns Medardus to flee, but that very night Medardus is summoned to administer the last rites to a dying man, and masked men lead him blindfolded into a subterranean vault, where, after performing this priestly function, he is forced to witness the execution of his old friend, the saintly Brother Cyrillus. An attempt is made upon his own life, and only by clever strategy does he turn the cup of poison from his lips.

Again Medardus flees, and this time he finds a place of changeless peace in the old cloister from which he has started on his strange journey into the great world. Broken in body, penitent in spirit, he now seeks admission in the cloister where he had once rebelled against the restrictions that he now longs to reverence and observe. But one trial still awaits him. The very day after his return, Aurelie is to take the vows and enter a near-by nunnery; the monks of the Capuchin cloister are to assist at the ceremony. Dressed as a bride, now the bride of Heaven, Aurelie advances to the altar of St. Rosalia, where the sacred act of consecration is to take place. Within Medardus a surge of memories wells up, a last full tide of earthly passion, a wild desire to leap from the rows of his Capuchin brothers and snatch Aurelie from the company of the nuns, to be his bride. Despite his constant prayers, a terrific struggle takes place between the good and evil powers within him. Only when Aurelie begins to speak the words of the vow, does Medardus feel that evil is at last conquered: "Every word of Aurelie's gave me new strength, and in the heated conflict I was soon victor . . . her vow was my consolation, my hope, and the serenity of Heaven arose bright within me."

But at this moment a man in the tattered robes of a Capuchin friar, with wild, distorted face, rushes into the foreground; before anyone can restrain him, he drives a dagger into Aurelie's breast. Aurelie is thus slain by Medardus' double—the fearful other self. He had appeared in the vicinity shortly before this, had been cared for at the monastery, had fallen into a deathlike trance, and then mysteriously had disappeared. A wild uproar fills the church; the crowds gather about the prostrate figure of Aurelie and cover her with roses. A miracle has taken place before their eyes, for they have witnessed the death of a martyr. No one prevents Medardus from kneeling beside the dying nun and begging her forgiveness, from seeking from her now hallowed lips some final explanation of the web that had bound them together. Suddenly the old painter appears; the crowd thinks he has descended from the altar piece which he himself had painted in the long ago. The circle is now complete. Medardus, over whom he has watched, has now returned forever to his real home, the House of God. A postscript in the hand of Father Spiridion, librarian of the Capuchin cloister in B., records the death of Medardus.

In *Die Elixiere des Teufels* Hoffmann has, in general, abandoned the exact-and detailed topography which marked *Der goldene Topf* and became an outstanding characteristic of his stories. Only in the Roman scenes does one find the mention of familiar streets and squares; the cloister of the "Heilige Linde" is also a real place of pilgrimage in East Prussia, and the walls of its church are adorned with paintings. But the location of the monastery where Medardus dedicated himself to conventual life and whither he returns in the end is not specified, nor are the industrial city and the princely residence which form the local background for the central events of the novel. They are situated in South Germany and the scenery, as Hoffmann describes it, is clearly that of the Bamberg region which he knew and loved—one may assume that "B" stands for Bamberg. Also contrary to his habit in so many of his tales, Hoffmann follows quite strictly the chronological order of events, beginning with the hero's birth and childhood and, by means of a postscript by another hand, ending with his death. The antecedent circumstances are for the most part accounted for bit by bit, usually in conversation, though now and then the information given in this form tends to become an independent narrative. The inserted manuscript of the old painter is the one striking violation of a normal chronology.

Most of the chief characters in the novel are related to one another, though in some important cases this relationship is unknown and unacknowledged. Both Maassen and Harich supply a family tree or graphic chart to disclose the legitimate, illegitimate, and even incestuous connections which lie behind the complex interrelations between Hoffmann's characters. The family stems, in part, from the old painter, who was once a favorite pupil of Leonardo da Vinci and now, as a strangely palpable spirit, walks the pathways of the world until his progeny shall become extinct. One may reasonably query whether the novel does not lose more than it gains by the introduction of this intricate pattern of kinship; Harich remarks that no one can hold the various relationships in mind without the aid of some such chart as he provides. Probably Hoffmann enjoyed fitting the pieces together; it is like the creation of an intricate crossword puzzle for others to solve; one may chuckle in anticipation over their perplexity. And yet the essential elements of the story are only slightly involved in this complicated web of family relationships. For the most part, matters which derive from these relationships are concessions to the interest and the taste of the superficial reader, perhaps even to the sensation seeker. In part doubtless the novelist invented the elaborate system of family connections as a unifying element, though this framework is by no means essential to his primary purpose. Schooled in the fiction of his times, even in sensational stories now largely forgotten, he sought to excite the reader's curiosity, to create a pleasing suspense, by covert suggestions as to mysterious connections between his characters. Even Goethe in *Wilhelm Meister* followed the example of his predecessors and contemporaries in fiction and at the end disclosed a considerable number of family connections which had been hitherto concealed. Hoffmann has not purged his system of the spell which the *Genius* of Julius Grosse and other tales of the type had cast upon him twenty years before.

Much of the plot of *Die Elixiere* depends upon the astonishing resemblance between Medardus and Viktorin—a virtual identity in all except the soul within. That they are half-brothers is in itself not sufficient to account for the extraordinary degree of likeness, and when offered as an explanation lessens rather than enhances the arresting mystery of their personalities. Hoffmann himself and others have made use of the motif of doubles very effectively where there is no family relationship. The presence of a double personality in an individual, the "divided ego," was a metaphysical and psychological problem which much intrigued Hoffmann's generation and indeed had already challenged the attention of an earlier day. The extension of the concept to two or more individuals belongs in the realm of insoluble mysteries, if not of the frankly supernatural. The artist might do well to leave it there and not invoke the aid of family relationship. That Euphemie is the half-sister of both Medardus and Viktorin, is further the half-sister of Aurelie and Hemogen, as well as their stepmother, are ultimate disclosures that may have been intended to startle the reader but nevertheless leave him quite unmoved. The discreditable conduct of Medardus' ancestors from the old painter down through the years holds the reader's attention only for the moment. Even the various transgressions of the old painter himself or of Francesco, the father of Medardus, and his relations with the princely family in the previous generation—running somewhat parallel to the guilt of Medardus—make little claim upon the reader's interest, partly, of course, because they are so tersely narrated in the style of a chronicle. Having once read the account and perhaps endeavored to retain it in memory as probably important for the life of Medardus, the reader is not likely to turn back to it. It is well that Hoffmann condensed this part of his story to relatively few pages. This criticism is admittedly invalid, if *Die Elixiere des Teufels* is, as some have maintained, a "fate-novel," showing the accumulated effect of the curse of sin upon a whole family. In time Hoffmann lays the scene of his novel only a few decades back, in the last years of the eighteenth century.[3]

Only in this story can one examine Hoffmann's control of a larger canvas, the novel as opposed to the short story or the "Novelle." The division of the novel into two volumes may be ignored as quite without significance; it was an accidental result of composition and publication. The two volumes really form one continuous narrative. At first glance the substance of the novel might seem to consist of several episodes, arranged in a somewhat artificial pattern, each ending with an escape—from the cloister, from the house of the Baron, from the unnamed industrial city, from the princely residence, and from Rome, and even, at the last, an escape from the world in Medardus' return to the cloister. Since Hoffmann was primarily a writer of shorter tales, some critics have been led to overemphasize the episodic form of the longer narrative[4] and consequently to discount the fundamental unity of the novel. But each of the episodes, though in itself a rounded whole, works naturally into the next following, is inextricably interlocked with what went before and what

[3] Hoffmann was ill-advised in giving in two instances more or less exact dates which may make the captious reader pause. The old painter was a pupil of Leonardo da Vinci who died in 1519, and yet he is the great-great-grandfather of Medardus, who died, a relatively young man, nearly three centuries later. Secondly, Aurelie has been reading Lewis' *The Monk* in a German translation; the translation of Friedrich von Oertel is dated 1797, and the death of Medardus is recorded as on September 5, 17—. Hoffmann leaves himself hardly space for the events that come in between these dates, even if Aurelie began to read the translation immediately upon its publication and the second date were 1799.

[4] Cf. O. Schissel von Fleschenberg: *Novellenkomposition in E. T. A. Hoffmanns Elixieren des Teufels*, Halle, 1910.

comes after; each has its part in the spiritual development of the hero, which gives unity to the whole.

The novel was, to be sure, written at a time when the so-called fate-drama was signally flourishing. In the early years of the Romantic Period the idea of fate had been explored by Tieck in *Karl von Berneck* and then had been given the authority of Schiller's great reputation in *Die Braut von Messina.* The immense popularity of Zacharias Werner's *Der vierundzwanzigste Februar* (The Twenty-fourth of February) did much to establish the contemporary concept of the fate-tragedy as a specific and important genre. The then prevailing popularity of the type and Hoffmann's personal acquaintance with Werner have led some critics to underscore heavily the fate element in *Die Elixiere* and interpret it as in essence a novel of fate corresponding to the contemporary drama of fate.[5]

In the narrative Medardus uses the word "Verhängnis" (destiny) and the derivative adjective with considerable frequency. The word "Schicksal" (fate), the term employed exclusively in connection with the "fate-drama," occurs occasionally in the conversation which Medardus records; Medardus uses it himself only once in the whole novel, and then in the most general sense—he has complicated his "Schicksal" by assuming a noble Polish name. It would seem reasonable to infer that Hoffmann, in the narrative of Medardus, consciously avoids the word "Schicksal," in order that his work, despite certain aspects of the story, should not be associated with the sensational and vulgarized concept of human destiny which pervaded the plays of the fate dramatists. One may recall a passage in a letter to Kunz: though we call the working of the unseen powers "chance," he wrote this novel to show that in the moral life there is no such thing as "chance." The fortunes of Medardus are ever in his own hands and his sins are the unmitigated action of his own free will. It may be acknowledged that Hoffmann makes use of certain trick devices common in the fate-drama: there is a dagger that mysteriously passes from hand to hand and brings its doom to members of a scattered family, as in Grillparzer's *Die Ahnfrau* (The Ancestress), or as the fatal knife in Werner's play. From the fate-tragedy he borrows the strange coincidence of dates, suggested by

---

[5] Werner's best-known colleague in the production of "fate-dramas," Ernst Houwald, was Contessa's closest friend, and Contessa lived the latter part of his life on Houwald's country estate; this was not far from Berlin, and Contessa often came to town to meet with his friends. From this connection, one may assume that Hoffmann was also personally acquainted with Houwald, though there is no mention of it in his correspondence.

the title of Werner's drama, and, further, the concept of a sin-
stained ancestor who bequeaths to his descendants the legacy of his
sins, as it were gathering strength and potency with the passing of
the years until the whole family, as far as the record goes, becomes
extinct. But all of this is purely external; Hoffmann uses the fate-
idea as an artistic device. He does not intend to fix the reader's
attention upon the hereditary transmission of evil tendencies. His
main purpose is something fundamentally different. *Die Elixiere
des Teufels* is a novel of Christian experience, of human sin and
divine redemption; the whole force of Hoffmann's thought is focused
on this problem. In two previous narratives, *Don Juan* and *Der
Magnetiseur*, he had considered the character of a man who gives
himself over to evil, even as Medardus, in the pride of power, but in
neither case had he provided for repentance and amendment of life.
From this point of view, *Die Elixiere* may be considered as a comple-
mentary study to the two earlier stories.

Franz, later the monk Medardus, was born in the very shadow
of a cloister, and his memories of childhood and early youth are
centered in places sacred to the ritual and the doctrines of the
Church. In the early pages Hoffmann foreshadows with fine perspi-
cacity and clarity the direction that the story is to take and indicates
the complex and contradictory elements in the character of Franz
which made his life's story what it was. Of course, the form he has
chosen, the reminiscences of Medardus himself, lends itself especially
to this type of self-revelation. He introduces at the beginning
certain features which link the narrative with sacred legends and
saints' legends—the story, then, is to be a kind of parable. Such,
for example, is the mysterious pilgrim who tells little Franz's
mother that her son is superbly equipped with many gifts; though
inherited sin boils and ferments within him, he can still become a
valiant warrior for the Faith. The pilgrim brings a wondrous child
to play with Franz, "to enkindle in him the spark of love." Only
through the mediation of a child, the Holy Child, does the human,
all too human, Franz understand the sanctity of the holy place where
his childhood was spent; the child plays with Franz's colored pebbles
and in the end always lays them in the form of a cross. In time the imprint of these experiences grows dim, but it is never completely erased.
One hardly needs the interpretation which Hoffmann himself supplies
in a letter to Kunz, that the pilgrim is St. Joseph and the little boy is
the Christ-child himself.

Akin to this intimation of saintly guidance is the figure of the

old painter who in the long ago had arrived mysteriously at the
monastery, executed the far-famed paintings in the cloister church,
and then as mysteriously disappeared. Again and again he appears
at critical moments in Medardus' life. He was Franz's great-great-
grandfather; the spirits of those who have sinned and have been
reconciled to God may watch over their descendants. His fixed and
sorrowful gaze completely disarms Medardus when in self-exalta-
tion he has forgotten the selflessness of his divine calling; his face
appears in vain warning when Medardus is about to unlock the
cabinet where the devil's elixir is kept. The exhibition of paintings
is a subtle but yet powerful admonition to the moral renegade—
scenes from the sacred precincts of his childhood, portraits of the
Abbess and of Aurelie. But when it seems that they have failed of
their purpose, the painter openly denounces Medardus before his
new friends. Immediately afterwards—as is disclosed later—the
painter and, more miraculously still, the paintings themselves have
vanished. He visits Medardus in prison, and this time he speaks words
of encouragement, though the reader is not yet aware that a turning
point in Medardus' life has been reached. In his distorted mental
processes, for a time completely under the control of evil, Medardus
interprets this ghostly messenger and mentor, this "good angel," as
his enemy; evil sees even the good as evil. At the martyrdom of
Aurelie the painter appears again, clad in his violet mantle, apparently stepping out of the St. Rosalia altar piece, which he himself
had painted; his benign presence marks the final emancipation from
the powers of evil. Though the cloister gates are locked, he steps out
of the cell of the dying monk: "the hour of release is no longer faraway," he says to the astonished Prior, and then disappears down
the dark corridor. The release was not only for Medardus but for
himself. As Schenck suggests, the role of the old painter has perhaps something in common with that of the "familiar spirit" in the
sensational novels of the time, such as Grosse's *Der Genius*,[6] but
this is incidental; Hoffmann is thinking primarily in terms of saints'
legends.

The incident of Medardus' first visit to the Abbess in the Cistercian
nunnery is a significant element in the development of the plot; as
the Abbess had known his father and shows an unfeigned interest
in the little boy, the reader suspects some hidden events in the past
which connect his fortunes to those of the princely house to which
the Abbess belongs. But the meeting has another, a spiritual, signifi-

[6] Cf. Schenck, *op. cit.*, pp. 278-79.

cance; the Abbess presses the boy to her bosom and the diamond cross which she is wearing makes an imprint, a wound, upon his neck; both his outcry of pain and the miraculous permanence of the scar are symbols of the life he is to lead. He has, though rebellious, received a kind of stigmata.

In boyhood Franz served as an acolyte, swinging the censer before the altar. He was transported in religious ecstasy when the tones of the organ swept down from the choir; his inmost soul was filled "with presentiments of the Highest and the Holiest." He was gifted with rare powers of the mind; even in childhood his personality exercised a strange fascination over others, even an uncanny authority. He was peculiarly responsive to aesthetic stimulus, and early displayed a premature eloquence; "as if inspired by a higher power" he described to the Abbess the beauty of the "Heilige Linde" and the glory of the paintings in the cloister church. But at the same time a susceptibility to sensual and erotic impulses showed its menacing presence, illustrated by an incident of his adolescence which is strongly reminiscent of Rousseau's *Confessions*: "In the beginning my spirit flowed with holy devotion, was turned entirely toward the world above, now the life of pleasure came over me and enveloped me with its variegated pictures."

It might, of course, be contended that the frail, repentant monk, transcribing his memories, views his childhood in its monastic environment in that wistful idealization with which most men veil the realities of youth. But his description of life in the Capuchin monastery is the fruit of mature observation, and is not less laudatory. In it Hoffmann, using the monk as his mouthpiece, pays an almost unqualified homage to the religious life, particularly as exemplified by the religious orders. Apart from the world, the chosen few lead their lives of devotion and adoration; ties of reverence bind them to the wise, tolerant, and understanding Prior, whose gentle spirit pervades the place, a spirit derived from the Divine Being to whom his days are dedicated. It is an exacting life indeed, of unremitting but beneficent discipline, shot through with the glory of the unseen Presence. In this companionship it is the privilege of Medardus to tarry a while and to listen to the ripe wisdom of those who have trodden the way before him. The function of the Church in uniting the world of sense with the unseen, supersensual world is finely expressed by Brother Cyrillus: it is the endeavor of the Church "to grasp those secret threads which bind the things of sense to the supersensuous, to animate our (human) organism, which is

developed for living an earthly existence, so that its origin steps
out as clearly derived from that higher spiritual principle, indeed
that its inward kinship to that Wondrous Being, whose strength penetrates all nature like a glowing breath, becomes manifest, and the
presentiment of a higher life, whose germ we bear within us, hovers
about us as with seraph's wings."[7]

The perplexities of a complex character, such as that of Medardus
—his real inner being as yet only touched by the Divine, but not
transformed—is neatly illustrated by the young monk's skepticism
as to the authenticity of the relics in the cloister treasury. He recalls
the vast accumulation of pieces of the true cross scattered about in
churches and monasteries, and, even some years after he has worn
the monk's cowl, confesses that he has always looked upon the
veneration of sacred relics as a kind of religious play (Spielerei).
But through the teachings of the Prior and Brother Cyrillus, he
begins to perceive the values inherent in these mute testimonials to
saintly lives: "The believer without oversubtle pondering [Grübeln]
may fasten his whole mind and spirit on them, and then soon be
filled with that heavenly exaltation which opens up to him the realm
of blessedness of which he has had only a vague conception."

Hoffmann follows the doctrine of St. Augustine in regarding
pride—Superbia, as the all-inclusive sin that leads all other offenses
in its train. Pride consumes every other impulse in the breast of
the young monk, and when the vision of the old painter in silent, uncomprehended warning deprives him of the powers upon which
his pride was built, he yields to temptation; the devil's elixir may
restore what he has lost. This first step leads to another, and another,
until he is engulfed in a maelstrom of sin and crime. Augustinian
also is the dogma that there can be no sin without freedom of the
will to choose the evil. The voice of conscience is stifled by the surge of
passion, but conscience is not dead, only temporarily inoperative:
"My mother seemed to bear a secret sorrow; I did not ask the cause of
it, because an obscure feeling placed the guilt for it on me myself,
though I was unable to unravel the matter more clearly." The
portrait of the Abbess startles and disturbs him, for she seems to be
begging forgiveness for his sins; emotions to which he has long been

---

[7] "Ist es nicht herrlich . . . , dass unsere Kirche darnach trachtet, jene geheimnisvollen Fäden zu erfassen, die das Sinnliche mit dem Übersinnlichen verknüpfen, ja
unseren zum irdischen Leben und Sein gediehenen Organism so anzuregen, dass sein
Ursprung aus dem höhern geistigen Prinzip, ja seine innige Verwandtschaft mit
dem wunderbaren Wesen, dessen Kraft wie ein glühender Hauch die ganze Natur
durchdringt, klar hervortritt, und uns die Ahnung eines höheren Lebens, dessen Keim
wir in uns tragen, wie mit Seraphsfittichen umweht." II, p. 24.

a stranger are evoked, and he sinks upon his knees in grief and repentance.

Elements of the plot, in themselves perhaps lurid and sensational, are skillfully employed in the account of Medardus' spiritual experience. The episode in the forester's house is a case in point. The insane monk is his other self, by some occult telepathy acquainted with every step of his moral downfall, even though in body he is still Viktorin. The hideously contorted face of the insane man, his memories of Medardus' misdeeds, which are now to him really his own, constitute a mirror in which Medardus sees himself. The "Magic Mirror" in whose reflection the real self is uncovered is familiar enough in story and legend; Schiller uses it in the doomsday dreams of Franz Moor. From the insane monk the forester has heard the story of his life, and now repeats it to Medardus. This is subtly contrived as a companion piece to Medardus' account of the same happenings—his own deeds seen now in their stark horror as if committed by this other self, who assumes responsibility for them, but filtered through the mind of the sturdy and upright forester. But the "Magic Mirror" is not sufficient to effect a fundamental change in Medardus. He is horrified to find that he, who thought himself free, is only moving about, as it were, in a cage; he is now ashamed of his conduct, and, for a time, he says in retrospect, he mistakenly regarded this "shame" as the genuine penitence he should have felt. The forlorn condition of the wretched "monk," again violently insane, bores into his very soul; how much does he owe to this mysterious "monk" for assuming his own guilt? At this juncture Medardus throws the now empty flask out of the window; even the stimulating odor he wishes to put far from him. This is, however, not the turning point of the story—as when Peter Schlemihl flings the inexhaustible purse into the chasm and the "Gray Man" torments him no more. Hoffmann has a much more complex problem to solve; Medardus has, to be sure, taken one step in the right direction, though it is not without significance that the flask is now empty.

Medardus has an uncomfortable feeling, new to him indeed, when on a hunting expedition with the forester and his sons, he brings down the flying birds without having aimed at them—this episode is evidently a reminiscence of Hoffmann's hunting days with Kunz in Bamberg. He hesitates to continue playing cards because his luck is so overwhelming—another reminiscence of personal experience. An alien power is working in him and through him, but he is already conscious of a "gradual budding" (Aufkeimen) of strength within him, becoming more capable of resisting the enemy. But his complete regeneration awaits another force outside himself.

After his arrest Medardus determines upon suicide; he can see no other way of atonement, no other method of atoning to Aurelie. He has begun to think of something other than himself, is willing to die in order to redeem himself in the eyes of someone else. But in the dream that arises from this resolve, his arm is mysteriously turned away from his breast, and the dagger is shattered in fragments on the cross-shaped scar. In dream also he sees the great cross in the cloister garden at B., and he longs to prostrate himself there in the dust and pay penance for his sins. After his release from prison an earthly heaven awaits him in Aurelie's love; this love, he thinks, has purified him of his sins: "Every wanton thought died in the thrill that passed through my inmost spirit." Through Aurelie his soul could be saved. But can he permit Aurelie to wed a monk who has broken his vows and committed deeds of nameless infamy? The whole night before the day appointed for the wedding he spends in prayer—for the first time, in really fervent prayer. In the Italian monastery he subjects himself to torturing penance, but as the sin of pride was the first downward step, so at the end a new type of pride assails him, a form of self-pity and hypocritical abasement which contaminates his real repentance and remorse.

Toward the final salvation of Medardus two separate lines of influence gradually converge, one within and one without: the purification of self in so far as the sinner himself can achieve it, and the Divine hand guiding and transforming through the intercessory power of the saints. St. Rosalia is the intercessor, using Aurelie as her chosen instrument; in her supreme self-immolation Aurelie merges her identity with that of the saint whose name she is to bear as nun. Theologically the salvation of Medardus is founded upon the twin doctrines of vicarious atonement and the intercession of the saints. Like Goethe's Iphigenie, Aurelie belongs to a family stained with sin; like Iphigenie, she may atone for the sins of others by her own stainless purity.

That the recent impact of the Julia Marc episode had some share in the creation of *Die Elixiere des Teufels* may be conceded. Love, such as he had never known and indeed never experienced again, had stirred Hoffmann's very being. The experience brought to him the conception of love as a mighty force which transmutes baser metal into gold, but it is a fundamental error to interpret the novel, as has been done, simply as an artificial structure, based on the analogy of religious experience but concealing merely his own quite individual misery and final renunciation in an affair of the heart. The Julia episode may have induced pondering upon another kind of love, higher than his own, transcending anything he could possibly have associated with Julia Marc.

The character of Belcampo the barber merits a few words of comment—a minor figure but still significant. His part in the unfolding of the plot is not inconsiderable; he aids Medardus in escaping from the city after the old painter has denounced him, saves the life of Medardus after the tragedy of the wedding day, visits him in the Italian hospital, and, a little later, after Medardus has found him delighting the Roman populace on the Piazza da Spagna with a marionette play, he tells Medardus of the plot against his life. At the requiem mass for the dead monk the perfume of roses fills the chapel, coming from a bouquet of rare flowers which, the Prior explains, had been placed before the picture of St. Rosalia by a tattered beggar. This beggar is Belcampo, who is now taken into the monastery as a lay brother, silent in the midst of the brothers but now and then delighting them with his harmless laughter. He is attracted to Medardus at their first meeting; with rare observation he recognizes the former monk by the manner of his walk and the fashion of holding his hands. He seems, however, unaccountably acquainted with past events and his devotion to Medardus would seem to have required further explanation. Generally Hoffmann is uncommonly careful in anticipating questions that might arise in the reader's mind. For example, how was it possible that Medardus in the Italian hospital was clothed in his own monk's robe which long ago he had hidden in a hollow tree? How did Viktorin come into possession of the monk's garments after he had physically recovered from the fall into the chasm? Not that he explains his real mysteries away, as was the practice of Mrs. Radcliffe; the occult and the seemingly supernatural are always left virtually untouched, but in the formation of his plots, in the narrative elements, he rarely leaves loose ends. If anything is unexplained, it is probably with conscious purpose—for example, the uncertainty as to the actuality of Aurelie's confession. It may be idle conjecture, but in view of the Italian origins of a part of Medardus' ancestry, Hoffmann may have intended to connect Belcampo in some way with the fortunes of the family to which Medardus belonged, and then inadvertently completed the novel without providing for it.

But Belcampo serves another and quite different purpose in the

novel. The old Prior says of him, "His light has been extinguished
by the mists of folly, into which, in his inmost being, the irony of life
has been transmuted." Hoffmann remembers his Shakespeare and
introduces a jester. The fools of Shakespeare, with their waggish
but often mordant comment on human life, were to Hoffmann
supremely important figures among the creations of the great
dramatist. He felt akin to them, and even as a youth, in a letter to
Hippel, called Trinculo his ancestor. Hence in this somber record
of mistaken ambition, passion, and crime, he introduces a jester
who with light or at times savage humor plays upon the surface of
grim reality and not infrequently probes deep beneath the surface.
Light-footed he pirouettes about the stage of action, accompanying
his nimble feet with equal nimbleness of tongue. From his lips flows
a stream of endless prattle, a flood of foolish-wise discourse, and as
Medardus tells him: "Often a deep meaning lies at the bottom of
your nonsense." Belcampo perceives at once the schism in Medardus' being: "You have not surrendered yourself to your real
nature; there is a compulsion in your actions, a conflict of contesting
natures."

Belcampo plays with current philosophical ideas. He queries, does
he exist simply because he is conscious of himself? The painter, he
says, is only a "base revenant," is merely an "idea," which can be
slain only by an "idea," can be exorcized only by a glowing, curling
iron, which will curl the idea, that he really is—or through an appropriate curling of the thoughts which he has to suck in, in order
to nourish the "idea."[8] Similar concepts he applies to himself:
"Reverend sir, inside me exists an infamous sinful fellow, and he
says, 'Peter Schönfeld, don't be a monkey and believe that you exist,
but I am really you, by name Belcampo, and am an original idea;
if you don't believe that, I will strike you down with a razor-sharp
idea. . . .' This Belcampo has made me, Peter Schönfeld, quite confused and all mixed up."[9] Or in a later passage: "I myself, I am the
folly which follows you everywhere, to aid your reason; you may

---

[8] "Ein schnöder Revenant, und durch nichts anders zu bannen, als durch ein
glühendes Lockeneisen, welches die Idee krümmt, welches eigentlich Er ist, oder
durch schickliches Frisieren der Gedanken, die er einsaugen muss, um die Idee zu
nähren, mit elektrischen Kämmen." ii, p. 94.

[9] "Ach, ehrwürdiger Herr, es steckt ein infamer sündlicher Kerl in meinem Innern,
und spricht: 'Peter Schönfeld, sei kein Affe, und glaube dass du bist, sondern ich
bin eigentlich *du*, heisse Belcampo und bin eine geniale Idee, und wenn du das nicht
glaubst, so stosse ich dich nieder mit einem spitzigen haarscharfen Gedanken. . . .
dieser Belcampo hat mich, den Peter Schönfeld, ganz verwirrt und konfuse gemacht." ii, p. 95.

realize it or not, but only in folly will you find your salvation, for your reason is a very miserable thing and cannot hold itself upright; it reels this way and that like a frail child, and must enter into partnership with folly, which helps her [reason] up again, and knows how to find the right way home—that is, the madhouse, where we both quite fittingly have arrived."[10] Life is so contradictory and unstable that folly alone can help one to endure it. But yet in his curious jargon, often studded with figures of speech from his profession as barber, Belcampo expresses his longing for something that would give meaning to life, some gleam out of another world.

Die Elixiere des Teufels is an expression of Hoffmann's longing for order in a world of kaleidoscopic disorder, for the stability that comes from unquestioning religious faith. Personally he has lost the key to the house of faith, as presented by the traditional dogma and the ritual of the churches, but he can still go back and peer into the uncurtained windows. Hoffmann was not sufficiently sure of himself to avoid introducing a Belcampo, not indeed as a religious unbeliever, a vulgar skeptic, but a being like himself, obsessed by the irony of life. And yet in the end Belcampo finds sanctuary in a cloister, an abode of untroubled peace, and where did he, a ragged beggar, get the miraculous wreath of roses?

In general Hoffmann maintains admirably the fiction of a monkish scribe recording the strange events of his life, albeit one especially gifted and unusually wise in the ways of the world. It is a tale of moral aberration and ultimate redemption, a sober chronicle, even if at times wildly exciting, and it is told in a style appropriate to the subject. One does not find—and does not expect to find—characteristics which mark most of Hoffmann's stories—the light tone of entertaining persiflage, the sly, genial humor, the merry twist and turn of phrase, in which Hoffmann delighted, or the frequent humorous conversations with his readers. When the monk addresses a possible reader, the tone is in keeping with the essential solemnity of his purpose. Only in the role of Belcampo do some of these common aspects of Hoffmann's narrative style appear. Once or twice, to be sure, in the course of the novel, Hoffmann seems to nod

---

10 "Ich selbst, ich selbst bin die Narrheit, die ist überall hinter dir her, um deiner Vernunft beizustehen, und du magst es nun einsehen oder nicht, in der Narrheit findest du nur dein Heil, denn deine Vernunft ist ein höchst miserables Ding, und kann sich nicht aufrecht erhalten, sie taumelt hin und her wie ein gebrechliches Kind, und muss mit der Narrheit in Compagnie treten, die hilft ihr auf und weiss den richtigen Weg zu finden nach der Heimat—das ist das Tollhaus, da sind wir beide richtig angelangt." ii, p. 206.

and introduces material which is pure episode, in no way contributing to the onward movement of the story—such, for example, as the
adventures of Medardus in the tavern, the two eccentric English-
men, and the discussion of the phenomenon known as an "Irish Bull."
Humor appears occasionally in the situations, though there is little
or no indication that the monk himself is aware of it. When Medardus, clad in Viktorin's clothes, arrives in a small town, he encounters a village magistrate, perhaps a first cousin to Mr. Justice
Shallow, a humorous figure whose inquiries as to Medardus' identity
are couched in picturesque language. He is persistent and even
threatening, and Medardus eventually has to take refuge in the
eloquence of Viktorin's well-filled purse. Medardus' departure from
the town is also attended by humorous incident: the bystanders
ridicule his inexpert horsemanship. "He rides like a Capuchin," they
shout in derision.

The autobiographical novel naturally tends to keep one character
in the center of action, though it may of course be employed to
describe a social milieu or to ventilate political or philosophical
theories. In Hoffmann's novel, the author concentrates his attention
rigidly upon the single theme—the character of Medardus in contact with the natural and the spiritual world. Everything else is
strictly subordinated to this purpose, and all the other figures of the
story are conceived only in their relationship to him. Such an
elimination of all other aspects of character or conduct which are
not useful from the author's narrowed point of view may easily
lessen the significance of the other figures in the narrative, or even
impair their validity as credible human beings. This stricture applies
especially to the two female characters chiefly involved in the "plot"
—Euphemie and Aurelie. Euphemie is a veritable embodiment of
evil; beauty of person and charm in social relations conceal an utter
depravity which knows no limits in seeking material advantages and
sensual satisfactions. She is doubtless intended to be a reincarnation
of her remote ancestress, the devil-woman who centuries before had
lured the painter to sin. The character of Aurelie is intentionally a
complete antithesis; it would be only a slight exaggeration to maintain that she consists largely of adjectives which in constant reitera-
tion on the lips of others attribute to her a childlike purity and
simplicity and an unexampled piety. Only in the problematical scene
of the confessional—whether it actually occurred or was only a vision—do qualities appear which disclose tendencies common to sin-
ning humanity. Her long letter to the Abbess, which Medardus in-

cludes in full, is hardly satisfying as a revelation of a more complex
personality, of a human being subject to the temptations to which
all flesh is heir. On the other hand, it may be noted that Hoffmann
has not even in this departed from his initial dependence upon the
style of the sacred legend or parable. Both Euphemie and Aurelie
are to a large extent personifications of abstract qualities, and the
personality of Aurelie is by implication gradually merged with that
of St. Rosalia. She resembles Tieck's Genoveva, in *Leben und Tod
der heiligen Genoveva* (Life and Death of St. Genevieve) ; only in a
few passages does Tieck allow purely human qualities to intrude
upon the saintliness of his heroine; she is a moral abstraction and
thus unfitted for her dramatic role as the bearer of a tragic conflict.

Hoffmann's remark in a letter to Kunz, March 8, 1818, that he
should not have had the first volume of *Die Elixiere* printed, has been
somewhat of a riddle to the commentators. And soon after Hoffmann's death Hitzig wrote in apparent confirmation, saying that the
whole work was one upon which Hoffmann himself placed no value.
He then went on to explain: "Between the composition of the first
and of the second parts he [Hoffmann] had through the change in
his conditions lost the connection; he sought artificially to regain
it and never succeeded in doing so." Harich's interpretation of the
passage in the letter seems inadequate or perhaps farfetched: that
the novel was by the way of being a first version of the Kreisler problem and was prematurely given to the world in the trappings of
a saint's legend, whereas the question at issue really belonged in the
world of music, as was later demonstrated in *Kater Murr*. It is also
difficult, indeed impossible, to agree with Maassen that the two volumes show a marked difference in the attitude toward the miraculous,
that the "mystic-romantic" elements are transformed "almost" into
the opposite. Unquestionably, as Maassen notes, the second volume
exhibits a deepening of interest in the psychology of character, that
of Medardus and of others, but this is precisely what the story requires as a record of the development of the hero.

As has been suggested, the early pages of the narrative give unmistakable indication of the main current of the story, and it seems
evident that Hoffmann had a complete plan at the outset, from
which, in essentials at least, he never swerves. In sending the manuscript of the first volume to Hitzig in the hope that Hitzig might find
a publisher, Hoffmann wrote: "The second part can be delivered in
five weeks, if it is required, since it needs only to be written out from
the rough draft [vom Konzept ins Reine bringen]." One needs, in-

cidentally, only a slight acquaintance with Hoffmann's promises
to editors to be very skeptical about the "five weeks," but the passage indicates plainly that the general plan for the novel, and probably most of the details, had been completely worked out in his
mind. Though the root idea of the story is carried out with utter
consistency, it may be admitted that the Roman scenes present a
somewhat altered picture of the Roman Catholic Church when compared with the earlier experiences of Medardus. The saintly lives,
the heavenly serenity of the Capuchin cloister, stand in striking
contrast to the intrigues of ecclesiastics, the thirst for temporal
power, the intrusion of worldly interests, even in the circle around
the Pope himself. Nothing, however, that is at all essential to Hoffmann's purpose, nothing that affects faith and dogma, is in any
way touched. The letter to Kunz was written four years after the
completion of the first part and nearly four years after his arrival
in Berlin. In writing the words in question, it may well have been
in Hoffmann's mind that the publication of the first volume committed him to a continuation of the novel in precisely the same tone,
and that years of residence in Berlin, skeptical but on the surface
rigidly Protestant, separated him from the impressions of the Roman
Church that he had gained in Bamberg. Yet in the second part of
the novel his implied condemnation is directed only against the unworthy representatives of the Church and not against the Church
itself or the faith upon which the Church is founded.

CHAPTER 12

KREISLER-HOFFMANN

THE "KREISLERIANA"

THE creation of Johannes Kreisler,[1] the Kapellmeister, was doubtless the result of a search, probably quite unconscious on Hoffmann's part, for an appropriate and congenial vehicle through which to express himself and his ideas. At the outset the Kreisler fiction provided simply an artistic method of presenting his opinions. Despite his technical equipment for analysis and appreciation of music, purely objective criticism ran counter to his nature; as an artist he could not prevent the creative imagination from intruding. It will be remembered that his first contribution to the *Allgemeine musikalische Zeitung* was a critique of Gluck in the guise of a story. In the course of time the figure of Kreisler developed and grew into a kind of self-portrait. Many artists have essayed self-portraiture, scanning their features in a mirror. Hoffmann not only drew his portrait but constructed the mirror as well, and thus the mirrored likeness is both Hoffmann and an imaginary personality, resulting from the peculiar mirror which he constructed.[2]

[1] In his *Kreislerbuch* (Leipzig, 1903) Hans von Müller has assembled Hoffmann's Kreisler writings between two covers: the Kreisler parts of *Kater Murr*; a selection from the *Kreisleriana* of numbers that seemed to him more definitely concerned with the character of Kreisler; an extract from *Berganza* in which the dog talks about his former master; the two fragments, *Der Freund* and *Lichte Stunden eines wahnsinnigen Musikers*; and the scores of four of Hoffmann's compositions which are mentioned in *Kater Murr*. In the case of *Kater Murr* he has not only separated the fragments of the Kreisler biography from the autobiography of the cat, but has rearranged the fragments and made minor alterations in the interest of coherence. To some admirers of Hoffmann's work this process may seem close to sacrilege.

[2] It is possible, perhaps probable, that the plan of inventing a character partly himself and partly imaginary, to serve as his mouthpiece, was suggested to Hoffmann by Wackenroder's Josef Berglinger in the *Herzensergiessungen eines kunstliebenden Klosterbruders*. When the new Romantic writings so captivated Hoffmann in Warsaw, it is difficult to believe that the work of Wackenroder was not included as well as that of Tieck, though at the time he makes no mention of it. The word "Herzensergiessungen" in a letter written at the time is of course no proof of acquaintance with Wackenroder, but later, as already noted, he took the name Berglinger (Berklinger) for the old artist in *Der Artushof*. Hoffmann was not in the habit of concealing his sources, and his literary admirations are spread broadly over the pages of his works. Whatever may have been the case, he was quite capable of creating Kreisler and probably would have done so, had Wackenroder never invented Berglinger. Ellinger first drew attention to the similarity between Kreisler and Berglinger and even suggested that the external form of Hoffmann's first published work, the *Sendschreiben eines Klostergeistlichen*, may owe something to the *Herzensergiessungen*, which would mean an acquaintance with Wackenroder previous to the residence in Warsaw. For a detailed examination of the similarities and divergences

The two cycles of the *Kreisleriana* were published in the first and second volumes of the *Fantasiestücke*, though most of the numbers had appeared previously in periodicals.[3] "Johannes Kreislers des Kapellmeisters musikalische Leiden" (The Musical Sufferings of Johannes Kreisler the Kapellmeister) was printed in the *Allgemeine musikalische Zeitung* for September 26, 1810, and with it a unique

between Kreisler and Berglinger, cf. Walter Jost, *Von Ludwig Tieck zu E. T. A. Hoffmann*, Frankfurt am Main, 1921.

In his obituary of Hoffmann (*Allgemeine musikalische Zeitung*, October 9, 1822) Rochlitz claimed some credit for the inception of the Kreisler plan, and many critics, even in very recent books, have taken him at his word. According to him, after the receipt of Hoffmann's letter describing his financial plight, Rochlitz sent him the score of Beethoven's *Symphony in C Minor* with the proposal that he should write about it, either a formal review or "eine Betrachtung darüber, eine Phantasie über die Phantasie, ein Kunstwerk über das Kunstwerk." Also on the basis of the humorous tone of Hoffmann's letter, he suggested that Hoffmann write for him "eine Erzählung oder Charakterschilderung" of an insane musician, "verworren und launenhaft, aber gross und kühn." This was written after Hoffmann's death, and it is impossible to reconcile Rochlitz' statements with indisputable facts. Though he says he has Hoffmann's letter before him as he writes, Hoffmann's first letter from Bamberg (January 12, 1809, *Briefwechsel*, II, pp. 62-63) contains nothing remotely corresponding to Rochlitz' description of it. And with this letter, expressing Hoffmann's desire for a connection with Rochlitz' journal and offering to write essays and reviews, he sent *Ritter Gluck* as a specimen of his work. From the letter itself it is plain that Hoffmann had not written to Rochlitz since May 1808, when he sent him from Berlin some musical compositions in the hope that the firm Breitkopf und Härtel might publish them. Hoffmann was accepted as a "Mitarbeiter" on the *Allgemeine musikalische Zeitung*, but the score of Beethoven's symphony was not sent to him then. In his letter of April 15, 1809, Hoffmann mentions several musical works sent to him at the beginning of March, but not the Beethoven symphony; indeed it could not have been sent as Rochlitz states, for it was not published till April 1809. Hoffmann's review of it appeared more than a year later, July 4 and 11, 1810. It is apparent that long after the event and when Hoffmann's Kreisler had become an established and favorite figure in literature, Rochlitz' memory played him false; of course, another and much less creditable interpretation could be made.

[3] Of the first cycle "Ombra Adorata" and "Der vollkommene Maschinist" were first published in the *Fantasiestücke*; the "Höchst zerstreute Gedanken" appeared in the *Zeitung für die elegante Welt*, January 1814; the paper on "Beethovens Instrumentalmusik," published in this journal in 1814, was put together out of reviews which had previously appeared in the *Allgemeine musikalische Zeitung*; "Johannes Kreislers des Kapellmeisters musikalische Leiden" was published in the *Allgemeine musikalische Zeitung*, September 26, 1810, and "Kreislers Gedanken über den hohen Wert der Musik," July 29, 1812, appearing there as "Dissertatiuncula" instead of "Gedanken," perhaps one of Rochlitz' various emendations of Hoffmann's texts. The seven numbers of the second cycle had all appeared previously, except *Kreislers musikalisch-poetischer Klub*. The "Nachricht von einem gebildeten Manne," "Der Musikfeind," and "Über einen Ausspruch Sacchinis" appeared in the *Allgemeine musikalische Zeitung*, March 16, June 1, and July 20, 1814. "Johannes Kreislers Lehrbrief" was adapted, with additions and alterations, from an article which Hoffmann sent to the publisher Cotta in the spring of 1814 for publication in the *Morgenblatt*; it was, however, not published in that periodical until February 21, 22, 1816, after the "Lehrbrief" had appeared in the *Fantasiestücke*; the article sent to Cotta was entitled "Ahnungen aus dem Reiche der Töne." The Wallborn-Kreisler letters appeared in 1814 in *Die Musen*, a magazine edited by Fouqué and Wilhelm Neumann, the latter a poet and also a friend of Hoffmann's.

figure in the history of fiction began its career. Early in 1812 a new plan was taking form in Hoffmann's mind, which was evidently an outgrowth of the Kreisler scheme—the *Lichte Stunden eines wahnsinnigen Musikers* (Lucid Hours of an Insane Musician). He wrote to Hitzig that he was occupied with an odd musical work; it was his purpose, he says, to express in the new work his views on music, particularly "on the inner structure of composition," and "in order to provide a place for any apparent eccentricity" the essays were to be written by an insane musician in his lucid hours. The spirit or "demon" within him evidently frowned upon a conventional musical treatise and would not let him write one. His diary records the beginning of formal composition and for several years there are references to the *Lichte Stunden* as a work in prospect.[4]

Among other fragments from Hoffmann's literary remains Hitzig published a fugitive page bearing the heading *Lichte Stunden eines wahnsinnigen Musikers, ein Buch für Kenner* and giving a list of subjects that Hoffmann intended to treat, probably a hasty sketch that would have been developed and extended in the process of composition. Thus what might have been, for the time at any rate, one of the world's great works of musical criticism exists only as a table of contents, probably incomplete: "Melody from the North," "Melody from the South," "Mysticism of the Instruments," "Musical Chiaroscuro," "The Secret of the Fugue," and various other titles. The first section was to be "Die Liebe eines Künstlers," the theme which in one form or another runs through so much of Hoffmann's subsequent work.[5]

Another fragment found among Hoffmann's papers and entitled

[4] Almost exactly a year after the first mention of the project Hoffmann notes: "Agreement with Kunz as to *Lichte Stunden*," apparently the publication of the work. Instead of the customary signature on the group portrait of the Kunz family, which he finished February 13, 1813, he placed a book opened at the title page: "Lichte Stunden eines wahnsinnigen Musikers: Ein Buch für Kenner, Bamberg bei C. F. Kunz." In the autumn of 1814 Kunz advertised the work among forthcoming books. After his removal to Berlin Hoffmann apparently bethought himself now and then of the plan for *Lichte Stunden*. On May 24, 1815, he wrote to Kunz, promising the manuscript in July, and as late as March 8, 1818, he wrote that the book would not be given to any other publisher; at the same time he remarks: "Das Buch ist ganz anders geworden als ich im Sinn hatte." By this time, however, Hoffmann's friendship for his former Bamberg companion had considerably cooled, and his promise as to the publication of *Lichte Stunden* has the flavor of an ironical jest. Probably some of the material prepared for *Lichte Stunden* passed over into the *Kreisleriana*.

[5] In the introduction to the second cycle of the *Kreisleriana* the author speaks of an essay left behind at Kreisler's death, "Die Liebe eines Künstlers," and goes on to say: "This essay as well as several others which form a cycle on the purely spiritual [reingeistig] aspects of music may perhaps appear soon under the title 'Lichte Stunden eines wahnsinnigen Musikers.'"

Der Freund (The Friend) has been thought by some to be the narrative introduction, or a part of it, which Hoffmann was preparing for the essays of the *Lichte Stunden.* A country gentleman writes a long letter from his estate to his friend Theodor, describing the arrival there of a mysterious stranger, at times violently and menacingly insane and at others gentle and subdued. Papers in his portfolio supply the initials ".J. K." and seem to indicate a professional musician, but he cannot bear the sound of music; hence it is apparent that some experience in which music played a part has unbalanced his mind. It would seem also possible that *Der Freund* was written as an introduction to the first cycle of the *Kreisleriana* when Hoffmann assembled the different numbers for inclusion in the *Fantasiestücke,* and was discarded in favor of the introductory sketch which appeared there. Perhaps Hoffmann decided to soften the impression of Kreisler's madness; the account of Kreisler as a raving maniac in *Der Freund* runs so radically counter to Hoffmann's conception of his hero that one is almost tempted, even against conclusive evidence, to doubt the authenticity of the fragment.[6]

All six numbers of the first cycle of the *Kreisleriana* are by inference the work of Kreisler himself. In the second cycle of seven numbers *Kreislers musikalisch-poetischer Klub* is a narrative in the third person—about Kreisler—and the *Nachricht von einem gebildeten Manne* is, after an introductory paragraph, presented as a letter from Milo, a learned ape; the letter of Baron Wallborn included in the series was written by Fouqué. In the *Kreisleriana* the figure of the musician is for the most part indirectly developed, as was inevitable from the nature of the scheme—a character whom Hoffmann might endow with some of his own qualities, to whom he might assign certain experiences analogous to his own and opinions subtly tinted in passing through the spirit of the imaginary Kreisler. A complete identification of himself with Kreisler would confine his imagination.

The one shattering emotional experience in the life of Hoffmann was the episode of his love for Julia Marc, and it was accordingly inevitable that a corresponding passage in the life of his "alter ego" should find a place in the *Kreisleriana.* In the first number there is a mere hint of a similar experience, a dim foreshadowing, in Kreisler's admiration for the niece of the privy councilor, whose girlish simplicity and superb voice attracted him to the councilor's house and led him to endure the agony of the aesthetic teas. That Kreisler's

---

[6] Hans von Müller regards *Der Freund* as the product of Hoffmann's early days in Bamberg.

mind was affected—whether it be called insanity or not—through hopeless love for one of his pupils is suggested both in the *Kreisleriana* and in the plans for the *Lichte Stunden,* but the facts are never really told. Some elements of the story are, to be sure, supplied in the *Nachricht von den neuesten Schicksalen des Hundes Berganza* which Hoffmann began in February 1813, two months after the marriage of Julia Marc—the figure of Cäcilia, endowed with all the beauty, the childlike charm, and the divine voice of Julia, her proud and ambitious mother, and the marriage to a brutal, lascivious moneybags, a marriage which the mother in financial straits forced upon her daughter. Kreisler has been the teacher of Cäcilia and has spoken of the mysterious magic of her song, which lives in his works, or rather really composes them. Yet the Dog Berganza knows but little of the passion that has taken possession of his master's very being. Now Kreisler, suspected of insanity, has fled to escape the confinement which he thinks is threatening him.

In the following years, Hoffmann incorporated "the love of an artist," the first theme he had suggested for treatment in the *Lichte Stunden,* in one story after another and viewed the problem from many angles. Yet the perpetual urge to treat the Julia episode in poetic form, to find a final sublimation for past experience, had never been fully satisfied, and left him no peace. During all this time *Berganza* remained the most definitely autobiographical, in detail the closest to the actual circumstances, but the Cäcilia episode was thrust incongruously into an amorphous product, and, despite passages of elevation and force, was without intrinsic dignity of conception. The figure of Cäcilia's mother was in part a vicious caricature of Konsulin Marc, and unquestionably at long last the story of his love for Julia should not have been marred by petty spite. At the time Hoffmann's resentment, however basically unfounded, distorted his vision, which was not ordinarily blind to defects of his own work, and he wrote to Kunz to leave the text of *Berganza* untouched; he feared the editorial pencil might take liberties with his manuscript. With the passing of time Hoffmann must have perceived that what he had written there was quite unworthy of the theme. The treatment in the *Kreisleriana* was fragmentary indeed, and the love of the artist variously presented in many of his tales, though subtly subjective, was never precisely his own. Hence for the ultimate version of the experience he would return to the old story of the eccentric musician and the maiden with the peerless voice. Thus the plan of *Kater Murr* came into being in the spring of 1819, and the first volume was pub-

lished late in that year. The long title suggests the vagaries of Jean
Paul: *Lebensansichten des Katers Murr nebst fragmentarischer
Biographie des Kapellmeisters Johannes Kreisler in zufälligen Maku-
laturblättern*, herausgegeben von E. T. A. Hoffmann (The Cat
Murr's Opinions of Life Together with a Fragmentary Biography
of the Kapellmeister Johannes Kreisler in Chance Wastepaper Leaves,
published by E. T. A. Hoffmann). The second volume bore the date
1822, but was probably issued toward the end of the previous year.

To the first cycle of the *Kreisleriana* Hoffmann prefixed an introductory note, containing a few words of biographical detail and
some elements of characterization. "Where did he come from? No
one knows. Who were his parents? It is unknown. Whose pupil is he?
A good master, for he plays superbly." He had been Kapellmeister
at a court theater but had been dismissed from his position because
he had obstinately refused to compose music for an opera, the text
of which the court poet had written. Indiscreetly also at the table in
the inn, he had spoken contemptuously of the "Primo Huomo" and
had ventured to prefer a girl whom he was instructing in music to
the prima donna. Johannes was tossed hither and thither by inner
visions and dreams as "on an eternally agitated sea." Traces of insanity had been noted, and one day he disappeared. The introduction
to the second cycle adds something: Johannes had long been regarded as insane, for his whole way of doing things was so in contradiction to everything reasonable and proper that there could hardly
be a doubt as to the disorder of his mind; his ideas had become more
and more eccentric and confused. He confessed his determination
to commit suicide, indeed a dagger thrust with "an augmented fifth."

One number of each cycle—the article on Beethoven's instrumental
music and the interpretation of a statement of Sacchini as applied
to church music and to the opera—are straight musical criticism,
though highly personal. Most of the other numbers are indeed directly or indirectly concerned with music and with the life of a musician. The satirical tone is strong if not actually predominant, and
satire appears in large measure in the form of irony. In *Gedanken
über den hohen Wert der Musik* and *Der vollkommene Maschinist*
the irony is sustained throughout the article, though by a neat turn
of phrase or sentence Hoffmann gives voice to his real opinions.

Music, says Kreisler in the first of these papers, provides a pleasing entertainment; it diverts a man agreeably from the employments
which are his proper sphere and give him bread and butter, so that
afterwards he can return to the real purpose of his existence as an

efficient cog in the treadmill of society. For this pastime reading is less effective, for in reading it is more or less necessary to think, and the contemplation of a painting is a transitory distraction, which loses its interest as soon as one has guessed what the picture is supposed to represent. With music one is entirely relieved of the obligation to think, and no one is prevented from carrying on a conversation with one's neighbors.

Children, even without the faintest musical talent, should be kept at their music, so that they may be able to contribute their bit to social life. Music has the further advantage of being moral, hence of no possible harm to tender youth; a police official once certified that a new musical instrument contained nothing detrimental to the state, to religion, or morals; and parents may rest assured that the new sonata contains not a single immoral idea. Naturally as mere purveyors of diversion musicians are looked upon by everyone of sound understanding and mature views as of less importance than a capable clerk or any solid workman, such as an upholsterer. If a well-to-do family of the upper classes is so unfortunate as to have a child with an inclination to the art of music, means should be sought to bring the child back from the error of his ways. Many unhappy enthusiasts awake all too late from their mistake and fall really into a kind of insanity, maintaining that art causes man to perceive his higher principles and leads him out of the foolish activities of everyday life into the Temple of Isis, where Nature speaks to him in sacred sounds, never as yet heard but still intelligible. "They call music the most romantic of all the arts, since its theme is only the infinite, the mysterious Sanskrit of Nature, expressed in sound, which fills the breast of man with endless longing, and only in music does one understand the song of songs, of the trees, the flowers, the animals, the stones, and the waters!"

In *Der vollkommene Maschinist* Kreisler explains that he has long intended to write a treatise for scene shifters and stage decorators, but, not having got around to it, he will pen a letter or address to them containing instructions for their advantage. He assumes that they are all fundamentally in conflict with the authors and composers whose works are to be presented, and suggests various means through which they can defeat the author's purpose. For example, when the author wishes to create an illusion, the scene shifter can easily frustrate the plan by inserting arbitrarily some element of incongruity to distract the spectator's attention. He gives illustrations of success in using this méthod and outlines other ways of obtaining satisfaction from one's natural enemy.

The letter of Milo, the educated ape, is also a sustained piece of satire. The ape has been taught to talk; he has listened to the speech of men, their thoughts, their clever ideas. He was concerned about his use of language, when once acquired, but his master reassured him: "You will be amazed how thoughts come to you while speaking, how wisdom will rise within you—you won't understand it yourself, but this will be of no consequence." He has devoted himself to music also; the size of his hands permits him to strike two octaves, and this, coupled with the extraordinary fleetness of his fingers, is the whole secret of piano-playing; as once he leaped about from tree to tree, he now springs about with trills and octaves, and has become a supreme virtuoso. In singing he has attained distinction and is always greeted with thunderous applause. Here there are original tricks, such as the insertion of notes not in the score of the composer—the "quintessence of all wisdom in the art of song." He is a composer as well, and though there are rules of musical composition, a genuine composer like himself regards them as tasteless and stupid.[7]

In *Kreislers musikalische Leiden* the irony is incidental. Hoffmann describes a tea at the home of Councilor Röderlein, who sets the tone in aesthetic matters in the town. While the older guests play cards, the younger members of the company beg the two daughters of the host to sing: Fräulein Nannette, who has been Kreisler's pupil for three years and a half, has accomplished so much in this short space of time that she can sing a melody which she has heard ten times in the theater and has tried at most ten times on the piano so that one knows what it is supposed to be; Fräulein Marie gets the melody at the eighth try, but often sings a quarter of a tone flat. The musical torture of the evening mounts to a climax in the singing of Frau Ebenstein, the wife of the Minister of Finance; Kreisler searches his vocabulary for words to describe her performance: "Schreie, quieke, miaue, gurgle, stöhne, ächze, tremuliere, quinkiliere." And there is chorus singing which he treats with similar sarcasm. Now the guests have gone, he has driven them away by playing Bach, and on the blank pages of Bach's variations for the piano he records the hellish torments he has endured. He is loath to go to his lodgings, for in

---

[7] Is Hoffmann thinking of his uncle Otto when the ape writes: "Vorzüglich liegt mir noch zuweilen unser alter Onkel (nach meinen Erinnerungen muss es ein Onkel mütterlicher Seite gewesen sein) im Sinn, der uns nach seiner dummen Weise erzog, und alles nur mögliche anwandte, uns von allem, was menschlich, entfernt zu halten"? I, p. 294.

this evening hour his neighbors are accustomed to display their interest in music—the shrill, discordant voices of the Oberjägermeister's daughters, the sound of flute and horn in "acoustic experiments," the dogs and cats participating, the landlord's amorous tomcat wailing the chromatic scale. In this entertaining trifle, it is easy to perceive Hoffmann's satire upon certain aspects of life in Bamberg.

Except in the letter of Milo, the learned ape, the satire of the first cycle is lessened quantitatively in the second, and is of a gentler, more reflective type. In *Der Musikfeind* Hoffmann-Kreisler gains a certain perspective on himself by assigning some of his own experiences to a friend who is regarded, paradoxically, as an "enemy of music." For the early part of the narrative he goes back to his own youth and adds significantly to the picture he has painted elsewhere, notably in *Kater Murr*. There is a highly entertaining glimpse of the musical evenings in the Doerffer household. He provides a first glimpse of Tante Füsschen, though he has not yet given her a name. She sings to the little boy, and, beneath his obstinacy and seeming perversity in his response to instruction in music, she perceives a higher understanding, though his father and the music master see only willful caprice and recalcitrance. Unlike the career of Kreisler-Hoffmann, his musical education comes to an early end, and on through life he passes as an enemy of music. Yet in the last analysis his appreciation far transcends that of those who may boast of superior understanding; often a single number, even the beginning of a piece of music, stirs him so mightily that he must seek refuge outside, in "loneliness, where the eternally ruling Power moves in the rustling of the oak leaves above my head, in the splashing of the springs, which entwine themselves with the sounds that lie within me, and now shine forth in glorious music."

Similar in tone is the last of the *Kreisleriana*, entitled, appropriately enough, *Johannes Kreislers Lehrbrief*. As if his "dear Johannes" were an apprentice about to start out into the world, Kreisler writes this body of instructions and recommends his pupil, really himself, to the "good masters" who are gathered at the portals of their workshops. The spirit of music is everywhere in nature, and the musician hears its tones, the rustle of the winds, the murmur of the watercourses, but the melodies which are the higher language of the spirit realm rest only in the human breast. Thus music unites the world without and the world within.

Hoffmann wrote *Ombra Adorata* as a kind of homage to Julia

Marc, either at the time of her betrothal in August 1812 or perhaps
after her marriage in December.[8] The little sketch, only three pages,
is, particularly when read in the light of the personal context, one
of the most moving and eloquent passages in Hoffmann's work, indeed
in the whole range of German literature. In its brevity *Ombra Adorata* resembles a lyric poem of a few stanzas, and in depth of emotion
it challenges the masterpieces of lyricism, such, perhaps, as the love
lyrics of Goethe or Heine. Kreisler has heard a voice of incomparable
beauty singing an aria from a now forgotten opera on the theme
of Romeo and Juliet; and he is lifted beyond all earthly pain and
sorrow; even though he will never hear that voice again, the memory
is eternal and will go with him to his life's end. Only in dreams can
he repeat the song: "Tranquillo io sono, fra poco teco saro mia vita."
It is a symbol of lofty resignation which Hoffmann perhaps enviously
attributed to Kreisler only a few weeks or perhaps months before he
wrote the venomous episodes in *Berganza*.

   With its revelation of Kreisler's disturbed mind and heart, subtly
interpreted in terms of music, *Kreislers musikalisch-poetischer Klub*
may take its place beside *Ombra Adorata* among the works of Hoffmann that are unique and most worthy of remembrance. The time
of the sketch is immediately before Kreisler's disappearance. The
members of the club, designated by their qualities, "The Jovial One,"
"The Indifferent One," "The Thoughtful One," "The Dissatisfied
One," and "The Faithful Friend," have gathered for their meeting.
Candle in hand, "The Thoughtful One" investigates the piano where
there had been trouble with an inoperative hammer during Hoffmann's playing, but he lets candle grease fall, ruining a dozen or
so of the strings. Kreisler is nothing daunted and proposes to im-
provise on the bass, where no damage has been done. He then begins
a long series of chords, accompanying them with a rhapsodical description of the emotional response: A flat major, pianissimo: "What
then rustles so wondrously, so strangely, about me? Invisible wings
sweep up and down. I float in fragrant aether. But the fragrance
gleams in flaming circles, mysteriously intertwined. They are fair
spirits who move their golden wings in rapturously glorious melodies
and chords."

   Other chords, A flat minor, E major sixth, E major third, A minor, and the like are similarly interpreted. The spirit evoked in
Kreisler becomes more and more uncontrolled. With the C major

   [8] The simple entry in his diary, August 25, "Ombra Adorata," would not seem
to be conclusive proof that it was written at that time.

third chord fortissimo, a frenzied ecstasy seizes him: "In mad joy let us dance over the open graves. Let us shout for joy—they don't hear it down there. Hurrah—Hurrah—dance and jubilation, the devil enters with drums and trumpets!" and then the C minor chord fortissimo: "Don't you know him? Don't you know him? See—with glowing claws he grabs for my heart! He disguises himself in all sorts of mad masks, a huntsman, a concertmaster, or a quack doctor—ricco mercante; he flings the candle shears into the strings so that I may not play. . . . Kreisler, Kreisler, pull yourself together. Do you see it, lying in wait, the pale specter with the red sparkling eyes—stretching toward you its bony, clawlike fists out of the torn cloak, shaking its crown of straw on its smooth, bald skull! It is madness! Be brave, Johannes . . . can I not escape from thee? Let me go, I'll be good. . . . I will curse song, music, I will lick your feet like drunken Caliban, only release me from this torment. Ay! Ay! cursed one, you have trodden down all my flowers—in the awful desert no blade of grass grows green any more—dead—dead—dead—"[9]

Kreisler has been playing in the dark, and at this juncture the "Faithful Friend" lights the candles to prevent further fantasies. Presently tea is brought in, but Kreisler's awesome chords, his horrible words, continue to resound in a far-off echo; the mood induced

[9] "Was rauscht denn so wunderbar, so seltsam um mich her? Unsichtbare Fittiche wehen auf und nieder—ich schwimme im duftigen Äther. Aber der Duft erglänzt in flammenden, geheimnisvollen verschlungenen Kreisen. Holde Geister sind es, die die goldnen Flügel regen in überschwenglich herrlichen Klängen und Accorden."

C dur Terz-Accord (Fortissimo)

"Aber in toller wilder Lust lasst uns über den offnen Gräbern tanzen. Lasst uns jauchzen—die da unten hören es nicht.—Heisa—Heisa—Tanz und Jubel, der Teufel zieht ein mit Pauken und Trompeten."

C moll Accorde (Fortissimo hintereinander fort)

"Kennt ihr ihn nicht? Kennt ihr ihn nicht?—Seht, er greift mit glühender Kralle nach meinem Herzen! er maskiert sich in allerlei tolle Fratzen—als Freijäger—Konzertmeister—Wurmdoktor—ricco mercante—er schmeisst mit Lichtscheren in die Saiten, damit ich nur nicht spielen soll!—Kreisler—Kreisler! raffe dich auf! Siehst du es lauern, das bleiche Gespenst mit rot funkelnden Augen—die krallichten Knochenfäuste aus dem zerrissenen Mantel nach dir ausstreckend?—die Strohkrone auf dem kahlen glatten Schädel schüttelnd! Es ist der Wahnsinn—Johannes halte dich tapfer . . . Kann ich dir nicht entfliehen? . . . Lass ab von mir! ich will artig sein! . . . ich verfluche den Gesang, die Musik—ich lecke dir die Füsse wie der trunkne Kaliban—nur erlöse mich von der Qual—hei, hei, Verruchter, du hast mir alle Blumen zertreten—in schauerlicher Wüste grünt kein Halm mehr—tot—tot—tot—" I, pp. 289-91.

In his reminiscences of his stay in Germany, the Danish author Adam Öhlenschläger gives an account of a visit at Hoffmann's house; Fouqué was the other guest: "Als unter anderm einmal Fouqué etwas erzählte, setzte sich Hoffmann ans Clavier, accompagnirte Fouqué's Erzählung, malte das Grässliche, Kriegerische, Zärtliche und Rührende mit Tönen aus, und machte es vortrefflich." *Briefe in die Heimat auf einer Reise durch Deutschland und Frankreich*, German translation by Georg Lotz, Altona, 1820; quoted by C. G. von Maassen: *Der grundgescheute Antiquarius*, I, pp. 119-20.

by them was not to be dispelled. One by one the guests depart—
except the "Faithful Friend." " 'I don't know what to make of you
today,' he says. 'You are so wrought up, and yet entirely without
humor, not at all as usual!' 'Ah, my friend,' Kreisler replies, 'the
gloomy shadow of a cloud passes over my life. Don't you believe that
a poor innocent melody, which does not wish any place at all on
earth, should be permitted to rove, free and inoffensive, through the
wide space of the heavens? O, I would like at once to pass out through
yonder window on my Chinese dressing gown as upon a cloak of
Mephistopheles.' 'As an inoffensive melody?' the 'True Friend' interrupted with a smile. 'Or as basso ostinato, if you prefer,' answered Kreisler, 'but in some way or other I must soon be off.' "10

The "Very Scattered Thoughts," *Höchst zerstreute Gedanken*,
were probably put in shape to fill so and so much space in the *Zeitung
für die elegante Welt* and to bring home to Hoffmann a corresponding honorarium. There are fourteen of them, separate paragraphs,
mostly concerned with music, anecdotes about Mozart and Rameau,
and a satirical account of a performance of Kotzebue's *Johanna von
Montfaucon* by a troupe of strolling actors. Personally more significant are the description of the strange synthesis of colors, tones,
and odors when he is falling asleep after hearing music, and the brief
discussion of the influence of alcoholic stimulants on artistic creation.

In the second cycle, the Wallborn-Kreisler letters were first published in Fouqué's magazine *Die Musen* (1814). Baron Wallborn
is the hero of Fouqué's story *Ixion*, who becomes insane through
hopeless love. Under the transparent fiction that a letter to Kreisler
had been found among Wallborn's papers, apparently never sent,
and similarly a letter to Wallborn among Kreisler's, Fouqué and
Hoffmann published the two letters with a brief foreword. The Wallborn letter, written by Fouqué, was by the nature of things inseparable from its companion, and Hoffmann included it with his own
Kreisler letter in the *Fantasiestücke*. The Baron has apparently read
Kreisler's description of the aesthetic tea and his essay on the value

10 " 'Ich weiss nicht,' sprach der treue Freund, 'wie du mir heute vorkommst,
Kreisler!—Du bist so aufgeregt, und doch ohne allen Humor, gar nicht so, wie sonst!'
—'Ach, Freund,' erwiderte Kreisler, 'ein düstrer Wolkenschatten geht über mein
Leben hin!—Glaubst du nicht, dass es einer armen unschuldigen Melodie, welche
keinen—keinen Platz auf der Erde begehrt, vergönnt sein dürfte, frei und harmlos
durch den weiten Himmelsraum zu ziehen?—Ei, ich möchte nur gleich auf meinem
chinesischen Schlafrock wie einem Mephistophelesmantel hinausfahren durch jenes
Fenster dort!'—'Als harmlose Melodie?' fiel der treue Freund lächelnd ein. 'Oder als
basso ostinato, wenn du lieber willst,' erwiderte Kreisler, 'aber fort muss ich bald
auf irgend eine Weise.' " I, p. 292.

of music, for he enters a plea for the performance of music by amateurs and by children. Though in accordance with the fiction which the two authors invented, the letters were never sent; Kreisler, by some act of clairvoyance, answers Wallborn's criticism. He was merely attacking pretense and insincerity, and can be moved to the depths by artless but heartfelt song.[11]

"KATER MURR"

The odd technique that Hoffmann employed in the Kreisler part of *Kater Murr*—chance fragments of a larger whole—sets perilous traps in the pathway of the narrator, though of course it forms a convenient method of skipping neutral passages in the lives of his characters. We have only the pages that the cat tore from the volume for his own uses, but the author of the whole biography acknowledges difficulties in the task he set for himself. His information has been obtained in part orally and in fragments which have to be pieced together, but despite the patchwork of the narrative he promises that the reader in the end will perceive a firm thread running through it all, binding it together. The first of the "wastepaper" fragments begins with a broken sentence: Meister Abraham is relating to Kreisler a long conversation between Prince Irenäus and himself, and then proceeds to describe the celebration of Princess Maria's name-day; the name-day of the princess happened to coincide with that of Julia, and the festivities took some notice of this fact.

Chronologically this interview belongs after Kreisler's return from the Abbey of Kanzheim at the close of the second volume, and in his *Kreislerbuch* Hans von Müller has placed it there—on the assumption that the cat's first plundering was from the latter part of the biography. The presence of this material at the beginning of the first volume proves that Hoffmann had his full narrative well in control at the outset. It was probably also not a mere whim to have the cat tear out this later portion of the narration; by this Hoffmann could anticipate the development of the relation between Kreisler and Julia, particularly in recording the musician's thrill at the very mention of her name. In the last part of the fragment, Hoff-

---

[11] In the first edition of the *Fantasiestücke* II, "Die Prinzessin Blandina" was inserted in Hoffmann's narrative of the meeting of the club. As he wrote to Kunz, he regarded this sketch in dramatic form as the weakest of his works hitherto and he omitted it from the second edition. Despite Hoffmann's own opinion of its merits, Harich has tried to rehabilitate *Prinzessin Blandina* as a work of deep significance, long neglected by students of Hoffmann. A discussion of the subject is not possible here, but most critics agree with the author's verdict.

mann joins the two narratives by introducing the cat Murr. Abraham has rescued the animal in circumstances that he himself acknowledges admit of comparison with the classic rescue of the dog in *Minna von Barnhelm*, has brought him up to maturity, and now presents him to Kreisler, who, though at first reluctant, takes him "into his service."

For the second fragment Murr made a very judicious selection, unwittingly tearing from the book the leaves that contain just the material which the reader requires in order to go on with the story. The scene is a minute mediatized principality; from the top of his castle the reigning prince had been able with a good telescope to view the whole realm. During the Napoleonic period the principality had been united with the neighboring Grand Duchy. The subjects were, however, hardly aware of the change, since neither in the past nor in the present was there any "governing" of which they were conscious. In retaining the ancestral title the present prince, Irenäus,[12] had chosen to retain as well the external trappings of sovereignty without its essence. The procedures of court etiquette were scrupulously observed; there was a prime minister (chancellor) and other court functionaries—the minister of finance, indeed, having no other duties sat up all night in a frenzy of activity over the laundry lists, and court balls were held, though there were hardly more than a dozen people whom the august rules governing eligibility admitted to the ballroom. The simple folk still looked upon Prince Irenäus as their sovereign and reverenced him as such, though he no longer had the slightest control over them.

Save for his insistence on princely prerogatives, Prince Irenäus is a nonentity, albeit a very entertaining one. The most influential persons at the tiny court are the Rätin Benzon and Meister Abraham. Rätin Benzon, widow of a former councilor, pulls the strings which control the activities of Sieghartshof, the princely residence. Over Hedwiga, the daughter of the Prince, she has exercised from babyhood a paramount influence, particularly since Princess Maria, the wife of the Prince, is a colorless, ineffectual figure. Beyond the boundaries of the realm, into the Grand Duchy, even into the Empire, the mysterious lines of Rätin Benzon's power spread out. She is a clever, dominating personality, a subtle and successful intriguer,

[12] Friedrich Holtze thinks that the characters of Prince Irenäus and his half-witted son Ignatius were suggested by the Bavarian Duke Wilhelm and his defective son Pius: cf. "E. T. A. Hoffmann als Hofmann," in *Mitteilungen des Vereins für die Geschichte Berlins*, XLII (1925), pp. 11-14.

and is possessed of an insensate ambition to regain for the mediatized principality its former sovereignty and to marry her daughter Julia to the half-witted Prince Ignatius, son and heir of Prince Irenäus. Julia Benzon is to be sacrificed to a mother's schemes even as Julia Marc had been.

The influence of Meister Abraham was of a more indirect and pervasive type; and it is apparent from the beginning that it is based in part upon his knowledge of secrets in the princely household. Originally an organ builder and musician, he had appeared many years before at Sieghartsweiler, the little town in the principality, as a sleight-of-hand performer, a dabbler, or adept, if you will, in mysterious arts; his wife Chiara, a clairvoyant of remarkable powers, was the miraculous voice of the "crystal ball." The father of Prince Irenäus had leaned toward the mysterious and the occult, and partly to flout two of his ministers whom he overheard talking about him, sought out Meister Abraham and became a devoted patron of the necromancer. According to popular rumors, the old prince and his new friend carried on secret experiments in alchemy and the like. On the death of his patron, Meister Abraham left Sieghartsweiler, but in time the new ruler, Prince Irenäus, called him back. The little court was suffering from ennui, and Abraham became a kind of "maître de plasir"; it was he who had arranged the gorgeous pageant, humorously described at the beginning of the first fragment. Through the connivance of Rätin Benzon, Chiara has been spirited away, and Abraham has no knowledge of her whereabouts or indeed that she is living, though he has sought her everywhere. In building his complex structure of mysteries, the novelist cultivates the suspicion that Rätin Benzon feared the clairvoyant powers of Chiara—they might disclose embarrassing secrets.

In the narrower sense, the story begins with the third fragment, but there are frequent pauses in the onward flow of the narrative; the immediate or the remoter past is accounted for by explanation on the part of the biographer or through the narration of the characters themselves. At the beginning of the third fragment Princess Hedwiga and Julia Benzon, who have been inseparable comrades since childhood, are walking towards evening in the park. The sound of a guitar is heard not far from them, the strings plucked with violence, and then the sonorous voice of a man, singing now with the tender sweetness of Italian song, now suddenly changing to solemn melody. Under cover of the shrubbery the two maidens creep nearer, discovering then a man dressed in black, his back turned to

them, who proceeds to tune the guitar, but after repeatedly testing
his work by a series of chords, is ever dissatisfied. He addresses the
instrument: "Tell me, little obstinate thing, where rests thy harmony, into what corner of thy inmost being has the pure scale crept
away?" Kreisler, for he is the stranger, is here asking similar questions to those which his spiritual kinsman, Rat Krespel, asked of
his violins. Eventually in exasperation he throws the perverse instrument into the bushes and goes his way.

Julia is fascinated by this brief episode; indeed, she was half
looking for some sort of adventure in the park, and, remembering
Rosalind and Celia in the forest of Arden, she thinks of the stranger
as a kind of melancholy Jacques whom chance has brought in their
way. Hedwiga, however, is terrified to the very roots of her being,
not merely by the admittance of strangers, perhaps dangerous characters, to the park toward nightfall, but the appearance of the man
himself had awakened in her the remembrance of the most horrible
experience in her young life. Hoffmann is an unsurpassed master in
the art of creating suspense, and as yet does not disclose what this
experience had been. Against the urgent protests of her companion,
Julia rescues the guitar, and then begins to play and to sing, "giving
full voice to the rich tones that rested in her breast." Presently the
stranger stands before them, his disheveled black hair filled with pine
needles, for he has forced his way through the thickest of the wood.
It is the first time that he has heard that voice, and he has to follow
it as if drawn by some elemental power of nature. Only a fugitive
glance does he cast upon Hedwiga, but his big dark eyes rest upon
Julia. "Are these heavenly tones silent simply at the sight of me?"
he says in a gentle voice. The Princess, naïvely conscious of her
rank, reproves the intruder, and proudly states her name and position. At her words the countenance of the stranger seems to become
a different one; the expression of melancholy longing, every trace of
a spirit stirred to its depths, was erased; a madly distorted smile
intensified the look of bitter irony till it turned to droll waggery—
and the Princess stops in the midst of her reproof. But Julia is ready
with words of apology; she has not only stolen the guitar but filched
the most excellent tones from it, and she tries to return it.

" 'It is,' the stranger said, 'a very rare melodious instrument,
coming down from the good old times, which only in my awkward
hands—yet what hands, what hands! The wondrous spirit of harmony which favors this strange little thing, dwells also in my breast
but in the form of a chrysalis, incapable of free movement; yet out

of your inmost being, my young lady, it soars up to the light celestial spaces in a thousand shimmering colors, like shining peacock's eyes. Oh, my lady! when you sang, all the longing pain of love, all the rapture of sweet dreams, hope, desire, surged through the forest and fell like refreshing dew into the perfumed chalices of the flowers, into the breast of listening nightingales. Keep the instrument; you have command over the magic which is locked up in it.' "[13]

The stranger has again become transformed, and in a high, strident voice a torrent of words, even with phrases in Latin and Italian, pours from his lips, expressing his regret at this unfortunate and premature meeting and indicating former acquaintance with personages of the court circle. On their return the two maidens relate the adventure to Rätin Benzon, who inquires into the minutest details of the stranger's appearance and manner, and then exclaims: "It is he; only too certainly it is he, he himself." But the fragment breaks off as she is about to relate happenings of five years before.

It seemed desirable to relate this initial episode somewhat at length, as containing what is virtually the introduction of the hero, his strange chameleonlike appearance, even the sudden changes in the tones of his voice, his emotions of a strength uncommon among mortals, the contradictory elements of his being, the passionate music within him, the droll irony, and seemingly bitter cynicism.

The character of Kreisler is further developed in the following section, in a long interview with Rätin Benzon. As an old acquaintance, who had once befriended him, she chides him for his eccentric conduct, which ever brings him into conflict with the conventions, "which once and for all exist." Her outspoken suspicion that his real name is not Kreisler provokes a long, ingenious, and entertaining analysis of the possible derivation of the word and its appropriateness to himself. In presenting the circumstances that caused his abrupt departure from the ducal city where he had been Kapellmeister, Kreisler analyzes his innate restlessness:

[13] " 'Es ist,' sprach der Fremde, 'ein sehr seltnes klangvolles Instrument, noch aus alter guter Zeit her, das nur in meinen ungeschickten Händen—doch was Hände, was Hände! Der wunderbare Geist des Wohllauts, der diesem kleinen seltsamen Dinge befreundet, wohnt auch in meiner Brust, aber eingepuppt, keiner freien Bewegung mächtig; doch aus Ihrem Innern, mein Fräulein, schwingt er sich auf zu den lichten Himmelsräumen, in tausend schimmernden Farben, wie das glänzende Pfauenauge. Ha, mein Fräulein! als Sie sangen, aller sehnsüchtige Schmerz der Liebe, alles Entzücken süsser Träume, die Hoffnung, das Verlangen, wogte durch den Wald und fiel nieder wie erquickender Tau in die duftenden Blumenkelche, in die Brust horchender Nachtigallen. Behalten Sie das Instrument; nur Sie gebieten über den Zauber, der in ihm verschlossen.' " x, pp. 54-55.

"A wild, insane longing often breaks forth for a something that in restless striving I seek outside of myself, since concealed in my inmost self there is a dark mystery, a confused, enigmatic dream of a paradise of highest satisfaction, a paradise which even the dream is incapable of naming, can only dimly suggest, and this presentiment distresses me with the torments of Tantalus."[14] Even in the most cheerful surroundings, in the company of good friends, suddenly everything appears wretched, worthless, colorless, dead, and only the spirit of music can silence the pains of earthly distress.

The following fragment carries the life of Kreisler back to his childhood. In the cottage of Meister Abraham, who had been a friend of Kreisler's father and the guide and mentor of his own youth, Kreisler gives a charming account of his boyhood days, often interrupted by his hearers, Meister Abraham himself and a privy councilor, so that the fiction of conversation is preserved and the account does not degenerate into an intercalated personal narration. Much of this material has passed over into biographies of Hoffmann, though of course much of it is also attested elsewhere. There are, however, many details that do not agree with the circumstances of Hoffmann's youth. These reminiscences are supplemented by the biographer, who says he has succeeded in finding information concerning the early acquaintance between Kreisler and Meister Abraham. For the figure of Abraham, Hoffmann seems to have made use of the organist Podbielski, his music teacher in Königsberg, transforming him from an organist into an organ builder. Once when Abraham (Liscov) came to tune Uncle "Ottfried's" piano he made the acquaintance of the little boy and in time they became devoted friends. Liscov, in his love of the eccentric, formed a counterbalance to the rigid conventionality of his uncle; the boy's love of music was widened and deepened; a love of curious inventions, mechanical tricks, indeed of so-called "natural magic," was also stimulated, but perhaps more abiding still was the contagious example of a highly original sense of humor. Meister Abraham saw in the boy a kindred soul in process of development, as if Johannes had been his own son. Like Hoffmann, Kreisler studied law, and under the aegis of an uncle entered governmental service. The temporary disruption of

14 "Ein wüstes wahnsinniges Verlangen bricht oft hervor nach einem Etwas, das ich in rastlosem Treiben ausser mir selbst suche, da es doch in meinem eignen Innern verborgen, ein dunkles Geheimnis, ein wirrer rätselhafter Traum von einem Paradies der höchsten Befriedigung, das selbst der Traum nicht zu nennen, nur zu ahnen vermag, und diese Ahnung ängstigt mich mit den Qualen des Tantalus." x, p. 67.

Hoffmann's legal career appears in somewhat altered form in the case of Kreisler. He had become "Legationsrat" in the royal capital, but "a mighty crowned colossus visited the monarch in his capital and embraced him so sincerely and cordially in his iron arms that the monarch lost the better part of the breath of life." Thus does Hoffmann begin his brief account of Napoleon's arrival in Prussia and its consequences for himself and his hero.

Kreisler is accepted as a temporary member of the court circle but not without the astute wire-pulling of Meister Abraham. If Kreisler is to remain, the Prince insists that he must abjure some irritating habits: when the Prince casts a withering look upon him, he does not lower his eyes, like other mortals, but looks the Prince directly in the eye with a strange smile; subtly, too, he conveys the impression that he does not regard what the Prince has just been saying as especially important. Hoffmann employs this interview between Meister Abraham and the Prince to cast a veil over Kreisler's past and to arouse further suspicion that there is some mystery as to his identity. Kreisler's eccentricities relieved the boredom of the tiny, really imaginary, court; with his sparkling wit, the sudden and startling change from extreme gravity of mien and word to turbulence and ebullient verbal fireworks, the ever-changing expression of his face, the odd contraction of the muscles of his brow—he was at times an irritating but ever a stimulating guest.

Almost at once he begins to instruct Julia in singing, accompanies her on the piano, and sings duets with her, in part Hoffmann's own compositions. For a time Hedwiga refuses to see Kreisler, for the impression of horror linked to something in the past is still too strong. Eventually at an evening musicale where Kreisler plays and Julia sings she approaches the musician and timidly, as if under some mysterious spell, asks him to instruct her also.

From this point on, the story centers largely in the relationship of these two girls to Kreisler. In ways subtly differentiated according to their characters, he absorbs their thoughts. Julia's love is deep and holy, is reverence, almost worship, without a taint of the material or physical; she dreams indeed of falling on Kreisler's breast, but only to seek there protection from the sinister forces that threaten her. Hedwiga's love is more capricious, effervescent, but not on that account superficial. In some occult fashion, even if love's fulfillment is eternally denied, is indeed never even thought of, they are both conscious of a strange protective power in Kreisler, which, like a magic cloak, might cover them in case of need. Hoffmann has never surpassed, indeed few novelists have equalled, the subtle revelation of character, the psychological insight, of the scene where Hedwiga and Julia again walk in the park and each in her own way gives voice to what lies deep within her.

Princess Hedwiga is by turns shy and retiring and at other times capable of unrestrained gaiety, of overstepping the proprieties demanded by her rank. She is subject also to nervous crises and swoons, to states of insensibility which the physicians call cataleptic; once in such a trance she acts as an automaton, raising her arms and letting them fall at the will of another. From the contact of her hand, Kreisler receives an electric shock, and on one occasion there is a suspicion of clairvoyant powers: "I see the bloody track of the murderer," she says long before Prince Hector's guilt is known to anyone but Meister Abraham. In earlier days, Hoffmann would perhaps have stressed these characteristics and have explained Hedwiga's conduct in terms of mesmerism and the like. Whether or not Hoffmann intended it as a psychological explanation, the modern psychologist might trace her nervous instability, her haunting dreams, to an event in her childhood which after a time she relates to Kreisler, to account for the terror she felt at his sudden appearance in the park. Years before, when she was a tiny girl, a painter named Ettlinger had resided at the court. He was fond of the little girl and she of him, but one day he was no more to be seen and they told her he was dead. Later as a raving madman he suddenly appeared before her, dragging broken chains; with frenzied words he seized her and was about to plunge a dagger into her throat when she was rescued by a servant and the madman's attendant. Much later still she learned that Ettlinger had become insane from love for her mother. At their first meeting in the park, Kreisler had resembled Ettlinger "as if he had been his brother." The story of the Princess prompts Kreisler to reflect upon the "love of the artist," and this relatively brief passage, wistfully melancholy and eloquent, we must accept as a surrogate for the more formal essay which he proposed as an introduction to the *Lichte Stunden*.

Remembering the words of a song in a comedy he has once heard, Kreisler, like the Great Judge at the world's end, divides all men into two classes, the "good people," who are poor musicians or rather no musicians at all, and the real musicians. The "good people" fall in love with a pair of beautiful eyes, encompass the fair one in an ever-narrowing circle, which turns into a wedding ring, and then bear the

loved one home into the marriage prison. It is quite different with
the "real musicians":

"It happens indeed that invisible hands suddenly draw aside the
veil which covered the eyes of the aforesaid musicians, and they behold walking on the earth the likeness of an angel, which as a sweet
unexplored mystery has silently rested in their bosoms. And now in
the pure heavenly fire, which only gleams and warms without destroying in ruinous flames, there blazes up all the rapture, all the
nameless bliss, of the higher life, springing forth from their inmost
being, and the spirit stretches out a thousand feelers in ardent longing and touches the one whom it has seen, but yet never possesses,
for the longing continues to exist in endless thirst. And *she, she*
herself, it is, the glorious one, which as a dream figure taking on living form, shines forth from the artist's soul, as song—picture—
poem! Ah! believe me, my lady, I beg you, be convinced, that the
real musicians who with their bodily arms and the hands grown to
them do nothing but make passable music, be it with the pen, the
brush, or otherwise, actually stretch out toward the one they really
love nothing but spiritual feelers which have no hands or fingers to
grasp a wedding ring with conventional delicacy and place it on the
finger of the one adored; . . . it matters rather little whether the
loved one who lives in the soul of the artist is a princess or a baker's
daughter, provided the latter is not a goose. These artists when in
love create glorious works, with the inspiration of Heaven, and
neither die wretchedly of consumption nor do they become insane."[15]

[15] "Es begiebt sich wohl, dass besagten Musikanten unsichtbare Hände urplötzlich
den Flor wegziehen, der ihre Augen verhüllte, und sie erschauen, auf Erden wandelnd,
das Engelsbild, das, ein süsses unerforschtes Geheimnis, schweigend ruhte in ihrer
Brust. Und nun lodert auf in reinem Himmelsfeuer, das nur leuchtet und wärmt,
ohne mit verderblichen Flammen zu vernichten, alles Entzücken, alle namenlose
Wonne des höheren aus dem Innersten emporkeimenden Lebens, und tausend Fühlhörner streckt der Geist aus in brünstigem Verlangen, und umnetzt die, die er ge-
schaut, und hat sie, und hat sie nie, da die Sehnsucht ewig dürstend fortlebt! Und
sie, sie selbst ist es, die Herrliche, die, zum Leben gestaltete Ahnung, aus der Seele
des Künstlers hervorleuchtet, als Gesang—Bild—Gedicht! Ach, Gnädigste, glauben
Sie mir, sein Sie überzeugt, dass wahre Musikanten, die mit ihren leiblichen Armen
und den daran gewachsenen Händen nichts tun, als passabel musizieren, sei es nun
mit der Feder, mit dem Pinsel oder sonst, in der Tat nach der wahrhaften Geliebten
nichts ausstrecken, als geistige Fühlhörner, an denen weder Hand noch Finger
befindlich, die mit konvenabler Zierlichkeit einen Trauring erfassen und anstecken
könnten an den kleinen Finger der Angebeteten . . . und scheint ziemlich gleichgültig,
ob die Geliebte, die in dem Innern des Künstlers lebt, eine Fürstin oder eine Bäckers-
tochter, insofern letztere nur keine Eule. Besagte Musikanten schaffen, sind sie in
Liebe gekommen, mit der Begeisterung des Himmels, herrliche Werke, und sterben
weder elendiglich dahin an der Schwindsucht, noch werden sie wahnsinnig." x, p. 141.
The comedy referred to in the introduction to this passage is Brentano's *Ponce de
Leon*; Hoffmann refers to this quotation also in *Seltsame Leiden*.

The external events of the story that follow after Hoffmann has thus liberally determined the setting are directly or indirectly connected with the arrival of Prince Hector, whom Prince Irenäus has chosen for his daughter's husband—events which might in less competent hands have become offensively melodramatic. The son of a mediatized prince, Hector had taken service in the French army and then in the Neapolitan, and had risen, "as can happen only to a prince," to the rank of general.[16] Prince Hector is handsome and gorgeously attired in his Neapolitan uniform; so opulent a figure had obviously never yet graced the Lilliputian court at Sieghartshof. With flattering impetuosity he unfolds before Princess Hedwiga "the many-colored, boastful peacock's tail of his gallantry," but in the midst of his "hymn" to her beauty and grace, Hedwiga suddenly takes flight and seeks sanctuary at Julia's side. The newcomer casts a long, strange look upon Julia, and the reader is prepared for the complication which fills the following pages of the novel.

While maintaining the outward show of his love for Hedwiga, the Prince begins to whisper to Julia that his words are really meant for her. Perceiving the baseness of Hector's character and his evil designs upon Julia, Kreisler is much concerned over the fate of the two young women, both of whom are dear to him. He confides in Meister Abraham, who gives him a medallion containing a picture and, in a secret compartment, a document; these he may use in case of need. Presently Kreisler seizes an opportunity to force Prince Hector to listen to a duet which he and Julia sing; but, since the spiritual intimacy or kinship thus symbolized and suggested as a barrier to Hector's plans makes no impression upon the Prince, Kreisler has recourse to the medallion, the Medusa head, as he later calls it. Hector turns pale, shrinks away, and flees abruptly. In the evening Kreisler walks back through the park in the direction of the little town, and soon Prince Hector's adjutant is seen going the same way. Before long a shot is heard in the far reaches of the wood; in the morning search is made, and Kreisler's hat is found with traces of blood on it, but Kreisler himself has disappeared.

With the beginning of the second volume (Part Third), the action of the story is somewhat retarded—as in the fourth act of a tragedy, though in the hands of the dramatist the substance presented should

---

[16] The figure of Prince Hector was probably suggested by the visit of an Italian officer in Bamberg; on September 1, 1812, Hoffmann records: "Dann zu Mark gebeten, weil ein Neapolitanischer Offizier St. Angelo da war."

betray no lessening of real significance; mighty happenings are
followed by a recoil and a covert preparation for a resumption of
the conflict. Rätin Benzon is no longer certain that she controls the
mechanism of the marionette show. In his confusion at the flight
of Prince Hector, who left only a brief word of apology for his host,
Prince Irenäus has consulted Meister Abraham, and Rätin Benzon is
suspicious. She is also confident that Kreisler's presence has been a
subtle but pervasive deterrent to the accomplishment of her plans.
She herself then visits Meister Abraham, hoping to discover the
content of his interview with Prince Irenäus. Her long conversation
with Abraham reveals Hoffmann as an unsurpassed master of con-
versational dialectic. Subtle and discreet, the organ builder and
magician spars with the wily lady of the court, and does not yield
a point; he perceives the cunning of his adversary but preserves his
outward composure, his courtly deference. More significant for the
later action of the story is the interview between Rätin Benzon and
Prince Irenäus. The position she occupies at the petty court is not
solely the achievement of her cleverness; she has a hold upon the
Prince, for she has once been his mistress and has borne him a daughter, Angela, who was secretly transported to Naples, where she is
liberally supported, and, as they suppose, carefully guarded. The
reader suspects, and is intended to suspect, some hidden connection
with Hector, the Neapolitan officer.

In the meantime Prince Hector has been hiding in a pavilion in
the park; both Hedwiga and Julia have been alarmed and excited
over mysterious lights in the building where no one dwelt. But his
ardent southern blood could not remain quiet long; he bribes a
servant and in the cover of darkness enters Rätin Benzon's apartments, and finding Julia alone he wildly clasps her to his breast.
Luckily the Rätin herself returns, and the gallant Prince escapes
through the window. Since he can now no longer remain in concealment, he appears again at the castle, and a formal betrothal is
celebrated. On this occasion Prince Hector sees Meister Abraham
for the first time, and he gazes upon him in unspeakable horror. It is
plain that Abraham is acquainted with dark secrets in the Prince's
past, but at the present moment he promises to remain silent, if the
Prince will cease molesting Julia.

Kreisler was indeed the target for the shot heard in the forest,
but the bullet only grazed his head. In the hand-to-hand conflict
which ensues, he strikes down his assailant with the dagger snatched
from his walking stick; but in the darkness he has no idea of the

assailant's identity. He rushes out of the park, sleeps during the
night in a forest, and in the early morning wanders on. Presently he
encounters the merry monk, Brother Hilarius, who urges him to
return with him to the Benedictine monastery of Kanzheim, where
Kreisler is well-known and beloved—the choir of the monastery is
desperately in need of music which Kreisler can compose. The first
part of the cloister idyll which follows is written with great charm.
The liberal-minded Abbot not only allows but fosters a reconciliation of religious devotion with the joys of living.[17] Kreisler even dons
the monk's habit, and rejoices in the intelligent and genial companionship of the Abbot and the brothers. It is the abode of peace; for
the time being his restless spirit is quieted, his longing stilled. Have
the monks really found the only pathway to peace?

But for Kreisler the serenity of the monastic walls is not without
disturbing interruptions. He is not beyond the reach of Rätin
Benzon's wiles; she suspects his place of refuge and writes to the
Abbot, whom she knows well, about Kreisler and his influence at
Sieghartsweiler. Presently also the monastery is disquieted and
annoyed by the arrival of Brother Cyprianus, who has been sent
from Rome, not, to be sure, to displace the liberal Abbot, but to in-
sist upon a more rigid observance of discipline. The new monk carries out his mission with fanatical zeal, insisting upon reforms
even in the music of the services. Before his arrival he had sent to
the monastery a large painting which the Abbot hung over a small
altar in the place of a Leonardo. The picture presented a young
man, mortally wounded, blood flowing from a deep gash in his breast;
dimly in the background another figure appears, obviously the murderer, dagger in hand, looking back at his victim, but, above, the
Virgin hovers, indicating the miracle of healing which took place.
Kreisler immediately recognizes Prince Hector in the picture of the
murderer, and the face of his victim, miraculously awakening again
to life, is vaguely familiar. When he sees the newcomer walking with
the Abbot, he recognizes in him the murdered man and the one
pictured on the medallion which Meister Abraham had given him.

[17] This may be illustrated by the invitation of Brother Hilarius when Kreisler
met him on the forest pathway; he asked him to partake of the luncheon he had
brought with him: "Ich kann Euch diese Feldhühner empfehlen, erst gestern schoss
sie unser ehrwürdiger Bruder Macarius, der, wie Ihr Euch wohl erinnert, alles trifft,
nur nicht die Noten in den Responsorien, und wenn Ihr den Kräuteressig vorschmeckt,
mit dem sie angefeuchtet, so verdankt Ihr das der Sorgfalt des Bruders Eusebius, der
sie selbst gebraten mir zu Liebe. Was aber den Wein betrifft, so ist er wert die
Zunge eines landflüchtigen Kapellmeisters zu netzen. Echter Bocksbeutel, carissime
Johannes, echter Bocksbeutel aus dem St. Johannis Hospital zu Würzburg, den wir
unwürdige Diener des Herrn erhalten in bester Qualität." x, p. 225.

Soon after the arrival of Brother Cyprianus, the cloister bell rings solemnly at midnight, summoning the monks to the chapel; Kreisler is awakened from sleep and joins them there. He is thus present at the obsequies of Prince Hector's adjutant, whom he himself has slain, though in self-defense. This dread midnight service, together with Kreisler's thoughts as he participates, forms one of the most moving scenes in the novel. At the end of the requiem a tattered, wild-eyed youth, who has gained entrance through a door which was supposed to be locked, springs forward and attacks Kreisler, crying out that he is there to avenge the death of "his brother." Kreisler is saved by the interposition of the new monk Cyprianus, who calls the youth by name and bids him be gone, though in words the precise meaning of which Kreisler does not understand. The following day Cyprianus orders Kreisler forthwith to leave the cloister with his unworthy, worldly music. Kreisler, however, is not intimidated; he defends his music as an expression of a sincere religious devotion, and then with stirring indignation he flings in the face of the monk his sinful past, acting indeed on a kind of intuition, and fortifies his charges by opening the medallion before the eyes of his now cowering antagonist. The monk acknowledges his identity and reveals the secret behind the painting he had sent.

Before taking the vows, the monk Cyprianus was Prince Antonio, the older brother of Prince Hector. In Naples he had become acquainted with Angela Benzoni, the daughter of Prince Irenäus and Rätin Benzon, partly through the strategy of her duenna, the mysterious Magdala Sigrun, who at times assumed the rags of an old gypsy and wandered in the streets of Naples. Though he had hitherto led the life of a libertine, he fell passionately and sincerely in love with Angela, and upon her insistence consented to a clandestine marriage. His brother Hector suspected his secret, tracked him to Angela's dwelling, and was then himself consumed with desire for his brother's wife. Antonio became insanely jealous, and poisoned Angela. Hector, seeking vengeance, stabbed his brother, who miraculously recovered, Antonio himself believed through the direct intervention of the Virgin. Repenting of his sins, Antonio entered a cloister. After his interview with Kreisler, the monk Cyprianus leaves the Cloister Kanzheim, and peace returns to the tormented Abbot and brothers. In his days in Naples Meister Abraham had known the two brothers, had indeed done them some service; he had entered into possession of family secrets, and Magdala Sigrun had given him the medallion.

At the end of the second volume Kreisler receives a letter from
Meister Abraham, urging him to return to Sieghartsweiler; a
catastrophe may perhaps be averted by his presence. Despite her
power at the little court, Rätin Benzon was still of dubious origins
from the standpoint of court eligibility, but now she has been
admitted to the august nobility of the empire and has become the
Countess Eschenau. Her plans are ripening to maturity; the court
will no longer frown upon the marriage of Prince Ignatius to Julia
Benzon as a misalliance. A double wedding is in prospect.

Kater Murr remained a torso; that Hoffmann never wrote the
third volume is one of the unforgivable mishaps of literary history.
He had arrived at the maturity of his powers as a storyteller. The
native endowment of the skillful narrator had been developed and
sharpened by experience; ready at his command were the ability to
create characters, vividly presented and convincingly alive, and
the knack of erecting a coherent, integrated structure as a plot in
which his characters might live their lives. His storytelling gives
the impression of that effortlessness which conceals perfect art. If
one separates for the time being the Kreisler material from the
autobiography of the cat, one finds a closely and neatly ordered
structure which bears its load with ease and grace. Or, to use Hoffmann's own figure, even without the third volume one is already
conscious of the "strong, firm thread running through the whole,"
which Hoffmann promised one would find at the end.

The more or less bare record of external happenings, the so-called
"argument" of *Kater Murr*, gives an inadequate and distorted idea
of the novel. Without Kreisler the story is an account of intrigue and
counter-intrigue in a petty principality, involving a generous
amount of secret happenings in the past which vitally affect the
present. Despite the use of the word in the text, it was not a
"biography" of Kreisler in the normal sense from which the cat tore
out the leaves; at best it was the relation of a period or an episode
in his life—albeit the most significant—with the inclusion of sundry
matters out of his past which are incidentally accounted for. At first
it might seem that Kreisler is only one of many characters of almost
equal importance; he is merely a visitor at the little court, in the
beginning not entirely welcome, and not definitely foreshadowing
a role other than that of an outside observer. Until Kreisler shows the
medallion to Prince Hector—and the story at that time is more than
half told—he has not acted in any overt way to affect the plot.

Hoffmann's dexterous artistry is shown in the gradual increase of focus upon Kreisler. From the moment of Kreisler's accidental meeting with Julia and Hedwiga in the park, his pervasive presence, his strangely dominating personality, are felt. Into a world of the everyday, as thoroughly mundane as if it were the household of a butcher or baker, instead of a prince, comes one whose "kingdom is not of this world." In his presence material things begin to lose their substance, to turn into shadows. A mere record of external events ignores the cumulative effect of Kreisler's influence, gradually, mysteriously, growing. The instruction he gives to Julia and later to Hedwiga is not merely technical—one may assume that he was master of that type of instruction; he gives them glimpses of that other world in which he lives, and moves, and has his being. Again and again he plays before the little court circle and accompanies Julia's matchless voice in songs he has taught her, some of them of his own making.[18] These experiences are not the happenings that make up an "argument," but they are more important, even as the world of the spirit is essentially more real than the material world. Whatever happens in the future, whatever fate circumstances force upon Julia and Hedwiga, their lives are forfeit to an abiding vision.

Hoffmann's novel presents a complex pattern of interrelated mysteries—secrets of the past, suspicions as to the identity of certain characters, and undiscovered family relationships. The retention of information is a constant and at times irritating device in the mystery story, often used capriciously or even perversely for the creation of suspense, but in Hoffmann there are usually quite plausible reasons why a complete revelation is not made. Hints, for example, are thrown out concerning the question of Kreisler's parentage: Rätin Benzon urges him to search his memory for his real name—he must have it somewhere hidden away in the recesses of his remembrance; it is plain that Meister Abraham has his own reasons for not telling more of what he knows. Events in the immediate or in the remoter past are disclosed naturally either in the conversation of the characters or in the narrative of the biographer, often under the fiction that he has just found them out and can record them. Kreisler tells of his childhood and youth; he informs Rätin Benzon of the circumstances responsible for his leaving his position as Kapellmeister in the Grand Ducal city—and naturally, since she was partly at least instrumental in securing him the place. The career

---

[18] Cf. Eugen Schmitz: "Musikhistorisches zu Hoffmanns 'Kater Murr'" in *Vom Geiste neuer Literaturforschung, Festschrift für Oskar Walzel*, Wildpark-Potsdam [1924], pp. 209-11.

of Meister Abraham and his early acquaintance with Kreisler are
accounted for in part directly by the biographer and in part by
Meister Abraham himself in conversation or in the so-called "interior
monologue." The elements of the plot that center in Naples are presented bit by bit with consummate artistry; it is foreshadowed when
Meister Abraham entrusts the incriminating medallion to Kreisler,
is in part disclosed in a conversation between Prince Irenäus and
Rätin Benzon, later by the Abbot in the monastery, and finally and
at length by Antonio, the monk Cyprianus himself.

One of the characters in *Kater Murr* is worthy to stand beside
the great figures of world literature—the hero Kreisler himself, to
the development of whom Hoffmann devoted an appreciable part of
his literary life. In his own way he is as uniquely interesting and
memorable a character as Werther, Don Quixote, or Hamlet.
Kreisler stands there fully realized, the classic portrait of the
artist in conflict with an unworthy and uncomprehending world, a
type doubtless, but much more than a type, since his personal
qualities are neatly and accurately balanced with the typical. In
Rätin Benzon, Hoffmann has presented a superb picture of the ambitious, scheming woman of the world. Her conversation with Meister
Abraham reveals one highly significant episode in her life; almost
at the very moment of her marriage to her husband she meets the
man whom she loves instantly, passionately, and singly, as—she
insists—a woman can love but once. That this man was the painter
Ettlinger, as Harich conjectures, seems an unwarranted inference;
there is nothing whatever to indicate his identity, and Hoffmann
includes the incident, in all probability, not to complicate the pattern of his plot still further, but as a clue to the development of her
character. From this point date the gradual atrophy of her finer
sensibilities and the substitution of ruthless personal ambition in
their place. Prince Irenäus is the only figure who approaches
caricature. Hoffmann employs him largely as a target for his
satirical thrusts at princely pride and privilege, and Hoffmann's
satire is enhanced by the insubstantial nature of the Prince's present
status; in his insistence on the exclusiveness of rank, the Prince is
embracing a shadow. Of the major characters at the court Princess
Maria is only slightly sketched; Hoffmann assigns to her a neutral
role.

The story of Kreisler in *Kater Murr* is told in a much lighter vein
than *Die Elixiere des Teufels*; at some points it may seem to approach
the gaiety of *Klein Zaches*. But the merriment lies only on the

surface; at bottom *Kater Murr* is a subtly tragic story. The letter from Meister Abraham which Kreisler receives at the end of the second volume may seem to promise a happy ending, resulting from Kreisler's influence upon his return to Sieghartsweiler, but the current has been flowing from the beginning in the opposite direction. Hoffmann could hardly have ignored the implications of the plan for the *Lichte Stunden* and the printed pages of the *Kreisleriana*, or indeed the personal experience of his Bamberg days. The Kreisler of the earlier essays had become at least intermittently insane—and through love for one of his pupils. The painter Ettlinger became insane through love for the wife of Prince Irenäus; for Kreisler this is a warning, prophetic finger, and on his way from the scene with Hedwiga where this was disclosed, Kreisler looks into the swan pool and sees, not himself, but his predecessor in madness. This episode accounts in part for the inclusion of Ettlinger in the narrative, but he is also used as the original source of Hedwiga's peculiar mental state. We can, it seems clear, assume that Kreisler is powerless to avert the catastrophe, the very thought of which is torture to him. As Julia Marc was married to Gröpel, the Hamburg merchant, as Cäcilia in *Berganza* weds the bestial George, so doubtless with great pomp Julia Benzon will be married to the imbecile Prince Ignatius. It is in this case, however, not merely a matter of analogy—which is hazardous inference; what are virtually parts of the story, though written earlier, leave no other conclusion.[19]

The union of the grave and the gay—the combination that Hoffmann so much admired in Gozzi—is achieved largely through the humor of Meister Abraham and the scintillating wit of Kreisler. The latter is spread widely over the pages of the novel; in brilliance his talk is hardly matched anywhere in fiction, and though his wit irradiates the whole narrative, the specter of distress and disaster is ever lurking in the background. Kreisler's jests are sometimes verbal, a playing with words, but more often they are in the nature of satirical thrusts, delicate and finely spun. His irony is for the reader frequently more effective when his victim does not see the point: a young lieutenant reads to the court circle the first act of a tragedy he has written and then asks Kreisler for an opinion of his work. Kreisler—the mildest expression of inward delight in his whole countenance—assures the young warrior-poet

---

[19] Schaukal's conjecture of Julia's death, like that of Antonie in *Rat Krespel*, perhaps thus averting the tragic marriage, is ingenious but has little if anything in the story to support it.

that the act contained superb thoughts and their originality as the work of a gifted young poet is proved by the fact that poets of recognized distinction, for example, Calderon, Shakespeare, and in modern times, Schiller, have come upon the same ideas. The youth is entranced by the answer and embraces Kreisler warmly.

Humor in *Kater Murr* is almost exclusively the humor of the mind; rarely does it take the form of a comic situation, apart from occasional incidents that provide brief satire on the court, perhaps only in one more extended scene. At the time when Prince Hector is concealed in the garden pavilion, and clandestine movements during the night are noticed and eventually brought to the attention of Prince Irenäus, he conceives the fantastic notion that there is a conspiracy on foot against him and his princely position. He questions his retainers, who are of course only his servants, and gives orders for the defense of the castle. All this provides a situation that might have interested Gilbert and Sullivan.

The two volumes of *Kater Murr* which we possess are in every respect so expert that the loss of the final volume seems doubly a tragedy. A Greek statue may acquire a new beauty in the baffling mystery of its mutilated members and challenge the imagination to a reconstruction, but a visual imagination is a much more common gift than a creative literary imagination. An unfinished book, particularly one containing a mystery, like Dickens' *Edwin Drood*, or, in the present instance, a whole set of skillfully articulated mysteries, is a tantalizing phenomenon.

Any reader may have his little game of solving the enigma and hazard a guess as to the content of the third volume. Hans von Müller has made a number of shrewd suggestions, but the most comprehensive design is supplied by Walter Harich in the recent biography of Hoffmann. Harich himself has written novels and here he finds ample scope for the exercise of his talents, adding a considerable number of new characters and providing, as in the case of *Die Elixiere des Teufels*, a graphic presentation of the intricate web of family relationships. The identity of several characters is called into question, and to account for his revelations, he posits the substitution of children in infancy, in one case even a double substitution. His various inventions are ingenious, and with considerable plausibility he extracts some of his "guesses" from a study of other stories by Hoffmann, notably *Die Doppeltgänger* and *Das öde Haus*, and from the curious unexplained situation in the house of Chancellor Hardenberg, which Hoffmann used in the latter of these tales. But it is dubious indeed to base a theory upon the analogy of other stories. It would seem probable that Hoffmann would have invented something quite different: he was at the height of his powers; the story was written from his heart as no other of his works; and he was in no haste to satisfy the demands of one of the annuals.

The major mystery is naturally that of Kreisler's identity. Hoffmann introduced memories of his own into the life of his hero, and much of Kreisler's career follows that of his creator, transformed and adjusted to his artistic purpose, but on the other hand there is much that does not correspond at all. Though Gönniesmühl, the city of Kreisler's childhood, is obviously Königsberg, though the little boy lived with an uncle and an aunt, there are covert hints to suggest that Kreisler does not entirely belong to the family, that there is something unexplained about his parentage. In time Meister Abraham, who is aware of the circumstances and had been a friend of Kreisler's father, would have disclosed the facts. That he was the son of the mad painter Ettlinger, as Harich conjectures, has merely the support of Hedwiga's testimony as to the extraordinary resemblance, but it is odd that a resemblance so striking as to overwhelm Hedwiga should not even have been noticed by the Prince and his wife; it was for love of the latter that Ettlinger became insane. Hedwiga was subject to neurotic spasms, and the resemblance may have been a temporary delusion; it is soon forgotten. Kreisler is, to be sure, much moved by Hedwiga's story and sees the face of the mad painter reflected in the swan pool instead of his own. In Kreisler's disturbed spirit the fact that Ettlinger, whom he outwardly resembles according to Hedwiga's relation, becomes insane from hopeless love, is sufficient to account for Kreisler's agitation. Later the Abbot, who apparently is well informed of past events at Sieghartshof, tells Kreisler that he has "nothing in common with Ettlinger."

That Prince Irenäus was an unconscious usurper and Ettlinger perhaps the real Prince is only one of Harich's conjectures dependent on the substitution of one infant for another. It seems possible that Princess Hedwiga also presents a mystery of descent, though the question of her parentage is never really raised. Hoffmann's occasional reference to her darker coloring arouses suspicion. That she is restive under the rigid etiquette of the court, is irritated by the constant presence of a "lady in waiting," does not in itself point to plebeian origins. Harich's interpretation or guess that she was the daughter of Meister Abraham and the gypsy Chiara has at least the support of Hedwiga's dark skin, and of the faint traces of clairvoyant powers. To account for this, Harich conjures up a double substitution; for the daughter of the Prince and Princess, Rätin Benzon substitutes her own daughter by the Prince, and sends the legitimate princely offspring to Naples as Angela, concealing this deception from the Prince; but Chiara then substitutes the child of her marriage with Meister Abraham for this alleged child of the Prince and Princess who is really the daughter of the Prince and Rätin Benzon. The latter, whom Harich christens Bianca, has been spirited away to grow up among Chiara's gypsy relatives. Presumably Harich assumes that she would have appeared and played a role in the third volume.

Was the veiled lady, who twice healed Hedwiga of her nervous ills, really the missing Chiara? If one queries why she does not return to her husband, who has long sought her in vain, there is a faint clue in the reference to an oath in the cryptic message of the crystal ball. The third volume would have explained why this oath kept her from her husband and the reasons which compelled her to submit to it. It is also evident that all of the secrets involved in the Neapolitan part of the story have not been revealed. The Abbot's statement concerning the papers concealed in the inner compartment of the medallion requires amplification. Who was Magdala Sigrun, the nurse and duenna of Angela? One is not content with the explanation that she is merely a faithful servant and a gypsy, though by some unexplained eccentricity she does like to play the role. And mystery still envelops the disheveled, wild-eyed youth, Giuseppe, who tries to avenge on Kreisler the death of Prince Hector's adjutant, calling him "brother." Antonio knows who he is and admonishes him in enigmatic words; the Abbot's explanation that he is a gypsy boy who has been annoying the countryside by his petty thievery is a transparent subterfuge.

After all, apart from the marriage of Julia—which is inevitable from the general context in Hoffmann's life and as the reason for Kreisler's insanity—it might be well to let Hoffmann's masterpiece stand as he himself unfortunately left it. Foolhardy would be any attempt at a continuation—Hoffmann left no spiritual kinsman to undertake the task with impunity; hardly less rash is the attempt to guess at the probable outcome of the plot.[20]

[20] The continuation by Hermann Schiff: *Nachlass des Katers Murr, eine Fortsetzung des Katers Murr von E. T. A. Hoffmann*, Leipzig, 1826, I have not been able

But the story of Kreisler at Sieghartsweiler was only accidentally interpolated in the autobiography of a cat. The title of the book as Hoffmann sent it out into the world is in itself a shrewd, perhaps cynical, comment on the relation between the two stories.

The eighteenth century delighted in criticizing Western civilization by recounting the European experiences of an Oriental. In *Die Geheimnisse* Hoffmann himself inserted a long letter of a Greek princess containing acid comment on German urban architecture. A new perspective is sought through this device. Older still is the use of animals in fictitious narrative to excoriate human vagaries and weaknesses. Early in his career Hoffmann stole the dog Berganza from Cervantes and made him the mouthpiece of his criticism. Pollux, the amiable dog of Frau Kauer, proprietress of the "Rose" in Bamberg, served as a kind of model for Berganza. Kater Murr was Hoffmann's own cat. Murr often sat on his table as he wrote, slept on his papers, or in a desk drawer which he knew how to open. Hoffmann was exceedingly fond of Murr, was much depressed by his last illness, and grieved over his demise as at the passing of an intimate friend. To announce Murr's departure from this life he sent black-bordered cards to his friends:

"During the night between the 29th and 30th of November of this year, my dear, much loved disciple Kater Murr passed away in the fourth year of his promising life, to awaken to a better existence. Whoever knew the departed youth, whoever saw him walking along the path of virtue and rectitude, will measure my grief and honor it by silence.

Hoffmann

Berlin, December 1, 1821."[21]

---

to examine. Schiff was a cousin of Heine, and Heine wrote to Moses Moser: "Hast du schon gehört, dass mein Vetter Schiff Hoffmanns 'Kater Murr' fortsetzt? Ich habe von dieser Schreckensnachricht fast den Tod aufgeladen." Cf. W. Siebert: *Heinrich Heines Beziehungen zu E. T. A. Hoffmann*, Marburg a/L (1908), p. 9. Willimczik's conjecture that *Kater Murr* is really finished, that Hoffmann did not intend to write a third volume, that there was no more to be said, runs counter to all the evidence.

[21] "In der Nacht vom 29. bis 30. November d.J. entschlief, um zu einem besseren Dasein zu erwachen, mein theurer geliebter Zögling der Kater Murr im vierten Jahre seines hoffnungsvollen Lebens. Wer den verewigten Jüngling kante, wer ihn wandeln sah auf der Bahn der Tugend und des Rechts, misst meinen Schmerz und ehrt ihn durch Schweigen.

Hoffmann

Berlin, d. 1. Decbr. 1821."

Facsimiles of the announcement of Murr's death are given in the *Briefwechsel* (II, p. 451) and in Hans von Müller's edition of *Kater Murr*.

August Klingemann, dramatist and director of the Brunswick theater, gives in his autobiography an account of a call he paid on Hoffmann in company with Devrient shortly before the death of Murr. After talking with Mischa he turned to Devrient

The Murr of Hoffmann's novel is, however, not a portrait of the cat he loved. In essentials the Kater Murr narrative is the obverse of the medal that Hoffmann has designed and executed in the Kreisler story, is the negative accompanying the positive. At times it is a parody of the other story, purposely placed in juxtaposition to it. Kreisler is an artist, bearing upon his brow the sign of divine gifts, to him the mark of Cain, separating him from his fellows. Murr is the reverse of Kreisler. He is an archbourgeois Philistine, self-satisfied, complacent and happy, inflated by the consciousness of his consummate endowment. Kreisler's "Kingdom is not of this world"; Murr is only a ridiculous pedant, bristling with learning but without a real glimmer of understanding. This mordant irony of self-criticism constitutes the main object of the strange inter-mingling of the two stories, but the device of an animal commentator affords opportunity for telling satire on a variety of topics—as in *Klein Zaches*, the practice of literature, pedantry, rationalism, patriotism, and politics.

In the period of Murr's life covered by the autobiography he is Meister Abraham's cat, not Kreisler's. At the end of the second volume the editor appends a note recording the death of Murr before he had completed the story of his life. Only some scattered notes and reflections were found among his papers, which apparently dated from his life with Kreisler, but a good part of the biography of Kreisler, which Murr had torn apart, was left intact. This remaining portion, together with selections from Murr's notes, would make up the third volume which the editor promises for publication the following Easter. As Hoffmann planned the third volume, it would thus have been for the most part a straight narrative of Kreisler's life. Hoffmann may have wearied of the form to which at the outset he had committed himself, or more probably the autobiography of the cat had already fulfilled the purpose of satirical negation and parody, and he saw no reason for continuing the fiction. It is also possible that the death of the real Kater Murr in

---

and Hoffmann, noting that Hoffmann's eyes, which just before had been sharply gleaming, were now gray and sad. "It was a question, as I saw at once, of a very sick person, of whose restoration to health the physicians were in doubt. . . ." After a pause the guest inquired sympathetically whether the patient belonged to the family or to the close circle of friends, and Hoffmann, opening the door to the next room, pointed to a couch on which Murr was lying. On the way back Devrient assured Klingemann that Hoffmann's worry was no satirical pose, that the situation was of serious moment to his friend. Hitzig relates an anecdote further confirming Hoffmann's devotion to his four-footed friend. The formal death notice was not a jest.

9. Portrait of Dr. Marcus and an Attendant Figure

10. Portrait of Hitzig and His Wife

the very days when he had just finished the second volume deterred him from further satirical use of his four-footed friend.

Meister Abraham had the habit of reading aloud, and Murr, looking over his shoulder at the printed page, had thus learned to read. This acquisition is followed by experiments in writing which were dubious at first in view of the difficulty of holding a pen in his paw. In the course of time Murr devours quite indiscriminately the contents of Meister Abraham's well-stocked library. Book after book is taken from the shelves and its content passes in helter-skelter fashion into Murr's mind, though most of it never takes root there and remains a miscellaneous mass of information and random book-lore upon which Murr draws when occasion seems to demand. The text is peppered with learned allusions, references, and quotations. Erudition thus appropriated is to Murr synonymous with both learning and wisdom, and he looks upon himself as an incomparable genius, though his ideas are all borrowed and the expression of them often borders on plagiarism. The "learned" ape Milo was a pre-liminary study for Kater Murr.

The seemingly insignificant details related of his babyhood (kittenhood) are excused by the rhetorical question: "Can indeed anything unimportant ever happen to a great genius?" and by his own answer: "Everything he undertook or did not undertake in his boyhood is of the highest significance and spreads a bright light over the deeper meaning, the real message, of his immortal works." Puffed up by his learning, Murr begins his career as an author, with a "philosophical, sentimental, didactic novel entitled *Thoughts and Premonition, or Cat and Dog*"; this was followed by a political work *Concerning Mousetraps and Their Influence on the Views and the Energy of Cathood*—mousetraps cultivate ignoble indolence— and a tragedy, *Kawdallor, the King of the Rats*. He started to write a heroic epic in twenty-four cantos, but it turned out to be some-thing quite different, for which "Tasso and Ariosto in their graves may thank Heaven," for no one would have continued to read them, "if a heroic epic had come forth under my claws." Some specimens of his poetry are inserted in the autobiography, one of them a sonnet entitled "Longing for What is Higher."

These poetical effusions bring Murr a temporary embarrassment. The professor of aesthetics in the Sieghartsweiler Upper School (Gymnasium) is a friend of Meister Abraham's and often calls upon him with his dog Ponto. A strong friendship springs up between the dog and the cat. Murr learns the speech of dogs. But one day Ponto runs away with several of Murr's poems in his mouth, and his master becomes convinced that Meister Abraham, whose experiments in the occult are well known to him, has been educating his cat; Murr's poems are of such merit, or at any rate of such a quality, that the professor fears to find in Murr a rival for the chair of aesthetics. He comes to Meister Abraham and challenges him with his discovery. Murr has been careful to conceal from his master the development of his abilities. In his childhood his mother had given him instruction on such matters; cats maintain their independence by concealment of their real intelligence. Murr is reminded of the passage in Tieck's *Der gestiefelte Kater*, where Hinz the cat comments upon the servitude to which the dog has submitted through the betrayal of his capacities; indeed Murr takes great pride in believing that he is descended from Tieck's Hinz. On this occasion the professor of aesthetics requires Abraham to put Murr out of the room lest he overhear the conversation, but Murr creeps stealthily back to a place of concealment. From this time on, Murr is even more discreet, and with reason, for the visit of the professor of aesthetics has suggested to Abraham the possibility of exhibiting Murr's accomplishments and earning more money than formerly with his famous crystal ball; or, that failing, he could perhaps spare himself the necessity of hiring a secretary or copyist.

Thus Murr's life runs by with varied adventures. After long separation he meets his mother, a spotted tabby, living, he is sad to discover, in much reduced circumstances. Though the encounter gives rise to eloquent reflections upon the beauties of motherhood, he himself eats the herring's head which he had intended to pass on to her: "One must obey the voice of nature." Murr's love affairs provide opportunity for burlesque, for the parody of popular romances. One day on the roof he encounters a young cat of extraordinary beauty and charm, dressed in white, and wearing a small black velvet cap and black stockings; out of grass-green eyes sweet fire sparkles, and the soft movements of her finely pointed ears suggest both virtue and understanding. Murr makes immediate advances and declares his love, but the progress of his suit is interrupted for the time being; he is about to embrace her (umpfoten) when two giant tomcats with devilish growls pounce upon him. In this crisis he seeks advice in Ovid's *Ars Amandi*, finding an appropriate passage:

"Venus otia amat. Qui finem quaeris amoris
Cedit amor rebus, res age, tuus eris!"

Accordingly, he seeks to bury himself in his studies, but in vain; he betakes himself to the cellar, hoping to find the "rebus" in a mouse hunt, and, quoting Goethe's *Jägerlied*, he wanders through the gloomy passages in vain. Once more he consults Ovid and, following a new and contradictory passage, he mounts again to the roof and sings a song of love. Miesmies, the white cat, walks gracefully from behind a chimney, and Murr's wooing is continued in words of ecstatic desire. Miesmies is also a gifted singer; in the aria "Di tanti palpiti" she mounts from the heroic strength of the recitative to the truly catlike sweetness of the Andante. And they sing duets together—"At my first glance, my heart flowed toward you." A black cat, an excellent bass singer, soon joins them, and the three make music until some barbarian throws a piece of slate roofing at them. After the marriage of Murr and Miesmies, matters go smoothly for a time, but husband and wife tire of one another, and Murr, though at first grieved and indignant, is at heart relieved when his friend Muzius informs him that his wife is having an affair with a Herculean tomcat recently returned from the wars—in him Harich sees a caricature of Prince Hector. Husband and wife part with a tender embrace and tears of rapture; they confess that they have long been bored in one another's company, and Miesmies goes her way. Murr returns to his studies: "I too was once in Arcady!"

At the time when Hoffmann turned to the writing of the second volume his mind was full of the loathsome task, which happily now lay behind him—his participation in the work of the Special Commission investigating alleged subversive elements in the Prussian state. This distressing and distasteful experience turned the course of his creative impulse from a parody of the Kreisler story, which hitherto informed the Murr autobiography, to satire upon the political situation. Thus, much of the satire in the second volume derives from the same frame of mind which prompted the objectionable and deleted passages in *Meister Floh*.

After the separation from his wife, Murr becomes fat and indolent, and his old friend Muzius, charging him with being a "cat Philistine" and an arrant bookworm, urges him to change his way of life. On Muzius' invitation Murr joins a society—expressly not a secret society—of young tomcats, attends their evening gatherings (Kommerse), suffering in the morning after from "Katzenjammer," and, following the habits of his new friends, fights a duel; the cat duel is a satirical masterpiece which one would like to quote in its entirety. This long section of Murr's memories is an extended satire upon the "Burschenschaften," the German student societies of the early nineteenth century; Hoffmann mocks at their crude German patriotism, their uncouth ways, their athleticism of the Father Jahn type. In the hysterical days of prosecution and real persecution of political offenders, the activities of these student organizations were highly suspect; and their very existence was a political issue, however trivial their outbursts, however silly the police interference with them may seem at the lapse of a century. The noisy meetings of the cat club to which Murr belonged were broken up and the members scattered through the activities of the watchdog Achilles, who, though himself chained, sets a pack of Spitz dogs upon them in their garret place of assembly. A terrific uproar breaks out, and the master of the house appears with a whip; when the dogs fawn upon him, he lets loose upon the offending cats. Traps are now set for the cats, and Muzius is one of the victims; the funeral services—including a long burlesque funeral oration, which Hoffmann describes with great gusto—form the last that we have of Kater Murr's autobiography. That all this is a parable of the governmental attack on the "Burschenschaften" is in itself quite obvious, but Hoffmann made the object of his satire even more unmistakable by including a very pointed conversation between Meister Abraham and the professor of aesthetics on the activities of the cats in the neighborhood, and in terms which are more immediately applicable to the case of the "Burschenschaften" than to any possible disturbance on the part of the cats.[22]

[22] For the use of the cat as character and satirical commentator, cf. F. Leppmann: *Der gestiefelte Kater, Kater Murr und seine Sippe*, München, 1908.

CHAPTER 13

THE TELLER OF TALES

D URING the brief period of Hoffmann's literary activity he was a prolific author, responding both to the call of the indwelling "demon" and to the urgency of financial need. Many of his tales do not fall readily into any rubric of classification. Though certain perpetual interests may appear in them—such as the problem of the artist or the phenomena of occultism—these elements are subordinate to the mere telling of a story. Some of these tales, as stories, are to be reckoned among his major achievements, but many of them also are the product of a lively imagination, working under the stimulus of a contract with a publisher.

To the former class *Das Majorat* (The Entail) indubitably belongs. It is not only one of the best of Hoffmann's stories but an outstanding work of German fiction. Some of the elements of this story have already been cited as exemplifying ideas or practices of the novelist. *Das Majorat* has also the distinction of being, together with *Der Sandmann*, the work upon which Sir Walter Scott based his one-sided appraisal of Hoffmann, and it offers perhaps the most plausible evidence for the influence of Hoffmann on Edgar Allan Poe (*The Fall of the House of Usher*). The autobiographical elements are especially significant, perhaps more directly derived from Hoffmann's life than in any other story except *Kater Murr*. The narrator, Theodor, accompanies his great-uncle V—as Hoffmann often did—to the estate of a nobleman whose legal affairs were under the supervision of the great-uncle; Theodor is a young lawyer with pronounced musical gifts, and he falls in love with the wife of another man, a reminiscence of Hoffmann's passion for "Cora" Hatt.

At the beginning the novelist evokes a mood of cheerlessness and impending doom, the dominant chord of the story—in the skillful description of the dreary, lifeless landscape through which the travelers pass before arriving at the castle. The arrival in night and storm, the battering at the gate, the final appearance of the shriveled old servant Franz, and the procession by flickering candlelight through empty corridors and apartments with their darkened portraits and wall paintings of wolf and boar hunt—all this intensifies the initial impression and transfers the mood of nature to a human habitation. The sense of decay and disintegration is still further underscored by Franz's information that the apartment is no longer available where hitherto the Justiciary has been wont to hold court, settling the legal questions arising between the landlord and his tenants or between the tenants themselves; the heavy, coffered ceiling has come crashing down.

Another room is, however, prepared and thither Franz leads the visitors. The one feature of this apartment to which the eye turns irresistibly is a walled-up door, the masonry of which has never been painted over, so that the bare spot stands in ominous contrast to the richly paneled and painted surfaces in the rest of the room. This walled-up door is the focus of the story, to which Hoffmann constantly and skillfully directs attention, though just what happened there is not fully disclosed until the "explanatory sequel." And there at midnight, the storm howling outside, Theodor sits before the fire, reading Schiller's *Der Geisterseher* (The Ghost-Seer) in unconscious preparation for what comes—the ghostly phenomena of the opened door, the shuffling steps across the room, and the strange scratchings upon the walled-up door. He hears sounds from outside, as if a horse were led into the courtyard and then led back again. And on the following night the intrepid old uncle bans the unseen visitor: "Daniel, Daniel, what are you doing here at this hour?"

Before the arrival at the castle the Justiciary had told his nephew something of the history of the baronial family, especially of the grandfather of the present Baron. Old Baron Roderich had been a gloomy recluse, converting the partly ruined castle for his solitary dwelling place, wandering at times by the sea and talking to the waves, watching sea and stars from the great tower that he had fitted out with a telescope and other instruments. According to popular rumor he not only practiced there astronomical and astrological observations, but also indulged in experiments of the black art. Now the castle was silent and deserted save for the old servant Franz and two old spinster aunts of the Baron who occupied a wing of the castle; other servants came by day from the village. But once a year the present Baron journeyed from his estates in Courland for a few weeks' stay, bringing with him his young wife and a company of friends; thereby he satisfied the terms of the entail and could also transact whatever business might have arisen. During this period the old Justiciary, who had served in a similar capacity as legal adviser to his grandfather, father, and uncle, was accustomed to come to the castle. Then the castle awakened to tumultuous merrymaking; the daytime pleasures of the chase were followed by dinners and balls in the evening to which the gentry of the vicinity and army officers of the garrison were bidden.

The account of life at the castle after the arrival of the Baron and his wife with their guests occupies nearly a third of the story. This may seem a technical blunder to the casual reader, a distortion of the real pattern of the tale, through the interpolation of a purely subjective interlude, the growth of Theodor's love for the Baroness, based in part on their common love of music. The old uncle interferes with ridicule and on one occasion with force, and one day remarks that their work is done and they are leaving the castle immediately; thus the whole episode might seem to lead nowhere. The story, in essence, relates the downfall and in the end the utter extinction of the whole baronial family, as the tragic events come directly or indirectly to the knowledge of the narrator, himself for a time a spectator on the perilous verge of some sort of participation in the doom of the family. This long episode contributes materially to an understanding of the nameless forces which are bringing the baronial family to its end. The castle of R - - - sitten bears the burden of some mysterious curse; physical disintegration of the fabric of the structure itself accompanies the gradual annihilation of the family. A malign influence seems to exude from the very walls. The Baron, who had formerly been a shy, gentle youth, grows stern, harsh, and arrogant when under the influence of the ancestral abode. He is afraid of the place and obsessed with the idea that something tragic is ever going to happen there. The gentle Baroness is even more timorous and finds in Theodor's music some alleviation for the unrest and fear that assail her there. Even Theodor himself is at times caught in the spell of the place and becomes headstrong and contentious. The interlude, if it can be called that, serves other purposes. On the analogy of music—and Hoffmann was a composer—it is simply another movement in the composition, written in another key and thus providing a contrast with the first movement, but at the same time introducing motifs that have been used there.

Before the death of the Justiciary nearly a year later—here Hoffmann is recalling his own grief at the passing of his great-uncle—he relates to Theodor the events in the life of the baronial family previous to Theodor's visit to the castle. This is the "explanatory sequel," for which, as was usual with him, the novelist adopted a more concise, more strictly factual style; Theodor is using, by and large, the very words of the old lawyer.

Whether or not by means of his astrological observations, old Baron Roderich had known beforehand the exact time of his approaching death and had summoned his two sons from a distance. The very night of his death the tower, where he and his faithful servant Daniel had carried on their mysterious investigations, had fallen in ruins. The elder of the sons, Wolfgang, arrived on the day his father was found dead. He was greedy and avaricious and insisted that his father must have had a larger store of gold than he found; suspecting that treasure might lie in the inaccessible ruins of the tower, he treated the old servant Daniel with scorn and physical brutality, for he conceived the idea that he was withholding information. On the arrival of the younger son, Hubert, the two brothers quarreled violently over the inheritance. The theme of the hostile brothers was a favorite with the Storm and Stress writers even before Schiller in *Die Räuber* (The Robbers) had given it its most memorable expression, and in drama and fiction the theme had retained its popularity.

One morning the servants looked in vain for Baron Wolfgang. At last he was found dead in the ruins of the great tower, one arm raised aloft bearing a candlestick. Evidence was produced that the Baron sometimes arose in the night, opened the door which once led into the tower, and gazed down into the rubble where he thought great treasure lay buried. This door was later walled up. Immediately before this Hubert had come to a financial agreement with his brother and was on the point of leaving the castle forever. Indeed it was shown that on the very night of Wolfgang's death a horse had been led out into the courtyard; a little later old Daniel and Hubert had been seen there in conversation, and the horse was then led back into the stables. Suspicious also was the fact that in the previous weeks Hubert and Daniel had often been observed in earnest talk together. But Hubert doggedly denied all culpability, and Wolfgang's death was declared to have been an accident. Hubert, though now apparently the sole heir, refused to live in the castle and administered the property from his place in Courland.

Wolfgang had, however, secretly married and had a son. Many years passed before this was brought to light; certain facts came to the attention of the old Justiciary and he followed up the clues with all the persistence and the ingenuity of a modern detective. Hoffmann as lawyer and judge was professionally interested in the legal intricacies of the lawsuit instituted in the course of time in behalf of the legal heir against the son of Hubert, who on his father's death laid claim to title and property. Upon this second Hubert all the impetuous arrogance and pride of the family inheritance had descended. After his defeat in the lawsuit he was killed in the Russian wars, as indeed a younger brother had been. But the new Baron, named Roderich like his grandfather, married his cousin, Hubert's daughter, the Baroness of the story. Through the somnambulism of old Daniel the Justiciary discovered that the servant, finding his hated master at the door of the former tower, had thrust him down into the ruins eighty feet below; night after night he wandered in his sleep to the scene of his crime, and after his death his ghostly self appeared there. This revelation is one of the steps leading to other discoveries—documents and the like—which form the evidence of Wolfgang's marriage and the birth of his son. Only two days after the departure of Theodor and his uncle from the castle, the Baroness was killed in an accident, the overturning of a sleigh; mysteriously, as if by supernatural agencies, the horses had taken fright. Through the death of the young Baron shortly afterwards, the family became extinct, and the ancestral acres fell to the state. Stones from the ruins of the castle were used to erect a lighthouse.

In *Das Majorat* Hoffmann has met squarely the two chief obligations which rest upon the storyteller, to create characters both convincing and interesting, and to construct a well-knit plot. Each character in the story is a firmly rounded, carefully developed individual. In some of his stories, it may be admitted, haste in fulfilling obligations to an editor led to careless methods and the inclusion of figures taken from stock, so to speak; but this is not the case in *Das Majorat*. The Justiciary is an example of the novelist's character-drawing at its best. Presumably his great-uncle stood in part as model for the character but with what modifications none can tell, for almost nothing is known of him beyond the love and reverence with which Hoffmann regarded him. He develops the character gradually and for the most part according to the epic tradition, through action; there is no general analysis of his qualities. Theodor mentions him first simply as the "splendid old uncle." Epithets are brought into direct connection with acts: he is vehement and irascible and hence is about to utter an oath when it seems that no proper preparation has been made for their reception at the castle; but he has himself under control and turns his wrathful oath into a ringing laugh, for he saw the humor of the situation. The phrase "inclined to merrymaking of all sorts" (zu allem Lustigen aufgelegt) introduces the amusing scene where the old man presents his nephew to the two eccentric old aunts of the Baron and then entangles them in an intricate web of ironical jesting. The support of religious faith gives him both courage and consciousness of power to face the dread phenomena of the unseen world without flinching: "like a commanding hero" he stands there, and there is something more than human in his mien after his triumph over the specter. Theodor's boyish love for the Baroness he opposes with good-humored ridicule or with blunt and telling sarcasm. He deflates Theodor's pride in his somewhat accidental slaying of the great boar; he laughs in his nephew's face: "God is mighty in the weak," he says. Whatever is sturdy, solid, and balanced in the young man he evidently owes to the old man's training. The Baron treats the Justiciary with almost childlike reverence, even with awe. The novelist develops a character through what others in the story think and say of him.

The mystery story, from Hoffmann's day to this, depends upon the skill of the author, first in presenting an enigmatic situation, the weaving of a complicated web of circumstances, and then the unraveling of the web through the ingenuity of the investigator. Hoffmann's story fulfills these conditions only in part, for *Das Majorat* is much more than the mere detection of Daniel's crime. As already noted, Hoffmann's eye is fixed on the fated family whose career of gradual disintegration he follows to its final doom. It is thus not a forerunner of the modern detective story in the same sense as *Das Fräulein von Scuderi*. Yet the technique of the detective story may be observed. The mystery story thrives through the creation of suspense—not only an initial sensation, but by frequent pinpricks of later stimuli. Most of Hoffmann's tales show a sovereign mastery of the technique of suspense. For example in *Das Majorat*: Old Franz leads the Justiciary and Theodor into the apartment which is to serve as the hall of justice—the room with the walled-up door. There is a bright fire on the hearth, and Theodor on entering feels cheered: "Yet my great-uncle remained standing in the middle of the room, looked about him, and said in a very serious, almost solemn, tone: 'So here, this is to be the courtroom?' Franz, holding the candle high so that a bright spot on the broad dark wall, the size of a door, struck one's eye, said in a muffled and pain-filled voice, 'Here judgment has already been given once,' " and to the query of the Justiciary he replies that the remark "only just slipped out." The question of the Justiciary was of course purely rhetorical; he knew what the old servant meant. When Wolfgang returns to find his father lying dead, he takes a piece of paper from his pocket and burns it by one of the great candles that stand at the four corners of his father's bier. This scene the reader holds in mind until he learns the content of the letter and why the new Baron burned it. Usually Hoffmann observes quite rigidly the rule that should govern the telling of a mystery tale; Theodor, as author, tells all he knows at the time—a feeling of suspense may be communicated to the reader of which the personal narrator is not conscious. *Das Majorat* was published in the second volume of the *Nachtstücke*, 1817.

From the time of its publication *Das Fräulein von Scuderi* has been one of the most popular of Hoffmann's tales, and deservedly so. Written in 1818, it was published in the *Taschenbuch für Liebe und Freundschaft auf 1820*; in the third volume of the *Serapionsbrüder* it was assigned to Sylvester-Contessa. Sylvester tells the companions of the brotherhood that he found the material for this story of Paris in the reign of Louis XIV, oddly enough, in Johann Christoph Wagenseil's *Chronicle of Nuremberg*.[1] Wagenseil's work appeared in 1697; the main body of the chronicle was written in Latin, but the appended account of the Meistersinger was in German. He had resided for a time in Paris and had paid a visit to the French authoress. The discursive style of the old chronicle permitted him to insert this somewhat incongruous episode in the story of his beloved Nuremberg.

Das Fräulein von Scuderi was the progenitor of a class of fiction which became immoderately popular in the later nineteenth century and in the twentieth has perhaps increased in respectability. Hoffmann's story is the first crime and crime-detection story in European literature. Hoffmann rather than Poe is the father of the modern mystery and detective story. To be sure, criminals and criminal deeds were recorded and exploited in earlier fiction, from exalted malefactors to thieving vagabonds, but as judge in criminal courts Hoffmann added a new angle of approach. In *Das Fräulein von Scuderi* the stuff out of which the normal detective story is fashioned first made its appearance: a series of mysterious murders, all with the same professional thrust of a knife or dagger, an energetic but still baffled police force, an innocent culprit against whom the evidence seems overwhelming, even to the bloody dirk in his possession, and finally the amateur detective who eventually proves the hero's in-

---

[1] *Joh. Christophori Wagenseilii De sacri rom. imperii libera Civitate Noribergensi Commentatio, accedit, De Germaniae Phonascorum Von der Meistersinger Origine, Praestantia, Utilitate, et Institutis sermone vernaculo liber*, Altdorfi-Noricorum, 1697.

nocence. There is even the record of a police detective who in disguise makes love to a female suspect in order to get her into his clutches. Thus Hoffmann's tale is a landmark in the history of fiction.

For a story of this type it would be difficult to conceive a more effective opening scene than Hoffmann has contrived. It is midnight, and on the outer door of Mlle. de Scudéry's dwelling there is a furious knocking. Her manservant is absent, and the timid maid, Martinière, is only too keenly aware of the fearful crimes, robbery and murder, which have been terrorizing Paris for months. From an upstairs window she converses briefly with the man at the door, and, concluding that he may really be seeking sanctuary, she admits an excited, frantically distracted youth, whose simplicity and honesty of countenance are disarming, but she stoutly refuses to awaken her aged mistress in spite of his pleading and even his threats. Then, placing a small casket in her hands, he rushes from the house. Presently Baptiste, the manservant returns; he had been held up by the police and released only when the chief of the police recognized him. As he approached the house, he had seen a cloaked figure, dagger in hand, storming away from the door. They are both convinced that some fearsome plot is on foot against their beloved mistress; at first they propose to throw the casket into the Seine, but more reasonably agree to lay the whole occurrence before Mlle. de Scudéry in the morning.

After this introductory scene, expertly conceived to arouse interest and tension, Hoffmann pauses in the main narrative to give a long account, perhaps too long, of the terror that had been gripping the French capital: the invention of a mysterious poison which slew its victims, leaving no trace, and the subsequent wave of horrible murders, creating fear in every heart and setting even members of families in terror of one another, since no one seemed safe. Then, coming closer to the story itself, he describes the chain of inexplicable murders on the streets at night, and the organization of a special body of police, hitherto foiled in their attempts to trace the murderer or the band of murderers. Desgrais, lieutenant of the police force, actually saw such a crime committed only a few yards from his place of watching. A cavalier walking blithely along the street was struck down by an assailant who seemed, as it were, to come from nowhere; Desgrais gave pursuit, but the swift-footed miscreant disappeared only a few yards ahead of his pursuer, as if he had melted into a long wall; other police officers appeared upon the scene but found no clue to the mystery.

It had been noted that those especially marked for the assassin's dagger were youthful cavaliers bearing gifts—jewels and the like—to their ladies. An appeal for protection, couched in verses and half in jest, was sent to the King by a group of these gallants. Mlle. de Scudéry, an intimate friend of Mme. de Maintenon and much revered by the King himself, happened to be present when the petition was read; her couplet of comment was soon quoted all over Paris:

> "Un amant qui craint les voleurs
> N'est point digne d'amour."

On the morning after the events related at the beginning Mlle. de Scudéry hears the report of her servants and with considerable trepidation opens the casket, to find jeweled bracelets and a necklace of wondrous workmanship, but she is horrified and humiliated to read the accompanying note—from the "Invisible One," thanking her for the sentiments in the lines just quoted. She drives at once to the apartments of Mme. de Maintenon, and in the jewels Mme. de Maintenon recognizes the work of Cardillac, the most gifted artificer of jewels in Paris, indeed in all Europe. Summoned to explain the mystery, he acknowledges his work, says that he has missed these jewels from his workshop, but is strangely embarrassed and furtive in his manner, insisting that Mlle. de Scudéry, whom he has long honored, should keep the jewels, and despite her remonstrances he succeeds in hurrying from the apartment, leaving the casket in her hands.

Some months later as Mlle. de Scudéry's carriage is crossing the Pont Neuf, an excited, impetuous youth elbows his way through the crowd and throws a note into her lap. Martinière, who accompanies her mistress, faints, recognizing in him the nocturnal visitor who brought the casket. The note implored Mlle. de Scudéry to return the jewels to Cardillac immediately, lest dire consequences should result. Circumstances prevent her fulfilling this demand for a day or two, and on arriving before Cardillac's house, she finds the street thronged and in uproar, and the house itself under guard of the police. Cardillac has been murdered, and his assistant Olivier, the betrothed of his daughter Madelon, arrested as the perpetrator of the crime. As the reader doubtless has inferred, he is the youth of the casket episode. Moved by pity for the sorrowing girl, who insists on her lover's innocence, Mlle. de Scudéry takes Madelon to her own home.

Then follow, as became the fixed tradition in detective fiction, the investigation of the police, the extended probing into the circumstances in Cardillac's household, the questioning of the culprit who has been arrested. Circumstantial evidence is strong against him, and it is easy to interpret the situation in such a way as to supply a motive. That Olivier, even in his assertion of innocence, is not telling all he knows seems patent and testifies against him. Even Mlle. de Scudéry wavers in her prepossessions, and against the dictates of her heart begins to believe in his guilt. The results of her first interview with the prisoner are unsatisfactory, but in the second, which he himself requests, the prisoner now facing torture and perhaps death puts his fate in her hands.

He discloses his identity, the son of an old friend and protégée of hers, whom she had caressed in her arms in his babyhood. In Geneva, whither his parents had gone, he had been apprenticed to a goldsmith and had become a master craftsman; he had then turned to Cardillac, to find a place with the greatest artist in his field in Europe. In time he accidentally discovers his master's secret. Cardillac's love of precious jewels, the product of his artistic skill, had become a mania, an insensate passion; now he cannot bear to part with them and invents endless excuses to delay the delivery of an order; once in alien hands, they form an irresistible lodestone, inciting him to robbery and murder. In view of this madness he resolutely refuses orders from those whom he personally reveres. To still his master's insane desires, Olivier has tried the experiment of getting these particular jewels into the hands of Mlle. de Scudéry, knowing Cardillac's regard for her. The plan works for a time; Cardillac is quiet and composed, but presently Olivier notes the signs of mental unrest, of frenzied excitement, and thus delivers the note requesting the immediate return of the jewels. On the night of the fatal tragedy Olivier had followed Cardillac, leaving the house by a secret door in the garden wall, had witnessed the attack upon his master, and had brought the dying man home. He acknowledges his own guilt in keeping silent for Madelon's sake; he could not destroy her life's happiness by revealing the crimes of her beloved father.

In the meantime the real slayer of Cardillac confides his story to Mlle. de Scudéry; a young nobleman, Comte de Miossens, he had ordered jewels of Cardillac but grew suspicious at Cardillac's questions as to the dwelling of his lady and the time he intended to visit her. He went over the accounts of previous murders, noted the kind of dagger thrust employed, and placed a piece of armor under his doublet. Cardillac's blow is thus deflected, giving Comte de Miossens an immediate advantage; in the conflict that ensues he kills Cardillac. For personal reasons he does not want his action bruited abroad, but is troubled at the thought that an innocent man might suffer for the deed.

In making his confession to Mlle. de Scudéry, Olivier had still insisted that for Madelon's sake her father's crimes must not come to light. The police officials to whom Mlle. de Scudéry can now reveal the whole story cannot in honor accede to her request; they cannot thwart the demands of justice or ignore Olivier's guilt in concealing the information he has so long possessed. Only the King can intervene, and this the King does. Olivier and Madelon are married, but after the torturing experiences of the last months he can no longer bear to remain in Paris, and returns to Geneva with his bride.

To a certain extent Hoffmann's story belongs in the group of artist tales. In Cardillac he has created the ultimate case of the artist versus society; his artistic passion, his frenzied love for the work of his own hands, make him not merely an eccentric though really harmless nonconformist but a criminal rebel against the social organism in which he lives. The development of this element in the plot doubtless interested Hoffmann, but in itself it forms only a central point about which the main story is constructed. The interest of the tale centers in the steps leading up to the slaying of Cardillac, the arrest of Olivier, and the activity of the police and of Mlle. de Scudéry to secure a solution for the crime. It is of small moment that the novelist introduces the moot question of prenatal influences to explain the character of Cardillac. Mlle. de Scudéry is, it may be admitted, as yet an imperfect example of the amateur detective as he appears in modern fiction, but in her the familiar role is clearly foreshadowed. In a modern detective story the plot of Comte Miossens to trick the murderer would be more integrally tied to the main plot, would probably be an idea of Mlle. de Scudéry's, though she would have had to employ someone to carry out the scheme, probably independent of police collusion. Yet by and large in Hoffmann's tale the detective story is born.

Meister Martin der Küfner und seine Gesellen (Master Martin the Cooper and His Assistants) is a story so worth-while in itself that one might resent the undue prominence sometimes given it simply as a source for Wagner's *Meistersinger*; it does not need to shine by reflected light. Hoffmann's love for southern Germany, halfway to Italy, the land of his longing, has found its expression in this little tale of Nuremberg in the latter part of the sixteenth century. Like other members of the Romantic brotherhood, he found in the old Bavarian towns a beauty, a lingering medieval charm, as nowhere else in German lands. During his stay in Bamberg he visited Nuremberg and here he has incorporated the memories of his enchantment. It is the city of Albrecht Dürer, of painters, sculptors, silversmiths, goldsmiths, and of the Meistersinger, and with loving devotion and the carefulness of a scholar Hoffmann recreates the past. Hoffmann's Nuremberg is, admittedly, a romanticized version of the sixteenth century German town, but the reader surrenders to his magic, and refuses to consider any possible inaccuracy in the focus of his picture. In the larger sense, perhaps such evocations of the past are more real than the labored and learned studies of the social historian, even as Velasquez' *Breda* and Rembrandt's *Night Watch* are essentially more eternally true than a photograph could have been. Hoffmann is indeed not entirely blind to matters that interest the historian of society. There are some hints of a period of transition in the old free city, more than a hint indeed of increasing self-confidence in bourgeois ways and bourgeois virtues, such as Hebbel in *Agnes Bernauer* portrayed in the Augsburg of an earlier century. But Hoffmann does not stress the point; it is all incidental to his narrative.

To Meister Martin's cooper shop orders come from far and near, for his workmanship is unrivaled. The accumulated wealth of his coffers might have enabled him to challenge the patricians of the old city or the neighboring noblemen in elegance of living. Though he maintained the old patriarchal system and housed some of his workers in his own spacious dwelling, he was still a patron of the arts and acquired things of beauty for his home. He was also an enthusiastic supporter of the Meistersinger. To him the craft of the cooper ranked with the noblest occupations of man, for the casks and hogsheads of his making were works of art comparable with other products of artistic genius in his own city. His love of his work was an obsession, and he had sworn to bestow his fair daughter only upon a cooper; in this resolve he was fortified by the cryptic prophecy of his dying grandmother, which he arbitrarily interprets according to his own prepossessions. The beauty of Rosa is such that the sons of patrician families or even of noblemen in the vicinity look upon her with favor—Hoffmann has not forgotten the first act of his beloved *Käthchen von Heilbronn*.

The story centers in the efforts of three suitors, the "Gesellen" of the title, to win the hand of Rosa. Each has abandoned, tempo-

11. Design for Stage-Set

12. Design for Stage-Set

rarily at any rate, the career in life already indicated for him, learned the trade of the cooper, and obtained work in Meister Martin's workshop; each intends to desert the fashioning of vats, barrels, and hogsheads as soon as the prize is won. Conrad, the nobleman's son, quits the workshop after a violent altercation with Meister Martin, in which pride of birth contends with pride of workmanship. Reinhold the painter, who has already gained a considerable reputation in Italy, wavers in his devotion to the "base" handiwork, and his devotion to Rosa he incorporates in a portrait at which he works secretly; when it is finished, his experiment is at an end—an idea that Hoffmann has employed elsewhere. Friedrich alone remains, but feigns illness, absents himself from the cooperage, and works with untold delight in the atelier of his former master, a goldsmith. The superb goblet which he makes as a present for Rosa is discovered to satisfy the wording of the great-grandmother's prophecy as well as a cask for bubbling wine.

For *Der Kampf der Sänger* one may reverse the statement made above concerning *Meister Martin der Küfner*; its share in the creation of Wagner's *Tannhäuser* is of greater interest than the story itself. Hoffmann has failed to conjure up even a romanticized picture of the Middle Ages which is satisfying. He could not follow in Fouqué's footsteps, though there are traces of Fouqué's style. The vision of the procession at the beginning of the story was evidently suggested by Tieck's *Aufzug der Romanze*, and there is an echo of Tieck (*Der Runenberg*) in the episode of the mysterious stranger whom Ofterdingen meets in the forest and the stranger's gift of a book that is missing when Ofterdingen awakes in the morning. It is clear that Hoffmann could enter more understandingly and more sympathetically into the bourgeois world of late sixteenth century Nuremberg than into the age of chivalry. The story proves also that the supernaturalism of medieval tradition lay largely outside of Hoffmann's domain. Though he makes quite abundant use of it in the necromancy of the great minstrel Klingsohr and in the diablerie of his demon representative Nasias, his interest is only halfhearted —he has come by it secondhand. The type of supernaturalism which Hoffmann correctly enough associates with medieval superstition was too bare-faced, forthright, and crude, and it lacked the tantalizing mystery of the borderland where the natural and the supernatural are indistinguishable.

Hoffmann provides a charming introduction to his tale of medieval love and song. While the rude winds of the spring equinox roar

and bluster outside, the author sits in his lonely room with Wagenseil's treatise on the Meistersinger open before him. To the tempest
he pays no heed, but, closing the book, he gazes raptly into the fire
on the hearth, lost in the magical picture of times long passed. In
the vision that follows he finds himself in a flowery meadow, surrounded by the twilight gloom of a dense forest; "the streams murmured, the bushes rustled as if in secret whisperings of love, and
sounding in the midst of it all a nightingale lamented his sweet woe."
Presently from a distance the joyful sound of hunting horns is
heard—the stags and roes peep out of the wood—and then the music
of harps and human voices blending in heavenly melody. From the
forest a train emerges, at the head huntsmen with shining horns;
then a stately gentleman in princely mantle, on a palfrey at his side
a lady of wondrous beauty; on six steeds of varied colors six riders
follow, playing on harp and lute and singing in wonderful, clear
tones; richly clad pages and servants bring up the rear of the procession. A stranger appears and accosts the dreamer; it is old Professor
Wagenseil himself, and he points out the figures in the train one by
one, the Landgraf von Thüringen, the Gräfin Mathilde von Falkenstein, and the six minstrels whom the Landgraf has gathered at his
court. These opening paragraphs arouse keen anticipation in the
reader which unhappily the author does not completely satisfy. To
the story of Heinrich von Ofterdingen that Hoffmann found in
Wagenseil and in other accessible sources, he made substantial additions, particularly in a closer definition of the hero's character. At
the beginning Heinrich von Ofterdingen is a youth of extraordinary
promise in the world of minstrelsy, sharing with the other singers the
purity of purpose and the exalted conception of the minstrel's
spiritual message. But he is moody and passionate, in love with the
beautiful widowed Countess Mathilde von Falkenstein, whose favor
he seeks through the power of song; he disappears from the court,
despairing and defeated, in perceiving that his lady looks with
greater favor upon his closest friend, the minstrel Wolframb von
Eschenbach. He turns away from the high ideals of his companions,
seeking the more robust but profane art of Klingsohr to raise his powers above his fellows, and returns to court in pride and boastful
arrogance, scorning the petty achievements of his old friends. For a
time the Countess falls under his spell, but again he meets defeat,
for however transcendent his skill, the evil he has learned creeps into
his song. Again he flees from his old home but this time for remorse
and spiritual regeneration.

That Hoffmann himself was doubtful of the story's merit may be inferred from the comment of the Serapion Brothers. To be sure, the tale is the work of Cyprian, one of the three Hoffmanns, but it is severely criticized by Theodor, Hoffmann's more essential self. Concretely, however, his criticism is beside the mark—that Cyprian's story has ruined for him the picture of Heinrich von Ofterdingen in Novalis' novel, that the minstrels, though ever making ready to sing, still never really sing. In reality Novalis' Heinrich von Ofterdingen has virtually nothing in common with the legendary minstrel except his name and his birthplace in Eisenach, and Ottmar demolishes the second objection by remarking that it was unreasonable to expect Cyprian to insert verses of his own as specimens of Wartburg minstrelsy. But Ottmar's own criticism is pertinent: Cyprian should guard himself against looking into old chronicles, since reading of this sort might easily entice him into an alien territory, in which an outsider with no special sense of direction would waver about on every false pathway, without ever being able to find the right one.

Hoffmann's longing to visit Italy was never fulfilled, but through ceaseless poring over books on Italy and views of Italian scenes he recreated Italy in his mind and heart as if he had really been there. As noted already, he used Italian backgrounds repeatedly in his stories—in *Prinzessin Brambilla*, and in parts of *Die Fermate, Das verlorene Spiegelbild, Die Jesuiterkirche in G., Der Artushof, Ignaz Denner, Die Elixiere des Teufels*, and *Kater Murr*, an amazing list for one who never saw the country. The scene of two other stories, *Signor Formica* and *Doge und Dogaressa*, is laid entirely in Italy.

That the "Signor Formica" of Hoffmann's tale is Salvator Rosa, the Italian artist, musician, and poet, would seem to offer him a peculiarly congenial theme. In the range of his professional and avocational activities, Salvator Rosa resembled Hoffmann, but the resemblance goes deeper. Not only in their versatility were they akin, but in their temperaments. Maassen quotes at length a passage from Lady Morgan's life of Salvator Rosa characterizing the artist as a man and remarks that it could be applied word for word to Hoffmann.[2] In the work of the Italian, Hoffmann found something not dissimilar to the qualities that he admired in Jacques Callot—for example, the small, grotesque, and agitated figures which Rosa placed against a background of mountain and forest. Despite the

---

[2] Maassen quotes from a German translation of 1825. The translation of the passage in Lady Morgan's book is not always accurate, and a considerable part of what he quotes as from Lady Morgan is from a quotation that she takes from Pascoli.

title, which refers to Salvator Rosa, Hoffmann is not writing a study of his artistic kinsman in seventeenth century Italy, and the specific problems of the artist are only incidentally touched upon. The story concerns two young people who are in love and Salvator Rosa's benevolent and intricate plotting to overcome the obstacles to their union. The title is justified since Rosa pulls the strings that control the action of the tale. One might say that Hoffmann's thinking on the problems of the artist passed over into *Kater Murr*, the first part of which was written at the same time. *Signor Formica* is a sprightly and diverting tale, and it is perhaps presuming to ask more of a storyteller.

Salvator Rosa has escaped from Naples to Rome after the insurrection of Masaniello. Desperately ill, he finds shelter in the home of a widow, where he had lodged years before when he was an unknown painter. His illness forms the novelist's scheme for introducing Antonio Scacciati, a young barber-surgeon, and the worthy Doctor Splendidiano Accoromboni, nicknamed the Pyramid Doctor because so many of his patients lie buried in the cemetery beside the pyramid of Caius Cestius. When summoned the Pyramid Doctor names one hundred and twenty diseases that Rosa did not have, but off-hand he is unable to find a name for his present malady; he returns, however, a few hours later, has found a nice name for it, and brings medicines that smell as if drawn from the River Acheron. Rosa continues to grow worse until he rises from his bed and throws the bottles out of the window upon the head of the doctor who happens to be entering. Dr. Accoromboni is hand and glove with the aged Pasquale Capuzzi, an eccentric miser, with whose niece Mariana the young barber-surgeon is in love; Capuzzi is a ridiculous fop, and regards himself as an illustrious composer and matchless singer. Accoromboni, only four feet tall and amply paunched, Capuzzi, tall and thin as a riding whip, with long pointed nose and chin, together with Capuzzi's dwarf servant Pitichinaccio, form an incomparable trio and should alone rescue the story from the disdain with which some critics regard it.

Antonio, though only a barber and blood-letter, is in secret an artist, has even been a pupil of Annibale Carracci and Guido Reni, but has been unable to gain any recognition from the hidebound guild of Roman painters. Rosa plays a trick on these arch-conservative critics; having conceived a warm liking for the young man, he exhibits one of his paintings, a Magdalen, as the work of a promising young Neapolitan artist, recently deceased. All Rome flocks to see the picture; critics and artists are unanimous in declaring it a masterpiece. The leading guild of artists, the Accademia di San Luca, elects the painter to posthumous fame as a member—all this when Salvator Rosa gleefully and sarcastically reveals the identity of the painter.

Capuzzi is in love with Mariana himself and obtains papal dispensation for the marriage in spite of the relationship. She is virtually a prisoner in his house, guarded by the dwarf Pitichinaccio. Plot and counterplot—Salvator Rosa and Antonio on the one side and Capuzzi and his two companions on the other—form an intricate and amusing, indeed often hilarious, pattern in Hoffmann's narrative. Eventually Mariana is abducted, and the young lovers flee to Florence. Involved in the plot is the establishment of a new theater in Rome where Rosa functions as manager and actor. The historical Rosa was an exceedingly clever actor; actually his participation in more or less impromptu street performances was well-known, but Hoffmann alters this and uses the mystery of Signor Formica's identity as a telling element in the plot. In this part of the story the novelist touches on conditions in the Roman theater that he portrays more brilliantly and effectively in *Prinzessin Brambilla*. He has in mind something of the scenery and the technique of the "Commedia dell' Arte" and visually perhaps some of Callot's little sketches called "Balli."

A painting by Wilhelm Kolbe in the Berlin exhibition of 1816 provided the initial stimulus for the story *Doge und Dogaressa*: the gray-bearded Doge Marino Falieri and his young bride are standing, accompanied by several attendants, before a balustrade, with a view of Venice as a background.[3] The sordid story of Falieri's conspiracy to gain sovereign power in the Venetian state was fused with romantic glow by the marriage of the eighty-year-old Doge to a beautiful girl of eighteen; it has stimulated the imagination of Byron, Otto Ludwig, and others, though before Hoffmann's story there is record of only one use of the theme in literature.[4] Presumably Kolbe heard the story in Venice; perhaps he could say with Byron that the Scala dei Giganti where Falieri was "crowned, discrowned, and decapitated struck forcibly my imagination." Hoffmann saw something in the painting that interested him, and he

[3] Reproduced in Maassen, vi.
[4] Cf. Maassen, vi, p. xlvi. Cf. also Maassen's notes for passages from Le Bret's history of Venice, Hoffmann's historical source.

sought sources of information. It can be shown that he transcribed
the historical facts of the story from Le Bret's history of Venice,
often with striking verbal correspondence.

But Le Bret's factual and rather pedestrian narrative supplied
only a limited amount of raw material out of which the novelist was
to fashion a beguiling and tragic story. The story is, indeed, Hoffmann's own; he takes historical events, develops a hint here and
there in his source, adds material entirely his own, and thus in complete mastery builds up the structure of his tale. A comparison of
Hoffmann's text with this one source illustrates the novelist's deft
and fertile methods of transforming his source into a work of art.
There is space for only a glimpse of all this.

Of the conspiracy itself in a political sense Hoffmann naturally
gives only a somewhat cursory account—only what is required; he
is telling the tragic story of two young lovers. That the beautiful
wife of the Doge had many admirers, that the Doge himself was "beside himself with jealousy" he found in Le Bret; further, that Michael
Steno, a young man of patrician family and a member of the Council
of Forty, was said to be one of these admirers, though other reports,
among them the source that Lord Byron used, maintained that
Steno's attentions were directed toward one of her ladies in waiting.
Hoffmann, however, weaves Steno's love for the Dogaressa into the
plot of his story. Le Bret does not mention the name of the Doge's
bride; Hoffmann calls her Annunziata; Byron uses the name Angiola. The hero is entirely Hoffmann's invention—a mere gondolier,
who nevertheless raises his eyes to the wife of the ruler. In his source
Hoffmann read the simple statement that one of the conspirators was
a German, Antonius Dalebinder; since he is writing a story for German readers, he takes the hint and makes his hero a German, though
Antonio has lived all his life, at all events since earliest childhood,
in Italy. As a humble gondolier he is obviously not one of the conspirators, though at the end, after discovering the circumstances
of his father's death, he seeks personal vengeance through a brief
participation in their activities.

The bare fact that the Bucentoro, bringing the newly elected
Doge home to Venice, is imperiled by a rising tempest, is noted in
Le Bret. Hoffmann turns the historian's bald record into an impressive picture: the gondolier rows his frail vessel out to the huge but
unseaworthy ship of state and rescues the Doge from death. The
rich reward that the Doge bestows upon him enables Antonio to
play another role than that of a gondolier. On the occasion of a great

procession Antonio and Annunziata see one another, and again on the following day when he uses an audacious stratagem to approach her, for he recognizes in her a playmate of his childhood days; the love that was then a mere seed in the soil is now by sudden miracle brought to full bloom.

The old beggar woman Margareta is an original and characteristic addition. She had been Antonio's nurse, and he is strongly drawn to her before his memories of the past are awakened. She has knowledge of secret remedies, precious salves, simples, and herbs, and had carried on her unofficial art of healing among the Venetian populace until ecclesiastical authority intervened; and she has strange mesmeric and prophetic powers. The novelist employs her to reveal something of Antonio's past and by her cryptic prophecies and warnings to foreshadow coming events, and thus bind the story together.

On the night when the Doge is executed Antonio finds his way into the palace; in the turmoil of that fatal night the lovers make their escape to a boat that a friend of Antonio's is holding in readiness for them, and they put out to sea, old Margareta with them. But a fierce storm arises and they are drowned: "The sea, the jealous widow of the beheaded Falieri, stretched up its foaming waves like giant arms and snatched them down into the bottomless deep."

The composition of *Das öde Haus* (The Deserted House) illustrates Hoffmann's response to a different type of stimulus. Although the material assembled by Hans von Müller and developed further by Harich is in part conjectural, it forms a neat and more than merely plausible pattern. In the very center of metropolitan life, on Unter den Linden, stood a house that was apparently deserted, its windows closed and the blinds drawn; rumors were indeed current that a woman lived there in mysterious seclusion. Such a house naturally excited Hoffmann's interest. During these days Hoffmann, who was occasionally invited to the houses of the socially prominent, even to the palace of Chancellor Hardenberg, was once seated at table beside the beautiful Helmina (Wilhelmina) Lanzendorf, who lived in the house of Chancellor Hardenberg as a protégée of Countess Pappenheim, the Chancellor's daughter. As noted above, the parentage of this famous figure in Berlin society has remained a mystery to this day. During the dinner she complained of a headache, and Hoffmann proposed the curious remedy of sipping the foam from a glass of champagne; in a letter to Graf Pückler he describes this

incident as occurring "on a desert island," a characteristically satirical designation for a formal dinner party. As Hoffmann brings into
his story both a Graf P. and a Dr. K., which patently stand for Graf
Pückler and Dr. Koreff, it is not an unreasonable conjecture that
the three participated in fanciful speculations as to the identity of
Helmina Lanzendorf and the mystery of the deserted house, perhaps
advancing the diverting possibility that she was the illegitimate
daughter of the unknown lady of Unter den Linden No. 9. Thus
Das öde Haus may have come into being. The material is promising,
but unfortunately Hoffmann tells his story in a rather awkward
fashion.

The personal narrative of Theodor occupies about two-thirds of
the story. He is drawn by a morbid fascination to the deserted house,
which is popularly regarded as haunted, watches its sightless windows from a park bench, once sees a woman's hand place a crystal
vase on the window ledge, and later catches a glimpse of a face that
in beauty corresponds to the arm and hand he has seen. A mirror that
he purchases from an itinerant peddler has, as he accidentally discovers, the magic power, when breathed upon, to reproduce this
face; that this is no mere hallucination is shown by his physician's
astonishment in seeing the face himself. Eventually Theodor forces
his way into the house and is met by an aged woman in bridal array
who greets him as her bridegroom.

Later at a dinner party an incident occurs corresponding to
Hoffmann's adventure with Helmina Lanzendorf. At dinner Theodor
is paired with a young lady, who, as Graf P. informs him, is a niece
of the insane woman in the deserted house; the latter is said to be
recovering from her madness under the ministrations of Dr. K. Then
from Dr. K. Theodor hears the story. This explanatory sequel, a
technical device that dogged Hoffmann's footsteps, is here singu-
larly ineffective. It does not explain all that the reader has a right
to learn, even allowing for inexplicable mysteries. The novelist has
really told his story and his interest slackens; even the style becomes
factual and colorless. The woman of the deserted house is Gräfin
Angelika von Z., who became insane when her lover Graf S. deserted
her for her younger sister, and retired to the long-untenanted family
house in town. In developing the narrative the novelist calls to his
aid secret connections between Angelika and members of a gypsy
band, especially with a tall and horrible old hag in a blood-red shawl;
from them she had apparently gained the telepathic power whereby
she lures her former lover to death in the deserted house. Hoffmann

seeks to mystify the reader as to the parentage of Edmonde, Theodor's companion at dinner; she had been secretly stolen by the gypsies but when she had been as mysteriously returned, Angelika claimed her as her child. In the first part of *Das öde Haus* Hoffmann runs more or less true to form; he succeeds admirably in endowing the mysterious, silent house with a ghostly fascination, in presenting the morbid, nervous state of a sensitive youth who allows the mystery of the house to enthrall him to the verge of mental unbalance. But in the explanatory sequel one sees the author too plainly at work manufacturing the antecedent circumstances to correspond to the eerieness of the house. Hoffmann himself thought the story an inferior work.

The predilection for the mysterious, even for the fearful, did not as a rule extend to "charnel-house horrors." The power of suggestion is more effective than a bald presentation of the horrible; to hint that there is something mysterious or terrible behind a closed door or one slightly ajar, works more potently on the nerves than to present the door wide open. Hoffmann's chief excursion into the field of the revolting is the short narrative embedded in the conversations of the Serapion Brothers to which editors have given such names as *Der Vampyrismus, Eine Vampyrgeschichte,* or *Die Hyänen*; the French translation calls it simply *Comte Hippolit.* It is the story of a man whose wife has a morbid appetite for human corpses, and the awful climax of the tale is reached in the scene where he finds her with several old hags in a cemetery devouring a body which they have exhumed from a newly filled grave.

Otherwise the closest approach to the horrible for its own sake is in the story *Ignaz Denner.* Hoffmann resented Kunz's rejection of the tale as unworthy of a place in the *Fantasiestücke* and later with pardonable malice called Kunz's attention to the publication of the story in the *Nachtstücke.* The scene of most of the story is the lonely cottage of Andres, a forest warden. Unwittingly Andres, though upright and God-fearing, falls into the toils of an infamous scoundrel, Ignaz Denner, who is possessed of mysterious and sinister powers. Denner is the head of a robber band, and Andres is actually on the scaffold, the arm of the executioner already raised, to suffer the penalty for participation in a robbery, when a witness provides an alibi. Denner escapes from prison, and though it was on Denner's false testimony that Andres was accused, Andres plays the part of the Good Samaritan to the outwardly repentant malefactor, but

later, when he comes upon Denner in the very act of murdering Andres' nine-year-old son, he shoots him. The explanatory sequel
is here inserted before the final events of the story. Ignaz is the son
of a Neapolitan doctor who was in league with the devil; this doctor
had murdered in succession one wife after another, then murdered
each child she had borne him, taking out the heart of the child and
preparing from the blood a secret life-giving elixir; the child must
be nine weeks or nine months old for the blood to have the proper
potency. The mother of Ignaz had succeeded in saving his life. The
doctor's crimes are revealed and he is condemned to death, but the
flames do not consume him and he disappears; the boy Ignaz escapes
equally miraculously from his father's burning house. The subsequent activities of father and son as heads of robber bands extended
over wide regions in Italy and Germany. All this the novelist fails
to inform with any real significance. At times he piles up the gruesome with heavy hands. But the youth in the fairy tale who went out
into the world to discover what shuddering meant would not experience it from Hoffmann's story.

Die Brautwahl (The Choice of a Bride) contains stuff out of
which Märchen are made—Hoffmann's own Märchen—but this material is on the whole so irrelevant that the story belongs rather
among the "Berlin Novellen." When Die Brautwahl was placed in
the setting of a meeting of the Serapion Brothers—in volume three—
Theodor himself criticizes sharply the role of the two "revenants"
who really lived in the sixteenth century but like the two magicians
in Meister Floh are still quite humanly alive; their share in the story
is forced, he says. Though they are often mildly entertaining, Hoffmann's imagination quite as often limps along without its characteristic swing: Tusmann, after an evening in a tavern with the two
"revenants," has a series of fantastic adventures on the way home,
spins about in a dizzy dance, sees himself standing before the door
of his own house, and on coming to himself discovers that he is seated
on the bronze horse of the Great Elector in Schlüter's famous equestrian statue. Leonhard the goldsmith moves from place to place with
magical speed; Albertine sees him in her room, where she had previously seen only the stove; the streaks of green paint which the
irate artist has smeared on Tusmann's face can be removed only by
Leonhard's magic handkerchief.

The story contains the germ of a companion piece to Der goldene
Topf, but the author was either too much in haste or too weary to

work it out. Edmund Lehsen is a promising young artist in Berlin. His awkwardness on first meeting Albertine Vosswinkel at an art exhibition might well have been one of the misadventures of Anselmus: he stoops to pick up Albertine's handkerchief, the two heads crash together, he starts back, and at the first step treads on the pug dog of an elderly lady and at the second on the gouty foot of a professor. Aroused by the tumult, people rush from the neighboring rooms and level their lorgnettes at Edmund. He is temporizing with his artistic equipment, which is as yet insecurely grounded; he longs to visit Italy, the "homeland of art," but still does not go. He falls in love, or thinks he does, with the pretty face of Albertine Vosswinkel, who is Veronika or Candida in a slightly different version. Leonhard the goldsmith, a pallid follower of the Archivarius Lindhorst or of Prosper Alpanus, has known Edmund from babyhood and concocts a plan to defeat Edmund's two rivals for Albertine's hand—the Geheimer Kanzlei-Sekretär Tusmann, a former schoolmate of her father, bald-headed and ugly, and Baron Dümmerl, the son of old Manasse, the other "revenant." He fills the Kommissionsrat Vosswinkel with abject terror by showing that Vosswinkel's pocketbook will be seriously endangered if he refuses his daughter's hand to either of these suitors, and thus induces the perplexed parent to approve of a solution of the problem taken directly from the casket scene in *The Merchant of Venice*.

All of this could have been accomplished without the use of supernaturalism. Obviously Edmund wins in the choice of the caskets, but the marriage is to be delayed until after Edmund has returned from a year in Italy. It is, however, plain that the separation will cure the young painter of his infatuation, and he will devote himself entirely to art. In the case of Edmund Lehsen, Hoffmann was more transparent than usual when introducing contemporary characters into his tales; the name "Lehsen" is obviously an anagram for Hensel (Wilhelm), whose sketch of Hoffmann is perhaps the most satisfactory likeness of the author; he was a brother of Luise Hensel, the poetess, whom Brentano loved in vain.[5]

In *Die Brautwahl* Hoffmann has created several figures which at the beginning give promise of a high place among his most memorable characters, but his creative powers became sluggish, and he

[5] It is probable that Leonhard's advice to Lehsen to study in Italy is an echo of Hoffmann's advice to his young artist friend. Hensel did not follow it, however, till three years after Hoffmann's death. On his return he became a prominent painter in Berlin, and married Fanny Mendelssohn, sister of the great musician.

failed to develop them into well-rounded portraits. Undue emphasis upon a single trait leads to "flat characters" or caricatures. Vosswinkel, the Kommissionsrat, is a businessman who with all his pretensions to cultural interests thinks only of money. When his portrait is to be painted, the artist suggests—in view of the somewhat grim likeness of him painted earlier—that he be portrayed in the happiest moment of his life, when his wife accepted his suit or when his beloved daughter was born. Vosswinkel is enthusiastic about the general principle, but chooses rather the hour when he received notice from Hamburg that he had won a large sum in the lottery, and insists on being painted with the letter in his hand, so displayed that its contents can be read. In Tusmann the novelist presents an inveterate pedant; his pockets are always filled with books, but it is a matter of indifference what they are, an algebra or cavalry exercise rules; in anticipation of marrying Albertine, he is studying a treatise on political wisdom translated from the Latin of Thomasius and published in 1710. In the casket he receives, not the portrait of Albertine, but a blank book which has the magic property of turning itself into any book he may wish to read.

Hoffmann had been for some years at home in Berlin, and he filled the story with local coloring and contemporary references; streets are mentioned familiarly—Friedrichstrasse, Königsstrasse, Spandauer Strasse; Albertine is studying the piano with Herr Lauska, a contemporary teacher, and sings in Zelter's Academy; Devrient has been playing Shylock, and Tieck's *Sternbald* is cited as an example to the young painter.[6]

At their meetings the members of the Serapion Club related anecdotes, some of which, as already noted, have been given names by editors of Hoffmann's works; others contain germs perhaps that Hoffmann never worked out into stories. Though *Aus dem Leben eines bekannten Mannes*, sometimes called *Der Teufel in Berlin*, was written and read aloud by its author, the manner in which the story

[6] "Die Brautwahl" was published late in 1819 in the *Berlinischer Taschenkalender auf 1820*, and in the autumn of the following year in the third volume of the *Serapionsbrüder*. The first version was more definitely planned for a Berlin audience, but with a wider circle of readers in view Hoffmann altered the text, toning down somewhat the purely local character of the tale. In the *Schriften des Vereins für die Geschichte Berlins*, Heft 43, 1910, Hans von Müller printed the original version from the *Taschenkalender* and Friedrich Holtze supplied an introduction explaining the many local and historical allusions and with considerable plausibility identifying some of the characters with people of those days in Berlin. Cf., also, Julius Rodenberg: *Bilder aus dem Berliner Leben* in *Deutsche Rundschau*, xxxvii (1883), pp. 96-166; liv (1888), pp. 86-106.

is introduced indicates that Hoffmann intended it to be judged somewhat informally. Theodor has found a copy of Hafftitz' *Microchronicon berolinense* on Lothar's desk, open at the point where one could read: "In this year the Devil walked openly on the streets of Berlin, followed funeral processions, behaving in a very sad manner, etc." Beside the book he found a manuscript in Lothar's hand which he confiscated, and now at the meeting of the club produces it to the dismay of Lothar himself. Lothar had supposed that he had long since destroyed this unsuccessful product of a jocular mood, and charges Theodor with playing a malicious joke upon him, but eventually he consents to read his story. This amusing trifle was published first in *Der Freimüthige* (May 1819), the same magazine in which sixteen years before Hoffmann had first seen his work in print.[7]

A stranger, well-dressed and of stately mien, appears suddenly in Berlin and through his charming manners, his extraordinary gallantries, makes himself popular in society in spite of some odd habits: he is slightly lame, but if one extends a helping hand, he is likely to leap several yards in the air with his helper and descend twelve paces away; he knocks at night on the doors of his acquaintances, dressed in white grave clothes and the next day excuses himself by saying that he merely wished to remind people of the transitoriness of life. Even the Elector becomes interested in him and offers him a place in the government. Apart from the general description, the single anecdote that makes up the story concerns the relations of the stranger with old Barbara Roloffen, a midwife, and he disappears in the form of a huge black bat when she is burned as a witch.

In the same year *Der Freimüthige* published another slight sketch by Hoffmann, *Die Haimatochare*, in which he contrives an amusing comedy about the jealousies of two rival scientists who hitherto have been devoted friends. Two entomologists, Menzies and Broughton, visit the island of O-wahu to study insect life there. Menzies, seeking a rare butterfly, finds "a dweller of the isles" (Insulanin) who becomes the entrancing object of his devotion. By use of the word "Insulanin" the storyteller reserves the point of his satire for a final disclosure, though he supplies hints enough for the nimble-minded. Broughton is insane with jealousy and lays claim to the treasure. A duel results in which both scientists are slain. The letter of Captain Bligh of the "Discovery," the ship on which the expedition was

[7] Cf. Otto Pniower: "E. T. A. Hoffmanns Erzählung 'Aus dem Leben eines bekannten Mannes'" in *Euphorion*, xiv (1907), pp. 714-17.

made, to the governor of New South Wales gives an account of the duel and the causes of it. The two scientists had quarreled over the possession of an insect which Davis, one of the ship's crew, called a louse, but from its bright colors the captain thinks it different from any known species. One of the scientists had shot the pigeon on whose wing (called "the carpet" in the correspondence of the scientists) the insect was concealed, but it was the other who discovered it there. In reply to Bligh's inquiry, the governor directs that "Haimatochare" should not be sent to a museum but buried at sea. This ceremony takes place with great pomp. The story is composed of letters which, Hoffmann says, were entrusted to him by Chamisso after his voyage around the world. Most of the letters are written by the two entomologists and develop both in brevity and fury as the altercation advances.[8]

Das steinerne Herz, published in the *Nachtstücke*, contains nothing to justify its inclusion under the title; there is not a solitary whiff of the uncanny. The chief character is an eighteenth century "original" such as adorned a multitude of novels, particularly those written under the influence of Lawrence Sterne. His early eccentricities had broken up a youthful love affair, and the lady in question had married a more reliable man. Reutlinger, the melancholy nobleman, incorporated his grief in a heart-shaped wood in the center of which he built a heart-shaped pavilion, and in the marble floor he set a red stone in the form of a heart. Now in the early nineteenth century he gives a great party, all the guests appearing in eighteenth century costume. The events of this festival, together with the necessary preliminaries, make up the story. The happenings of the day bring about a reconciliation between Reutlinger and his nephew, whom years before he had cast out into the rude world for a childish offense, and the union of the nephew and a daughter of Reutlinger's former loved one. Hoffmann's treatment of this rather trivial theme is appropriately lighthearted, and the story is lengthened by obvious padding—such as the account of the tailor's wedding and the nephew's misadventures with a caricature, an echo of Hoffmann's indiscretion long ago in Posen.

[8] That Chamisso gave the letters to Hoffmann is, of course, a transparent fiction, but he did ask Chamisso for a "charakteristischen Namen des Schiffs sowie ein paar tüchtige englische *nomen; propr* für die handelnden Personen" (letter of February 28, 1819), and in a later letter (May 21) he queries: "Welchen Rang, welchen Titel hat der Befehlshaber auf Port Jakson [sic], der die Expedition nach O-Wahu ausrüstet?" Cf. C. G. von Maassen: "Aus E. T. A. Hoffmanns Briefwechsel; Sieben Billets an Chamisso und ein Brief an Fouqué," in *Hyperion*, III (1908), pp. 123-26.

The short story *Spielerglück* (Gambler's Luck) is chiefly interesting for the fictional use of an incident in Hoffmann's early years, which was the origin of a curious vagary that he maintained through life. On his journey from Glogau over the mountains to Dresden, Hoffmann stopped for the night at a watering place where there were gaming tables. Under the influence of his traveling companion he took a hand at the play, and with amazing success; every venture on his part brought in golden returns. He became terrified—was some malign power taking possession of him?—and from that time on he never touched a playing card. This experience is the basis for *Spielerglück*. In the case of the gambler in question, whose first experience follows Hoffmann's very closely, the passion for gambling, though once satisfactorily resisted, becomes deeply ingrained. In the end, having lost all material possessions, he consents to play for his wife as a final stake, not knowing that his opponent had once been in love with her.

In Richer's *Causes Célèbres*[9] Hoffmann found the story of *Die Marquise de la Pivadière*, the account of an alleged crime together with the detailed testimony of various witnesses, the opinions of magistrates and judges, and quotations from French laws of the time covering legal procedure. He supplied an introductory narrative, carried the story farther back into the past, and deepened the psychological problems involved. The Marquise and her father confessor are tried for the murder of her worthless and faithless husband. Though the circumstances and the seemingly incontrovertible evidence of eyewitnesses point to their guilt, the body of their victim cannot be found. Even after the Marquis comes forward alive and well, with plausible reasons for his disappearance, there are certain subtle legal questions calling for solution, such as the testimony of the eyewitnesses and the investigation of illegitimate influences behind their falsified evidence. That the identity of the man now claiming to be the missing Marquis is called into question complicates the case still further. In view of Hoffmann's interest in "doubles" and his use of the motif in his tales, it may seem odd that he makes little of this aspect of the case. He was particularly concerned with the psychology of the heroine, building up her character as determined by the peculiar upbringing of an austere and eccentric father. To enhance the interest of the story he invents an

---

[9] M. Richer: *Causes célèbres et intéressantes avec les Jugemens qui les ont decidés* (Amsterdam, 1773), IV, pp. 431-578, "Histoire de la Pivadière."

episode in the early life of the Marquise and Charost, now her priest and confessor. As young people they had fallen in love with one another at first sight, and intrigue on the part of the Marquise's father had separated them. The story is one of the novelist's minor performances, but more than any other of his stories it shows the intrusion of his professional interests as a lawyer into his literary work.

CHAPTER 14

HOFFMANN AS A CRITIC OF LITERATURE

THE number of literary references not only in Hoffmann's critical writings but in his stories is likely to strike the eye of the reader.[1] Such abundance of allusion to authors and works of literature conveys the impression that Hoffmann was very widely read, in spite of Kunz's statement that in his Bamberg days he read "very little" and his own confession that later in Berlin he had no time for reading. In some cases Hoffmann's acquaintance with books may have been secondhand, derived from reviews or extracts in periodicals, or again he may have taken pleasure in hoodwinking the reader by reference to obscure works.[2] A survey of the allusions in Hoffmann's works and in his letters, particularly of the earlier period, demonstrates clearly the essential subjectivity of his attitude toward literature and thus the early and continued presence of a psychological factor that played a significant part in his own literary work. That is, the subjectivity of his own works, obvious in some cases—as in *Das Majorat*, where he openly makes use of experiences of his own—but subtly pervasive in others, is simply the obverse of the medal. The impulse to project himself into the works of others has found another outlet; he projects himself into his own works.

Much of Hoffmann's reading was directly or indirectly "professional" and hardly enters into the balance in the survey suggested. He was diligent in assembling material for his stories and intent upon the accuracy of historical events when he required them, upon the correct topography of places with which he was personally unacquainted, upon the establishment of historical and local atmosphere. This conscientious endeavor greatly extended the scope of his reading. Hoffmann's interest in the occult, in curious phenomena of the mind, in pathological states, covers another conspicuous category of the books he read. He possessed a native bent in this direc-

---

[1] Cf. Max Pirker: "E. T. A. Hoffmann als Bücherfreund," in *Jahrbuch deutscher Bibliophilen für 1918* (Wien, 1918), pp. 19-28.

[2] Max Pirker has shown (*Euphorion*, xvii, p. 444) that the list of works to which Hoffmann refers in *Der Elementargeist* is found one and all in Villars' *Gabalis*, with which Hoffmann was surely acquainted. This does not in itself prove that he had no firsthand knowledge of the books in question. If he found them in *Gabalis*, his curiosity may well have been aroused to look them up himself, and one may assume that he would probably have done so. Yet unquestionably the list in this case may have been a playful display of erudition.

tion which unquestionably supplied a subjective foundation for his reading of works dealing with such topics, but he also needed definite information for the writing of his stories. His frequent allusions to works on magic, mesmerism, curious medical lore, and the like do not form a mere parade of erudition, but give a quasi-scientific foundation for some of his mysterious incidents. The Biblical and classical allusions that are fairly numerous are the inevitable result of his schooling; in his day they formed the stock in trade of the educated man.

Most significant in a consideration of Hoffmann's reading are the works to which his youth paid special devotion, some of which remain ineradicable influences throughout his career. His youthful attitude is naïve, his approach purely subjective. In effect, he unconsciously tests the value of a book by its power to invite or compel him to project himself into its substance, to identify himself with a character, to find parallels to his own mind and experience. Psychologically this process is closely allied to the play or daydreams of childhood, which Hoffmann never completely outgrew. Another body of allusions, similar in their subjective basis, is to authors whom Hoffmann recognized as kindred spirits—either in their view of life or their method of expression—even though there is no documentary proof that he interpreted an individual work purely through an imaginary participation in its contents.

This particular type of admiration led him early to Jean Paul, Sterne, and Rousseau, and a little later, though still early, to Cervantes, Tieck, and Gozzi; Lichtenberg also, as satirist and humorist, awakened a kindred response, in the beginning apparently through his penetrating commentary on Hogarth's engravings. In the early correspondence, allusions to Jean Paul are frequent; Jean Paul was the most popular author of the day, and his mingling of sentiment and humor found a response in Hoffmann's youthful nature. Later he saw Jean Paul with more critical eyes, and, if not ready openly to satirize his former master, he did not hesitate to ridicule the excesses of his admirers (*Das steinerne Herz*).

Among the books that Hoffmann most admired in his youth, Rousseau's *Confessions* occupies a unique place. In his sketch of Hoffmann's life Hippel relates how the two fourteen-year-old youths, supposedly reading Cicero or Xenophon, plundered the bookshelves of Hoffmann's uncle to relieve the tedium of study, choosing particularly Rousseau's *Confessions* for this purpose. Kreisler-Hoffmann in *Kater Murr* states that he was only twelve years old when his acquaintance with Rousseau began. Years later Hoffmann wrote in his diary, February 13, 1804: "I am reading Rousseau's *Confessions* perhaps for the thirtieth time—I find myself like him in many things. My thought also becomes confused when it comes to putting feelings into words." The impression of kinship with Rousseau was perhaps in the early days supported by certain chance similarities: an older brother who was actually or virtually "lost" from the family, an aunt resembling Rousseau's description of one of his own, a friendship with Hippel which paralleled the tie between Rousseau and his cousin Bernard. The praise of country life, particularly "at the side of a friend," owes much to Rousseau's account of the days at Bossey with his cousin. The plan of the two youths to dig a tunnel into the garden of the neighboring school for young ladies may have had its origin in the trench which the two Swiss youths dug to the willow tree. That both Rousseau and Hoffmann showed ability in music and drawing provided another bond of recognized kinship; as young men they gave instruction in music. Kreisler-Hoffmann in *Kater Murr* gives an account of his boyish attempt, without adequate technical equipment, to imitate Rousseau in composing music, imitating Rousseau even to the point of working in bed. In a letter to Hippel, spring of 1803, Hoffmann mentions hypothetically the writing of an "autobiography with the conscientiousness of Rousseau." When in the *Kreisleriana* Kreisler's friends say of him: "In forming him Nature tried a new recipe, and the experiment was a failure," it is probably a reminiscence of the words at the beginning of the *Confessions* with which Rousseau expressed the unique quality of his character: "Si la nature a bien ou mal fait de briser le moule dans lequel elle m'a jeté, c'est ce dont on ne peut juger qu'après m'avoir lu." Hoffmann's ability to project himself into the *Confessions* and identify himself with the author was, of course, not dependent entirely upon fortuitous resemblances.

In his youth Hoffmann came under the spell of Shakespeare. As early as 1795, when Hoffmann was nineteen, he signed some satirical sketches "Ewald Trinkulo," and he speaks of Trinculo, the jester in *The Tempest*, as his "ancestor." This is chronologically the first Shakespeare reference—the letters begin only the year before—but it implies an already enthusiastic acquaintance. The early letters contain numerous allusions to Shakespeare, and somewhat later (1803), at the end of a letter to Hippel, Hoffmann remarks that he has already quoted the English dramatist three times.

Allusions to Shakespeare are more numerous than to any other author. Hoffmann mentions seventeen of the plays in all, some of them, to be sure, only once, and often without special significance. From a statistical survey, it seems plain that *Hamlet* and *As You Like It* were his favorite plays; more than a third of all the references are to *Hamlet*, and *As You Like It* stands in second place. The reason for this preference seems equally clear: Hoffmann "read himself" into the substance of the dramas, saw himself mirrored in certain characters, identified himself with Hamlet and with Jacques in *As You Like It*. With keen perception he characterizes these roles, incidentally describing himself and his relationship to his world:

"The feeling of disparity between the inner spirit and all the external mundane activity about it, brings forth the morbid excess of irritation which breaks out in bitter, scornful irony. . . . Such characters are the Fool in *Lear*, Jacques in *As You Like It*, but the supreme example of them is doubtless the incomparable Hamlet."[3]

This identification Hoffmann acknowledges in *Kater Murr*. Meister Abraham tells the Prince that Kreisler, though just as little crazy as Abraham himself, "yet at times behaves somewhat queerly and falls into a state, that almost might be compared to that of Prince Hamlet." The case of *As You Like It* is analogous. To Hoffmann apparently the center of interest lies not so much in the charming love idyll in the Forest of Arden as in the character of Jacques, with whom he feels a kinship of spirit. "Misanthropisch, humoristisch" are adjectives he applies to Jacques, really thinking of himself. Oddly enough, as with Hamlet, passages in *Kater Murr* confirm Hoffmann's identification of himself with Jacques. Julia declares that she does not regard Kreisler as insane, only as "an ironical wag [Schalk], really a kind of Monsieur Jacques," and later, when Rätin Benzon informs Kreisler of Julia's characterization, he exclaims: "O thou perceptive child of heaven" (O du ahnendes Himmelskind).

A striking example of Hoffmann's subjective approach to literature is his youthful admiration for *Don Carlos*. He wrote to Hippel, January 23, 1796, that he was reading Schiller's play for the seventh time:

"Nothing moves me more than Posa's friendship with the Prince— I can hardly believe that a more sublime and at the same time more

---

[3] "Das Gefühl des Missverhältnisses, in dem der innere Geist mit allem äussern irdischen Treiben um ihn her steht, erzeugt den krankhaften Überreiz, der ausbricht in bittre höhnende Ironie. . . . Solche Charaktere sind der Narr im Lear, Jacques in: Wie es euch gefällt, aber auf der höchsten Spitze derselben steht wohl der unvergleichliche Hamlet." IV, pp. 51-52.

attractive and touching picture of friendship has ever been presented than this—I read into the night—the scene changes. H[att] is Don Philip, she [Frau Hatt] Elisabeth, I Don Carlos, you Posa."[4]

In other words, Schiller's play is transformed into a mirror of his own personal relationships. In *Der Elementargeist*, written about a year before Hoffmann's death, Viktor is reported as giving his friend Albert an account of the development of his youth—and one may reasonably infer that Hoffmann is thinking of his own early years. Among the books that influenced him he mentions Goethe's *Werther*. On this point the early letters are silent, but the problem in Goethe's novel offered a challenge to subjective interpretation, similar to that recorded of *Don Carlos*.

Similar evidence of this psychological projection of himself into the books he read is afforded by passages referring to Grosse's novel *Der Genius*. In February 1795 Hoffmann records the reading of the work and the impression it made upon him. Inevitably the prominence of the mysterious or supernatural attracted Hoffmann. But Hoffmann's letter places the emphasis elsewhere, on his sense of a parallel between his friendship with Hippel and the tie that binds the two chief male characters in the novel; and the female characters are blended into one and identified with his own loved one (Frau Hatt). In the *Elementargeist* he includes *Der Genius* among the books of prime influence, noting his youthful fondness for the mystic and the miraculous. Though by implication he now classifies Grosse's novel among the works "of slight value" (von geringerem Gehalt), he says he is not ashamed of his early enthusiasm, and comments on the vividness of the narration and the skillful handling of the material. Thus the mature Hoffmann looks back and with critical insight explains and in part justifies the fervent admiration of other days.

In hearing Iffland's play *Der Herbsttag* or Salieri's opera *Axur* Hoffmann's enjoyment consisted, at any rate in part, in seeing parallels to the friendship between Hippel and himself. His early admiration for Lawrence Sterne, which remained with him through life, was similarly subjective; the friendship between himself and Hippel was conceived in terms of the Sterne-Eugenius relationship.[5]

---

[4] *Briefwechsel*, I, pp. 87-88. A second letter, March 31, 1796, repeats the identification of himself with Don Carlos and Hippel with Posa.

[5] Cf. *Briefwechsel*, I, pp. 116, 128, 189. For an amusing brief parody of Sterne's style—and incidentally also of Jean Paul—cf. the fragments from Hoffmann's "Nachlass," published by Hans von Müller in *Nord und Süd*, cxxxiii (1910), pp. 344-63.

Inevitably the subjective approach becomes obscured, less palpable, as Hoffmann grows more mature, as his sphere widens, and his personal contacts with the world of letters become more numerous and complex. The purely personal reactions are checked and neutralized. He became keenly aware of Shakespeare's universal genius, the comprehensive scope of Shakespeare's world. Yet the purely personal is not eliminated when he stands in awe before Shakespeare's genius. The appeal of Shakespeare still lies in the union of the tragic and the comic, in the tragic undertones of outwardly comic or humorous characters, the mingling in a single character of disparate, irreconcilable qualities—where indeed he sees himself. In the Bamberg years his admiration for Kleist's *Käthchen von Heilbronn* is in part determined by his contemporary passion for Julia Marc, and his advocacy of Calderon had a strong subjective basis in his attitude at the time toward the Roman Catholic Church. If he still indulged in naïve daydreaming of participation and identification, he was discreet enough to conceal it.

Though there is no documentary evidence, it is probable that his interest in *Rameaus Neffe* was in part founded on a partial identification. Hoffmann read Diderot's dialogue in Goethe's translation soon after its publication (1805), and Kunz records that it was one of Hoffmann's favorite books in Bamberg. There are several later references to it, and Hoffmann also refers to Diderot's *Jacques le Fataliste*. Though Hoffmann was no parasite and lived a life of honest effort, he often felt that his physical inferiority and certain eccentric qualities of his nature placed him in a position apart from society. He was acutely aware of the buffetings in human existence, the inequalities of life, the unreliability of earthly fortune, and could in his pessimistic moods perhaps envy the parasite, however base and unworthy, who was able to snap his fingers impertinently at the world and be triumphantly indifferent to all that most people regard as essential in human living. Rameau's nephew was also musical and relates an experience as a teacher of music which must in those days have seemed to Hoffmann a fragment of his own biography. Hoffmann's fondness for the dialogue form as a vehicle for the expression of his opinions may owe something to *Rameaus Neffe*. In the Bamberg days he read and reread James Beresford's *Miseries of Human Life* translated into German under the title *Menschliches Elend* (Bayreuth, 1810). But his intensely subjective reactions form now a spur to the creative imagination, and later enter into the composition of *Der goldene Topf*.

Save for the dramatic criticism in the dialogues of *Berganza,* *Der Dichter und der Komponist,* and *Seltsame Leiden eines Theater- direktors,* Hoffmann wrote no formal appraisals of men of letters or works of literature. His opinions must be inferred—and often with hesitation—from his letters, the conversation of the Serapion Brothers, and chance allusions in his stories. Often the only clue to his evaluation is a single adjective, which expresses approval or disapproval but has otherwise no critical value; for example, the adjective "herrlich" (glorious or splendid) is a favorite vehicle of the esteem that he applies repeatedly to Tieck, and twice to Kleist.

In the days of his maturity the great reputations of the classical period stand largely unchallenged or at least unexamined. Allusions to the work of Goethe and Schiller are numerous, but for the most part of slight value as criticism. Goethe and Schiller have become "classic" in the sense that quotations from them, like, "Das Land, wo die Zitronen blühn" or "Die schönen Tage in Aranjuez," have become "geflügelte Worte." Goethe's supreme greatness, one may say, Hoffmann took for granted. The early Goethe inspired him to some of his first musical compositions, and it may be assumed that he read Goethe's poems, plays, and novels, even those to which he makes no reference. He regarded Goethe as possessing the first requisite of a writer of tragedy: "the spirit [Gemüt] of such an author must be completely healthy, free from every kind of sickliness, whether from physical weakness or poisoned inheritance"; it was with such "unweakened powers and inner cleanness" he created *Götz* and *Egmont.* The lifelong devotee of Shakespeare apparently found less to admire in the classic formalism and studied restraint of *Iphigenie,* which he never mentions.[6] He could accept with enthusi- asm Goethe's interpretation of *Hamlet* and openly adapt a Mignon figure to his own uses, confessedly in *Der Zusammenhang der Dinge* and possibly in the Chiara of *Kater Murr,* but there is little evidence that he was influenced by Goethe's thought or appreciated the range of Goethe's message to his age. They never met, but one can assume that they would not have seen eye to eye—the serene, balanced mind of the Weimar sage and the restless, turbulent spirit of Romanti-

6 Rochlitz tells of "ein ernstes und ausführliches Gespräch über Goethes *Iphigenie*" between himself, Hoffmann, and another friend on an evening in the winter of 1812. Rochlitz introduces the incident to show Hoffmann's reaction, then to him inexplicable, when the line of *Iphigenie* was quoted: "Wohl dem, der seiner Väter gern gedenkt"; this is used to underscore the misfortunes of Hoffmann's youth. Either Rochlitz' date is incorrect or the interview must have taken place on the occasion of an otherwise unrecorded visit to Bamberg. Cf. Rochlitz: *Für Freunde der Tonkunst,* ii, pp. 8-9.

cism.[7] Hoffmann was bold enough to write a scathing criticism of the version of *Romeo and Juliet* that Goethe prepared for the Weimar stage.

The case of Schiller is somewhat different. The passage in *Der Elementargeist* referred to above includes *Der Geisterseher* (The Ghost Seer) and *Die Räuber* (The Robbers) among the books to which Viktor attributes a role in his early development. Schiller's unfinished story, *Der Geisterseher*, appealed to Hoffmann's love of the mysterious and the supernatural; Theodor in *Das Majorat*, in part a self-portrait, had a copy of *Der Geisterseher* in his pocket, like, he said, "all youths of the time who were interested in romanticism." Schiller's first play continued to make a strong impression on Hoffmann when he saw it on the stage, especially in later years by the acting of his friend Devrient in the role of Franz Moor; and his own story *Die Räuber* boldly appropriates much of Schiller's plot and then remodels both characters and situation. The fate element in *Wallenstein* seems to have struck a peculiarly receptive chord when Hoffmann was in a fatalistic humor. It will be remembered that Hoffmann's first appearance in print was a rather hesitating query as to the use of the ancient chorus in modern drama, prompted by Schiller's experiment in *Die Braut von Messina*.

As Hoffmann condemned the imitators of Goethe's *Götz*, he had only contempt for the followers of Schiller: they have no conception of the truly dramatic, are satisfied with composing respectable iambics—"those animals with one short and one long foot"; they can only fumble with Schiller's exalted rhetoric since they are incapable of inventing dramatic situations where it might be appropriate. As he criticized Goethe's version of *Romeo and Juliet*, he berated soundly Schiller's adaptation of Gozzi's *Turandot*. His attitude toward Schiller is indeed somewhat ambiguous. He speaks of him as a "highly gifted spirit" (Genius), of his greatness and excellence (Grösse und Herrlichkeit) ; "Schiller the hero," he says, "in his greatness can never pass away" (Der Heros Schiller bleibt ewig unvergänglich). And yet when advancing from such rhetorical epithets to concrete criticism, he whittles away something from his encomium. Schiller possessed a power over language such as is rarely granted to anyone, but at the same time "a certain fertility was characteristic of him so that verses gave birth to verses." That is, he finds in Schiller a rhetorical redundancy which, at any rate in his dramatic work, had a pernicious influence upon his imitators.

[7] For Goethe's opinion of Hoffmann, cf. *Epilogue*, pp. 380-81.

Though *Die Räuber*, a favorite in early days, apparently maintained something of its position in his esteem, *Don Carlos*, now that the subjective appeal has lost its force, appears entirely undramatic. Indeed, according to Hoffmann a debate would be possible as to "how far Schiller can be called a real dramatic poet." With his great gifts he "must have borne within him profound knowledge of the genuinely dramatic"; his "striving for the really dramatic in his last years is unmistakable," but Hoffmann implies that Schiller's success in this striving is still qualified. However, he admits that *Wilhelm Tell* is a "real drama at least in the first acts," and regards the exposition as a masterpiece. It is apparent that Hoffmann regarded Schiller as a great poet, but in the field of his highest endeavor, the drama, great only with strong reservations. Of Lessing Hoffmann mentions only *Minna von Barnhelm* and *Emilia Galotti*, in each case, however, a mere allusion without critical significance; in his strictures upon German ineptitude in comedy, it is perhaps surprising that he does not make an exception of *Minna von Barnhelm*.

Hoffmann's esteem for his predecessors in the Romantic Movement, especially for Tieck and Novalis, has already been recorded, and it remained unchanged through the years. If Tieck had but overcome his aversion for the "boards," he says, he might have given the degenerate German theater a turn in a new and wholesome direction and become a German Gozzi. Tieck's fanciful satirical comedies, notably *Der gestiefelte Kater*, offer indisputable proof of his abilities. It was quite within his power (es lag nur an ihm) to batter down that "wretched house of cards," the contemporary German theater. He is certain of Tieck's place among the immortals; indeed he prophesies that only posterity will recognize his lofty eminence (hohe Vortrefflichkeit), "while quick-flaming will-o'-the-wisps, capable of blinding the eye for a moment with borrowed glow, are extinguished again just as quickly." There is no record that Hoffmann read the two "Novellen" which Tieck published after a long silence the year before Hoffmann's death.

Hoffmann was one of the few contemporaries of Heinrich von Kleist who appreciated fully his rare genius. As previously noted, Kleist's *Käthchen von Heilbronn* was in the whole range of dramatic literature one of the plays that most impressed him—partly, one must admit, for purely subjective reasons. The first performance of *Käthchen* in Bamberg was on September 1, 1811, but by February 3 of that year he had begun his references to Julia Marc under the cover name of Käthchen (Ktch). It is possible that Hoffmann knew only this one drama. He sincerely lamented the dearth of German comedy, and *Der zerbrochene Krug* (The Broken Pitcher) should have given him encouragement, and the tragic power of *Penthesilea* would have held him spellbound. It is likely that these plays did not come into his hands. *Die Hermannsschlacht* and *Prinz Friedrich von Homburg* were not published until 1821. He spoke with enthusiasm of Kleist's essay on the "Marionettentheater."

Hoffmann may have read some of Kleist's stories as they appeared in periodicals prior to the publication of the two volumes of *Erzählungen* in 1810-1811, but his first reference to them is in a letter of July 1, 1812; he says, "Kleist's stories I know well; they are worthy of him." He mentions, however, only two stories *Das Bettelweib von Locarno* and *Michael Kohlhaas*. In *Das Bettelweib von Locarno* Kleist "knew how not only to dip into the paint pot [of which the Serapion brothers have been speaking] and draw from it his colors with the power and originality of a perfected master, but as no one else he could create a living picture." Hoffmann admired Kleist's skill in gaining effects with simple means: an old beggar woman in a story of a few pages can produce a sensation of terror that the lurid description of vampire activities could not evoke—this evaluation of Kleist's story follows the "Vampire" narrative in the *Serapionsbrüder*. Though the bare facts in *Michael Kohlhaas* are taken from Hafftitz' *Microcronicon*, Kleist has made the story of the sixteenth century rebel completely his own, creating it out of the "meager and unsatisfactory material" that Hafftitz offered. As Hoffmann himself rummaged in ancient chronicles for subjects for his stories—indeed in this very one—he is inevitably arrested by Kleist's creative use of the old chronicle: "No one has shown so superbly how material can be worked over or rather formed into life"; the crude narrative of Hafftitz has been transformed into a living thing. As a matter of fact the word "lebendig" (living or alive) appears repeatedly in Hoffmann's criticism as the supreme touchstone of literary values. A few months after Kleist had committed suicide, Hoffmann asked Hitzig for information concerning "glorious Kleist and his heroic end." Hoffmann is disgusted with current gossip, "by the stupid prattle in the public prints written by people who before a beam [Strahl] of Kleist's powers [Genius] would have crawled away into their own wretched nutshells which they look upon as a palace with seven towers."

Of the later Romanticists, Fouqué and Brentano were friends of Hoffmann, and Arnim, it may be assumed, at least an acquaintance.

In his Warsaw days Hoffmann was sufficiently interested in Brentano's *Die lustigen Musikanten* to compose music for it—probably the Gozzi flavor of the little play attracted him; of Brentano's other work he mentions only *Ponce de Leon*. In Bamberg he records trying to read Arnim's drama *Halle und Jerusalem*, but "it wouldn't go" (wollte nicht von statten gehen); later he mentions *Isabella von Ägypten*; the use of folk superstition in Arnim's story probably intrigued him. Despite the paucity of allusion, it may be assumed that he read much more widely both in Brentano and Arnim. To Fouqué Hoffmann repeatedly applied his favorite adjective "herrlich." He is placed beside Novalis in true poetic feeling and in childlikeness of spirit. With rare power he has touched the harp of the North; with genuine consecration and inspiration he has summoned the hero Sigurd into life, "so that his splendor outshone the pale twilight lamps of the times and before his mighty tread all the suits of armor which one had formerly taken for heroes fell down of themselves, hollow and bodiless." As unlimited master he controlled the realm of the miraculous; "its strange forms and phenomena followed willingly his magic call" (*Berganza*). To Hoffmann, Fouqué's *Undine* was incomparably lovely, and he spent years in the effort to give it a musical setting worthy of its beauty. *Das Galgenmännlein*, a little Märchen, the novel *Der Zauberring*, and the short story *Ixion* were among Hoffmann's best-loved books. In Berlin he composed choruses for Fouqué's *Tassilo*, a "prologue" performed at a festival in honor of the four hundredth anniversary of the Hohenzollerns in Brandenburg. The warm personal regard for the man Fouqué, however, did not prevent Hoffmann from noting the gradual deterioration and flattening out of Fouqué's work.

Naturally Hoffmann had no thought of supplying a future investigator with a list of the books he read, but in the whole record of Hoffmann's contact with literature—in full acknowledgment of its incompleteness—there are unaccountable gaps. One outstanding genre of literature, especially of German literature, he almost completely ignores: he says almost nothing of lyric poetry. Two of the most popular lyricists, much esteemed at the time, were his intimate friends, Chamisso and Fouqué. Though he delighted in *Peter Schlemihl*, Hoffmann never mentions Chamisso's poetry, and only twice does he refer to Fouqué's lyric poems: in a letter to Hippel he says that Fouqué's *Gedichte aus den Jünglingsjahren* (Poems from Youthful Years), contain much that is beautiful, and in *Die Brautwahl* he quotes two stanzas of a poem by Fouqué—but in a context rather depreciatory than complimentary. Uhland is mentioned only once: he knows that Hippel will like his poems—which says very little. Eichendorff appears once in Hoffmann's diary, merely the record of his visit to Berlin. He mentions the music for Körner's patriotic lyric *Lützows wilde Jagd*. Otherwise, the lyricism of the period receives not a word. Hoffmann confessed his own inability to write respectable verse; was lyric poetry a blind spot in his make-up, except in so far as it served the composer as material for his harmonies? Did he feel that the lyric in words needed music to give intensity?

Though Hoffmann himself was not a dramatist, save in a few early and unsuccessful efforts, the drama was the literary form to which he chiefly directed his criticism, and from the angle that he would recognize as alone valid—the drama as performed on the stage. He had been keenly interested in the theater from childhood. His letters abound in references to the plays he has seen. When in the winter of 1804 he visited Königsberg from his forlorn exile in Plock in the hope of claiming for himself something from the estate of his Aunt Sophie—though perhaps he did not expect to be understood literally—he wrote to Hippel that he was "daily" in the theater, and even in a stay of a few weeks he established friendly relations with the actors of the local troupe. In Bamberg, Dresden, and Leipzig the theater, including both drama and opera, was his profession. And in Berlin, outside of his work at the courts and his activities as an author, the theater and all that concerned the theater occupied his attention more absorbingly than any other aspect of life in the Prussian capital. The relations between the composer of an opera and the author of the text he examined in *Der Dichter und der Komponist*, written in Dresden. In the spring of 1817 he published in the *Dramatisches Wochenblatt* (Dramatic Weekly) a dialogue entitled *Die Kunstverwandten* (Kinsmen in Art), which he rewrote, enlarged substantially, and published in 1818 as *Seltsame Leiden eines Theaterdirektors* (Strange Sufferings of a Theater Director). For a work on the drama Hoffmann was well equipped. In addition to his practical experience in the theater, his acquaintance with dramatic literature was most comprehensive, and though there are only a few references to works of dramatic criticism, he unquestionably established his own opinions and theories in part through examination of his predecessors. He knew Lessing's critical work, and an entry in his diary, Bamberg, January 12, 1811, is significant: "Read much in Schlegel's *Lectures on Dramatic Art*: I will copy out the most important definitions from this work ad usum." He was also acquainted with what Tieck up to that time had written on the drama.

The frame which Hoffmann has invented for the *Seltsame Leiden* is highly diverting and throughout the whole long dialogue the pleasing fiction is skillfully maintained. An elderly gentleman dressed in brown—incidentally Hoffmann's favorite costume—enters the public room of an inn, orders a bottle of wine, and busies himself with a manuscript. Presently a younger man, dressed in gray, arrives in extreme agitation; his whole appearance and demeanor betray vexation, anger, and despair. He orders oysters and wine, tears a letter to bits, apparently the immediate cause of his agitation, and stamps the fragments under his feet. After a while the "Brown One" approaches the "Gray One"—they continue to be thus designated throughout the dialogue—and engages him in conversation. The "Brown One" is a theater director of long experience, now in charge of a traveling company, and the "Gray One" is director of the local theater, according to him one of the most important in the whole country. In his preface Hoffmann warned the reader against the attempt to interpret the dialogue in personal and local terms—a warning that most commentators have flagrantly disregarded. Unquestionably Hoffmann drew upon his own experiences and observations, and the "Brown One" expresses by and large Hoffmann's opinions, but at times the "Gray One" voices them also; some critics have identified the "Gray One" with Holbein.

The occasion for the "Gray One's" misery is the long series of exasperating difficulties encountered in producing a new opera *Guzmann der Löwe* (Guzmann the Lion), culminating in the refusal of the bass to continue with his role, even though the preparations for the production are far advanced and he has himself until now taken part in the rehearsals. The work has been carried on at great expense, and unremitting labor has been involved, particularly in the toilsome process of training a dog to take the part of the lion. These circumstances as the "Gray One" relates them introduce a long and entertaining exchange of experiences on the part of the two directors: the interminable wrangling among the actors, their jealousies, intrigues, and back-stage gossip, their insane vanities, their interest in costumes, their greed for applause, their capricious stubbornness, and inconceivable pettiness. At times the two directors have controlled untoward situations by flattery, hidden strategy, and neat little intrigues of their own. But the troubles of a director do not end with the actors, scene shifters, costumers, and the like, for they still have to deal with the authors of the plays, the composers, and the orchestral leaders; then the treasurer of the theater, the critics, and the general public, enter upon the scene to provide each a peculiar type of annoyance.

Hoffmann's work is in essence a profoundly interesting, stimulating treatise, and his comment has by no means lost its pertinence today. The artistic device of a dialogue between two directors is peculiarly effective; the give-and-take of the two men, skillfully individualized, the numerous excursions into personal experience, the easy transitions from one phase of the subject to another, enliven the solid matter under discussion; in the flow of conversation, topics are taken up, dropped, and then resumed later. Hoffmann's constructive work gains rather than loses by not being cast in the mold of a formal treatise. Though quite overlooked or ignored by historians of dramatic theory and criticism, Hoffmann's book is incomparably more alive than Freytag's *Technique of the Drama*, or many another later work written to displace Freytag.

To the decay of the German theater many causes have contributed. The beneficial influence of earlier works on dramaturgy has vanished. The new theatrical journals and the newspapers provide no really enlightened guidance, for the belief has gained currency that anybody, no matter how slenderly equipped, can write theatrical criticism; the sheets are filled with shallow reviews of insipid plays and obscure comedies, and worthless plays are accorded the same critical attention as the work of the masters. Hoffmann acknowledges to the full the values of intelligent, disinterested criticism. In the end the director brings ruin upon himself, if he seeks by subtle bribery of one sort or another to influence the critics. The "Brown One" had once succeeded by clever strategy in getting a goodly portion of the local critics on his side, but with disastrous results; both he and his company ceased to be on their toes; the actors became negligent and arrogant, they lost their interest, while the critics poured forth a flood of laudatory nonsense and no longer thought it worth-while to exert themselves in intelligent appraisal. The whole enterprise slumped completely, and the intelligent public stayed away. Another experience illustrates the invaluable service of thorough, disinterested criticism; during his whole stay in the town, the director never found out the identity of his helpful though merciless critic.

The present generation of actors is, in general, unworthy of the traditions of a great art. Many do not act at all; they merely declaim. Too many of them are simply intent upon popular approval and distort their roles to gain immediate applause from the unthinking, applause which is then used as a lever to demand increased pay. If they wish to portray a hero "they shriek, or roar, beat their foreheads, smash a few glasses, or break a chair." Even actors of real distinction yield to the temptation of this rewarding type of exhibitionism; an actor recently deceased (meaning Iffland) "often sacrificed the truth and the harmony of a play for the stormy applause of the moment." That an actor was called before the footlights was once a rare mark of honor accorded to a deserving and beloved artist. If this distinction is limited to a recognition of genuine merit—not merely for a single passage in his role but for success in the whole part—the actor may justly bask in such recognition of his accomplishment (Verdienst), but much too frequently all meaning is drained from praise thus bestowed by the subsequent demand for the appearance of an actor who has really played the fool (sich recht toll gebärdet) or has merely shrieked vigorously. But the real artist will discriminate between false and true applause. The radically different response of the audience to tragedy and to comedy he will know how to appraise. The experience of an actor friend (Devrient) illustrates the actor's emotional contact with the audience in a tragic scene.

The accomplished actor taking a relatively minor role must not feed his vanity by trying to outshine his fellows; this will destroy the harmony of the play. On the other hand, the great actor should not submit to the dictates of a director who would constantly cast him in insignificant roles; the "Gray One's" "little Garrick," as he calls him, accepts minor character parts without a word of protest —Hoffmann is doubtless reading a lecture to his friend Devrient, who, Hoffmann thought, was prostituting his great talents in mediocre roles. Since Hoffmann himself gives a detailed account of the acting of certain accomplished actors in important roles, apparently without disapproval of differences in interpretation, there is a touch of inconsistency in his emphatic dictum that the actor must follow the author's obvious intention. It is sometimes said that an actor has created a character markedly different from the author's text, but in such a case the actor is seriously at fault. An actor does not "create" a role, except in a confessedly weak play, where the author has not really done the creating himself.

In Hoffmann's opinion the actor, like the poet, is born and not made, though he would by no means minimize the necessity of rigid training. For the real artist he sets up a truly exalted standard: "Within the true artist as an actor there must dwell the special power of mind and spirit, to represent the person which the author has given him, endowed with life and with the colors of life, that is, with all the inward springs of action that determine the external appearance in speech, gait, and gesture."[8] In addition to this power of the mind the actor must possess that gift, rarely vouchsafed by Heaven, to control his outward appearance so completely that even the slightest movement is conditioned by the inner will. "Speech, gait, position, and gesture belong no longer to the individual actor but to the person that, as the creation of the poet, has risen within him true and living and now shines forth so blindingly that his own self vanishes in the process like some colorless, empty thing."[9] The utter denial of one's self, or rather complete forgetfulness, is hence the very first requisite in the art of acting.

But the genuine actor is not merely an intelligent, perhaps superintelligent mimic. He must be one who comprehends the deepest depths of human nature. If he lacks this, the realm of the real poet is forever closed to him; without this comprehension he will regard "the strangely distorted marionettes of some capricious puppet player as truly living men and women." That no company can be composed of this supreme type of actor Hoffmann readily admits— it is the ideal—but even the lesser talents who must be called in to take the numerous parts, for example, in a Shakespearean play, must still be such as can be animated by the spirit of the master.

Hoffmann relies primarily on Shakespeare for his illustrations of real greatness in the drama and comments on the acting of great actors in Shakespearean roles. The supreme eminence of Shakespeare, which he had felt rather than really apprehended in his youth, he is now capable of demonstrating. "No author," he says, "has ever so comprehended human nature in its depths and known how to present it, and on that account his characters belong to the world

[8] "Dem wahren darstellenden Künstler muss die besondere geistige Kraft inwohnen, sich die von dem Dichter gegebene Person beseelt und lebendig gefärbt, das heisst, mit allen innern Motiven, die die äussere Erscheinung in Sprache, Gang, Gebärde bedingen, vorzustellen." IV, p. 34.

[9] "Sprache, Gang, Haltung, Gebärde gehören nicht mehr dem individuellen Schauspieler, sondern der Person an, die, die Schöpfung des Dichters, wahr und lebendig in ihm aufgegangen und die nun so blendend herausstrahlt, dass sein Ich darüber wie ein farblos nichtiges Ding verschwindet." IV, p. 34.

and will persist as long as human beings exist"; he speaks of the power of Shakespeare's "gigantic creations." The "Brown One" is so unqualified in his homage that the director in "gray" remarks: "I note that you will not allow a single flaw in your favorite." The frequent lack of success in staging Shakespeare's plays is attributed to lack of reverence for the text. Hoffmann condemns all changes—the omission of words, passages, or scenes, and the transposition of scenes. All mutilation of the text is the work of ignorant bunglers: "One begins to make changes, one makes omissions, the next one changes what has been changed, and that does not satisfy the third who adds something of his own" to the point where "the name of Shakespeare on the playbill becomes a wretched [heillos] irony." Shakespeare was a conscientious craftsman; his plays are subtly and thoroughly integrated, and there is nothing superfluous. Hoffmann comments with special emphasis on the masterly exposition in Shakespeare's dramas; it is evident that he regards the exposition as the most difficult problem for the dramatist, the touchstone of mastery. In Shakespeare the exposition is always a part of the action—action commences with the first words—and he praises Goethe's *Egmont* as worthy of Shakespeare in this regard.

The two directors discuss several of Shakespeare's plays and actors whom they have seen in Shakespearean roles. Most interesting is the debate on the versatility of actors in assuming both tragic and comic parts. After the "farcical" has been clearly distinguished from the "comic"—and the farcical may have its place—the kinship, indeed the virtual identity, of the comic and the tragic is postulated, as coming from an identical source. Irony lies deep in human nature, determines human nature in its inmost being, and from this sense of irony, "jest, wit, and waggery [Schalkheit] beam forth [strahlen], but with profound seriousness." "The convulsive quiverings of pain, the most piercing tones of lament in despair stream out into that laughter of the wondrous joy which has just been born of pain and despair. The complete perception of this strange organic process in human nature may well be just what we call humor, and thus the deep inner essence of the humorous, which in my way of thinking is one and the same as the genuinely comic, may be defined. Now I will go still farther and maintain that just this perception or really this humor is at home in the breast of the actor who draws his playing of roles from the depths of human nature. It follows then as a matter of course that *this* highly gifted actor can present comic and tragic roles with equal power and truth; they are beams from a single focus."[10] In this connection Hoffmann mentions King John, King Lear, Malvolio, and, finally, Falstaff as "the quintessence of this superb irony, this abounding humor." Later he adds Hamlet to the list. A penetrating comparison of Othello and Molière's Harpagon serves to demonstrate the kinship of the tragic and the comic. It is only "the individual shaping of the passion," the peculiar form it takes, which in each case brings about the difference in the manner of its appearance and determines the tragic or the comic. Both of them, Othello and Harpagon, "attacked in their inmost soul, in the essence of their being, wounded in life and happiness [Leben und Heil] break forth in full rage, and in this rage, in the climax of its manifestation, the beams come together in a focus, streaming forth from within in different refraction, and enkindle in the breast of the spectator, in one case, tragic amazement, in the other laughter and scorn."[11] The character of Shylock—incidentally one of De- vrient's most successful roles—provides a further illustration of the union of the tragic and the comic. In addition to Shakespeare, the works of Calderon and of Gozzi are discussed in relation to stage production, of the latter *Turandot*, and especially *Die drei Pomeran- zen* (L'Amore delle tre melarance).

In one place or another Hoffmann touches upon most problems in the production of a play—the size of the theater for different types of drama (tragedy, comedy, opera, or spectacle), the lighting of the stage, costuming, and stage settings. In the matter of stage sets he condemns the contemporary effort to obtain illusion by ex- aggerated attention to the visibly concrete. We cannot, he admits, return to the bare simplicity of the Shakespearean stage, which de- manded everything of the spectator; the creative imagination of the audience in those days must have given a response, impossible to expect now, when such passages were spoken as the chorus in the Prologue to *Henry V*. Hoffmann quotes a long selection in Schlegel's translation to illustrate his point. But we are sorely at fault if we do

---

[10] "Die krampfhaften Zuckungen des Schmerzes, die schneidendsten Klagetöne der Verzweiflung strömen aus in das Lachen der wunderbaren Lust, die eben erst von Schmerz und Verzweiflung erzeugt wurde. Die volle Erkenntnis dieses seltsamen Organism der menschlichen Natur möchte ja eben das sein, was wir Humor nennen und so sich das tiefe innere Wesen des Humoristischen, welches meines Bedünkens mit dem wahrhaftig Komischen eins und dasselbe ist, von selbst bestimmen. Nun gehe ich weiter und behaupte, dass eben jene Erkenntnis oder recht eigentlich der Humor in der Brust des Schauspielers heimatlich ist, der seine Darstellungen aus der Tiefe der menschlichen Natur schöpft. Hieraus folgt denn aber wieder von selbst, dass *dieser* hochbegabte Schauspieler mit gleicher Kraft und Wahrheit komische und tragische Rollen, Strahlen aus einem Fokus geworfen, darstellen wird!" iv, pp. 47-48.
[11] iv, p. 50.

not leave something to the imagination. Hoffmann illustrates his idea of what is appropriate and effective in a stage set by describing two different sets for the garden scene in *The Merchant of Venice.*

At various points in the dialogue the "Brown One" has hinted at the excellence of his troupe of actors: rivalries, jealousies, contentions, are unknown among them; they are even content with very modest salaries. Such unprecedented conditions in the theater arouse incredulity in the breast of the other director. With sly artistry Hoffmann has reserved a surprise for the end of his essay, a kind of "curtain" at the close of the drama. The "Brown One" is willing to satisfy the curiosity of his companion; he takes him upstairs in the inn to the room he is occupying, opens a chest, and discloses his troupe of actors—a set of marionettes.

It would lead too far afield to enter further than has already been done into the possible or probable interpretation of Hoffmann's concealed references to current dramatic history. The refusal of the bass singer to continue in his part in *Guzmann the Lion* is patently a jibe at Joseph Fischer, who declined to sing the role of Kühleborn in Hoffmann's opera *Undine.* The play itself, with an animal in the leading part, is a satire upon the famous case of *Der Hund des Aubry* which resulted in Goethe's resignation from his connection with the Weimar theater. The "Gray One" says that the spirit of the times demands dogs on the stage; "it is praiseworthy to educate this wise animal for higher roles [Repräsentationen], from the ordinary courtesy of the drama to the romantic chivalry of tragedy and heroic opera. One theater director wished to go even further and, attempting the sublime, to bring on the stage a small, well-formed donkey in the role of a lover, but it was generally observed that this would be nothing new, and the plan was dropped."

Apart from Schiller, who died in 1805, the two chief dramatic talents in the first decades of the nineteenth century were Heinrich von Kleist and Zacharias Werner. It may be an oversimplification to say that Kleist's potentialities as a great dramatist were checked, not by his own fault but by those who stifled his genius in refusing to give it recognition, that Werner was his own enemy and singlehanded brought about his own defeat. Hoffmann's personal relations with Werner have already been described. In a letter to Hippel from Warsaw, he describes Werner's new play, *Die Brautnacht* (The Bridal Night), the first part of *Das Kreuz an der Ostsee* (The Cross on the Baltic Sea), in so far as he was at the time writing incidental music for it. He regards the play as inferior to Werner's previous drama *Die Söhne des Tals* (The Sons of the Valley), as rather crude, and occasionally in poor taste, though strokes of real genius mark it here and there. The play tortures the reader with every conceivable innovation that the Romanticists have introduced into the drama, "assonance, alliteration," and various verse forms, "tercets, sonnets, and the like"; it is something quite different, Hoffmann says, when Tieck illustrates the movement in *Genoveva* and *Octavian*.

Werner was accustomed to read his work aloud to a group of friends in Warsaw, and the theatrical, rhetorical, and pompous reading of his own lines, and the odd, indescribable grimaces which accompanied it, lessened the hearer's appreciation of the drama's merits. In the *Serapionsbrüder* Hoffmann relates a diverting anecdote. The friends were gathered to hear Werner read *Das Kreuz an der Ostsee*; they knew fragments of the play already and were filled with keen anticipation. After elaborate preparations and amid the breathless silence of his friends, Werner began to read the first scene of the play, where the ancient Prussians, gathering amber on the shore of the sea, invoke one of their gods named Bankputtis: "Bankputtis! Bankputtis! Bankputtis!" In the rhetorical pause that Werner permitted himself after these vocables, one of the company, doubtless Hoffmann himself, remonstrated in soft accents: "My dear, dear friend, most excellent poet, if you have composed the whole work in this cursed language, no one of us will understand the very deuce of it, and I beg of you rather to begin at once with the translation."[12] Of Werner's later plays Hoffmann has a word or two of comment: he thought *Kunegunde* could be recommended for performance on the Bamberg stage, and on its merits as a drama, not merely on the historical Kunegunde's connection with the town; in *Attila* he found splendid features, though the play was interwoven with trivialities and guilty of poor taste; on the strength of rumors he has heard, he thinks that *Wanda* "must be a highly fanciful work but one of originality."

Hoffmann's final estimate of Werner, close to the end of his life, is more discriminating. Not only does he revise his opinion of Werner's character in the mitigating light of Werner's confession in the preface to his *Die Mutter der Makkabäer*, but he also states more clearly his appreciation of Werner's astounding gifts as a dramatist. Hoffmann would assent to the general verdict which he puts in the

---

[12] Fouqué relates that among the Berlin friends the phrase "Es ist Bankputtis" became a "Generalbezeichnung mancherlei seltsamer, ob sonst an sich auch verschiedenartiger Literaturerscheinungen." Cf. Hitzig (1839), III, p. 221.

mouths of the Serapion Brothers: in Werner's characters there is true greatness, true strength, the genuinely tragic, but, mingled with it, something strange, fantastic, often something vulgar or ordinary (gemein), which proves that he had arrived at no entirely clear conception of his hero, that he lacked the perfect health of the inner spirit which is unconditionally essential to the writer of tragedy.

An exception is made of one drama, the second part of *Das Kreuz an der Ostsee,* and of one particular character in it. For the sake of varying the discussion, Hoffmann divides the characterization of the play between Theodor and Cyprian, as if two of his three selves had been on friendly terms with Werner in Warsaw. From what he then heard of the play Theodor declares his conviction that Werner's drama would rise in greatness and power not only to the level of his other work but of anything written by anyone in recent times (neuere Zeit). And Cyprian contends that since the days of Shakespeare no such character has trodden the stage as the old king of the ancient Prussians, Waidewuthis, "this superhuman, terrible, frightful old man" (fürchterlich grauenhaft); the poet, "capable of powerful magic," "seemed to have conjured him up out of the shuddery depths of the subterranean realm." Several scenes are described in support of these opinions. Werner's drama was intended to be a glorification of Christian victory over the pagan world in old Prussia, and "with amazing power and originality" the poet conceived this demon, so great, mighty, and gigantic that he appeared to be quite worthy of this conflict, and the victory, the glory of Christianity, could but shine forth the more resplendently; "to use the words of Dante," the old king seemed to be the "imperador del doloroso regno" wandering upon earth. Hoffmann did not know how Werner had conceived the end of the play, an ending commensurate with the foregoing, even surpassing it in awful sublimity. Vinzenz suggests that the play grew beyond its author's powers, and that accordingly he never finished it. The second part of *Das Kreuz an der Ostsee* was at any rate never published, and the skeptical might smilingly suggest that Hoffmann was safe in thus lauding a play that did not exist.

It seems strange that Hoffmann in speaking thus at length of Werner's dramatic work does not mention the one play that has really kept his name alive, *Der vierundzwanzigste Februar* (The Twenty-fourth of February). In another place Hoffmann speaks contemptuously of the fate drama, of which Werner's play is the most famous example: "The muse which had recently been so tender, weak-nerved, suddenly became friendly with Satan and hell, and with a grotesquerie that she called fate, and the gallows and the wheel became the playthings of her toilette. . . . So we saw nights in February, ancestresses, devil conjurors, fractricides bewitched by gypsies, and the humbug [Schwindel] of the time spirit really kept this stuff for a moment on top."[13] "The nights in February" refers to Werner's drama and to Müllner's companion thriller *Der neunundzwanzigste Februar* (The Twenty-ninth of February). The third of the famous triumvirate in the fabrication of fate-tragedies, Ernst Houwald, was Contessa's most intimate friend. Hoffmann regrets that Contessa is squandering his own excellent talents in helping his friend to prepare his "well-meant tragedies, which are however, sapless and weak"; in this censure Hoffmann includes other dramatic work of Houwald's than his fate-plays. In *Der Zusammenhang der Dinge* Hoffmann gives a most entertaining description of an aesthetic tea at which a youthful poet read from his new fate-tragedy, which "was tedious and tasteless enough to be quite appropriate for the occasion."

In the *Seltsame Leiden* Hoffmann has little to say specifically of contemporary dramatic authors. The audience for whom he was writing did not require definite mention of authors and plays, and Hoffmann left no doubt as to his estimate when he censured so unsparingly the theater of his day. Kotzebue and Iffland, in his opinion, simply pandered to the uninformed, if not downright depraved, taste of the time. Tieck's approximation to the style of Gozzi in *Der gestiefelte Kater* was not the only aspect of the play which delighted Hoffmann; Tieck's pungent satire upon Iffland and Kotzebue and their now forgotten comrades struck a responsive chord. The boards were flooded with insipid plays of family life, cast in a conventional mold; the characters were stock figures—the blustering father, the vain but goodhearted mother, the fair but simple-minded daughter, the worthy and the unworthy lover. These were shuffled and reshuffled, and the domestic trials stimulated the tear ducts of the audience until, as Hoffmann says, these plays were submerged in the flood of tears they had brought forth. The purely mechanical drama Hoffmann viewed with scorn, and Kotzebue, as if with the turn of a crank, is said to have produced over two hundred

---

[13] "Die jüngst noch so zarte, nervenschwache Muse befreundete sich plötzlich mit dem Satan, der Hölle, mit einer Fratze, die sie Schicksal nannte, und Galgen und Rad wurden ihr Toiletten-Spielwerk. . . . So sahen wir Februarsnächte Ahnfrauen, Teufelsbeschwörer, von Zigeunern behexte Bruder-Mörder, und der Schwindel des Zeitgeistes hielt ordentlich dieses Zeug einen Augenblick oben." xv, p. 187.

plays. That these dramas were supposed to elevate public morals increased Hoffmann's disgust.

In Kotzebue Hoffmann admits a genuine talent for the theater, a cleverness in manipulating his material, an ease of diction, though in one passage he speaks of Kotzebue's "greasy prose" (schmierige Prosa). But a single dramatic situation, says Lothar in the *Serapionsbrüder*, however happily invented, does not make a real drama. He has personally heard Kotzebue describe his own method of procedure—though there is no record of Hoffmann's personal acquaintance with Kotzebue. He took some good dramatic situation which had occurred to him; then, merely to fit this situation, he pasted some sort of canvas together and hung the canvas around it. These were Kotzebue's own words, and Lothar applies the process to Kotzebue's plays—a good situation, often invented with genuine mastery, and around it the scenes which toilsomely drag along their thin, commonplace material, woven like a loose, slack web, "yet in the technique the practiced hand of the weaver is not to be denied." The degeneration of comedy into a mere series of farcical notions (Einfälle) arbitrarily thrown together, Hoffmann lays at Kotzebue's door. Kotzebue's occasional excursions into romantic fields Hoffmann treats with unmitigated scorn. *Johanna von Montfaucon,* a play of medieval chivalry, enjoyed considerable popularity, but in an unintentionally burlesque performance of the play by a troupe of strolling actors Hoffmann sees the real essence of the drama—a delightful farce. The actors comprehended the "deep meaning" of the play, the intent of the author to ridicule false sentiment, and poetry that is not poetic. In other words, Kotzebue was a gifted mechanician of the theater but no poet in any real sense of the word; he had no conception of the poet's lofty function as an interpreter of life. Kotzebue's *Opern-Almanach*[14] Hoffmann looked upon as an impertinent invasion of a territory in which the author was, to say the least, not at home. The attempt to prepare texts for operas, even though in response to multitudinous requests from would-be composers, was an absurd fiasco, for he had not "the remotest suspicion of the real nature of true opera." At the end of a letter to Hitzig (autumn 1812), Hoffmann exclaims: "Pereat Kotzebue, vivat Schlegel"; he has evidently been reading A. W. Schlegel's clever lampoon on Kotzebue, *Ehrenpforte und Triumphbogen für den Theater-Präsidenten von Kotzebue bei seiner gehofften Rückkehr*

[14] Hoffmann reviewed Kotzebue's *Opern-Almanach* in the *Allgemeine musikalische Zeitung,* October 26 and November 2, 1814.

ins Vaterland (Gateway of Honor and Triumphal Arch for the Theater-President von Kotzebue on the Occasion of his hoped-for Return to the Fatherland).

Iffland was both actor and dramatist, and for a number of years also was manager of the theater in Berlin; he died only a few days before the arrival of Hoffmann for the final Berlin residence. During the dreary year that Hoffmann spent in Berlin, 1807-1808, his friends tried to interest Iffland in his as yet largely untested talents. Hoffmann's rather sharp criticism of Iffland can hardly be attributed to Iffland's failure to listen; Hoffmann had no reason for harboring resentment against Kotzebue, and Iffland stands condemned on much the same charge, perhaps receiving a somewhat lighter sentence. In Hoffmann's opinion, Iffland was incapable of creating real living characters; he had a lively conception of individual traits of character, but he fitted them together like a strange garment, cutting them out himself and adorning them with frills—inner poetic truth was not attained. To Iffland more than to Kotzebue, Hoffmann attributes that decay of the stage which resulted from the false notion that the theater justified its existence primarily by giving lessons in morality.

With the exception of Shakespeare, Hoffmann's references to English literature are meager. He mentions none of the other Elizabethan dramatists, but his admiration for Tieck and Tieck's opinions on the drama might have led him to Tieck's early versions of Ben Jonson and his *Alt-Englisches Theater* (1811), though, to be sure, Tieck attributed most of the plays in the collection to Shakespeare; *Shakespeares Vorschule* appeared the year after Hoffmann's death. There were, however, fairly numerous plays of the seventeenth and eighteenth century in translation, and some were produced in the theaters but often so thoroughly adapted and mutilated that their English origins were obscured. The novel of the eighteenth century Hoffmann probably read casually, as the volumes happened to come his way. Sterne, as noted above, was an early favorite. He shows acquaintance with Smollett—*Roderick Random, Peregrine Pickle*, and *Humphrey Clinker*; to Smollett he applied his favorite adjective of commendation, "lebendig," "alive" rather than merely "lively." There is no mention of either Richardson or Fielding.[15] In view of the immense popularity of the *Vicar of*

---

[15] From certain similarities between Belcampo and the "barber" (Partridge) in *Tom Jones*, Wilhelm Horn thinks that Hoffmann knew Fielding's novel; cf. "Über das Komische im Schauerroman: E. T. A. Hoffmanns *Elixiere des Teufels* und ihre

Wakefield in Germany, Hoffmann could hardly have escaped reading it, but he does not mention Goldsmith. He speaks of the brilliant fire of Swift's humor.

In the last years of Hoffmann's life, Sir Walter Scott was more widely read in Germany than any other English author. The youthful Heine wrote in 1822 that Scott's novels were being read by everyone, high and low, from morn till night; several of Scott's novels were then available in translation, and Heine stated that of Scott's latest work, *The Pirate*, four different translations were already announced. Hoffmann had apparently resisted the current until January 1821, only a year and a half before his death, though he must have been aware of Scott's popularity and of the critical acclaim. He may have been deterred by a prejudice against historical fiction in general, derived from acquaintance with the hack work of certain German novelists, Veit Weber and his kind, of whom he speaks scathingly.

Hitzig, the candid and solicitous friend, often tried to turn Hoffmann not only from his convivial habits, regarding them as a menace to his friend's health, but from the imaginative type of writing which he never understood. He has often seen him, he says, "upon the wrong path, that of a foggy and wavering occupation with empty shadows [Nebeln und Schwebeln]" but never yet so decidedly as in *Prinzessin Brambilla*, and now as a corrective he recommends the reading of Scott, noting especially *Guy Mannering* (in German, *Der Astrolog*). The very next day after Hoffmann received this advice, Dr. Koreff called in the morning, and at Hoffmann's request sent him a copy of Scott's novel later in the day. To Hitzig, Hoffmann then wrote that he was "not only reading it but devouring it": "a most excellent book; with the greatest simplicity, stirring vivid life, but this spirit lies far from me, and I should do ill to feign a calm which for the present at any rate is not granted me."[16] The Serapion Brothers discuss Scott on the basis of this one novel. Ottmar praises the masterly exposition, which as by a stroke of magic places the reader at once *in medias res*, the descriptions of Scottish life and customs, so vividly presented that one totally unacquainted with them is struck by the freshness of life imparted to everything he creates. The novelist possesses the rare power of presenting his figures with a few strokes so that they emerge alive from the frame

Beziehungen zur englischen Literatur," in *Archiv für das Studium der neueren Sprachen und Literaturen,* cxlvi (1923), pp. 153-63.

[16] Cf. letter of January 8, 1821, in *Der Sammler,* Heft 42 (1921), p. 249.

of the picture and act in accordance with the character assigned to them. Vinzenz-Koreff comments on the skillful management of the plot; it progresses in methodical fashion, like the quiet unwinding of a skein; the firmly spun thread is never broken. Yet except for the "sublimely fearsome" (grauenhaft) figure of the gypsy woman (Meg Merrilies) he finds the female characters in the novel pallid and flat; the two girls have no real life, no "divinely animating breath." It is perhaps significant that no one of Hoffmann's three personal representatives expresses an opinion; one would have expected Cyprian to make some comment on the use of the supernatural.[17] Hoffmann knew something of Byron and calls him more powerful and solid (gediegen) than Thomas Moore. He wrote a review of Spontini's music composed for a kind of "opera ballet" founded on Moore's *Lalla Rookh.*

Hoffmann read both French and Italian with ease, and there is evidence of some knowledge of Spanish, though his acquaintance with Spanish literature was primarily based on translations. With French literature he was probably more extensively acquainted than with English, but the scattered references to French authors afford slight reward to the investigator. His interest in Rousseau probably did not end with the *Confessions*, though there is no documentary proof of further reading. Rabelais he knew in his early days, and there is evidence that he did not forget him. He mentions both Corneille and Racine, implying acquaintance, but the classical form, the unquestioned acceptance of convention, were doubtless uncongenial if not actually repugnant to him, as a Romantic free lance and a Shakespearean. The case of Molière was different. One may censure Hoffmann's blindness in not seeing "life" in the characters of Racine, however confined in classic forms, but in Molière he could find characters to whom he could apply his supreme criterion of values, expressed in the adjective "lebendig"; in Molière's satire upon the foibles of his time he could perceive a kindred spirit. The more recent French drama Hoffmann doubtless knew well; it flooded the German stage in translation and adaptation; he mentions, however, only Beaumarchais and Picard.

---

[17] A passage in Hoffmann's formal defense in the *Meister Floh* affair, written only a little over a year later, suggests a much wider acquaintance with Scott's novels. The inclusion of juridical questions in his novels was perfectly natural, he maintains, that "jeder Schriftsteller von seinem Metier nicht ablässt, sondern sich an Schilderungen daraus ergötzt," and he gives as an example: "der neue berühmte Walter Scott, einer der ersten Rechtsbeamten in Edinburgh, hat es beinahe in jedem seiner Romane mit Prozessen zu thun." Cf. Ellinger in *Deutsche Rundschau*, cxxviii, p. 98.

He called Voltaire's *Candide* the model of a good novel;[18] the philosophical principle that is implicit throughout is concealed behind a curtain of caricatures; the spice is human stupidity (Albernheit) presented in vivid coloring. His admiration for *Gil Blas* and *Le Diable boiteux* derives from qualities in Le Sage which he had also found in Sterne and Smollett; further, in *Le Diable boiteux* he found an alluring array of hundreds of little anecdotes, glimpses of characters, or human situations, each of which might challenge his imagination, to be perhaps the germ of a story he might tell himself.[19] J. Cazotte's *Le Diable amoureux* interested him both for the supernatural elements involved and for the vividness of the narration, and he built his own story *Der Elementargeist* in part upon it.[20] He quotes a line from Boileau's *L'Art poétique*, but he may have looked it up simply as an appropriate insertion in *Das Fraulein von Scuderi*; one cannot imagine that Boileau would otherwise have had a remote interest for him.[21] The "Cousin" of *Des Vetters Eckfenster* Hoffmann likens to Scarron, both in the physical misfortune of invalidism and in his type of humor. Scarron's wit departed from the common French groove, and the cousin, like Scarron, was endowed with a peculiar, lively fancy and indulged in a strange type of humorous jesting all his own; but, unlike Scarron, the cousin never regarded it as necessary to spice his piquant little dishes with asafetida to tickle the palate of his German readers.

Hoffmann's scorn of literary ladies included Mme. de Staël. Mlle. de Scudéry was, to be sure, the heroine of his story, but he is interested only in her activity in a field quite alien to her profession, and it is not evident that he ever looked into one of her interminable romances. Women, he thought, have no sense of humor, and humor, in his conception of it, is a prime essential in an author's equipment.

The Italian and Spanish lists are brief, though in the case of Italian one may assume a wider acquaintance with literature than is actually evidenced by references to such authors as Dante, from whom he could quote, Boccaccio, whom he unquestionably knew well, Ariosto, or Petrarch. An intimate acquaintance with Italian drama

[18] This is according to Hitzig's reading of an illegible word in Hoffmann's diary. The sentence seems to call for the word "Roman," but Hans von Müller deems "Roman" an orthographic impossibility, though he offers no satisfactory substitute.

[19] In *Der Dey von Elba* he borrows admittedly from the technique of Le Sage's narrative.

[20] Cf. note 3, Part II, Chapter 7.

[21] Hoffmann quotes an opinion from Boileau in *Prinzessin Brambilla*. Cf. Ellinger, x, p. 278.

stands behind the partisanship for Gozzi in *Prinzessin Brambilla* and elsewhere. Hoffmann's admiration for Gozzi and the influence of Gozzi upon his own work have already been mentioned. In Hoffmann's writings on the art of the drama, he speaks—or rather the characters who voice his opinions speak—of "glorious Gozzi," comments on the effective combination of the serious and the comic; his plays contain more powerful situations than many modern tragedies that are highly praised. Among Gozzi's dramas, *Turandot*, *L'Amore delle tre melarance,* and *Il (re) Corvo* are analyzed at length with quotations either in the original or in translation. In the *Seltsame Leiden* the director "in brown" defends Gozzi with valiant enthusiasm against the skepticism of his colleague in "gray."

In Spanish two names stand in brilliant light. Cervantes was one of Hoffmann's best-loved authors, a companion of his whole life, both in *Don Quixote* and the *Novelas ejemplares.* Calderon he places close beside Shakespeare. Three plays by Calderon were performed at Bamberg under his direction: *Die Andacht zum Kreuz* (La Devoción de la Cruz), *Der standhafte Prinz* (El Príncipe constante), and *Die Brücke von Mantible* (La Puente de Mantible); he wrote an interesting account of the performances for Fouqué's magazine, *Die Musen, Über die Aufführung der Schauspiele des Calderon de la Barca auf dem Theater in Bamberg* (Concerning the Performance of the Plays of Calderon de la Barca at the Theater in Bamberg). Both in *Berganza* and in the *Seltsame Leiden* he pays tribute to Calderon's greatness. Calderon is a "romantic dramatist," "romanticism in its highest sense," but in Hoffmann's opinion only a few in Germany were capable of entering into the "deep romanticism" of the Spanish dramatist, only those "who with true poetic spirit [Gemüt] confess their allegiance to the invisible church which with divine power fights against the vulgar and the common." He acknowledges Calderon's limitations, as compared with Shakespeare —he is emphatically Spanish and Roman Catholic. The signal success of these plays on the Bamberg stage Hoffmann attributes in part to the specialized understanding of a Roman Catholic community, the ingrained traditions which assured a devout hearing for the dramas, solid burgher families and priests who otherwise never entered the theater following the play with reverent attention. *Die Brücke von Mantible* and *Die grosse Zenobia* (La gran Cenobia) Hoffmann recommends for production in places where no specially prepared audience is available, though the view of the Middle Ages in the former would be difficult to present to a German audience;

it demands the appropriation (Aneignung) of romantic taste, a comprehension of the spirit of chivalry as a substitute for what in a Roman Catholic community is supplied by upbringing and religious faith. But the purely spectacular which Calderon's drama contains may attract many for its own sake; incidentally, they will hear and see much which in the end will have its appeal and give pleasure, just as many who are "spiritually petrified" awake from their torpidity when listening continuously to fine music.

Soon after his first reading of Schlegel's translations from Calderon, Hoffmann wrote to Hitzig from Warsaw, April 1807, that he was working with renewed strength on an operatic version of *Die Schärpe und die Blume* (La Vanda y la Flor); in this "superb play" he sees arias, duets, trios, tercets, as if "born there"; the comic elements of the play are highly poetic, and the music accompanying them should be in the vein of Mozart's *Cosi fan tutti* and *Figaro*. A year later in the drab Berlin days he wrote to Hippel of the solace he found in work on this opera, which he renamed *Liebe und Eifersucht* (Love and Jealousy). Ten years later (1817) he planned an opera founded on Calderon's *El Galán fantasma*, for which his friend Contessa had prepared the text.[22] In *Die Genesung*, dictated on his deathbed, Hoffmann placed a song from Calderon on the lips of Wilhelmine. He mentions further *Arzt seiner Ehre* (El Médico de su Honra) and Calderon's Faustian play *Der grosse Magus* (El Mágico prodigioso); from the latter he probably took the name Cyprian for one of his selves in the *Serapionsbrüder*.

Hoffmann had no rigid canons of literary criticism, no dogma of literary values. His attitude toward literature, in the beginning naïvely subjective, remained largely personal and idiosyncratic; it was a matter of instinctive taste into the workings of which for the most part he did not probe. In this sense he was essentially romantic. In literature as elsewhere he was a relentless foe of all pretense and sham; he abhorred the conventional, the superficial, and the falsely sentimental. For formal classicism he had no appreciation, form for form's sake. Literary values were inseparable from the personality of the author, and hence imitative works presented only a second-

---

[22] Helmina von Chézy resented Hoffmann's failure to use her German version of this Calderon play. Hitzig arranged an evening meeting at which it was read aloud in Hoffmann's presence, and she thought him sufficiently impressed, yet unaccountably he turned to Contessa. She was deeply indebted to Hoffmann for his activities in her behalf when she was accused and threatened with imprisonment for "slandering" the "Invalidenprüfungscommission." Cf. Helmina von Chézy: *Unvergessenes* (Leipzig, 1858), ii, pp. 157, 179.

hand and diluted personality; his disapproval of all imitation is registered early, indeed in his first published work, the essay on the use of the ancient chorus in modern drama. As noted above, Hoffmann involuntarily tested every work of the creative imagination by the impression it gave of life, of being alive, even though life thus vividly presented might not correspond to normal human experience. Though he liked swift-moving action, the anecdotal or the picaresque, it was only as an index of what went on within the mind of man: "the human spirit is the most wonderful of all Märchen." Ideally action is only the externalization of the inner life; the mere deed is meaningless unless it can be related to the spirit of the doer.

Circumstances forced Hoffmann to think more critically and to apply certain standards when he considered the drama. And yet his dramatic criticism—though he studied the great critics of the drama, Lessing, Schlegel, and Tieck—remained personally empirical. In the last analysis it was his own personal response which formed the test of values. He judged a play by what he knew and felt personally from seeing it on the stage, or he tested its availability for stage production by an imagined presentation with its effect upon his mind and his emotions.

EPILOGUE

(I)

MORE than a century has passed since Hoffmann's death. Outside of his own homeland he leads an elusive existence in Offenbach's charming opera *The Tales of Hoffmann* and a more shadowy existence still, perhaps, in Schumann's *Kreisleriana*. In 1851 Jules Barbier and Michael Carré published *Les Contes d'Hoffmann*, "drame fantastique en cinq actes," upon which in 1881 Offenbach based his opera text. With considerable skill the two authors had taken elements from *Der Sandmann, Das verlorene Spiegelbild*, and *Rat Krespel* and woven them together; the "framework" about these "dreams" they placed in the familiar wine room of Lutter and Wegner. Though Hoffmann's work is much altered— distorted, if you will—the admirer of Hoffmann finds much of the real Hoffmann in the opera, and Offenbach's music lulls his criticism to silence.[1] Schumann composed his *Kreisleriana* in 1838 and explained the title to an admiring correspondent as derived from "a creation of E. T. A. Hoffmann's, an eccentric, wild, gifted conductor."[2]

In Germany during the half century after Hoffmann's death little was written about him save Hitzig's biography, which was generally regarded as authoritative, and the volume of reminiscences by Kunz; these were the product of the first few years. And there the matter rested for decades. With the important work of Georg

---

[1] Cf. Martin Lesser: "Zur Psychologie in 'Hoffmanns Erzählungen'" in *Neue Musikzeitung*, xxxviii (1917), pp. 119-21. With fine discernment Lesser shows the skill of the two French dramatists in weaving the three separate stories into a unity, yet holding Hoffmann as the hero and interpreting his "dreams" in terms of his life. In *Hoffmanns Erzählungen* (Leipzig, 1922), Max Mell brought together the different "Vorlagen" for the opera, and with the same title Hans von Müller has published the opera, both text and music, with an introduction.

[2] Cf. *Robert Schumanns Briefe*, Neue Folge, herausgegeben von F. Gustav Jansen (Leipzig, 1886), letter of March 15, 1839. Schumann's motley group, the "Davidsbündler," quite possibly owes its inception to Hoffmann's Serapion Brothers; and Schumann composed not only the *Kreisleriana* but *Phantasiestücke* and *Nachtstücke*. In a letter to Hauptmann von Fricken, September 1834, Schumann says that a dilapidated musician (Johann) Ludwig Böthmer served Hoffmann as a model for his Kapellmeister Kreisler (*Robert Schumanns Jugendbriefe*, Leipzig, 1885, p. 254), and this is repeated in the latest life of Schumann, *Florestan*, by Robert Haven Schauffler (New York, 1945). This exceedingly dubious origin of Kreisler rests solely on this unsupported statement of Schumann's. In admiration for Hoffmann, Brahms called a collection of quotations which he had compiled for his own pleasure "Des jungen Kreislers Schatzkästlein"; it has been published by the Deutsche Brahmsgesellschaft, Berlin, 1909.

Ellinger (1894) the storyteller entered upon a new epoch of his posthumous career. Since that date Hoffmann bibliography has grown unconscionably. Extensive research has revealed many facts of his life previously unknown—some relatively insignificant, others of prime importance, such, for example, as his engagement to Minna Doerffer. Studies of his mind and art have come from the presses in large numbers, mostly academic performances, but contributing in most cases something to the understanding and the appreciation of Hoffmann's storytelling and of the views of life that are incorporated in his tales.

Yet when all is said and done, many of Hoffmann's secrets he carried with him to his grave. Perhaps this is true of more men than we are wont to think or are willing to believe. The epitaphs and the obituaries in the public prints are amplified into stately volumes of formal biography. The mind and spirit of the dead man are an open book; it is all there in black and white, built up in accurate dependence upon his oral and recorded utterances. But what of the things he never said, and did he really mean all he said? Hoffmann had many acquaintances but few friends, and even to the latter there was much he left unuttered.

Physically Hoffmann was a diminutive figure, perhaps half comic and gnomelike, with prominent nose and chin and bushy hair growing far down on his forehead; if one perchance were inclined to smile, one met the forbidding challenge of searching, sparkling eyes. He was acutely conscious of his lack of comeliness. And this odd physical organism was constantly in motion; even the facial muscles, especially those of the forehead, moved in rapid and agitated change. The countenance of the old witch woman in Tieck's *Der blonde Eckbert* was so perpetually in movement that Bertha could never tell precisely what her features were; in Tieck's Märchen this was perhaps an attempt to suggest the uncertain and wavering outlines of dream phenomena. But in Hoffmann's case the mobile face was the mirror of his spirit. If it were possible for the artist to fasten the muscles of the face into a temporary immobility, a portrait might be drawn, but it would still be inaccurate, a transitory likeness. The constant changes in his countenance corresponded to the abrupt shifting of his moods, as is repeatedly recorded of Kreisler, but it was more fundamental than a mere matter of mood, deeper than a kaleidoscopic whimsicality. The whims of a man are the ripples on the surface while the main body of water responds to the ebb and flow of cosmic laws, the essential character of the man.[3]

In Hoffmann it was more than a change of mood; it was a radical shift of character. Long before he used the romantic concept of "doubles," either in a divided personality in the breast of an individual or the mysterious sharing of a personality between two or more persons, the idea tormented him. As early as 1804 he noted in his diary the excitement of his nervous organism and the consciousness of a divided self, and a few years later (1809) he wrote: "I fancy [seeing] myself through a multiplying glass—all forms that move around about me are myselfs [ichs], and I am vexed at what they do and leave undone." In him was an unusual capacity for detachment which led to self-criticism. This talent for analysis of self was early developed; what other youth of nineteen in the throes of his first violent love affair could stand off and look at himself as Hoffmann did in his letters to Hippel?[4] It was through the process of detachment and inspection that a consciousness of a disintegrated personality began to disturb him. The harmony of one's nature is undermined. That a double nature is a house divided against itself was an initial tragedy in Hoffmann's being, and the consciousness of it leaves a trail over all his works.

When the fairy Rosabelverde takes final leave of her dead protégé Klein Zaches, she calls him a "stepchild of nature." In inventing the phrase, Hoffmann must have felt a pang of identification, not only in the unloveliness of his person, but in the buffetings of fortune. One may imagine Hoffmann comparing himself with Novalis, whom he really revered as perhaps no other of his Romantic predecessors. Novalis had served as a young lawyer and was indeed, like Hoffmann, efficient and punctilious in his tasks; in the legal documents that he drew up he never failed to dot an "i" or cross a "t." But neither as assistant to a magistrate nor later as a mining engineer did he regard his professional work as a penal servitude. With envy perhaps, Hoffmann perceived that Novalis was not "a stepchild of nature"; it was not that he was a nobleman with all that such distinc-

---

[3] Dr. Klinke regards Hoffmann's nervous mobility as a sign of degeneration, like St. Vitus's dance; cf. *E. T. A. Hoffmanns Leben und Werke*, p. 8. The unfriendly Gubitz wrote: "Seine eigenen Verzerrungen und Krampfverzuckungen, die sich sogar in Hoffmanns Antlitz tummelten, aus seinen unaufhaltsam unruhig beweglichen Gesichtszügen, liessen sich Muster zu Spott- und Hohn-Larven entnehmen." *Op. cit.*, I, p. 25; cf. note 11, Chapter 5.

[4] "Zur jeder Empfindung für Cora . . . hab' ich gleich irgend eine komische Posse zur Surdine (Sourdine)." *Briefwechsel*, I, p. 51.

tion meant in those days—this Hoffmann would have ignored—but the unusual, ethereal beauty of his person was a symbol of the harmony within, and through the harmonious integration of his personality Novalis could unite the real world with the dream world. He prepared the legal paper or studied geology and mineralogy, but this activity did not interrupt his dreams. As Browning said of Lazarus, returned to life after three days in the tomb:

> "He holds on firmly to some thread of life . . .
> Which runs across some vast distracting orb
> Of glory on either side that meagre thread,
> Which, conscious of, he must not enter yet—
> The spiritual life around the earthly life;
> The law of that is known to him as this,
> His heart and brain move there, his feet stay here."

A common source may be found for Hoffmann's tragic brooding, for the disharmony of his being, for homelessness in the world about him and in himself. All is covered by one fatal flaw, the doubt as to reality—is there anything that really is, instead of merely seeming to be? He applies this dubiety to himself and doubts the validity of his own being. This doubt forms the intellectual basis for the nervous consciousness of a divided personality. In one character after another the question of identity arises; as Medardus in *Die Elixiere des Teufels* cries out: "I wanted to confess openly all that I had done that was sinful and wanton, but to my horror what I said was not at all what I thought and wanted to say." Every man wears a mask, perhaps several of them, not merely on the streets of Rome at carnival time. This feeling is doubtless the very brink of madness, and Hoffmann knew it.

The people of Hoffmann's world, the characters in his stories, he classified somewhat loosely according to a feudal system of his own invention which scoffed at the remnants of historical feudalism in the Germany of his day. Pride in hereditary rank, the mania for titles of distinction, the display of wealth, were to Hoffmann ridiculous absurdities. Not precisely in accordance with purely intellectual gifts did he erect his unrecognized aristocracy—Leander was rejected for membership in the Serapion Club; he had uncommon intellectual powers under perfect command, but he lacked the real spark. "Men are blind their whole life long," said Mephistopheles to the aged Faust, and it was with this blindness that Hoffmann showed a perhaps ignoble impatience. Most men spend their lives in

contact with trivial, material things. One may recall Hugo von Hofmannsthal's lovely *Ballade des äussern Lebens* (Ballade of the External Life). The world is full of things that have or seem to have
no meaning and of those who pass their lives with them and find no
meaning in them, and hence see no real goal to strive for, are themselves then merely meaningless objects, are like fruits that fall at
night time, lie a while, and then decay:

> "Und Kinder wachsen auf mit tiefen Augen
> Die von nichts wissen, wachsen auf und sterben
> Und alle Menschen gehen ihre Wege

> "Und süsse Früchte werden aus den herben
> Und fallen nachts wie tote Vögel nieder
> Und liegen wenig Tage und verderben. . . .

> "Was frommt dies alles uns und diese Spiele
> Die wir doch gross und ewig einsam sind
> Und wandernd nimmer suchen irgend Ziele?"

While Hofmannsthal distills a pensive melancholy from the vacuity
of most human lives, Hoffmann is sometimes irritated and scornful, at
others merely amused, and at times a little envious. One may regret
his lack of a more sympathetic understanding of human frailty; his
impatience with dullness brought him an undeserved reputation
for vanity. And one may censure the inconsistency in his own life, for
he often took the lower road when the higher was plainly in sight,
often busied himself with meaningless things, and knew it was so.

And then there are those who are in the world but not of it. The
one undebatable reality that Hoffmann acknowledged and to which
he paid homage was the world of dreams. Deep in his contradictory
nature lay a fixed belief in an eternal and invisible world which envelops all our ignorances and our futilities. The "Invisible Church"
consists of all those who at times lift their eyes above the dust. But
there are many subtle gradations in worldliness and otherworldliness. "Uncle" Drosselmeier has unquestionably caught glimpses of
another world than that of our everyday, but he does not really live
there, for he says to little Marie: "More has been given to you than
to me or to all the rest of us; you are like Pirlipat, a born princess,
for you reign in a beautiful and shining kingdom" (*Nussknacker
und Mausekönig*). And some are disobedient to the heavenly vision
when it has once been vouchsafed: as a boy Herr von Brakel had also

seen the "stranger child," but he had forgotten all about it until the adventures of his children brought it to remembrance; even so the father of Heinrich von Ofterdingen had once beheld the "Blue Flower," but the vision becomes dim in his memory, he is not sure of the color of the flower. "And the thorns grew up and choked it."

And this world of dreams is not a child's make-believe, a diversion for an idle hour or an opiate for those in distress. It is more real than sea and sky. A relationship to this world can be established. To human eyes and ears its being is concretely made manifest through things of beauty seen and heard—the melody that the musician hears and then repeats is the witness of a Divine Presence. The artists are the messengers and revealers of the Divine. Though perhaps introduced in part for dramatic effect, the consciousness of this relation to the Divine is often associated with a single concrete experience or a series of related experiences. In the flash of sunlight reflected on a metal dish of common domestic use, Jakob Boehme, the Silesian mystic, suddenly beheld a vision of nature's deepest mystery. After his dream of the "Blue Flower" Heinrich von Ofterdingen encounters an old miner in an inn: "The words of the old man had opened a concealed door within him; he saw that his little living room was built beside a sublime cathedral."[5] These concepts lie at the root of Hoffmann's Märchen and are constantly present in his other tales.

(II)

The Märchen form Hoffmann's most characteristic achievement; they are a unique product of the creative imagination. He was an observer in two worlds and in the Märchen he fused these two worlds with sovereign skill. With Hoffmann the reader walks up and down the streets of Dresden, Berlin, and Frankfurt, enters perhaps in his company into familiar restaurants and cafés; and these experiences are as realistically and vividly portrayed as in the realistic novel of a later day. But in the Dresden café the Archivarius Lindhorst, who is really a salamander, talks of his ancestors, the lily and the youth

---

[5] In his monograph *E. T. A. Hoffmann: die drei Reiche seiner Gestaltenwelt* (Berlin, 1939), Kurt Willimczik analyzes in detail this so-called "Durchbruch," this experience on the road to Damascus. But his insistence on discovering a "Durchbruch" becomes a runaway hobbyhorse, in one case at any rate leading to the unintentionally comic: Ännchen in *Die Königsbraut* accidentally hits her betrothed, the would-be poet Amandus, over the head with a garden spade and makes a sensible man out of him; this is a "Durchbruch." A parallel weakness is the author's ingenious but often unconvincing effort to fit all the characters in Hoffmann's stories into his ready-made scheme of the "three realms."

Phosphorus; the coat tails of the old gentleman may perhaps become wings and bear him away. Anselmus sits at an everyday tea table in the house of the schoolmaster and talks to Veronika, who wants to marry a "Hofrat," live in a fine house in the Moritzstrasse, have beautiful clothes, and meet the "best people," but later, perhaps on the same day he listens to Serpentina, who tells him the strange story of her family and arouses in him a longing for that fabulous isle of bliss to which in the end they fly. Peregrinus Tyss stands in an everyday shop in everyday Frankfurt buying Christmas toys to distribute among the children of a humble bookbinder, but beside him stands Dörtje Elverdink, who is really the Princess Gamaheh; for the time being she is a bit hazy as to her identity, for she has passed through an intermediary stage in the pollen of a tulip.

In endless succession the children of Hoffmann's exuberant and unique fancy rise to one's mind—the aesthetic tea in the house of Mosch Terpin where Klein Zaches makes his first appearance in society, the telescope duel between the two magicians in *Meister Floh*, the adventures of "Geheimer Kanzleisekretär" Tusmann in the café with the two "revenants," the final contest between the Archivarius Lindhorst and his ancient enemy the old apple woman while Anselmus is imprisoned in a bottle on the shelf. It would seem that fanciful gaiety and rollicking humor could go no further. The satirical sallies of Hoffmann's wit are directed against contemporary follies and foibles and at times may need a commentary for complete understanding, but the contemporary absurdity that he ridicules has still a timelessness; only its accidental qualities are contemporary. But all this is only one aspect of the Märchen, and a superficial one, however diverting. To Hoffmann the Märchen was the vehicle in which he could express, however concealed by vagrant fancies, his profound and often tragic pondering upon human life in its relation to a material and to an immaterial world.

An appreciable part of his storytelling is directly concerned with the artist and the artist's contacts and conflicts with the everyday world, with his aspirations, discouragements, and now and then with his triumphs. These stories constitute an interpretation of the artist's spirit—the artist as a phenomenon, one may say—which it might be difficult to match. And they find a culmination in the creation of one character, the musician Kreisler, who stands unsurpassed in literature, as an individual unique but nevertheless an eternal portrait of a type. The occult and the frankly supernatural had been the themes of fiction before Hoffmann's day, but he took this material and so transformed it as to create a new type of mystery story. In the first place he reduced the excessive length of earlier mystery tales, like *Der Genius*, to manageable quantity and through such concentration achieved a unified and effective impact of the occult upon the lives of his characters; Poe carried this concentration still further. By loose connection with the scientific thought of his time, allowing it to impinge gently upon his mysterious happenings, Hoffmann really heightened in subtle fashion the conception of the supernatural.

In other ways Hoffmann was a pathfinder. The germs of much that has characterized narrative fiction since his day may be observed in his stories. To his credit—some may maintain, to his eternal discredit—he created the story of crime and crime detection; not fully developed, one may admit, but in essence *Das Fräulein von Scuderi* is the first unmistakable example of the popular genre. The sensational happenings in his tales, which caught the attention of the casual and unthinking reader, are not there for their own sake; they are the externalization of what transpired in the human spirit. The more significant scene of action Hoffmann transfers to the mind and spirit of man. In the first two decades of the nineteenth century the psychological novel became through Hoffmann a challenging reality. In part by study of contemporary medical science, still in matters of the mind fumbling and rudimentary, but more through an intuition that is hardly less than miraculous, Hoffmann explored the normal and the abnormal mind of man. He anticipated much that the modern psychologist or psychoanalyst has brought to light and foreshadows the work of present-day novelists who investigate the relation between the character of a man and his conscious or unconscious remembrance of things past. Long before the twentieth century novelist had exploited the phenomena of schizophrenia, Hoffmann had been acutely aware of them and had probed their deeps. In all the tricks of the profession—in clever retardation of movement, in the introduction of information at points where it is most effective—Hoffmann could give instruction to the twentieth century storyteller. A striking technical innovation was the contrapuntal arrangement of material, as exemplified in *Kater Murr*; he breaks up his material into fragments and then presents it in a marvelous pattern of fictional counterpoint.

(III)

In literature Hoffmann left no direct heirs, though collateral relatives in many lands are numerous indeed, some of them doubtless quite ignorant of their kinship.[6] Inevitably an author whose work was much sought by the "annuals," the popular magazines of the day, invited imitation. Carl Weisflog, for example, a long-forgotten storyteller, thought that the mantle of the prophet had fallen on his shoulders; he even had the audacity to publish a collection of tales as *Phantasiestücke und Historien.*[7] After a dedicatory poem to Hoffmann's Dresden acquaintance Theodor Hell (Winkler), he adds a kind of secondary dedication in the form of a long letter from his private secretary, Jeremias Kätzlein, "an den Kön. Preuss. Kammergerichtsrath E. T. A. Hoffmann in Dschinnistan, zwei Treppen hoch, vorn heraus"; Hoffmann, he suggests, has touched his master with the magic wand of Prosper Alpanus. A story, *Der Nautilus*, in the seventh volume Weisflog calls a "Nachtstück," and in *Der Denkzettel* he boldly introduces himself as an intimate companion of Hoffmann's during the summer of 1819 in Warmbrunn.[8] The case of Wilhelm Hauff is different; he combined discreet borrowing from Hoffmann with some very admirable qualities of his own.[9] Similarly, Heine's indebtedness to Hoffmann is demonstrable, particularly in his early career, though not merely there, but Heine likewise could combine certain characteristics derived from Hoffmann with a markedly individual style.[10] To what extent the banalities of many of his imitators contributed to the decline of Hoffmann's reputation it would be impossible to determine.[11]

There are doubtless few students of cultural history who cherish any illusions as to the permanence of aesthetic judgments. The pathway of literature is strewn with discarded masterpieces which, it

[6] An interesting brief survey of Hoffmann's reputation in other lands is to be found in the first chapters of Arthur Sakheim's *E. T. A. Hoffmann: Studien zu seiner Persönlichkeit und seinen Werken*, Leipzig, 1908. The present account is indebted to Sakheim for several suggestions.

[7] Carl Weisflog: *Phantasiestücke und Historien*, Wien, 1827, 7 vols.

[8] For further use of Hoffmann as a figure in German fiction cf. Albert Ludwig: "E. T. A. Hoffmanns Gestalt in der deutschen erzählenden Dichtung," in *Archiv für das Studium der neueren Sprachen und Literaturen*, CXLVII (1924), pp. 1-29.

[9] Cf. J. F. Haussmann: "E. T. A. Hoffmanns Einfluss auf Hauff," in *Journal of English and Germanic Philology*, XVI (1917), pp. 53-66.

[10] Cf. W. Siebert: *Heinrich Heines Beziehungen zu E. T. A. Hoffmann*, Marburg, 1908; Heinrich Uhlendahl: *Fünf Kapitel über H. Heine und E. T. A. Hoffmann*, Berlin, 1919.

[11] Cf. Erich Guttmann: *Die deutsche romantische Musikerzählung nach E. T. A. Hoffmann: ein Beitrag zur Geschichte des historisch-biographischen Künstlerromans und der Künstlernovelle in Deutschland*, Breslau, 1934.

may be, a later generation rehabilitates. Perhaps the fashion that
once produced them has come around again in the whirligig of time.
Of this Hoffmann is an interesting example. It would be possible to
quote from the standard histories of German literature during the
greater part of the nineteenth century, from Vilmars, Gervinus, and
Koberstein to Wilhelm Scherer, all of whom in varying degrees clas-
sify Hoffmann with the mere entertainers, the purveyors of cheap
fiction for the unintelligent.[12] They are not all entirely blind to his
gifts as a storyteller and find something to praise in the less fanciful
of his tales, such as *Meister Martin der Küfner*, but his more characteristic productions appear to them morbid and grotesque, to one of
them indeed a "literary bedlam."

In the decades when many of Goethe's works were viewed askance
as not contributing to standardized views of morality—if not actually
immoral—it was natural that the critics failed to perceive in
Hoffmann any substantial support for traditional ethics. It should
be remembered also that Hoffmann stood close to the end of a period;
some authorities even date the end of the German Romantic Epoch
with Hoffmann's death. From this point of view, the later years
brought only echoes, growing fainter and fainter—the dying rever-
berations of an orchestra that has really ceased to play. Again, it is
natural that the protagonists of the new movement in German literature should see in Hoffmann little worthy of their regard, for in their
new literary creed the practice of letters was an adjunct to social
and political thinking. Of this they found nothing in Hoffmann. In
1853 Julian Schmidt could write of the Romantics, specifically of
Hoffmann: "One lived in an artist's world of dreams; one did not
even read the newspaper."[13]

Goethe regarded Hoffmann's influence as injurious. In his review
of Sir Walter Scott's article "On the Supernatural in Fictitious
Composition" Goethe agrees with Scott's censure of Hoffmann and
exclaims: "What man who is really concerned about our national culture has not observed with sadness that the morbid works of this sick
man have for many years had an influence in Germany and such aber-
rations have been inoculated upon healthy spirits as highly beneficial
innovations."[14] In the conversations with Eckermann he classifies

    [12] Cf. Sakheim, *op. cit.*, pp. 249–52.
    [13] Cf. Julian Schmidt: *Nationalliteratur des 19. Jahrhunderts* (Leipzig, 1853), II,
pp. 396–98.
    [14] "Wir können den reichen Inhalt dieses Artikels unsern Lesern nicht genugsam
empfehlen; denn welcher treue, für Nationalbildung besorgte Teilnehmer hat nicht
mit Trauer gesehen, dass die krankhaften Werke jenes leidenden Mannes lange Jahre

Hoffmann among the lesser storytellers. It was about this time indeed that Eckermann recorded Goethe's much debated apothegm that "classic" is synonymous with "healthy" and "romantic" with "sickly."[15] Tieck, whom Hoffmann placed among the immortals, to whom he was indeed indebted for many an inspiration, was chary in recognizing the merits of his admiring pupil. In the literary allegory of *Das alte Buch und die Reise ins Blaue hinein* he casts a subtly negative glance upon Hoffmann, simply implying that Hoffmann is not one of those into whom the spirit of "Hannes," the hostile gnome, has entered. Late in life in his conversations with Köpke Tieck admits Hoffmann's narrative skill but dismisses his work on the whole as "caricature": "almost all of his stories are grotesque."[16] The most devastating criticism came from the pen of the poet Eichendorff; to him Hoffmann's lack of religious faith not only blackened his character but besmirched all his works.[17] Yet there were ever here and there throughout the nineteenth century those who did not forget him, who found both delight and inspiration in his stories. Otto Ludwig dramatized *Das Fräulein von Scuderi*[18] and his many plans for dramatic work included a *Doge und Dogaressa* and a *Signor Formica*; his *Die wahrhaftige Geschichte von den drei Wünschen* is confessedly patterned on Hoffmann's Märchen. In both

in Deutschland wirksam gewesen und solche Verirrungen als bedeutend fördernde Neuigkeiten gesunden Gemütern eingeimpft worden!" (*Goethes Werke*, Hempel edition, xxix, p. 774.) Till shortly before Hoffmann's death Goethe had read none of his works. On April 10, 1822, Karl August sent him a copy of *Meister Floh*, then recently published, with information, partly incorrect, as to Hoffmann's satire and the resultant investigation by the authorities; he comments on the story as "sehr munter und artig zusammengestellt, besonders wegen der Wahl der bekannten Localität." Two days later Goethe replied: "Ew. Königliche Hoheit haben durch gnädige Mittheilung des dankbarlichst zurückgehenden Buches mir sehr viel Vergnügen verschafft; es war das erste was ich von Hoffmann las, und es ist nicht zu läugnen, dass die wunderliche Art und Weise, wie er das bekannteste Locale, gewohnte, ja gemeine Zustände mit unwahrscheinlichen, unmöglichen Vorfällen verknüpft, einen gewissen Reiz hat dem man sich nicht entziehen kann." (*Briefwechsel des Herzogs-Grossherzogs Carl August mit Goethe* herausgegeben von Hans Wahl [Berlin, 1918], iii, p. 62.) Thus Goethe's first recorded opinion was not unappreciative; there is no further record of his reading of Hoffmann.

15 Cf. *Gespräche mit Goethe* (Düntzer's edition, sechste Auflage, Leipzig, 1885) i, p. 119 (December 3, 1824); and ii, p. 63 (April 2, 1829).

16 Cf. Rudolf Köpke: *Ludwig Tieck: Erinnerungen aus dem Leben des Dichters* (Leipzig, 1855), ii, p. 206.

17 *Über die ethische und religiöse Bedeutung der neueren romantischen Poesie*, Leipzig, 1847.

18 Cf. Karl Werner Barthel: *Die dramatischen Bearbeitungen der Novelle "Das Fräulein von Scuderi" und ihre Bühnenschicksale*, Greifswald, 1929. Including two operas, the author counts eight different dramatic works based on Hoffmann's story and nine stage versions of Ludwig's play.

Keller and Storm there are recognizable traces of Hoffmann's influence, though with writers of such originality one cannot speak of imitation.[19]

"Ancient Germany, mother of us all, land of Goethe and of Schiller, country of Hoffmann!" were the words of Gerard de Nerval on first treading German soil (1836). However flattered by the apostrophe, the German of those days would have raised a scornful eyebrow at the inclusion of Hoffmann's name. But in the middle decades of the nineteenth century Hoffmann was in France accorded a position among the greatest of foreign authors.[20] The limited praise and outspoken detraction in Heine's *Romantische Schule* seem almost the only discordant note; and Heine, a German exile in Paris, was writing his account of recent German literature for the enlightenment of the French.

During his lifetime Hoffmann was utterly unknown in France. In 1823 a version of *Das Fräulein von Scuderi* was published, apparently a much garbled version, and without the original author's name. In that year Dr. Koreff arrived in Paris. From his previous residence there he had retained an extensive acquaintance with political and literary circles, and it is reasonable to assume that he began at once his service as an intermediary between German literature and French readers; in this service of propaganda he would not have ignored an author who had been an intimate personal friend in Berlin. Koreff was at all events a friend of Loève-Veimars, who was soon to begin his translation of Hoffmann's stories.[21] The *Globe* pub-

[19] Cf. Hermann Todsen: *Über die Entwicklung des romantischen Kunstmärchens*, Berlin, 1906; also Wilhelm Fehse: "Wilhelm Raabe und E. T. A. Hoffmann," in *Der Türmer*, xxii, pp. 504-8; and E. Guttmann, *op. cit.*, note 11; Karl Wittmann: *Der Einfluss E. T. A. Hoffmanns auf Friedrich Hebbel*, Arnau, 1908.

[20] For details as to the fortunes of Hoffmann's works in France, cf. Gustav Thurau: "E. T. A. Hoffmanns Erzählungen in Frankreich," in *Festschrift zum 70. Geburtstag Oskar Schades* (Königsberg, 1896), pp. 239-88; Marcel Breuillac: "Hoffmann en France," in *Revue d'histoire littéraire de la France*, xiii (1906), pp. 427-57; xiv (1907), pp. 74-105; Ernst Hofmann: *E. T. A. Hoffmann et la littérature française*, Dresden, 1913; Gerhard Pankalla: "E. T. A. Hoffmann und Frankreich," in *Germanisch-Romanische Monatsschrift*, xxvii (1939), pp. 308-18. Thurau, and especially Breuillac, describe at length the many works in which they find evidence of Hoffmann's influence. Hofmann presents some divergent opinions, analyzes the work of several added authors, and supplies a valuable, if incomplete, list of French translations from 1829 to 1910. Cf. also Kurt Otto Weise: "Die Wirkung einer Synästhesie Hoffmanns in Frankreich," in *Archiv für das Studium der neueren Sprachen*, clxx, pp. 106-8; Hoffmann's statement concerning the effect of wine upon himself (*Höchst zerstreute Gedanken*) as reproduced by Baudelaire, Massenet, and Huysmans; Kurt Schönherr: *Die Bedeutung E. T. A. Hoffmanns für die Entwicklung des musikalischen Gefühls in der französischen Romantik*, München, 1931.

[21] Adolphe Jullien, in "Le Romantisme et l'éditeur Renduel," in *Revue des deux Mondes*, cxxxii (1895), p. 657, implies that the Loève-Veimars translation owes its

lished in 1828 a long review of Hitzig's life of Hoffmann by J-J. Ampère, son of the great scientist; he was an admirer of German literature, and had traveled in Germany, meeting both Goethe and Tieck.[22] In his review Ampère introduced Hoffmann's works to French readers with almost unbounded enthusiasm, finding their chief characteristic in "le merveilleux naturel," a phrase which appears constantly in subsequent French criticism. Whatever may have been the exertions of Dr. Koreff in his friend's behalf, the year 1829 ushered in what might be called a Hoffmann "boom" in France. It witnessed a translation of *Die Elixiere des Teufels* by Jean Cohen, two articles on Hoffmann by Saint-Marc Giradin in the *Revue de Paris* with partial translation of two stories, and six other translations from Hoffmann in the same journal, an article by Loève-Veimars entitled "Les derniers années et la mort d'Hoffmann," and, more important still, the first volumes of Loève-Veimars' translation of the *Contes fantastiques et nocturnes*. By 1833 Loève-Veimars was ready with his *Oeuvres complètes*, though the title is a misnomer. In 1836 the translation by Henry Egmont appeared and in 1843 the *Contes fantastiques d'Hoffmann* in the version of Xavier Marmier. The *Contes posthumes*, translated by Champfleury (1856), contained a considerable amount of critical and biographical material, much of the latter taken from Hitzig's *Life*.

In 1843 Gautier wrote that Hoffmann was "popular in France, more popular than in Germany," and unquestionably Hoffmann's position was such that critical journals were constantly referring to him and most of the outstanding authors—Saint-Beuve, George Sand, Musset, Gautier, Baudelaire, and others—acknowledged his prominence by expression of opinion or in many cases reflected something of Hoffmann's influence in their own work, either directly in the use of some theme or in a subtle betrayal of Hoffmann's presence in their thought.[23] Thurau and Breuillac, two scholars who have investigated the reception of Hoffmann's works in France and the extent of his influence there, both present evidence to show the persistence of an interest in the fantastic and the supernatural, coupled

---

origin to this publisher, who, "l'ésprit séduit et charmé par les contes d'Hoffmann," decided to have all the tales translated, and appealed to Loève-Veimars for "cette tâche délicate."

[22] Cf. Ampère's letters to Tieck: K. von Holtei: *Briefe an Ludwig Tieck* (Breslau, 1864), I, pp. 1-4.

[23] Cf. B. Payr: *Théophile Gautier und E. T. A. Hoffmann*, Borna-Leipzig, 1927; Jean Pommier: "Baudelaire et Hoffmann," in *Mélanges de philologie, d'histoire, et de littérature offerts à Joseph Vianey* (Paris, 1894), pp. 259-477.

often with a humorous and skeptical detachment, from the Middle Ages down through the classical period and the rationalism of the eighteenth century; this interest stood ready to greet the type of story that Hoffmann wrote. Indeed, it is suggested that J. Cazotte's *Le Diable amoureux*—which Hoffmann himself admired—and perhaps certain other tales had already anticipated Hoffmann's style; at any rate, Cazotte's story may have prepared the ground for Hoffmann's outstanding popularity. A marked decline in Hoffmann's French fortunes is definitely dated from the publication of Baudelaire's translation of Edgar Allan Poe in 1855. The French saw in Poe's tales the use of similar material but greater artistry; in Poe's mysteries they admired the working out of "logical, mathematical deduction." Detractors arose, such as Philarète Chasles, who contended that Loève-Veimars had through the modifications of the original text really created a new author, and had "invented" Hoffmann,[24] but there were those who protested against these new views of Hoffmann's merits.

In the last part of the eighteenth century and the beginning of the nineteenth, German fiction bulked large among English translations of foreign books, and the list included some of the sensational stories and tales of the supernatural which might have paved the way for Hoffmann's very different treatment of similar material.[25] In 1824, a translation of *Die Elixiere des Teufels* appeared, the work of R. F. Gillies, an indefatigable translator of German books. Two years later, Gillies published a translation of *Das Fräulein von Scuderi* and of *Das Majorat* under the title *Rolandsitten or the Deed of Entail*, G. Soames translated *Meister Floh*, and there was another translation of *Das Fräulein von Scuderi* by R. Holcraft. The following year Scott's paper *On the Supernatural in Fictitious Composition* appeared in the July number of the *Quarterly Review*, possibly promoted by the spate of translations in 1826; it is presented, however, as a review of Hitzig's life of Hoffmann, *Die Serapionsbrüder*, and the *Nachtstücke*.

In his historical survey of the supernatural in fiction at the beginning of his essay, Scott makes some very sound remarks on the use of the supernatural: it must be "managed with considerable deli-

[24] For the problem of translating Hoffmann's diction and style into French, cf. Thurau, *op. cit.*, pp. 250-52; X. Marmier: "De tous les romanciers allemands, l'auteur de *Mademoiselle Scudéry*, des *Frères Sérapion*, etc. est peut-être le plus intraduisible" in "Hoffmann et Devrient" in *Revue des deux Mondes*, Seconde Série (1833), IV, pp. 466-75.

[25] Cf. V. Stockley: *German Literature in England, 1750-1830*, London, 1929.

cacy"; "the interest it excites is peculiarly subject to be exhausted by coarse handling and repeated pressure"; "the exhibition of supernatural appearances in fictitious narrative should be rare, brief, and indistinct"; even the second appearance of the ghost in *Hamlet* is less impressive than the first.[26] Thus, before he mentions Hoffmann, Scott is setting up a standard that he thinks Hoffmann egregiously violates. To Hoffmann Sir Walter attributes the leadership in a new "species of composition," the "Fantastic Tale," which knows "no restraint save that which it may ultimately find in the exhausted imagination of the author"; "our English severity of taste will not easily adopt this wild and fantastic tone into our literature; nay, perhaps will scarce tolerate it in translations." The modern reader may perhaps be startled by Scott's comparison of Wordsworth and Hoffmann—in the effect of petty incidents upon their sensibility: Wordsworth's "virtuous and manly, and well-regulated disposition" leading him to "derive pleasing, tender, and consoling reflections," while Hoffmann's reactions are of a quite different character. "Observers of poetical imagination [like Wordsworth and Hoffmann] are the chemists who distill them [the petty incidents] into cordials or poisons." "It is impossible," he says of Hoffmann's stories, "to subject tales of this nature to criticism. They are not the visions of a poetical mind; they have scarcely even the seeming authenticity which the hallucinations of lunacy convey to the patient; they are the feverish dreams of a lightheaded patient, to which, though they may sometimes excite by their peculiarity, or surprise by their oddity, we never feel disposed to yield more than a momentary attention."

Throughout the essay Scott treats Hoffmann somewhat in the manner of a considerate and sympathetic physician who diagnoses the maladies of a deceased patient and regrets that they prevented the achievement of success in his chosen profession. "Notwithstanding the dreams of an overheated imagination, by which his taste appears to have been so strangely misled, Hoffmann seems to have been a man of excellent disposition, a close observer of nature, and one who, if this sickly and disturbed train of thought had not led him to confound the supernatural with the absurd, would have distinguished himself as a painter of human nature, of which in its realities he was an observer and an admirer." And Hoffmann's unusual power in creating real and admirable character is illustrated

---

[26] Compare Hawthorne's caution as to the use of the supernatural in his introduction to *The House of Seven Gables*.

by the Justiciary in *Das Majorat*; the supernatural happenings in the story are well-narrated, but our chief admiration is reserved for the exhibition Hoffmann gives us of "unsullied masculine honor and integrity." As a contrast Scott analyzes the character of Nathanael in *Der Sandmann*, a "wild and absurd story," which in some measure is redeemed by the substantial and sane traits in the character of Clara. And the physician speaks out at the end: "Phlebotomy and cathartics, joined to sound and deliberate observation, might . . . have brought to a healthy state a mind which we cannot help regarding as diseased, and his imagination soaring with an equal and steady flight might have reached the highest pitch of the poetical profession."

Carlyle's appreciation of Hoffmann in the introduction to his translation of *Der goldene Topf* appeared in the same year as Scott's essay; it was a real distinction that two outstanding figures in the world of letters should concern themselves with him. His main, if not his only, source for the life of Hoffmann was Hitzig's recently published work, which drew attention to aspects of his life and character that Carlyle would be particularly prone to censure. In spite of very limited critical material to assist him in forming his opinions, Carlyle's evaluation of Hoffmann was in some respects strangely perceptive; though it is sprinkled here and there with half-truths or occasionally with downright errors, it is still for the time a considerable achievement in comprehending the mind and utterance of a foreign man of letters. He agrees with Scott that Hoffmann failed to control his talents and did not attain the greatness that might have been his; here Carlyle naturally stresses moral greatness. It was not weakness of will, for he demonstrated the contrary; nor was it lack of diligence, but—and here Carlyle perceives the center of the issue—"he found no sure principle of action; no Truth adequate to the guidance of such a mind." In the midst of work, of social enjoyments, he "longed for some worthier home. This home, unhappily, he was not destined to find. He sought for it in the poetry of Art; and the aim of his writings, so far as they have any aim, as they are not mere interjections, expressing the casual moods of his mind, was constantly the celebration and unfolding of this the best and truest doctrine which he had to preach." His love for art was deep but scarcely pure; art was not a fountain of beauty but of refined enjoyment; "he demanded from it not heavenly peace but earthly excitement." One admires Carlyle's discernment when he says: "It was not things but 'the shows of things,' that he saw; and the world and its business, in which he had to live and move, often hovered before him like a perplexed and spectral vision." Carlyle's critical perceptions are further exemplified in his choice of *Der goldene Topf* for translation instead of *Meister Martin der Küfner*, which, he says, the critics regard as the most perfect of Hoffmann's "shorter performances," because *Der goldene Topf* "exhibits a much truer picture of his individuality."

Of authors writing in English, Edgar Allan Poe doubtless shows the closest affinity with Hoffmann, though their kinship is confined to limited aspects of their work.[27] To what extent Poe was indebted to the German storyteller is a moot point among critics. In general the biographers of Poe either admit a casual borrowing of non-essential details or are inclined to deny the influence outright. Special investigators have discovered a much more extended influence than the biographers allow, and unquestionably certain correspondences go beyond the possibility of mere coincidence and present a broader base for establishing the influence; the cumulative evidence is very strong and is not met by the assumption that Poe read Scott's review and that alone. In Sakheim's brief survey he mentions also Washington Irving's *Tales of a Traveller*. In contrast with Poe, Irving's acquaintance with the language, literature, and folklore of Germany is fairly well documented. In the early 1820's he traveled extensively in Germany and spent eight months in Dresden, associating with both court circles and the literary world.[28] An enthusiasm for German legends and German Romantic literature he had acquired before this German residence, perhaps derived in part from his personal acquaintance with Sir Walter Scott. In Irving's stories the German influence is unmistakable, but on the whole would seem to be general rather than specific, though use of specific legends is demonstrable.

[27] Cf. Gustav Gruener: "Notes on the Influence of E. T. A. Hoffmann upon Edgar Allan Poe," in *Publications of the Modern Language Association*, xix (1904), pp. 1-25; Palmer Cobb: *The Influence of E. T. A. Hoffmann on the Tales of Edgar Allan Poe*, Chapel Hill, 1908. Any "tiefgehende Beeinflussung" is categorically denied by Dr. Karl Ferdinand van Vleuten in an article on Poe in *Die Zukunft*, xliv (1903), pp. 181-90; the author does not enter upon an investigation of details, but bases his opinions on medical grounds: Poe was epileptic and dipsomaniac, and Hoffmann was neither. Friedrich Schneider in "Edgar Allan Poe und E. T. A. Hoffmann" (*Über den Wassern*, ii [1909], pp. 37-42, 73-76) assembles interesting parallels in the life and work of the two authors, but makes no attempt to establish the influence.

[28] Cf. Stanley T. Williams: *The Life of Washington Irving*, New York, 1935; H. A. Pochmann: "Irving's German Tour and Its Influence on His Tales," in *Publications of the Modern Language Association*, xlv (1930), pp. 1150-87 and "Irving's German Sources in the Sketch Book," in *Studies in Philology*, xxvii (1930), pp. 477-507; E. H. Zeydel: "Washington Irving and Ludwig Tieck," in *Publications of the Modern Language Association*, xxviii (1931), pp. 946-47.

The most recent biographer of Irving (Williams) remarks with reference to his use of "Gothic material": "It should be noticed that almost invariably there is in his description of this kind an underlying note of the burlesque." It is possible that Irving derived this note from Hoffmann. But in general the quality of the supernatural in Irving's work is simple and traditional as compared with Hoffmann's complex and original use of supernatural elements. With Bulwer-Lytton Sakheim is perhaps on firmer ground but less in the tales he mentions, such as *Paul Clifford* and *Eugene Aram*, than in *Zanoni* and *A Strange Story*, though in any case it was only the outer shell of Hoffmann's supernaturalism that the English novelist appropriated. That Scrooge in Dickens' *Christmas Carol* sees the face of old Marley in the door-knocker, as Anselmus in *Der goldene Topf* is horrified by a parallel apparition, one can probably write down as pure coincidence; and considerable ingenuity is required to see anything of Hoffmann in Oscar Wilde's *Portrait of Dorian Grey*, even more in the clumsy imaginings and turgid rhetoric of D'Israeli's *Alroy*.

The emergence of Russia in the nineteenth century as the producer of a major literature counted Hoffmann among the directive forces.[29] The great names of the period, Pushkin, Dostoevski, Lermontov, Turgenev, Gogol, Chekhov, Andreev, and others, all stand in some demonstrable relation to the German master, often by influences shaping recognizable elements in their work. In translation Russia stood only slightly behind England and France, and her critics early called attention to Hoffmann's literary importance. The account given both by Gorlin and Sakheim of Alexander Herzen's criticism of Hoffmann is striking evidence of Russian appreciation only

---

[29] Cf. M. Gorlin: "Hoffmann en Russie," in *Revue de littérature comparée*, xv (1935), pp. 60-76 and "N. V. Gogol und E. T. A. Hoffmann," in *Veröffentlichungen*, Slavisches Institut, University of Berlin, ix, Leipzig, 1933. Gorlin asserts that among German authors Hoffmann exercised the greatest influence in Russia, more than Goethe or Schiller; beginning about 1830 Hoffmann became a "passion," a "cult," one critic saying: "I do not comprehend why Europe does not place him beside Shakespeare and Goethe." According to Gorlin, the availability of French translations delayed somewhat the rendering of Hoffmann's works into Russian. He quotes a historian of Russian literature to the effect that no Russian author of the 1830's was without knowledge of Hoffmann, "zwar das Gesamtbild seines Schaffens." In the early period the Russians saw in Hoffmann not merely the fascinating teller of uncanny tales, but the delicate analyst of the artist soul. Later they turned more to the realistic tales. Though Gorlin does not mention it, they were probably influenced by French criticism; the French were apparently more interested in the stories that combined something of the marvelous with more outspoken realism. Dostoevski thought *Kater Murr* Hoffmann's masterpiece; it has been pointed out that *Crime and Punishment* follows closely the psychology of *Die Elixiere des Teufels*.

slightly later than Carlyle's, and much more comprehensive and penetrating. When Dostoevski wrote to his brother in 1838 that he had read all of Hoffmann and in 1840 that "our conversation [was] of Homer, Schiller, and Hoffmann," it is eloquent proof that the German storyteller occupied an undisputed place of eminence among the very great in the world's literature. The Scandinavian literatures of the nineteenth century also took counsel of Hoffmann,[30] and his tales were translated into Dutch, Czech, Italian, and Spanish.[31]

(IV)

An evaluation of Hoffmann's work as an artist and as a musician is beset with almost insuperable difficulties, especially for the layman. Only a few of his paintings have been preserved, and they are widely scattered, mostly in private possession. His designs for book covers, the vignettes for title pages and end pieces, and a few illustrations for his stories offer a more satisfactory basis for study; they are still available in the form in which Hoffmann intended them to be seen, even though the original drawings may be lost. Some of the caricatures may also be studied in published form, for example, the Napoleonic series or the series of Berlin actors and actresses in certain roles; these represent a finished product that he was willing to have published as his work. Otherwise, the scattered evidences of Hoffmann's draftsmanship are mostly mere sketches, hastily executed, many of them caricatures such as he was wont to turn out by the score for the entertainment of his friends. The caprice of fate has preserved a few of them. Hoffmann's musical work presents a similar pattern. Many of his compositions are lost, perhaps irretrievably, though the quite recent finding of *Aurora* and of *Saul* is encouraging; some exist only in manuscript, a considerable number in the Berlin Library. In the last two decades several of his scores have been republished,[32] but, save for the expert, music must be heard, not merely

---

[30] Cf. Friedrich Holtze: "E. T. A. Hoffmann und H. Chr. Andersen," in *Mitteilungen des Vereins für die Geschichte Berlins*, xxxv (1918), p. 20. The author asserts that Andersen owed "einen guten Teil seiner Entwicklung" to Hoffmann. The Danish work of Hans Brix (Copenhagen, 1907) upon which Holtze bases his account I have not been able to examine.

[31] Cf. Franz Schneider: "E. T. A. Hoffmann en España: Apuntes bibliográphicos e históricos" in *Estudios Eruditos in memoriam de Adolfo Bonilla y San Martín* (Madrid, 1927), Tomo i, pp. 279-87. An Italian translation of Hoffmann's tales appeared in 1835: *Raconti di Ernesto Teodoro Hoffmann. Premesso un discorso di Gualtiero Scott*, Prima versione italiana (Milano, 1835), 4 vols.

[32] Hans von Müller in *Die Musik* i, *Quartal* iii (1902), pp. 1651-66, gives a list of Hoffmann's compositions (a) published during his lifetime and (b) known to be existing in manuscript at the time of his death. E. Kroll in his monograph *E. T. A. Hoffmann* provides a similar list with the present location of the manuscripts. H.

seen. The centennial of Hoffmann's death in 1922 witnessed the performance of some of his music, and other works have been revived in the following years. An awakened interest in Hoffmann's place in musical history is evidenced by the increase of references to his compositions and to his musical criticism.

The paintings of Hoffmann's youth—those, for example, that he aspired to sell to Hippel's uncle—were doubtless the imitative product of a gifted amateur. The Dresden Gallery, which he visited from Glogau, convinced him of his temporary incompetence and sent him back to first principles—the study of drawing as a condition of progress. At times, as in Plock, Hoffmann applied himself diligently and with confidence to his development as an artist, though discouragement soon stayed his hand. While in Warsaw he designed and, for the most part, executed the decoration of the Mniszek Palace which the new Academy of Music had acquired. Apparently he covered the walls with arabesque designs and fabulous beasts of his own imagining; according to Hitzig, he painted one room in the Egyptian style: "among the marvelous pictures of Egyptian deities he contrived to weave in caricatures of members of the Society, disguised by tails of animals, wings, and the like." The Altenburg, a picturesque ruin with a tower in a good state of preservation on a height outside of Bamberg, had been bought by his friend Dr. Marcus, and Hoffmann adorned the walls of the tower with frescoes—the capture of Graf Adalbert von Babenberg to whom the tower had once belonged; he portrayed himself among the knights, a liberty for which, of course, he had excellent precedents in the history of painting. These mural paintings have long since vanished, as well as such more intrinsically ephemeral work as the curtain he designed for the Würzburg theater. Some of the designs for stage scenery, however, have been preserved. Cf. Illus. 11, 12.

Two formal portraits, painted in *gouache*, are still extant. The portrait of the Kunz family has already been mentioned. Hoffmann had evidently studied carefully the conventional portraiture of the

---

Pfitzner published in 1906 a transcription of *Undine* for the piano, and in 1922 Gustav Becking began the publication of the *Musikalische Werke*; three volumes were issued, containing: "Vier Sonaten für Pianoforte," "Quintett für Harfe oder Pianoforte und Streichquartett," and "Sechs geistliche Chöre für gemischten Chor." A few other pieces have been published, such as a duet from the opera "Aurora" in *Zeitschrift für Musikwissenschaft*, IV, pp. 550-52, and in Hans von Müller's *Kreislerbuch*: "Agnus Dei" from the *Mass in D*, the hymns "Ave maris Stella" and "O sanctissima" and the duet "Ah che mi manca l'anima," all of these are connected with the Kreisler story.

time. The design is perhaps too obviously calculated, but it is executed with considerable skill. The four figures are somewhat stiffly
posed in a pyramidal pattern; the drapery of a heavy curtain covers
part of a large window at the left and extends across the remainder
of the wall, forming a diagonal line in the background of the picture. The window presented a problem of light and shadow with
which the artist refused to cope. Kunz himself sits beside a small
table; his wife stands behind it, her right hand apparently on the
back of his chair; a small child stands at Kunz's right, and he grasps
her arm as if he were feeling her pulse; an older woman, mother or
mother-in-law, sits on the other side—incidentally the most successful
of the four figures, though the artist was, it would appear, especially
interested in the statuesque pose of Frau Kunz and the classic dra-
peries of her costume. As painting, if one may judge from a reproduction, Hoffmann seems to have excelled in the still life of rummer
glass, carafe, and plate of fruit on the table. The coloring of the
portrait was, at the time, called excellent. Since it has remained in
the possession of the family, one may hope that Kunz was pleased
with the portrait, but the expression on the faces suggests a mild
family misunderstanding; this may or may not have been a sly intention on Hoffmann's part.

The other large painting is in the Library (Staatsbibliothek) in
Bamberg. It presents Dr. Marcus and an attendant figure, supposed
to be Hoffmann himself, against a forest background, an opening
in the trees at the extreme right affording a more distant prospect;
this is presumably the scenery in the neighborhood of the Altenburg.
The portrait of Dr. Marcus would seem to be a superior piece of
work; he stands in a lifelike position, and Hoffmann has caught a
genuine and individual facial expression, though, of course, the
accuracy of the likeness cannot be attested. If the attendant figure
really represents Hoffmann, it was indeed a curious fancy to depict
himself as a kind of sybil in long, trailing, white garments and a
white cap, one bare arm and index finger pointing the way to his
companion. The grouping of the two figures, as has been noted, is
reminiscent of Dante and Virgil at the beginning of the *Inferno*,
but this hardly lessens the mystery of the composition (Illus. 9).

More successful, perhaps, in view of its simplicity, is the small
aquarelle of Hitzig and his wife (Illus. 10). The portrait of Julia in
his miniature of the three Marc children is the one work of Hoffmann
that one would most like to see, but no one knows what has become of

it.[33] These more formal efforts in portrait painting offer evidence of a genuine talent, but in themselves hardly point to latent greatness. With the exception of some instruction when he was a youth, Hoffmann was self-trained, learning as the years went by something here and there from association with artist friends, for instance from Molinari in Glogau. An exclusive absorption in the art of painting and study under acknowledged masters, perhaps in the Italy of those days, would have unquestionably raised the level of his accomplishment, but in all probability a really great painter was not lost in Hoffmann.

In one field, however, he showed an uncommon gift. Caricature is in itself a subordinate form of art, which must be supported by other qualities, as in the case of Goya or Daumier, to achieve a permanent place in the history of art. As a serious effort Hoffmann cultivated the art of caricature only spasmodically, though the impishness of his nature often found vent in casual sketches. He had a keen eye for salient features or peculiarities that can be stressed for humorous or satirical effect. The single figures seem more telling than the groups, and to modern taste the Napoleonic caricatures may appear cluttered and forced. In viewing some of the elongated, thin-legged figures, one thinks perhaps of Cruikshank's drawings (Illus. 3). Most of the sketches are mementos without artistic pretension. In a few cases Hoffmann made little drawings in his diary or letters; for example, on Sunday, January 15, 1804, he records having dinner at the house of K(riegs) R(at) Hakenek, "with Reichenberg and a red-faced, well-nourished parson [Pfäfflein] . . . he looked *circiter* as follows"; below is an amusing sketch of a plump ecclesiastic. His marked decorative sense, his feeling for symbolic values, is evident in the designs for book covers and the vignettes, such, for example, as the border of curious masks, joined by a flowing line of flowering twigs, which frames the aquarelle "Pasquin" (Cf. Illus. 5, 8).[34]

[33] Cf. Speyer's letter to Hitzig in Hans von Müller's: "Aus E. T. A. Hoffmanns Kapellmeisterzeit," in *Neue deutsche Rundschau*, XIV (1903), p. 44. Unless it were marked, who would recognize this miniature, in case it is still somewhere in existence? The portrait of Julia in later life would probably offer no clue; cf. the reproduction of a pencil drawing of Julia Marc at forty-eight (1844) by Friedrich Kaulbach, in Maassen, I.

[34] Hornbogen's dissertation *E. T. A. Hoffmann und die bildende Kunst* (Maschinendruck, Jena, 1922) I have not been able to examine. An excellent outline of Hoffmann's occupation with the fine arts is provided by Hans von Müller's introduction to *Handzeichnungen E. T. A. Hoffmanns in Facsimilelichtdruck nach den Originalen*, Berlin, 1925 (Propyläen-Verlag). Müller gives a chronological list of all of Hoffmann's paintings, drawings, designs for stage sets, and the like. Reproductions are to be found in books on Hoffmann and in editions of his works; cf. Heil-

As a musician Hoffmann presents a curious and paradoxical contrast with the man of letters.[35] He was influenced in each field both by past and contemporary masters, and in some ways is a representative of his times. In literature he absorbed philosophical ideas and literary methods from his environment and with apparent ease made them so thoroughly his own that his work bears the imprint of a strong and unique personality; Hoffmann's tales are Hoffmann speaking in his own voice. In music, on the other hand, he never succeeded in achieving a thoroughly individual and characteristic note, though here and there something may be marked as pure "Hoffmann."

He was equipped with a technical control of musical media that might have aroused the envy of many a great master. He knew all

---

born, Sakheim (including the "Pasquin") and the editions of Maassen and Hirschberg. The latter contains fifty-seven reproductions, and Hirschberg has also published a separate volume, *Die Zeichnungen E. T. A. Hoffmanns* (Potsdam, 1921), containing sixty-two reproductions; five numbers reproduced in the *Werke* are not included in this volume. The work of Hans von Müller referred to above contains fifty drawings, mostly from the collection of Walter Steffen. Hirschberg published also several of the caricatures made in Berlin 1807-1808; cf. note 22, Part I, Chapter 7. Cf. H. von Müller: "Die neueren Sammlungen von E. T. A. Hoffmanns Werken und Aufzeichnungen," in *Zeitschrift für Bücherfreunde*, N.F. XVIII (1926), pp. 1-16.

[35] The attempt at a formal evaluation of Hoffmann as a musician began with A. B. Marx's essay in Hitzig's biography; this was followed by Hieronymus Truhn's "E. T. A. Hoffmann als Musiker," in *Der Freihafen*, II (1839), pp. 66-105. In recent years the essays on Hoffmann as musician and critic of music have been very numerous: cf. Erwin Kroll: *Ernst Theodor Amadeus Hoffmann* in Breitkopf und Härtel's series of *Musikbücher*, Leipzig, 1923; *E. T. A. Hoffmanns musikalische Anschauung*, Königsberg, 1909; "Über den Musiker Hoffmann," in *Zeitschrift für Musikwissenschaft*, IV (1922), pp. 530-52; "E. T. A. Hoffmann als Bühnenkomponist," in *Die Musik*, XV (1922), pp. 99-115; "E. T. A. Hoffmann als Musikkritiker," in *Signale für die musikalische Welt*, LXVIII (1910), pp. 289-92, 332-33, 411-14; Hugo Conrat: "E. T. A. Hoffmann als Musiker," in *Allgemeine Musikzeitung*, XXX (1903), pp. 641-43, 659-61; Edgar Istel, "E. T. A. Hoffmann als Musikschriftsteller," in *Neue Zeitschrift für Musik*, XCIX (1903), pp. 569-72; M. Steuer: "E. T. A. Hoffmann als Musikschriftsteller," in *Signale für die musikalische Welt*, LX (1902) pp. 451-52; Gerald Abraham: "Hoffmann as Composer," in *The Musical Times*, LXXXIII (London, 1942), pp. 233-35; Paul Moos: "E. T. A. Hoffmann als Musikästhetiker," in *Die Musik*, XXIII (1907), pp. 67-84; and, more specialized, Hans Pfitzner: "E. T. A. Hoffmanns *Undine*," in *Süddeutsche Monatshefte*, III (1906), pp. 370-80; Edgar Istel: "E. T. A. Hoffmanns *Undine*," in *Die Musik*, XXI (1906), pp. 105-9; R. Bottacchiari: "Hoffmann e Beethoven," in *La Cultura*, II (1923), pp. 198-204.

Steuer remarks that "die ganze romantische Clavier-Musik . . . ist so eng mit E. T. A. Hoffmann verknüpft, dass volles Verständnis nur gewinnen kann, wer mit E. T. A. Hoffmann vertraut ist." Kroll notes a schism in all of Hoffmann's musical criticism: when he is speaking of the nature and effect of music, he is rooted in Romantic soil, but when he turns from general aesthetic reflections to definite artistic judgments, they always rest on classical formalism. Carl Schaeffer in *Die Bedeutung des Musikalischen und Akustischen in E. T. A. Hoffmanns literarischem Schaffen* provides an excellent account of Hoffmann's life as a musician and a résumé of his views on music, as an introduction to the specific theme of his monograph.

the pathways and the hidden byways of musical composition, but in the main he failed to fuse his musical scores with his own personality as an artist. To the musical critic of today there is something "studied" about the major part of his musical production; it seems strange that the charge of "formalism" could possibly be brought against any attempt of Hoffmann at artistic expression of himself. This inability spells tragedy for one who looked upon music as the supreme method of expressing the highest in human aspiration, as man's wistful plea for admittance into the Divine Presence.

And yet in the history of music Hoffmann's compositions are by no means negligible, and his musical criticism is of great significance. A recent German critic, Erwin Kroll, who has busied himself much with Hoffmann the musician, has said that Hoffmann must be regarded as the "father of the modern view of music [Musikanschauung], as the first real herald of Palestrina, Bach, and Beethoven, the co-creator of the Romantic opera, and the forerunner of the reform in the music of the Roman Catholic Church."[36]

Hoffmann's attention was early called to Bach, even by his first teacher in Königsberg, and the contrapuntal idea clung to him tenaciously throughout his career as a composer. The experience of Theodor in *Die Fermate* is presumably autobiographical; after a thorough grounding in traditional Northern forms of musical expression he encounters the two Italian singers who bring to him the melody, the bel canto, of Italian song. Kroll remarks that the peculiar mingling of melodic structure and playful (spielerisch) polyphony is a typically Romantic trait. In this connection one is inclined to seek a parallel between the musician and the man of letters. Hoffmann possessed a highly emotional, that is, a lyrical, nature, but he never wrote a real lyric. His songs, such as the six Italian duets dedicated to Julia Marc, are said to be very competent, even distinguished, examples of music to accompany words, yet there is in them only a "breath" of his own participation in the emotions involved, though they were written for soprano and tenor, for Julia's voice and his own. He never wrote his own life, his love for Julia, into a song; the *Ombra Adorata* is in prose. Only in the imagination could such an experience as he puts in the words of Donna Anna (*Don Juan*) be realized: "I have sung *you* just as *I* am your melodies."

---

[36] Cf. Eugen Schmitz: "E. T. A. Hoffmann und die Reform in der katholischen Kirchenmusik," in *Musica Divina*, IV (1916), pp. 63-65. Schmitz says that Hoffmann's essay on church music contains the "Kern, alles dessen was das ganze 19. Jahrhundert hindurch bis zum Motu proprio Pius X. immer wieder für die Reform der katholischen Kirchenmusik ins Treffen geführt wurde."

There are indeed competent and melodious arias in his operas and, according to Pfitzner, in *Undine* some passages in the form of a *Lied* which "if presented as by Mozart would deceive many an orthodox devotee of beauty." Hoffmann would, however, seem to have been more interested in the ensemble pieces; the same critic calls the sextet in that opera "a really masterly opera number," "perfect in form, nicely in keeping with the character of the individual roles, maintaining unaffectedly a genuine dramatic temper, and as music exceedingly charming." In *Liebe und Eifersucht*, which Hoffmann began in Warsaw to the text of Schlegel's translation of Calderon, there are numerous duets, quartets, quintets, a sextet, and three finales "broadly worked out," but only five arias.

His musical composition was influenced by Gluck, Mozart, Beethoven, and other masters. Among the critics Ellinger, especially, finds traces of Mozart in Hoffmann's work, often following the suggestions of Mozart's style step by step through a symphony or sonata, yet at the same time, in his analysis of the composition, he notes divergences and comments upon individual musical ideas, some of which point to Schubert, Schumann, and Mendelssohn. Despite this emphasis on Mozart's influence, Ellinger is more confident of Hoffmann's independence and originality as a composer than any other of the critics.[37] *Aurora*, the chief operatic work of the Bamberg period, is apparently the beginning of German romantic opera and in *Undine*, which followed after a short interval, the romantic opera became a reality. It is also demonstrable that the idea of a "music-drama" in contradistinction to the "opera" was more or less definitely before his mind's eye.[38] Also, though the "leitmotif" in rudimentary state is found before Hoffmann, his use of it, especially in *Undine*, is a long step forward toward its recognition as a basic musical form. In imitative music, or "Tonmalerei," the interpretation in musical terms of events or of the moods of the characters, Hoffmann was a pathfinder; this appears very early in his work, for example in the music he composed for Werner's *Kreuz an der Ostsee*, where he used such devices to imitate the roar of the sea and the outcries of the heathen and barbarian East Prussians. Apart from *Undine*, perhaps Hoffmann's most distinguished musical compositions were written

---

[37] Nearly thirty years later in an article entitled "E. T. A. Hoffmann als Musiker," Ellinger seems somewhat less assured of Hoffmann's position as a composer (*Mitteilungen des Vereins für die Geschichte Berlins*, xxxix (1922), pp. 65-67.

[38] Cf. Hans von Wolzogen: *E. T. A. Hoffmann und Richard Wagner, Harmonien und Parallelen*, Berlin (without date), and "E. T. A. Hoffmann, der deutsche Geisterseher," in *Bayreuther Blätter*, xvi, pp. 11-22; xvii, pp. 62-70; xviii, pp. 11-29.

for the services of the Roman Catholic Church. They form an eloquent testimony to the depth of his religious feeling, which has been
so often overlooked, or indeed categorically denied. Ellinger mentions with especial praise the five *a cappella* choruses that Hoffmann
composed in Bamberg, following in part the style of the great Italian
composers of church music; the *Miserere* written during the same
period he regards as one of Hoffmann's most beautiful and memorable compositions.

In the history of musical criticism, however, Hoffmann's place is
not in doubt. An eminent musicologist wrote a few years ago: "One
more generation and with E. T. A. Hoffmann, one of the master
novelists of the Romantic movement and musician of no mean talent,
we reach the beginnings of an era which produced the most enlightened and truly 'professional' musical criticism."[39] Numerous similar
utterances could be quoted from other authorities. In the account of
Hoffmann's life mention has already been made of his reviews of
musical works for the *Allgemeine musikalische Zeitung*. Only three
of these did he himself incorporate into his other writings, and all
three were concerned with Beethoven. Two of them, the reviews of the
Fifth Symphony and of the Trios in D Major and E Major, he re-
worked into the essay on *Beethovens Instrumentalmusik* in the first
cycle of the *Kreisleriana*, and the third, on Beethoven's Mass in C
Major he used in the essay on *Alte und neue Kirchenmusik*. For this
reason, as well as for the eminence of the composer in question, these
musical criticisms of Hoffmann's are the best known. It may be added
that the review of the *Fifth Symphony* drew from the great master
himself a note of appreciation, a signal mark of distinction as coming from Beethoven. Other reviews in considerable numbers are, however, now available in the editions of Hoffmann's works and in several collections of his writings on music. In recent years scholarly
research has added a number of reviews to the list, some of which may
perhaps be attributed to Hoffmann only with caution. Hoffmann's
reviews are unsurpassed models in the field of musical criticism. With
his unusual command of the technique of music he analyzes both the
structure and the details of a musical composition, his wide knowledge of music permitting frequent and illuminating reference to
kindred works of other composers. But he does not forget the principles that the Schlegels applied to literary criticism and with sympathy he seeks to understand and interpret the intent of the com-

Cf. P. H. Lang: "Ecce Criticus," in *The American Scholar*, VII (1938), p. 479.

poser. For to Hoffmann music was not an ingenious arrangement of sounds founded on mathematical and physical laws; it was the voice of a human spirit interpreting the highest that man knows or dreams.[40]

[40] The statement, often encountered, that Hoffmann studied music with Reichardt during his first residence in Berlin rests on rather uncertain foundation. It was first made in Brockhaus' *Conversations-Lexicon* (Real-Encyclopädie für gebildete Stände) 1819, IV; according to Hans von Müller, this volume appeared November 1, 1818. That Hoffmann wrote the biographical record himself, as has been inferred (Schenck), is open to question. From Hoffmann's letter of May 7, 1818, it would seem that Brockhaus had consulted him with reference to the biography to appear in the Encyclopedia: "Um mich meines Versprechens Rücksichts der gewünschten Notizen für das Convers L zu entledigen, erwarte ich nur nähere Bescheidung auf meine Anfrage" (*Briefwechsel*, II, p. 308). In view of Hoffmann's habits of procrastination, it seems probable that Brockhaus did not receive Hoffmann's biographical data in time for inclusion in vol. IV, and turned for information to former friends of Hoffmann in Leipzig. Support for this interpretation is afforded by the incorrect date of his birth (1778), which error could not have occurred in any notes that Hoffmann sent. Kroll is somewhat guarded in saying that Hoffmann "seems to have frequented [verkehrt in] Reichardt's hospitable house," but the statement is more than dubious. During these years Reichardt did not reside continuously in Berlin; he came there at times for musical performances. It is also to be noted that Tieck married a sister of Reichardt's wife in 1799, his *Sternbald* had just been published, and in the circumstances it is inconceivable that Hoffmann could have been a familiar visitor in Reichardt's home without knowing of Tieck, and it is almost certain that he knew nothing of him until his days in Warsaw. Harich (*Hoffmanns Werke*, XII, p. vi) says that Hoffmann "nennt sich einmal an versteckter Stelle einen Schüler Reichardts," but the passage to which he refers in *Alte und neue Kirchenmusik* expresses only an approval of Reichardt's efforts to bring works of the old masters to the attention of the modern world. Doubtless Harich intended to refer to Hoffmann's review of Spontini's *Olympia* where he quotes Reichardt's advice to his pupils to write ballets in order to clarify in their minds the function of rhythm in music: "Der Verfasser dieses Aufsatzes gehörte unter diese Schüler." It seems probable, however, that Hoffmann uses the word "Schüler" in a general sense, referring to ideas communicated through Reichardt's writings; or, on the other hand, Hoffmann may have participated as a singer in the chorus of a musical performance that Reichardt conducted, and owed his "discipleship" to Reichardt's oral instruction as to the value of rhythm; the use of the plural rather than the singular is pertinent to this conjecture. Reichardt was, to be sure, born in Königsberg (1752), and might as a consequence have had an interest in his fellow townsman, in case Hoffmann had been presented to him. The episode of *List, Scherz und Rache* (cf. note 9, Part I, Chapter 1) adds no real confirmation of Hoffmann's music lessons with Reichardt; Hoffmann's score could easily have been submitted for Reichardt's comment by any one of the circle in Berlin who might be interested in Minna Doerffer's betrothed.

LIST OF HOFFMANN'S LITERARY WORKS

This list includes the few pieces of musical criticism that Hoffmann incorporated in the *Kreisleriana* and in the *Serapionsbrüder* and gives the dates
of publication: (1) in the annuals or periodicals and (2) in the collections.

Die Abenteuer der Sylvester-Nacht. Fantasiestücke, iv, 1815 (Spring).

Ahnungen aus dem Reiche der Töne. Morgenblatt, February 21, 22, 1816.
(Cf. *Johannes Kreislers Lehrbrief.*)

Alte und neue Kirchenmusik. (1) *Allgemeine musikalische Zeitung,* August
31; September 7, 14, 1814. (2) *Die Serapionsbrüder,* 1819 (Autumn).

Der Baron von B. (*Der Schüler Tartinis*). (1) *Allgemeine musikalische*
tumn). (2) *Die Serapionsbrüder,* i, 1819 (Spring).

Die Automate. (1) Extract in *Allgemeine musikalische Zeitung,* February
9, 1814; *Zeitung für die elegante Welt,* April 7-16, 1814. (2) *Die
Serapionsbrüder,* ii, 1819 (Autumn).

Der Baron von B. (*Der Schüler Tartinis*). (1) *Allgemeine musikalische
Zeitung,* March 10, 1819. (2) *Die Serapionsbrüder,* iii, 1820 (Autumn).

Beethovens Instrumentalmusik. (1) *Zeitung für die elegante Welt,* December
9, 10, 11, 1813. (2) *Fantasiestücke,* i, 1814 (Spring).

*Nachricht von den neuesten Schicksalen des Hundes Berganza. Fan-
tasiestücke,* ii, 1814 (Spring).

Die Bergwerke zu Falun. Die Serapionsbrüder, i, 1819 (Spring).

Prinzessin Blandina. Fantasiestücke, iv, 1815 (Spring).

Prinzessin Brambilla. 1821 (published late in 1820).

Die Brautwahl. (1) *Berlinischer Taschenkalender auf das Schalt-Jahr
1820,* 1819 (Autumn).

Datura Fastuosa. (1) *Taschenbuch für das Jahr 1823. Der Liebe und
Freundschaft gewidmet,* 1822 (Autumn). (2) *Die letzten Erzählungen,*
ii, 1825.

Der Dey von Elba. Freimütige Blätter für Deutsche, May 1815.

Der Dichter und der Komponist. (1) *Allgemeine musikalische Zeitung,*
December 8, 15, 1813. (2) *Serapionsbrüder,* i, 1819 (Spring).

Doge und Dogaressa. (1) *Taschenbuch für das Jahr 1819. Der Liebe und
Freundschaft gewidmet,* 1818 (Autumn).

Don Juan. (1) *Allgemeine musikalische Zeitung,* March 31, 1813. (2)
Fantasiestücke, i (Spring).

Die Doppeltgänger. (1) *Feierstunden,* 1822. (2) *Die letzten Erzählungen,*
i, 1825.

Der Elementargeist. (1) *Taschenbuch zum geselligen Vergnügen auf das
Jahr 1822,* 1821 (Autumn).

Die Elixiere des Teufels, i, ii, 1816.

Erscheinungen. (1) *Gaben der Milde,* ii, 1817. (2) *Die Serapionsbrüder,* iv,
1821 (Spring).

Die letzten Erzählungen, i, ii, 1825.

Fantasiestücke in Callots Manier. i, ii, 1814 (Spring); iii, 1814 (Autumn);
iv, 1815 (Spring).

Der Feind. Frauentaschenbuch für das Jahr 1824, 1823 (Autumn).

Die Fermate. (1) *Frauentaschenbuch für das Jahr 1816*, 1815 (Autumn).
(2) *Die Serapionsbrüder*, i, 1819 (Spring).

Meister Floh. 1822.

Signor Formica. (1) *Taschenbuch zum geselligen Vergnügen auf das Jahr 1820*, 1819 (Autumn). (2) *Die Serapionsbrüder*, iv, 1821 (Spring).

Ein Fragment aus dem Leben dreier Freunde. (1) *Der Wintergarten*, 1818.
(2) *Die Serapionsbrüder*, i, 1819 (Spring).

Der unheimliche Gast. (1) *Der Erzähler*, ii, 1819. (2) *Die Serapionsbrüder*, iii, 1820 (Autumn).

Die Geheimnisse. (1) *Berlinischer Taschenkalender auf das Gemein-Jahr 1822*, 1821 (Autumn). (2) *Die letzten Erzählungen*, i, 1825.

Das Gelübde. *Nachtstücke*, i, 1817.

Die Genesung. *Der Zuschauer*, July 4, 6, 1822.

Haimatochare. *Der Freimüthige*, June 24, 26, 29, 1819.

Das öde Haus. *Nachtstücke*, ii, 1817 (Autumn).

Das steinerne Herz. *Nachtstücke*, ii, 1817 (Autumn).

Ignaz Denner. *Nachtstücke*, i, 1817 (published late in 1816).

Die Irrungen. (1) *Berlinischer Taschenkalender auf das Gemein-Jahr 1821*, 1820 (Autumn).

Die Jesuiterkirche in G. *Nachtstücke*, i, 1817 (published late in 1816).

Der Kampf der Sänger. (1) *Urania. Taschenbuch auf das Jahr 1819*, 1818 (Autumn). (2) *Die Serapionsbrüder*, ii, 1819 (Autumn).

Lebensansichten des Katers Murr. i, 1820 (published late in 1819) ; ii, 1821.

Das fremde Kind. (1) *Kindermärchen*, ii, 1817. (2) *Die Serapionsbrüder*, ii, 1819 (Autumn).

Klein Zaches genannt Zinnober, 1819.

Die Königsbraut. *Die Serapionsbrüder*, iv, 1821 (Spring).

Kreisleriana. *Fantasiestücke*, i, 1814 ; iv, 1815.

(Kreislers) Gedanken über den hohen Wert der Musik. (1) *Allgemeine musikalische Zeitung*, July 29, 1812. (2) *Fantasiestücke*, i, 1814.

(Kreislers) Höchst zerstreute Gedanken. (1) *Zeitung für die elegante Welt*, January 4, 6, 7, 8, 1814. (2) *Fantasiestücke*, i, 1814.

Johannes Kreislers Lehrbrief (Reworking of *Ahnungen aus dem Reiche der Töne*). *Fantasiestücke*, iv, 1815 (Spring).

Johannes Kreislers des Kapellmeisters musikalische Leiden. (1) *Allgemeine musikalische Zeitung*, September 26, 1810. (2) *Fantasiestücke*, i, 1814.

Kreislers musikalisch-poetischer Klub. *Fantasiestücke*, iv, 1815 (Spring).

Rat Krespel. (1) *Frauentaschenbuch für das Jahr 1818*, 1817 (Autumn). (2) *Die Serapionsbrüder*, iv, 1819 (Spring).

Die Kunstverwandten (Preliminary version of *Seltsame Leiden eines Theaterdirektors*). *Dramatisches Wochenblatt*, February 18, 22 ; March 8, 29 ; May 3, 10, 17, 1817.

Seltsame Leiden eines Theaterdirektors. 1819 (published late in 1818).

Der Magnetiseur. *Fantasiestücke*, ii, 1814.

Das Majorat. *Nachtstücke*, ii, 1817.

Aus dem Leben eines bekannten Mannes (*Der Teufel in Berlin*). (1) *Der*

Freimüthige, May 25, 27, 1819. (2) *Die Serapionsbrüder,* III, 1820 (Autumn).

Nachricht von einem gebildeten jungen Mann (Schreiben Milos, eines gebildeten Affen). (1) *Allgemeine musikalische Zeitung,* March 16, 1814; *Fantasiestücke,* IV, 1815 (Spring).

Meister Martin der Küfner und seine Gesellen. (1) *Taschenbuch zum geselligen Vergnügen auf das Jahr 1819,* 1818 (Autumn). (2) *Die Serapionsbrüder,* II, 1819 (Autumn).

Der vollkommene Maschinist. Fantasiestücke, I, 1814.

Der Musikfeind. (1) *Allgemeine musikalische Zeitung,* June 1, 1814. (2) *Fantasiestücke,* IV, 1815 (Spring).

Nachtstücke. I, 1817 (published late in 1816); II, 1817 (Autumn).

Nussknacker und Mausekönig. (1) *Kindermärchen,* I, 1816. (2) *Die Serapionsbrüder,* I, 1819 (Spring).

Ombra Adorata. Fantasiestücke, I, 1814.

Die Marquise de la Pivadière. Taschenbuch zum geselligen Vergnügen auf das Jahr 1821, 1820 (Autumn).

Die Räuber. (1) *Rheinisches Taschenbuch auf das Jahr 1822,* 1821 (Autumn). (2) *Die letzten Erzählungen,* I, 1825.

Ritter Gluck. (1) *Allgemeine musikalische Zeitung,* February 15, 1809. (2) *Fantasiestücke,* I, 1814.

Über einen Ausspruch Sacchinis. (1) *Allgemeine musikalische Zeitung,* July 20, 1814. (2) *Fantasiestücke,* IV, 1815 (Spring).

Das Sanctus. Nachtstücke, I, 1817 (published late in 1816).

Der Sandmann. Nachtstücke, I, 1817 (published late in 1816).

Das Fräulein von Scuderi. (1) *Taschenbuch für das Jahr 1820. Der Liebe und Freundschaft gewidmet,* 1819 (Autumn). (2) *Die Serapionsbrüder,* III, 1820 (Autumn).

Sendschreiben eines Klostergeistlichen an seinen Freund in der Hauptstadt. Der Freimüthige, September 9, 1803.

Die Serapionsbrüder. I, 1819 (Spring); II, 1819 (Autumn); III, 1820 (Autumn); IV, 1821 (Spring).

Spielerglück. (1) *Urania. Taschenbuch auf das Jahr 1820,* 1819 (Autumn). (2) *Die Serapionsbrüder,* III, 1820 (Autumn).

Eine Spukgeschichte. Die Serapionsbrüder, II, 1819 (Autumn).

Der goldene Topf. Fantasiestücke, III, 1814 (Autumn).

Der Vampyr (Eine Vampyrgeschichte). Die Serapionsbrüder, IV, 1821.

Des Vetters Eckfenster. Der Zuschauer, April 23-May 4, 1822.

Vision auf dem Schlachtfeld bei Dresden, 1814.

Meister Johannes Wacht. (1) *Geschichten Märchen und Sagen von Fr. H von der Hagen, E. T. A. Hoffmann und Heinrich Steffens,* 1823. (2) *Die letzten Erzählungen,* II, 1825.

Des Kapellmeisters Johannes Kreislers Brief an den Baron Wallborn. (1) *Die Musen,* 1814; *Fantasiestücke,* IV, 1815 (Spring).

Der Zusammenhang der Dinge. (1) *Wiener Zeitschrift für Kunst, Litteratur, Theater und Mode,* February 15-March 2, 1820. (2) *Die Serapionsbrüder,* IV, 1821 (Spring).

BIBLIOGRAPHY

Soon after Hoffmann's death, Hitzig began to collect material for a biography of his friend, which he published the following year under the title: *Aus Hoffmann's Leben und Nachlass* (2 vols., Berlin, 1823). As an aid to Hitzig in the task of preparation Hippel sent not only the invaluable, "Erinnerungen an Hoffmann," especially important for Hoffmann's youth, but also copies of Hoffmann's letters to him; Dr. Speyer supplied reminiscences of the Bamberg period. For the Warsaw residence and the second and third periods in Berlin, Hitzig could, of course, rely in part on his own memories, and for the intermediate years his correspondence with Hoffmann was available. Hoffmann's diaries had come into his possession with the "Nachlass." As "Beilagen" Hitzig published many of Hoffmann's letters, either complete or in part, and included fragments from the "Tagebuch," also some miscellaneous items from the "Nachlass." In order to obtain a purely "objective judgment," he invited two young friends who had not been intimate with Hoffmann (fern gestanden) to cooperate by providing special articles, Willibald Alexis (Häring) for Hoffmann's literary work, and A. B. Marx on his music; to the latter, Hitzig added Weber's review of *Undine* from the *Allgemeine musikalische Zeitung* (March 19, 1817).

With the publication of *Die letzten Erzählungen* in 1825, Hitzig issued supplementary material to the above. An "enlarged and revised" edition of the *Leben und Nachlass* appeared with the *Erzählende Schriften in einer Auswahl*, ostensibly published by Hoffmann's widow but really by Hitzig in 1831, and still a third edition with the *Ausgewählte Schriften* in 1839; a considerable amount of new material was included in this edition, for example, Fouqué's reminiscences of Hoffmann and notes by Kunz; the *Leben und Nachlass* was subjected to a further revision. Hitzig's work remains an indispensable source for the study of Hoffmann, though it must be used with caution; he took unwarranted liberties with the text of Hoffmann's letters and though a Jew by birth he had become a devout Protestant of a rather austere Puritanical type and he viewed the vagaries of Hoffmann's character and conduct with jaundiced eyes.

Under the pseudonym "Z. Funck," an anagram of his own name, Hoffmann's friend in Bamberg, C. F. Kunz, published in 1836 *Aus dem Leben zweier Dichter: Ernst Theodor Wilhelm Hoffmann's und Friedrich Gottlob Wetzel's* as the first volume of his *Erinnerungen aus meinem Leben in biographischen Denksteinen*; his reminiscences of Hoffmann are pp. 1-172. Though not entirely reliable, Kunz's book is of value for the Bamberg period. The letters and memoirs of many of Hoffmann's contemporaries add important details and interesting glimpses of his character: Helmina von Chézy, Wilhelm Dorow, Gubitz, Holbein, Rochlitz, Varnhagen von Ense, A. Klingemann, F. Laun (Schulze), Stephan Schütze, the Danish author Öhlenschläger, and others.

The modern, more scholarly approach to the study of Hoffmann began with Georg Ellinger's: *E. T. A. Hoffmann: Sein Leben und seine Werke* (Hamburg und Leipzig, 1894). Later researches have corrected and amplified some of the data presented, and some of his critical conclusions are decidedly debatable, but, in general, no subsequent work surpasses Ellinger's *Hoffmann* in sympathetic understanding of an enigmatic personality; as a trained critic of music Ellinger could include an intensive and authoritative survey of Hoffmann's musical compositions, not to be found in any other biography. In *E. T. A. Hoffmann: Das Leben eines Künstlers* (Berlin, without date, "Vorrede" dated 1920) Walter Harich produced the most extensive account of Hoffmann's life and work. Harich made some use of the scholarly research of others, particularly the work of Hans von Müller and C. G. von Maassen, and, himself a novelist, put together a story of Hoffmann's life of absorbing interest and considerable charm. An excellent brief life is that of Richard von Schaukal: *E. T. A. Hoffmann: Sein Werk aus seinem Leben* (Zürich-Leipzig-Wien, 1923). Schaukal interprets both Hoffmann's character and his works with sympathy and fine discrimination, often using Hoffmann's own words, which he weaves together with admirable skill.

Most important for the student is the monumental publication of Hoffmann's letters by Hans von Müller with the title: *E. T. A. Hoffmann im persönlichen und brieflichen Verkehr* (Berlin, 1912); the first volume is *Hoffmann und Hippel: Das Denkmal einer Freundschaft*, and the second contains the letters to other correspondents. Both volumes are supplied with excellent critical apparatus, such as explanatory notes, the determination of dates, factual information concerning Hoffmann's correspondents and his relations with them, and the like; the appendices are especially important, providing minute bibliographical data of publications after Hoffmann's death and supplementary material. Since the publication of the *Briefwechsel*, letters of Hoffmann have been found and published in various books and periodicals, but unfortunately not collected as yet into a supplementary volume.

In the present generation of scholars Hans von Müller has been the most indefatigable and resourceful research worker. For his articles he has directly or indirectly investigated archives, town and church records, newspapers, court reports, and family papers and letters, and has followed up clues with tireless zeal. Unfortunately, his findings are less accessible than one might wish—some of them published privately and others widely scattered in periodicals. They constitute the spade-work for a life of Hoffmann that has not yet been written. But every student of Hoffmann is profoundly indebted to Hans von Müller.

The most useful editions of Hoffmann's works are those of Ellinger, Grisebach, Harich, and Maassen, either for completeness of the texts or for the value of the introductions and notes. It is a matter for real regret that the comprehensive edition of Carl Georg von Maassen is incomplete. The volumes that have been published are invaluable both for the introductions and for the extensive—perhaps too extensive—notes. Ellinger's edition is also thoroughly and helpfully annotated, and both Ellinger and Maassen give variant readings and omitted passages. There have been numerous editions of selections from the works, and individual stories have been issued with introductions and notes. Hoffmann's musical criticism has also been published in separate volumes.

(For the general bibliography, the reader is referred to the footnotes, but for convenience a selected list of titles is given here.)

HOFFMANN BIBLIOGRAPHY

Gerhard Salomon (Hans Roger Madol). *E. T. A. Hoffmann: Bibliographie.* Berlin-Leipzig: 1924. 2nd edition, 1927 (only through 1871).

EDITIONS OF HOFFMANN'S WORKS

E. T. A. Hoffmanns sämtliche Werke, herausgegeben von Eduard Grisebach. Leipzig: 1900. 15 vols.

E. T. A. Hoffmanns sämtliche Werke. Historisch-kritische Ausgabe mit Einleitungen, Anmerkungen und Lesarten von Carl Georg von Maassen. München: 1908-1928. Vols 1, 2, 3, 4, 6, 7, 8, 9-10.

E. T. A. Hoffmanns Werke. Auf Grund der Hempelschen Ausgabe neu herausgegeben, mit Einleitungen und Anmerkungen versehen von Georg Ellinger. Berlin: 1912. 15 vols.

E. T. A. Hoffmann Dichtungen und Schriften, herausgegeben von Walter Harich. Weimar: 1924. 15 vols.

E. T. A. Hoffmanns Musikalische Schriften, herausgegeben von H. von Ende. Köln-Leipzig (without date).

E. T. A. Hoffmanns Musikalische Schriften, herausgegeben von Edgar Istel. Stuttgart (without date).

BIOGRAPHIES

Ellinger, Georg. *E. T. A. Hoffmann: Sein Leben und seine Werke.* Hamburg und Leipzig: 1894.

Funck, Z. (C. F. Kunz.) *Aus dem Leben zweier Dichter.* Leipzig: 1836.

Harich, Walter. *E. T. A. Hoffmann: Das Leben eines Künstlers.* Berlin (without date, preface dated 1920).

Heilborn, Ernst. *E. T. A. Hoffmann: Der Künstler und die Kunst.* Berlin: 1926.

Hitzig, Julius Eduard. *Aus Hoffmann's Leben und Nachlass.* Herausgegeben von dem Verfasser des Lebens-Abrisses Friedrich Zacharias Werners. Berlin: 1823. 2 vols. Supplementary material published with *Die letzten Erzählungen* (Berlin, 1825); enlarged and revised edition published with the *Erzählende Schriften in einer Auswahl* (Stuttgart, 1831); further revision with the *Ausgewählte Schriften* (Stuttgart, 1839).

Klinke, Otto. *E. T. A. Hoffmanns Leben und Werke.* Vom Standpunkte eines Irrenarztes. Braunschweig-Leipzig: 1903.

Von Schaukal, Richard. *E. T. A. Hoffmann: Sein Werk aus seinem Leben.* Zürich-Leipzig-Wien: 1923.

Von Schenck, Ernst. *E. T. A. Hoffmann: Ein Kampf um das Bild des Menschen.* Berlin: 1939.

LETTERS AND DIARIES

E. T. A. Hoffmann im persönlichen und brieflichen Verkehr: sein Brief-wechsel und die Erinnerungen seiner Bekannten. I: Hoffmann und Hippel. II: Hoffmanns Briefwechsel mit Ausnahme der Briefe an Hippel, gesammelt und erläutert von Hans von Müller. Berlin: 1912. (Referred to as *Briefwechsel.*)

E. T. A. Hoffmanns Tagebücher und literarische Entwürfe mit Erläuterungen und ausführlichen Verzeichnissen, herausgegeben von Hans von Müller, Erster Band. Berlin: 1915.

GENERAL WORKS

Benz, R. *Märchendichtung der Romantiker.* Gotha: 1908.

Buchmann, R. *Helden und Mächte des romantischen Kunstmärchens.* Leipzig: 1910.

C(z)erny, J. *Jean Pauls Beziehungen zu E. T. A. Hoffmann.* Mies: 1907-1908.

Cohn, Hilda. *Realismus und Transzendenz in der Romantik, insbesondere bei E. T. A. Hoffmann.* Heidelberg: 1933.

Dahmen, Hans. *E. T. A. Hoffmanns Weltanschauung.* Marburg: 1929.

Egli, Gustav. *E. T. A. Hoffmann: Ewigkeit und Endlichkeit in seinem Werk.* Zürich: 1927.

Ellinger, Georg. "Das Disziplinarverfahren gegen E. T. A. Hoffmann," *Deutsche Rundschau,* cxxviii (1906), pp. 79-103.

Fife, Robert Herndon Jr. "Jean Paul Friedrich Richter and E. T. A. Hoffmann," *Publications of the Modern Language Association,* xxii (1907), pp. 1-32.

Fischer, Ottokar. "E. T. A. Hoffmanns Doppelempfindungen," *Archiv für das Studium der neueren Sprachen und Literaturen,* cxxiii (1909), pp. 1-22.

Floeck, Oswald. *Die Elementargeister bei Fouqué und anderen Dichtern der romantischen und nachromantischen Zeit.* Heidelberg: 1909.

Glöckner, Ernst. *Studien zur romantischen Psychologie der Musik, besonders mit Rücksicht auf die Schriften E. T. A. Hoffmanns.* München: 1909.

Grahl-Mögelin, Walter. *Die Lieblingsbilder im Stil E. T. A. Hoffmanns.* Greifswald: 1914.

Jost, Walter. *Von Tieck zu Hoffmann.* Frankfurt am Main: 1921.

Krauss, Wilhelmine. *Das Doppelgängermotiv in der Romantik.* Berlin: 1930.

Kuttner, Margot. *Die Gestaltung des Individualitätsproblems bei E. T. A. Hoffmann.* Düsseldorf: 1936.

Ljungdorff, Vilhelm. *E. T. A. Hoffmann och Ursprunget till hans Konstnärskap.* Lund, 1924.

Maassen, Carl Georg von. *Der grundgescheute Antiquarius,* ii (München: 1923), pp. 33-100. Twelve articles on Hoffmann.

Mausolf, Werner. *Hoffmanns Stellung zu Drama und Theater.* Berlin: 1920.

Müller, Hans von. *Neues über E. T. A. Hoffmann.* Berlin: 1901.

———. "Aus E. T. A. Hoffmanns Flegeljahren," *Frankfurter Zeitung,* June 14, 1901.

————. *E. T. A. Hoffmann und sein Leihbibliothekar.* Leipzig: 1904.

————. *E. T. A. Hoffmann in Dresden und Leipzig.* Leipzig: 1905.

————. *Materialien zu einer Biographie E. T. A. Hoffmanns.* Berlin: 1907.

————. *Hoffmann und Härtel: Neue Mitteilungen über ihren Verkehr in den Jahren 1799-1819.* (Without date, published 1908.)

————. *E. T. A. Hoffmanns Tagebuchaufzeichnungen über seinen Leipziger Aufenthalt im Frühjahr 1813.* Leipzig: 1910.

————. *Fragment einer Biographie E. T. A. Hoffmanns. I: Letzte Monate in Posen und Aufenthalt in Plock.* Berlin: 1914.

————. *Aus den Materialien zu einer Biographie E. T. A. Hoffmanns.* München: 1915.

————. *Fragment einer Biographie E. T. A. Hoffmanns.* Berlin: 1916.

————. *Das künstlerische Schaffen E. T. A. Hoffmanns.* Leipzig: 1926.

————. *E. T. A. Hoffmann und Jean Paul: ihre Beziehungen zu einander und zu gemeinsamen Bekannten.* Köln: 1927.

(For articles in periodicals, cf. references in the footnotes. Most of the publications listed above are made up from magazine articles, revised and often enlarged.)

Ochsener, Karl. *E. T. A. Hoffmann als Dichter des Unbewussten.* Frauenfeld-Leipzig: 1935.

Pfeiffer-Belli, W. "Mythos und Religion bei E. T. A. Hoffmann," in *Euphorion,* xxxiv (1933), pp. 305-40.

Pirker, Max. Review of Sucher's *Les Sources du merveilleux chez E. T. A. Hoffmann,* in *Euphorion,* xx (1913), pp. 261-76. Review of Paul Margis' *E. T. A. Hoffmann: Eine psychographische Individualanalyse* in *Euphorion,* xx (1913), pp. 255-61.

Raydt, Olga. *Das Dämonische als Stilform in den literarischen Werken E. T. A. Hoffmanns.* München: 1912.

Reimann, Olga. *Das Märchen bei E. T. A. Hoffmann.* München: 1926.

Roehl, Martin. *Die Doppelpersönlichkeit bei E. T. A. Hoffmann.* Rostock: 1918.

Sakheim, Arthur. *E. T. A. Hoffmann: Studien zu seiner Persönlichkeit und seinen Werken.* Leipzig: 1908.

Schaeffer, Carl. *Die Bedeutung des Musikalischen und Akustischen in E. T. A. Hoffmanns literarischem Schaffen.* Marburg: 1909.

Schmerbach, Hartmut. *Stilstudien zu E. T. A. Hoffmann.* Berlin: 1929.

Sucher, Paul. *Les Sources du merveilleux chez E. T. A. Hoffmann.* Paris: 1912.

Thalmann, Marianne. *Der triviale Roman im 18. Jahrhundert und der romantische Roman.* Berlin: 1923.

Todsen, Hermann. *Über die Entwicklung des romantischen Kunstmärchens.* München: 1906.

Willimczik, Kurt. *E. T. A. Hoffmann: die drei Reiche seiner Gestaltenwelt.* Berlin: 1939.

INDEX

OF NAMES AND OF HOFFMANN'S WORKS